2018-2019
SEPTEMBER–AUGUST
KJV

Standard LESSON
COMMENTARY®

KING JAMES VERSION

EDITORIAL TEAM

RONALD L. NICKELSON
Senior Editor

JANE ANN KENNEY

MARGARET K. WILLIAMS

ANDREW SLOAN

Volume 66

Standard®
PUBLISHING
part of the David C Cook family

IN THIS VOLUME

INDEX OF PRINTED TEXTS

The printed texts for 2018–2019 are arranged here in the order in which they appear in the Bible.

KJV Deluxe Edition

Get the eCommentary download from Logos!

The *Standard Lesson eCommentary*®, for either PC or Mac, is included with purchase of a deluxe edition. After purchasing a deluxe edition, just go to www.logos.com/redeem to enter the unlock code that is printed on the survey stub. If you do not have a deluxe edition, you can purchase the SLeC separately at www.logos.com. If you have questions regarding the download, registration, activation, or other technical issues of the SLeC, go to www.logos.com and click on the support link. Support is also available by phone at 1.800.875.6467.

. . . and don't forget the visuals!

The thumbnail visuals in the lessons are small reproductions of 18″ x 24″ full-color posters that are included in the *Adult Resources* packet for each quarter. Order numbers 1629118 (fall 2018), 2629119 (winter 2018–2019), 3629119 (spring 2019), and 4629119 (summer 2019) from either your supplier, by calling 1.800.323.7543, or at www.standardlesson.com.

CUMULATIVE INDEX

A cumulative index for Scripture passages used in the STANDARD LESSON COMMENTARY
for September 2016–August 2019 (of the 2016–2022 cycle) is provided below.

✝

STUDY THE BIBLE LIKE NEVER BEFORE

With study notes derived from 60 years of the best-selling Standard Lesson Commentary, this Bible is the perfect complement to enhance your study of Scripture. Whether you're in Sunday school, with a small group, or doing your own personal study—this Bible will help you discover, reflect on, and discuss Scripture in a new and powerful way.

What you'll find:

- Study notes from the best of 60 years of Standard Lesson Commentary
- Cross-references to other relevant passages
- Discussion questions with "talking points" for deeper understanding
- In-text maps showing the world of the Bible
- Harmony of the Gospels

- Introductions to each book in the Bible
- Illustrated time line of Bible events
- Pronunciation Guide to help pronounce those hard-to-say names and places
- Concordance of key words throughout the Bible
- Easy-to-read font
- Daily Bible reading plan

NIV® Standard Lesson®
Study Bible Hardcover
978-0-7847-7686-5
Price: $49.99

NIV® Standard Lesson®
Study Bible DuoTone
978-0-7847-7685-8
Color: Desert Sand / Navy
Price: $59.99

KJV Standard Lesson®
Study Bible Hardcover
978-0-7847-7478-6
Price: $49.99

KJV Standard Lesson®
Study Bible DuoTone
978-0-7847-7477-9
Color: Desert Sand / Saddle Brown
Price: $59.99

KJV Standard Lesson®
Women's Study Bible
978-0-7847-7736-7
Color: Lydian Purple/ Maroon
Price $59.99

Standard®
PUBLISHING
part of the David C Cook family

Notes

FALL 2018
KING JAMES VERSION

GOD'S WORLD AND GOD'S PEOPLE

Special Features

Lessons

Unit 1: God Creates the World

Unit 2: God Destroys and Re-creates

Unit 3: God Blesses and Re-creates Regardless

QUARTERLY QUIZ

Use these questions as a pretest or as a review. The answers are on page iv of This Quarter in the Word.

Lesson 1

1. The earth had no form, and _____ was above the deep. *Genesis 1:2*

2. The first recorded spoken words of God are "Let there be _____." *Genesis 1:3*

Lesson 2

1. God created water animals and birds one day and land animals the next. T/F. *Genesis 1:20-24*

2. God told the living creatures He made to be fruitful and _____. *Genesis 1:22*

Lesson 3

1. God gave the animals to man for food at the outset. T/F. *Genesis 1:29*

2. God breathed into man's nostrils the breath of what? (soul, life, immortality?) *Genesis 2:7*

Lesson 4

1. During Adam's deep sleep, God took one of his _____. *Genesis 2:21*

2. Which son of Adam and Eve was a keeper of sheep? (Cain, Abel, Seth?) *Genesis 4:2*

Lesson 5

1. God told the serpent that the woman's seed would bruise his _____. *Genesis 3:15*

2. God stationed armed _____ at the edge of Eden to bar the way to the tree of life. *Genesis 3:24*

Lesson 6

1. God told Noah that the earth was filled with what? (people, knowledge, violence?) *Genesis 6:13*

2. How many stories, or decks, was the ark to have? (two, three, four?) *Genesis 6:16*

Lesson 7

1. Who was Abram's father? (Terah, Nahor, Nimrod?) *Genesis 11:27*

2. How old was Abram when he left Haran for Canaan? (70, 75, 90?) *Genesis 12:4*

Lesson 8

1. When a visitor said Sarah was going to have a baby, she _____. *Genesis 18:12*

2. Abraham was 120 years old when Isaac was born. T/F. *Genesis 21:5*

Lesson 9

1. Rebekah offered to draw water for the _____ of Abraham's servant. *Genesis 24:19*

2. Rebekah covered herself before meeting Isaac. T/F. *Genesis 24:65*

Lesson 10

1. Describing the boys struggling in Rebekah's womb, the Lord told her that the _____ would serve the _____. (pick two: elder, taller, younger, smarter, quicker, slower?) *Genesis 25:23*

2. As Jacob emerged from Rebekah's womb, his hand took hold of what part of Esau? (head, finger, heel?) *Genesis 25:26*

Lesson 11

1. Isaac told Esau to prepare him a meal so Isaac could give Esau what? (birthright, blessing, inheritance?) *Genesis 27:6-8*

2. When Jacob came near to Isaac, Isaac said the voice was that of _____ but the hands were those of _____. *Genesis 27:22*

Lesson 12

1. Jacob sacrificed an animal on the stone he used for a pillow. T/F. *Genesis 28:18*

2. Jacob named the place where he had his dream _____. *Genesis 28:19*

Lesson 13

1. What did Rachel name her first son? (Benjamin, Joseph, Judah?) *Genesis 30:24*

2. Who told Jacob, "The Lord hath blessed me for thy sake"? (Rachel, Leah, Laban?) *Genesis 30:27*

QUARTER AT A GLANCE

by Doug Redford

THE WORD *creation* is applied to accomplishments in various fields of endeavor. Likewise, the word *recreation* has a wide range of uses, applying primarily to leisure activities that provide a break from stressful routines.

The lessons for this quarter focus on the uniquely creative and re-creative activity of the Lord God. The lessons are drawn from Genesis, the Bible's book of beginnings. Genesis is rightly associated with God's work as Creator. But Genesis also emphasizes God's power to *re-create*, to address what happened when His "very good" creation (Genesis 1:31) became very bad due to sin.

The Creator

The first unit of studies consists of five lessons drawn from the first three chapters of Genesis. The opening chapter (covered in lessons 1–3) moves from the general statement of God's creation of "the heaven and the earth" (Genesis 1:1) to the day-by-day record of specific items created, climaxed by the crowning glory of the Creator's handiwork: the man and the woman created "in the image of God" (Genesis 1:27)—which launches God's gift of the family as well (lesson 4).

Sadly, the Creator must become the confronter in response to the first humans' sin (lesson 5). The intimacy with God that was Adam and Eve's privilege to experience was shattered by their choice to heed the destroyer rather than the Creator.

The Re-creator

Even in the midst of confronting Adam and Eve with their wrongdoing, the Creator announced His plan to re-create and to reverse the effects of sin's curse (also covered in lesson 5). Indeed, the remainder of the Bible is the account of God's longing to re-create and humanity's stubborn desire to follow its own path. God had commanded the first couple to fill the earth (Genesis 1:28). By Noah's time it was indeed "filled"—with violence (6:13)! God destroyed the world by means of the flood and established a covenant with Noah, who "walked with God" (Genesis 6:9), as part of His re-creating program (lesson 6).

Another step in God's re-creation was His covenant with Abraham (lesson 7). God promised to make of this man a "great nation" (Genesis 12:2). But 25 years passed from the time Abraham and his wife Sarah left home for Canaan to the time when the promised son, Isaac, was born (lesson 8). God then continued to provide for Isaac by guiding Abraham's servant to Rebekah, who became Isaac's wife (lesson 9).

The Re-creator's Challenge

Isaac and Rebekah's son Jacob appears to put the Re-creator's expertise to the test. The "sibling rivalry" that began in Rebekah's womb became much more serious and personal when Jacob negotiated the birthright away from Esau and later (with Rebekah's assistance) obtained the blessing intended for Esau (lessons 10 and 11).

But the Re-creator's purposes weren't thwarted, even by such a clever schemer as Jacob. As Jacob fled from Esau's revenge, God appeared in a dream and assured Jacob of His continual presence and

> *Genesis also emphasizes God's power to re-create.*

also promised to bring him back to his homeland (lesson 12). And God *was* with Jacob, even during the often stormy years in Haran, keeping His word in spite of the maneuvers of Laban, who was every bit the conniver that Jacob was (lesson 13).

Jacob's life reminds us that the Re-creator has often had to work with some truly "damaged goods." Let's be humbly grateful that He is still making "new creatures" (2 Corinthians 5:17) out of the most improbable candidates.

GET THE SETTING

by Lloyd M. Pelfrey

WHY DID Moses write Genesis? How did he know so much about the people and the events that go back to creation? Why were these things important to the new nation of Israel or to future generations? With all the other things he had to do, how did Moses find time to write Genesis, one of the books of the Pentateuch? Was Moses even able to write?

Why Did Moses Write Genesis?

First, other nations had explanations about the origins of the universe and man—offering similarities and vivid contrasts to the simple record in Genesis 1. God wanted the people of Israel to know the facts in a permanent, written format.

Second, the people of Israel had just spent 430 years in Egypt (Exodus 12:40, 41). Some of the Israelites had probably heard the differing accounts of creation that were associated with Egyptian gods. They needed what the Lord gave through Moses—the short, factual explanation that would be understandable through the ages.

Third, it was important that the people of Israel know the promises God made to the patriarchs (Abraham, Isaac, and Jacob) about their descendants. God therefore deemed it essential that there be an accurate account about the patriarchs, plus other events that affected all of humanity (the fall, the flood, and the diversification of languages).

It was in Genesis that God promised the land of Canaan to Israel. There were divine reasons for the migration from Canaan to Egypt, and the Israelites could not return until everything was ready (Genesis 15:16). The generations of Moses and beyond needed to know why they were in Canaan—that it was because the Lord had promised Canaan to their ancestors.

How Did Moses Know?

How did Moses know the events, the conversations, and the specific prophecies or promises that are documented in Genesis? Several possibilities have been given, and the best answer may be a mixture of them. First, 2 Peter 1:21 establishes that prophecy came as godly men were moved by the Holy Spirit. This could include information about creation, the flood, and other historical events. God therefore prompted Moses and revealed to him what he wrote.

Second, oral traditions were important for the ancients, and Moses may have blended the gift of inspiration with what he had heard from others.

Third, other nations had records of major events, especially in the lives of their former kings. The history of Israel is different in that it tells not only of great accomplishments by figures of the past but also of weaknesses in the lives of its heroes. Israel records its history, but it is history that is moving toward divine goals.

Was Moses Able to Write?

The hieroglyphic writing of Egypt had about 1,000 different characters. Moses, however, was quite familiar with "all the wisdom of the Egyptians" (Acts 7:22). Recent discoveries show that primitive alphabetic writing with a Semitic influence can be dated as early as 1850 BC. Moses lived about 1526–1406 BC. The Israelites were Semitic, and the evidence combines to say that Moses could write, using an alphabet.

Did Moses Have Time to Write?

Yes, he did. In Numbers 33 there is a total of only 40 sites for the wilderness camping, plus the beginning and ending places. The length of stay could be for short or long periods of time at any one place (Numbers 9:22).

The evidence is clear. The Bible repeatedly indicates that Moses wrote the Law, including Genesis. The testimony of history is that it was possible, likely, and necessary for him to write Genesis, the first book of the Bible.

THIS QUARTER IN THE WORD

Answers to the Quarterly Quiz on page 2

Lesson 1—1. darkness. 2. light. **Lesson 2**—1. true. 2. multiply. **Lesson 3**—1. false. 2. life. **Lesson 4**—1. ribs. 2. Abel. **Lesson 5**—1. head. 2. Cherubims. **Lesson 6**—1. violence. 2. three. **Lesson 7**—1. Terah. 2. 75. **Lesson 8**—1. laughed. 2. false. **Lesson 9**—1. camels. 2. true. **Lesson 10**—1. elder, younger. 2. Esau's heel. **Lesson 11**—1. blessing. 2. Jacob, Esau. **Lesson 12**—1. false. 2. Bethel. **Lesson 13**—1. Joseph. 2. Laban.

LESSON CYCLE CHART

International Sunday School Lesson Cycle, September 2016–August 2022

Year	Fall Quarter (Sep, Oct, Nov)	Winter Quarter (Dec, Jan, Feb)	Spring Quarter (Mar, Apr, May)	Summer Quarter (Jun, Jul, Aug)
2016–2017	**The Sovereignty of God** (Isaiah, Matthew, Hebrews, Revelation)	**Creation: A Divine Cycle** (Psalms, Luke, Galatians)	**God Loves Us** (Psalms, Joel, Jonah, John, Romans, Ephesians, 1 Peter, 1 John)	**God's Urgent Call** (Exodus, Judges, Prophets, Acts)
2017–2018	**Covenant with God** (Pentateuch, 1 & 2 Samuel, Nehemiah, Jeremiah, Ezekiel, 1 Corinthians, Hebrews)	**Faith in Action** (Daniel, Matthew, Acts, Ephesians, 1 Timothy, James)	**Acknowledging God** (Pentateuch, 2 Chronicles, Psalms, Luke, John, 2 Corinthians, Hebrews, Revelation)	**Justice in the New Testament** (Matthew, Luke, Romans, 2 Corinthians, Colossians)
2018–2019	**God's World and God's People** (Genesis)	**Our Love for God** (Deuteronomy, Joshua, Psalms, Matthew, Luke, Epistles)	**Discipleship and Mission** (Matthew, Mark, Luke, Acts, Romans)	**Covenant in God** (Ruth, 1 Samuel, Matthew, Mark, Ephesians, Colossians, Hebrews)
2019–2020	**Responding to God's Grace** (Pentateuch, 1 Samuel, 1 Kings, Luke, Epistles)	**Honoring God** (1 Kings, 1 Chronicles, Matthew, Luke)	**Justice and the Prophets** (Esther, Prophets, 1 Corinthians)	**Many Faces of Wisdom** (Proverbs, Ecclesiastes, Gospels, James)
2020–2021	**Love for One Another** (Genesis, 1 Samuel, Luke, John, Acts, Epistles)	**Call in the New Testament** (Gospels, Acts, Romans, 1 Corinthians, Hebrews)	**Prophets Faithful to God's Covenant** (Deuteronomy, Joshua, 1 & 2 Kings, Ezra, Nehemiah, Lamentations, Prophets)	**Confident Hope** (Leviticus, Matthew, Luke, Romans, 2 Corinthians, Hebrews, 1 John)
2021–2022	**Celebrating God** (Exodus, 2 Samuel, Psalms, Mark, Acts, Revelation)	**Justice, Law, History** (Pentateuch, 2 Samuel, Ezra, Job, Isaiah, Nahum)	**God Frees and Redeems** (Deuteronomy, Ezra, Matthew, John, Romans, Galatians)	**Partners in a New Creation** (Isaiah, John, Revelation)

CHECK THE BLUEPRINT

Part 1 of Building Bible Literacy   *Teacher Tips by Jim Eichenberger*

IF SOMEONE were to ask why you lead a Bible study, the answer would be obvious. You want your students to understand God's Word; you want to build Bible literacy. But if you were asked to explain exactly how Bible literacy can be imparted, that question may give you pause. This article begins a series of four quarterly teacher tips that will help you answer that query.

In explaining how to build Bible literacy, let us use the metaphor of building a house. This article will deal with the first step: checking the blueprint. The blueprint for a house reveals the architect's vision for the structure to be completed. In building Bible literacy, we help fellow Bible students examine God's blueprint for His revelation to humankind.

God's plan has a story arc—a saga that begins at creation and ends at the culmination of this present age. In helping fellow Bible students understand the message of Scripture, a teacher must assist them in putting the content of the Bible into an understandable chronology. This article will suggest some practical ideas.

Take Advantage of Time Lines

Post Bible time lines in your classroom. Though available commercially, you can easily create your own time lines using a roll of shelf paper, a marker, and the chronology that appears in a study Bible. Post an Old Testament time line at eye level, using two adjacent classroom walls (the wall to the left of your group and the wall facing them). Since New Testament chronology is much more compact, you could draw and post a New Testament time line on the wall to the right of your group.

Having these ever-present charts in your classroom has two benefits. First, your group members can be constantly reviewing Bible chronology when they are in the room. Second, the charts will allow you to place every Bible lesson in historical context with a mere gesture of your hand.

Approach the Bible Chronologically

Prepare a devotional reading plan for your group that will help them study the Bible chronologically. Books of the Bible are not arranged in chronological order, but by literature type. Chronological Bibles, which present biblical content in the order in which events occurred, are available. Daily chronological reading plans are easily downloaded. As the new year approaches, why not make such a plan available to your group and tackle it together?

Make a game of it. Quick team-building exercises are a good way to start a class occasionally. One such activity is to divide into small groups, then see which group can put a list of 5 to 10 Bible people or events in chronological order in the least amount of time. You wouldn't necessarily want to do this every week, but rather work it into a regular schedule. For example, use it on the first Sunday of a quarter, on the fifth Sunday of a month (whenever those occur), etc. Develop a schedule in such a way that the activity is anticipated without becoming a tired routine.

Consider a Crash Course

The preceding suggestions are ways of helping learners grasp the story arc of the Bible over time. They are easily implemented and sustainable. But there is a more comprehensive way of teaching the blueprint of Scripture: a Bible survey course. Such a course could be taught in your classroom or as a special whole-church offering. *Training for Service*, a time-tested resource, is available for purchase at www.sundayschool.com or from your bookstore. Like most Bible surveys, this course requires a long-term commitment (26 sessions).

One would not build a house without consulting the blueprint, the architect's vision of what the completed structure will be. Likewise, the first step in building Bible literacy is exposing your class to a panoramic view of God's plan.

GOD CREATES HEAVENS AND EARTH

DEVOTIONAL READING: Psalm 33:1-9
BACKGROUND SCRIPTURE: Genesis 1:1-13

GENESIS 1:1-13

1 In the beginning God created the heaven and the earth.

2 And the earth was without form, and void; and darkness was upon the face of the deep. And the Spirit of God moved upon the face of the waters.

3 And God said, Let there be light: and there was light.

4 And God saw the light, that it was good: and God divided the light from the darkness.

5 And God called the light Day, and the darkness he called Night. And the evening and the morning were the first day.

6 And God said, Let there be a firmament in the midst of the waters, and let it divide the waters from the waters.

7 And God made the firmament, and divided the waters which were under the firmament from the waters which were above the firmament: and it was so.

8 And God called the firmament Heaven. And the evening and the morning were the second day.

9 And God said, Let the waters under the heaven be gathered together unto one place, and let the dry land appear: and it was so.

10 And God called the dry land Earth; and the gathering together of the waters called he Seas: and God saw that it was good.

11 And God said, Let the earth bring forth grass, the herb yielding seed, and the fruit tree yielding fruit after his kind, whose seed is in itself, upon the earth: and it was so.

12 And the earth brought forth grass, and herb yielding seed after his kind, and the tree yielding fruit, whose seed was in itself, after his kind: and God saw that it was good.

13 And the evening and the morning were the third day.

KEY VERSES

In the beginning God created the heaven and the earth. And the earth was without form, and void; and darkness was upon the face of the deep. And the Spirit of God moved upon the face of the waters. —**Genesis 1:1, 2**

GOD'S WORLD AND GOD'S PEOPLE

Unit 1: God Creates the World

LESSONS 1–5

LESSON AIMS

After participating in this lesson, each learner will be able to:

1. List what was created on each of the first three days in Genesis 1.

2. Explain the meaning of the *firmament*.

3. Write a prayer praising God for who He is and for His works of creation.

LESSON OUTLINE

Introduction

A. Many, One, or None?

Ironically, polytheism (belief in many gods) and atheism (denial of any god) both seem to be growing in popularity in Western democracies. Neither viewpoint is new. Scholars have identified more than 2,000 named deities in the ancient Near East, the region of biblical events. As for atheism, the psalmist from centuries ago wrote, "The fool hath said in his heart, There is no God" (Psalm 14:1).

Polytheism leads to a chaos of competing, fickle gods of equal or shifting strength, and mortals must try to get on the side of the one(s) who will win. One feature of polytheism is the absence of a singular basis of moral absolutes; atheism ends up in the same place. The inevitable results in both cases are moral relativism and the rule of the powerful over the powerless.

Genesis 1 reveals, however, that there is only one true God. Only in the existence of a personal God can there be a designed, absolute standard that governs all human behavior and makes sense of the universe. This great truth forms the doctrinal foundation for the rest of Scripture.

B. Lesson Context

Cosmology refers to one's concept of the universe. The cosmology of the ancient Near East, which was the historical and cultural context of the Old Testament, was different from popular cosmologies today. Michael S. Heiser has described the ancient cosmology as envisioning three realms: (1) the heavens, the place where the gods are; (2) the earth, the place of humans and other creatures; and (3) the region below the earth. (For a variant that took into account only immediate sense experience, see commentary on Genesis 1:20 in lesson 2.)

This three-tier concept was held by the peoples of Egypt, Mesopotamia, and Canaan; it was also assumed by the writers of the Old and New Testaments (see Psalm 33:6-8; Proverbs 8:27-29; Philippians 2:10; Revelation 5:3). This cosmology may be compared with a flat plate that has an upside-down bowl atop it. People and animals lived on the plate underneath the bowl. The arc of sun, moon, and stars across the sky (the surface of the bowl) marked where the gods lived. The depths and supports of the earth were below the plate; the dead were located there as well.

The basis of this cosmology was how the earth appeared in relation to everything else as one stood on the ground, not as one looking at the earth and galaxies from the vantage point of an orbiting space station. For ancient peoples, the mountains seemed to reach up to the heavens and support it (2 Samuel 22:8). Bars and roots of the mountains formed the lower regions to support the earth and provide depth for the seas (Jonah 2:5, 6).

Such language is not meant to describe the geology of creation in a scientific way, but rather its appearance. This is no different from our speaking of the sun's "rising" when we've known since childhood that the sun does not actually rise but only appears to do so from our vantage point on the earth. When we speak of the sun's "rising," we are not speaking untruthfully from ignorance; rather, we (and the Bible authors) are speaking phenomenologically.

Skeptics often put Genesis in the same category as ancient Near Eastern myths. But Genesis does not borrow from those myths; the Genesis creation account stands alone, in stark contrast to rival accounts of the ancient world.

I. The Big Picture
(GENESIS 1:1, 2)
A. Attribution (v. 1)
1a. In the beginning.

Neither the peoples of the ancient world in general nor the Scriptures in particular assert innumerable beginnings. Only one beginning is in view, and it is that which commences in the first verse of the Bible. The concept of *the beginning* is not limited to a singular point of time, but rather includes the span of events that are described through Genesis 2:4.

1b. God created.

The Hebrew word translated *God* is actually plural in form. Some well-meaning believers, knowing that Scripture clearly teaches there is only one true God (Isaiah 46:9; etc.), assert that

this plural form demonstrates that God is a trinity. Unbelievers claim that this plural form indicates that the Old Testament teaches the existence of many gods.

Neither view is necessarily supported by this plural form, for two reasons. First, though a plural noun in Hebrew may indicate "more than one," a noun may be plural to signify honor; this is similar to the royal "we" spoken by a king or queen. Second, the Hebrew behind the verb *created* is singular, indicating only one subject. The best explanation is that God is viewed as a single essence who is honored above all other beings.

1c. The heaven and the earth.

This expression is roughly equivalent to our term *universe*. In Hebrew, two words with opposite senses are often paired to indicate a totality. For example, "great and small" in 2 Chronicles 34:30 means all kinds of people. Therefore Genesis 1:1 is expressing quite clearly that all we call "matter" today is not coeternal with God. Rather, God brought it into existence.

❧ THE WONDER OF IT ALL ❧

The Great Wall of China, Christ the Redeemer Statue in Brazil, and India's Taj Mahal are prestigious landmarks among the Seven Wonders of the Modern World. Each architectural masterpiece showcases ingenuity and artistic achievements. Yet as we turn to the first page of history, we do not find detailed prototypes, world-class construction engineers, or tireless artisans.

Instead, we encounter nothing—nothing, that is, except God.

HOW TO SAY IT

Canaan	*Kay*-nun.
cosmology	koz-*mol*-uh-jee.
Galileo	*Gah*-luh-**lee**-oh.
Mesopotamia	*Mes*-uh-puh-**tay**-me-uh.
Micah	*My*-kuh.
phenomenologically	
	fih-*naw*-meh-nuh-**law**-jih-kuh-lee.
polytheism	**paw**-lee-thee-*ih*-zum.
Taj Mahal	*Tawzh* Meh-**haul**.
Zephaniah	Zef-uh-*nye*-uh.

Worship the
CREATOR

Visual for Lesson 1. *Point to this visual as you ask, "How would your life be different if you didn't believe God created the heavens and the earth?"*

Then in a mere five words, the Bible announces one colossal moment: "In the beginning God created." God's divine word ordered our world into structured being. He created it to stand fast (Psalm 33:9) until He commands otherwise. Within the hitherto lifeless void, the all-powerful Creator precisely shaped the heavens and earth.

God did not use a trial and error method to perfect creation. He did not rely on guesswork to create. Rather He relied on His unfathomable wisdom, which the books of Job and Psalms extol (Job 38, 39; Psalm 104:24).

Given that inanimate creation proclaims God's glory and wise knowledge (Psalm 19:1, 2), how much more are *we* obligated to do so! Each new day invites us to celebrate visibly our loving, majestic maker of the heavens and the earth (Job 9:8, 9; 38:4–39:30; etc.). —B. L.

> **What Do You Think?**
> What are some specific things for which you can praise God as you observe creation?
> **Digging Deeper**
> For ideas, skim through Psalms 1–41 to identify passages that include the theme of creation.

B. The Earth in the Universe (v. 2)

2a. And the earth was without form, and void.

We move to the description of the situation after the creation of matter in verse 1. The exact phrase (in the original Hebrew) of earth's description *without form, and void* also occurs in Jeremiah 4:23. There it describes the moral chaos of a chosen people who do not know the Lord, who do not know how to do good, and who are wise only in knowing how to do evil. The phrase seems to describe a situation that is without moral boundaries. In parallel, Genesis 1:2 implies that physical boundaries are not yet fully defined (compare 1:4).

2b. And darkness was upon the face of the deep.

Here, the word *darkness* communicates the absence of light in a physical sense. Later writers and Jesus himself will use this word to communicate the absence of light in a moral sense (Isaiah 9:2; 50:10; Matthew 4:16; John 1:5; 12:46; etc.). It also comes to be used in contexts that call for the punitive acts of God (Amos 5:20; Zephaniah 1:15).

Regarding Genesis 1, the literal, physical sense is clear. But as we read the Old Testament in light of the New Testament, our understanding of figurative uses of the word *darkness* is enhanced.

2c. And the Spirit of God moved upon the face of the waters.

The word translated *Spirit* is elsewhere translated "breath" (Genesis 6:17), "wind" (8:1), "spirit" (45:27), "courage" (Joshua 2:11), and others. Regarding a choice between translations of *Spirit* or *spirit*, the translators were faced with a difficulty in that the Hebrew language does not distinguish between uppercase and lowercase letters. So translators must interpret the meaning, and they capitalize when the reference is to God personally as divine being.

As a result, the phrases *Spirit of God* and *spirit of God* occur 10 and 4 times respectively in the *King James Version* of the Old Testament. Many Christians think the phrase *Spirit of God* always refers to the Holy Spirit. But passages where the identical Hebrew is properly not translated that way are 1 Samuel 16:15, 16, 23; 18:10.

The phrase *Spirit of God* in the passage before us refers to the same one known as "the Spirit of the Lord." This Spirit can be present (Judges 11:29), take action (13:25), speak messages (2 Samuel

23:2), and depart (1 Samuel 16:14). These are the qualities of a personal being, not an impersonal force.

II. Day One
(Genesis 1:3-5)
A. Creating Light (v. 3)

3. And God said, Let there be light: and there was light.

Creation begins! The phrase *And God said* occurs at the beginning of each day of creation, and here it serves to separate Genesis 1:3 and following from 1:1, 2. *Let there be* is a command or desire for something to take place. Presumably those hearing this command are the inhabitants of Heaven, the abode of God.

> *What Do You Think?*
> What steps can you take to be more attentive to what God says?
> *Digging Deeper*
> With reference to Psalm 19:1-3 and Romans 1:18-20, consider how and what God communicates in Scriptures is different from how and what He communicates through creation.

The first thing created is light. Since the sun, moon, and stars are not created until the fourth day, some think that the light referred to here may be what scientists call energy. Perhaps this light-as-energy, if that is what it is, is a new creation out of nothing. Or perhaps matter that God previously created is now turned into energy, a concept absent from the ancient mind. Addressing such an issue is not the aim of the book of Genesis. The stress, rather, is that light stands in positive contrast to darkness (next verse).

B. Dividing Light from Darkness (v. 4)

4. And God saw the light, that it was good: and God divided the light from the darkness.

God acts in and on His creation, and His light pushes back the darkness. The word *good* describes the value of *the light*. It may also include the excellence of figurative ideas associated with light. The Scripture may be using the acts of creation to teach a spiritual lesson in addition to the material events of creation. If that's the case, then the lesson is that there is a difference between good and evil just as clearly as there is a difference between physical light and darkness. Foolish, sinful humans will later blur those distinctions. "Woe unto them that call evil good, and good evil" (Isaiah 5:20).

> *What Do You Think?*
> What more can your church do to participate with God in dispelling moral darkness with the light of the gospel?
> *Digging Deeper*
> Using a concordance, find occurrences of the word *light* in the Gospel of John and Epistle of 1 John to inform your answer.

C. Naming Light and Darkness (v. 5)

5. And God called the light Day, and the darkness he called Night. And the evening and the morning were the first day.

From the perspective of the ancient world, naming brings things into existence; unnamed things do not exist. Modern, scientific ideas about the nature of light are not in view. Just as darkness is merely the absence of light, and light is the creation of God, so also *Day* and *Night* are portrayed as impersonal creations rather than as rival gods or the forces used by other gods. In naming *light* and *darkness*, God exercises His authority and power as Creator.

The meaning of *day* has been interpreted in various ways to calculate the age of the earth. The word *day* in some contexts refers to the part of a 24-hour period that has light (Exodus 13:21). In other contexts it refers to entire 24-hour periods of time (Genesis 7:10). In still other contexts, *day* refers to a longer period of time (Genesis 2:4). The proposal that the phrase *the evening and the morning* naturally suggests a 24-hour day is met with the observation that the sun—the rising and setting of which establish evening and morning—is not created until the fourth day.

One commentator has identified 20 creation accounts in the Bible. In so doing, he notes that the main emphasis across these is "the who" of creation

—namely God. Secondarily, the Bible writers address "the how" of creation. Of least importance to them is "the when." The goal of the authors is not to describe the age of the earth, but rather to describe the orderliness of creation and the lordship of the Creator over all that exists.

> **What Do You Think?**
> How do we ensure that discussions on the age of the earth promote the gospel?
> **Digging Deeper**
> Inform your answer by researching the differences between the "old earth," "young earth," and "ultra-young earth" viewpoints as held by creationists in those camps.

❧ LIGHT FOR THE WORLD ❧

Galileo (1564–1642) labored to calculate the speed of light, but his experiments fell short. Danish astronomer Olaus Roemer (spelled variously) is credited with successfully measuring the speed of light, in 1676. Today's scientists calculate that light travels at 186,000 miles per second.

Cosmic gamma rays, quantum gravity, black holes—while humans theorize to probe the origins of the universe, God is already there. He created light and its speed. He knows where every ray of sunlight and moonlight will fall on earth at any given nanosecond (compare Isaiah 38:8).

The psalmist declares that the Lord covers himself with light (Psalm 104:2). Jesus announced himself to be "the light of the world" (John 8:12). Light sustains life, both physical and spiritual. Light is part of God's essence (1 John 1:5). God delights in light. Do we? (See Romans 13:12; 1 Peter 2:9; 1 John 2:11.)   —B. L.

III. Day Two
(GENESIS 1:6-8)
A. Creating Firmament (v. 6a)

6a. And God said, Let there be a firmament in the midst of the waters.

The word *firmament* refers to the bowl-like dome mentioned in the Lesson Context; see discussion there.

B. Dividing Waters (vv. 6b, 7)

6b, 7. and let it divide the waters from the waters. And God made the firmament, and divided the waters which were under the firmament from the waters which were above the firmament: and it was so.

Of particular interest here is the firmament's function as a boundary to *divide the waters from the waters.* Those *waters which were under the firmament* are all the bodies of water on the earth and below the earth (rivers, lakes, oceans, aquifers). *The waters which were above the firmament* refer to the clouds from which rain falls.

C. Naming Firmament (v. 8)

8. And God called the firmament Heaven. And the evening and the morning were the second day.

The word translated *Heaven* can be used for the air where the birds fly (Genesis 1:20); the location of sun, moon, and stars (Deuteronomy 4:19); or the abode of God and other heavenly beings (1 Kings 22:19; compare 2 Corinthians 12:2). In any case, again God asserts His authority by naming. Paul Kissling notes that this serves to oppose the ancient Near East belief that creation of *the firmament* is a battle between warring gods. Instead, the Bible depicts the unique Creator God calmly forming everything as He alone wills.

IV. Day Three
(GENESIS 1:9-13)
A. Gathering Waters (v. 9)

9. And God said, Let the waters under the heaven be gathered together unto one place, and let the dry land appear: and it was so.

The gathering of *the waters . . . unto one place* refers to the seas on the surface of the earth. The result is that landforms appear. Again, the account does not say how, or how quickly, God does this. It simply happens at His command.

B. Naming Land and Waters (v. 10)

10. And God called the dry land Earth; and the gathering together of the waters called he Seas: and God saw that it was good.

One of the deities of the ancient world was Yam, a name equivalent to the Hebrew word for *seas*. The verse before us stands in sharp contrast with such a myth as it credits the one, true God as Creator of the seas. The seas are simply inanimate water, neither sentient nor divine.

> *What Do You Think?*
> How would you teach truth about God to some-one who believes in a fictitious god or gods?
> *Digging Deeper*
> Consider how Paul's technique in Acts 17:16-31 (which does not use Scripture) should be modified in various modern contexts.

C. Establishing Vegetation (vv. 11-13)

11, 12a. And God said, Let the earth bring forth grass, the herb yielding seed, and the fruit tree yielding fruit after his kind, whose seed is in itself, upon the earth: and it was so. And the earth brought forth grass, and herb yielding seed after his kind, and the tree yielding fruit, whose seed was in itself, after his kind.

Various kinds of plant life appear. This continues the preparation of the earth for human habitation, for now there is renewable sustenance of the earth necessary for survival of humans and animals.

The phrase *after his kind* is important and remarkable in indicating that watermelon seeds result in watermelons, etc. If we pause to consider the consistency of this, it is remarkable yet today.

12b, 13. And God saw that it was good. And the evening and the morning were the third day.

The account of *the third day* concludes with a refrain found throughout the first chapter of Genesis: God approves of what He has created (1:4, 10, 18, 21, 25, 31).

Conclusion

A. The Game Maker

My son-in-law loves to play board games. I am amazed at the creativity of the people who invent the games. The inventor designs the game board, playing pieces, and rules of play. The players are free to choose to ignore the rules, but then they are not playing the game as intended by its creator.

There are really only two viewpoints regarding the ultimate source of all things. In one view, the ultimate source is eternally existing *matter*, the substance of which all things consist. Such a "god" is impersonal—without will or purpose, unable to possess or impose morals. In the other viewpoint, the ultimate source is a *person*. A person has qualities such as self-awareness, will, morality, and the power to act.

The difference is profound. In the universe of an impersonal god, there can be no absolute standard of right and wrong. Humans have no eternal destiny; they do not suffer eternal consequences for behavior. But in the real universe of the personal God, it is He who decides what is right and wrong. The uncreated God of the Bible is the Creator of all that exists, and His creation is obligated to obey Him.

The Scriptures tell us about the designer of the universe. Like the game maker, God has sent us instructions of how to live, the rules of right and wrong, and the consequences of breaking the rules. Humankind has been granted freedom to choose whether or not to obey the rules, but humankind has not been given the right to decide what the rules are.

B. Prayer

Dear God, Creator of the universe, we thank You for making yourself known to us. We also thank You for providing Christ, Your Son, as our means becoming a new creation after breaking Your rules. Help us to submit to Your Spirit. We pray in Jesus' name. Amen.

C. Thought to Remember

Praise the Creator!

VISUALS FOR THESE LESSONS

The visual pictured in each lesson (example: page 12) is a small reproduction of a large, full-color poster included in the *Adult Resources* packet for the Fall Quarter. That packet also contains the very useful *Presentation Tools* CD for teacher use. Order No. 1629118 from your supplier.

INVOLVEMENT LEARNING

Enhance your lesson with KJV Bible Student (from your curriculum supplier) and the reproducible activity page (at www.standardlesson.com or in the back of the KJV Standard Lesson Commentary Deluxe Edition).

Into the Lesson

Divide learners into groups of three or four. Ask them to recall things they have accomplished that were completed in steps (examples: making a cake, building a model car). Ask them to share the major steps of completing the task, allowing about five minutes.

As you reassemble the group, ask for a few of the tasks or accomplishments that were discussed. Remind learners that none of the accomplishments they described could be completed without someone following the necessary steps. Make a transition by saying, "Nothing that is made happens without someone to create it. This huge and complicated universe also had a beginning. Let's find out how it all started."

Into the Word

Read Genesis 1:1, 2 aloud. Invite learners to talk about the pictures these verses paint in their minds. Say, "The phrase *the heaven and the earth* is a collective expression similar to our term *universe*. Imagine a universe without order and light! But then, the Spirit of God moved, and His creating of order and beauty was about to begin."

Divide learners into three groups of no more than four each. If you have more than a dozen students, form more groups and duplicate the assignments to follow. Provide each group with a handout (you prepare) of its assignment, several large index cards, and (if learners don't have student books) relevant portions of the commentary.

First-Day Group: Use Genesis 1:3-5 and the commentary to discover important events regarding the first day of creation. Write discoveries on separate index cards. Be prepared to discuss how there can be light when sun and stars are not created until the fourth day.

Second-Day Group: Read Genesis 1:6-8 and the commentary to discover important events regarding the second day of creation. Write discoveries on separate index cards. Be prepared to explain the meaning of "firmament."

Third-Day Group: Read Genesis 1:9-13 and the commentary to discover important events regarding the third day of creation. Write discoveries on separate index cards. Be prepared to explain what the gathering of the waters signifies.

As groups work, write the following headers on the board:

Day One   *Day Two*   *Day Three*

After no more than 10 minutes, call time, collect the completed index cards, shuffle them, and place them blank side up on the table. Form learners into two teams to take turns drawing a card, revealing its fact, and affixing it under the correct header from memory only.

When all cards have been placed, ask learners to reposition incorrectly placed cards. *(Expected placements: Day One—God created light / declared it good / separated light from darkness / called the light "Day" and darkness "Night"; Day Two—God created a firmament / used it to divide waters above from waters below / called the firmament "Heaven"; Day Three—God separated water from land / called the land "Earth" and the gathered waters "Seas" / caused the earth to produce vegetation.)*

Wrap up this section by calling for explanations of the other topic assigned to each group.

Into Life

Say, "In our hurry to ask God for things, we neglect to praise Him for who He is and for His works of creation. Take a minute to write a brief prayer in which you do so." Invite volunteers to read theirs. Suggest that the prayers be incorporated into devotional times in the week ahead.

Options. Distribute copies of the "Picture This!" and/or "Say What?" activities from the reproducible page, which you can download, to be completed as indicated. Close with a prayer of praise.

God Creates
Lights and Life

Devotional Reading: Psalm 136:1-9
Background Scripture: Genesis 1:14-25

Genesis 1:14-25

14 And God said, Let there be lights in the firmament of the heaven to divide the day from the night; and let them be for signs, and for seasons, and for days, and years:

15 And let them be for lights in the firmament of the heaven to give light upon the earth: and it was so.

16 And God made two great lights; the greater light to rule the day, and the lesser light to rule the night: he made the stars also.

17 And God set them in the firmament of the heaven to give light upon the earth,

18 And to rule over the day and over the night, and to divide the light from the darkness: and God saw that it was good.

19 And the evening and the morning were the fourth day.

20 And God said, Let the waters bring forth abundantly the moving creature that hath life, and fowl that may fly above the earth in the open firmament of heaven.

21 And God created great whales, and every living creature that moveth, which the waters brought forth abundantly, after their kind, and every winged fowl after his kind: and God saw that it was good.

22 And God blessed them, saying, Be fruitful, and multiply, and fill the waters in the seas, and let fowl multiply in the earth.

23 And the evening and the morning were the fifth day.

24 And God said, Let the earth bring forth the living creature after his kind, cattle, and creeping thing, and beast of the earth after his kind: and it was so.

25 And God made the beast of the earth after his kind, and cattle after their kind, and every thing that creepeth upon the earth after his kind: and God saw that it was good.

Key Verse

God said, Let there be lights in the firmament of the heaven to divide the day from the night; and let them be for signs, and for seasons, and for days, and years. —**Genesis 1:14**

GOD'S WORLD AND GOD'S PEOPLE

Unit 1: God Creates the World

LESSONS 1–5

LESSON AIMS

After participating in this lesson, each learner will be able to:

1. Relate what came into being on the fourth, fifth, and sixth days of creation.

2. Explain the permanent patterns of created order as found in Genesis 1.

3. Write a personal "Creation Declaration" that describes a way he or she will honor God for His creation.

LESSON OUTLINE

Introduction
  A. "Where Did We Come From?"
  B. Lesson Context
I. Day Four (GENESIS 1:14-19)
  A. Seasonal Cycle Created (vv. 14, 15)
  B. Sun and Moon Created (vv. 16-19)
    Drawn to the Light
II. Day Five (GENESIS 1:20-23)
  A. Avians and Aquatics Created (vv. 20, 21)
    Light and Life
  B. Abundant Supply Created (vv. 22, 23)
III. Day Six (GENESIS 1:24, 25)
  A. Animals Created (v. 24)
  B. Animal Categories (v. 25)
Conclusion
  A. For the Beauty of the Earth
  B. Prayer
  C. Thought to Remember

Introduction

A. "Where Did We Come From?"

Almost all cultures attempt to answer the question above. But as we saw in last week's lesson, every proposed answer ultimately takes one of two positions: we trace our origins either (1) to eternally existing impersonal matter or (2) to an eternally existing personal being.

Explanations that fall into the latter category are often labeled "myths," a term that injects an air of untruth into the story. If an explanation is mythical, it can be consigned (some think) to the area of religion and therefore marginalized. Secular culture tells us to keep our religious views separated from the larger issues of our culture.

Today this is seen in the apparent conflict between those who adopt a scientific viewpoint that disallows supernatural explanations and those who accept the Bible as God's revealed Word. *Where did we come from?* We want to know, and competing explanations are set in opposition.

One side explains origins through a theory of a spontaneous "big bang" and billions of years of development. While this theory draws on certain facts derived from scientific investigation, it cannot explain where the matter for a so-called big bang came from. It cannot explain why there are laws of nature that allow this bang and subsequent development. Can there be laws of physics without a lawgiver?

The other side listens to the account given in Genesis plus other Bible texts that speak of creation by a Creator. These accounts will not answer every question a scientist might want to ask, but that is not their intent. The biblical account of origins reveals an orderly plan for the creation of the heavens and the earth.

What Do You Think?
  What resources have you found valuable for resolving tensions between faith and science? Which will you recommend to others?
Digging Deeper
  Research the concept of "evidential faith" at www.coldcasechristianity.com.

B. Lesson Context

Christians look to Genesis to explain God's orderly creation of the universe, and this it certainly does. We should not forget, however, that Genesis is also a part of a five-volume set: Genesis, Exodus, Leviticus, Numbers, and Deuteronomy. This collection of books, sometimes called the Pentateuch, is associated with Moses. He is the great hero of ancient Israel, and he is the primary character in the books beginning with Exodus (see Luke 24:44). These books answer the question of human origins from the perspective of the nation of Israel.

As these books relate the origin and history of Israel, the early chapters of Genesis go all the way back to the origins of humanity as a whole, because the people of Israel have common ancestors with all other peoples. Genesis gives an account of the origins of the world and the universe that surrounds us.

Last week's lesson took us through the third day of creation. To summarize: day one related the creation of light and its separation from darkness. Day two told of the creation of a firmament, a barrier that separates the waters above it from those below it. And day three described the emergence of dry land and the furnishing of this land with vegetation.

I. Day Four
(Genesis 1:14-19)
A. Seasonal Cycle Created (vv. 14, 15)

14a. And God said, Let there be lights in the firmament of the heaven to divide the day from the night.

As with the other days of creation, this one, the fourth, begins with God speaking. Having created "light" (singular) on the first day, God now creates *lights* (plural; compare Psalms 74:16; 136:7). These are physical objects that serve specific purposes. For them *to divide the day from the night* speaks to the need for cyclical illumination of the earth.

14b. And let them be for signs.

This illumination goes hand in hand with the lights' being *signs*: things that attest to divine power at work. The idea is to give credit to God for His active role in the world. This is the word used to state the significance of the rainbow, given as a sign in the sky that God will not again destroy the earth by a flood (Genesis 9:12-15, same Hebrew word translated "token"). While there might be the occasional extraordinary sign, the ordered nature of earthly cycles is a daily reminder of God's provision and presence.

14c. And for seasons, and for days, and years.

Beyond the signs, we now see three derivative manifestations of God's order. First, the celestial lights also give us *seasons*. We may naturally think of seasons in terms of spring, summer, fall, and winter. That idea may be included (see below), but the idea as it develops throughout the Old Testament is more along the lines of time periods longer than 24 hours in general and the religious festivals of Israel's calendar in particular. These become appointed times (example: Exodus 23:15) as determined by phases of the moon (compare Psalms 81:3; 104:19.)

Hand in hand with such periods of time are the *days* and *years*. These are the familiar periods of 24 hours and 365 days, respectively. The yearly cycle is what gives us the seasons of fall, winter, spring, and summer (or, in some areas, the rainy season and the dry season).

All these provide order and regularity. We are created to thrive within this system. For example, astronauts who leave the earth still try to regulate their activities in 24-hour cycles. God has designed a world to fit us and created us to fit His world.

> **What Do You Think?**
> Since God is the author of the calendar, what are some ways to manage time that will honor Him for that fact?
>
> *Digging Deeper*
> Which of the three *M*s of *m*odifying your environment, *m*aking a commitment to another, and *m*onitoring your behavior would work best for you in overcoming time management challenges? Why?

15. And let them be for lights in the firmament of the heaven to give light upon the earth: and it was so.

We should catch a little of the wonder and awe of the ancient author here. He understands the value and purpose of light (created on day one), of heavenly *lights* (created on day four), and of the need for *light upon the earth*. We are created to be creatures of light, both physically and spiritually. The more science learns about sunlight, the more we realize our dependence on it for life.

Without the God-provided light that bathes our world on a regular basis, we would lead a sad existence—if any existence at all. The lighting of our world is a testimony to God's love and care for us. It is an exciting comparison, then, for Jesus to take the role of "light of the world" (John 8:12), God's loving answer to our spiritual darkness.

B. Sun and Moon Created (vv. 16-19)

16. And God made two great lights; the greater light to rule the day, and the lesser light to rule the night: he made the stars also.

The created order has three classifications of observable heavenly *lights*. First we have *the greater light*, the sun, which rules *the day*. This does not imply that the sun comes out when there is daylight. Rather, it's the other way around: the sun defines and causes the day.

Likewise, *the lesser light*, the moon, defines a darker period, *the night*. Nights are not without some light, given the shadows we observe when the moon is bright. Even on nights of a new moon, *the stars* provide light, although dimly.

While we see God's intentional patterns in creation here, we should also notice that the descriptions are observational, from the perspective of the author or any other human. It is silly to criticize this portrayal by saying that some of the stars we see are far bigger and brighter than our sun. It doesn't appear that way from the author's viewpoint, nor from any other unaided human viewpoint today. Stars are tiny in the amount of light they shed on the earth. This is the point.

HOW TO SAY IT

Deuteronomy	Due-ter-*ahn*-uh-me.
Leviticus	Leh-*vit*-ih-kus.
Pentateuch	*Pen*-ta-teuk.

17, 18. And God set them in the firmament of the heaven to give light upon the earth, and to rule over the day and over the night, and to divide the light from the darkness: and God saw that it was good.

These celestial lights—sun, moon, and stars—are placed *in the firmament of the heaven* by God to provide various degrees of *light upon the earth*. Their intensity causes the distinction between daytime and nighttime. All of them counteract *darkness*, the absence of light. In this sense, they are testimonies to the presence of God in our world, for we are never without a heavenly light source.

As at the end of the previous day of creation, the author notes that God observes what He has created and approves by designating it as *good*. It is pleasing to Him and beneficial to us.

What Do You Think?
What responsibilities do we have to distinguish between moral light and darkness?
Digging Deeper
What are some dangers that come with accepting this task? How do we manage them?

❧ DRAWN TO THE LIGHT ❧

Missionaries who live off the grid have a unique appreciation for light and for the creatures that are drawn to it. I remember huddling at night under a mosquito net with my old e-reader, reading with a small light. Every little bug that could fit through the mosquito net's holes would join me, irrepressibly drawn to the light. One time a battalion of tiny spiders began spinning their webs on the little light in my hands.

Another time my wife came stumbling into the room. "There's something in my ear!" she cried. She had been in a deep sleep and wasn't fully coherent, but I heard her say, "I can hear it breathing!"

I didn't see anything. I tried carefully probing with tweezers (which was difficult as she kept freaking out with shuddering spasms). As I held the flashlight over her ear, I tried to suggest that perhaps she had been dreaming and hadn't yet fully awoken. Then the insect's legs emerged from her ear, and a little beetle finished its journey out toward the flashlight. After it had found a more appropriate habitat, my wife thought the beetle, which had intricate colored markings on its tiny shell, was quite beautiful.

God's creation is amazing in its diversity. I shared an unlikely camaraderie with the creepy crawlies as we clustered around my little light under the mosquito net. We were fellow creatures created by God, attracted to the mysterious phenomenon of light that He created first. More importantly, we remember that spiritually we are "the children of light, and the children of the day: we are not of the night, nor of darkness" (1 Thessalonians 5:5). —D. G.

19. And the evening and the morning were the fourth day.

As before, the cycle of what makes up a day is noted. The Bible's way of marking a day begins with sundown, a pattern still observed by Jews. It is not so much that night commences the new day as that the setting of the sun ends the old day. On the various possible meanings of *day*, see commentary on Genesis 1:5 in lesson 1.

> *What Do You Think?*
> What one improvement can you make to imitate better God's deliberate and rhythmic approach to work and creativity?
> *Digging Deeper*
> What forces make it difficult for you to maintain a creative rhythm? What strategies can you adopt to overcome those challenges?

II. Day Five
(GENESIS 1:20-23)

A. Avians and Aquatics Created (vv. 20, 21)

20. And God said, Let the waters bring forth abundantly the moving creature that hath life, and fowl that may fly above the earth in the open firmament of heaven.

The ancient person sees the world in three parts: the watery world of seas, lakes, and rivers; the habitable world of dry ground; and the above-ground world of the atmosphere. Day five of creation begins, as the others have, with God speaking. On this day, God speaks into existence the living animals for the watery world and the sky. As before, this is presented from an observational perspective—what the author or any reader could see.

21. And God created great whales, and every living creature that moveth, which the waters brought forth abundantly, after their kind, and every winged fowl after his kind: and God saw that it was good.

The unpolluted and unfished *waters* of the ancient world teem with life. This includes water creatures of massive size, something the author (Moses) is aware of on some level. Has he heard of *great whales* that have breached the surface of the ocean or washed up on a beach? God's creation has variety that is barely imaginable for us. After hundreds of years of study, scientists are still discovering and classifying new water creatures (compare Psalm 104:25).

The author also acknowledges creation of the creatures of the atmospheric world, the birds. He knows that most creatures do not have the capability of flight—only those with wings. These make up a special and wonderful category of God's *good* created animals.

The author also gives another insight into the wonder and awe of the ancient person when it comes to beholding God's created order: the reproductive capability of water creatures and birds. This is their ability to produce offspring *after his/their kind*. Why does a sparrow always reproduce sparrows, not eagles sometimes? Why does a trout always reproduce trout, not barracudas sometimes? This is part of God's created order as observed by the author, and it is marvelous for him. As we appreciate the enormous variety of God's creatures, we should also understand the boundaries for variation He has built into each one.

❧ LIGHT AND LIFE ❧

There is a clear relationship between light and life in the creation account of Genesis. I recently stumbled across a book by scientist Michael Gross that explores this relationship from the perspective

Visual for Lesson 2. *Start a discussion by pointing to this visual as you ask, "Where is your favorite place to marvel at the wonders of God's creation?"*

of modern secular science. After noting the vital linkage between light and life, he further reflects that even reading the page requires light reflecting onto retinas and being converted into nerve signals.

Given modern humanity's reliance on light for energy, information, and guidance, Gross concludes that it's quite understandable that ancient cultures worshipped the sun. But despite his tone of wonder as he contemplates light, Gross takes a nonreligious stance himself.

I share this sense of wonder at the complex relationship between light and life. But for me, these observations elicit praise for the Creator of light and life. When I read of the outpouring of God's creative activity in Genesis 1, from the great lights of the heavens to the vast diversity of life in the land, sea, and sky, my heart joins the ancient psalmist's in thanking the Lord, the Creator of all. See Psalm 136:1-9.   —D. G.

B. Abundant Supply Created (vv. 22, 23)

22. And God blessed them, saying, Be fruitful, and multiply, and fill the waters in the seas, and let fowl multiply in the earth.

How many of each type of fish or bird does God create to get things started? We don't know, but we do see that His plan includes multiplication of these creatures. He intends that the salt waters and fresh waters be filled with appropriate creatures. God intends that His created variety of birds *multiply* and spread throughout *the earth*

(compare Genesis 8:17). It is a tragedy when a species becomes extinct because of human behavior.

23. And the evening and the morning were the fifth day.

As the day ends by marking the cycle of *the evening and the morning*, the sustaining earth has been stocked in its waters and its air.

III. Day Six
(GENESIS 1:24, 25)
A. Animals Created (v. 24)

24a. And God said, Let the earth bring forth the living creature after his kind.

God speaks again, on day six, to call into existence specific components of His overall created order. On this day God addresses the dry land, the earth itself. This will be the home of God's ultimate creation, human beings, later in this same day (Genesis 1:26-30).

24b. Cattle, and creeping thing, and beast of the earth after his kind: and it was so.

There are three general categories of land animals presented. The first, *cattle*, is a generic term that means more than cows. It generally refers to herded animals, and here it has the sense of domesticated livestock as distinct from wild animals (see below; also see the distinction in Leviticus 25:7). This may include goats and sheep, which are popular choices among cultures dependent on herding. Later in the history of Israel, it will be animals from this category that are considered ritually clean for food or sacrifice (see Leviticus 11).

The second category, the *creeping thing*, refers to creatures that live on the ground, including reptiles and snakes. Such animals will not be considered clean when the food laws are instituted for Israel (Leviticus 11:42). It is also likely that the tempting serpent of a coming story (Genesis 3:1) is included in this category.

The third category, the *beast of the earth*, refers to wild animals. We might divide these into carnivores (example: lions), herbivores (example: gazelles), and omnivores (example: bears). Such animals might be hunted for food, but they are not part of a nomadic herd or a located farm.

B. Animal Categories (v. 25)

25. And God made the beast of the earth after his kind, and cattle after their kind, and every thing that creepeth upon the earth after his kind: and God saw that it was good.

As with the creatures of the sea and air, the land creatures are made with the capacity to reproduce *after his/their kind*. Again, God finishes creating these three categories and sees His work as *good*.

We should notice there are many missing, undiscussed animals. These categories are quite general and not intended to be exhaustive. What about rodents—are they creeping things? What about insects? What about worms? Or, some might ask, what about dinosaurs?

The silence of the text on such matters is just that: no information. It does not imply ignorance or avoidance. The author tells the story he wants to tell; and just as he does not divide the "stars" into planets, comets, meteors, and distant suns, he does not give more than a brief description of the creative activities of God on each of the days.

What Do You Think?
Where will you unhurriedly allow creation to inspire you to worship the Creator this week?
Digging Deeper
Which of the following texts speak to you most forcefully regarding the need to worship God as Creator: Job 9:9; 38:31; Psalm 19:1-3; 95:4-6; 104:5-24; Isaiah 40:26; Amos 5:8; Romans 1:20? Why?

Conclusion

A. For the Beauty of the Earth

The old hymn "For the Beauty of the Earth" was a favorite in years past. This hymn spoke to me when I was a child growing up in remote, mountainous Idaho. We can see God's power, wisdom, and intellect in the lofty mountains, the sparkling streams, the lush forests, the soaring fir trees, the tranquil lakes, the majestic deer, the glorious eagles, and many other features of our earth.

The second line of the hymn is "for the glory of the skies." This is one of the lessons of Gene-

sis 1, that God's glory is shown in His creation of the heavens as well as the earth. More recent worship songs such as "God of Wonders" continue this tradition of celebrating God as Creator of a universe filled with endless marvels for human observers.

Science, rather than being the enemy of faith, has shown us the wonders of the heavens in breathtaking pictures from the Hubble Space Telescope. Going the other direction, advanced microscopic technology of "inner space" has shown the intricate designs of God on the tiniest levels.

The Genesis account of creation is brief and beautiful (unlike scientific treatises of our day). It gives us a hint of the wonder and awe that ancient men and women experienced when they contemplated the world they inhabited. They were convinced that this ordered and beautiful universe came into being through the acts of a Creator (Job 9:9; Psalm 8:3; Proverbs 3:19; Isaiah 40:26; etc.).

The marvels of creation were not only the visible, tangible things, but also the systems of days, months, and years that followed patterns that could be analyzed and then predicted. It was for later observers to understand that the angle of the earth's axis, its period of daily rotations, and its yearly circumnavigation of the sun were all essential to sustaining the ecosystems that permit life.

There would be no life without God's plan and provision. Genesis, however, teaches us that life did not arise on our planet as random adaptations to existing conditions, but that the earth was created to sustain the life that God intended and designed. That includes us human beings, the topic of next week's lesson.

B. Prayer

Creator God, we are learning about our world at a furious pace. May we channel our increased knowledge into more opportunities to contemplate You and Your marvelous designs. You are truly the God of wonders, and we give You praise and glory. We pray in Jesus' name. Amen.

C. Thought to Remember

If creation is not an endless wonder to you, you're not paying attention!

INVOLVEMENT LEARNING

Enhance your lesson with KJV Bible Student *(from your curriculum supplier) and the reproducible activity page (at www.standardlesson.com or in the back of the* KJV Standard Lesson Commentary Deluxe Edition*).*

Into the Lesson

Provide each participant with a portion of clay or drawing paper; challenge students model or draw a creature of their own design. After a few minutes, have students describe their creatures, including how they move and communicate.

Then pose this question: "What do these creatures teach you about their creators?" (Expect humorous responses.) Make a transition by saying, "Learning about things God created is good; learning what they imply about their Creator is even better. Let's do both."

Into the Word

Say, "Genesis explains God's orderly creation of the universe. Last week's lesson described the first three days of creation. Now it's time to consider the next three." Write these headings on the board:

Creation   *Purpose*   *God*

For each section of the lesson's text below, jot students' responses under the appropriate heading.

Have a volunteer read Genesis 1:14-19. Ask students to (1) identify what is created, (2) describe their purposes, and (3) explain what this aspect of creation reveals about the character of God. If students are slow to respond to the third, don't jump in to fill the silence too quickly! Eventual responses should be along the lines of how light testifies of God's love and presence.

Have a volunteer read Genesis 1:20-23. Then challenge students to identify, describe, and explain as above. Inquire whether any students have unique experiences with creatures of the sea or sky, and invite sharing of those experiences. Ask students to describe how these creatures reveal the character of God.

Move to the next segment of text by saying, "The skies and seas have been filled. Next is the provision for animals on dry land. Our lesson will cover only the first part of the sixth day of creation. The new day begins as God speaks again."

Have another student read Genesis 1:24, 25. Then challenge students to identify, describe, and explain as before. Ask participants to describe the three categories of land animals; use the commentary to correct misperceptions. Note that the categories are not meant to be exhaustive.

Option. Distribute copies of the "Six Days of Creation" activity from the reproducible page, which you can download. Form students into small groups to complete as indicated. This activity will help learners see the bigger picture of six days of creation by connecting last week's lesson with this week's.

Sum up by saying, "Genesis teaches us that life did not arise on our planet as a random adaptation of preexisting material. Rather, the earth was created to sustain the life that God intended and designed."

Into Life

Go to a window or lead class members outside to a place where they will have a striking view of God's creation. (*Alternative.* Provide pictures of scenery and animals.) Say, "When God declared aspects of His creation to be 'good,' that carried a sense of something's being excellent, just right, as God intended. What do you see that strikes you as particularly 'good'?" Encourage free discussion.

Brainstorm reasons to be good stewards of God's creation. For each reason, ask students to state a way they can make that reason a reality. After returning to your classroom (if your class went outside), ask each student to write a "Creation Declaration" that describes a way he or she will honor God for His creation in the coming week.

Alternative. Distribute copies of the "For the Beauty of the Earth" activity from the reproducible page. Allow time to complete as indicated. Encourage sharing of results.

God Creates People

Devotional Reading: Psalm 103:1-5, 11-14
Background Scripture: Genesis 1:26–2:7

Genesis 1:26-31

26 And God said, Let us make man in our image, after our likeness: and let them have dominion over the fish of the sea, and over the fowl of the air, and over the cattle, and over all the earth, and over every creeping thing that creepeth upon the earth.

27 So God created man in his own image, in the image of God created he him; male and female created he them.

28 And God blessed them, and God said unto them, Be fruitful, and multiply, and replenish the earth, and subdue it: and have dominion over the fish of the sea, and over the fowl of the air, and over every living thing that moveth upon the earth.

29 And God said, Behold, I have given you every herb bearing seed, which is upon the face of all the earth, and every tree, in the which is the fruit of a tree yielding seed; to you it shall be for meat.

30 And to every beast of the earth, and to every fowl of the air, and to every thing that creepeth upon the earth, wherein there is life, I have given every green herb for meat: and it was so.

31 And God saw every thing that he had made, and, behold, it was very good. And the evening and the morning were the sixth day.

Genesis 2:4-7

4 These are the generations of the heavens and of the earth when they were created, in the day that the LORD God made the earth and the heavens,

5 And every plant of the field before it was in the earth, and every herb of the field before it grew: for the LORD God had not caused it to rain upon the earth, and there was not a man to till the ground.

6 But there went up a mist from the earth, and watered the whole face of the ground.

7 And the LORD God formed man of the dust of the ground, and breathed into his nostrils the breath of life; and man became a living soul.

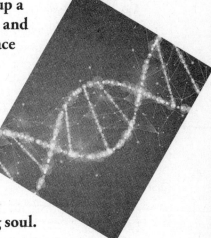

Key Verse

God created man in his own image, in the image of God created he him; male and female created he them.
—**Genesis 1:27**

God's World and God's People

Unit 1: God Creates the World
Lessons 1–5

Lesson Aims

After participating in this lesson, each learner will be able to:

1. Identify aspects of the image of God in humanity.

2. Contrast biblical with nonbiblical notions of the nature of humanity.

3. Express one way he or she will honor the dominion mandate.

Lesson Outline

Introduction
    A. Identity Crisis
    B. Lesson Context
I. Plan for Humans (Genesis 1:26-31)
    A. God's Image (vv. 26, 27)
       Children of Promise
    B. God's Blessing (v. 28)
    C. God's Provision (vv. 29, 30)
       Because God Said
    D. God's Assessment (v. 31)
II. Life for the First Human (Genesis 2:4-7)
    A. Absence of Water and Man (vv. 4, 5)
    B. Presence of Water and Man (vv. 6, 7)
Conclusion
    A. Identity Confirmed
    B. Prayer
    C. Thought to Remember

Introduction

A. Identity Crisis

In the mid–twentieth century, psychologist Erik Erikson coined the term "identity crisis" to describe a developmental issue that occurs during adolescence. That phrase has since been used to describe the common plight of people wrestling with the questions "Who am I?" and "Why am I here?" The early theologian Augustine of Hippo (AD 354–430) addressed this issue as he prayed, "You have made us for yourself, O Lord, and our hearts are restless until they find their rest in you" (*Confessions* 1.1).

Augustine's words reflect the biblical texts we are exploring today. Genesis 1:26-31 and 2:4-7 teach us that God created people in His image at the apex of His creation. As His image bearers, we are precious in God's sight, having received an extraordinary status and role within creation.

B. Lesson Context

The first 25 verses of Genesis 1 narrate concisely God's forming of the cosmos through His spoken word. In successive days, God created light (1:3-5); the heavenly firmament (1:6-8); the seas and dry land (1:9-13); the sun, moon, and stars (1:14-19); living creatures that inhabit the waters and the heavens (1:20-23); and land animals (1:24, 25). The text's focus throughout is on the planet Earth, either directly or indirectly.

The recounting of the first through fourth days in Genesis grows longer with successive days. A reversal of sorts occurs with the fifth day of creation, as the narration becomes shorter (Genesis 1:20-23). The narration then lengthens dramatically to relate what happens on the sixth day: creation of land animals and people. By allotting only two verses to the creation of land animals on this day (1:24, 25), the author appears in a hurry to get to his focus: the creation of humanity (1:26-31). Not included in the record are any blessings or commands God gave the land animals to multiply, as He had done to creatures of the air and sea in 1:22; compare 8:17).

The author (Moses) presents God's seeing the creation of land animals as "good" even though, like on day three, he has not finished describing the creations of the day. God has created some good things during the sixth day, but there is more and greater yet to come.

I. Plan for Humans
(Genesis 1:26-31)

The focus of the narrative up to Genesis 1:26 has narrowed from the vast universe God created to things of the planet Earth specifically. The pace of the narrative now seems to slow down as the author narrates the pinnacle of creation.

A. God's Image (vv. 26, 27)

26a. And God said, Let us make man in our image, after our likeness.

Something new and significant is happening as God now speaks in a new manner. Up to this point, His words on each new day have begun with "Let there be . . ." (Genesis 1:3, 6, 14) or "Let the . . ." (1:9, 11, 20, 24). But now His creation declaration is more reflective in nature: *Let us make man in our image, after our likeness.*

Many new-covenant believers have understood these plural pronouns as trinitarian in nature. But the original audience lacked the revelation we have to understand them that way. The Old Testament is essentially silent on the triune nature of God.

It is the New Testament record that ultimately reveals God as being three-in-one (John 1; etc.). That record will make it possible for believers in the first century and later to contemplate a plurality in the oneness of God's essence (compare Deuteronomy 6:4; Isaiah 44:8; 45:5, 14).

That leaves open the question of how the earliest readers interpret the plural pronouns. One proposal is that God is speaking to angelic beings in His heavenly court. Another view is that the plurals are to be understood as a "plural of majesty" by which God refers to the fullness of His power and identity. An illustration of this type of plural is the quotation "We are not amused," supposedly uttered by Queen Victoria after hearing a story that was not as funny as the storyteller thought it to be (compare Genesis 11:7; Isaiah 6:8).

An enduring issue is determining what it means to be created in God's image, after His likeness. That the words *image* and *likeness* refer to different things is unlikely. First, there is no *and* between *image* and *likeness* in the original text. Second, the same Hebrew words translated *image* and *likeness* appear in Genesis 5:3 to refer to the same thing. Thus the two words should be seen as synonyms combined to add intensity.

It is problematic to identify the image of God with one of God's specific qualities. God is complex, so His image must also be complex. But we are able to get a better grasp if we approach the topic from two angles: those of *form* and *content*.

The form of the image of God is personhood. This speaks to the intellectual, volitional, moral, creative, and religious capacities that animals do not have. As God exercises His creative will, so also human beings alone among earth's creatures have the ability to think of complex things that don't exist, then take deliberate steps to make them a reality. A beaver may go through a sequence of steps to make a dam, but stacking a pile of sticks is not the same as building a hospital!

Content, for its part, speaks to relationship with God (in terms of servants-in-fellowship) and relationship to the world (in terms of dominion-in-stewardship). It is the form part of the image that makes the content part of the image possible.

Regarding the servant aspect, the portrayal of God in the creation narrative highlights a certain correspondence between humans and God that allows us to have a relationship with Him. Regarding the dominion part of the content part of the image, that's addressed in our next verse.

26b. And let them have dominion over the fish of the sea, and over the fowl of the air, and

HOW TO SAY IT

Augustine	*Aw*-gus-*teen* or Aw-*gus*-tin.
Elohim *(Hebrew)*	El-oh-*heem*.
euthanasia	*yoo*-thuh-**nay**-zhuh.
Nyssa	*Nee*-sah.
Rafflesia arnoldii	Reh-*flee*-zhuh ar-*nol*-dee-eye.
sequoia	sih-*kwoi*-uh.
Yahweh *(Hebrew)*	*Yah*-weh.

Visual for Lesson 3. *Start a discussion by pointing to this visual as you pose the* What Do You Think? *question on this page.*

over the cattle, and over all the earth, and over every creeping thing that creepeth upon the earth.

God bids us to rule over His creation, a task elegantly described as having *dominion*. David will reflect further on this centuries later in Psalm 8:6-8. In creating, the Lord worked and exercised dominion, and He invites us to participate with Him in exercising that dominion as we ourselves work. This is an issue of stewardship. (On understandings of *cattle* and *creeping thing*, see commentary on Genesis 1:24 in lesson 2.)

27. So God created man in his own image, in the image of God created he him; male and female created he them.

The image of God in which humanity is created includes *male and female*. That we exist in community reflects the communal nature of God that we see taught more clearly in the New Testament. The Father, Son, and Spirit are one, yet they are clearly distinct persons. And though male and female together form one humanity, there is a clear, God-intended distinction between male and female.

God's statement identifying us as being in His image points to humanity's exalted place. Some students also see the triple-usage of the verb *created* as significant. The word in the original language being translated thus occurs only eight times between Genesis 1:1 and 5:1, and fully half of those are connected with the final and most sig-

nificant aspect of creation: the creation of God's image bearers (three times here and once in 5:1).

It is difficult to overstate the significance of "the image of God" within Judeo-Christian ethics. Without the belief that humans are morally endowed creations of a morally good God, there is nothing to ensure the dignity and value of any and every person—born or unborn, healthy or ill.

Whatever value humans possess comes from the sovereign Creator, to whom we are accountable and responsible. The physical, economic, social, and cultural criteria by which secular humanism establishes and defends personhood are arbitrary, changing, and unreliable. Christians must shape their response to moral issues such as abortion, euthanasia, and racism on the foundation of humanity's value and special status of being made in the image of God.

> **What Do You Think?**
> How will being created in God's image affect how you treat people you dislike?
> *Digging Deeper*
> Which New Testament passages do you find most helpful in that regard? Why?

❧ *CHILDREN OF PROMISE* ❧

An online search of "baby names" produces over 33 million results. Expectant parents the world over eagerly hunt for the ideal name for their new arrival (or arrivals). Emma, Olivia, Ava, Caleb, Liam, Noah . . . To this eagerness is added the anxiety with regard to the various uncertainties that parents-to-be experience.

Given the fact that God has emotions (Numbers 22:22; Psalm 59:8; etc.), have you ever wondered what He was experiencing when He was ready to announce the arrival of His first children, the first humans? Scripture does not give us the backstory details, but the written account of creation does declare the achieved ideal after the fact of creation.

God had hardwired divine values into the first people, and those innate values are passed down to all humans, including us today (see Romans 1:18, 19; 2:15). Christians are "heirs of God, and

joint-heirs with Christ" (8:17). We are the "children of promise" (Galatians 4:28). What a reason to rejoice in the "glory of his inheritance in the saints" (Ephesians 1:18)!
—B. L.

B. God's Blessing (v. 28)

28. And God blessed them, and God said unto them, Be fruitful, and multiply, and replenish the earth, and subdue it: and have dominion over the fish of the sea, and over the fowl of the air, and over every living thing that moveth upon the earth.

God's blessing-command spoken over humanity reflects what He has already spoken over creatures of sea and sky (Genesis 1:22). It resembles a number of other fruitfulness-blessing statements found throughout this book (9:1, 7; 17:20; 28:3; 35:11; 48:4). Together these demonstrate that rearing children is an integral part of God's plan for humanity. God desires that the whole earth be inhabited (Isaiah 45:18) and experience His glory (40:5; 42:10-13).

To the notion of *dominion* used earlier, God now adds the verb *subdue*. The word in the original language appears elsewhere in a positive sense in contexts of order and security resulting from the subjugation of enemies (Numbers 32:20-22; 1 Chronicles 22:18; etc.). It also occurs in a negative sense of bondage and enslavement (2 Chronicles 28:10; Jeremiah 34:11). All this suggests that the focus is the idea of control. Those who are granted this control are, naturally, accountable to God for stewardship in ordering and developing the resources available.

What has come to be called "the dominion mandate" forms a basis for science and technology; it should never be thought a license for careless and abusive use of natural resources. We exercise dominion only as the image or representatives of God in the world, not as creation's owners. Because we don't own creation (Psalm 95:5), we have no right to exploit it in such a way that brings discredit on God. We should exercise the responsibility toward the environment that God expects (contrast Deuteronomy 20:19, 20 with 2 Kings 3:18, 19; God's expectations are different because of subsequent uses anticipated for the resources).

The extent to which we are able to exercise this dominion is now limited because of sin (see lesson 5). However, Christ, who is the image of the invisible God (2 Corinthians 4:4; Colossians 1:15), has come as the last Adam to achieve dominion (1 Corinthians 15:22, 45-49; compare Hebrews 2:5-18). In Him we have put on the new self and are growing into the image and likeness of God (Colossians 1:15; 3:9, 10).

> *What Do You Think?*
> What steps should you take to determine your responsibilities in the stewardship of God's creation?
> *Digging Deeper*
> What resources will you consult for understanding those responsibilities?

C. God's Provision (vv. 29, 30)

29, 30. And God said, Behold, I have given you every herb bearing seed, which is upon the face of all the earth, and every tree, in the which is the fruit of a tree yielding seed; to you it shall be for meat. And to every beast of the earth, and to every fowl of the air, and to every thing that creepeth upon the earth, wherein there is life, I have given every green herb for meat: and it was so.

The repetition of *every* highlights the fact that God is the faithful and generous provider of sustenance to both man and animals. Humans will eat from *seed*-bearing plants and *fruit* trees, and animals will consume *every green* plant. After the flood, people will receive authority from God to eat animal flesh as well (Genesis 9:3), a new source of protein.

> *What Do You Think?*
> How will awareness of God's generosity result in one specific change in the way you live?
> *Digging Deeper*
> At what times are you more aware of God's generosity than at others? Why? Explain your answer in light of Proverbs 22:9; Matthew 5:45; 20:1-16; and 2 Corinthians 9:6-15.

The largest flower in the world, the Rafflesia arnoldii, can reach three feet in diameter. In California's Sequoia National Park, the giant redwoods stretch up to 280 feet in height. We can trace all the features of our planet's vegetation back to two words: "God said."

With an exacting "God said," sky, land, and seas stood to attention. Plants and trees took root in God's care. Seed-bearing plants and fruit trees flourished. God had already planned their purposes and futures, including those of the enormous Rafflesia arnoldii and giant redwoods. Better yet, He planned the ideal purpose and future of His children.

When the timeless Creator spoke the world's first foliage into life, He had already pictured not only their ranges of sizes and features, but ours as well. The Creator knows all the details of each person's being, having tenderly formed us in our mothers' wombs (Psalm 139:13). What a joy to know that above all plants and animals, we are precious in His sight!   —B. L.

D. God's Assessment (v. 31)

31. And God saw every thing that he had made, and, behold, it was very good. And the evening and the morning were the sixth day.

God had previously assessed elements of creation as "good" (Genesis 1:4, 10, 12, 18, 21, 25). He now evaluates His creation in light of the addition of humanity, and He pronounces it *very good*. The exclamation *behold* both expresses God's excitement and invites the reader also to view creation from God's perspective. Creation, before the intrusion of human sin in Genesis 3, fully reflected God's intent. Humanity now awaits the new heaven and new earth, to appear when God's redemptive purposes, initiated in the work of Christ, are consummated (Revelation 21:1-5).

II. Life for the First Human
(Genesis 2:4-7)

The intervening text not included in today's lesson summarizes what God does on the seventh day: nothing! He rests from His work.

A. Absence of Water and Man (vv. 4, 5)

4. These are the generations of the heavens and of the earth when they were created, in the day that the Lord God made the earth and the heavens.

We come to what many characterize as a second account of the creation of man. This section, however, is better thought of as a more detailed account of what Genesis 1 described in the format of panorama.

The phrase *these are the generations* is a formulaic section-header (compare Genesis 5:1; 10:1; 11:10; 25:12, 19; 36:1, 9; 37:2). This introductory statement carries the sense of "This is what happened concerning . . ."

A feature of the Bible, first occurring in the verse before us, is the use of the divine name *Yahweh*; this is traditionally rendered, in small capitals, as Lord in our English Bibles. Previously, God has been called only by the Hebrew name *Elohim*, a title conveying His transcendence and power. The name *Yahweh*, on the other hand, emphasizes His eternal existence and covenantal presence with His people. The combined name—seen three times in Genesis 2:4-7 and dozens of times elsewhere as "Lord God"—is thus particularly powerful.

> *What Do You Think?*
> How might the doubled name "Lord God" influence how you relate to Him?
>
> *Digging Deeper*
> Does the triple designation "Lord God Almighty" in Revelation 4:8; 11:17; 15:3; 16:7; 21:22 change your answer? Why, or why not?

5. And every plant of the field before it was in the earth, and every herb of the field before it grew: for the Lord God had not caused it to rain upon the earth, and there was not a man to till the ground.

The language here suggests that the writer is not looking back to the creation of vegetation in Genesis 1, but rather is previewing the cultivation that will occur in the Garden of Eden and after the fall. Two features lend support for this view. First, the phrase *herb of the field* appears again in

Genesis 3:18 to designate what humanity will eat after the fall. Second, whereas the *rain* anticipated in verse 5 will be a blessing, it is an instrument of judgment in Noah's day (7:4). These verses thus may set the stage for the more detailed account of man's creation that follows, which complements the general description in 1:26, 27.

B. Presence of Water and Man (vv. 6, 7)

6, 7a. But there went up a mist from the earth, and watered the whole face of the ground. And the LORD God formed man of the dust of the ground.

The exact nature of the *mist* that rises *from the earth* is unclear. The underlying Hebrew word occurs in the Old Testament only here and in Job 36:27, there translated "vapour." Taken together, the idea may be that of evaporated water that condenses to a liquid state to water *the whole face of the ground*. Perhaps the water mixed with *dust* provides clay *the Lord God* uses to create man (compare Job 10:9; 33:6; Isaiah 45:9; Romans 9:21).

The sound of the Hebrew word for *man*, which is *Adam* (Genesis 2:19), resembles closely the word for *ground*. Thus the lofty image of being created in God's likeness (1:26) is now tempered with the reality of what constitutes the human body, its humble origin. "The first man is of the earth, earthy" (1 Corinthians 15:47).

7b. And breathed into his nostrils the breath of life.

Some have proposed that for God to breathe *the breath of life* into the man is to place a tiny portion of God's very own essence into a human. This is wrong. When 2 Peter 1:4 speaks of being "partakers of the divine nature," the meaning is that we share in those attributes of God that He grants us as His image bearers (example: 1 Peter 1:15, 16). No part of our essence as humans is uncreated.

7c. And man became a living soul.

On first reading, this phrase may lead one to believe that it is at this point that the first human receives that element of his nature that sets him apart from the animals: the soul. But the original language behind the translation *became a living soul* is identical in the descriptions of other crea-

tures in Genesis 1:20, 24, 30; 2:19). We are indeed a combination of physical and spiritual (Matthew 10:28), but that fact cannot be established from this verse.

Conclusion

A. Identity Confirmed

The following is attributed to Gregory of Nyssa (AD 335–395):

> In this world I have discovered the two affirmations that man is nothing and that man is great. If you consider nature alone, he is nothing and has no value; but if you regard the honor with which he has been created, man is something great.

Christians should view themselves and others as special creations of God and objects of His love and concern. Because all are made in our Lord's image, all deserve respect, dignity, honor, and care, regardless of social status, accomplishments, etc. Moreover, as God's image bearers, our work is a cooperative enterprise with Him. Our work is exalted, holy, and spiritual. May we treat it as such!

> **What Do You Think?**
> What will the expression "of Christ, who is the image of God" in 2 Corinthians 4:4 motivate you to do differently in the week ahead? Why?
> *Digging Deeper*
> Consider how we are like and unlike Christ as image bearers.

B. Prayer

Father, we praise You as ones having been formed in your image, unique and loved. Grant us to see the value You have already bestowed abundantly on us and others. Give us eyes to see the stewardship we have from You in our work. We pray this in the name of the one into whose image You are transforming us—our Lord Jesus. Amen.

C. Thought to Remember

Live up to the meaning
of Romans 8:29.

INVOLVEMENT LEARNING

Enhance your lesson with KJV Bible Student *(from your curriculum supplier) and the reproducible activity page (at www.standardlesson.com or in the back of the* KJV Standard Lesson Commentary Deluxe Edition*).*

Into the Lesson

Display the letters *E, E, L, O, P, P*. Ask learners to suggest as many words as they can create; jot responses on the board.

When responses are no longer forthcoming, say, "Creating these words was probably easy for most of you, as easy as it was for God to take elements of His creation and bring *people* into existence. In creating words from random letters, you demonstrate you share an attribute of God, having been made in His image: the ability to form words. Let's explore further the idea of being made in God's likeness."

Into the Word

Recruit four students to read the text aloud: two to alternate verses of Genesis 1:26-31 and two to do the same with 2:4-7. Then pose this question for whole-class discussion: *What does it mean and not mean to be created in the image of God, in His likeness?* Jot responses on the board. After a few minutes, offer these observations: "We should not identify the image of God with one specific quality. God is complex, so His image must also be complex. The core concept in an image, or likeness, is correspondence. God created someone who would correspond to and relate to Him in ways other elements of creation cannot. A likeness is in some sense a similarity, but it is not an exact duplicate."

After summarizing the issues of form and content of the image from page 27 ask, "Do these factors cause you to modify your responses or add to them?" Encourage free discussion. (Expect responses that address the abilities to exercise creative willfulness, language, moral discernment, etc.) Request clarification and Scripture backup where appropriate. (*Option.* This can be a small-group discussion.)

Option. Distribute copies of the "In His Own Image" activity from the reproducible page, which

you can download. Have students work individually for not more than one minute to complete. Then call time and discuss.

Next, divide the class in half and give each group a handout (you create) with one of the following summary statements of an ancient school of philosophy. Have group members compare and contrast the view with the text for today.

Epicurean Group: Modest pleasure, meaning the absence of bodily pain and troubles of the soul, is the end and aim of life. *Stoic Group:* Freedom from suffering through being objective and exercising clear judgment is the purpose of life.

If your class is larger than eight learners, form more groups and give duplicate assignments. Have group spokespersons summarize how their philosophical summary contrasts with today's text. Point out the interaction between Paul and advocates of these philosophies in Acts 17:18-34. Wrap up by quoting Colossians 2:8.

Alternative. Distribute copies of the "Potter and Clay" activity from the reproducible page. Have learners complete as indicated.

Into Life

Say, "God has given humanity dominion over other earthly creatures. What are some synonyms for the word *dominion*? (Possible responses: control, rule, jurisdiction, authority, etc.) Ask, "How does the dominion mandate apply to you personally?"

After a time of personal sharing, give each learner an index card (you prepare) on which appears the following:

My dominion over animals and plant life implies that I should _____. So to glorify God and submit obediently to Him, I will _____.

Suggest that learners place this card where they will see it daily in the week ahead.

God Creates the Family

DEVOTIONAL READING: Leviticus 19:11-18
BACKGROUND SCRIPTURE: Genesis 2:18-24; 4:1, 2

GENESIS 2:18-24

18 And the LORD God said, It is not good that the man should be alone; I will make him an help meet for him.

19 And out of the ground the LORD God formed every beast of the field, and every fowl of the air; and brought them unto Adam to see what he would call them: and whatsoever Adam called every living creature, that was the name thereof.

20 And Adam gave names to all cattle, and to the fowl of the air, and to every beast of the field; but for Adam there was not found an help meet for him.

21 And the LORD God caused a deep sleep to fall upon Adam, and he slept: and he took one of his ribs, and closed up the flesh instead thereof;

22 And the rib, which the LORD God had taken from man, made he a woman, and brought her unto the man.

23 And Adam said, This is now bone of my bones, and flesh of my flesh: she shall be called Woman, because she was taken out of Man.

24 Therefore shall a man leave his father and his mother, and shall cleave unto his wife: and they shall be one flesh.

GENESIS 4:1, 2

1 And Adam knew Eve his wife; and she conceived, and bare Cain, and said, I have gotten a man from the LORD.

2 And she again bare his brother Abel. And Abel was a keeper of sheep, but Cain was a tiller of the ground.

KEY VERSE

Therefore shall a man leave his father and his mother, and shall cleave unto his wife: and they shall be one flesh. —**Genesis 2:24**

GOD'S WORLD AND GOD'S PEOPLE

Unit 1: God Creates the World

LESSONS 1–5

LESSON AIMS

After participating in this lesson, each learner will be able to:

1. Describe the situation that led to the creation of woman.

2. Explain God's larger purposes in creating a woman for the man.

3. Express appreciation to a member of his or her family in light of today's text.

LESSON OUTLINE

Introduction

A. From Matrimony to Multiplication

Few occasions in life bring as much joy and hope as a wedding. Though unmarried myself, I have had the privilege of officiating five weddings. Especially with a close-up view, the sense of wonder, love, and anticipation is palpable. In these extraordinary moments, bride and groom become a new family; and in most weddings the potential for children to expand the family only enhances the excitement.

God commanded humankind to "be fruitful, and multiply, and replenish the earth" (Genesis 1:28), and by all indications people have accepted the challenge. After topping 1 billion sometime in the early 1800s, the human population has risen seven times that amount in the ensuing 200 years. According to the 2015 United Nations' official projections, the world population will grow to 8.5 billion in 2030 and 9.7 billion in 2050.

If He had so chosen, God could have created billions of people to fill the earth from the start. But His mode of operation is to use human beings to partner in His plans. So in remote antiquity, God created a man and a woman. The result was a family to get those plans going. Today's lesson continues our study of God's creative work in the early chapters of Genesis.

B. Lesson Context

In one mythical account from ancient Mesopotamia, humans were created largely to do work that the gods themselves did not want to do. In this scenario, human population growth was desirable for a time. Eventually, though, the multitudes of people became a noisy nuisance to the gods, who grew frustrated and found ways to reduce human population growth.

The Genesis account contrasts sharply with this picture. In Genesis 1, God gave function, order, and meaning to His creation. He consistently saw that His work was good. The pinnacle of His creative efforts was human beings, male and female, in His own image. The "image of God" entails a number of aspects, and among them is being granted dominion over the fish, birds, and all other animals, wild and domesticated (1:26). Though all life on earth is valuable, human life alone is sacred because of God's image.

Also in contrast to the mythical account, God desires people to multiply to the ends of the earth. He created humans out of His goodness, not out of whim or necessity. Human population growth was never a problem; it was a command! God desired humans to flourish, thrive, and give Him glory in abundance.

I. Family Not Possible
(Genesis 2:18-20)
A. Problem Stated (v. 18)

18a. And the Lord God said, It is not good that the man should be alone.

After seven evaluations of creation's elements being "good," we come to something that is *not good*: the solitary existence of *the man*. We glean from this passage that God creates us to interact within a context of companionship and community of our own kind. This aspect of the human makeup also relates to the above-stated directives to multiply and replenish the earth. We do so as we relate to mutual benefit in a wider circle of family, friends, and humanity as a whole. Our quality of life is found in relationships.

The divine assessment *It is not good that the man should be alone* therefore doesn't count the fact that the man is technically not alone given that he already has the companionship of God and the creatures of the garden. The assessment we see here must involve additional purpose of God that the man is unable to fulfill by himself. To "multiply, and replenish the earth" (Genesis 1:27, 28) won't happen if there is only one human.

What Do You Think?
What factors will you consider when determining whether a context of life indicates that being alone for a time is a good thing or not?
Digging Deeper
Use Matthew 6:6; 14:23; Luke 22:41; John 6:15; 1 Corinthians 7:5; etc., to inform your conclusions.

18b. I will make him an help meet for him.

This description establishes both the woman's similarity to the man and her equality with him. In the older English of the *KJV*, the word *meet* carries the idea of "appropriate" (compare Matthew 3:8). The woman to be created will possess all the qualities of humanity and personhood that the man does and will likewise be distinct from every other animal or vegetable.

The description of her as a helper to the man in no way diminishes her dignity or standing, for "help" is a term also used to describe God in relation to people (see Exodus 18:4; Deuteronomy 33:29; Psalm 121:1, 2). The woman will be equal in personhood though complementarily opposite in her procreative role.

B. Solution Pending (vv. 19, 20)

19. And out of the ground the Lord God formed every beast of the field, and every fowl of the air; and brought them unto Adam to see what he would call them: and whatsoever Adam called every living creature, that was the name thereof.

The sequence of events here appears to differ from the account of creation in Genesis 1, in which the animals are created before humans. Questions have therefore arisen about the relationship between the two versions of the story.

A reasonable solution is that one chapter or the other presents a thematic account that is not intended to be taken as chronological. Yet another possibility is that Genesis 2 narrates an additional, special act of creation undertaken for the purpose of presenting the animals for naming. The latter view has a very long history.

Though the animals are *formed* from *the ground* just as the man is, none of them is created in God's image. By naming the animals, the man assigns a function and place to each one, thereby exercising the ruling authority that bearers of the divine image possess (Genesis 1:26). In the process of observing the animal world, Adam certainly recognizes that he is not like them; he undoubtedly realizes his superior nature.

20. And Adam gave names to all cattle, and to the fowl of the air, and to every beast of the

Visual for Lesson 4. *Point to this visual as you ask, "What difference does it make that marriage and family is God's idea and plan, not ours?"*

field; but for Adam there was not found an help meet for him.

The text reveals that the parade of animals involves not only naming them but also searching among them for a suitable companion. Even though all the animals are formed from the same material as the man and by the same good Creator, no animal is adequate as a proper *help*.

We reasonably speculate that the man eventually becomes aware of what God already knows: none of the animals can stand beside the man as his equal, to partner with him in his assigned roles. As Adam gives *names to all cattle, and to the fowl . . . and to every beast,* he presumably observes the complementary nature of male and female among them. For him, something is missing!

II. Family Now Possible
(Genesis 2:21-24)
A. Flesh Divided (vv. 21, 22)

21. And the Lord God caused a deep sleep to fall upon Adam, and he slept: and he took one of his ribs, and closed up the flesh instead thereof.

In the Old Testament, God sometimes works while people are in a divinely induced sleep (see Genesis 15:12; 1 Samuel 26:12). Here, Adam needs to be under heavy anesthesia while God removes a certain part of him. The Hebrew term that is behind the word *ribs* occurs over two dozen

times in the Old Testament, but it is translated "rib(s)" only in the verse before us and the next. Nowhere else in the Old Testament does it have anatomical significance.

Instead, the term's other usages frequently describe the side or sides of objects (example: Exodus 25:14). With those instances as a guide, we are confident in concluding that God uses the man's side and/or something from it in what happens next.

22. And the rib, which the Lord God had taken from man, made he a woman, and brought her unto the man.

In keeping with the pattern in Genesis 1, the high point of which is 1:26, 27, God saves the best of His creation for last. From the records of Israel's neighbors later on, we sometimes find alternative accounts of human origins, but none of them includes special mention of the creation of women in particular. In Genesis 1 and 2, women bear the image of God as men do, serve as corulers of God's creation, and play equally important roles in advancing God's purposes.

It is intriguing that the original word behind the translation *made* is used elsewhere as an architectural term to describe the construction of cities and altars (examples: Genesis 4:17; 12:7). What the author describes with a bare minimum of detail is in fact more profound than any construction project that humans themselves can undertake—ever.

B. Flesh United (vv. 23, 24)

23. And Adam said, This is now bone of my bones, and flesh of my flesh: she shall be called Woman, because she was taken out of Man.

Perhaps the seeming delay in creating the woman was intended by God to allow Adam time to sense the depth of his need for a companion of his own kind. After considering the animals first and finding himself yet wanting, *Adam* is now positioned (as are we) to experience the greatest possible appreciation of the creation of woman. We can almost hear the jubilant outburst "At last!"

We should not overlook the fact that the verse before us is the first record of a human's words. It is also humanity's first recorded play on words, as the terms for man and woman sound even more alike in Hebrew than they do in English. The sound-alike quality of the two words reflects Adam's awareness of the source of the woman: *she was taken out of Man.*

Adam's mention of both *flesh* and *bone* confirms the nature of the man's bodily material used to form the woman. Whereas we today use the phrase "flesh and blood" as a reference to family members, the Old Testament likes to use "flesh" and "bone(s)" together to indicate the same (examples: Genesis 29:14; Judges 9:2; 2 Samuel 5:1). In Hebrew poetry, "flesh" and "bone" often stand in parallel to each other to refer to things that are the same or nearly so (examples: Job 10:11; Psalm 38:3).

Adam's declaration also serves as a foil for what God declares in the next verse.

❧ THE FEASIBILITY OF FUNCTIONAL FAMILIES ❧

My preacher just finished a sermon series called "The Functional Family." We have a minister who practices what he preaches. While clearly the leader in his home, his wife has every confidence that what's important to her will never be ignored. Their three children have very different personalities, so each one is being reared according to his or her bent. On a day off, this minister is completely focused on the interests of his family—those he serves in the church can usually wait a day for his attention. His success in ministry begins with his success at home.

The very first marriage happened in a sinless environment. When the first man was introduced to the first woman, there was immediate acceptance. The Genesis text does not tell us how long after this first meeting that the fall (actually, the jump) into sin occurred. But for that interval of time, it's easy to imagine husband and wife working together in a harmony not experienced since.

HOW TO SAY IT

anatomical	*an*-uh-***tom***-i-kuhl.
Deuteronomy	Due-ter-*ahn*-uh-me.
Mesopotamia	*Mes*-uh-puh-***tay***-me-uh.
paradigm	***pair***-uh-*dime*.

Thriving, functional marriages and families are still possible today, any popular opinion to the contrary aside. Of course, we must wrestle with the presence of sin in our hearts, which can have a profound effect on how well we get along with family members. Even so, families can flourish in peaceful homes by the power of the Holy Spirit. In such, God takes great delight.   —D. C. S.

24. Therefore shall a man leave his father and his mother, and shall cleave unto his wife: and they shall be one flesh.

Whereas the creation of the woman involved a surrender of part of the man's physical person, the joining of the two in marital union serves as a reunification. In that light, the account of the first meeting between a man and a woman ends with an affirmation (by the narrator rather than by the man) that the first marriage is to be viewed as a paradigm for all subsequent marriages in at least two ways.

First, marriage is to demonstrate the enduring reality that marital love surpasses even the love between parent and child. Family commitments remain important, but the commitment inherent in marital vows supersedes them.

What Do You Think?
  What lessons will you pass on to others regarding lessons learned from observing marriages where one person did not honor that relationship above other family relationships?
Digging Deeper
  How do you decide which of those lessons apply to yourself and which do not?

Second, marriages are to reenact, in a sense, the joining that took place between the first man and woman. Every married man is to embrace *his wife* not only sexually but also in the sharing of property, plans, and purpose. Marriage is intended from the outset to be lifelong and monogamous (Matthew 19:4-6).

On a further note, the text also implies that the first marriage is consummated soon after God presents the woman to the man. God is the author of the institution of marriage, and He grants to the first couple the gift of sexuality. In effect, God creates the original family. The male-female basis for marriage as instituted by God is apparent in this passage and is taught and assumed thereafter in Scripture.

So important is Genesis 2:24 that it is quoted four times in the New Testament. Jesus cites it in His teaching on marriage and divorce, thus, among other things, reaffirming the male-female basis for marriage (Matthew 19:3-9; Mark 10:2-12). Paul, quoting Genesis 2:24 twice, also implies that a male-female union is necessary for becoming one flesh (1 Corinthians 6:16; Ephesians 5:31).

> **What Do You Think?**
> Which of the four New Testament passages that quote Genesis 2:24 speaks most forcefully of a change you need to make? Why?
> *Digging Deeper*
> How will you allow that most forceful usage to make a difference in what you model?

The Bible nowhere provides support for a supposed marriage between members of the same sex. Those who enter into such unions do so under solely human authority and at great risk of divine displeasure. The apostle Paul likens those who disregard nature's biological clues to those who overlook the obvious signs of a Creator (Romans 1:18-32). Marriage between one man and one woman is the only proper context for sexual relations. While it is right and Christian to show great love and grace to those tempted by same-sex attraction, the church must continue to uphold the biblical model of marriage.

Remaining single, a pathway chosen by a few but undesired by most, is the only biblically approved lifestyle alternative to marriage. Jesus and Paul both affirm exceptional situations in which an individual remains unmarried and celibate (Matthew 19:10-12; 1 Corinthians 7:7, 8). This lifestyle may be prompted by troubled times (compare Jeremiah 16:1-4; 1 Corinthians 7:26-28) and/or a desire to devote more time to serve God (Matthew 19:12; 1 Corinthians 7:32-35). Such a lifestyle prefigures the future situation in which there will be no marriage (Matthew 22:30).

> **What Do You Think?**
> Should churches develop programming and ministries specifically for those who are single? Why, or why not?
> *Digging Deeper*
> How will your answer change, if at all, when you consider the needs of single people in these demographics: young, middle-age, elderly, divorced, never married, widowed, with children, without children?

❧ SECURE MARRIAGE BOUNDARIES ❧

My wife and I experienced the deaths of both mothers within days of each other. The memorial services brought together siblings who hadn't seen each other in years.

The reunions were unexpectedly delightful. With the passing of the families' matriarchs, everyone's guard was down. We simply enjoyed one another's company. The Lord brought opportunities for restoration and reconciliation through this otherwise sad experience.

Without going into details, let's just agree that the marriage covenant is sacred, and its boundaries must not be tested, even by (especially by?) well-meaning relatives. With those boundaries respected and secure, family members (including in-laws) can continue to build strong bonds with their adult children—and the siblings with one another. These are the God-honoring bonds upon which strong families are built.   —D. C. S.

III. Family Expanded
(GENESIS 4:1, 2)
A. Son Number One (v. 1)

1. And Adam knew Eve his wife; and she conceived, and bare Cain, and said, I have gotten a man from the LORD.

Our lesson text now jumps past the account of the fall in Genesis 3 to the conception and birth of Cain. The majority of interpreters see all the events of Genesis 4 as occurring after Adam and Eve's expulsion from the Garden of Eden (3:23, 24). Against this understanding, however, is a proposal that the construction in the original language has the author backtracking (at least briefly) to events that occur prior to the expulsion. This theory means that Eve's future punishment noted in Genesis 3:16 connects with childbearing already experienced.

Whether what is recorded in the verse before us happens before or after the fall may affect interpretation. If the birth of Cain takes place before the fall, then Eve's words *I have gotten a man from the Lord* are seen as giving the Lord credit. If the birth of Cain takes place after the fall into sin, however, Eve's words are understood by some to be a boast in that she is claiming to have created a man just as the Lord did.

In either case, we see underway the God-ordained imperative to multiply. The sexual function between husband and wife is God-ordained. Sexual expression neither resulted *in* nor resulted *from* the fall into sin by Adam and Eve. The name *Cain* occurs 20 times in 17 verses in the *KJV*, and all but one of these (Joshua 15:57) refers to the individual in the verse before us. Three of the occurrences are in the New Testament (Hebrews 11:4; 1 John 3:12; Jude 11).

B. Son Number Two (v. 2)

2. And she again bare his brother Abel. And Abel was a keeper of sheep, but Cain was a tiller of the ground.

The designation *Abel* occurs 16 times in 13 verses in the *KJV*, although some refer to a stone (1 Samuel 6:18) or a city (2 Samuel 20:14, 15, 18). Four of the references to Abel the man are in the New Testament (Matthew 23:35; Luke 11:51; Hebrews 11:4; 12:24). To be either *a keeper of sheep* or *a tiller of the ground* is a common occupation in antiquity.

Conclusion

A. Spouse Comes First

God bestows on us many blessings and gifts, the best of which (after salvation through Jesus) is the capacity to have relationships. Aloneness is not good for us. Life is about relationships—with God and with each other. Relatives, friends, and acquaintances can partner with us in God's work. Animals can provide meaningful company, but the marriage relationship stands above all.

God desires that humanity flourish through the marriage relationship. Procreation is never stated as a requirement for each and every marriage, nor is it the only purpose of marriage. But it is the means by which God has established that people fill the earth. The family unit is not only a precious social gift but also a means for teaching children and spreading God's Word throughout the world.

God's ideals for marriage are always under attack, and recent attempts to redefine marriage comprise but the latest example. Sinful humans are up to their old tricks again. To be sure, God has left much about marriage up to us. Prenuptial customs, wedding ceremonies, legal recognitions and benefits, and many other specifics may be determined (for better or worse) by one's society, laws, and culture. But the male-female basis and the lifelong exclusive commitment are parameters set by God, not earthly powers.

The church must continue to uphold the biblical ideals for holy matrimony and to celebrate it as a gift from God. May those who enter into this most sacred of earthly unions remain faithful to their spouses and give glory to their Creator.

What Do You Think?
   What are some things that husbands and wives can do to glorify God through their marriage?
Digging Deeper
   Make your answer pointedly specific by (1) avoiding generalities such as "love each other" and (2) focusing on positive things to do, not sins to avoid doing.

B. Prayer

Father, whether married or not, we give You thanks for the gift of marriage and resulting relationships. May we give You the glory as we honor marriage and family. In Jesus' name we pray. Amen.

C. Thought to Remember

Through marriage, family, and community, God advances His purposes.

INVOLVEMENT LEARNING

Enhance your lesson with KJV Bible Student *(from your curriculum supplier) and the reproducible activity page (at www.standardlesson.com or in the back of the* KJV Standard Lesson Commentary Deluxe Edition*).*

Into the Lesson

Place in each chair, for learners to work on as they arrive, a copy of the following handout (you create) of contemporary "marriage" practices: 1–Common-law marriage; 2–Same-sex unions; 3–Producing wedding spectaculars; 4–Ignoring divorce status; 5–Living together as a "test"; 6–Parent-arranged marriage; 7–Prenuptial agreements; 8–Eloping. Have out to the side of each item the following scale: 1 = Fully comfortable; 4 = Indifferent; 7 = Completely uncomfortable. Above the scale (which is repeated eight times, once for each entry), have this heading: *My Comfort Level.*

After allowing time for completion and discussion, make a transition by having learners cross out the word *My* on the heading and replace it with the word *God's.* Ask whether any of the results have changed. If an awkward silence ensues, let it continue for at least 15 seconds. (Just because your learners have stopped talking doesn't mean it's your turn to start talking.)

Offer this observation as a transition to Bible study: "Today we study the model for the closest of human relationships, which God established at the beginning. The question should always be, What is the holy God 'comfortable' with?"

Into the Word

Have class members take turns reading Genesis 2:18-24; 4:1, 2 aloud. Immediately announce a closed-Bible test on what was just read. Then give each learner a copy of the following True/False quiz. Announce a time limit of one minute. Assure your learners that they will score their own quizzes and that you will not collect them.

1. One result of God's creation was not good.
2. Man was designed to be in relationship.
3. God introduced Adam to the animals and birds and told Adam their names.
4. As Adam slept at night, God showed him a dream of the ideal mate.

5. God created Adam's wife from the dust of the ground, just as He had created Adam.
6. Adam could not obey God's command to multiply and fill the earth on his own.
7. Man's first recorded words were his complaint about not having an acceptable mate.

Read and discuss each after having the text read aloud again. *[Answers: 1–True (2:18); 2–True (2:18); 3–False (2:19); 4–False (2:21, 22); 5–False (2:22); 6–True (by inference); 7–False (2:23).]*

Draw attention to statement 6. Read it aloud and ask, "How does this truth relate to God's need to provide an appropriate helper for the man?" The likely response of the need of a partner for procreation is obvious. Anticipate that your sharper students will infer something the text doesn't mention: the man had undoubtedly observed the two genders of the animal world.

Option 1. Distribute copies of the "Family" activity from the reproducible page, which you can download. Have learners complete it for an alternative way to look at the plan God has for the family in His creation of man and woman.

Option 2. For broader study, distribute copies of the "Two Sexes" activity from the reproducible page. Have your learners complete and discuss it in pairs or threes as indicated.

Into Life

Say, "This will be a good week to honor God by honoring members of your family that God has given you as a relationship blessing. What is one thing you can do to demonstrate your appreciation of spouse, parent, etc.?" Encourage several suggestions. Anticipate ideas such as an unexpected phone call, a small gift, or a "thank you" or "thinking of you" card. Ask learners to consider also their church family.

Option. Use the "Another Family" activity on the reproducible page for an additional look at the church family.

GOD CONFRONTS SIN

DEVOTIONAL READING: Psalm 51:1-12
BACKGROUND SCRIPTURE: Genesis 3

GENESIS 3:8-17, 20-24

8 And they heard the voice of the LORD God walking in the garden in the cool of the day: and Adam and his wife hid themselves from the presence of the LORD God amongst the trees of the garden.

9 And the LORD God called unto Adam, and said unto him, Where art thou?

10 And he said, I heard thy voice in the garden, and I was afraid, because I was naked; and I hid myself.

11 And he said, Who told thee that thou wast naked? Hast thou eaten of the tree, whereof I commanded thee that thou shouldest not eat?

12 And the man said, The woman whom thou gavest to be with me, she gave me of the tree, and I did eat.

13 And the LORD God said unto the woman, What is this that thou hast done? And the woman said, The serpent beguiled me, and I did eat.

14 And the LORD God said unto the serpent, Because thou hast done this, thou art cursed above all cattle, and above every beast of the field; upon thy belly shalt thou go, and dust shalt thou eat all the days of thy life:

15 And I will put enmity between thee and the woman, and between thy seed and her seed; it shall bruise thy head, and thou shalt bruise his heel.

16 Unto the woman he said, I will greatly multiply thy sorrow and thy conception; in sorrow thou shalt bring forth children; and thy desire shall be to thy husband, and he shall rule over thee.

17 And unto Adam he said, Because thou hast hearkened unto the voice of thy wife, and hast eaten of the tree, of which I commanded thee, saying, Thou shalt not eat of it: cursed is the ground for thy sake; in sorrow shalt thou eat of it all the days of thy life.

. . . .

20 And Adam called his wife's name Eve; because she was the mother of all living.

21 Unto Adam also and to his wife did the LORD God make coats of skins, and clothed them.

22 And the LORD God said, Behold, the man is become as one of us, to know good and evil: and now, lest he put forth his hand, and take also of the tree of life, and eat, and live for ever:

23 Therefore the LORD God sent him forth from the garden of Eden, to till the ground from whence he was taken.

24 So he drove out the man; and he placed at the east of the garden of Eden Cherubims, and a flaming sword which turned every way, to keep the way of the tree of life.

KEY VERSE

The LORD God sent him forth from the garden of Eden, to till the ground from whence he was taken.
—Genesis 3:23

GOD'S WORLD AND GOD'S PEOPLE

Unit 1: God Creates the World

LESSONS 1–5

LESSON AIMS

After participating in this lesson, each learner will be able to:

1. Relate the sequence of events that led to Adam and Eve's expulsion from the Garden of Eden.

2. Identify elements of the story of sin's origins similar to his or her own experiences with temptation and sin.

3. State an action that will be a step toward repairing a personal relationship damaged by sin.

LESSON OUTLINE

Introduction

A. The Perfect Marriage

When we think of the Garden of Eden, we have visions of perfection. We imagine perfect weather. We think of friendly animals. We envision pristine water and air. *Oh, to return to the garden*, we think! Plenty of space. No crowds. Direct access to God. How could it be any better?

Yet in Genesis the garden is both a place and a story, and the story has a tough ending. Any good story has the tension of a crisis that must be resolved, and Genesis is no exception. In chapter 3 we read of a series of deepening crises that end with Adam and Eve losing paradise. It is a drama that shakes the foundations of God's created order and changes the trajectory of human relationships with the Creator, a change we still cope with today.

This story of the first couple and the first sins is archetypal, a pattern repeated many times in the Bible. First, an opportunity to violate God's commands (temptation) seems a good thing. Then the violation occurs (sin) with short-term pleasure. The consequences of breaking God's laws (punishment) that follow bring regret (repentance). But people don't seem to learn!

B. Lesson Context

Genesis 3 begins a different style of presentation. Up until this point, the book has been largely narrative in format (a story told by a narrator). But in Genesis 3 we encounter a drama (a story told through the dialogue of the characters). By the time we arrive at today's lesson text, two characters have already spoken: the serpent and the woman.

Earlier in Genesis 3, the serpent used the fruit to entice the woman by its visual appeal and the promise of wisdom. She ate and then shared her sin with her husband. So he ended up being a willing accomplice. Immediately they were overcome with shame and attempted to cover their nakedness with makeshift fig-leaf garments. Covering their nakedness was not enough, though, so when their regular time with the Lord God arrived, they attempted to hide.

I. Confrontation

(Genesis 3:8-13)

A. Avoiding God (vv. 8-10)

8. And they heard the voice of the Lord God walking in the garden in the cool of the day: and Adam and his wife hid themselves from the presence of the Lord God amongst the trees of the garden.

Our picture of what the garden looks like is far from complete. But we get a small insight here when we learn that *Adam and his wife* in their shame (contrast Genesis 2:25) attempt to hide *from . . . the Lord God amongst the trees of the garden.* Some think this implies a dense, lush forest with areas open enough to permit walking for pleasure. That's a nice mental image, but ultimately it is speculation. It is reasonable to infer, however, that the two humans find what they think is enough foliage to block the Lord's view, while still being close enough to a path to be able to hear God (next verse).

9. And the Lord God called unto Adam, and said unto him, Where art thou?

The Lord arrives at the customary meeting place, but His two human creations are not present. The Lord's question *Where art thou?* does not indicate a lack of knowledge on His part; He is not fooled by the clumsy attempt to hide. His question, rather, is an invitation to meet. It's been said that God's search for people is a unique feature of Christianity, inherited from Judaism. In other religions, man searches for God.

Our "sanctified imaginations" tell us that the Lord's *Where art thou?* pierces the hearts of the couple as it has the effect of asking "Why are you hiding?" or, even more so, "What have you done?" The Lord's question implies an accusation of guilt, a conviction of sin.

God does not hesitate to show us our sins. He shatters delusions that ungodly behavior is acceptable or inevitable. As the Lord's question pierces the hearts of Adam and Eve, so it pierces ours as well. Centuries later, David will acknowledge the impossibility of hiding from God (Psalm 139:7-12). Whether Adam fully realizes this truth in his day, we are obligated to realize that fact fully.

But what we hold as truth in terms of "head knowledge," we do not always model in practice. We cannot hide from God, yet we do try. For example, we may have sins we are afraid to share with God in our prayers of confession, when in our minds we understand that God knows these sins already.

> ### What Do You Think?
> What guardrails can you (and have you) put in place to help ensure that you don't try to hide from God?
> ### Digging Deeper
> What guardrails might work for you but not for others? How about the reverse? Why?

10. And he said, I heard thy voice in the garden, and I was afraid, because I was naked; and I hid myself.

Adam, within earshot of the Lord's summons, does not simply come forth and say, "Here I am" (contrast Genesis 22:1, 11; 46:2; Exodus 3:4; Isaiah 6:8). Instead, he explains his hiding in an attempt to excuse it.

The explanation is true but misleading. Yes, Adam had been *naked* (Genesis 2:25), and his fear is self-evident in the fact that he has attempted to hide. He offers an explanation of the latter as being due to the former, but the explanation doesn't hold water as we realize that his nakedness hasn't resulted in hiding before now. He is afraid because of his disobedience.

The audacity and stupidity of the sin is amazing. As far as we know, there was only one rule in the Garden of Eden: don't eat the fruit of one special tree (Genesis 2:15-17). Adam and Eve, given spectacular freedom from rules and laws, managed to break this one command.

B. Shifting Blame (vv. 11-13)

11. And he said, Who told thee that thou wast naked? Hast thou eaten of the tree, whereof I commanded thee that thou shouldest not eat?

Again, the questioning by the Lord does not indicate a lack of knowledge on His part. He knows what has happened. But He gives Adam a chance to confess his sin. He does this in a way that confronts Adam with the obvious as God says, in effect, "Let's talk about your discomfort with being naked. You didn't feel this way yesterday when we met. What changed? Did you eat the forbidden fruit? That would do it."

12. And the man said, The woman whom thou gavest to be with me, she gave me of the tree, and I did eat.

When confronted, Adam seems to realize there is no hiding his sin. Yet he does not say, "Yes, Lord, I ate the forbidden fruit, but I regret it deeply. Please forgive me." Instead, Adam attempts to dodge his guilt by redirecting the blame. In one of the saddest moments of all Bible accounts, Adam points the finger of guilt in two directions. First he points that finger toward his beloved wife. Then in the same breath Adam indicts the Lord as well with the phrase *whom thou gavest to be with me*. Adam's admission *I did eat* comes with no acceptance of personal responsibility.

13. And the LORD God said unto the woman, What is this that thou hast done? And the woman said, The serpent beguiled me, and I did eat.

Following the model just set by her husband, *the woman* admits *I did eat*, but attempts to shift full blame elsewhere: to *the serpent*. There is no repentance, no asking for forgiveness.

What Do You Think?
Which have you found more useful: to fixate on Satan's role in tempting you or to ignore his role altogether? Or does the key lie somewhere between those extremes? Why?
Digging Deeper
Consider contexts of occurrences of the word *Satan* in the New Testament.

❧ DEFLECTING RESPONSIBILITY ❧

Bill would never cheat on his wife. But he maintains a "just friends" texting relationship with a woman from work. Bill would never hit his wife. But the way he belittles her appearance has a similar humiliating effect. Of course, Bill would never move out. But he refuses to connect on any emotional level with his wife.

Bill may think that any resulting divorce that his wife initiates will allow him to blame her for it, since he himself will not have created a biblical basis for divorce. But as our text establishes, attempts to shift blame are nothing new. God knows! Although the one through whom temptation comes is not let off the hook (Luke 17:1), the bottom line is that each person is held responsible for his or her sin (Ezekiel 18:4).

There are no victimless sins. Willful disobedience always affects relationships with God and others, even those sins committed in private or in the dark sanctuary of our minds. When looking for the promised way of escape from temptation (1 Corinthians 10:13), look first at how your decisions may damage someone else's soul—then go in the other direction.   —D. C. S.

What Do You Think?
What responsibility will you accept in helping others in your church to be free of blame?
Digging Deeper
Consider 1 Timothy 3:2; 5:7; 6:14; Titus 1:6-8 in their contexts as you form your reply.

II. Judgment
(GENESIS 3:14-17)
A. On the Serpent (vv. 14, 15)

14. And the LORD God said unto the serpent, Because thou hast done this, thou art cursed above all cattle, and above every beast of the field; upon thy belly shalt thou go, and dust shalt thou eat all the days of thy life.

God, knowing precisely what has taken place earlier at the tree, does not question *the serpent*. If the questioning of the two humans indicates opportunities to repent, we see no such opportunity being offered to the tempter. The Lord merely passes judgment and declares the penalty. The penalty reflects the categories of land creatures from Genesis 1:24, 25: domestic animals, wild animals, and creeping-on-the-ground animals.

The apostle John identifies "that old serpent" as being "the Devil, and Satan" himself (Revelation 12:9; 20:2). Because of his ability to speak and his intelligence (Genesis 3:1-5), he is more like the man and the woman than any other creature in the garden.

Whatever his form before God's sentencing, the serpent is now to be included among the lowest and despised of the land animals: the ground-creepers. The description gives us the picture of a snake as we are familiar with today, that of a slithering, dust-eating belly-dragger. We assume this also includes the loss of speech and cunning intelligence.

15a. And I will put enmity between thee and the woman, and between thy seed and her seed.

This verse, sometimes called the *protevangelium* (meaning "first gospel"), is the first prophecy in the Bible about a future Savior. Until this story there has been no need for a Savior because there has been no sin. But now there is.

The pronouncement in this verse, given directly to the serpent, has three parts. First, there is a promise of *enmity*—fear and loathing—between *the woman* and *her seed* (descendants) plus the serpent and his *seed*. This reflects a coming battle related to the serpent and his agenda to undermine God's authority and entice humans to sin (compare John 8:44; Acts 13:10; 1 John 3:8; Revelation 12:17). This is spiritual warfare, the struggle for the hearts and souls of men and women (Ephesians 6:10-12).

15b. It shall bruise thy head.

The coming Savior will strike some kind of blow to the serpent and his power. From this side of the cross, we realize that Jesus accomplished this when He rose from the dead and thereby defeated the power of death (compare Romans

HOW TO SAY IT

Augustine	*Aw*-gus-teen or Aw-*gus*-tin.
archetypal	*ahr*-kih-*tie*-pull.
beguiled	bih-*giled*.
Cherubims	*Chair*-uh-bims.
Euphrates	You-*fray*-teez.
Mesopotamia	*Mes*-uh-puh-*tay*-me-uh.
protevangelium	proat-ee-van-*jel*-ee-uhm.
Tigris	*Tie*-griss.

16:20; 1 Corinthians 15:54-57; Hebrews 2:14; Revelation 1:18).

15c. And thou shalt bruise his heel.

The coming Messiah will be wounded by Satan's efforts, but not defeated. He will experience death, but not remain dead (Revelation 1:18; 5:6).

> *What Do You Think?*
> What Scriptures do you turn to when wrestling with temptation?
> *Digging Deeper*
> How has the answer to the question above changed over the years for you? Why?

B. On Humanity (vv. 16, 17)

16a. Unto the woman he said, I will greatly multiply thy sorrow and thy conception; in sorrow thou shalt bring forth children.

God's pronouncements continue, now with regard to difficulties that lie in the future of *the woman* in particular and that of women in general. Childbearing and childbirth will become unpleasant and painful, something all mothers today can verify.

16b. And thy desire shall be to thy husband, and he shall rule over thee.

Furthermore, the woman will also be tied to her *husband* in ways that are not always joyful. She will fulfill her *desire* by marriage, but will also have a new master who will *rule over* her (compare 1 Corinthians 11:3; Ephesians 5:22). This dependency has not yet existed in the case of the first man and woman, but it will haunt humankind in the future. The Hebrew behind the translation *rule over* is translated that way as well in Genesis 1:18.

17. And unto Adam he said, Because thou hast hearkened unto the voice of thy wife, and hast eaten of the tree, of which I commanded thee, saying, Thou shalt not eat of it: cursed is the ground for thy sake; in sorrow shalt thou eat of it all the days of thy life.

The pronouncement *unto Adam* is the strongest and longest of all. First, God states the basis for His judgment. Yes, the temptation had come through his wife, but he still bears responsibility

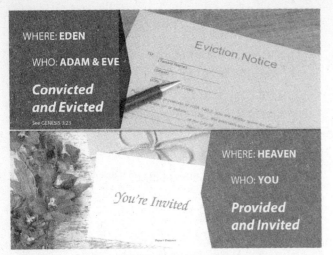

Visual for Lesson 5. *Use this visual to explore emotional responses to the two scenarios suggested; this can be a small-group exercise.*

for his sin. As a consequence, the man will no longer have access to the blessed, perfect fertility of the garden. He will now have to scratch out a living from *ground* that is in some way *cursed*. Life will be difficult and tenuous.

The unpredictable nature of farming is still with us. Despite great advances in technology and methodology, we still have drought and famine. People die every day from malnutrition and hunger. There is no end in sight for this until we enter the New Jerusalem, where there no longer will be any curse (Revelation 22:3). This will be paradise restored, with direct access to both the Lord and the tree of life, access lost because of the sin in the garden.

III. Banishment
(GENESIS 3:20-24)
A. Provision (vv. 20, 21)

20. And Adam called his wife's name Eve; because she was the mother of all living.

The story ends with some final arrangements. The woman needs a name, and *Adam* served as the namer-in-chief earlier (Genesis 2:19, 20). He gives her a hopeful name, one based on the word for *living*. Adam understands that *Eve* will produce babies and multiply the number of humans (1:28).

21. Unto Adam also and to his wife did the LORD God make coats of skins, and clothed them.

The garments provided by God replace the flimsy and temporary fig-leaf apparel (Genesis 3:7). The author presents this as a gracious and loving act by God. He knows that Adam and Eve will need more than mere coverings for their nakedness, once outside the garden.

B. Expulsion (vv. 22-24)

22. And the LORD God said, Behold, the man is become as one of us, to know good and evil: and now, lest he put forth his hand, and take also of the tree of life, and eat, and live for ever.

The author gives a divine detail at this juncture: the gist of God's rationale for expelling the two from the garden. Things have changed, and sin has caused a loss of innocence for the man and his companion. God foresees that Adam has *become as one of us*. The "us" is not specified. Some see this as God's addressing His heavenly council of angels (compare Job 1:6). Others see it as conversation between the three persons of the Trinity. Still others see it as the "plural of majesty" (see the commentary on Genesis 1:26 in lesson 3 on page 27).

To lose access to *the tree of life* signs the death warrant of Adam and Eve. Instead of living forever, they will age and eventually die. Another future feature of the New Jerusalem is year-round access to the tree of life, planted in or straddling the river of life (Revelation 22:2).

23, 24. Therefore the LORD God sent him forth from the garden of Eden, to till the ground from whence he was taken. So he drove out the man; and he placed at the east of the garden of Eden Cherubims, and a flaming sword which turned every way, to keep the way of the tree of life.

The Lord takes extraordinary measures to prevent contact with the precious *tree of life*, posting a guard of heavenly beings known as *Cherubims* (compare Ezekiel 10:20). Although stated as guarding the *east* side of *Eden*, the implication is that the Cherubims prevent any approach to the special tree. This raises a question: Why didn't God just destroy the garden and its location.

The Bible does not address this issue specifically. Given that *the garden of Eden* is not to be found anywhere today, God either did destroy it eventually or allowed forces of nature to overtake it. Traditionally, the garden is located in Mesopotamia between the Tigris and the Euphrates Rivers. We search in vain, though, to find this exact spot. We will only see it restored as the New Jerusalem of Revelation 21 and 22.

❧ SELF-DECEPTION ❧

In his *Confessions*, the early-church theologian Augustine told a story from his younger years. He and a group of friends snuck into an orchard to steal some pears—not to eat them, but for the mere pleasure of doing something forbidden. Centuries later, a young friend of mine felt a similar urge. So he wandered into a convenience store, took a ball of string, and put it into the back of his jacket. He didn't need the string, but that wasn't the point.

As he walked out of the store, he half expected to be tackled by the owner and held down while the police arrived. But nothing happened. All he could think was, *I got away with it!*

But his conscience began to weigh on him as he rode home on his bike. The thrill was gone, and all that remained was guilt. The next day, he snuck the ball of string back into the store and determined that he would never do something like that again.

Did Adam and Eve wrestle with dark desires before they made the first sinful decision in history? We don't know. But we know all too well that we do. We would do well to question our assumptions and run our expectations by trusted people who will tell us the truth. Otherwise, like Adam and Eve, we can get caught up in a type of self-deception and blame-shifting that have lifelong consequences. —D. C. S.

> *What Do You Think?*
> What steps can you take to help keep sin out of your church?
> *Digging Deeper*
> Under what circumstances, if any, would "more Bible study" not be the best way to keep sin from infecting your church? Why?

Conclusion
A. The Pattern Then as Now

Think about the pattern: First, one partner allows sin to enter the marriage. Second, the person involves the other partner. Third, the realization of the presence of sin causes shame. Fourth, the couple withdraws and tries to hide from God. Fifth, the shame becomes blame. Finally, God resolves these crises by expelling the couple from the garden. They lose their home. This is not the way we want this story to end.

The actions of the first couple is archetypical, a pattern repeated many times in the Bible. An opportunity to violate God's commands seems a good thing (temptation), the violation occurs with short-term pleasure (sin), then the consequences of breaking God's laws (punishment) bring regret (repentance). We see this several times in Genesis alone. Think of Cain and Abel, Judah and Tamar, and Joseph and his brothers.

B. The Solution Now as Then

The ideal is, of course, not to sin in the first place. But we do sin. And when we do, we have a choice to make: let shame lead to repentance, or let shame become blame.

We might reasonably infer that Adam and Eve would have been expelled from the garden even with immediate repentance, without having tried to shift blame. But we might also reasonably infer that the fact that they tried to shift blame caused tensions in their marriage down the road. Even so, they endured together and established a family. When tragedy struck again with Cain's murder of Abel, they stayed together and had a third son, Seth (Genesis 4:25). Will we learn from the first family's defeats and triumphs?

C. Prayer

Lord God, help us see our own weaknesses in the story of the first sin. We pray deliverance from daily temptations through the one who bruised the head of the serpent: Jesus Your Son. Amen.

D. Thought to Remember
Shifting blame delays repentance.

INVOLVEMENT LEARNING

Enhance your lesson with KJV Bible Student *(from your curriculum supplier) and the reproducible activity page (at www.standardlesson.com or in the back of the* KJV Standard Lesson Commentary Deluxe Edition*).*

Into the Lesson

Pose this question for whole-class response: "What is your perfect earthly place in terms of people, weather, scenery, food, etc.?" Jot responses on the board. Then ask, "What would disturb or disrupt such a place?"

After responses, make a transition by saying, "When God created the world, everything was perfect. Within this perfect world, God placed the blissful Garden of Eden, which we imagine to have been complete with friendly animals, pristine water, etc. But sin disturbed this perfection. The result was the breaking of relationship between God and people. Let's explore the enduring consequences."

Into the Word

Prior to class, print four copies of Genesis 3:8-17, 20-24. Highlight on one copy the part of narrator, on another the part of Adam, on another that of Eve, and on the one remaining the part of God. Distribute these to four volunteers, one each, to give a dramatic reading of the account.

Say, "In Genesis 3, the perfect place is the scene of a crisis. In this story of the first sin, a pattern is established that is repeated many times in the Bible: an opportunity to violate God's commands (temptation) seems like a good thing, the violation (sin) occurs with short-term pleasure, then the consequences of breaking God's laws (punishment) bring regret (repentance)."

Write the following four words on the board as headings of columns: *Temptation / Sin / Punishment / Repentance*. Ask students to identify how Adam and Eve were tempted to violate God's command. Jot answers below that column heading. Continue similarly in turn with the remaining three column designations as you identify what the sin was, the punishment for it, and the demonstrations of repentance, if any. This can be either a whole-class or small-group exercise.

If you choose the latter, create handouts with the four words as column headers; include written instructions.

Either during the whole-class discussion or after small groups wrap up, make sure also to discuss how both Adam and Eve attempted to dodge guilt by redirecting blame. Explore how that finger-pointing may have affected their marriage. Jot responses on the board to affirm participation.

Option. Begin the Into the Word segment by distributing copies of the "A Tree and a Temptation" activity from the reproducible page, which you can download. This will provide the background to today's text. Assign small groups to complete as indicated.

Into Life

Say, "We too can tell our own stories of temptation, sin, punishment, and repentance." Divide the class into small groups of four or five. Give each group handouts (you create) with the following questions about the pattern of temptation, sin, punishment, repentance. 1–How does wanting something you should not have heighten your desire for it? 2–What strategies help you resist temptation? 3–What or whom do people blame for their sin? 4–What are some common consequences for sin? 5–How can we demonstrate repentance?

Say, "Sin destroys relationships. It destroyed the perfect relationship between God, Adam, and Eve." Discuss as a class the following questions: 1–How do our sins affect other people? 2–How do our sins affect our relationship with God?

Give each student a piece of paper and pencil. Ask them to write down how they will repent and seek to restore a relationship this week. Close by praying for the restoration of relationships.

Alternative. Distribute copies of the "Confession and Repentance" activity from the reproducible page to be completed as indicated in quiet reflection. Read Psalm 51:1-14 to close.

THE RIGHTEOUSNESS OF NOAH

DEVOTIONAL READING: Matthew 24:36-44
BACKGROUND SCRIPTURE: Genesis 6; 8:19

GENESIS 6:9B-22

9b Noah was a just man and perfect in his generations, and Noah walked with God.

10 And Noah begat three sons, Shem, Ham, and Japheth.

11 The earth also was corrupt before God, and the earth was filled with violence.

12 And God looked upon the earth, and, behold, it was corrupt; for all flesh had corrupted his way upon the earth.

13 And God said unto Noah, The end of all flesh is come before me; for the earth is filled with violence through them; and, behold, I will destroy them with the earth.

14 Make thee an ark of gopher wood; rooms shalt thou make in the ark, and shalt pitch it within and without with pitch.

15 And this is the fashion which thou shalt make it of: The length of the ark shall be three hundred cubits, the breadth of it fifty cubits, and the height of it thirty cubits.

16 A window shalt thou make to the ark, and in a cubit shalt thou finish it above; and the door of the ark shalt thou set in the side

thereof; with lower, second, and third stories shalt thou make it.

17 And, behold, I, even I, do bring a flood of waters upon the earth, to destroy all flesh, wherein is the breath of life, from under heaven; and every thing that is in the earth shall die.

18 But with thee will I establish my covenant; and thou shalt come into the ark, thou, and thy sons, and thy wife, and thy sons' wives with thee.

19 And of every living thing of all flesh, two of every sort shalt thou bring into the ark, to keep them alive with thee; they shall be male and female.

20 Of fowls after their kind, and of cattle after their kind, of every creeping thing of the earth after his kind, two of every sort shall come unto thee, to keep them alive.

21 And take thou unto thee of all food that is eaten, and thou shalt gather it to thee; and it shall be for food for thee, and for them.

22 Thus did Noah; according to all that God commanded him, so did he.

KEY VERSE

Thus did Noah; according to all that God commanded him, so did he. —**Genesis 6:22**

GOD'S WORLD AND GOD'S PEOPLE

Unit 2: God Destroys and Re-creates

LESSONS 6–9

LESSON AIMS

After participating in this lesson, each learner will be able to:

1. Describe the situation that led God to destroy human society.

2. Explain why Noah and his family were protected from the flood.

3. Identify a personal characteristic to develop or strengthen for the glory of God and make a plan to do so.

LESSON OUTLINE

Introduction

A. Control-Alt-Delete

Many of us have become familiar with a term that would have seemed nonsensical before 1981: Control-Alt-Delete. When a Windows-based computer freezes up and you can't do anything or just can't stand to wait, the keystroke combination Control-Alt-Delete will bring up the Task Manager. That feature allows the user to shut down a frozen program or reboot the operating system; for Mac users, the equivalent is Command-Option-Esc.

In a perfect world, computers would always run without a hitch. But since we don't live in a perfect world, we sometimes have to stop and start over when a system doesn't do what it's supposed to.

Our lesson today involves a "Control-Alt-Delete" scenario from early history. God had created a perfect world, and He created humans to share it sinlessly with Him. But Adam and Eve spoiled the system by eating the forbidden fruit. That started history's downward spiral. God realized the only way forward was a reboot, a fresh start with a renewed creation.

B. Lesson Context: History

The first four lessons of this quarter considered the biblical account of creation. Because all things were made by God and were consistent with His purposes, they all were inherently "good" (Genesis 1:12, 18, 21, 25, 31). The situation changed, however, when sin entered the picture. The period described in Genesis 4:1–6:7, between expulsion from the garden and Noah's lifetime, was characterized by a dramatic population expansion and a corresponding increase in evil. Over time, God's hopeful plans for a perfect world were so spoiled by wickedness that only one option remained: to destroy humans and animals (6:5-7).

C. Lesson Context: Legends

Legends of a great flood were widespread in the ancient world. The two most commonly cited as parallels to Genesis 6–9 are the Babylonian epics *Gilgamesh* (composed over 2,000 years ago) and *Atrahasis* (a late version of which was written about 1700 BC). Similar to Genesis, both works attribute the flood to a divine cause, show the gods warning a select human being of the destruction to come, and advising him to build a boat. These works portray the hero rescuing animal life by bringing animals onto the boat and include the hero offering sacrifices to the gods after the boat settles on dry land (compare Genesis 8:20, 21).

In *Gilgamesh*, as in Genesis 8:6-12, the hero tests the receding of the waters by releasing several birds from the boat. Noting these similarities, some scholars have suggested that the biblical story of Noah is based on these pagan legends.

Yet while the Genesis flood story is like other ancient accounts of a great flood in certain respects, there are key differences. The Babylonian epics locate the flood within a larger narrative about a running conflict between the many pagan gods of early Mesopotamia. They portray humans as servile pawns to capricious deities. The Genesis account, by contrast, portrays the flood as a consequence of human sin and connects it with God's larger creation and re-creation of the world. The differences are telling!

I. Faithful Man
(Genesis 6:9b-12)
A. Noah Described (vv. 9b, 10)

9b. Noah was a just man and perfect in his generations, and Noah walked with God.

This characterization of Noah creates a sharp contrast with the description of the world at large in Genesis 6:5. Of course, Noah sinned like every other human being (compare 9:21). But clearly he

HOW TO SAY IT

Atrahasis	*A*-truh-***hay***-sis.
Babylonians	Bab-ih-*low*-nee-unz.
Gilgamesh	***Gill***-guh-*mesh*.
hygriscence	*hi*-grih-sense.
Japheth	*Jay*-feth.
Mesopotamia	*Mes*-uh-puh-***tay***-me-uh.
Noahic	No-*ay*-ik.
Septuagint	Sep-*too*-ih-jent.
serotiny	suh-*rot*-nee.

did not participate in the general moral decay into which the society around him had fallen. Noah was a follower of the Lord rather than idols. But the language and context here distinguish him from other people more on the basis of his character than on the object of his worship. While others are violent, abusive, and self-centered, Noah acts with justice toward others.

The word *perfect* emphasizes his outstanding reputation for doing good. Noah's faithfulness explains God's selecting him to play a part in the renewal of the earth (see Genesis 6:8).

10. And Noah begat three sons, Shem, Ham, and Japheth.

Noah's *three sons* are significant for the role they will play in repopulating the earth after the great flood. As survivors of the catastrophe, *Shem, Ham, and Japheth* will become the forefathers of all ethnic groups (Genesis 10). Presumably, they follow their father's moral example and avoid the sins of the culture around them.

B. Humanity Decried (vv. 11, 12)

11. The earth also was corrupt before God, and the earth was filled with violence.

This verse summarizes the more detailed description of society in Genesis 6:4-7. As seen earlier, God intends for humans to manage the earth and all living things responsibly by following His instructions. While God had commanded Adam and Eve to produce new life (1:28), the darker human capacity to murder was introduced in the second generation of the human race (4:8). The tendency now seems to be to take life rather than multiply it.

12. And God looked upon the earth, and, behold, it was corrupt; for all flesh had corrupted his way upon the earth.

The breadth of the problem is stressed in that the phrase *all flesh* includes all descendants of Adam and Eve. Everyone except Noah has become corrupt. (Regarding the status of Noah's immediate family, see on Genesis 6:18 below.) This implies many self-centered sins: violent struggles for power, no regard for the common stewardship of the earth's resources as God originally commanded (1:16-28; 2:15), etc. People have come to realize that control of the world at the expense of others can produce great material wealth.

What Do You Think?
If we viewed our world the way God does, in what ways should our prayer lives, priorities, and behavior change?
Digging Deeper
How does your answer change, if at all, after comparing and contrasting John 3:16 with 1 John 2:15?

II. Divine Plan
(GENESIS 6:13-21)
A. For the Wicked (v. 13)

13. And God said unto Noah, The end of all flesh is come before me; for the earth is filled with violence through them; and, behold, I will destroy them with the earth.

By the time Noah comes on the scene, the situation has become so bad that God sees no other solution than to *destroy* what He has made. Theoretically, Genesis 6:7 could signal a return to the timelessness that existed before Genesis 1 after God destroys the universe and all humans with it. Then He could start over. Or God could keep all the inanimate elements of creation intact, then bring new humans into existence.

But since Noah is an exception to the rule of wickedness, God decides to work with him and his family rather than starting from scratch. God's decision to reveal His plan to Noah further stresses the quality of Noah's character.

To what extent Noah shares this dire warning with others outside his family is unknown. Noah is characterized as "a preacher of righteousness" in 2 Peter 2:5, but it is unclear whether that means Noah actually speaks to his contemporaries about the coming judgment and the need to repent.

What Do You Think?
What would you say to someone who believes that a loving God would never judge sin so harshly?
Digging Deeper
What Old Testament passages (only) would you use in that response?

B. For an Ark (vv. 14-16)

14. Make thee an ark of gopher wood; rooms shalt thou make in the ark, and shalt pitch it within and without with pitch.

Having warned Noah of the impending flood, God now tells him how to survive it. Notably, God's instructions require Noah to demonstrate faith. While God could miraculously protect Noah and his household inside a magic underwater bubble, He instead requires Noah to create his own means of survival at his own expense long before the first drop of rain falls.

Noah's salvation is to take the form of a boat—*an ark*. The Hebrew word used to describe the vessel is somewhat unusual, appearing in the Bible only here in the story of Noah and at Exodus 2:3-5. In the latter, it refers to the container in which Moses' mother set him afloat on the Nile River. Some commentators think the word, deriving from an Egyptian term, means "chest" or "box"; others think it means "palace." In Noah's context, it perhaps implies the special role the ark will play as a container of the precious life within.

The precise kind of *wood* is uncertain since the word *gopher* is not a translation but a transliteration (that is, a literal rendering of the sounds of the original Hebrew word). The fact that this is the only place in the Old Testament where this word is used adds to the uncertainty.

15. And this is the fashion which thou shalt make it of: The length of the ark shall be three hundred cubits, the breadth of it fifty cubits, and the height of it thirty cubits.

The dimensions of the ark are impressive, even by modern standards: conversion of 18-inch cubits to feet yields a length of 450 feet, a breadth of 75 feet, and height of 45 feet. At first glance, the 33,750 square feet of floor space is impressive enough, but Genesis 6:16b (below) has more to add to this.

The total volume computes to more than 1.5 million cubic feet. This equates to the capacity of about 375 modern tractor trailers! Note that Noah's ark is conceived as a free-floating barge, not as a steerable ship. Therefore none of its capacity will be occupied by any kind of propulsion system.

16a. A window shalt thou make to the ark, and in a cubit shalt thou finish it above.

The Hebrew word translated *window* occurs only here in the Old Testament, so the problem of exact meaning is similar to that of "gopher" in verse 14, above. The translators of the old Greek version known as the Septuagint, who lived two centuries before Christ, seem to have been just as perplexed in their translation: "By an assembling, you shall make the ark; and by a cubit you shall complete it from above." Presumably, the ark is to have many openings below an overhanging roof for light and ventilation (see Genesis 8:6).

16b. And the door of the ark shalt thou set in the side thereof; with lower, second, and third stories shalt thou make it.

The *door of the ark* will allow the loading of cargo and animals. It is likely sealed with pitch before the journey. Because the ark is to include three habitable *stories*, its floor space will exceed 100,000 square feet.

❧ IN NEED OF A MASTER BUILDER ❧

One of the high school courses I enjoyed most was mechanical drawing. While it wasn't a drawing class in the artistic sense, mechanical drawing definitely is an art. The course started me on a lifetime of doodling with geometric shapes. And it gave me the skill to draw, 25 years later, the plans for our family's first home of our own after living in several church parsonages.

Our contractor graciously complimented my drawing. He told me, however, that we would

Visual for Lesson 6. *Point to this visual as you ask, "What part of God's monologue would a person of lesser faith have found hardest to accept? Why?"*

still need an architect to draw a set of plans that reflected a professional's knowledge of engineering principles and county building codes.

Noah was undoubtedly capable of building a boat. But he had never built one that could carry such a massive and unique cargo as the ark would be required to accommodate.

Most of us who have a few decades of life experience believe we can manage whatever problems life presents to us. This is our pride talking, though. Like my attempt at drawing house plans, the plans we have for our lives often do not mesh with the realities we face. That's when we need our master builder's instructions. The question is, however, whether we will be wise enough to recognize the need and be humble enough to set our plans aside and follow His!　　　—C. R. B.

C. For a Covenant (vv. 17, 18)

17. And, behold, I, even I, do bring a flood of waters upon the earth, to destroy all flesh, wherein is the breath of life, from under heaven; and every thing that is in the earth shall die.

Having provided instructions for the ark, God now identifies its purpose: the judgment He has decreed (Genesis 6:13) will take the form of a devastating flood. The scale of the destruction parallels the scale of the sin: 6:5, 13 indicate that violence and evil had become universal, and the verse at hand prescribes a universal *flood* as the remedy.

Scholars debate whether the term *all flesh* should be taken to mean that the flood was to be global (covering the entire earth) or regional (confined to one specific part of the world). The latter interpretation emphasizes the fact that judgment is pronounced on and targeted at humanity. And at this point, humans seem confined to a specific area of the world, signifying that all human life can be destroyed by a flood that affects only that region. In either case, the scope of the devastation to come is clear: God intends to wipe out the entire human race, with just a few exceptions (next verse).

18. But with thee will I establish my covenant; and thou shalt come into the ark, thou, and thy sons, and thy wife, and thy sons' wives with thee.

The term *covenant*, appearing here for the first time in the Bible, is used in a way that specifically distinguishes faithful Noah and his family from the rest of the human race that will be destroyed. *Covenant* means "contract." This covenant implies that obedience to a sovereign ruler (in this case God) will result in protection and provision. The terms of the agreement presuppose that Noah, as a servant of God, must follow the command to build and enter *the ark*; the implied reward is protection from the deluge, which Noah receives as a result of his obedience. The explicit terms of the Noahic covenant are listed in Genesis 8:20–9:17.

> *What Do You Think?*
> How will the Bible's concept of *covenant* affect how you live this week?
> *Digging Deeper*
> Moving from abstract concept to concrete details, how does Hebrews 8 cause you to modify your conclusion, if at all?

D. For Creatures (vv. 19, 20)

19, 20. And of every living thing of all flesh, two of every sort shalt thou bring into the ark, to keep them alive with thee; they shall be male and female. Of fowls after their kind, and of cattle after their kind, of every creeping thing of the earth after his kind, two of every sort shall come unto thee, to keep them alive.

The terms of Noah's obedience to God's covenant continue, now regarding the plan for preserving animal life. These instructions cover the full range of creatures.

It will be physically impossible for Noah to capture a mating pair of each and every species. The fact will leave room for another miraculous display of God's power as He will compel healthy representatives to come into the ark. The note that the animals will come in pairs of *male and female* reflects their purpose of repopulation. These instructions are further clarified in Genesis 7:1-3.

Skeptics who doubt the truth of the biblical narrative question the ark's ability to accommodate eight humans (1 Peter 3:20) and representatives of all animal species of land and air. They generally approach the question by noting the number of species extant today and arguing that Noah's ark was not big enough to hold them all. The biblical account, however, takes the opposite approach: only those animals who travel on the ark will survive the flood.

E. For Sustenance (v. 21)

21. And take thou unto thee of all food that is eaten, and thou shalt gather it to thee; and it shall be for food for thee, and for them.

As a final instruction, Noah is commanded to stock the ark with supplies for his family and the animals. Comparing Genesis 7:11 with 8:3-14 indicates that they were in the ark for more than a year.

III. Obedient Man
(GENESIS 6:22)

22. Thus did Noah; according to all that God commanded him, so did he.

Now aware of the forthcoming reality of the annihilation of the human race, Noah proceeds with God's intricate instructions. The action God intends to take is unprecedented, and we wonder if this quickens the pace of construction. We don't know. This part of the story merely concludes with a simple statement of Noah's obedience. Just as he has distinguished himself throughout his life by his righteous conduct, he now distinguishes himself by his full and unquestioning obedience to God's commands. This aspect of Noah's story is highlighted in Hebrews 11:7, part of a listing known as the Faith Hall of Fame:

> By faith Noah, being warned of God of things not seen as yet, moved with fear, prepared an ark to the saving of his house; by the which he condemned the world, and became heir of the righteousness which is by faith.

What Do You Think?
What is one thing you can do in the week ahead to prepare yourself to be responsive to God's promptings?
Digging Deeper
How do you guard against the possibility of confusing your own desires with God's will?

❧ WATER AS AN INSTRUMENT OF LIFE ❧

On January 15, 2009, US Airways Flight 1549 ended up in the Hudson River a few minutes after takeoff from LaGuardia Airport. Pilot Chesley "Sully" Sullenberger had decided to ditch the plane in the river after simultaneous bird strikes in both engines caused them to fail.

The relatively soft landing surface of the water, compared with the surrounding terrain, served as an instrument of life. Such a landing also helped ensure no fire, and all 155 passengers and crew survived as the damaged airliner stayed afloat long enough be something of an "ark." The incident has come to be called the Miracle on the Hudson.

Commenting on the great flood, the apostle Peter says that "in the days of Noah . . . eight souls were saved by water" (1 Peter 3:20). But wait—with the word *by* correctly understood as meaning "by means of" (instrumentality), shouldn't Peter have written that "eight souls were saved by the ark"?

The fact that Peter does *not* say that may indicate that something vital in the bigger picture must not be overlooked: the fact that in addition to escaping physical death, the eight souls also escaped spiritual death.

Think about the wholesale wickedness of the surrounding culture in Noah's day. If that wickedness had not been extinguished, would it not just have been a matter of time before some, most, or all of those eight souls succumbed to the temptation to join the party? The death of the wicked by water meant removal of that temptation so righteousness could flourish unfettered. The ark allowed the saving of the physical; the flood waters allowed the saving of the spiritual.

Don't leave the analysis there, however, because what the apostle says about the flood in 1 Peter 3:20 serves as an analogy or parallel with the significance of Christian baptism in 3:21. You should read that now. —C. R. B.

Conclusion
A. Starting Over

While we normally think of floods, forest fires, and hurricanes as "natural disasters," these events can also serve positive purposes in the larger picture. Many plants and trees, for example, exhibit an adaptation called *serotiny*. That means that they release seeds only in reaction to an environmental trigger. One such tree is the giant sequoia, which produces seed cones that open only under great heat. This allows these trees to take advantage of the ground opened up by a forest fire.

Other forms of plant life evidence *hygriscence*. That means that they release their seeds only after a heavy rain, thus allowing survival in a desert. Fire and flood in these cases become contexts for the generation of new life.

Noah's flood, terrible as it was, served a similar purpose. It was humanity's first, but not last, "Control-Alt-Delete." The last one is noted in 2 Peter 3:10-13.

B. Prayer

Lord, give us the strength to be faithful when the world around us is crumbling. Protect us from evil, even when everyone around us turns away from You. We pray in Jesus' name. Amen.

C. Thought to Remember

God protects the righteous at all times.

INVOLVEMENT LEARNING

Enhance your lesson with KJV Bible Student *(from your curriculum supplier) and the reproducible activity page (at www.standardlesson.com or in the back of the* KJV Standard Lesson Commentary Deluxe Edition*).*

Into the Lesson

As class starts, do your best imitation of someone using lingo from the 1980s as you say this: "So who like remembers, like, phrases of the '80s? Totally. Like rad. Let's take, like, a few minutes and see how many '80s words and phrases we can list." *(Possible responses among many: awesome, bad, da bomb, chill, even/not even, gag me with a spoon, gnarly, psych, radical, righteous.)*

Next, invite the class to come up with as many sentences as they can, using the popular '80s word *righteous* as used to indicate something that was genuine or excellent. Use this discussion to compare and contrast culture's use of the word *righteous* with its use in the Bible, particularly with regard to Noah. Emphasize his blameless reputation and faithfulness in walking with God.

Into the Word

Say, "God determined that Noah was a righteous, blameless man living in a violent, corrupt world. Noah continued to obey God even when all those outside of Noah's immediate family turned their backs on God. Let's look at what it means to be faithful in following God."

Have students pair up, and give each a copy of a handout (you prepare) that has the warning-sign messages below (but leave off the answer verses). Ask learners to work "two by two" to find verses in Genesis 6:9-22 that match the sign phrases on the handout.

> *Slow!* Animal Crossing . . . . v. 20
> *Beware!* Deep Water . . . . .v. 17
> *Wash Hands!* Food Storage Area . . . . . . .v. 21
> *Caution!* Construction Zone . . .vv. 15, 16
> *Warning!* Violence Ahead . . . . .v. 11
> *No Lone Zone!* Proceed 2 by 2 . . . . . . .vv. 19, 20
> *Danger!* Don't Touch Wet Pitch . . . .v. 14
> *No Entrance!* Use Side Door . . . . .v. 16

Option. For some competitive fun, the first pair to finish wins either two boxes of animal crackers (to represent animals saved) or bottles of water (to symbolize the flood).

Make a transition as you say, "Staying obedient to God regardless of what the world around is doing is not always easy. But as Noah models, careful attention to God's Word is how the Christian maintains a right relationship with Him."

Into Life

Discuss ways it is tempting to go along with the crowd. Talk about ways that God warns us to steer clear of troublesome thoughts, actions, places, and people.

Give each student an index card and pen. Instruct: "In 60 seconds, jot down as many character attributes as you can that reveal faithfulness in following God—no matter what others are saying or doing." Discuss results; explore Scripture passages that support the proposals (example: the fruit of the Spirit in Galatians 5:22, 23). Invite students to take their cards home and reflect this coming week on the qualities that they would most like God to develop in their hearts and lives.

Alternative. Distribute copies of the "Warning Signs for Today" activity from the reproducible page, which you can download, for learners to complete as indicated in small groups. If groups are slow getting started, give an example. Call time after eight minutes. Use a method that is appropriate for your class of rotating among groups and through the eight signs in discussing possibilities.

Close the lesson with prayer. Share, "Lord, thank You for understanding our weaknesses and the things that can trip us up in following wholeheartedly after You. Right now, I want to give You this area of my life where I am I tempted to ignore Your warning signs. *[Pause to allow students to name silently the area where they struggle most.]* Thank You for giving me Your Word to help me, like Noah, stand strong and obedient. In Jesus' name I pray. Amen."

THE CALL
OF ABRAM

DEVOTIONAL READING: Hebrews 11:4-10
BACKGROUND SCRIPTURE: Genesis 9–12

GENESIS 10:1

1 Now these are the generations of the sons of Noah, Shem, Ham, and Japheth: and unto them were sons born after the flood.

GENESIS 11:10, 27, 31, 32

10 These are the generations of Shem: Shem was an hundred years old, and begat Arphaxad two years after the flood.

. . . .

27 Now these are the generations of Terah: Terah begat Abram, Nahor, and Haran; and Haran begat Lot.

. . . .

31 And Terah took Abram his son, and Lot the son of Haran his son's son, and Sarai his daughter in law, his son Abram's wife; and they went forth with them from Ur of the Chaldees, to go into the land of Canaan; and they came unto Haran, and dwelt there.

32 And the days of Terah were two hundred and five years: and Terah died in Haran.

GENESIS 12:1-4

1 Now the LORD had said unto Abram, Get thee out of thy country, and from thy kindred, and from thy father's house, unto a land that I will shew thee:

2 And I will make of thee a great nation, and I will bless thee, and make thy name great; and thou shalt be a blessing:

3 And I will bless them that bless thee, and curse him that curseth thee: and in thee shall all families of the earth be blessed.

4 So Abram departed, as the LORD had spoken unto him; and Lot went with him: and Abram was seventy and five years old when he departed out of Haran.

KEY VERSES

I will make of thee a great nation, and I will bless thee, and make thy name great; and thou shalt be a blessing: And I will bless them that bless thee, and curse him that curseth thee: and in thee shall all families of the earth be blessed. —**Genesis 12:2, 3**

GOD'S WORLD AND GOD'S PEOPLE

Unit 2: God Destroys and Re-creates

LESSONS 6–9

LESSON AIMS

After participating in this lesson, each learner will be able to:

1. Explain the purpose of the genealogical tables in Genesis.

2. Describe the purpose and terms of Abram's covenant with God.

3. Describe his or her role in the fulfillment of God's promise to Abram (Abraham).

LESSON OUTLINE

Introduction
    A. The Family Tree
    B. Lesson Context
I. Legacy (GENESIS 10:1; 11:10, 27)
    A. Line of Noah (v. 1)
    B. Line of Shem (v. 10)
    C. Line of Terah (v. 27)
II. Journey (GENESIS 11:31, 32)
    A. Departure from Ur (v. 31a)
    B. Sojourn in Haran (v. 31b)
    C. Death of Terah (v. 32)
III. Promise (GENESIS 12:1-4)
    A. Call to Be Blessed (vv. 1-3)
      Searching for Something Better
    B. Departure at 75 (v. 4)
      Daddy, Are We There Yet?
Conclusion
    A. Inheriting a Legacy
    B. Leaving a Legacy
    C. Prayer
    D. Thought to Remember

Introduction

A. The Family Tree

Documenting one's family tree used to involve days of searching through family albums and old courthouse records. Now various websites place historical records at our fingertips. For $99, one such site promises a personal genetic profile from a saliva sample. The site also promises to help you connect with long-lost relatives whose DNA matches yours in some way. Clearly these services have hit a nerve: one reports 2.5 million monthly subscribers and 3 million total customers!

Our ancestry is interesting to us because our family tree gives us a sense of our roots. Individuals and groups identify themselves and understand how they are like and unlike others by appealing to the past. For example, my mother's parents are Coxes and Wallaces. The former are descendants of horse thieves from the English town of Bath, who were given the choice of going to prison or emigrating to the American colonies. The latter are descendants of the Scottish reformer William Wallace (of *Braveheart* fame), who fought for the freedom of his people. While these people lived generations ago, knowing who they are and what they did gives our children a sense of where they came from—but that's a double-edged sword!

B. Lesson Context

Our lessons this quarter focus on the themes of creation, God's identity as Creator, and the role human beings play in God's fulfillment of His promises across generations. Last week we looked at God's covenant with Noah, a person of outstanding faith in an era of wickedness (Genesis 6:1-6). Because Noah was faithful, he was granted a special role in God's renewal of the world following the great flood (6:7, 8, 18-22).

Genesis 10, a chapter often referred to as the Table of Nations, provides a lineage of Noah's descendants. The Tower of Babel event caused the various clans to scatter, resulting in social separation and corresponding isolation. As part of this process, Shem's descendants gradually settled in Mesopotamia (modern Iraq and Iran), where Abram (Abraham) was born (11:27-32).

While passages like Genesis 10 may seem tedious to modern readers, genealogies were extremely significant to ancient people groups. Tribal societies preserve records of ancestors to establish distinct identities for themselves and for the other clans with which they interact. These social identities, in turn, served as the basis for claims to land ownership, political and military alliances, channels of trade, patterns of intermarriage, and common religious observances.

I. Legacy

(GENESIS 10:1; 11:10, 27)

A. Line of Noah (v. 1)

1. Now these are the generations of the sons of Noah, Shem, Ham, and Japheth: and unto them were sons born after the flood.

Genesis 10 opens and closes with verses that bracket the genealogies between them and reveal their purpose. Verses 1 and 32 both refer to the chapter as a record of *the sons of Noah . . . after the flood,* and verse 32 states that these lines of descent and the geographical distribution of the respective clans ultimately produce "nations" (people groups living in specific territories) that Abram and the patriarchs encounter later.

The chapter rehearses the genealogies of Noah's three sons, beginning with *Japheth,* who seems least influential of the three in history. Next comes *Ham* and then *Shem,* the latter being our next focus.

> *What Do You Think?*
> How will the renewed realization that we all descend from the "sons of Noah" affect your participation in global evangelism?
> *Digging Deeper*
> What negative influences from your ancestral heritage and/or cultural traditions will you need to guard against, lest they hinder global evangelism?

B. Line of Shem (v. 10)

10. These are the generations of Shem: Shem was an hundred years old, and begat Arphaxad two years after the flood.

The Tower of Babel incident of Genesis 11:1-9 is tied to the genealogical table of chapter 10 by the reference to Nimrod, a grandson of Noah's son Ham, at 10:8-12. The Babel narrative serves to explain what has preceded and what will follow by connecting the development of distinct nations and cultures to the corresponding distribution of languages. Following this story, the author resumes the account of the line of Noah's son Shem.

The list in Genesis 11 shows that God's earlier promise in 3:15—that Eve's "seed" would bruise the head of the serpent, an allusion to Christ's victory on the cross—ultimately could not be stopped by the chaos following Babel. Even though Noah's descendants are scattered and divided, God's purpose to redeem His creation through a chosen line is not compromised.

C. Line of Terah (v. 27)

27. Now these are the generations of Terah: Terah begat Abram, Nahor, and Haran; and Haran begat Lot.

Now we see why the author focuses on Shem: it is his line that leads to *Terah,* the father of *Abram.*

II. Journey

(GENESIS 11:31, 32)

A. Departure from Ur (v. 31a)

31a. And Terah took Abram his son, and Lot the son of Haran his son's son, and Sarai his daughter in law, his son Abram's wife; and they went forth with them from Ur of the Chaldees, to go into the land of Canaan.

Terah's clan had settled in the city of *Ur* (Genesis 11:28)—likely located in southern Mesopotamia at the mouth of the Euphrates River by the Persian Gulf (in modern Iraq). Modern archaeological research has revealed that this was among the most advanced civilizations in antiquity, with a well-developed legal and political system and a strong economy. Ur was a major trade center, and its archaeological remains are impressive for the sophistication of its buildings and infrastructure. The city was one of the wealthiest in the world at the time Abram was born there.

Some think that Abram received his initial call from God to leave home while still in Ur. They base their conclusion on Genesis 15:7; Nehemiah 9:7; and especially Acts 7:2, 3.

On the other hand, Genesis 12:1-4 (in the context of 11:31, 32,) suggests that God appeared to Abram in the town of Haran. And 12:1 refers specifically to Abram's need to leave his "father's house," which he proceeds to do by leaving Haran with only Lot and the respective families. A trip from Ur would not be entirely consistent with this command, since Abram's father, Terah, left Ur with him. Perhaps God had already appeared to Abram in Ur and then came to him again after his father died (11:32).

A command to depart from Ur would be consistent with the larger story line of God's creation and re-creation that runs through the early chapters of Genesis. After the creation was ruined by sin (Genesis 6:1-7), God worked through Noah's family to renew the world following the flood. While God had intended for humans to spread out and populate the earth (1:28; 9:1, 7), various clans attempted to stay together and build a large city, including the Tower of Babel (11:4).

God foiled this plan by scattering them (Genesis 11:5-9). Generations later, however, major cities like Ur emerged, with advanced political and economic systems and religions with a multitude of deities (see Joshua 24:2). Another solution to human rebellion was needed.

B. Sojourn in Haran (v. 31b)

31b. And they came unto Haran, and dwelt there.

After leaving Ur, Terah decides to stop in *Haran*, a town that later becomes a major stop on the caravan trade network. Haran is located in what is now southern Turkey, near the border of Syria. While this appears to be an indirect route from Ur to Canaan, it reflects the practice of traveling northwest around the Syrian desert and then southwest near the Mediterranean coast.

C. Death of Terah (v. 32)

32. And the days of Terah were two hundred and five years: and Terah died in Haran.

Terah's death leaves Abram, apparently the oldest of his children (Genesis 11:26, 27), as the head of the clan.

What Do You Think?
> What lessons did you learn from a period of life when it seemed that you were just marking time at an in-between "Haran"?

Digging Deeper
> How did God use that experience to prepare you for now? What parts of that experience are usable by others? Why?

III. Promise
(Genesis 12:1-4)
A. Call to Be Blessed (vv. 1-3)

1. Now the LORD had said unto Abram, Get thee out of thy country, and from thy kindred, and from thy father's house, unto a land that I will shew thee.

As in the days of Noah, God chooses to break the cycle of rebellion by working through an individual: *Abram*. He is to leave the post-Babel population centers and journey to a new land of promise.

As with Noah following the flood (Genesis 9:8-17), Abram's commission emphasizes God's ongoing plan to re-create people as a way of preserving a faithful "seed" that will undo the work of Satan (3:15). Also as with Noah, God accomplishes this purpose by entering into a covenant, or contract, with an individual of outstanding faithfulness, someone who will pass the promise through the line of his descendants.

God's covenant with Abram is patterned after ancient suzerain-vassal treaties. In these arrangements, a great king declared sovereignty over a weaker subject king and demanded absolute loyalty in exchange for military protection and overall security. The terms of these agreements could be extended across generations, provided that the vassal king's heirs agreed to fulfill the conditions of obedience. Covenants of this kind were typical of ancient empires such as Egypt and Assyria, which ruled vast regions through local client kings.

In the present case, the supreme sovereign, God, offers a local tribal leader, Abram, blessings in exchange for obedience to God's unilateral terms. These terms in the verse before us are that Abram must leave everything—including his *country*, his *kindred* (ethnic/tribal group), and even some of his more immediate relatives (his *father's house*)—and undertake a journey to an unspecified location. God's terms suggest that this is a permanent migration; there is no indication that Abram will ever return to his homeland.

2. And I will make of thee a great nation, and I will bless thee, and make thy name great; and thou shalt be a blessing.

God continues by stating the benefits of the covenant. First, the promise that God will produce through Abram *a great nation* means that Abram will have many descendants. Moreover, they will form a distinct and influential people group (see also Genesis 15:5; 17:2-4). This aspect of God's promise is notable in that Abram's wife, Sarai, has been unable to conceive children to this point in time (11:30). This problem will become a driving theme in Abram's story (15:1-8; 16:1-6; 17:15-18; 18:9-15).

The benefits of the covenant require supernatural intervention, a reality that will further demonstrate God's power to fulfill His plans and purposes. The term *great nation* further implies what will be stated explicitly later: Abram is leaving his current homeland to occupy a new territory, Canaan, which will belong to his descendants (Genesis 12:7; 13:14-17; 15:7; 17:8).

The remaining benefits to Abram emerge from the first. *I will bless thee* stresses the divine protection Abram will enjoy as he travels and as his influence expands. Further, even though he has no children as of yet, the size of Abram's clan will expand his reputation and renown (*thy name great*) dramatically.

Abram and his descendants will also bless others, not only in the political and economic sense but also, and more particularly, through their witness to the faithfulness of the one true God.

3. And I will bless them that bless thee, and curse him that curseth thee: and in thee shall all families of the earth be blessed.

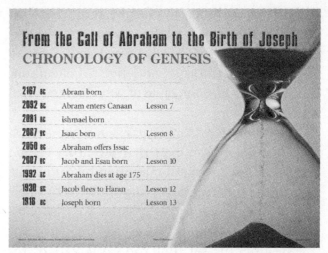

From the Call of Abraham to the Birth of Joseph
CHRONOLOGY OF GENESIS

2167 BC	Abram born	
2092 BC	Abram enters Canaan	Lesson 7
2081 BC	Ishmael born	
2067 BC	Isaac born	Lesson 8
2050 BC	Abraham offers Issac	
2007 BC	Jacob and Esau born	Lesson 10
1992 BC	Abraham dies at age 175	
1930 BC	Jacob flees to Haran	Lesson 12
1916 BC	Joseph born	Lesson 13

Visual for Lesson 7 & 9. *Display this chart for the remainder of the quarter to provide a timeframe for significant events covered in the lessons.*

More benefits that will proceed from God's covenant are revealed. The first implies that God will relate to other nations as those nations choose to relate to the nation that is to come from Abram. Those who ally themselves with God's people will be rewarded for doing so, but those who stand in opposition will be fighting against God. Such language is again typical of suzerain treaties, where the great king pledges to send aid and military support to defend the vassal king's homeland.

Another benefit reflects God's ultimate purpose: all people groups will ultimately *be blessed* somehow. What is unknown to Abram is known to us: that blessing is Christ (see Acts 3:25, 26; Galatians 3:8). Abram's descendants will thus serve to fulfill God's original plan to create a world that Satan cannot destroy (Genesis 3:15; 6:18; 9:1, 9).

What Do You Think?
In what specific ways can you help your church be a blessing to those outside its walls?
Digging Deeper
What does the connection between Abraham's obedience and his being a blessing have to say about your obligations?

❧ SEARCHING FOR SOMETHING BETTER ❧

In search of a better life, my ancestors made their way from the British Isles to the Appalachian

Mountains and then to southwestern Missouri. Several generations lived there before my grandfather and his growing family moved, first to Idaho and then to California. So I like to joke about descending from a long line of very distinguished hillbillies!

My family was simply part of a population shift that had begun more than a century earlier. America's great western migration began in earnest in the nineteenth century. In 1800, 10 percent of Americans lived west of the Appalachians; by 1825, 30 percent did!

The impetus for migration was varied: for some, it was escape from the crowded cities of the East; for others, it was commerce, land for homesteading, and the prospect of a better life—enhanced by the discovery of gold in the West. What Theodore Roosevelt called "the great leap Westward" continued into the twentieth century, as Americans collectively and individually sought to implement the "manifest destiny" mantra of the nineteenth century regarding that westward expansion.

It may be that some of those same interests caused Abram to perk up his ears when God called him to move west from Ur and then Haran. But for Abram, there was more. That something more was faith—faith that God would deliver on a glorious promise. And because of Abram's faith, we all are beneficiaries! Who will your faith benefit today?

—C. R. B.

HOW TO SAY IT

Arphaxad	Ar-*fax*-add.
Babel	*Bay*-bul.
Chaldees	*Kal*-deez.
Euphrates	You-*fray*-teez.
Haran	*Hair*-un.
Japheth	*Jay*-feth.
Nahor	*Nay*-hor.
Nimrod	*Nim*-rod.
Sarai	*Seh*-rye.
suzerain	*soo*-zuh-rin.
Terah	*Tair*-uh.
Ur	Er.
vassal	*vas*-uhl.

B. Departure at 75 (v. 4)

4. So Abram departed, as the LORD had spoken unto him; and Lot went with him: and Abram was seventy and five years old when he departed out of Haran.

Apparently without hesitation, *Abram* sets out for Canaan (Genesis 12:5). This trip is the start of a nomadic existence, with Abram moving his family members, servants, and livestock from place to place while receiving no specific indication from God that the land through which he travels will belong to him in his own lifetime. The author of Hebrews refers to Abraham (Abram's later name) as a model of faithfulness because he departed without knowing where he was going and lived as an alien in a land not his own (Hebrews 11:8-10).

> **What Do You Think?**
> How should the factor of Abraham's age when called affect your reaction to modern culture's view of "retirement age," if at all? Why?
>
> *Digging Deeper*
> Explain which elements of these passages are relevant and irrelevant to your answer: Exodus 4:13 (relating to Deuteronomy 29:5; 34:7); Numbers 8:23-26; 2 Samuel 19:32; 1 Kings 11:4; Psalms 71:18; 92:14; Luke 13:6-9

❧ DADDY, ARE WE THERE YET? ❧

It's the beginning of a long-anticipated vacation trip. Weeks of planning have gone into the coming excursion. Finally, the day has come for the journey to begin. The bags are packed and loaded into the family's SUV. The smaller children are strapped into their car seats. Dad, Mom, and the older children are buckled in, and the vacation starts. An hour later, teenaged Sally is totally engrossed in social media on her smartphone. Already bored, 5-year-old Johnny asks, "Daddy, are we there yet?" What parent hasn't heard this question?

On Abram's journey from Haran to Canaan, he didn't have to deal with teenagers isolating themselves from the family adventure or with bored little ones wishing the destination had been reached. He was not troubled by holiday traffic at favorite tourist spots. However, he also did not have the advantages we modern travelers have. Unlike us, he had no maps, paper or electronic. He had neither campgrounds with civilized amenities nor roadside motels offering "all the comforts of home, including WiFi." In fact, he didn't even know where he was going!

All Abram knew was that God was calling him on the trip of a lifetime. It required that he set aside his fears of the unknown and trust in the wisdom and power of God to lead and protect him and his family. Does that sound like God's call for our lives?   —C. R. B.

Conclusion

A. Inheriting a Legacy

For Christians, the Old Testament genealogies are significant because they demonstrate how Jesus fits into God's grand plan of salvation. The detailed records of Christ's lineage in Matthew 1:1-17 and Luke 3:23-38 demonstrate His connection with David, Abraham, Noah, and Adam. Genesis 11:10-26 is summarized in Luke 3:34-36; Genesis 11:31–12:1 is cited in Stephen's speech in Acts 7:2-4; Genesis 12:3 is quoted by Paul in Galatians 3:8; Genesis 12:1-15 is alluded to in Hebrews 11:8-10 to portray Abraham as a model of faithfulness.

As we modern readers struggle to pronounce the ancient Hebrew names in these passages, let us not overlook what the Bible authors strive to show. They show us how God's purposes are fulfilled from creation through the flood through Abraham and Israel and, ultimately, in Christ. That's the legacy Christians inherit. It is a legacy pointing to eternal life.

B. Leaving a Legacy

The decisions of parents can dramatically affect their descendants, sometimes for generations. These impacts are sometimes referred to as "generational curses." A more biblically accurate term might be "generational consequences."

This principle is reflected most explicitly in Exodus 20:5, which states that God visits the sins of the parents to the third and fourth generation of their descendants. Later generations used this to blame their ancestors for the suffering of descendants (Ezekiel 18:2). But God does not punish the innocent (Jeremiah 31:29, 30; Ezekiel 18:4). Even so, children and grandchildren suffer natural consequences of ancestral sins. They also are likely to imitate the sinful behaviors of older family members. When people worship idols, no one can be surprised when their children and grandchildren grow up to do the same.

One is reminded of the scene from the movie *A Christmas Story,* in which 9-year-old Ralphie utters a bad word and his mother demands to know who taught him to say such a thing. Ralphie blames one of the neighbor kids, when in fact he actually learned it from his father.

The world portrayed in the early chapters of Genesis is one in which parents trained their children to be experts in evil. But just as parents can leave a legacy of sinfulness for their children, they can also leave a legacy of faith that will last through the generations.

God planned for people to teach their children to love Him. The lineage of Noah to Shem to Abraham shows this system working at its best: faithful people passing truth down through generations in the midst of a dark world. Their commitment has become our blessing in Christ.

> *What Do You Think?*
> What steps can you take to ensure the legacy of Christ in your family?
> *Digging Deeper*
> Considering passages such as Matthew 3:9, 10; 1 Timothy 1:3, 4; and Titus 3:9, what guardrails should you put in place to prevent legacy-building from taking a wrong turn?

C. Prayer

Lord, help us find our place in Your plan to save the world, being faithful in the legacy we leave. We pray for this in Jesus' name. Amen.

D. Thought to Remember

"Every man is a quotation from all his ancestors."
                                —Ralph Waldo Emerson

INVOLVEMENT LEARNING

Enhance your lesson with KJV Bible Student *(from your curriculum supplier) and the reproducible activity page (at www.standardlesson.com or in the back of the* KJV Standard Lesson Commentary Deluxe Edition*).*

Into the Lesson

Write the following on the board:

Our ancestors are totally essential to our every waking moment, although most of us don't even have the faintest idea about their lives, their trials, their hardships or challenges. —A. Lennox

Ask students to volunteer stories about their ancestors. See who can go back the furthest in their family tree. Make a transition by saying, "Today's lesson takes us to the family tree of Abraham. We know the stories of some people listed, but nothing about others. This much is true: every name listed in any biblical genealogy represents a story as rich and complex as our own." Encourage students to elaborate on how the values of their ancestors may have influenced them.

Alternative. Distribute copies of the "Famous Ancestors" activity from the reproducible page, which you can download. Have students work in pairs, trying to match celebrities with their famous ancestors. Ask, "From what you know about [pick a name], how may this person have been influenced by knowing about his [or her] famous ancestor?"

Into the Word

Before class, write the 11 names from Genesis 10:1; 11:10, 27, 31 on slips of paper, one each. Distribute the slips randomly, making sure that each learner has at least one. (If you have more than 11 learners, include also the 7 additional names of Genesis 10:2.)

After allowing a quick glance at today's text, have everyone attempt to arrange the names in their correct genealogical order on a table. When they are done, make any needed corrections. Ask for volunteers to tell what they know about those people. When the stories are exhausted, call out the remaining names, the ones about whom little or nothing was said. Ask why God may have chosen to list people in genealogies but not give us further information about them.

Divide the class in half and distribute the following assignments. *Abraham's Responsibility Group:* Read Genesis 12:1-4 and identify Abraham's responsibility in the covenant described. *God's Responsibility Group:* Read Genesis 12:1-4 and identify God's responsibility in the covenant described. After group discussions, pose these questions: 1–How did the successful completion of this covenant depend on Abraham's obedience? 2–What was God's promised response to Abraham's obedience? 3–What promises of God are conditioned on our obedience?

Into Life

Read the following promise made by a famous world leader.

We choose to go to the moon in this decade . . . not because [it will be] easy, but because [it will be] hard; . . . because that challenge is one that we are willing to accept, one we are unwilling to postpone, and one which we intend to win.

Ask, "Which world leader made this promise?" *(John F. Kennedy)* Ask, "Was this promise fulfilled?" *(Yes)* Continue: "The promise God gave to Abraham in Genesis 12:3 is of eternally greater importance than going to the moon. As spiritual descendants of Abraham, we all have roles in the fulfillment of that promise. What words would you use to describe your role in the fulfillment of God's promise to Abraham?"

Pause for a time of whole-class discussion. *(Possible responses: hard, time-consuming, challenging, surprising, etc.)* Push deeper by inviting specifics, but don't put anyone on the spot.

Option. Distribute copies of the "Promise Search" activity from the reproducible page as a take-home. Encourage students to use it to consider the impact of God's promises on their lives.

THE BIRTH OF THE PROMISED SON

DEVOTIONAL READING: Luke 1:26-38
BACKGROUND SCRIPTURE: Genesis 18:9-15; 21:1-7

GENESIS 18:9-15

9 And they said unto him, Where is Sarah thy wife? And he said, Behold, in the tent.

10 And he said, I will certainly return unto thee according to the time of life; and, lo, Sarah thy wife shall have a son. And Sarah heard it in the tent door, which was behind him.

11 Now Abraham and Sarah were old and well stricken in age; and it ceased to be with Sarah after the manner of women.

12 Therefore Sarah laughed within herself, saying, After I am waxed old shall I have pleasure, my lord being old also?

13 And the LORD said unto Abraham, Wherefore did Sarah laugh, saying, Shall I of a surety bear a child, which am old?

14 Is any thing too hard for the LORD? At the time appointed I will return unto thee, according to the time of life, and Sarah shall have a son.

15 Then Sarah denied, saying, I laughed not; for she was afraid. And he said, Nay; but thou didst laugh.

GENESIS 21:1-7

1 And the LORD visited Sarah as he had said, and the LORD did unto Sarah as he had spoken.

2 For Sarah conceived, and bare Abraham a son in his old age, at the set time of which God had spoken to him.

3 And Abraham called the name of his son that was born unto him, whom Sarah bare to him, Isaac.

4 And Abraham circumcised his son Isaac being eight days old, as God had commanded him.

5 And Abraham was an hundred years old, when his son Isaac was born unto him.

6 And Sarah said, God hath made me to laugh, so that all that hear will laugh with me.

7 And she said, Who would have said unto Abraham, that Sarah should have given children suck? for I have born him a son in his old age.

KEY VERSE

The LORD visited Sarah as he had said, and the LORD did unto Sarah as he had spoken. —**Genesis 21:1**

GOD'S WORLD AND GOD'S PEOPLE

Unit 2: God Destroys and Re-creates

LESSONS 6–9

LESSON AIMS

After participating in this lesson, each learner will be able to:

1. Explain how the birth of Isaac fits the larger framework of Abraham's covenant.

2. Discuss ways that the manner in which God fulfilled the promise required patience on the part of Abraham and Sarah.

3. Identify situations in which their own faith has been challenged by God's apparent delay in fulfilling His promises.

LESSON OUTLINE

Introduction

A. Slow and Steady

"The Tortoise and the Hare" is a fable attributed to the Greek sage Aesop (believed to have lived about 600 BC). In this tale an arrogant rabbit berates a tortoise for being so slow. Embarrassed, the tortoise finally challenges the hare to a race. The rabbit is so confident that he pauses on the course to allow the slow tortoise to catch up so that he will be forced to see the hare win.

The hare falls asleep, however, and during his nap the plodding tortoise passes him to cross the finish line first. While this story carries much wisdom, its moral is communicated in the still-famous punch line, "Slow and steady wins the race."

"The Tortoise and the Hare" is still a popular subject of modern children's books. Perhaps the most significant lesson speaks to the value of patience. Though some tasks take a long time, the solution is to not give up in the face of obstacles, but rather to pace oneself and keep moving forward.

Today's lesson emphasizes the value of, and the need for, a "slow and steady" approach to faith. Whether we like it or not, God moves on His own timetable toward the fulfillment of His plans. Sometimes the pace seems to be frustratingly slow as we wait for God to act. And very often the finish line seems so far ahead that we can't even see where we are going. Real faith calls us to keep moving steadily forward in the knowledge that victory will come if we don't give up.

B. Lesson Context

We saw last week God's promise to make Abram "a great nation" and make his "name great" (Genesis 12:2). Abram was to have many descendants who together would form a formidable and respected people group.

Working against this outcome, however, was the fact that Abram and Sarai had not been able to have children (Genesis 11:30). Abram may have assumed that God would correct this problem sooner rather than later. Support for this supposition may be seen in the fact that God told Abram on more than one occasion that his descendants would possess the land of Canaan, which at that time was occupied by other tribes (Genesis 12:6, 7; 13:14-17; 15:18-21).

Yet despite all these promises, nothing happened. Abram and Sarai prospered financially (Genesis 13:2), and their clan was feared for its military power (Genesis 14), but no son was born. How could God's plan be fulfilled if His promise remained unfulfilled?

> ### What Do You Think?
> What are some things we can do to maintain faith when fulfillment of Bible promises seems too distant to happen in our lifetimes?
>
> *Digging Deeper*
> Considering the same issue in the lives of Bible characters, which one or two do you most relate to? Why?

Abram raised this point with God explicitly in Genesis 15:1-3. That time when God appeared to him, Abram observed that it would be impossible for God's plan to work: since Abram had no male heir, at death all his assets would revert to his oldest male servant, Eliezer, who was not related to him by blood (15:2). In response, God reaffirmed the promise (15:4, 5).

Yet more time passed, and no child came. In desperation, elderly Abram and Sarai decided to take matters into their own hands: they produced an heir through a surrogate mother, Hagar (Genesis 16). But then some 13 years later, with Abram nearing the century mark, God again made His intentions clear (Genesis 17). Abram (meaning "exalted father") would be known as Abraham ("father of many"; 17:4, 5). Abraham and Sarah (renamed from Sarai) would have many descendants, who would indeed conquer and possess the land (17:6-8). Having heard this same story many times before, Abraham could only laugh (17:17).

I. Human Impossibility
(Genesis 18:9-15)

Our reading picks up near the beginning of a long episode that culminates in the deliverance of Abraham's nephew, Lot (Genesis 11:27), from the destruction of the city of Sodom. Abraham is now 99 years old (17:1, 24). He and Sarah still have no children, and God has instructed them to circumcise all the men in their household as a sign of His plan to make a covenant with their heirs (17:9-14, 23-27).

Somewhere along the line, God has decided to destroy the towns of Sodom and Gomorrah, where Lot was then living (Genesis 13:5-13). Before He does this, however, He has a message for Abraham and Sarah. As our passage for today opens, the couple has been told several times over a period of many years that they will become the ancestors of a great and powerful nation. Working against God's promise is the hard reality of infertility and menopause.

A. God Promises (vv. 9, 10)

9. And they said unto him, Where is Sarah thy wife? And he said, Behold, in the tent.

The word *they* refers to the "three men" of Genesis 18:2. Their identity is often proposed to be the Lord and two angels, who disguise themselves in human form. They have stopped by the home of Abraham and Sarah to confirm once again God's promise regarding a child.

To this point in the story, Abraham has hosted the three men by providing a meal and rest (Genesis 18:1-8). These are standard gestures of hospitality offered to traveling guests. The Lord apparently does not disclose His identity to Abraham until later, so Abraham may not realize at this point that he is talking to the Lord and His angelic messengers. The author of Hebrews seems to allude to this story when he urges, "Be not forgetful to entertain strangers: for thereby some have entertained angels unawares" (Hebrews 13:2).

Sarah has assisted in the preparation of the food (Genesis 18:6), but has not shared in the meal. Instead, she has remained *in the tent* while the men dined outside. In that time, as in some cultures today, it is considered inappropriate for a married woman even to talk with men outside her family, much less dine with them. The mysterious strangers' inquiry about Sarah is doubtless unsettling, since they should have no way of knowing the name of Abraham's wife.

10a. And he said, I will certainly return unto thee according to the time of life; and, lo, Sarah thy wife shall have a son.

The plural "they" of the previous verse changes to singular *he*, which further changes to "the Lord" in Genesis 18:13, below. If Abraham believes it inappropriate for strangers to ask about his wife, he must be shocked by this statement. Abraham is clearly an old man; even if his wife were half his age, she is past the point of childbearing.

If nothing else, the declaration might be taken as a sort of prophetic confirmation of what God has said already on previous occasions. Yet this time there is a key difference: while all of God's earlier promises about Abraham's descendants have oriented toward a distant future (Genesis 12:1-3, 7; 13:14-17; 15:1-21; 17:1-21), this one is specific: *according to the time of life*—that is, about this same time next year—the promised son will come (compare 2 Kings 4:16). The importance of this prediction is acknowledged in Romans 9:9.

10b. And Sarah heard it in the tent door, which was behind him.

We wonder if Sarah is intentionally eavesdropping, or if the message is intentionally spoken loudly enough so that it's impossible for her not to hear. The text doesn't say.

B. Sarah Doubts (vv. 11-15)

11. Now Abraham and Sarah were old and well stricken in age; and it ceased to be with Sarah after the manner of women.

This verse underscores the human impossibility of what the stranger is saying. It has already been stated numerous times that Sarah is unable to become pregnant (Genesis 11:30; 16:1; 17:17). The physical challenge clearly lies with her, because Abraham was able to father a child with Hagar (16:1-4). Even if Sarah had already borne a dozen children, she is now 90 years old (17:17) and well past menopause.

12. Therefore Sarah laughed within herself, saying, After I am waxed old shall I have pleasure, my lord being old also?

Whether Sarah realizes this is God talking or simply thinks their guest is offering a blessing on Abraham's household for the hospitality,

this verse reveals the state of her own faith. Her earlier scheme to produce an heir through Hagar has already revealed her assumption that God's promise can only be fulfilled through some natural means (16:1-4).

Compounding the problem, she thinks, is the fact of Abraham's advanced age. The whole scenario has devolved, for her, into grim humor; all she can do is laugh in God's face, as Abraham himself had done a few months earlier (Genesis 17:17).

> **What Do You Think?**
> What are appropriate ways to respond to news that is hard to believe, yet is from a reliable source?
>
> **Digging Deeper**
> Categorize responses in the following texts as "appropriate," "inappropriate but understandable," or "inexcusably inappropriate": Judges 6:11-40; Jeremiah 1:4-6; Luke 1:8-18, 26-34.

13. And the LORD said unto Abraham, Wherefore did Sarah laugh, saying, Shall I of a surety bear a child, which am old?

The stranger, now revealed to the reader as not being a mere mortal, knows that Sarah has "laughed within herself." His question implies feeling insulted.

14a. Is any thing too hard for the LORD?

This rhetorical question states a premise of the Bible in a way that demands faith. The God who created the universe can do anything He wants and has proven so time and again. The question, then, is not whether God does what He says but whether Abraham and Sarah believe that He can and will.

> **What Do You Think?**
> What spiritual strategies can you adopt to not allow physical limitations to determine what God can and cannot do through you?
>
> **Digging Deeper**
> To what extent does (or should) the reality mixture of belief and unbelief in Mark 9:21-24 influence your response?

14b. At the time appointed I will return unto thee, according to the time of life, and Sarah shall have a son.

This restatement of the promise is not worded in such a way as to imply contingency on faith. The unconditional *I will return* asserts that this will be an occasion when God's will cannot be negated by lack of faith (contrast Luke 13:34).

15. Then Sarah denied, saying, I laughed not; for she was afraid. And he said, Nay; but thou didst laugh.

Realizing that she has been caught red-handed, perhaps offending their guests and embarrassing her husband, Sarah whips up a quick lie to get off the hook. Her fear may simply reflect the social awkwardness of the situation. But perhaps it is driven by something deeper: this strange man clearly knows something about God and what God has promised them. The men leave (Genesis 18:16) with the prophecy unretracted. Sarah will have a son within about a year, whether she believes it or not.

> **What Do You Think?**
> What are some proper ways for a Christian to respond when embarrassed by a lack of faith?
> *Digging Deeper*
> In determining whether lying is ever a proper reaction, consider Genesis 12:10-20; 20:1-12; 31:33-35; Joshua 2:1-6 (compare James 2:25); Matthew 26:69-75; Revelation 21:8.

❧ SARAH'S LAUGH ❧

What makes us laugh? The answer seems obvious: when something is funny! But maybe not.

We've all heard nervous giggles, and we've seen villains in movies laugh at the diabolical plots they've conceived. Psychological research shows that no more than 20 percent of our laughs are in response to something that could be considered a joke. Babies, as well as people born deaf and blind, laugh—demonstrating that laughter is not learned behavior. And most of us have experienced fits of uncontrollable laughter, usually in a group setting, to the point of saying (with a bit of exaggeration), "I nearly died laughing!" So the

laughter of others can stimulate us to laugh, as can nervousness and fiendish glee, as well as the occasional good joke.

When Sarah heard the mysterious visitor's prediction that she would bear a son, she laughed, perhaps at the irony of what seemed to be such an impossible suggestion. Of course, she was looking at the idea from a human perspective. Even today, some people find it laughable to think that God performs miracles. But they are not viewing the world through the eyes of faith.

For those willing to set aside human wisdom, the appropriate response when God does the seemingly impossible is . . . delight.   —C. R. B.

II. Divine Reality
(GENESIS 21:1-7)

Two interventions by the Lord are recorded between the two primary segments of today's lesson text. First, He destroys Sodom and Gomorrah (Genesis 19:1-29). After that, God corrects a situation brought on by Abraham's lack of faith (Genesis 20).

A. Promise Fulfilled (vv. 1-5)

1, 2. And the LORD visited Sarah as he had said, and the LORD did unto Sarah as he had spoken. For Sarah conceived, and bare Abraham a son in his old age, at the set time of which God had spoken to him.

Sarah becomes pregnant and gives birth at the age of 90 (see Genesis 17:17). This fact answers the rhetorical question of Genesis 18:14a, above. Clearly, nothing is impossible with God! After decades of Abraham and Sarah's childlessness, God acts miraculously within the exact time frame specified.

3. And Abraham called the name of his son that was born unto him, whom Sarah bare to him, Isaac.

Both Abraham and Sarah had laughed when promised a child, reflecting their doubt (Genesis 17:17; 18:12). In response to Abraham's laughter, God directed that the child's name be *Isaac* (17:19), which means "he laughs" when translated. Thus the child's name serves as an enduring reminder of God's faithfulness in the face of human doubt.

Isaac's name thus speaks volumes. To his parents, it condemns their "we know better" impatience with God's timetable. At the same time, the name symbolizes the great joy their son is bringing them. For Isaac himself, it serves as a lifelong reminder of his status as the promised child of the covenant (Genesis 17:19) and of his obligation to remain faithful to the God who has given him life.

4. And Abraham circumcised his son Isaac being eight days old, as God had commanded him.

A year before Isaac's birth, God had directed Abraham to seal the covenant by circumcising the male members of his household (Genesis 17:9-14). Further, God had commanded that Abraham's future descendants also should be circumcised. This is a known medical practice in Egypt in Abraham's time. Abraham may have first become aware of it during his brief sojourn there during a period of famine (12:10-20).

Circumcision in the current context is symbolic of the fact that God has promised to bless Abraham, and through him the world. That is to happen via the production of offspring (Genesis 12:1-3). God's earlier commands to Adam (1:28) and Noah (9:1) to populate the earth obviously involved natural sexual reproduction; and God's covenant with Abraham assumes that his descendants will pass along not only Abraham's bloodline but also his faith.

In this sense, circumcision is to serve as a powerful symbol of the passing of the blessings of the true God from one generation to the next. As Abraham's descendants are circumcised a week

HOW TO SAY IT

Aesop	*Ee*-sop.
Eliezer	El-ih-*ee*-zer.
Gomorrah	Guh-*more*-uh.
Hagar	*Hay*-gar.
Maasai	Mah-*sigh*.
Sarai	*Seh*-rye.
Sodom	*Sod*-um.
Tanzania	Tan-zuh-*nee*-uh.

after birth (Genesis 17:12; 21:4), they are literally, physically marked for God's service while still in the cradle.

❧ *RITE OF PASSAGE?* ❧

Growing up in Minnesota in the 1950s, I couldn't wait for my fifteenth birthday. That day I would be ready for a rite of passage: getting my driver's license. Throughout the year before that birthday, my friends and I emotionally wrestled with the perennial rumors that the age of eligibility would be increased to 16 before we reached the magic age. Looking back, I suspect 15 was too early an age at which to entrust someone with such a responsibility.

Every society has rites of passage. For example, Maasai boys in Kenya and Tanzania begin a many-year initiation process with a night spent in the forest. The next day's ceremony involves singing, dancing, drinking a concoction of various liquids, and eating large quantities of meat.

Then comes circumcision, the symbol of becoming men and warriors. They are not to cry out or even flinch, because this would show they are not brave warriors. The next 10 years are spent at warrior's camp, learning skills in preparation for the senior-warrior ceremony, which also entitles young men to get married.

God's intent for circumcision to Abraham was much different. Rather than being a rite of passage into adulthood, it was "a seal of the righteousness of the faith which he had yet being uncircumcised" (Romans 4:11). Today, circumcision for religious purposes is irrelevant (Galatians 6:15). What is important is circumcision of the heart (Romans 2:28, 29). But you may be surprised to learn that that is not a new thing for the new covenant era. See Deuteronomy 10:16; 30:6; Jeremiah 4:4.

—C. R. B.

5. And Abraham was an hundred years old, when his son Isaac was born unto him.

This verse is significant to Abraham's story for two reasons. First, it again stresses the miraculous nature of Isaac's birth, which occurred far beyond the time when his parents would naturally be able to have children. Second, it stresses the patience that God required of Abraham and Sarah. The two were age 75 and 65, respectively, when they departed Haran for Canaan (see Genesis 12:4; 17:17) with expectation of being made into "a great nation" there (12:2). But the two had to wait another 25 years to see the promise fulfilled. Their story is usually a model of persistent faithfulness; on a few occasions, however, they model the opposite.

B. Sarah Praises (vv. 6, 7)

6. And Sarah said, God hath made me to laugh, so that all that hear will laugh with me.

Though Sarah had earlier laughed at God's promise, to her credit she praises Him when she sees it finally fulfilled. Here again, the word *laugh* has more than one implication. God's prediction of the humanly impossible had previously provoked Sarah's laughter as an expression of doubt. Now she laughs with joy at God's fulfilling His promise. Sarah clearly intends to share her testimony with others, who will laugh with her as they share her joy and marvel with her at God's power.

> *What Do You Think?*
> How should the church as a body respond when God shows His faithfulness?
> *Digging Deeper*
> In what ways, if at all, should that response differ in the sight of unbelievers and fellow believers? Why?

7. And she said, Who would have said unto Abraham, that Sarah should have given children suck? for I have born him a son in his old age.

Sarah now indicates the reason people will laugh in amazement with her. Clearly she had given up, coming to a point where she didn't believe it possible for God's promise to be fulfilled. Her words also reflect the social pressure she had been under for decades, living in a world where a woman's primary responsibility was providing male heirs for her husband. Whereas people had previously whispered about her shame, they can now rejoice with her for God's provision.

Visual for Lesson 8. *Point to this visual as you ask, "What was a blessing you received that was so unlikely that it could only have come from the Lord?"*

Conclusion

A. Remember to Say "Thank You"

People seem to have a natural tendency to take things for granted. "Please" is easy to remember because we use that word to help us get something we want. "Thank you" takes more thought because we already have what we want and are ready to move on. Many believers find the same scenario to be true of their relationship with God. We know how to ask with "please," but don't invest much time in saying "thank You."

Sarah can serve as a good model for doing better on our thank-yous to God. Once her desire for a child was honored, she remembered to give God the credit—a special kind of "thank You." This told the whole world how grateful she was for what the Lord had done for her.

Genuine faith always expresses itself in gratitude. Does yours?

B. Prayer

Heavenly Father, help us realize anew that You expect us to adopt Your timetable, not the other way around. May times of Your silence be times of increasing faith as we await Your perfect timing. We pray in Jesus' name. Amen.

C. Thought to Remember

"With God all things are possible."
—Matthew 19:26

INVOLVEMENT LEARNING

Enhance your lesson with KJV Bible Student *(from your curriculum supplier) and the reproducible activity page (at www.standardlesson.com or in the back of the* KJV Standard Lesson Commentary Deluxe Edition*).*

Into the Lesson

Say, "It is likely that all of us know at least one couple that has struggled with infertility. What are some occasions that may be especially difficult for a couple that is unable to conceive?" *(Potential responses: a baby shower, births to close friends, Mother's Day.)*

After discussing the need for compassion and support, make a transition by pointing out that there are occasional "happy endings" when a child indeed comes along after many years of waiting and praying. Say, "Today's lesson is about just such a happy ending."

Alternative. Distribute copies of the "That's Impossible!" activity from the reproducible page, which you can download. Allow students to complete as indicated. After no more than one minute, call time, go over the answers, and discuss. Then ask, "What commonplace things do we experience today that were once considered impossible?" and/or "How have you seen God accomplish the impossible during your lifetime?"

Into the Word

Have students take turns reading aloud Genesis 18:9-15; 21:1-7. Then divide the class into three groups, giving each group pen and paper. Instruct them to create journal entries that focus on a particular character in the story. Provide the following questions on handouts that you create.

Sarah's Perspective Group: 1–With what was Sarah struggling? 2–Why did she laugh at the messenger's news? 3–Why did she deny laughing? 4–Why did she feel free to laugh once Isaac arrived?

Abraham's Perspective Group: 1–What was the only response Abraham made during the entire conversation with the messengers? 2–What is the significance of Abraham's giving his son a name that means "laughter"? 3–What covenantal act did Abraham perform after Isaac was born?

Messengers' Perspective Group: 1–What was the message they delivered? 2–How did the Lord feel about Sarah's response? 3–Why was Sarah confronted?

After no more than 15 minutes, allow groups to share entries with the class as a whole. Then pose the following questions, pausing after each one for discussion. 1–Why had Sarah resigned herself to being barren? 2–Why did the messenger speak to Abraham's knowing that Sarah would overhear the conversation? 3–Why did the messenger not respond directly to Sarah in verse 15? 4–Beyond the obvious biological reasons, how were Abraham and Sarah going to have to work together to see God's promise fulfilled through them?

Option. Distribute copies of the "Bible Babies" activity from the reproducible page. Have students work in pairs to complete as indicated. As a transition to Into Life, ask, "How does God's intimate knowledge of every human being, from the very moment of conception, change your understanding of how the Lord values you?"

Into Life

Say, "Today's Bible text describes the fulfillment of a promise from God in the midst of an impossible circumstance." Then, depending on the nature of your class, pose one or both of the following questions for discussion. 1–What do you desire from God that requires the seemingly impossible? 2–What promises from God do you especially depend on as you wait for the Lord's answer to your prayers? Encourage free discussion.

Option. Provide learners with pen, paper, and envelopes. Have them write short letters to themselves describing their hopes. When finished, have them put the letters in envelopes that they address to themselves. Collect the sealed envelopes; stamp and mail them a year from now so your learners can be reminded about how God has worked in their lives over the previous 12 months.

THE MARRIAGE OF ISAAC

DEVOTIONAL READING: Ephesians 5:21-33
BACKGROUND SCRIPTURE: Genesis 24

GENESIS 24:12-21, 61-67

12 And he said, O LORD God of my master Abraham, I pray thee, send me good speed this day, and shew kindness unto my master Abraham.

13 Behold, I stand here by the well of water; and the daughters of the men of the city come out to draw water:

14 And let it come to pass, that the damsel to whom I shall say, Let down thy pitcher, I pray thee, that I may drink; and she shall say, Drink, and I will give thy camels drink also: let the same be she that thou hast appointed for thy servant Isaac; and thereby shall I know that thou hast shewed kindness unto my master.

15 And it came to pass, before he had done speaking, that, behold, Rebekah came out, who was born to Bethuel, son of Milcah, the wife of Nahor, Abraham's brother, with her pitcher upon her shoulder.

16 And the damsel was very fair to look upon, a virgin, neither had any man known her: and she went down to the well, and filled her pitcher, and came up.

17 And the servant ran to meet her, and said, Let me, I pray thee, drink a little water of thy pitcher.

18 And she said, Drink, my lord: and she hasted, and let down her pitcher upon her hand, and gave him drink.

19 And when she had done giving him drink, she said, I will draw water for thy camels also, until they have done drinking.

20 And she hasted, and emptied her pitcher into the trough, and ran again unto the well to draw water, and drew for all his camels.

21 And the man wondering at her held his peace, to wit whether the LORD had made his journey prosperous or not.

· ·

61 And Rebekah arose, and her damsels, and they rode upon the camels, and followed the man: and the servant took Rebekah, and went his way.

62 And Isaac came from the way of the well Lahairoi; for he dwelt in the south country.

63 And Isaac went out to meditate in the field at the eventide: and he lifted up his eyes, and saw, and, behold, the camels were coming.

64 And Rebekah lifted up her eyes, and when she saw Isaac, she lighted off the camel.

65 For she had said unto the servant, What man is this that walketh in the field to meet us? And the servant had said, It is my master: therefore she took a vail, and covered herself.

66 And the servant told Isaac all things that he had done.

67 And Isaac brought her into his mother Sarah's tent, and took Rebekah, and she became his wife; and he loved her: and Isaac was comforted after his mother's death.

KEY VERSE

Rebekah arose, and her damsels, and they rode upon the camels, and followed the man: and the servant took Rebekah, and went his way. —**Genesis 24:61**

GOD'S WORLD AND GOD'S PEOPLE

Unit 2: God Destroys and Re-creates

LESSONS 6–9

LESSON AIMS

After participating in this lesson, each learner will be able to:

1. Explain how the story of Isaac and Rebekah fits into the larger creation/re-creation cycle in the book of Genesis.

2. Discuss the correct biblical perspective on the practice of seeking signs from God.

3. Write a commitment statement to take the next bold step of faith that presents itself.

LESSON OUTLINE

Introduction
  A. Putting Out a Fleece
  B. Lesson Context
I. Answered Prayer (GENESIS 24:12-21)
  A. Sign Requested (vv. 12-14)
  B. Sign Granted (vv. 15-21)
II. Answered Call (GENESIS 24:61-67)
  A. Journey of Faith (vv. 61-65)
    Stepping Out on Faith
  B. Fulfillment of Hope (vv. 66, 67)
    The Blessings of a Good Marriage
Conclusion
  A. God's Choices and Ours
  B. Prayer
  C. Thought to Remember

Introduction

A. Putting Out a Fleece

When facing an important decision, sometimes we may ask God for a sign to help us decide what to do. Based on a famous story involving Gideon in Judges 6, such requests are often referred to as "putting out a fleece." Gideon's story has been taken as evidence that God will grant signs of His will to those who ask for them.

While it is essential that we are open to God's leading and while the Bible does record instances of individuals asking God for signs and receiving them, it is important to note the contexts of these biblical accounts. In each case the requested sign related to something God had already commanded or promised would happen. In the story of the fleece, for example, God had already called Gideon to save the Israelites from oppression and had given specific instructions on what to do (Judges 6:1-16, 33-35). These instructions did not involve Gideon's personal well-being, but rather pertained to God's larger plan for the redemption of His people. Gideon was requesting tangible signs to prove that he had not merely imagined that God had spoken to him. We also note what Jesus had to say about seeking signs in Matthew 12:39; Luke 11:29.

Our story today illustrates some principles in a context that frequently drives Christians to ask God for a sign: choosing a spouse. God had decided to preserve a chosen people by making a covenant with Abraham and his descendants. Obviously, that plan could be fulfilled only if Abraham had faithful descendants. With stakes so high, it would be critical for God to be involved in the process.

B. Lesson Context

Our lessons this quarter have focused on God's plan to create a perfect world populated with human beings who would live in fellowship with Him and one another (Genesis 1:26-31). Sin spoiled this plan, but God did not give up. When the world was all but completely corrupted, God cleansed the earth through the flood and started the cycle of creation afresh with Noah and his family (6:1–7:1; 9:1-7). The line of faith continued through Noah's son Shem and his descendants, even after the scattering of the nations following the Tower of Babel incident (11:1-9). Generations later, Abraham (as Abram) was called to leave his homeland. He did so carrying the promise of becoming a great nation (12:1-3, 6, 7; 13:14-17; 15:1-7; 17:1-16).

Many years after receiving this promise, Abraham and Sarah miraculously conceived Isaac, who would be heir to his father's possessions and blessing (Genesis 21:1-7). After Sarah passed away (23:1, 17-20), Abraham was left with a final task: finding Isaac a wife who would continue his bloodline and pass along the promise that God would one day crush Satan through one of his descendants, Jesus (Genesis 3:15).

Since Abraham was a wealthy and respected clan leader (Genesis 12:1, 2, 16; 21:22, 23; 23:1-6; 24:1), it would have been easy for him to broker a lucrative match for his son among the nobility of the local people groups. But recalling the nature of his covenant with God, Abraham instead determined that Isaac's wife should come from his own relatives. He therefore sent a servant to choose a wife for Isaac, a wife whose family was willing to release her to relocate to Canaan (23:2; 24:1-9).

Finding such a young woman was no small task, for Abraham had been away from Haran in his homeland for more than 60 years (compare Genesis 12:4 with 17:17 and 23:1). There is no record of his having been in contact with his brother during the interim, except for the information received in 22:20-24. Further, there was no guarantee that Abraham's relatives would allow one of their marriage-eligible daughters, if they even had any, to leave home with a stranger and move hundreds of miles away to marry a man she had never seen or heard of.

I. Answered Prayer

(Genesis 24:12-21)

As today's lesson begins, the servant has arrived with 10 camels in the land of Abraham's family (Genesis 24:10). There the servant stops by a well outside the town of Nahor, apparently named after Abraham's deceased brother (11:27-30; 22:20-24). The servant needs to water his animals, and it is providential that he is there at "the time of the evening . . . that women go out to draw water" (24:11).

Wells are a major gathering place for women of the time—one of the few places where they can meet regularly with friends from other households. Since women were generally not permitted to interact with men outside their families (see Genesis 24:65), the village well is the only place a traveling stranger might encounter local women. The servant seems to have chosen this location and time (see 24:11) strategically as a good place to seek a sign from God.

A. Sign Requested (vv. 12-14)

12, 13. And he said, O LORD God of my master Abraham, I pray thee, send me good speed this day, and shew kindness unto my master Abraham. Behold, I stand here by the well of water; and the daughters of the men of the city come out to draw water.

Marriage is viewed primarily as a business and political transaction in this era. In that light, the servant would seek out the leader of the local clan to initiate negotiations. Earlier, however, Abraham had told the servant that God would guide the proceedings (Genesis 24:7). As the servant begins to pray in that regard, he postures himself as a wealthy traveling merchant.

What Do You Think?
Considering the servant's alertness to an opportunity to fulfill his mission, what steps can our church take to develop alertness for opportunities to fulfill the church's mission?
Digging Deeper
What will be your own contribution to that task?

14a. And let it come to pass, that the damsel to whom I shall say, Let down thy pitcher, I pray thee, that I may drink.

At the same time, the servant prays that God will fulfill the covenant promise to Abraham by giving a sign that will reveal which young woman he should choose for Isaac. In so doing, the servant states the criteria of the sign he is seeking. Three aspects of his prayer are notable.

First, he does not assume that the first woman he talks to will be the one God has chosen. Since it will be inappropriate for a woman to initiate conversation, he plans to do so himself. But he realizes that he may need to ask several women before receiving a positive response.

14b. And she shall say, Drink, and I will give thy camels drink also: let the same be she that thou hast appointed for thy servant Isaac.

Second, in order to avoid a "false positive," the servant's test involves two elements: the chosen young lady will not only respond to his request by giving him a *drink* but will go beyond what he asks and offer to water his *camels* as well. Such a task would normally be relegated to his own servants. The latter condition makes it impossible for the servant to lead prospects toward an answer he might want, since the woman to whom he speaks will have to offer to water the camels on her own initiative.

As a side note, this test will identify the chosen woman as a person of unusual generosity: a single camel can consume up to 30 gallons of water, and the servant has 10 camels (Genesis 24:10). So this aspect of the sign will require many, many draws from the well.

14c. And thereby shall I know that thou hast shewed kindness unto my master.

Third, it is important to note that the servant's requested sign is tied to a divine commission that he has already received. It is not tied to any personal desire to know God's plans for the future. By this time, God has told Abraham numerous times that his son by Sarah would carry the promises of the covenant (see Genesis 17:15-19). This charge necessitates that Isaac, Sarah's only son, must marry a woman of the Lord's approval.

> **What Do You Think?**
> In what circumstances, if any, should we seek a sign from God today? Why?
> *Digging Deeper*
> How do texts such as Matthew 4:7; 12:38, 39; 16:1-4; and 24:3 affect your answer, if at all?

B. Sign Granted (vv. 15-21)

15. And it came to pass, before he had done speaking, that, behold, Rebekah came out, who was born to Bethuel, son of Milcah, the wife of Nahor, Abraham's brother, with her pitcher upon her shoulder.

Even before the servant finishes stating the criteria of the sign he is seeking from God, a young woman appears at the well. The text immediately identifies her as a person meeting Abraham's standards for his son's bride (Genesis 24:3-8). First, *Rebekah* is a relative of Abraham: his grandniece, being the granddaughter of his brother *Nahor* (see also 22:20-23). She is therefore of the right bloodline, not of a Canaanite tribe (24:3).

16. And the damsel was very fair to look upon, a virgin, neither had any man known her: and she went down to the well, and filled her pitcher, and came up.

Second, she is an unmarried *virgin*, eligible to marry and bear legitimate children as heirs to Isaac. As an added bonus, she also happens to be physically attractive, although that is by no means essential for God's purposes.

17. And the servant ran to meet her, and said, Let me, I pray thee, drink a little water of thy pitcher.

The servant does not hesitate to approach Rebekah. We may wonder how much the slow pace of the long journey influences the quickness of his step at this point, but the text doesn't say. We rightly infer that he is focused on applying as quickly as possible the criteria he has established.

> **What Do You Think?**
> What are some times that impel (or should impel) us to move more quickly than others in doing the will of God? Why?
> *Digging Deeper*
> Considering Hebrews 6:12; 12:1; and 2 John 9, what sins most seem to keep Christians from moving at best speed to do the will of God? What is the evidence for your conclusion?

18. And she said, Drink, my lord: and she hasted, and let down her pitcher upon her hand, and gave him drink.

The first test (Genesis 24:14) is immediately passed as Rebekah offers Abraham's servant a *drink* from *her pitcher*. This is significant in view of what the servant, and Abraham, will ask Rebekah to do. Since she will need to leave her home and travel hundreds of miles to join a family she has never met, she will need to feel comfortable with strangers.

19, 20. And when she had done giving him drink, she said, I will draw water for thy camels also, until they have done drinking. And she hasted, and emptied her pitcher into the trough, and ran again unto the well to draw water, and drew for all his camels.

Without prompting, Rebekah proceeds to fulfill the second test by also watering the servant's *camels*. At this point, she is unaware of the significance of her actions.

21. And the man wondering at her held his peace, to wit whether the LORD had made his journey prosperous or not.

Although—or because—his mission is urgent, the servant is careful not to jump to conclusions. In the first place, he has asked God that the proper candidate would water his camels (Genesis 24:14), and that task is not yet complete. He has 10 of them (24:10), and watering will take quite some time. Further, the servant has had no confirmation that God has agreed to his request for a sign. He is therefore appropriately cautious and seems to wait to see whether Rebekah's actions are simply coincidental gestures of hospitality.

II. Answered Call
(GENESIS 24:61-67)

In the intervening text that is not part of today's lesson (Genesis 24:22-60), Abraham's servant concludes that Rebekah is the one he seeks. So he reveals his identity and mission. The leaders of Rebekah's family agree that she can go.

A. Journey of Faith (vv. 61-65)

61. And Rebekah arose, and her damsels, and they rode upon the camels, and followed the man: and the servant took Rebekah, and went his way.

In certain respects, Rebekah's story parallels that of Abraham. Both are called by God to leave a comfortable life (see Genesis 11:27–12:5); both are given a chance to participate in God's formation of a people-group; and both are required to migrate to Canaan in order to fulfill their calling.

> *What Do You Think?*
> How will you decide if embarking on a trip to an unknown future is a step of faith or a step of foolishness?
> *Digging Deeper*
> In what way, if any, do the two episodes in Ruth 1:16-18 and 3:1-6 plus the illustrations in Luke 14:28-33 provide direction for your conclusions?

Because the circumstances of this proposal are unique, it may seem at first glance that Rebekah's family ultimately leaves the decision to her (Genesis 24:55-58). But such a procedure would be quite out of the ordinary in the ancient world, since women of the time do not participate in making major decisions (compare 24:50, 51). Some propose, therefore, that Rebekah's decision is actually limited either to leaving with the servant immediately or to leave after spending 10 days with her family (24:55). Her choice to leave immediately illustrates her confidence in God's plan.

❧ STEPPING OUT ON FAITH ❧

Some years ago, I was invited to join a former college professor of mine on a trip to survey the feasibility of starting a new mission in Africa. He wanted me to help him evaluate the situation. After my wife and I prayed about it, we decided I should make the trip. The circumstances we found there were positive, and I made a commitment to return.

At the time, my wife and I had just entered new teaching careers. We had been preparing for those careers for years, yet we felt led to go. Saying yes to God's call meant risking our future and vacating our first new home. And then there was the matter of raising thousands of dollars to support a family of four and to launch the yet-to-be-birthed mission.

2167 BC	Abram born	
2092 BC	Abram enters Canaan	Lesson 7
2081 BC	Ishmael born	
2067 BC	Isaac born	Lesson 8
2050 BC	Abraham offers Isaac	
2007 BC	Jacob and Esau born	Lesson 10
1992 BC	Abraham dies at age 175	
1930 BC	Jacob flees to Haran	Lesson 12
1916 BC	Joseph born	Lesson 13

Visual for Lesson 7 & 9. *Point to this chart as you ask, "Given that Isaac was 40 years old when he married Rebekah, what year would that have been?*

And God provided! Others joined us in this journey of faith. Some went with us in the venture and some faithfully supported us with prayer and finances during our time in Africa.

The decision on the part of Rebekah and her family to accept the call to go to a land unknown undoubtedly took more faith than was required of us. She left home to travel with a man she had just met, to marry a man she had never met, and to live the rest of her life in an unfamiliar land and society about which she knew little or nothing. In Africa, we could stay in touch with home through mail, telephone, and ham radio. Today it's even easier with video streaming, etc. Rebekah wasn't assured of ever again having contact with her family of origin.

Whatever our situation, the essence of faith is trusting God to care for us in His calling for us. Do you live that truth?   —C. R. B.

62, 63. And Isaac came from the way of the well Lahairoi; for he dwelt in the south country. And Isaac went out to meditate in the field at the eventide: and he lifted up his eyes, and saw, and, behold, the camels were coming.

The scene switches to the end of Rebekah's long journey, as she and the servant return to Abraham's territory. *Isaac* is 40 years old at this time (Genesis 25:20). Apparently he has accumulated significant livestock herds of his own and is grazing them near *the well Lahairoi*.

This location is significant to Isaac's family as the site where God appeared to Hagar, Ishmael's mother, to tell her to return to Sarah (Genesis 16:7-14). The Hebrew name of the well means "well of the Living One [God] who sees me." This may explain why Isaac is meditating.

64, 65. And Rebekah lifted up her eyes, and when she saw Isaac, she lighted off the camel. For she had said unto the servant, What man is this that walketh in the field to meet us? And the servant had said, It is my master: therefore she took a vail, and covered herself.

Upon learning that the man approaching the caravan is her betrothed husband, *Rebekah* covers her face with *a vail* (veil) as customary for unmarried women at the time.

B. Fulfillment of Hope (vv. 66, 67)

66, 67. And the servant told Isaac all things that he had done. And Isaac brought her into his mother Sarah's tent, and took Rebekah, and she became his wife; and he loved her: and Isaac was comforted after his mother's death.

The servant's complete disclosure regarding *all things that he had done* convinces *Isaac* that Abraham's requirements have been met. Isaac's marriage to a woman of the bloodline of Shem and Noah demonstrates that God's promise to Abraham to become the father of a great nation is being fulfilled.

> *What Do You Think?*
> Considering the full disclosure from the servant to Isaac, how do we know when that's a model for us, as opposed to times when we should keep silent?
>
> *Digging Deeper*
> What lessons have you learned the hard way in this regard?

❧ THE BLESSINGS OF A GOOD MARRIAGE ❧

"And they lived happily ever after." So goes the clichéd description of a so-called fairy-tale marriage. Many people today don't believe in such idealistic marriages—or in marriage period. The concept of traditional marriage has fallen on hard times. A high percentage of marriages don't last, although the good news is that the divorce rate has been decreasing in recent years.

The bad news, however, is that more people are choosing cohabitation rather than marriage. In the process, they are depriving themselves of the opportunity for growth that the challenges of marriage provide.

Isaac's marriage to Rebekah came about in a way that seems strange to our culture. The romantic idea of "falling in love" seems to have been absent (at least in the way we think it should come about). However, that may be what is wrong with many relationships. If a relationship is based solely on physical desire and the light-headed thrill of "being in love," the partners may be blind to the fact that the satisfaction of an enduring love is possible.

We read that Isaac loved Rebekah, a woman he had married according to God's leading. Although they were personally as imperfect as we are, their life together reflected their commitment to the plan of God. And following the death of Isaac's mother, it was his marriage to Rebekah that brought him comfort. Sometimes God meets more than one need at a time, doesn't He? —C. R. B.

Conclusion

A. God's Choices and Ours

One of the greatest doctrinal debates in history concerns the tension between God's sovereignty and humanity's free will. Obviously, God is all-powerful, knows everything, and works all things according to His purposes. At the same time, the Bible provides many examples of people who made a godly difference, or who attempted to subvert God's plans, through their choices.

In either case, we are bound to hear someone say, "Well, it was God's will." But what does that mean? The answer lies in seeing God's will in terms of three categories. First, there's God's *purposive will*. These are actions God takes unilaterally of His own volition. Deciding to create the earth is an example.

Second is God's *prescriptive will*. These are things God wants us to do (He prescribes them), but allows us a choice to obey or not. Third is God's *permissive will*. These are things God desires that we do not do, but He permits us free will to disobey; sin falls in this category.

Our lesson today illustrates what happens when God's desires and our choices align to fulfill His purposes. Centuries before Abraham, God had decreed that He would destroy the work of Satan (Genesis 3:15) and had worked through Seth, Noah, and their descendants to maintain a family line of faithfulness. He then made a covenant with Abraham to create a chosen race and caused Abraham and Sarah to have a child, Isaac, to fulfill this plan. Clearly, God had planned that Rebekah would play a key role in this story long before she had ever heard of Isaac.

What if Rebekah's family had refused to let her go? Would that have ruined God's plans? No. God can always find a different way. Even so, today's story is one of obedience, not of rebellion. It is a story of what can happen when we align our plans with God's purposes.

B. Prayer

Lord, help us to be alert to what Your purposes are and to Your desires for how we can advance the cause of Christ. Grant that we will step out on faith when called. We pray this in Jesus' name. Amen.

C. Thought to Remember

"We want big directional signs from God. God just wants us to pay attention."

—Lysa TerKeurst, President, Proverbs 31 Ministries

HOW TO SAY IT

Babel	*Bay*-bul.
Bethuel	Beh-*thew*-el.
Canaan	*Kay*-nun.
Hagar	*Hay*-gar.
Haran	*Hair*-un.
Ishmael	*Ish*-may-el.
Lahairoi	Luh-*hi*-roy.
Nahor	*Nay*-hor.
Rebekah	Reh-*bek*-uh.

INVOLVEMENT LEARNING

Enhance your lesson with KJV Bible Student (from your curriculum supplier) and the reproducible activity page (at www.standardlesson.com or in the back of the KJV Standard Lesson Commentary Deluxe Edition).

Into the Lesson

Have this request displayed on the board as learners arrive:

List one to three things that popular culture tells us to do or have in order to be happy.

Ask volunteers to read their lists aloud. *(Expect responses that involve food, fashion, achievement, physical fitness, beauty, status, wealth, power, etc.)* After acknowledging the diversity of responses, ask, "What do *you* think we need to do in order to be happy?" Encourage free discussion. *(Possible responses: trust in God, faithfulness to Him and our families, loving service to others.)*

Make a transition by asking, "The old hymn 'Trust and Obey' declares that there is no other way to be happy in Jesus, but to trust and obey. So why are those two things so difficult at times?"

Into the Word

After a time of free discussion on the preceding question, ask a student to read Genesis 24:12-21, 61-67 aloud. Break the class into two groups: the *Trust Group* and the *Obey Group*. Distribute handouts (you prepare) to the groups with the instructions below; have enumerations of the lesson's 17 verses down the left side. (If your class is larger, create additional groups so that group sizes are from three to five.)

Trust Group: List next to the verse references the times in Genesis 24:12-21, 61-67 that someone had to trust God, another person, and/or themselves.

Obey Group: List next to the verse references the times in Genesis 24:12-21, 61-67 that someone had an opportunity to obey God or another person who was working to a godly end.

After groups complete their tasks, have a member from each read its list to the class. *(Sample responses to anticipate:* for *trust,* verse 14, the servant trusted that God would honor his request for a sign; for *obey,* verse 67, Isaac obeyed his father's plan for an arranged marriage.)*

Then ask, "What would be different if Rebekah, her family, and/or Isaac had chosen not to trust or obey in their story today?" *(Possible responses:* If Rebekah's family had said *no* to leaving, she wouldn't have been a part of the lineage of Christ. If Isaac had chosen a bride from among the peoples where he lived, it could have disqualified him from being a patriarch of Israel.)*

Into Life

Then say, "Even if Rebekah's family had said no, she still could have led a life that honored God. But she would have missed out on the epic role God had in mind for her." Ask the class to use the back of the handout from the Into the Word activity to list one to three instances when they faced an epic choice. Then have them reflect on whether they made the *epic choice*—to trust and obey God, following Him to something great—or if they made a safe choice. Assure them that (1) they won't be asked to share their lists and (2) a *safe* choice isn't necessarily a *sinful* choice—it may simply be to miss an epic opportunity that God had for them.

After a few minutes, ask, "How will the call to trust and obey influence the next time you are faced with an epic choice?" Encourage free discussion. *(Possible responses:* It will grow my faith as I trust the Lord even when it is scary. I will have to consciously consider what "obeying" looks like when faced with the choice. I will consider whether or not the Lord is calling me to something greater in making the choice one way or the other.)*

Alternative. Distribute copies of the "Trust and Obey" activity from the reproducible page, which you can download. Have students work in pairs or trios to complete it as indicated. Encourage them to use this to ponder the mandate to *trust* and *obey* as they face choices in the week ahead.

SIBLINGS' RIVALRY

DEVOTIONAL READING: Matthew 16:13-20
BACKGROUND SCRIPTURE: Genesis 25:19-34

GENESIS 25:19-34

19 And these are the generations of Isaac, Abraham's son: Abraham begat Isaac:

20 And Isaac was forty years old when he took Rebekah to wife, the daughter of Bethuel the Syrian of Padanaram, the sister to Laban the Syrian.

21 And Isaac intreated the LORD for his wife, because she was barren: and the LORD was intreated of him, and Rebekah his wife conceived.

22 And the children struggled together within her; and she said, If it be so, why am I thus? And she went to enquire of the LORD.

23 And the LORD said unto her, Two nations are in thy womb, and two manner of people shall be separated from thy bowels; and the one people shall be stronger than the other people; and the elder shall serve the younger.

24 And when her days to be delivered were fulfilled, behold, there were twins in her womb.

25 And the first came out red, all over like an hairy garment; and they called his name Esau.

26 And after that came his brother out, and his hand took hold on Esau's heel; and his name was called Jacob: and Isaac was threescore years old when she bare them.

27 And the boys grew: and Esau was a cunning hunter, a man of the field; and Jacob was a plain man, dwelling in tents.

28 And Isaac loved Esau, because he did eat of his venison: but Rebekah loved Jacob.

29 And Jacob sod pottage: and Esau came from the field, and he was faint:

30 And Esau said to Jacob, Feed me, I pray thee, with that same red pottage; for I am faint: therefore was his name called Edom.

31 And Jacob said, Sell me this day thy birthright.

32 And Esau said, Behold, I am at the point to die: and what profit shall this birthright do to me?

33 And Jacob said, Swear to me this day; and he sware unto him: and he sold his birthright unto Jacob.

34 Then Jacob gave Esau bread and pottage of lentiles; and he did eat and drink, and rose up, and went his way: thus Esau despised his birthright.

KEY VERSE

The LORD said unto her, Two nations are in thy womb, and two manner of people shall be separated from thy bowels; and the one people shall be stronger than the other people; and the elder shall serve the younger.

—Genesis 25:23

GOD'S WORLD AND GOD'S PEOPLE

LESSON AIMS

After participating in this lesson, each learner will be able to:

1. Summarize the account of Rebekah's pregnancy, the birth of her twin boys, and the account of how Jacob obtained the birthright from Esau.

2. Explain what contributed to the sibling rivalry between Jacob and Esau and which influences today create such rivalries.

3. Take the first step to resolve a family rivalry.

LESSON OUTLINE

Introduction

A. Lucy and Jacob

The classic *Peanuts* comic strip often featured a theme centered around a promise that Charlie Brown's nemesis, Lucy, makes to hold a football on the ground so he can kick it. Charlie is wary; he knows that Lucy will pull the ball away. Lucy pleads for another chance, claiming that she has changed. She gives Charlie her "bonded word" that she will not pull the ball away. So Charlie backs up, runs toward the ball, and (of course) Lucy yanks it away. Charlie is seen flipping into the air with his predictable exclamation of "Aaugh!" Then he lands on his back with a *Wump!*

Lucy's clever, deceptive behavior is similar to that of Jacob, the focus of our next four lessons. In today's Scripture passage we see him taking advantage of his brother Esau's hunger in order to pull away from him something much more significant than a football: the family's birthright. But this was no cartoon; it was a series of events with tragic consequences for Jacob and his family.

B. Lesson Context

Today's lesson begins a new unit of lessons that continues our studies from Genesis this quarter. The unit's theme of "God Blesses and Re-creates Regardless" highlights God's ability to work through the life of one flawed man in particular: Jacob.

Initially, Jacob had very little regard for anyone except himself. He was a man who lived by his wits, by his ability to outwit and outmaneuver anyone who crossed his path. Eventually he learned to acknowledge God, not himself, as the one in control, though the consequences of his deceitful tactics dogged him through much of his life.

"Siblings' Rivalry," the title of this lesson, could serve as a subtitle for the book of Genesis as a whole. Before we read of Jacob and Esau's tension, we read of Cain and Abel and of Ishmael and Isaac (Jacob's father). Later in Genesis, we see the friction between the two sisters Leah and Rachel. Then there is that of Jacob's sons. Thus today's account doesn't lack for company!

I. Distressed Mother
(Genesis 25:19-23)
A. Big Picture (vv. 19, 20)

19. And these are the generations of Isaac, Abraham's son: Abraham begat Isaac.

The book of Genesis is arranged by the use of the phrase *the generations of* (compare Genesis 2:4; 5:1; 6:9; 10:1; 11:10, 27; 25:12; 25:19; 36:1, 9; 37:2). The verses just prior to this one record "the generations of Ishmael," Abraham's son through Hagar. But that account lasts only through verse 18. By contrast, the record of *the generations of Isaac* that begins here continues through Genesis 35:29—more than 10 chapters! That speaks to the relative significance of these half brothers.

20. And Isaac was forty years old when he took Rebekah to wife, the daughter of Bethuel the Syrian of Padanaram, the sister to Laban the Syrian.

Genesis 24 records the arranged marriage of Isaac to Rebekah (last week's lesson). *Bethuel* is the son of Abraham's brother Nahor. Her brother *Laban* eventually becomes father-in-law of Jacob, son of Isaac and Rebekah, through Jacob's marriages to Leah and Rachel, Laban's daughters.

The term *Syrian* is a geographical designation rather than an ethnic one. The term *Padanaram* means "plain of Aram" (another name for Syria). It is a part of Mesopotamia, to which Abraham had sent his servant to find a wife for Isaac (Genesis 24:10).

HOW TO SAY IT

Aram	*Air*-um.
Bethuel	Beh-*thew*-el.
Esau	*Ee*-saw.
Hagar	*Hay*-gar.
Haran	*Hair*-un.
Isaac	*Eye*-zuk.
Jacob	*Jay*-kub.
Laban	*Lay*-bun.
Mesopotamia	*Mes*-uh-puh-***tay***-me-uh.
Nahor	*Nay*-hor.
Padanaram	*Pay*-dan-*a*-ram.
Rebekah	Reh-*bek*-uh.

B. Barrenness (v. 21)

21. And Isaac intreated the LORD for his wife, because she was barren: and the LORD was intreated of him, and Rebekah his wife conceived.

Barrenness is a characteristic of three prominent women in the book of Genesis: Sarah, Rebekah, and Rachel. This condition, viewed as shameful in biblical times (Genesis 30:23; Luke 1:25), becomes the backdrop for God to show His power to reverse such circumstances. But God does not grant this request simply to relieve heartache. He is committed to let nothing—not even a seemingly irreversible condition like barrenness—prevent Him from keeping His covenant with Abraham (Genesis 12:2).

Isaac, distraught over his wife's condition, turns to the Lord in prayer. Thus did his father Abraham express to the Lord his own concern over Sarah (Genesis 15:2, 3). In each case the barren woman is empowered to conceive.

> *What Do You Think?*
> How can we ensure that life's difficulties drive us closer to God rather than further from Him?
> *Digging Deeper*
> Analyze motives and spiritual maturity of Bible characters who made wrong choices in this regard (Matthew 13:20, 21; 26:69-75; etc.).

C. Battle (vv. 22, 23)

22a. And the children struggled together within her; and she said, If it be so, why am I thus?

An expectant mother can often feel the baby inside kick. Rebekah, however, seems to be experiencing an unusual amount of such activity. She does not yet know that she is carrying twins; she is only questioning why the movement within her is so intense. Perhaps she suspects that there is more than one child responsible for this. In truth, though, the sibling rivalry has begun!

22b. And she went to enquire of the LORD.

Just what this action consists of is difficult to determine. It appears that she goes to a specific place as opposed to simply praying, which is what

Isaac has done. Perhaps it is a place that has come to be associated with the presence of the Lord for some reason, much as is the case later with Bethel (Genesis 28:16-19). What is most important is that Rebekah is going to the right source with her question.

23a. And the LORD said unto her, Two nations are in thy womb, and two manner of people shall be separated from thy bowels; and the one people shall be stronger than the other people.

In some clear and unmistakable manner, the Lord speaks to Rebekah and answers her inquiry, just as He has answered Isaac's prayer for a child. Rebekah is carrying twins, but they are described as *two nations*. The nations are not specifically named; all that Rebekah is told involves the future of each.

23b. And the elder shall serve the younger.

The prophecy then focuses on the children themselves. The promise here is not the norm in the Old Testament world. Typically, the older sibling is to be given greater prominence within the family. The Law of Moses later stipulates that the firstborn son be given a "double portion" of the family's wealth (Deuteronomy 21:15-17). But in Genesis, the younger sibling is generally more favored. In addition to Jacob, this is true with Abel, Isaac, Rachel, and Joseph.

This illustrates what the Lord will later say through the prophet Isaiah: "My thoughts are not your thoughts, neither are your ways my ways" (Isaiah 55:8). One may also see the preference for the younger sibling as illustrating the principle of grace at work: the individual who does not deserve prominence or blessing (the younger) receives it nonetheless.

II. Distinctive Boys
(GENESIS 25:24-28)
A. Esau's Birth (vv. 24, 25)

24, 25. And when her days to be delivered were fulfilled, behold, there were twins in her womb. And the first came out red, all over like an hairy garment; and they called his name Esau.

A child's name in the Bible often reflects some detail in the circumstances of the birth itself (Genesis 38:27-30; 1 Samuel 4:19-22) or includes a statement of hope or vindication (Genesis 30:8, 20). In this case the unusually *hairy* appearance of the firstborn son yields the name *Esau*, from the Hebrew for "hairy."

Also quite striking is the redness of his skin. Both details will play an important role in the sibling rivalry that will characterize these boys: the color *red* (of Jacob's stew) will figure in Jacob's act of cunning in obtaining Esau's birthright, and the hairy appearance will enter into the deception of Isaac in Genesis 27.

B. Jacob's Birth (v. 26)

26a. And after that came his brother out, and his hand took hold on Esau's heel; and his name was called Jacob.

The second of Rebekah's twins is marked not by his appearance but by a rather curious action for a newborn: *his hand* seizes *Esau's heel*. From this he is given the name *Jacob*, from the Hebrew word for "heel." At this point, no one can anticipate what kind of "heel-grabbing" this infant will eventually engage in. Nor can anyone anticipate how the characteristics of Esau will play themselves out in his life someday. Whoever names these twins (probably their parents) may be chuckling as they do so. But deceit and heartbreak await this family, not laughter.

Jacob's heel-grabbing will come to have a much more sinister connotation to it: grabbing the heel as if to pull a rival back and impede his progress so that the heel-grabber can move ahead of him. This is what Jacob will become known for doing—especially and tragically to his own brother and father.

26b. And Isaac was threescore years old when she bare them.

Isaac married when he was 40 (Genesis 25:20, above), and now he is age 60. Thus he has had to wait 20 years for his sons' births.

❧ *When Siblings Struggle* ❧

For years, twins Alexandria and Anastasia Duval shared the ups and downs of life, experiencing together business enterprises, bankruptcies, and moves to various places. On May 29, 2016, the sisters were seen in a parked vehicle on a cliff 200 feet above the ocean in Hawaii. Alexandria was in the driver's seat. Witnesses saw a fight break out between them, with Anastasia pulling Alexandria's hair. Then, according to witnesses, the vehicle accelerated and made a sharp left turn over the cliff. Alexandria was injured, and Anastasia was killed in the crash at the bottom of the cliff.

Shortly thereafter, police charged Alexandria with second-degree murder, alleging that she intentionally drove off the road. But a judge said there was not sufficient evidence for the charge. Four months later, however, a grand jury accepted the murder charge, and Alexandria was arrested in New York and held for extradition to Hawaii.

The Bible also includes tragic tales of siblings who struggled against each other. We know about the later struggles of Jacob and Esau, but today's passage tells us the problem began early—before birth! Many of us wonder how we can work with God to overcome family strife. Let us pray we do better at it than Jacob and Esau did. Perhaps God gave us their story to encourage us to strive not to be like them!   —C. R. B.

C. Boys' Preferences (v. 27)

27. And the boys grew: and Esau was a cunning hunter, a man of the field; and Jacob was a plain man, dwelling in tents.

The account now moves forward in time, though no specific number of years is given. The text simply reads that *the boys grew.* Of more importance is how different the boys become, though they are twins: *Esau* becomes an outdoorsman, a *cunning hunter* and a *man of the field. Jacob* is more of a homebody. The Hebrew word ren-

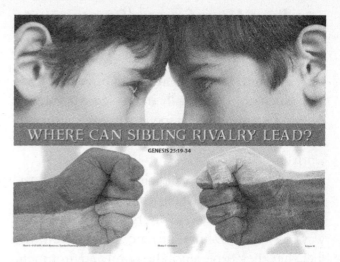

Visual for Lesson 10. *Start a discussion by pointing to this visual as you ask, "What's at the heart of sibling rivalry?"*

dered *plain* describes someone who is orderly and methodical, more of a quiet and private person. Jacob is certainly not the rugged, robust individual his brother is.

D. Parents' Preferences (v. 28)

28. And Isaac loved Esau, because he did eat of his venison: but Rebekah loved Jacob.

Not only are these boys different, but their differences affect the attitudes of their parents toward them. *Isaac* is drawn toward *Esau*, while *Rebekah* favors *Jacob*. With Isaac a reason is given for his preference: he likes the kind of food Esau prepares from what he captures when he hunts. Although *venison* refers to deer meat in modern English, the Hebrew word can designate any kind of game obtained by hunting.

No reason is given for why Rebekah becomes especially fond of Jacob, but this is likely because he spends so much time among the tents where Rebekah presumably spends most of her days. If there is already any degree of sibling rivalry between Esau and Jacob, the fact that the parents play favorites can only exacerbate the problem.

> *What Do You Think?*
> How can parents ensure they do not exhibit favoritism regarding their children?
> *Digging Deeper*
> Consider both dos and don'ts.

I was born 4 years before my first brother, 8 years before the second, and 12 years before our sister. We differ in many ways, but others see us as very much alike, especially in our sense of humor. At family reunions, our spouses make a game out of simultaneously cringing at our puns and time-worn stories.

Some psychologists call sibling differences a matter of divergence: when one child excels in an area, the others seek to excel in divergent ways. A second way to explain sibling differences comes from the fact that they experience the family environment differently. If their parents divorce, siblings of varying ages will react differently. A third explanation comes from exaggerated comparisons. Though two siblings might both be friendly, the extremely outgoing child will be labeled the family's extrovert while the other is seen as the introvert.

Esau and Jacob differed in appearance from birth, and soon their personality differences became apparent. Their differences were likely exaggerated by the dysfunctional way their parents responded to them. Many of the difficulties the two brothers experienced later in life might have been mitigated if they had received wiser parenting. Rearing children is difficult, but we can make it less stressful if we use godly wisdom in doing so.

—C. R. B.

III. Despised Birthright
(Genesis 25:29-34)
A. Offer Given (vv. 29-31)

29. And Jacob sod pottage: and Esau came from the field, and he was faint.

The word *sod* is an old past tense of the verb *seethe*, which originally meant "to boil." We still speak of someone seething with rage as "boiling mad." The usage here describes Jacob as boiling or cooking *pottage*, or stew. As Esau comes *from the field*, the text does not say whether he has been working or hunting. But he is *faint*, or weak. Apparently it has been some time since his last meal.

30. And Esau said to Jacob, Feed me, I pray thee, with that same red pottage; for I am faint: therefore was his name called Edom.

The *red* coloring of the food may come from the lentils (Genesis 25:34) in the stew. Esau's craving for this food leads to another name for him: *Edom*, meaning "red." (Remember that verse 25 tells us that Esau came out of the womb "red.") Esau's second name, Edom, is eventually used to identify his descendants: Edomites.

> **What Do You Think?**
> How can we ensure that our decisions are driven by a sense of right and wrong rather than self-gratification?
> *Digging Deeper*
> Distinguish between those who make selfish choices intentionally and those who do so because of ignorance or blind spots.

31. And Jacob said, Sell me this day thy birthright.

To this point, the idea of a *birthright* has not been mentioned in the book of Genesis. The Hebrew word behind this translation appears a total of 10 times in the Old Testament in reference to humans, and 5 of them are in the account of Jacob and Esau. The other 5 occur in Genesis 43:33; Deuteronomy 21:17 (discussed earlier); and 1 Chronicles 5:1, 2.

Obviously, *Jacob* is well aware of the birthright's importance. Esau may have returned from a hunting expedition, but Jacob is now the hunter who sees his prey, and his "heel-grabbing" skills go into action. He sees in his brother's appetite an opportunity to offer a deal and thus take the lead within the family hierarchy.

B. Offer Accepted (vv. 32-34)

32. And Esau said, Behold, I am at the point to die: and what profit shall this birthright do to me?

Esau exaggerates his condition, claiming to be *at the point* of death, and thereby reasons that a *birthright* is worthless to a dead man. In his mind, if the birthright cannot keep him from starving to death, then what good is it?

33. And Jacob said, Swear to me this day; and he sware unto him: and he sold his birthright unto Jacob.

Abraham's servant had sworn an oath that he would carry out Abraham's desire that he find a wife for Isaac from Abraham's relatives in Haran. The oath was accompanied by a specified gesture (Genesis 24:1-9). With Esau and Jacob, the two may exchange a verbal agreement accompanied by a gesture (something similar to a handshake). The deal is finalized: the *birthright* has been *sold*.

> *What Do You Think?*
> What can we do to protect ourselves from those who use our weakness to take advantage?
> *Digging Deeper*
> Consider how Psalm 55:20, 21; Proverbs 7:21; Romans 16:17, 18; 2 Timothy 3:6; 1 John 2:18-27; and 3:7-10 help identify characteristics and tactics of manipulative personalities.

34. Then Jacob gave Esau bread and pottage of lentiles; and he did eat and drink, and rose up, and went his way: thus Esau despised his birthright.

The word *lentiles* refers to a member of the pea family, whose seeds are often used even today in making soups or stews. But the contents of the stew are not nearly as noteworthy as the contents of its eater's heart. Esau has no qualms whatsoever about what he has just agreed to. He has *despised his birthright*, something that involves far more than mere material possessions or wealth.

This birthright is linked to a spiritual legacy that Esau should have viewed as a sacred trust. Instead he has bargained it away for a bowl of stew. He may walk away with a full stomach, but his heart is pitifully empty.

Conclusion

A. The Real Rivalry

While "Siblings' Rivalry" is the title for today's study, that is not the only rivalry on display. In fact, it is not really the main rivalry. Both Esau and Jacob fought another battle even more intense than the one that developed between them. This battle was *within* each man.

The Scriptures place special emphasis on Esau's treatment of the family birthright. Both Old and New Testaments are equally grim in their evaluation of his actions. Our text says that Esau "despised his birthright" (Genesis 25:34). One can see why the writer of Hebrews uses the word profane to describe Esau (Hebrews 12:16). He is not using profanity in his language, but his interests and actions are linked solely to what gratifies his desires.

Jacob had his own battle, as demonstrated by his actions in today's lesson. He could have simply given Esau what he wanted—a bowl of stew. But Jacob, the schemer and "heel-grabber," saw an opportunity to further his own standing; and he took full advantage of it. Just like Esau, he too was looking out for number one (himself).

Eventually Jacob's craftiness yielded a bitter harvest of additional deception and heartache. The remainder of Genesis tells us of the conflicts that the practice of deception produced within his wives and his sons. While there was certainly sibling rivalry between Esau and Jacob, each man was his own worst rival. Each gave in to the temptation to make himself and his desires of supreme importance.

Esau and Jacob are not the only competitors in this battle. Paul knew this struggle as well. He describes its intensity in Romans 7:7-25. He desires to do what is good and right before God, but he is constantly at war with "the law of sin which is in my members" (7:23). However, he also knows the key to victory in this battle: "Who shall deliver me from the body of this death? I thank God through Jesus Christ our Lord" (7:24, 25). That is the key for us as well.

B. Prayer

Father, our world today encourages us to be very Esau-like and Jacob-like in our thoughts, words, and actions: to live for the moment and to make the achievement of our personal desires and wishes more important than anyone else's. Deliver us from such a self-centered point of view. Keep our minds on higher, holier pursuits. We pray in Jesus' name. Amen.

C. Thought to Remember

Live for the Master, not for the moment.

INVOLVEMENT LEARNING

Enhance your lesson with KJV Bible Student (from your curriculum supplier) and the reproducible activity page (at www.standardlesson.com or in the back of the KJV Standard Lesson Commentary Deluxe Edition).

Into the Lesson

Distribute handouts (you prepare) with the following statements:

* My birth order: I am the ___ of ___ children.
* I agree/disagree [circle one] with this observation: "Comparison is a death knell to sibling harmony" (Elizabeth Fishel).
* My parents did/did not [circle one] play favorites, and it affected me this way: _____.

Lead into the Bible study by saying "When parents favor one child over another, the result is usually deep hurt and resentment that negatively affect the relationships between those siblings. Let's look at the devastation that resulted when Rebekah and Isaac played favorites."

Alternative. Distribute copies of the "What's Your Family's Conflict Style?" activity from the reproducible page, which you can download. Have students work on it in small groups and discuss their answers.

Into the Word

Say, "Jacob and Esau each seemed to feel entitled to the rights of the firstborn for differing reasons. The fact that their parents played favorites didn't help."

Divide the class in half. Designate one as *Team Jacob* and the other as *Team Esau*. Distribute handouts (you create) with these identical instructions: Read Genesis 25:19-34. Then answer these questions: 1–Why would the brother for which your team is named consider himself to be deserving of the birthright? 2–Which parent favored him? 3–What can we tell about his moral character?

Anticipated responses (do not distribute) for *Team Jacob:* 1–God stated that the older would serve the younger; besides, Esau traded it to him fair and square. 2–Rebekah. 3–Jacob was willing to exploit his brother's vulnerable state. *Team Esau:* 1–Esau deserved the birthright because he

was older; a trade undertaken in a moment of vulnerability isn't valid. 2–Isaac. 3–Esau was impulsive and naïve.

Allow several minutes for group discussion; then ask the two teams to share their answers.

Option. Distribute copies of the "Conflict in Scripture" activity from the reproducible page. Assign Scripture references to small groups to read and discuss as indicated. In the ensuing whole-class discussion, decide which conflict styles were used by the people in today's text.

Into Life

Move to close the class by saying, "When siblings get along, they can have a profound impact on one another. Over the course of history, these famous siblings have made a significant impact in the world." Read the following list.

Orville and Wilbur Wright changed the nature of transportation.
Venus and Serena Williams have both won Olympic gold medals.
The Marx Brothers became influential comedic entertainers in the early twentieth century.
The Lennon Sisters entertained audiences for some six decades.
John and Charles Wesley became famous for preaching and hymn writing.

Conclude: "When siblings work together, there's no telling what they can accomplish."

On the board, write "When you said or did _____, it made a significant impact on me; I would like to hear your perspective on what happened." Ask, "What would happen if you were to say this to a sibling or family member with whom you were in conflict (customizing the sentence to your situation)? How could you see the resulting conversation moving you closer to the resolution of the conflict?"

JACOB'S DECEPTION

DEVOTIONAL READING: Psalm 24:1-6
BACKGROUND SCRIPTURE: Genesis 27:1–28:5

GENESIS 27:5-10, 18, 19, 21-29

5 And Rebekah heard when Isaac spake to Esau his son. And Esau went to the field to hunt for venison, and to bring it.

6 And Rebekah spake unto Jacob her son, saying, Behold, I heard thy father speak unto Esau thy brother, saying,

7 Bring me venison, and make me savoury meat, that I may eat, and bless thee before the LORD before my death.

8 Now therefore, my son, obey my voice according to that which I command thee.

9 Go now to the flock, and fetch me from thence two good kids of the goats; and I will make them savoury meat for thy father, such as he loveth:

10 And thou shalt bring it to thy father, that he may eat, and that he may bless thee before his death.

· · · · · · · · · · · · · · · · · · · ·

18 And he came unto his father, and said, My father: and he said, Here am I; who art thou, my son?

19 And Jacob said unto his father, I am Esau thy firstborn; I have done according as thou badest me: arise, I pray thee, sit and eat of my venison, that thy soul may bless me.

· · · · · · · · · · · · · · · · · · · ·

21 And Isaac said unto Jacob, Come near, I pray thee, that I may feel thee, my son, whether thou be my very son Esau or not.

22 And Jacob went near unto Isaac his father; and he felt him, and said, The voice is Jacob's voice, but the hands are the hands of Esau.

23 And he discerned him not, because his hands were hairy, as his brother Esau's hands: so he blessed him.

24 And he said, Art thou my very son Esau? And he said, I am.

25 And he said, Bring it near to me, and I will eat of my son's venison, that my soul may bless thee. And he brought it near to him, and he did eat: and he brought him wine, and he drank.

26 And his father Isaac said unto him, Come near now, and kiss me, my son.

27 And he came near, and kissed him: and he smelled the smell of his raiment, and blessed him, and said, See, the smell of my son is as the smell of a field which the LORD hath blessed:

28 Therefore God give thee of the dew of heaven, and the fatness of the earth, and plenty of corn and wine:

29 Let people serve thee, and nations bow down to thee: be lord over thy brethren, and let thy mother's sons bow down to thee: cursed be every one that curseth thee, and blessed be he that blesseth thee.

KEY VERSE

He discerned him not, because his hands were hairy, as his brother Esau's hands: so he blessed him.

—Genesis 27:23

GOD'S WORLD AND GOD'S PEOPLE

Unit 3: God Blesses and Re-creates Regardless

LESSONS 10–13

LESSON AIMS

After participating in this lesson, each learner will be able to:

1. Recount how Isaac was deceived into blessing Jacob rather than Esau and what the blessing consisted of.

2. Tell why human beings resort to deception so often instead of telling the truth.

3. Identify and correct one thought process that tends to produce words and actions intended to deceive.

LESSON OUTLINE

Introduction
 A. Dress-Up for Grown-Ups
 B. Lesson Context: Family Dynamics
 C. Lesson Context: Patriarchal Blessing
 I. Deception Suggested (GENESIS 27:5-10)
 A. Overhearing Isaac (v. 5)
 B. Advising Jacob (vv. 6-10)
  Parenting Pathology
 II. Deception Starts (GENESIS 27:18, 19)
 A. Addressing Isaac (v. 18)
 B. Lying to Isaac (v. 19)
 III. Deception Succeeds (GENESIS 27:21-29)
 A. Isaac's Doubt (vv. 21-24)
  Not a "Little White Lie"
 B. Isaac's Declaration (vv. 25-29)
Conclusion
 A. Two Laws
 B. One Solution
 C. Prayer
 D. Thought to Remember

Introduction

A. Dress-Up for Grown-Ups

One of the games children often used to play was "dress-up." (Today it has lost much of its appeal, a casualty of our digital, high-tech age.) A little boy would try to wear what Dad wore, especially if some kind of special clothing or uniform was involved. A little girl would dress up like her mother, possibly using some of Mom's makeup without her permission. The parents laughed at how "grown-up" the child looked.

Jacob was a grown man, not a child, when he (with his mother Rebekah's help) dressed up like Esau. But this was no game for Jacob and Rebekah. The stakes were enormously high; the patriarchal blessing, associated with future prosperity and security, was on the line. The outcome of Jacob and Rebekah's deception of old, blind Isaac was not laughter, the meaning of Isaac's name. Rather, it was anger, sorrow, and the eventual self-exile of Jacob.

B. Lesson Context: Family Dynamics

Last week's lesson covered the birth of Jacob and Esau, their parents' favoritism, and Esau's willingness to sell his birthright to Jacob to satisfy his hunger. Genesis 26 then chronicles Isaac's dealings with the Philistines, during which time God came to him at Beersheba and reaffirmed the covenant promises (26:23, 24).

Nothing is said in Genesis 26 about Jacob. For Esau's part, he is mentioned only at the end of the chapter: when Esau was 40 years old, he married two Hittite women (26:34). This hurt both Isaac and Rebekah greatly. Once again (as he did with selling his birthright) Esau demonstrated contempt for his heritage, this time by marrying outside the covenant people.

C. Lesson Context: Patriarchal Blessing

By the time Genesis 27 begins, Isaac had grown old and nearly blind. Believing it was time to set his house in order, he called son Esau to come before him. He expressed his desire to give Esau the special patriarchal blessing. Such blessing is essentially a prophecy of what the future holds for the individual or people being blessed. Near the conclusion of Genesis, Jacob blessed his sons in a similar fashion just before his death (Genesis 49:1-28).

It is also important to note that a blessing (or a curse for that matter) once spoken cannot be reversed, even if that blessing was given unintentionally to the wrong person. This is especially so in a solemn setting such as the one in our text.

Blessing should not be confused with *birthright*. The birthright (already obtained by Jacob; see last week's lesson) dealt primarily with passing down the greatest share of the family's material wealth to the oldest son. The blessing involved the family patriarch's (in today's case, Isaac's) participation more directly as he requested divine favor on the person being blessed so that future prosperity and abundance would be his.

I. Deception Suggested

(Genesis 27:5-10)

The preface to today's lesson is Isaac's sense that his time is short. His plan is to grant Esau, elder of the two sons, his blessing. Surely Isaac is aware of the words that the Lord spoke to Rebekah when her twins were jostling within her: "The elder shall serve the younger" (Genesis 25:23). Yet in spite of that declaration, he attempts to ensure that Esau (his older and favored son) receives the blessing. But first Isaac desires a favorite meal from Esau's hands (27:1-4).

A. Overhearing Isaac (v. 5)

5. And Rebekah heard when Isaac spake to Esau his son. And Esau went to the field to hunt for venison, and to bring it.

If *Isaac* believes his meeting with *Esau* is private, he is badly mistaken. Wife *Rebekah* is eavesdropping. Perhaps she has seen Esau go into Isaac's tent and is curious as to what is going on. Once Esau has gone out to fulfill his father's wishes, she knows she must act—and quickly.

As in last week's lesson, the Hebrew word translated *venison* refers to any kind of game obtained by hunting. It need not refer only to deer meat as modern English designates.

B. Advising Jacob (vv. 6-10)

6. And Rebekah spake unto Jacob her son, saying, Behold, I heard thy father speak unto Esau thy brother, saying.

It is interesting to consider the description of Esau as "his [Isaac's] son" in verse 5, while here *Jacob* is referred to as *her* [Rebekah's] *son*. This may highlight the favoritism noted in last week's lesson (Genesis 25:28). Reference to neither son is in terms of *their*. Rebekah now proceeds to tell Jacob what she has heard.

7. Bring me venison, and make me savoury meat, that I may eat, and bless thee before the Lord before my death.

When Isaac had spoken to Esau earlier, he had requested him to bring *savoury meat* "that my soul may bless thee before I die" (Genesis 27:4). Rebekah, however, includes a sacred element in her version of Isaac's words: she depicts Isaac's plan as being to *bless* Esau *before the Lord before my death*. Perhaps this use of the Lord's name is intended to heighten the sense of urgency with which Jacob must carry out his mother's unfolding plan. He must be sure to do whatever is necessary to obtain the blessing. Jacob himself will use the Lord's name in a deceptive way later (27:20).

8. Now therefore, my son, obey my voice according to that which I command thee.

Just as Esau has gone out to fulfill Isaac's wishes, Jacob is now ordered to carry out the plan devised by Rebekah.

> *What Do You Think?*
> How should we handle a situation where someone in authority attempts to include us in an unethical plan?
> *Digging Deeper*
> How would your response change, if at all, if the unethical plan requires only your passive acceptance rather than active participation?

9, 10. Go now to the flock, and fetch me from thence two good kids of the goats; and I will make them savoury meat for thy father, such as he loveth: and thou shalt bring it to thy father, that he may eat, and that he may bless thee before his death.

Many cooks try to prepare a dish "just like Mother makes." Rebekah's plan is to duplicate what son Esau intends to make. Jacob is to secure the ingredients by which Rebekah will make Isaac's favorite dish. Food will be the tool to trick Isaac, in something of a repeat of food being used by Jacob to nab Esau's birthright.

> ### What Do You Think?
> What are some ways to determine whether someone's kind words, gifts, or acts of service are selfless or self-seeking?
>
> ### Digging Deeper
> How do we avoid Pilate's error of correctly recognizing wrong motives but reacting wrongly anyway (Mark 15:9-15)?

❧ PARENTING PATHOLOGY ❧

"Mom always liked you best." That famous line from a Smothers Brothers TV skit became a continuing theme—either spoken or implied—in their comedy routine.

In the original interchange, Dick, supposedly the more intelligent of the two, ran through a litany of criticisms of Tommy, who played the role of a dense, socially inept fellow. Dick would say something like "You're stupid; you're dumb" in a series of put-downs. Running out of insults, he paused, and Tommy (in an unscripted moment of inspired comedic genius) said, "Yeah, and Mom liked you best."

The audience roared. In addition to giving voice to the ongoing undercurrent of the act, it also touched a nerve in audience members. Every person who has had a brother or sister has probably entertained an occasional thought that the other sibling(s) was treated better.

The struggle between Jacob and Esau is only one in a series of sibling rivalries in Genesis. But their story portrays most vividly the negative power of parental favoritism. Isaac and Rebekah's greatest parenting fault was the failure to see Esau and Jacob as "ours" rather than "my son," etc. They were part of a multigenerational parenting pathology. We can learn an important lesson from their failure! —C. R. B.

II. Deception Starts
(GENESIS 27:18, 19)

In the intervening verses not in today's lesson (Genesis 27:11-17), Jacob's reaction to Rebekah's scheme is understandable. Normally the pronouncement of a blessing involves some kind of physical contact. The food Rebekah prepares may resemble what Esau fixes; but if Isaac touches Jacob in the process of blessing him, he won't need eyes to know this isn't Esau!

But as Rebekah cooks food, she also cooks up a plan: she covers Jacob's smooth skin with the skins of the goats. She also provides him with some of Esau's clothing to wear. Jacob is now prepared to see his father, though he must be the proverbial nervous wreck.

A. Addressing Isaac (v. 18)

18a. And he came unto his father, and said, My father.

Another part of the ruse must involve convincing Isaac that Jacob sounds like Esau. Part of the plan may be for Jacob to speak as little as possible. Jacob's short *my father* is only one word in Hebrew. Some suggest that since Jacob and Esau are twins, their voices are somewhat similar.

18b. And he said, Here am I; who art thou, my son?

Although Isaac's vision is gone, his sense of hearing seems to be in good working order—perhaps more so than Rebekah and Jacob realize. Isaac's ears tell him something is amiss, thus he questions the identity of the son before him, as if asking, "Which of my sons are you?"

B. Lying to Isaac (v. 19)

19. And Jacob said unto his father, I am Esau thy firstborn; I have done according as thou badest me: arise, I pray thee, sit and eat of my venison, that thy soul may bless me.

Jacob continues the deception in making the two claims we see here. Then Jacob immediately throws in the proofs of requested food and expected blessing. As long as Isaac doesn't suspect eavesdropping, he will assume that those two subjects are known only to him and Esau.

III. Deception Succeeds
(GENESIS 27:21-29)

Jacob then uses the Lord's name as part of the cover-up (Genesis 27:20, not in today's lesson text) to assuage Isaac's doubt. But it isn't enough.

A. Isaac's Doubt (vv. 21-24)

21. And Isaac said unto Jacob, Come near, I pray thee, that I may feel thee, my son, whether thou be my very son Esau or not.

Now comes the part of the ceremony that Jacob must be dreading the most (see again Genesis 27:12). *Isaac* is not convinced that the man before him is indeed *Esau*. So he shifts from the senses of seeing and hearing to that of touch.

22. And Jacob went near unto Isaac his father; and he felt him, and said, The voice is Jacob's voice, but the hands are the hands of Esau.

Isaac may be blind (Genesis 27:1), but he is not deaf! Yet his sense of touch now contradicts what his sense of hearing reports.

Jacob's degree of anxiety at this point is easy to imagine. It must be all he can do to keep from trembling with fear of being discovered as an impostor.

23. And he discerned him not, because his hands were hairy, as his brother Esau's hands: so he blessed him.

The scheme apparently works as Isaac resolves the contradictory evidence by trusting his sense of touch over his sense of hearing. Almost.

24. And he said, Art thou my very son Esau? And he said, I am.

Still doubting, Isaac again questions the identity of the individual before him. Jacob seems to perceive that a short response at this point is better than a long one, and his *I am* is just a single brief word in Hebrew. He speaks as little as possible, trying not to create any further doubt in Isaac's mind. This is the final time Jacob speaks in the blessing procedure.

✖ NOT A "LITTLE WHITE LIE" ✖

Evaluate this situation: A friend's loved one is gravely injured or deathly ill. You know the truth, but your friend doesn't. Are you tempted to hedge the truth when you call your friend to report the injury or illness? Do you diminish the seriousness of the person's condition with a "little white lie"?

We're occasionally tempted to tell such lies. That designation makes them sound so innocent. But lies by their very nature are attempts to deceive. Many people rationalize a supposed difference between little lies and big lies by appealing to the difference in consequences. We may assume that the results of so-called little white lies are relatively harmless. Or we may think that a little lie is justified because harmful consequences of telling the truth will be greater than harmful consequences of telling the lie. This appeal to good intentions is an easy one.

When Rebekah conspired with Jacob, she probably convinced herself of her good intentions. Perhaps she thought "her" son was far more worthy of Isaac's blessing than "his" son was. But as the further record of Genesis reports, the consequences of the birthright exchange and blessing deception were quite profound. Relationships and history changed courses. We feel those aftershocks yet today. Unintended consequences put the lie to the idea of "little white lies."   —C. R. B.

B. Isaac's Declaration (vv. 25-29)

25. And he said, Bring it near to me, and I will eat of my son's venison, that my soul may bless

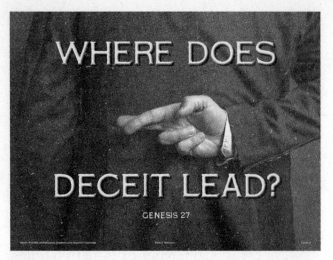

Visual for Lesson 11. *Point to this visual as you ask, "Is the outcome of today's story typical of where deceit ends up? Why, or why not?"*

thee. And he brought it near to him, and he did eat: and he brought him wine, and he drank.

What we might call the "identity confirmation phase" is over—Isaac is convinced. But the "chance of getting caught phase" is still underway. Esau can return at any moment. It's easy to imagine Jacob trying to hurry the meal along in subtle ways.

26. And his father Isaac said unto him, Come near now, and kiss me, my son.

Jacob must again come before Isaac to be touched, so the anxious moments drag on. A *kiss* is a common part of greeting someone or saying farewell in Bible times (Genesis 31:28, 55; 33:4; 48:10; Ruth 1:9; Mark 14:44; 1 Peter 5:14; etc.). Here it may be part of the ceremony of blessing.

27a. And he came near, and kissed him: and he smelled the smell of his raiment, and blessed him.

All five of Isaac's senses (or lack thereof) have come into play in this account. His sight is gone (which affects how the deception is carried out), he hears a voice, he touches the imposter, he tastes the food, and now he smells the clothing (*raiment*) of Esau that Jacob is wearing.

27b. And said, See, the smell of my son is as the smell of a field which the LORD hath blessed.

These words are certainly appropriate for a "man of the field" such as Esau (Genesis 25:27), so the deception is solidified. Isaac proceeds to pro-

nounce the blessing the imposter desires to have so badly. Regarding credit to the Lord for agricultural blessing, compare Psalm 65:9-13.

28. Therefore God give thee of the dew of heaven, and the fatness of the earth, and plenty of corn and wine.

The contents of the blessing include the promise of material abundance. In a few minutes, Isaac will mention these same things in something of an anti-blessing to Esau (Genesis 27:39, 40).

29a. Let people serve thee, and nations bow down to thee.

The blessing then turns to matters of authority and influence. This promise may indicate how Jacob's descendants (the Israelites) will at times dominate the surrounding *nations* (as during David's reign).

29b. Be lord over thy brethren.

Isaac is unintentionally fulfilling the prophetic word the Lord gave to Rebekah when she was still expecting: "the elder shall serve the younger" (Genesis 25:23).

29c. And let thy mother's sons bow down to thee.

Jacob's *mother's sons* may refer to Esau's descendants (although Isaac doesn't intend it that way), which will be the Edomites. Their demise before God's covenant people will be foreseen particularly by the prophet Obadiah (Obadiah 1-4, 15-21; see also Genesis 27:40; 2 Samuel 8:14).

29d. Cursed be every one that curseth thee, and blessed be he that blesseth thee.

The final statement in Isaac's words of blessing reflects the final statement in God's original covenant with Abraham (Genesis 12:3).

We do not read of any further exchange of words between Isaac and Jacob after Isaac offers the blessing. Jacob has likely been wishing that the ceremony will end as soon as possible, aware that Esau can return at any moment.

As it turns out, Jacob scarcely leaves before Esau returns, prepares a meal for his father, and enters the tent—expecting a blessing from him. One cannot fathom the degree of sadness and despair that Isaac feels and the degree of anger and bitterness that Esau experiences when they realize what has happened.

But God's sovereign purpose is still being carried out. His plan is moving forward, even in the midst of the deception and heartbreak that we see in the events of this chapter of Scripture.

Conclusion

A. Two Laws

Sociologists have identified a concept called *the law of unintended consequences.* Unintended consequences are outcomes that are not foreseen or intended by a certain action. According to Wikipedia, these consequences fall into three categories:

1–Unexpected benefits (when positive results exceed expectations); this has also been referred to as a *windfall*

2–Unexpected drawbacks (which can occur in addition to any benefits gained from an action); this is also known as *doing more harm than good*

3–Perverse results (when the consequences of a course of action make a given problem worse); this is also known as a *backfire* in some contexts

The difference between number 2 and number 3 can be hard to see. But it's easy to see how both descriptions of *doing more harm than good* and *backfire* can certainly be applied to what happened in the aftermath of Jacob and Rebekah's deception of Isaac when the unfolding events of Genesis 27:41 and following are considered. While God's higher purpose *was* carried out in spite of the chicanery, this series of events brought further havoc into a family where sibling rivalry and parental favoritism had already created significant friction.

The law of unintended consequences is both a sociological and spiritual concept. It is grounded in scriptural principles such as "Be sure your sin will find you out" (Numbers 32:23); "He that soweth iniquity shall reap vanity" (Proverbs 22:8); and "Be not deceived; God is not mocked: for whatsoever a man soweth, that shall he also reap" (Galatians 6:7). This is known as *the law of sowing and reaping.*

The two laws are similar but not identical. The similarities seem more profound than the differences, however, and we've all experienced those negative similarities. Lying begets more lies as we dig ourselves deeper and deeper into a hole. Eventually the avalanche of sin catches up with us.

B. One Solution

The solution starts with recognizing the problem. And that problem is one of taking the short view instead of the long view. When we focus on the potential long-term effects, the temptation to grab shortsighted, short-term fixes will diminish. The Bible has the correct long-term view for everyone: "Let us hear the conclusion of the whole matter: Fear God, and keep his commandments: for this is the whole duty of man" (Ecclesiastes 12:13).

C. Prayer

Father, may we extend hands not to grab another's heel but to lend genuine assistance. May we be the hands and feet of Jesus to our broken, hurting world. We pray this in His name. Amen.

D. Thought to Remember

The law of sowing and reaping applies to both crops and character.

HOW TO SAY IT

badest	*bad*-est.
chicanery	shi-*cane*-ree.
Edomites	*Ee*-dum-ites.
Esau	*Ee*-saw.
Hittite	*Hit*-ite or *Hit*-tite.
Jacob	*Jay*-kub.
Obadiah	O-buh-*dye*-uh.
Philistines	Fuh-*liss*-teenz or *Fill*-us-teenz.

INVOLVEMENT LEARNING

Enhance your lesson with KJV Bible Student *(from your curriculum supplier) and the reproducible activity page (at www.standardlesson.com or in the back of the* KJV Standard Lesson Commentary Deluxe Edition*).*

Into the Lesson

Give each person an index card. Say, "Let's play Two Truths and a Lie. In this game, each of us will write three things about ourselves, two of which are true and one is false. Then we will guess which statements are false. Write your three statements on the card in random order."

When everyone is ready, ask for volunteers to read their cards and have others guess which statement is false. Conclude by asking, "Why do people sometimes make false claims about themselves? For what reasons are some people tempted to create a persona on social media that does not reflect their true nature?"

Alternative: Distribute copies of the "How Not to Be Scammed" activity from the reproducible page, which you can download. Have students pair off to discuss their own experiences.

After either activity, lead into the Bible study by saying, "Sometimes we are tempted to use white lies in order to get out of an awkward situation or to protect someone's feelings. But other types of deception can have serious consequences. Let's look at what happened when Rebekah and Jacob deceived Isaac into giving Jacob his irrevocable blessing."

Into the Word

Have students take turns in reading aloud Genesis 27:5-10, 18, 19, 21-29. Then divide the class into two groups (or multiples of two), the *Deceivers Group* and the *Duped Group*. Give these two questions to the *Deceivers Group:* 1–How was Rebekah complicit in Jacob's deception? 2–In what ways did Jacob lie to his father? For the *Duped Group:* 1–What were Esau's reasonable expectations after he came back from hunting? 2–In what ways did Isaac try to prevent himself from being deceived?

Anticipated responses (do not distribute) for the *Deceivers Group:* 1–Rebekah overheard Isaac's instructions to Esau to get prepared to receive his father's blessings; she then exploited the time Esau was away in order to get Jacob to impersonate his brother. 2–Jacob claimed to be Esau, pretended to have followed his father's instructions, lied when asked if he were really Esau, and deceived his father's sense of touch and smell. *Duped Group:* 1–Esau expected to receive his father's irrevocable blessing. 2–Isaac questioned Jacob's voice, felt his son's hairy arms, and smelled the garments.

Allow several minutes for group discussion; then ask the teams to share their answers. Use the commentary to fill in any gaps.

Into Life

Say, "Social media has made it easy to post fake news stories. People do so for a variety of reasons: to push an agenda, support political candidates, or just to see if they can get away with it. Christians can be tempted to pass along these fake news stories if they appear to be supporting the gospel. In the end, however, these believers lose credibility when many of these compelling stories turn out to be hoaxes." Allow some time for participants to suggest ways that Christians can confirm the truthfulness of news stories before they pass them along.

Before class, write the following five phrases on index cards, one each: My Vocation / My Family / My Friendships / My Money / My Ministry. Distribute the cards so that each learner has one (for larger classes, create duplicate cards). Say, "Let's close our class today in prayer, committing to the Lord that we will never practice any level of deception in the area of life described on the cards in our hands."

Alternative: Distribute copies of the "Deceptive Excuses" activity from the reproducible page. Briefly discuss some possible truthful alternatives to the deceptive excuses listed. Encourage students to be honest in their communications with others in the week ahead.

Jacob's Dream

DEVOTIONAL READING: Psalm 42:1-5
BACKGROUND SCRIPTURE: Genesis 28:10-22

Genesis 28:10-22

10 And Jacob went out from Beersheba, and went toward Haran.

11 And he lighted upon a certain place, and tarried there all night, because the sun was set; and he took of the stones of that place, and put them for his pillows, and lay down in that place to sleep.

12 And he dreamed, and behold a ladder set up on the earth, and the top of it reached to heaven: and behold the angels of God ascending and descending on it.

13 And, behold, the LORD stood above it, and said, I am the LORD God of Abraham thy father, and the God of Isaac: the land whereon thou liest, to thee will I give it, and to thy seed;

14 And thy seed shall be as the dust of the earth, and thou shalt spread abroad to the west, and to the east, and to the north, and to the south: and in thee and in thy seed shall all the families of the earth be blessed.

15 And, behold, I am with thee, and will keep thee in all places whither thou goest, and will bring thee again into this land; for I will not leave thee, until I have done that which I have spoken to thee of.

16 And Jacob awaked out of his sleep, and he said, Surely the LORD is in this place; and I knew it not.

17 And he was afraid, and said, How dreadful is this place! this is none other but the house of God, and this is the gate of heaven.

18 And Jacob rose up early in the morning, and took the stone that he had put for his pillows, and set it up for a pillar, and poured oil upon the top of it.

19 And he called the name of that place Bethel: but the name of that city was called Luz at the first.

20 And Jacob vowed a vow, saying, If God will be with me, and will keep me in this way that I go, and will give me bread to eat, and raiment to put on,

21 So that I come again to my father's house in peace; then shall the LORD be my God:

22 And this stone, which I have set for a pillar, shall be God's house: and of all that thou shalt give me I will surely give the tenth unto thee.

KEY VERSE

Behold, I am with thee, and will keep thee in all places whither thou goest, and will bring thee again into this land; for I will not leave thee, until I have done that which I have spoken to thee of. —**Genesis 28:15**

GOD'S WORLD AND GOD'S PEOPLE

LESSON AIMS

After participating in this lesson, each learner will be able to:

1. Tell what Jacob saw in his dream, what God told him, and how Jacob responded.

2. Compare and contrast how people memorialize things with how Jacob did so.

3. Share with the class one way God has provided for him or her.

LESSON OUTLINE

Introduction

A. From Scripture to Song

The Scripture text today from Genesis 28 records Jacob's experience with God via a dream one night as he was departing from Canaan. The passage has prompted two well known songs over the years. One is the African American slave spiritual "We Are Climbing Jacob's Ladder." The other is the hymn "Nearer, My God, to Thee." The latter is perhaps best known as the song that the musicians on board the *Titanic* purportedly began to play as the ship plunged into the icy waters of the Atlantic Ocean on that tragic April night in 1912. Much of the content of this hymn is based on the incident found in today's text.

While the words and melody of this hymn are comforting to hear or sing, we must remember that Jacob's circumstances in Genesis 28 were very uncertain. He was on the run from his angry brother, Esau. Jacob's self-exile had him traveling to a place he had never been, and moving beyond the territory of the promised land for the first time.

When would he be able to return home? What did the future hold? Jacob came to realize that what he was leaving behind did *not* include the blessing and protection of God. God had his future well in hand.

B. Lesson Context

When Esau realized that he had been outwitted by his brother Jacob (for the second time), he determined to kill Jacob, though not until after Isaac's death. Rebekah learned of Esau's plan and urged Jacob to flee northward to Haran (Genesis 27:41-45). This was the place where Abraham stopped and stayed for a time on his way from Ur of the Chaldees to Canaan. Abraham's father, Terah, had died in Haran (11:32), and apparently Abraham's brother Nahor had decided to remain there. Jacob was thus being sent to stay with family, specifically with Rebekah's brother Laban (see lesson 9).

Rebekah then spoke to Isaac about her dislike for the Hittite women in the region (two of whom Esau had previously married) and her concern that Jacob might marry one of them (Genesis 27:46). This persuaded Isaac to do what his father Abraham's servant had done for him years before: secure a wife for Isaac from his family in the area of Haran. Isaac, however, did not send a servant to do this; he sent Jacob himself (28:1, 2). Isaac may well have been aware of Esau's intentions to kill Jacob.

Genesis 28:6-9 notes that when Esau recognized that Isaac had sent Jacob away to find a wife, Esau married a daughter of Ishmael (Abraham's first son by Hagar). Thus Esau married someone with closer family ties. He seems to have desired to lessen Isaac and Rebekah's disappointment with him on account of the Hittite women he had married.

I. Moving Away
(Genesis 28:10-15)
A. Jacob's Departure (v. 10)

10. And Jacob went out from Beersheba, and went toward Haran.

Beersheba is the town where Isaac had eventually settled, following a series of disputes with the Philistines over the ownership of certain wells (Genesis 26:15-33). A journey from Beersheba to *Haran*, where Jacob's relatives live, is approximately 550 miles. This is quite a journey for someone who is used to "dwelling in tents" (25:27)!

Genesis 26:34 states that Esau to be 40 years old when he marries two Hittite women. Jacob's age when he leaves his parents to find a wife is not stated. Circumstantial data based on subsequent events are used by some scholars to suggest him to be age 77 when he leaves his parents. An alternative viewpoint calculates an age of 57.

B. Jacob's Dream (vv. 11-15)

11a. And he lighted upon a certain place, and tarried there all night, because the sun was set.

Later we learn that the *certain place* where Jacob stops for the *night* is the town of Luz (Genesis 28:19). It is approximately 60 miles north of Beersheba, so it may take Jacob a few days to reach that point in his travels. With no streetlights or flash-

lights available to illuminate the way, travelers of the era must stop when *the sun* sets. Even if the moon were full, walking would be problematic.

Two meals per day are customary, and perhaps Jacob has the second of these before bedding down for the night. His meal may be something his mother prepared for him, which is possible at this stage of the journey. But Jacob will have to live off the land as the journey progresses.

What Do You Think?
What "at a minimum" preparations should we make before embarking on a physical, emotional, and/or spiritual transition?

Digging Deeper
How do we know where and when to draw the line between preparations God expects us to make and stuff we are to trust Him for?

11b. And he took of the stones of that place, and put them for his pillows, and lay down in that place to sleep.

We may wonder how Jacob intends to get much sleep if he is using *stones . . . for his pillows*! We will discover the importance of this detail when we get to Genesis 28:18, below. And this will be no ordinary night of *sleep* in any case.

12a. And he dreamed, and behold a ladder set up on the earth, and the top of it reached to heaven.

The *ladder* of which Jacob dreams is generally believed not to be the type of runged ladder familiar to us. Rather, it is likely part of a structure known as a ziggurat.

A ziggurat resembles a pyramid in shape, but includes steps that one climbs until reaching a platform at the top. An altar or shrine may be there, used by worshippers for sacrifices or other religious ritual.

12b. And behold the angels of God ascending and descending on it.

Probably more captivating to Jacob than the structure is what he sees on it. *Angels* will play an important part in the account of Jacob's life, particularly from the standpoint of his spiritual pilgrimage (Genesis 32:1, 24). In the case before us, he dreams of them.

Centuries later, Jesus seems to comment on this incident very early in His ministry. It happens during His first meeting with Nathanael, who becomes one of His disciples. Expressing astonishment at what Jesus knows about him, Nathanael declares Jesus to be both the Son of God and the King of Israel (John 1:49). In response, Jesus declares that Nathanael will witness "greater things" (1:50).

One such thing will be seeing "heaven open, and the angels of God ascending and descending upon the Son of man" (John 1:51). The implication is that Jesus will serve the function of a ladder as He bridges the gap between Heaven and earth, between the holy God and sinful humanity. This happens through His death and resurrection.

13a. And, behold, the LORD stood above it.

Archaeologists have discovered that the steps of pagan ziggurats are for gods to descend to earth. What Jacob sees, however, is different: *the Lord* stands *above* the ladder and makes no move to descend. What exact form Jacob sees is unknown to us. But it is likely more awe-inspiring and glorious than the angels.

13b. And said, I am the LORD God of Abraham thy father, and the God of Isaac: the land whereon thou liest, to thee will I give it, and to thy seed.

As *the Lord* speaks to Jacob, it is worth noting that He says nothing whatsoever about Jacob's deceptive actions toward his father and his brother. That is not what this wanderer from home needs to hear at this point. Instead, God reaffirms the covenant promises made to grandfather *Abraham* and father *Isaac*.

The promise embraces two important elements: the *land* and Jacob's descendants (*seed*). The fact that the land will be given to Jacob's seed means that he will have a wife and at least one child. Such an affirmation is likely intended to provide much-needed assurance to Jacob, since he will soon be leaving the territory of the land of promise to go to Haran. Perhaps Jacob has been wondering if and how the promise will be affected by his departure from the land (or by his treatment of his father and brother). If he harbors any such doubts, God has come to ease them.

14a. And thy seed shall be as the dust of the earth, and thou shalt spread abroad to the west, and to the east, and to the north, and to the south.

This language reflects God's promises to Abraham. The phrase *shall be as the dust of the earth* was used when Abraham separated from Lot and as Abraham was promised all the land he could see (Genesis 13:14-18). Jacob may have heard about this from his grandfather personally, for Jacob was 15 when Abraham died (computed from 21:5; 25:7, 20, 26).

14b. And in thee and in thy seed shall all the families of the earth be blessed.

This part of the message was first stated in Genesis 12:3, when Abraham was leaving Haran (the place Jacob is now headed). To bless *all the families of the earth* has been God's larger plan all along. It is not a new element.

> *What Do You Think?*
> What are some ways our church can better participate in fulfilling God's promises in Genesis 28:14 in light of Matthew 28:19, 20?
> *Digging Deeper*
> Evaluate how Acts 3:24-26 and Galatians 3:7-9 should direct your efforts.

15. And, behold, I am with thee, and will keep thee in all places whither thou goest, and will bring thee again into this land; for I will not leave thee, until I have done that which I have spoken to thee of.

God's promise *I am with thee* is one of the most common and reassuring statements in Scripture (see Genesis 26:24; Isaiah 41:10; 43:5; Jeremiah 1:8, 19; 15:20; 42:11; 46:28; Haggai 1:13; 2:4; Matthew 28:20; Acts 18:10). For Jacob these words provide further encouragement as he embarks on life as a fugitive and a sojourner. In pagan thinking, gods are local, not global. They are limited to the territory or country that they rule. But Jacob, though he is moving away from the land promised to his grandfather and father, is not moving away from the presence or protection of God. Finding a place outside of God's "jurisdiction" is impossible (Psalm 139:7-12).

The landscape covered by God's promises to Jacob is quite extensive: the Lord will *keep* him throughout his travels, *bring* him back to his homeland, and fulfill everything He has promised to Jacob. In fact, God says *I will not leave thee, until I have done that which I have spoken to thee of.* This does not mean that once God's promises have been fulfilled, Jacob is on his own. It expresses the degree of God's commitment to keeping His word.

❧ LEAVING HOME ❧

I grew up in the Midwest, then moved to California several decades ago, where I quickly adapted to Western culture. Six years later I was invited to interview for a ministry in the Midwest.

As my plane flew over the Sierra Nevada, I looked down on Yosemite National Park, which had become one of my favorite places in God's creation. I wondered if it was a good idea to leave California's diverse natural beauty, which I had

HOW TO SAY IT

Beersheba	Beer-*she*-buh.
Bethel	*Beth*-ul.
Canaan	*Kay*-nun.
Chaldees	*Kal*-deez.
Ebenezer	*Eb*-en-*ee*-zer.
Esau	*Ee*-saw.
Hagar	*Hay*-gar.
Haran	*Hair*-un.
Ishmael	*Ish*-may-el.
Laban	*Lay*-bun.
Melchizedek	Mel-*kiz*-eh-dek.
Nathanael	Nuh-*than*-yull (*th* as in *thin*).
Terah	*Tair*-uh.
ziggurat	*zih*-guh-*rat*.

grown to love. Then I reminded myself might be calling me, and I should be ope.. invitation.

The interview went well until a member of the church board said, "It looks to me like you've moved around a lot." In that moment, I knew a "city feller" from California would have an uphill battle relating to, and winning the hearts of, these fine people. Their outlook had been shaped by the fact that many had never lived anywhere but the small town in which they'd been born! We mutually agreed that I could more effectively minister in my new home in the West.

When Jacob left home, we easily imagine his mixed feelings, since he was leaving familiar land and people. But one night he had a magnificent dream in which the Lord promised to be with him. We should not expect such a dream today (Hebrews 1:1, 2). God sometimes communicates His will through doors He opens (1 Corinthians 16:9; 2 Corinthians 2:12; Colossians 4:3). But we should not overlook the fact that the declarations and examples in Scripture are our primary source of assurance. And one of those examples is God's providential protection of Jacob. —C. R. B.

II. Marking the Place
(GENESIS 28:16-19)
A. Acknowledging God (vv. 16, 17)

16. And Jacob awaked out of his sleep, and he said, Surely the LORD is in this place; and I knew it not.

Jacob seems to awaken as soon as the dream ends, while it is yet night. His amazement that *the Lord is in this place* is probably due to the fact that the spot seems very ordinary. There is nothing especially holy about it. Jacob is learning that God can make the most ordinary location holy by His presence; this is a truth that Moses will come to realize in his day (Exodus 3:5).

17. And he was afraid, and said, How dreadful is this place! this is none other but the house of God, and this is the gate of heaven.

Fear kicks in. The word *dreadful* indicates a place to be dreaded or feared. (The words *afraid* and *dreadful* are derived from the same Hebrew word.) Many today express desire to have a face-to-face discussion with God. But Jacob's experience is cautionary. The phrase *the house of God* is considered in Genesis 28:19, below.

B. Anointing the Stone (vv. 18, 19)

18. And Jacob rose up early in the morning, and took the stone that he had put for his pillows, and set it up for a pillar, and poured oil upon the top of it.

Perhaps Jacob lies awake the rest of the night, reflecting on the contents of the dream, replaying it over and over in his mind. Any paralysis in that regard gives way to action when he arises *early in the morning*.

The stone that he had put for his pillows now serves a different purpose. The *oil* he pours *upon the top of it* serves to consecrate the place. Oil is often used in the Old Testament to set apart priests and kings. But it will also come to be used on objects (example: Exodus 30:22-29); the one we see here is the first such. A single stone may not constitute a *pillar* to our thinking today; but the important point is commemorating an event, not the size of the memorial.

19. And he called the name of that place Bethel: but the name of that city was called Luz at the first.

Bethel means in Hebrew "house of God," which reflects Jacob's earlier declaration in verse 17. Ironically and sadly, Bethel later becomes the site where the first king of the northern kingdom of divided Israel builds one of his golden calves to keep the people from going to Jerusalem to worship at the temple there (1 Kings 12:28, 29). Archaeologists have not been able to determine with certainty the location.

> *What Do You Think?*
> How can we improve the ways we use (or don't use) naming practices to remind us of things and actions of God?
> *Digging Deeper*
> Give an example of when a naming or renaming practice was successful in this regard and one when it wasn't. Explain why in both cases.

III. Making a Vow
(GENESIS 28:20-22)

A. God's Provision (vv. 20, 21a)

20, 21a. And Jacob vowed a vow, saying, If God will be with me, and will keep me in this way that I go, and will give me bread to eat, and raiment to put on, so that I come again to my father's house in peace.

Vows have not been seen prior to this point in Old Testament history. Regulations for making vows will later be included within the Law of Moses (Numbers 30:1-16). Jacob's vow echoes the words God had spoken to him in his dream (Genesis 28:15).

B. Jacob's Pledge (vv. 21b, 22)

21b, 22a. Then shall the LORD be my God: and this stone, which I have set for a pillar, shall be God's house.

Jacob's *vow* should be viewed as different from vows that are sometimes made to God in the heat of a crisis or emergency. Jacob is making his vow based on what God has revealed to him.

One must also keep in mind that this vow is coming from someone who is just beginning to understand what trusting in God means. Jacob has a lengthy journey ahead of him, in terms of both miles and spiritual maturity. When Jacob promises *then shall the Lord be my God*, he is pledging that at the end of his journey his personal relationship with the Lord will be far deeper than what it is now.

> *What Do You Think?*
> How can we create ways to remember and celebrate what God has promised and done?
> *Digging Deeper*
> What dangers present themselves by adding memorial aids to those God has already provided (example: the Lord's Supper)?

22b. And of all that thou shalt give me I will surely give the tenth unto thee.

Jacob's additional promise to *give the tenth* has a precedent in Genesis 14:17-20, where Abraham offered a tenth to Melchizedek. As with vows, tithing will also be covered in the Law of Moses (Numbers 18:21-29; Deuteronomy 14:22-29).

The tithe, or tenth, in the ancient world was usually a tax given to a ruler. The context shows that Jacob's desire to give a tenth to God is in appreciation for God's working through him to accomplish God's purposes.

❧ TAKING VOWS SERIOUSLY ❧

"I take thee to my wedded wife, to have and to hold from this day forward, for better for worse, for richer or poorer, in sickness and in health." So begin the traditional wedding vows spoken by millions of couples in days gone by. Today, however, we might hear something like this: "I promise to love and cherish you as much as I do our dog, Spot." Or this: "I promise to grab your toes with my toes when we cuddle at night, and when old age has robbed my toes of their monkey-like dexterity, I will just place my feet gently against yours until we fall asleep together like we always have." (Yes, both of these can be found on the Internet as serious suggestions!)

The first of these comes from the stilted Old English of the Episcopal *Book of Common Prayer*. The second may be an example of how pets have come to replace children in the family plans of many couples. And the third may be seen as a clever way of saying, "My love for you isn't based on the agile, youthful bodies we have today."

Jacob's vow to follow God may have been stated in common language, but he was serious in what he was promising. He based his vow to God on his solemn trust in God's faithfulness. Whatever our vows, in whatever circumstances, we should make them just as seriously.   —C. R. B.

Conclusion

A. "Stopping" Stones

We have seen in our study today how something very common, a stone, became something very special for Jacob as he marked the place where God appeared to him. Years later, he stopped at the same place and used a stone yet again to remember God's faithfulness to him through very turbulent years. The prophet Samuel used a

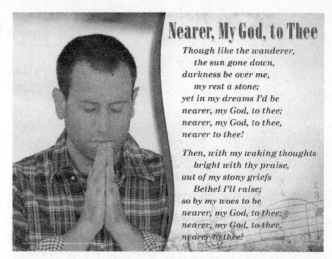

Nearer, My God, to Thee

Though like the wanderer,
*   the sun gone down,*
darkness be over me,
*   my rest a stone;*
yet in my dreams I'd be
*   nearer, my God, to thee;*
nearer, my God, to thee,
*   nearer to thee!*

Then, with my waking thoughts
*   bright with thy praise,*
out of my stony griefs
*   Bethel I'll raise;*
so by my woes to be
*   nearer, my God, to thee;*
nearer, my God, to thee,
*   nearer to thee!*

Visual for Lesson 12. *Point to this visual as you ask, "How do these lyrics connect the story in Genesis 28 with our own experience as believers?"*

stone to commemorate the Lord's deliverance of His people during a battle. He called the stone "Ebenezer," meaning in Hebrew "stone of help" (1 Samuel 7:12).

It is important for us to stop and mark times when the Lord has demonstrated His faithfulness to us or answered our prayers. Our memorial does not have to be a stone (it probably will not be), nor do we have to pour oil on it. It could be a card someone sent, a picture, a gift, a copy of an e-mail. In fact, any object, though as common as a stone, can serve the purpose—if it reminds us to stop at a specific time during our busy schedules and thank God for blessing us.

To pause and remember spiritual landmarks can be a source of great reassurance and encouragement to us. That is especially so when our own times become as turbulent as Jacob's did.

B. Prayer

Father, thank You for the many ways You have shown the unfailing nature of Your love. You have been abundantly faithful to us; yet in the hectic pace of life we often fail to stop and acknowledge our gratitude. May we do that not only in private settings but also before those who need our testimony. We pray this in Jesus' name. Amen.

C. Thought to Remember

Remember God's faithfulness to you
—in tangible ways.

INVOLVEMENT LEARNING

Enhance your lesson with KJV Bible Student (from your curriculum supplier) and the reproducible activity page (at www.standardlesson.com or in the back of the KJV Standard Lesson Commentary Deluxe Edition).

Into the Lesson

Open the session by starting a discussion about how we commemorate major holidays. Call out a few of those holidays and ask participants to discuss how they observe those days. Then divide your class into groups of four or five and ask them to invent a holiday. Instruct them to come up with a list of customs to honor the meaning of the day.

Lead into the Bible study by saying, "Holidays are important because they cause us to remember things that we value, including relationships that are dear or milestones of various types. In today's lesson, we are going to discover the importance of commemorating key moments in our relationship with God."

Alternative. Distribute copies of the "Too Busy to Remember?" activity from the reproducible page, which you can download. Group students into pairs to complete it as indicated. Lead into the Bible study by saying, "Lord Ashley was aware of our tendency to forget about God in the midst of our busy lives. However, our lives can go off the rails when we fail to remember and respond to God's character. In our Bible study today, we'll see how one man made sure that he'd never forget a life-changing encounter with God."

Into the Word

Divide the class in half. Have one group read Genesis 28:10-22 and make a list of everything that God promised to do for Jacob. Instruct the second group to read the passage and make a list of everything that Jacob promised to do for God in return. Lead a discussion of how the dream changed the trajectory of Jacob's life. Point out that God had already made this same promise to Abraham in Genesis 12:1-3; however, God deemed it necessary to remind Jacob of his spiritual heritage by renewing the promise directly to him in a dream.

State the following hypothetical situation: "Imagine that the next day Jacob decided to disregard the dream. What outcomes different from those promised in the dream might have become reality?"

As students brainstorm, remind them to consider Jacob's character flaws and that he was on a long journey into a kind of self-exile, away from his family. Ask them to imagine how those facts would affect their answer.

Begin a transition by writing "Spiritual Forgetfulness" on the board and asking, "What are some dangers of this?" Lead whole-class discussion while jotting responses on the board. If students are slow to respond, use passages such as Isaiah 17:10, 11; 65:11, 12 as discussion prompts.

Into Life

Connect the above with specific customs and traditions of your church that are intended to keep everyone mindful of God. Ask what those customs are and discuss how they are like and unlike Jacob's "stone . . . pillar" in Genesis 28:22. Let this lead to a discussion of ways your congregation can become better at collectively remembering God's goodness.

Follow with a minute of silence for students to reflect on their personal history with God. Have them write down (1) one thing that God has done for them for which they are particularly grateful and (2) one thing they can do to create a reminder of what God has promised yet to do. (*Option.* Provide small craft stones for the second step; have permanent markers available for students to write on their stones a word or symbol as a blessing reminder for the future.)

Alternative. Distribute copies of the "Table of Blessing" activity from the reproducible page for whole-class completion. Introduce the activity by telling the class that it's time to plan a mini-holiday to celebrate God's history with them.

GOD'S BLESSING

DEVOTIONAL READING: Psalm 46
BACKGROUND SCRIPTURE: Genesis 30

GENESIS 30:22-32, 43

22 And God remembered Rachel, and God hearkened to her, and opened her womb.

23 And she conceived, and bare a son; and said, God hath taken away my reproach:

24 And she called his name Joseph; and said, The LORD shall add to me another son.

25 And it came to pass, when Rachel had born Joseph, that Jacob said unto Laban, Send me away, that I may go unto mine own place, and to my country.

26 Give me my wives and my children, for whom I have served thee, and let me go: for thou knowest my service which I have done thee.

27 And Laban said unto him, I pray thee, if I have found favour in thine eyes, tarry: for I have learned by experience that the LORD hath blessed me for thy sake.

28 And he said, Appoint me thy wages, and I will give it.

29 And he said unto him, Thou knowest how I have served thee, and how thy cattle was with me.

30 For it was little which thou hadst before I came, and it is now increased unto a multi-tude; and the LORD hath blessed thee since my coming: and now when shall I provide for mine own house also?

31 And he said, What shall I give thee? And Jacob said, Thou shalt not give me any thing: if thou wilt do this thing for me, I will again feed and keep thy flock.

32 I will pass through all thy flock to day, removing from thence all the speckled and spotted cattle, and all the brown cattle among the sheep, and the spotted and speckled among the goats: and of such shall be my hire.

· ·

43 And the man increased exceedingly, and had much cattle, and maidservants, and menservants, and camels, and asses.

KEY VERSE

God remembered Rachel, and God hearkened to her, and opened her womb. —**Genesis 30:22**

GOD'S WORLD AND GOD'S PEOPLE

Unit 3: God Blesses and Re-creates Regardless

LESSON AIMS

After participating in this lesson, each learner will be able to:

1. Recount the instances of God's blessing of individuals in today's text.

2. Compare and contrast the deceptive personalities of Laban and Jacob.

3. Acknowledge with gratitude one or more blessings from God.

LESSON OUTLINE

Introduction

A. ASAP

In our fast-paced world where everything is required to happen ASAP (as soon as possible), delays can be especially frustrating. At the time this lesson is being written, the road I usually take to our church is under repair. Detour signs let drivers know they have to take an alternate route.

Delays seem to be a common part of God's modus operandi in Scripture. He appears to prefer operating by another kind of ASAP: as slowly as possible. Consider the patriarchs in the book of Genesis. Abraham entered Canaan at the age of 75 (Genesis 12:4), having received God's promise that he would be the source of a great nation (12:2). Yet his covenant son, Isaac, was not born until Abraham had reached age 100!

Isaac was 40 when he married Rebekah, but their sons Jacob and Esau did not arrive for another 20 years (lesson 10). Jacob had to wait 7 years before he could marry Laban's daughter Rachel; even then he ended up married to her sister Leah. Laban allowed him to marry Rachel provided that he worked another 7 years.

Rachel also spent time in God's "waiting room" as she struggled with the disappointment of her inability to conceive (Genesis 29:31). It is hard to imagine the depths of her frustration at seeing the other women in her household bearing children while she remained barren. It is hard at times for us to explain or fully understand why God delays answering certain prayers or fulfilling certain promises. This is where faith provides another outlook (or "uplook"). We trust that God will do what He has said, by accepting another interpretation of ASAP: as sure as promised.

B. Lesson Context

Following Jacob's dream at Bethel (last week's study), he traveled on to Haran. There he met Rachel, Laban's daughter (and Jacob's cousin) when she came to water her father's sheep. Rachel ran back home to tell her father about Jacob's arrival; and Laban hurried to meet Jacob, welcoming him with great excitement. Then followed the series of events that resulted in the master deceiver, Jacob, being deceived in turn by Laban. As a result, Jacob first married Leah, then Rachel (whom he truly loved).

The Bible then records how Jacob began to build a family that would grow to 12 sons and a daughter (Dinah), with the sons becoming the source of the 12 tribes of the nation of Israel. Leah gave birth to Jacob's sons Reuben, Simeon, Levi, and Judah (Genesis 29:31-35). Then Rachel, who was barren, determined that she would build a family through her servant Bilhah, who gave birth to Dan and Naphtali (30:4-8). Leah's servant Zilpah then gave birth to Gad and Asher (30:9-13). Later, Leah gave birth to sons Issachar and Zebulun plus daughter Dinah (30:17-21).

Rachel voiced her anguish to Jacob with great emotion (Genesis 30:1). She must have grown increasingly discouraged as she watched the three other women in her household provide children for Jacob while she remained barren. The sibling rivalry between Rachel and sister Leah (30:7, 8, 14-16) must have reminded Jacob of the friction that had developed between him and Esau back home. But circumstances were about to change.

I. Increase of Family
(Genesis 30:22-24)
A. God's Sustenance (v. 22)
22a. And God remembered Rachel.

When Scripture says *God remembered* something or someone, that does not imply something that had slipped His mind now pops back

HOW TO SAY IT

Asher	*Ash*-er.
Bilhah	*Bill*-ha.
Gad	*Gad* (*a* as in *bad*).
Haran	*Hair*-un.
Issachar	*Izz*-uh-kar.
Laban	*Lay*-bun.
modus operandi	*mow*-duhs *ah*-puh-**ran**-dee.
Naphtali	*Naf*-tuh-lye.
Simeon	*Sim*-ee-un.
Zebulun	*Zeb*-you-lun.
Zilpah	*Zil*-pa.

to memory. God does not need to have His memory jogged as we do. He needs no reminders. Rather, when the text says that God remembers, the meaning is that He is about to act to fulfill a promise (compare Genesis 8:1; 19:29; Exodus 2:24, 25; etc.).

22b. And God hearkened to her, and opened her womb.

It is interesting to compare this statement with Genesis 25:21. There the text says that God listened to the prayer of husband Isaac on behalf of his barren wife, Rebekah. Here, however, God responds to the barren wife's own expression of anguish. Perhaps she has been praying about her condition, but the text does not specifically say that.

B. Rachel's Son (vv. 23, 24)
23. And she conceived, and bare a son; and said, God hath taken away my reproach.

Barrenness is a source of *reproach* in biblical times (compare Isaiah 49:21; 54:1; Galatians 4:27). When Elisabeth is allowed to conceive in her old age, she declares, "Thus hath the Lord dealt with me in the days wherein he looked on me, to take away my reproach among men" (Luke 1:25). With the birth of a *son*, an especially heavy burden has been lifted from Rachel's shoulders, and she is grateful.

> *What Do You Think?*
> What are some ways that the church can help alleviate the shame people feel about their circumstances?
> *Digging Deeper*
> How, if at all, should the church's approach to the issue depend on whether the shame is due to voluntary or involuntary circumstances?

24. And she called his name Joseph; and said, The Lord shall add to me another son.

The name *Joseph* comes from a Hebrew word meaning "to add." Rachel hopes that her childbearing prowess is not limited to bearing him. Her statement may also be seen as a prayer request, that God will be gracious enough to add yet *another son*. In either case, Rachel recognizes *the Lord* as the source of the son she now holds.

II. Increase of Flocks

(GENESIS 30:25-32, 43)

A. Jacob's Proposal (vv. 25, 26)

25. And it came to pass, when Rachel had born Joseph, that Jacob said unto Laban, Send me away, that I may go unto mine own place, and to my country.

Joseph's birth seems to serve as a signal to Jacob that it is time that he should return to Canaan, his homeland. A woman's status is very uncertain if she has no children. A barren woman is probably in better surroundings if she remains among family members who will care for her; otherwise she risks being ostracized and possibly mistreated. But now that Rachel has a son of her own, Jacob seems to feel more at ease about making the request we see here.

26. Give me my wives and my children, for whom I have served thee, and let me go: for thou knowest my service which I have done thee.

Another factor influencing Jacob's desire to return home at this point is that the 14 years for which he had agreed to work in order to marry both Rachel and Leah have apparently been fulfilled. That work represents what Jacob has "paid" for both Leah and Rachel: 7 years initially for Rachel (only to be given Leah instead) and then 7 additional years for Rachel, though Jacob was allowed to marry Rachel before his second 7-year obligation was carried out (Genesis 29:18, 26-28).

❧ DECISION POINTS ❧

"Having children will bring a couple closer together." Don't believe it. It's a myth! At least that's what many psychological studies show.

On the other hand, even though research says marital happiness may decline with the birth of the first child, a couple is less likely to divorce at that point. Apparently, when that "little bundle of joy" comes along, the primary focus is no longer on efforts that reinforce the pleasure the couple experiences with each other. Rather, the new dynamic focuses on that innocent stranger that has come to live with them.

Parenting adds a dimension to the relationship that calls for selfless actions such as feeding, bathing, and diapering the baby. The emotional weight of being responsible for a little one can be a decision point in forcing a parent to realize that it's time to grow up emotionally in accepting responsibility. This is often especially true of fathers.

Jacob already had 10 sons before Joseph—who would be his favorite son—was born. However, the birth of this son by the wife he loved seems to have resulted in a decision point: it was time for him to ponder anew his promised role in the nation through which God would bless the world.

An occasion, a precipitating event, may come to each of us that causes us to realize that it's time to take seriously our roles in fulfilling the Great Commission (Matthew 28:19, 20). But, of course, that time is not now because we have so much else to do. Right?　　　　　—C. R. B.

> **What Do You Think?**
> What questions are helpful to ask ourselves when considering a major transition?
> **Digging Deeper**
> How might issues of body and issues of spirit affect one another during such a transition?

B. Laban's Plea (vv. 27, 28)

27. And Laban said unto him, I pray thee, if I have found favour in thine eyes, tarry: for I have learned by experience that the LORD hath blessed me for thy sake.

Laban has been as much of a deceiving "heel-grabber" as Jacob. This is seen in Laban's sister-swap of Leah in place of Rachel (Genesis 29:23). His deception has been rewarded by 14 years of labor from Jacob, and Laban is hesitant to let good help get away.

Laban's deceiving and manipulative ways cause us to be suspicious about the sincerity of his declaration that he has *learned by experience that the Lord* has *blessed* him for Jacob's *sake*. Is Laban merely "playing the Lord card" as a further attempt to manipulate Jacob?

The Hebrew word translated *experience* is an interesting one. Its nine uses in the Old Testament are variously translated "enchantment(s)" (Leviticus 19:26; 2 Kings 17:17; 21:6; 2 Chronicles 33:6) and divinations (Genesis 44:5, 15). These suggest attempts to discover hidden information by means that are tied to pagan religious practices. This is the first time the term is used in the Bible; the practice will later be clearly spelled out as forbidden in the Law of Moses (Deuteronomy 18:9-14).

We do not know what rituals Laban has engaged in to determine what he says he knows. Even so, it appears that some elements of superstition or pagan religion are practiced in his household. This is seen by the use of mandrake plants to induce pregnancy (Genesis 30:14-18). It is also apparent given the presence of the "images," or "gods," that Rachel later takes from Laban and hides (31:19, 30-35).

This provides another example of God's guiding or superintending human efforts (as misguided as they may be) to accomplish His sovereign will. Just as God can use pagan rulers to further His divine program (as He used Pharaoh during the exodus), so He can use a sinful human practice such as divination (whatever it may have involved) to accomplish His ultimate plan. That plan is to return Jacob to his homeland as God promised He would (Genesis 28:15).

Of course, the real reason for Laban's being blessed has nothing to do with divination. The blessing that Isaac had given to Jacob (under the assumption he was Esau) included these words: "Blessed be he that blesseth thee" (Genesis 27:29). Ultimately that promise is rooted in the Lord's covenant with Abraham (12:3).

28. And he said, Appoint me thy wages, and I will give it.

Jacob's presence has been very profitable for Laban; he is reluctant to lose that expertise. So he uses the promise of a blank check in an attempt to persuade Jacob to stay. The offer we see in the verse before us is the same as the one Laban made after Jacob had been in Laban's household a month (Genesis 29:14, 15). The offer that had worked before may work again, or so Laban seems to hope.

C. Laban's Prosperity (vv. 29, 30)

29, 30. And he said unto him, Thou knowest how I have served thee, and how thy cattle was with me. For it was little which thou hadst before I came, and it is now increased unto a multitude; and the Lord hath blessed thee since my coming: and now when shall I provide for mine own house also?

Once again Jacob mentions the service he has already rendered Laban. Jacob repeats Laban's observation regarding credit to be given to *the Lord* for the blessing that has resulted. Laban has indeed prospered well because of the Lord's blessing after Jacob's arrival. But Jacob adds that he needs to think about his family and what is best for them.

> **What Do You Think?**
> How do you know when you've met your responsibility to assist others given your responsibility to meet the needs of your own family?
>
> **Digging Deeper**
> What are some ways to determine if your motives are selfish?

D. Jacob's Pay (vv. 31, 32, 43)

31. And he said, What shall I give thee? And Jacob said, Thou shalt not give me any thing: if thou wilt do this thing for me, I will again feed and keep thy flock.

Laban again offers Jacob a blank check, giving the appearance of being more than fair. *Jacob* responds with a proposal that will allow Laban to keep Jacob in his service for an unspecified amount of time.

This immediately makes us wonder why Jacob yields to Laban's desire after Jacob has voiced his desire to return to his homeland. Does the "heel-grabber" see at this point an opportunity to enhance his own wealth by means of the plan (scheme?) he is about to propose? Is Jacob already thinking ahead to what he will do to outsmart Laban at his own game? It is tempting, with someone like Jacob or Laban, to try to discern some ulterior motive for his actions. Perhaps Jacob simply has had a change of heart.

Visual for Lesson 13. *Ask your class members to discuss how this visual connects with Genesis 30:22, 23 and incidents in their lives.*

32. I will pass through all thy flock to day, removing from thence all the speckled and spotted cattle, and all the brown cattle among the sheep, and the spotted and speckled among the goats: and of such shall be my hire.

Sheep (and lambs) are usually all white, while *goats* are all black. *Speckled* or *spotted* animals (and *brown sheep*) are far fewer in number. Essentially, Jacob is proposing to keep for himself the least numerous animals among the livestock for his *hire*, or pay; Laban is to retain all the rest.

In the verses that immediately follow those in our lesson text, Jacob further proposes that any unspeckled or unspotted livestock found among Jacob's flocks will be assumed to be stolen. Laban immediately (and understandably!) agrees to Jacob's suggestion (Genesis 30:33, 34).

43. And the man increased exceedingly, and had much cattle, and maidservants, and menservants, and camels, and asses.

The ultimate result—when Jacob uses a combination of selective breeding and superstitious beliefs (Genesis 30:37-42)—is that Laban is outsmarted, and Jacob increases his holdings greatly at Laban's expense. Laban's desire to retain Jacob's expertise proves the validity of the old warning, "Be careful what you ask for because you may just get it!"

The man (Jacob) later acknowledges to Rachel and Leah that God has been the source of the blessings and the abundance he has received (Genesis 31:9-12). It appears that the tree branches

Jacob uses in 30:37-42 have an impact similar to mandrakes on the ability of females to become pregnant (30:14-16, 22). However such things work (or people believe they work), God is, in truth, the source of the desired fertility. Both Rachel and Jacob attest to this fact (30:23, 30).

The results God desires are obtained, above and beyond what Rachel and Jacob do or desire. Throughout all of this, God has been keeping the promise He made to Jacob in his dream (Genesis 28:14, 15). That increase will also apply to Jacob's descendants, the children of Israel, while in Egypt (47:27).

> **What Do You Think?**
> How can we can determine if God is pleased with our plans and decisions?
> *Digging Deeper*
> Consider 2 Corinthians 6:4-10 and the characters of Hebrews 11 in your conclusion.

Genesis 31 records how Laban's sons begin to complain about all that Jacob has obtained at the expense of their father. The relationship between Laban and Jacob becomes much more strained. Genesis 31:3 includes a detail that is missing from Jacob's earlier plan to return home: the Lord's personal command for him to do so. Included with the command is repetition of the promise given to Jacob during his dream of last week's lesson: "I am with thee" (28:15). Much still lies ahead for Jacob. He has a vow to keep (28:20-22) and a brother to encounter.

❧ HUMAN SCHEMES OR GOD'S HELP? ❧

Jacob's bargain with Laban shows us that animal husbandry folklore was part of ancient culture. But the custom has continued for centuries since. For example, changing the name of an animal will cause it to die, according to an old Pennsylvania belief. On the other hand, an Illinois proverb held that if you get a horse on trade, you *must* change its name to have good luck with it.

A North Carolina belief promised that nailing a horseshoe over the stable door will prevent witches from stealing your horses. Are you a chicken farmer? A Maryland proverb assured that eggs set in the morning will result in male chicks. But in Alabama, eggs needed to be set in the afternoon to get the same result. In Kentucky, your chickens would be protected from hawks if you put a round rock in a fire—causing the hawk's claws to draw up in that shape so it couldn't grab your chickens.

Animal husbandry folklore may have been in play as Laban and Jacob connived to outsmart each other when determining Jacob's wages. But we know from prior readings in Genesis that God planned to bless Jacob and his descendants. So it's far more likely that the real reason for Jacob's success in breeding his flocks was that God had His hand in the process.

The principle is still valid: Our blessings are due more to God's actions than to our own plans (however noble) or schemes (however devious).

—C. R. B.

> ### What Do You Think?
> What guardrails can we put in place to keep our motives above reproach?
> ### Digging Deeper
> Distinguish between guardrails that all Christians should adopt vs. guardrails that are specific to your own past and personality.

Conclusion

A. Facing Labans

We've all heard the quip "When life gives you lemons, make lemonade." That lighthearted advice offers perspective in surviving difficult circumstances that are not of our own making. The idea is to try to make the best of a bad situation.

What do we do when life gives us "Labans"? We have seen Jacob's "heel-grabbing" ability on display in the previous lessons of this unit, but Laban was just as crafty as Jacob. Each man learned to live by his wits, to "do unto others *before* they can do unto you." Having two "heel-grabbers" in such proximity to one another was bound to create a constant atmosphere of tension. Even Laban's own daughters, Leah and Rachel, admitted that he had not treated them fairly in denying them what they

were entitled to receive as an inheritance. They felt more like "strangers" than daughters in the household (Genesis 31:14, 15).

We may come across people who remind us of Laban. We may meet them in the workplace, at school, or perhaps (sadly) even in the church. They are always looking to gain an advantage over others. They may even use the Lord's name as Laban did with Jacob. We want to think the best of people, but the track record of some may cause us to be cautious.

When life gives us Labans, what do we do? Our main desire should be to maintain a God-honoring attitude and conduct. We do so as we are "wise as serpents, and harmless as doves" (Matthew 10:16). Spiritual maturity and tact are important in knowing when and how to confront a Laban in a way that does not make matters worse.

It is easy to allow life's Labans to sour our relationship with God and with other people. We may think that we have to become Labans in order to survive. We end up leaning on our own understanding rather than trusting in the Lord, contrary to Proverbs 3:5. True, life's Labans are not easy to face or easy to love. Perhaps a long, hard look in the mirror will remind us that at times we are not all that easy to love or deal with either. We all need God's grace on a daily basis—grace to avoid being like Laban and grace to love the Labans who cross our paths.

B. Being Jacob

Jacob would not seem to be someone to emulate as we face life's Labans. But we should not allow Jacob's massive flaws to cause us to miss what was right about him: his awareness that God was watching over him to fulfill His promises. The same is true for us.

C. Prayer

Father, the manipulative people in our broken world discourage us! Keep us from becoming one of them. Let people see Christ in us. We pray this in Jesus' name. Amen.

D. Thought to Remember

Count your blessings and thank the blesser.

INVOLVEMENT LEARNING

Enhance your lesson with KJV Bible Student *(from your curriculum supplier) and the reproducible activity page (at www.standardlesson.com or in the back of the* KJV Standard Lesson Commentary Deluxe Edition*).*

Into the Lesson

Lead a conversation about everyone's best and worst jobs. Ask participants to identify specifically what made certain jobs desirable and other jobs draining. Encourage them to explore what had the biggest impact on their attitude toward these jobs—the work itself, the wages and benefits, or something else.

Alternative. Distribute copies of the "What Each Generation Wants from Work" activity from the reproducible page, which you can download. Form students into groups of no more than four to complete the activity as indicated. After about four minutes of sharing, have a spokesperson from each group share their conclusions.

After either opening, make a transition to Bible study by saying, "In today's lesson we're going to investigate an intriguing discussion involving wages and benefits. What will be different from such discussions as we typically hear of them in the news is the role of God and His blessings."

Into the Word

Use the Lesson Context to remind participants of how Laban had deceived Jacob, the result being more long years of hard work. Set the stage further by reminding the class that Rachel's inability to conceive was a barrier for Jacob to receive God's promise of uncountable offspring.

Read Genesis 30:22-32, 43 aloud, then form the class into groups of four to six. After distributing index cards and pens, instruct groups to (1) identify, with one entry per card, the specific ways that God had blessed Jacob and then (2) group those blessings into two general categories and name those categories.

After no more than five minutes, have a reporter from each group share discoveries of specific blessings. *(Anticipated responses: God's provisions of healing for Rachel, the birth of a child, wages for livelihood, etc.)*

Next, call for groups' discoveries of the two general categories of those blessings. *(Anticipated responses: (1) the category of covenantal blessings [birth of Joseph to help fulfill the promises of Genesis 28:13, 14; see last week's lesson] and (2) he category of material blessings [as summarized in Genesis 30:43].)* Be ready to add information that groups miss.

Collect the cards and shuffle them. Pick a card, read it, and pose this question for whole-class discussion: "Would this blessing have been obvious to Jacob as coming from God or not?" Have respondents explain their conclusions. If a disagreement is not quickly forthcoming, ask, "Does anyone disagree?" Play the two responses off one another to enhance the discussion.

Repeat this sequence with the remaining cards, discarding cards that list blessings already considered. Throughout this process, jot on the board the blessing under consideration and bullet-point summaries of participants' responses.

As a transition to the Into Life segment, pose this question for whole-class discussion: "Which of these blessings resonates with you most strongly?" Ask the follow up "Why?" as appropriate.

Into Life

To groups of no more than six, distribute handouts (you prepare) with the word *Gratitude* printed vertically down the middle. Have these instructions printed at the top: "Create an acrostic of ways that God has provided for those in your group." After a few minutes, have group spokespersons present results for whole-class discussion.

Alternative. Distribute copies of the "How Gratitude Changes Us" activity from the reproducible page to be completed as indicated by groups of three. Allow time for whole-class discussion.

After either activity, lead a time of prayer to thank God for all the ways that He has provided for you and members of your class.

OUR LOVE
FOR GOD

Special Features

Lessons
Unit 1: God Is Worthy of Our Love

Unit 2: Loving God by Trusting Christ

Unit 3: Songs That Glorify the God of Love

QUARTERLY QUIZ

Use these questions as a pretest or as a review. The answers are on page iv of This Quarter in the Word.

Lesson 1

1. "Hear O Israel, the Lord our God is _____ Lord." *Deuteronomy 6:4*

2. We are to love the Lord with all our heart, soul, and _____ . *Deuteronomy 6:5*

Lesson 2

1. Near the end of his life, Joshua gathered the leaders of Israel at Shechem. T/F. *Joshua 24:1*

2. Abraham's father, Terah, worshipped other gods. T/F. *Joshua 24:2*

3. Joshua said, "As for me and my house, we will serve the _____." *Joshua 24:15*

Lesson 3

1. Forgiven sins are removed as far as what from what? (east from west, Jerusalem from Damascus, mountains from the sea?) *Psalm 103: 12*

2. The Lord's mercy is from everlasting to _____. *Psalm 103:17*

Lesson 4

1. Nazareth was located in what region? (Judea, Galilee, Egypt?) *Luke 1:26*

2. The angel who visited Mary is unnamed in the text. T/F. *Luke 1:26*

Lesson 5

1. The final judgment is presented as separating sheep from _____. *Matthew 25:32*

2. The saved will enter a kingdom prepared since the founding of the world. T/F. *Matthew 25:34*

Lesson 6

1. Paul said that all people have some faith. T/F. *2 Thessalonians 3:2*

2. John's command "from the beginning" was that Christians love _____ _____. *2 John 5*

3. According to John, one who denies the human nature of Jesus is a what? (heretic, teacher, antichrist?) *2 John 7*

Lesson 7

1. A friend of the world is an enemy of God. T/F. *James 4:4*

2. God gives comfort and support to proud people. T/F. *James 4:6*

Lesson 8

1. While imprisoned in Rome, Paul was unable to witness to his guards. T/F. *Philippians 1:13*

2. For Paul, to live is Christ and to die is ____. *Philippians 1:21*

Lesson 9

1. Coming in human likeness, Christ took the form of a servant. T/F. *Philippians 2:7*

2. In the end, only believers will confess that Jesus is Lord. T/F. *Philippians 2:11*

Lesson 10

1. Paul said he wanted to know Christ and the power of His _____. *Philippians 3:10*

2. Paul advised his readers to forget the things of the past. T/F. *Philippians 3:13*

Lesson 11

1. Jerusalem was considered to be built on a holy mountain. T/F. *Psalm 48:1*

2. Jerusalem is described as the city of the great what? (priest, king, army?) *Psalm 48:2*

Lesson 12

1. Only Israel is to make a joyful noise to the Lord. *Psalm 66:1*

2. The people had been tested like what? (gold, silver, iron?) *Psalm 66:10*

Lesson 13

1. To dwell in "the shadow of the Almighty" is a good thing. T/F. *Psalm 91:1*

2. "Pestilence" is something to be welcomed as a gift from the Lord. T/F. *Psalm 91:3*

QUARTER AT A GLANCE

by Tom Thatcher

Our Love for God, the title of this quarter's studies, can be a rather humbling subject. While the Lord's love is "everlasting" (Jeremiah 31:3), ours is inconsistent and "never-lasting." Still, the command to love God is, as Jesus stated, "the first and great commandment" (Matthew 22:36-38). Lessons this quarter are drawn from both the Old and New Testament, since loving God is seen throughout Scripture as humanity's principal response to God.

A Nation's Foundation

It is only fitting that this quarter begins by studying the passage where the original command to love God is found: Deuteronomy 6:4, 5. The Israelites were preparing to enter the land promised to them by God when Moses spoke his farewell address that makes up the book of Deuteronomy. Joshua spoke his own farewell address to the Israelites who had entered the land and triumphed over the residents there. He challenged God's people to discard any gods that remained among them, and he made his own choice unmistakably clear: "As for me and my house, we will serve the Lord" (Joshua 24:15, lesson 2).

Love Songs

Four lessons are taken from the book of Psalms, the collection of songs that express God's love for us and our reciprocal love for Him. Psalm 103 (lesson 3) encourages us not to forget the Lord's abundant blessings. The other lessons from Psalms form the final unit of the quarter, "Songs That Glorify the God of Love." Lesson 11 highlights expressing love for God in the primary place of worship for Old Testament believers: "mount Zion, . . . the city of the great King" (Psalm 48:2). Lesson 12 focuses on God's mighty deeds (66:3-7) and answered prayers (66:16-20). Lesson 13 invites readers to praise God for the protection and security found in "the shadow of the Almighty" (91:1).

The Ultimate Gift of Love

Our love for God takes on a whole new meaning when we come to the New Testament. And why shouldn't it? Here we see, as did Simeon, the salvation brought about by the Lord's Christ (Luke 2:26, 30). This is the focus of lesson 4, which falls on the Sunday before Christmas Day.

The other lessons from the New Testament (5–10) challenge students to love God in a manner befitting such a marvelous gift. Lesson 5, the final study of the year, may provide a source of New Year's resolutions in calling students to loving acts that demonstrate their love of Jesus. In lesson 9 Paul exhorts us to imitate the Savior's sacrificial love as we esteem others (Philippians 2:1-11).

We show our love for God essentially the same way that Old Testament believers were to show theirs: by a life of obedience. "This is love," writes John, "that we walk after [God's] commandments" (2 John 6, lesson 6). We must not allow our love to erode by becoming too closely attached to this world. James is clear about that: "Whosoever therefore will be a friend of the world is the enemy of God" (James 4:4, lesson 7).

> *Our love for God took on new meaning when God came to live in our world.*

Furthermore, our love for God is meant to deepen even in the midst of this world's difficult circumstances. Paul's chains in Rome could not hinder either the progress of the gospel (lesson 8) or his personal walk with the Lord (lesson 10). In fact, not even death can shake the Christian's confidence. As Paul so beautifully states, "For to me to live is Christ, and to die is gain" (Philippians 1:21, lesson 8). Our love for God took on new meaning when God came to live in our world; it will certainly take on new meaning when we go to live in His!

GET THE SETTING

by Tom Thatcher

OUR LESSONS this quarter focus on "love," an oft-used and much abused word. While the word *love* itself takes on many cultural connotations that shift every few years, the biblical outlook on love is grounded in God's unchanging nature. Our acts of love toward Him and others are responses to this aspect of His identity.

God as Love

The Bible portrays love as a defining characteristic of God—so much so that He can be equated with love (1 John 4:8). God's love is seen in His creation, sustenance, protection, and offers of redemption of people. These expressions of God's love are unconditional; examples of such expressions are found in Psalm 33:5; Matthew 5:45; Acts 14:17; John 3:16; and 1 John 2:2; 4:10.

We hasten to caution against confusing the unconditional expressions of God's love with the conditional acceptance on the part of people. A vital example is John 3:16. There the word *whosoever* makes clear the unconditional nature of God's making redemption possible for all. But whether or not a person actually receives redemption is conditioned on his or her accessing it only through Jesus (John 3:18-20; 14:6). See both sides on the chart on page 119.

Love for God

God's love is often unrequited —many people simply reject Him. But the Bible's view is that we should love God in return (1 John 4:19). Such love is portrayed as tangible rather than simply emotional.

Love for God expresses itself in praise and worship, in obedience to His commands (John 14:15; 1 John 5:3), and in service to Him

(Deuteronomy 10:12; Matthew 25:31-46; etc.). Just as God visibly and publicly communicates His love by sustaining us, believers are expected to act on their love for Him.

Love Like God

Both the Old and New Testaments stress that love for God should express itself through love for others. This is logical: since God loves and cares for other people, He wants us to love and care for them as well, just as parents rejoice to see their children caring for one another.

God's love, especially as expressed through the act of giving His Son (John 3:16), is the model for all human relationships. Jesus exemplified this divine standard in His own ministry, and commanded His disciples to do the same (Mark 12:28-31; John 13:34-35). The apostle Paul says that God transforms us for the very purpose of doing good works, which primarily involve acting for the good of others (Ephesians 2:8-10; Philippians 2:1-11).

Love Like No Other

While the above principles are familiar to most Christians, they were unique in the biblical world. Ancient pagan religions included "love gods" such as Venus but did not promote the idea that gods love people (often the opposite), did not expect worshippers to love the gods (just to serve them), and did not teach that loving others was an aspect of religious life (that was a subject for philosophy).

The notions that God loves us, we love God, and we love others because God loves us reflect the distinct biblical conception of the God we serve, the only God there is!

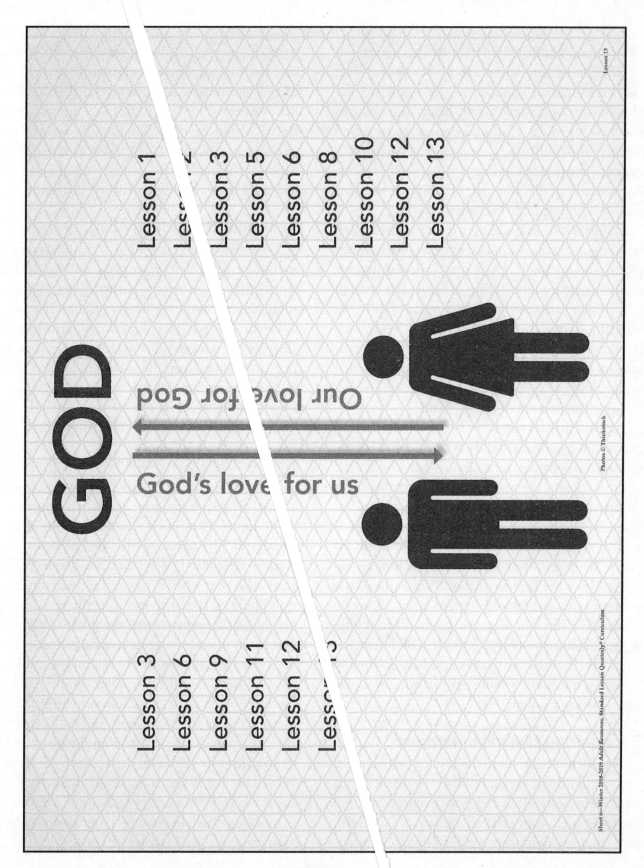

GOD

Our love for God

God's love for us

Lesson 1
Lesson 2
Lesson 3
Lesson 5
Lesson 6
Lesson 8
Lesson 10
Lesson 12
Lesson 13

Lesson 3
Lesson 6
Lesson 9
Lesson 11
Lesson 12
Lesson 13

Lesson 13

Photos © Thinkstock

Sheet 6—Winter 2018-2019 Adult Resources, Standard Lesson Quarterly® Curriculum

RECOGNIZING MATERIALS

Part 2 of Building Bible Literacy   *Teacher Tips by Jim Eichenberger*

IN THE PRECEDING article in this series, we compared the story arc of Scripture with the blueprint of a house. By knowing the plot line of God's revelation, Bible students can place each passage read and each lesson studied into its proper historical context. As a blueprint is essential for understanding the architect's intent, understanding the story line of Scripture is essential for building Bible literacy.

The next step in building a house is assembling building materials—lumber, drywall, brick, wires, pipes, and so forth. Each material is different, requiring an understanding of how each is used. In a similar fashion, the Bible is made of different building materials—historical narrative, letters, poetry, and even types of literature with no parallel in Western writings. The Bible student must understand each type to grasp the literary context of any given portion of God's Word.

Although this may sound like an intellectual exercise, recognizing literary types is a skill we use every day. Consider the sentence "My love is a red rose." We know the words are meant symbolically, comparing the beauty of a loved one with a fragrant flower. But the same words on the cover of a gardening magazine tell us to take the words literally. We expect the author to explain how to cultivate his or her favorite blooms. The same words on a supermarket tabloid warn us to anticipate an outlandish story of a crazed horticulturist who wants to marry a plant! A skilled Bible teacher can help a class better understand God's Word by pointing out literary hallmarks in whatever passage is being studied.

Recognizing Historical Narrative

A work of fiction may be set "once upon a time" or "in a land far, far away." But historical narratives identify the time and place events occur. For example, alert your class to the phrase "unto this day" that often appears in Old Testament narratives as a way to tell the original reader, "Check it out; you can see the evidence with your own eyes." The 12 stones set up as a memorial after the Israelites crossed the Jordan (Joshua 4:9), the presence of Rahab of Jericho in the land (6:25), and the ruins of the city of Ai (8:28) were given as verifiable evidence to the first readers of the book of Joshua that the events described were history, not fantasy.

Recognizing Spiritual Allegory

Fictional stories are told in Scripture to explain a divine truth. Help your class distinguish such stories from history by pointing out the much more general language used in them. This is very evident in the parables of Jesus. He introduced the story of the Good Samaritan saying, "A certain man went down from Jerusalem to Jericho" (Luke 10:30). Likewise, we know the parable of the sower is allegorical by the introduction, "Behold, a sower went forth to sow" (Matthew 13:3).

Recognizing Symbolism

Some Bible literature, such as books of poetry and some prophecy, use words as symbols. The depiction of Jesus in Revelation 1:13-16 is meant to portray His nature with word pictures rather than to describe His appearance literally. Warn your class that when symbols are common in certain books, it is wise to examine the text carefully before ascribing face-value meaning to numbers, descriptions, or even geographical references.

These are just a few of the building materials of God's Word. A skillful teacher should use commentary (such as in every lesson in this book) to assist learners in identifying and properly interpreting them. Just as a skilled builder knows how to treat lumber differently than drywall, a skilled Bible teacher is quick to point out which passages are promises and which are proverbs. This is building Bible literacy by "rightly dividing the word of truth" (2 Timothy 2:15).

Love and Obey God

DEVOTIONAL READING: Mark 12:28-34
BACKGROUND SCRIPTURE: Deuteronomy 6:1-9

DEUTERONOMY 6:1-9

1 Now these are the commandments, the statutes, and the judgments, which the LORD your God commanded to teach you, that ye might do them in the land whither ye go to possess it:

2 That thou mightest fear the LORD thy God, to keep all his statutes and his commandments, which I command thee, thou, and thy son, and thy son's son, all the days of thy life; and that thy days may be prolonged.

3 Hear therefore, O Israel, and observe to do it; that it may be well with thee, and that ye may increase mightily, as the LORD God of thy fathers hath promised thee, in the land that floweth with milk and honey.

4 Hear, O Israel: The LORD our God is one LORD:

5 And thou shalt love the LORD thy God with all thine heart, and with all thy soul, and with all thy might.

6 And these words, which I command thee this day, shall be in thine heart:

7 And thou shalt teach them diligently unto thy children, and shalt talk of them when thou sittest in thine house, and when thou walk-est by the way, and when thou liest down, and when thou risest up.

8 And thou shalt bind them for a sign upon thine hand, and they shall be as frontlets between thine eyes.

9 And thou shalt write them upon the posts of thy house, and on thy gates.

KEY VERSE

Thou shalt love the LORD thy God with all thine heart, and with all thy soul, and with all thy might.
—Deuteronomy 6:5

Our Love for God

LESSON AIMS

After participating in this lesson, each learner will be able to:

1. Recount the instructions from Moses to the Israelites found in today's text.

2. Tell why the intentional teaching of the faith to the next generation is so crucial in today's world.

3. Suggest practical ways to apply the commands of Deuteronomy 6:6-9 in a contemporary setting.

LESSON OUTLINE

Introduction
    A. Sunday School Every Day
    B. Lesson Context
 I. Priority of Obedience (DEUTERONOMY 6:1-5)
    A. Great Responsibility (vv. 1, 2)
    B. Great Promise (v. 3)
    C. Great Commandment (vv. 4, 5)
 II. Priority of Teaching (DEUTERONOMY 6:6-9)
    A. Private Devotion (v. 6)
    B. Persistent Discussion (v. 7)
     Monsters and Opportunities
    C. Personal Discipline (vv. 8, 9)
     The Crucial Factor
Conclusion
    A. Intentional Instruction
    B. Prayer
    C. Thought to Remember

Introduction

A. Sunday School Every Day

A 7-year-old boy who had never been to church was invited by a friend to come along with him one Sunday morning. The boy found himself quite taken by the Bible lesson, the activities, and other features of the class. So excited was he that when the class was over, he told the friend who invited him, "This was great! I wish there could be Sunday school every day!"

That boy's wish is very similar to what Moses proposed to the Israelite parents in today's lesson text from Deuteronomy 6. The principle at issue there is still valid and vital for Christians today.

B. Lesson Context

The book of Deuteronomy records Moses' farewell address to the second generation of Israelites following the exodus from Egypt. The first generation had perished in the wilderness because of unbelief that God could lead them to conquer the inhabitants of the land of their destination (Numbers 14). With the first generation having passed from the scene, the second generation—on the verge of entering the promised land of Canaan—needed the Law of Moses explained anew. Indeed, the word *Deuteronomy* comes from two Greek words that mean "second law," in the sense of "repetition."

Portions of Deuteronomy are similar to what we find earlier in the Pentateuch (the first five books of the Old Testament). This is to be expected since God had established His covenant with the first generation of Israelites at Mount Sinai and had given His commandments and laws through Moses to the people (Exodus 24:3-8, 12). For example, the Ten Commandments, which were foundational to the covenant, are recorded both in Exodus 20:1-17 and Deuteronomy 5:6-21. Other laws in Deuteronomy reflect the circumstances that the people would face once they entered Canaan (such as the laws regarding war in chapter 20).

Deuteronomy begins with Moses' review of the history of the nation to the present, including the first generation's disobedience. But Moses also reminded the people of God's faithfulness and of the power He had previously demonstrated in helping a portion of the people conquer lands east of the Jordan River (Deuteronomy 2:24–3:11). That same power was to guide the second generation in completing the conquest of the territory west of the Jordan.

Those of the second generation, however, were required to avoid the unfaithfulness of their predecessors. Deuteronomy 5 concludes with an exhortation to the people to obey the Lord faithfully and "not turn aside to the right hand or to the left" (5:32). The exhortation continues in today's lesson text.

I. Priority of Obedience
(DEUTERONOMY 6:1-5)
A. Great Responsibility (vv. 1, 2)

1. Now these are the commandments, the statutes, and the judgments, which the LORD your God commanded to teach you, that ye might do them in the land whither ye go to possess it.

It's possible to draw technical distinctions among *the commandments, the statutes, and the judgments* of the Lord, but it's their cumulative weight that is intended. Two crucial responsibilities regarding this totality of the Lord's desires are stressed. The first involves Moses' obligation *to teach* the people. In that and other senses, Moses has served as the mediator between them and God. The people even had requested this because of their terror at hearing the Lord's voice speak the Ten Commandments "out of the midst of the fire" (Deuteronomy 5:22, 26).

The other responsibility is placed on the people themselves: they must actually *do* what God has

HOW TO SAY IT

Boaz	*Bo-az.*
mezuzah	muh-*zoo*-zuh.
Papua New Guinea	*Paw*-pyoo New *Gih*-nee.
Pentateuch	*Pen*-ta-teuk.
phylacteries	fuh-*lak*-tuh-reez.
shema *(Hebrew)*	shih-*mah.*

said, in faithful obedience to His words. Similar twin duties are found in the Great Commission, where Jesus commanded His followers to teach those whom they make disciples to "observe all things whatsoever I have commanded you" (Matthew 28:19, 20).

2a. That thou mightest fear the LORD thy God, to keep all his statutes and his commandments, which I command thee.

Today's lesson text is perhaps best known for the command to love the Lord (see Deuteronomy 6:5, below). But it is noteworthy that here, just three verses before that command is given, the importance of fearing the Lord is emphasized.

The *fear* mentioned in the verse before us implies a deep reverence for who God is. He, the God of Scripture, is holy, loving, righteous, faithful, and all-knowing—to name just a few of His attributes. Fear of the Lord acknowledges that we must come to Him on His terms, not ours.

2b. Thou, and thy son, and thy son's son, all the days of thy life; and that thy days may be prolonged.

The commands God has given are not for the second generation of Israelites alone. They are intended to be taught to succeeding generations. Every generation will need to see itself as having the solemn responsibility of conveying the faith to those who follow them. That will be the teaching generation's most important and enduring legacy.

> *What Do You Think?*
> How will your commitment differ, if at all, between teaching natural descendants and descendants "in the faith" (1 Timothy 1:2)?
> *Digging Deeper*
> How will teaching methods be the same and different for those two types of descendants?

The promise of long life is specifically tied to honoring one's father and mother in Deuteronomy 5:16. In the verse at hand, it is linked to the people's general obedience to God's commandments. This promise may be understood not so much in terms of an individual's life span but of the nation's span of existence in the promised land (compare Deuteronomy 4:26; 11:9; etc.).

B. Great Promise (v. 3)

3a. Hear therefore, O Israel, and observe to do it; that it may be well with thee, and that ye may increase mightily, as the LORD God of thy fathers hath promised thee.

While obedience will be the key factor in the people's continued residence in the promised land, the primary reason they are going there at all is because of what the covenant-keeping God *hath promised*. That promise goes back to God's covenant with Abraham (Genesis 12:1-3).

What Do You Think?

What steps can we take to help us continue in the Lord's commands?

Digging Deeper

Which Scriptures have you personally found most helpful in this regard? Why?

3b. In the land that floweth with milk and honey.

This particular description of *the land* occurs 18 times in the Old Testament in a positive sense of a promise and/or description. This is the eighth such usage. The first is found in Exodus 3:8, where God spoke to Moses at the burning bush and commissioned him to lead the Israelites out of Egyptian bondage. The characterization *milk and honey* highlights the abundance that awaits the Israelites in the promised land of Canaan in contrast with the "iron furnace" of Egypt (Deuteronomy 4:20; 1 Kings 8:51). Amazingly, rebellious Israelites applied the description "land that floweth with milk and honey" to the Egypt of their servitude rather than the land of their destination (Numbers 16:13, 14)!

C. Great Commandment (vv. 4, 5)

4. Hear, O Israel: The LORD our God is one LORD.

This verse is of supreme importance in the Old Testament (see on v. 5, next). It is still referred to as "the shema," which is the Hebrew verb for *hear*.

Because the Hebrew verse does not contain any verbs for "is," the exact rendering of the verse has been subject to much discussion. (The need to supply the word *is* for smooth English is indi-

cated by that word's appearing in italics in most editions of the *King James Version*.) As it appears in Hebrew, the verse literally says, "Hear, Israel, the Lord, our God, the Lord, one."

Some students suggest that the word for *one* may also be rendered *alone*; however, *one* is the most accepted translation. Certainly the oneness of God that this verse declares implies that He alone is God, and there is no other.

This is affirmed elsewhere in Scripture (Psalm 18:31; Isaiah 44:8; 45:22; 1 Corinthians 8:4-6; Ephesians 4:6). Such a belief stands in stark contrast to the pagan religions of the Old Testament world, which are characterized by belief in many gods. The fact that the singular God has clearly revealed His will eliminates the guesswork and uncertainty that accompanies belief in many gods.

What Do You Think?

How can we guard ourselves against living as though there are, in effect, many gods?

Digging Deeper

In that regard, what choices will you have to make concerning your responsibility to warn others vs. your need to pay attention to your own temptations? (Resources: Ezekiel 33:7-9; Matthew 7:1; Romans 14:4, 10, 13; 1 Thessalonians 4:11; 2 Thessalonians 3:14, 15; 1 Timothy 5:20; Titus 3:10; James 4:11, 12.)

5. And thou shalt love the LORD thy God with all thine heart, and with all thy soul, and with all thy might.

This, the appropriate human response to God, is what Jesus declared to be "the first and great commandment" (Matthew 22:38): to love Him without any reservation, to love Him with the totality of one's *heart* and *soul* and *might*. Indeed, on this and the command to love one's neighbor "hang all the law and the prophets" (22:40).

The commandment to *love the Lord thy God* is foundation for maintaining residence in the promised land. The word *heart* in Hebrew usually refers to the center of human life, and that is the sense here. The heart is seen as the seat of the intellect and the will. One is often said to think or reason in the heart (Proverbs 23:7; Mark 2:6-8).

Scripture also uses the term *soul* differently than how most understand it today. In Scripture, the word often describes one's entire identity. The parallelism in Psalm 103:1 (lesson 3) is insightful:

Bless the Lord, ⤬ O my soul:

all that is within me, bless his holy name.

As is typical of Hebrew poetic parallels, the two thoughts of the first line are reflected again in the second line using different words.

The Hebrew word behind the translation *might* is frequently rendered "very" in other passages (example: Deuteronomy 30:14). This sense of "exceedingly" is present here as well. One will never achieve fully this objective in this life, but the blessing comes in the quest.

II. Priority of Teaching
(DEUTERONOMY 6:6-9)
A. Private Devotion (v. 6)

6. And these words, which I command thee this day, shall be in thine heart.

To love God with the devotion described in the previous verse implies keeping His *words* treasured within one's *heart*. The psalmist recognized the importance of this when he wrote, "Thy word have I hid in mine heart, that I might not sin against thee" (Psalm 119:11).

Some students propose that the Old Testament is concerned primarily with an individual's outward actions and with conformity to a rigid code of rules, and that there is very little concern for the inner person. This verse disproves such thinking. God has always been concerned about the condition of a person's heart (compare Isaiah 29:13; Ezekiel 33:31; Joel 2:13; etc.).

B. Persistent Discussion (v. 7)

7. And thou shalt teach them diligently unto thy children, and shalt talk of them when thou sittest in thine house, and when thou walkest by the way, and when thou liest down, and when thou risest up.

God's words are not a treasure to be hoarded in one's heart. This treasure is to be communicated to others, specifically to the *children* in a household. The expressions concerning how this is to be done are framed as opposites: (1) sitting indoors vs. walking outdoors and (2) lying *down* to sleep vs. awakening from sleep. These imply that any time a parent has the opportunity to offer further instruction in the ways of the Lord, he or she should not let it slip away.

Virtually any set of surroundings can serve as a classroom in which children can be taught God's words. An atmosphere of constant teaching will eventually spark questions from the children, a scenario described in Deuteronomy 6:20-25.

What Do You Think?
What changes can our church make in its teaching of children so they won't abandon the faith when they leave for college?
Digging Deeper
Which is better: to shelter children from exposure to false beliefs or to allow the exposure in order to inoculate the young minds against the falsehood? Explain.

❧ MONSTERS AND OPPORTUNITIES ❧

"Daad-dy," called the little voice at 2 a.m. "I'm scared." After I painfully dragged myself out of bed, I discovered that our 5-year-old son was afraid of monsters in the closet.

I tried the scientific approach first: "Joshua, you know there's no such thing as monsters. Have you ever seen one?" It didn't work, so I tried the practical approach: "Joshua, if you see a monster come out of your closet, just yell and I'll come running in. I'll beat up that monster. I'll kick it right out of the house!" He giggled, but quickly turned serious again: "I'm still scared."

Finally the text of Deuteronomy 6:7 flashed through my sleep-deprived mind. I winced. These were the precious, irreplaceable opportunities I had to teach my son about God and about walking in faith. Where should he turn when he felt vulnerable and afraid? to science? to pragmatism?

"Joshua, you know that God loves you. And He is bigger and more powerful than everything. He hears us when we ask Him for help, and He will never leave us alone. He tells us that we don't have to be afraid of anything, because He will be right with us no matter what."

After I reminded Joshua of a few comforting verses of Scripture and rubbed his back, he fell asleep. Then I offered a prayer for myself: *Lord, next time help me to think of You first, so my children will learn to think of You first too!*   —D. G.

C. Personal Discipline (vv. 8, 9)

8. And thou shalt bind them for a sign upon thine hand, and they shall be as frontlets between thine eyes.

As the years passed, some practiced this imperative in a literalistic way: they placed passages of Scripture in small leather boxes (called phylacteries) and wore them on arms and foreheads. By the time of Jesus, this practice had become a way to flaunt one's devotion to God publicly (Matthew 23:5).

This verse has its intended (and much more powerful) impact when interpreted symbolically. The word *hand* represents one's actions, which are to be guided by God's words. The phrase *between thine eyes* means allowing His words to be a constant source of instruction.

What Do You Think?
   What steps can you take today to implement the principle of verse 8?
Digging Deeper
   How will you ensure that your witness (see Matthew 5:14-16; 1 Timothy 4:12; etc.) does not become holier-than-thou showmanship (see Matthew 6:1, 2, 5, 16; 23:5; etc.)?

---

9. And thou shalt write them upon the posts of thy house, and on thy gates.

This commandment also came to be interpreted in a literalistic way. Some Jews today attach near the entrance of their home a mezuzah, which is a small container in which Scriptures are placed. (The word *mezuzah* is the Hebrew word translated here as *the posts of thy house*.)

As with the previous verse, this imperative has its intended (and much more powerful) impact when applied symbolically. To write God's commands on the posts of one's house means living

by them consistently at home in the family setting so that children can learn from their parents' example.

The word *gates* may refer to the place in town where business is typically conducted and where important decisions are made. An example is found in Ruth 4:1-10, where Boaz meets with elders at the city gate to announce his intentions to marry Ruth. Thus, the key message of the verse is this: apply God's commands in everyday circumstances, not just in "religious" settings.

The power of the symbolic interpretation should not lead us to think that a more physically literal interpretation is of no value. Indeed, the two approaches may interact in positive ways. Smartphones serve as "posts" and "gates" of our lives in various ways. Various apps can be used to "write" a Bible verse of the day as a pop-up on one's smartphone "gate" for the user to read as the day begins.

Parents need creative ways to impress God's words on the minds of their children, and today's technology can be used to reinforce important spiritual principles and Bible lessons. The more that parents can keep God's words before their children, the more likely those words will be remembered and obeyed.

❧ THE CRUCIAL FACTOR ❧

In 1971, the leadership of the Summer Institute of Linguistics initiated 510 Bible translation projects. The projects resulted in varying degrees of success in producing growth in churches, so an in-depth study was undertaken to identify what methods were the most fruitful. The methodology involved four years of investigating reports from 15 translation programs in Mexico, the Philippines, and Papua New Guinea.

One factor was discovered to have been crucial to all the successful programs; that factor was *per-*

VISUALS FOR THESE LESSONS

The visual pictured in each lesson (example: page 127) is a small reproduction of a large, full-color poster included in the *Adult Resources* packet for the Winter Quarter. That packet also contains the very useful *Presentation Tools* CD for teacher use. Order No. 2629119 from your supplier.

sonal relevance. When people saw that God and His Word were relevant to them and their needs, they responded to the gospel. People began to see this relevance when Christians lovingly pointed to the God of the Bible in ways that connected with those needs. That's the power of seeking guidance from Scripture in every circumstance of life.

How well are you living this out as an example to others? Behind that, how well are you living it out when no one but God can see? —D. G.

Conclusion

A. Intentional Instruction

God's desire for the Israelites was that His commandments be passed from generation to generation. This was to happen through the faithful, consistent teaching and modeling of those commandments in various settings. This is a key principle within today's text.

Western culture at one time was characterized by such a respect for teaching biblical principles. I grew up in the late 1950s and the 1960s, when much of children's television programming featured occasional references to the teachings of the Bible. One example is the old "Mickey Mouse Club." I can remember playing records of songs from that show on our phonograph at home. Those songs included titles such as "Do What the Good Book Says" and "Proverbs" (referring to the biblical Proverbs). The lyrics of such songs can be heard on file-sharing websites. Many of us are aware that the Charlie Brown Christmas special of 1965 featured a discussion of Luke 2:8-14. Of course, no such material would be permitted on a network children's program today!

Some have offered this comparison: the church at one time possessed the "home-field advantage" where the culture for the most part was "on our side." Today, the church is in the position of the "visitors," and it is often treated with great contempt and scorn. The increasing secularization of Western culture has made the teaching of biblical principles more challenging, but certainly not impossible. It means that parents must become much more deliberate and intentional in seeing to it that their children are exposed to the virtuous

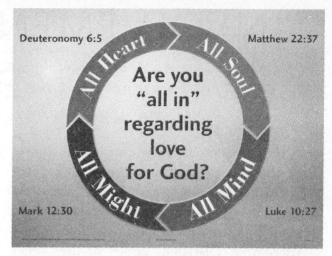

Visual for Lesson 1. *Start a discussion by pointing to this visual as you ask, "What has to happen for Christians to improve in these areas?"*

and praiseworthy things that Paul, in Philippians 4:8, says should characterize a Christian's thought life. This includes exercising discernment regarding what children are allowed to watch on television, how they use social media, etc. So much that is available for public viewing is clearly at odds with the principles of loving God and His words that are emphasized in today's text.

In these times that are awash in spiritual darkness and confusion, it is critical that Christian parents take Moses' instructions in today's text to heart—using every opportunity available to reinforce biblical truth to their children and help them see its relevance to daily living. The most influential translation of the Bible for children is the one they see communicated by their parents' example and speech. We should remind ourselves that today's lesson is from the passage that sets forth what Jesus declared to be the "greatest commandment," the focus of which is our love for God (compare Matthew 22:34-40; Mark 12:28-34).

B. Prayer

Father, we pray for Christian parents to possess the strength and resolve to stand firm in their faithfulness in teaching their children. May they do so for Your glory. We pray in Jesus' name. Amen.

C. Thought to Remember

The best way to keep the faith
is to give it away.

INVOLVEMENT LEARNING

Enhance your lesson with KJV Bible Student *(from your curriculum supplier) and the reproducible activity page (at www.standardlesson.com or in the back of the* KJV Standard Lesson Commentary Deluxe Edition*).*

Into the Lesson

As the class gathers, invite everyone to enjoy a snack of honey graham crackers and milk. (Provide substitutes for those with food allergies.) As learners enjoy their treats, ask several to share a childhood memory regarding a favorite food.

Alternative. Distribute copies of the "Like-minded" activity from the reproducible page, which you can download. Ask learners to complete as indicated.

After either activity, introduce the Bible study by saying, "We are all devoted to various things, whether to certain foods, hobbies, etc. By the time of today's lesson text, God had already promised to honor the Israelites' devotion to Him by prospering them with a new land 'flowing with milk and honey' (Exodus 3:8)." Hold up a honey graham cracker and cup of milk. Continue: "The Bible's reference to *milk and honey* symbolizes an abundant land brimming with goodness. Let's see some implications of that."

Into the Word

Read Deuteronomy 6:1-9 aloud, then divide the class into halves that sit opposite each other. Ask one side to role-play being parents and grandparents. The other group will pretend to be young children through teenagers. Read Deuteronomy 6:7 aloud again and say, "We are going to act out conversations we might have about God with our children and grandchildren as we sit together on the sofa or go for a walk. Use ideas from the text for inspiration."

Invite someone from the *Parents/Grandparents Group* to pose a question or make a statement about following God; then let two or three from the *Children Group* respond with answers or questions. Alternate back and forth on the conversations, allowing opportunity for all the learners to voice a question or answer. If they have trouble knowing what to say, give each group the appro-

priate handout (you prepare). For the *Parents/Grandparents Group:* 1–What are some of the commandments God wants us to obey? 2–What do you know about God's promises? 3–Why does God want us to love Him with all our hearts? Hand these suggestions to the *Children Group:* 1–Why does God say we're supposed to fear Him? 2–Why are there so many commandments? 3–Why do we have to obey all the time?

Wrap up by saying, "God encourages us to find opportunities in everyday life to talk about the importance of loving and obeying Him."

Into Life

Ask learners to cite some challenges and benefits of loving God and following after Him; jot responses on the board. Then ask the learners to cite Scripture passages that encourage or command a love of God. (Those with smartphones may find the following: Deuteronomy 6:5; 11:1, 13, 22; 13:3; 19:9; 30:6, 16, 20; Joshua 22:5; 23:11; Psalms 31:23; 97:10; 116:1; Matthew 22:37; Mark 12:30; Luke 10:27 [negatively, 1 Corinthians 16:22].) Talk about the connection between loving God and obeying His commands. Ask students to share times when they've been able to have meaningful spiritual discussions with their children and grandchildren.

Alternative. Distribute copies of the "Famous Farewell Addresses" activity from the reproducible page for learners to complete as indicated. Remind the class that parting words from those who are wise are instructive for moving forward.

End with prayer. Share: "O Lord, thank You for loving us so deeply and steadily. Help us each day to love and obey You with all our entire beings. Remind us to talk about You and model a devoted faith in You. We present to You these young people we want to help follow You wholeheartedly. *[Pause to allow students to name them silently.]* In the matchless name of Jesus we pray. Amen."

Love and Serve God

DEVOTIONAL READING: Psalm 81
BACKGROUND SCRIPTURE: Exodus 20:1-11; Joshua 24

JOSHUA 24:1-3A, 13-15, 21-24

1 And Joshua gathered all the tribes of Israel to Shechem, and called for the elders of Israel, and for their heads, and for their judges, and for their officers; and they presented themselves before God.

2 And Joshua said unto all the people, Thus saith the LORD God of Israel, Your fathers dwelt on the other side of the flood in old time, even Terah, the father of Abraham, and the father of Nachor: and they served other gods.

3a And I took your father Abraham from the other side of the flood, and led him throughout all the land of Canaan, and multiplied his seed

· ·

13 And I have given you a land for which ye did not labour, and cities which ye built not, and ye dwell in them; of the vineyards and oliveyards which ye planted not do ye eat.

14 Now therefore fear the LORD, and serve him in sincerity and in truth: and put away the gods which your fathers served on the other side of the flood, and in Egypt; and serve ye the LORD.

15 And if it seem evil unto you to serve the LORD, choose you this day whom ye will serve; whether the gods which your fathers served that were on the other side of the flood, or the gods of the Amorites, in whose land ye dwell: but as for me and my house, we will serve the LORD.

· ·

21 And the people said unto Joshua, Nay; but we will serve the LORD.

22 And Joshua said unto the people, Ye are witnesses against yourselves that ye have chosen you the LORD, to serve him. And they said, We are witnesses.

23 Now therefore put away, said he, the strange gods which are among you, and incline your heart unto the LORD God of Israel.

24 And the people said unto Joshua, The LORD our God will we serve, and his voice will we obey.

KEY VERSE

If it seem evil unto you to serve the LORD, choose you this day whom ye will serve; whether the gods which your fathers served that were on the other side of the flood, or the gods of the Amorites, in whose land ye dwell: but as for me and my house, we will serve the LORD. —**Joshua 24:15**

OUR LOVE FOR GOD

Unit I: God Is Worthy of Our Love

LESSON AIMS

After participating in this lesson, each learner will be able to:

1. Summarize the portion of today's text regarding Joshua's farewell challenge to the Israelites and their response.

2. Explain what rejecting false gods means in the twenty-first century.

3. Identify a cultural "god" and make a plan to resist its influence.

LESSON OUTLINE

Introduction

A. A Veteran Speaks

Many nations observe a day each year to honor their military veterans. Such days feature expressions of appreciation to the men and women who have placed themselves in harm's way in defense of the nation. Societies deem it important that the next generation learn to acknowledge and appreciate the sacrifices that veterans have made on their behalf.

In today's lesson, from the final chapter of the book of Joshua, Joshua presents to the nation of Israel what amounts to his farewell address. By this time, Joshua was an old man and a true "veteran" whose career included a host of experiences, serving first as Moses' apprentice and then leading the Israelites in the conquest of the promised land. It was important, before Joshua's death, that the next generation hear his testimony and learn to appreciate the wisdom that he had to offer God's people.

B. Lesson Context

Joshua had seen it all. The first time he is mentioned in the Bible is when Moses commanded him to choose some men to fight the Amalekites who had attacked Israel not long after the exodus from Egypt (Exodus 17:8-13). Exodus 24:13 describes Joshua as Moses' *minister*, a word that could be considered the equivalent of an assistant or an apprentice.

Joshua was with Moses when the two came down from Mount Sinai after Moses had received God's laws written on tablets of stone by "the finger of God" (Exodus 31:18). They found the Israelites taking part in sinful, degrading actions that sparked Moses' anger (32:15-20). Along with Caleb, Joshua was one of the two spies who voiced confidence that the Lord would lead the Israelites into the promised land (Numbers 14:6-9). Tragically, their voices were drowned out by the defiant unbelief of the other 10 spies.

Given this background, it seems inevitable that Joshua would be selected as Moses' successor to lead the nation into the promised land and complete the task Moses had begun. Deuteronomy

31:1-8 records Moses' charge to Joshua to assume the leadership of the people. The final chapter of Deuteronomy tells us that "Joshua the son of Nun was full of the spirit of wisdom; for Moses had laid his hands upon him: and the children of Israel hearkened unto him, and did as the Lord commanded Moses" (34:9).

The book of Joshua then chronicles the conquest of Canaan under Joshua's leadership and the allotment of territory to the various tribes. By the time of today's text, Joshua had "waxed old" and was "stricken in age" (Joshua 23:1). It was in this condition that he called an assembly.

I. Looking at the Past

(Joshua 24:1-3a, 13)

A. Public Assembly of Tribes (v. 1)

1. And Joshua gathered all the tribes of Israel to Shechem, and called for the elders of Israel, and for their heads, and for their judges, and for their officers; and they presented themselves before God.

The city of *Shechem* first appears in the Bible in connection with Abraham. It is the first place mentioned upon his arrival in the land of Canaan, and he built an altar there (Genesis 12:6, 7). Ironically (and sadly) Shechem is later the location where the nation becomes divided into two king-

HOW TO SAY IT

Amalekites	*Am*-uh-leh-kites or Uh-*mal*-ih-kites.
Amorites	*Am*-uh-rites.
Baal	*Bay*-ul.
Balaam	*Bay*-lum.
Balak	*Bay*-lack.
Chaldees	*Kal*-deez.
Euphrates	You-*fray*-teez.
Moab	*Mo*-ab.
Nachor	*Nay*-kor.
Shechem	*Shee*-kem or *Shek*-em.
Sinai	*Sigh*-nye or *Sigh*-nay-eye.
syncretic	sin-*kre*-tik.
Terah	*Tair*-uh.
Ur	Er.

doms (1 Kings 12:1-20). In Joshua's time, however, Shechem is a place where a unified nation is *gathered*.

The various leaders are present as well; the terms used indicate that the spiritual, judicial, and military leaders are in attendance to present *themselves before God*. Thus this is not a political or legislative assembly; it is primarily spiritual in nature. Joshua may be the person calling the gathering and addressing it, but the one truly in charge is the Lord.

> *What Do You Think?*
> What preparations can we make before we present ourselves before God in worship?
> *Digging Deeper*
> Which of those preparations, if any, should be the practice of all Christians? Why?

B. God's Blessings to Abraham (vv. 2, 3a)

2a. And Joshua said unto all the people, Thus saith the LORD God of Israel.

While the leaders are given special emphasis in the previous verse (and in Joshua 23:2), here it is noted that Joshua addresses *all the people*. Moses had spoken to "all Israel" east of the Jordan River (Deuteronomy 1:1); now Joshua does so west of the Jordan, with the conquest of the promised land having been largely accomplished. As Joshua prefaces his words with *thus saith the Lord God of Israel*, the focus will be on the Lord's words and deeds, not those of any person.

2b. Your fathers dwelt on the other side of the flood in old time, even Terah, the father of Abraham, and the father of Nachor: and they served other gods.

Joshua begins by recounting the history of the nation up to this point. It has now been several hundred years since the *old time* of Abraham. The Hebrew word translated *flood* often indicates a river (examples: Genesis 2:13, 14), and most likely refers here to the Euphrates River. The Euphrates formed a natural boundary between Ur of the Chaldees, Abraham's original home, and the land of Canaan to which God guided him. Israel's problematic heritage is to have had ancestors who *served other gods*. How Abraham came to embrace faith in one God, the true God, is not clear from Scripture. Yet the man who became the father of the Israelite nation severed ties with his upbringing by choosing to exercise faith in God and follow His leading (compare Joshua 24:23, below).

> *What Do You Think?*
> What are some ways our church can reflect on its roots in times of growth and change?
> *Digging Deeper*
> Why is it important to do so, considering Genesis 1:1-31; Psalm 78, 106; Acts 7:2-53; and 1 Corinthians 15:1-8?

3a. And I took your father Abraham from the other side of the flood, and led him throughout all the land of Canaan, and multiplied his seed.

Joshua now alludes to the Lord's call of Abraham, which is recorded in Genesis 12:1-3. God's covenant with Abraham *took* him from his life on *the other side of the flood* (east of the Euphrates River) and brought him into *the land of Canaan*. The two most important elements of God's covenant are highlighted here: the *land* God promised and Abraham's *seed*, which God promised to multiply.

In Joshua 24:3b-12, not included in today's text, Joshua continues his review of the history of God's people. His primary focus is God's deliverance of the people by means of the exodus and His protection of them from those such as Balak, king of Moab, who hired Balaam to curse the people. This allowed the nation to enter the land of Canaan, where God provided victory in battle over the peoples residing in the promised land so that His people could dwell there.

C. God's Blessings to Israel (v. 13)

13. And I have given you a land for which ye did not labour, and cities which ye built not, and ye dwell in them; of the vineyards and oliveyards which ye planted not do ye eat.

A frequently repeated theme whenever the *land* is discussed is the fact that it has been *given* by God to the people (Exodus 6:4, 8; 12:25; 13:5; 20:12; 32:13; Leviticus 23:10; 25:2; Numbers 13:2; 15:2; Deuteronomy 1:8, 25; 8:10; 11:31). A related point is the fact that the people have done nothing to produce the wealth or abundance found within this land. Others have done the hard work to build the *cities* and plant the crops; the Israelites have been granted the privilege of enjoying these blessings. Moses had spoken similar words to the Israelites in his message recorded in Deuteronomy 6:10, 11.

> *What Do You Think?*
> How will life be different as we become more grateful for the Lord's material provisions?
> *Digging Deeper*
> What Scriptures help you most to recall your dependence on God and His provisions?

II. Living in the Present
(JOSHUA 24:14, 15, 21-24)
A. Joshua's Challenge (vv. 14, 15)

14. Now therefore fear the LORD, and serve him in sincerity and in truth: and put away the gods which your fathers served on the other side of the flood, and in Egypt; and serve ye the LORD.

The Israelites should not think that the blessings of the promised land are unconditionally guaranteed, with no obligation on their part. God has given them the land, but to continue residence there the people must follow the terms set down by the giver.

Moses had also urged the people to "*fear the Lord* thy God, and *serve him*" (Deuteronomy 6:13) and had warned the people not to forget the Lord's goodness and not to pursue other *gods* (6:10-15). Now Joshua echoes this same appeal. The Lord is to be their only God, not only in what they profess but in how they behave.

To achieve such a challenge requires that the people *put away* whatever *gods* they may yet have among them. No matter whether these gods are from their ancestors in the more distant past (*on the other side of the flood*; see commentary on Joshua 24:2b, above) or from their more recent experience *in Egypt*, allegiance to the one true God is top priority.

It may be difficult to grasp how some Israelites can still be holding on to false gods after all that the Lord had done for them. The previous generation of Israelites, however, had been guilty of idolatry as well, building a golden calf at the foot of Mount Sinai. This happened not long after being delivered from their bondage in Egypt and protected at the Red Sea (Exodus 32:1-6). As someone has observed, it was one thing to get Israel out of Egypt but quite another to get Egypt out of Israel.

15. And if it seem evil unto you to serve the Lord, choose you this day whom ye will serve; whether the gods which your fathers served that were on the other side of the flood, or the gods of the Amorites, in whose land ye dwell: but as for me and my house, we will serve the Lord.

The Hebrew word rendered *evil* can be used of something that is not necessarily evil in a moral sense (as in good versus evil). Sometimes it carries a sense of "unpleasant" or "disagreeable." That is probably the case here. Joshua's challenge is thus along these lines: if you Israelites find it unpleasant *to serve the Lord*, then consider whom you will end up serving instead.

Joshua's proposal reflects a principle that remains true: we must serve someone or something. The Israelites before Joshua must choose whether they will serve the false *gods* of their ancestors or the gods of the peoples in the *land* of Canaan where they now reside. The *Amorites* are one of several peoples who have lived in Canaan (Deuteronomy 7:1; Joshua 24:11). But in some places the word is used to designate the peoples of the land in general (examples: Genesis 15:16; Amos 2:9, 10).

The history Joshua has recounted should be reason enough for choosing to serve the Lord. One must keep in mind that this history is not something that Joshua is relating as a body of facts that have no personal meaning to him. This history includes much that Joshua himself has experienced. He witnessed the events surrounding the exodus from Egypt and the rescue at the Red Sea. He saw firsthand the tragic results of idolatry when he descended from Mount Sinai with Moses (Exodus 32:17-20). Joshua himself knows for certain that the Lord is the one true God.

And yet he cannot *choose* for those who are assembled before him. Each person must choose for himself or herself whom to serve. But Joshua, as the nation's leader, as the one who has directed their conquest of the promised land, will make absolutely clear where he stands: *as for me and my house, we will serve the Lord.*

We should note that Joshua's challenge offers the people essentially only two choices: either the Lord or other gods. Moses had spoken in similar terms to the Israelites, setting before them a choice between "life and death, blessing and cursing" (Deuteronomy 30:19). Jesus also described two ways, a broad way and a narrow way, and of building wisely or foolishly (Matthew 7:13, 14, 24-27).

In Joshua 24:16-20, not in our lesson text, the people respond with a passionate desire to follow Joshua's lead and to serve the Lord above any other gods. Joshua then warns them not to take their promise lightly. Their commitment to the Lord must involve more than just voicing good intentions or pious-sounding words; it must be supported by actions.

❧ IDOLS OF THE HEART ❧

Coming back from a budding career on the mission field for medical reasons uncovered idols in my heart.

I had gotten used to the accolades. "Wow, you lived in a mud hut in Africa?" "You saw giraffes and zebras and elephants on the way to work?" "You could hear bombs across the border from the refugee camp?" We could mesmerize our friends back home with our exploits: tales of exotic cultures and music and food, hilarious language blunders, and austere living conditions.

One of my most cherished idols was the image of myself being a spiritual hero on the front lines of the cosmic battleground. "We could never do that," whispered many voices back home. My life held eternal significance, a cut above the rest.

Our infant daughter's traumatic brain injuries from birth and extensive ongoing medical care brought us home from the field and uncovered my idols. No one applauds when we administer her medicine or give her a bath. No one drops their jaw when I tell them about my current ministry role.

Whom will I serve? Will I try to seek out and bow down to my old idol of pride? Or will I choose this day to serve God, who brought me through dangers and deserts? Will I content myself in Him alone? Today will I serve myself or will I serve Him, wherever He may lead me?

That's the choice I must make. What about you? —D. G.

What Do You Think?
  Be still for a moment. What choice or decision is the Lord setting before you today?
Digging Deeper
  How do Matthew 7:13, 14, 24-27; Romans 6:16-19; and 1 John 1:5-10 convict you of a choice you must make?

B. Israel's Choice (v. 21)

21. And the people said unto Joshua, Nay; but we will serve the LORD.

Again *the people* declare their loyalty to *the Lord*. The scene is reminiscent of what transpired at Mount Sinai when the Lord established His covenant with the Israelites there and the people said, "All that the Lord hath said will we do, and be obedient" (Exodus 24:7).

C. Choice Reaffirmed (vv. 22-24)

22. And Joshua said unto the people, Ye are witnesses against yourselves that ye have chosen you the LORD, to serve him. And they said, We are witnesses.

In a solemn proceeding such as this, where the people have "presented themselves before God" (Joshua 24:1) and pledged their loyalty to Him alone, there is a need for *witnesses*. In this case Joshua calls upon the people themselves to serve as witnesses *against* themselves. They have chosen to follow Joshua's example and *serve* the Lord; but if they turn away from Him and worship other gods, they will bring upon themselves the punishment that Joshua has said must follow (24:20). The people agree to Joshua's terms: *We are witnesses.*

23. Now therefore put away, said he, the strange gods which are among you, and incline your heart unto the LORD God of Israel.

Joshua urges the people before him to make a break with the *gods* that remain in their midst. In so doing, he repeats the command he issued earlier (Joshua 24:14). But as important as that action is, genuine commitment to the Lord (the kind that must accompany the pledge that the people have just made) has to include the hearts of the people. They must *put away* other gods internally as well as externally. The word *incline* is often used in Scripture of one's ear being tuned to hear sound instruction (Proverbs 4:20) or refusing to hear it (Jeremiah 25:4).

❧ PICKING AND CHOOSING ❧

"We go to the foreign doctors to cure our malaria," the ladies told us. "We go to the witch doctors if we have hepatitis or other problems."

Having close access to modern health care was new to these North African refugees. They had walked for days as they fled the war in their homeland. In the refugee camp, multiple aid organizations were operating medical clinics for the refugees. They could let the foreigners diagnose them and give them medicine for any of their health issues, or they could pay their traditional healers who practiced witchcraft. Several witch doctors had also fled their homeland and continued to offer their services to their fellow refugees.

With options available, the ladies quickly tabulated the perceived success rate of each faction in treating various ailments. Before long they had decided under what circumstances they would go to the witch doctors or to the foreign doctors.

The Israelites under Joshua may have been tempted to employ similar syncretic tactics. "The God of Abraham is good at wars, but Baal is good at crops," they might decide. They could pick and choose which "god" to follow when. But Joshua would have none of it. In reminding them of God's incomparable greatness, Joshua forced them to choose. Would they serve God with all their hearts—or not?

Have you been doing any picking and choosing recently? Do you trust God with your spiritual needs but break His commands in your efforts to meet your physical or emotional needs? Will you choose to follow Him with all your heart and trust Him to provide everything you need?   —D. G.

24. And the people said unto Joshua, The LORD our God will we serve, and his voice will we obey.

This is the third time *the people* have expressed a desire to *serve* the Lord (see Joshua 24:18, 21). Anyone who knows the history of Israel that follows in the book of Judges may well think, "If only the people had followed through on their words and promises." As promising as the conclusion to the book of Joshua is, the conclusion to the book of Judges is disheartening. Its final verse is one of the saddest in the Bible: "In those days there was no king in Israel: every man did that which was right in his own eyes" (Judges 21:25).

It is easy in the midst of a throng of like-minded believers (such as the gathering in Joshua 24) to voice allegiance to the Lord; it is quite another to translate that pledge into everyday actions and choices that are consistent with that allegiance. That remains true today.

Conclusion

A. Joshua and Jesus

It is noteworthy that the names Joshua and Jesus come from the same Hebrew verb, meaning "to save." As Joshua brought the Israelites into the promised land of Canaan, Jesus, the "captain of [our] salvation" (Hebrews 2:10), leads us toward our promised land of Heaven. And as one ponders Joshua's words in our text and the degree of

Visual for Lesson 2. *Start a discussion by pointing to this visual as you ask, "How do you turn this verse into an action that witnesses to others?"*

commitment to the Lord that he called the Israelites to demonstrate, it is not difficult to recognize similarities to Jesus' teaching about what is required to be His disciple (Luke 14:25-33). One must "count the cost," as Jesus put it, and that is what Joshua encouraged the Israelites to do.

For us as Christians to say that "We will serve the Lord" means we will honor Jesus as Lord and demonstrate that commitment by serving Him faithfully every day. Like Joshua's audience, we too must reject the "gods" that threaten to undermine that commitment. Those gods may not be statues or images of pagan deities; they can be material objects (money and possessions) or a degree of devotion to a career, to sports, to education, or something else that has claimed, for all intents and purposes, the status of a "god" in our lives.

In whom or what are we placing our trust? Where is *our* heart inclined? The words of Joshua still issue a resounding call to New Testament believers: "Choose you this day whom ye will serve."

B. Prayer

Father, in a world abounding with "gods" that vie for our allegiance, help us never to treat lightly the need to choose daily whom we will serve. In the name of Jesus we pray. Amen.

C. Thought to Remember

"Choose this day" applies to every day.

INVOLVEMENT LEARNING

Enhance your lesson with KJV Bible Student *(from your curriculum supplier) and the reproducible activity page (at www.standardlesson.com or in the back of the* KJV Standard Lesson Commentary Deluxe Edition*).*

Into the Lesson

Say, "Let's see how many names of servants, maids, butlers, governesses, and household staff we can remember from popular movies, TV shows, and books. It also counts if you know the names of the actors or actresses who played servants." (*Possible responses among many: Downton Abbey*—Mrs. Hughes, Mr. Carson, Anna, Mr. Bates; *The Sound of Music*—Maria; *Driving Miss Daisy*—Hoke Colburn; and *The King and I*—Anna.)

Invite learners to share what character qualities they most appreciate about those who serve others. Use this discussion to elaborate on tough choices that servants must sometimes make. Conclude the introductory time by saying, "Servants must often choose what they personally would like to do versus following the directives of those in authority. We face similar choices with God."

Into the Word

Read Joshua 24:1-3, 13-15, 21-24 aloud. Explain: "In Joshua's final address to the leaders and citizens of Israel, he called for the people to banish any ties to others gods and choose to serve only the Lord."

Form learners into study pairs; give each pair a handout (you prepare) printed with the lesson text. Let the two students in each pair decide which of them will go first for a word-find activity. At your "ready, set, go," the first participants have 20 seconds to circle how many times *Lord* is listed in the Joshua passages. After you call "Switch!" the other member of each pair must take the handout and has 20 seconds to circle all the references to *serve(d)*.

Have the pairs add up their total of circled words and see how many found all the *Lord* and *serve(d)* words. (*Expected responses:* 9 occurrences of *Lord* [vv. 2, 14 (twice), 15 (twice), 21, 22, 23, 24]; 11 occurrences of *serve(d)* [vv. 2, 14 (three times), 15 (four times), 21, 22, 24].)

Option. Distribute copies of the "Serve the Lord" word-search activity from the reproducible page, which you can download. Have the class work together to solve the search by calling out each word they spot and revealing its position.

After the first or both activities, explain an essential point of the Bible: "Sometimes when we are in a group, it's easy to join in a collective 'yes' to follow God's best; but what really matters is the individual choices we make to serve God day-in and day-out."

Into Life

Ask learners to identify subtle and not-so-subtle "other gods" of today's world. Discuss how they entice us away from loving and serving the true God. Talk about how we can practically "put away" cultural gods and idols without appearing judgmental or standoffish to the people around us who don't follow Jesus.

Next, hand everyone a blank sheet of paper and a pen or marker. Direct each learner to draw a large heart in the center of the paper. Ask everyone to write down things that can incline hearts to serve self-centered purposes instead of God's. Discuss and name Scriptures that can help overcome areas of self-serving distraction.

Alternative. Distribute copies of the "Signs of Your Faith?" activity from the reproducible page for learners to complete in small groups. Allow about five minutes.

Close with this prayer: "Lord, forgive us for falling short at times in loving and serving You. Help us to stand firm in faith and put away anything that keeps us from choosing You first. In this quiet moment, we come to you with our own other gods and distractions that keep us from loving and serving You. *[Pause to allow learners time to name silently their distractions.]* Thank You for helping us start fresh because of Jesus. In His all-powerful name we pray. Amen."

LOVE AND WORSHIP GOD

DEVOTIONAL READING: Psalm 86:1-7
BACKGROUND SCRIPTURE: Psalm 103:1-17a, 21, 22

PSALM 103:1-17A, 21, 22

1 Bless the LORD, O my soul: and all that is within me, bless his holy name.

2 Bless the LORD, O my soul, and forget not all his benefits:

3 Who forgiveth all thine iniquities; who healeth all thy diseases;

4 Who redeemeth thy life from destruction; who crowneth thee with lovingkindness and tender mercies;

5 Who satisfieth thy mouth with good things; so that thy youth is renewed like the eagle's.

6 The LORD executeth righteousness and judgment for all that are oppressed.

7 He made known his ways unto Moses, his acts unto the children of Israel.

8 The LORD is merciful and gracious, slow to anger, and plenteous in mercy.

9 He will not always chide: neither will he keep his anger for ever.

10 He hath not dealt with us after our sins; nor rewarded us according to our iniquities.

11 For as the heaven is high above the earth, so great is his mercy toward them that fear him.

12 As far as the east is from the west, so far hath he removed our transgressions from us.

13 Like as a father pitieth his children, so the LORD pitieth them that fear him.

14 For he knoweth our frame; he remembereth that we are dust.

15 As for man, his days are as grass: as a flower of the field, so he flourisheth.

16 For the wind passeth over it, and it is gone; and the place thereof shall know it no more.

17a But the mercy of the LORD is from everlasting to everlasting upon them that fear him.

. . . .

21 Bless ye the LORD, all ye his hosts; ye ministers of his, that do his pleasure.

22 Bless the LORD, all his works in all places of his dominion: bless the LORD, O my soul.

KEY VERSE

As far as the east is from the west, so far hath he removed our transgressions from us. —**Psalm 103:12**

OUR LOVE FOR GOD

Unit I: God Is Worthy of Our Love

LESSONS 1–5

LESSON AIMS

After participating in this lesson, each learner will be able to:

1. Give the reasons for praising the Lord found in today's text from Psalm 103.

2. Tell how these reasons apply to Christians living under Jesus' new covenant.

3. Compose a psalm to the Lord, combining an acknowledgment of the Lord's character with an awareness of the blessings He has given.

LESSON OUTLINE

Introduction
    A. Praying It Upward
    B. Lesson Context
I. Opening Exhortation (Psalm 103:1-5)
    A. Reasons to Praise (vv. 1, 2)
    B. Remembrance of Blessings (vv. 3-5)
II. God's Character (Psalm 103:6-17a)
    A. Righteous (vv. 6, 7)
    B. Gracious (vv. 8-12)
       Abundant Mercy
    C. Compassionate (vv. 13-17a)
       Prairie Grass
III. Closing Exhortation (Psalm 103:21, 22)
    A. To the Hosts of Heaven (v. 21)
    B. To Every Place on Earth (v. 22)
Conclusion
    A. What's Your Story?
    B. Prayer
    C. Thought to Remember

Introduction

A. Praying It Upward

Sometimes when a person is the recipient of a kind deed, the individual will talk about "paying it forward." The idea is that anyone who has been helped should "forward" that kindness to someone else. This way of thinking is meant to counter a self-centered, "me first" frame of mind.

The principle of paying it forward can be drawn from certain biblical passages. When sending His disciples to preach and do miracles in His name, Jesus said, "Freely ye have received, freely give" (Matthew 10:8; compare Romans 15:25-27).

Scripture also encourages the practice of "praying it upward," of acknowledging that "Every good gift and every perfect gift is from above, and cometh down from the Father of lights" (James 1:17). Offering praise to the Lord does not mean ignoring the needs of others around us; if anything, it encourages us to bless others as we have been blessed and to thus "pay forward" the goodness we have received from God.

The Bible includes dozens of commands to praise the Lord. The book of Psalms witnesses many such imperatives and a variety of expressions of praise to God. One such is the source of today's lesson text.

B. Lesson Context

The book of Psalms has often been described as "Israel's hymnal." It is replete with expressions of emotions directed to God. These range from praise (as in today's passage from Psalm 103) to extreme frustration and anger at how God appears to be addressing (or not addressing) the problems of a broken world. Often there is disappointment and confusion expressed over how God's own covenant people are being mistreated while evildoers seem to suffer no consequences in doing as they please (see Psalms 73 and 74). No sentiment seems to be off-limits in the Psalms. This makes the book of immense value to God's people when they pray.

The above factors and others have resulted in Bible scholars noting various types of Psalms. These include hymns, psalms of thanksgiving, laments, royal psalms, wisdom psalms, and messianic psalms. Certainly some of these can overlap, so one must be careful not to be too rigid with such classifications. A writer can go from lament to praise in the same brief psalm (as in Psalm 13).

Like any hymnal, the book of Psalms includes contributions by different authors and covers a wide span of time. The oldest psalm is by Moses (Psalm 90), and there is at least one psalm that comes out of the setting of the captivity of God's people in Babylon (Psalm 137). These two benchmarks are separated by approximately 900 years.

About half of the psalms are attributed to King David, known as the "sweet psalmist of Israel" (2 Samuel 23:1). Today's passage from Psalm 103 is one of those psalms. While some psalms include a superscription that provides the setting (example: Psalm 51), there is no such background given for Psalm 103. It simply notes the association with David.

I. Opening Exhortation
(PSALM 103:1-5)

A. Reasons to Praise (vv. 1, 2)

1. Bless the LORD, O my soul: and all that is within me, bless his holy name.

The word *bless* is used in Scripture both of what God does for people and what they offer up to Him. God's blessings are His gifts to His people, what the psalmist (David) calls "his "benefits" (Psalm 103:2, next). The people's blessing of God is expressed in praise of Him and gratitude for those benefits. Indeed, the Psalms often use the words

HOW TO SAY IT

Babylon	*Bab*-uh-lun.
Colossians	Kuh-*losh*-unz.
Ecclesiastes	Ik-*leez*-ee-*as*-teez.
Hosea	Ho-*zay*-uh.
Immanuel	Ih-*man*-you-el.
Micah	*My*-kuh.
parallelism	*pair*-uh-le-li-zum.
paralytic	pair-uh-*li*-tik.
Sinai	*Sigh*-nye or *Sigh*-nay-eye.

bless and *praise* rather interchangeably, as parallel thoughts (examples: Psalms 34:1; 104:35; 145:2).

David's blessing of the Lord is not a casual, half-hearted sentiment. It comes from his very *soul*. In the Old Testament, the word *soul* is often used to signify a person's being or essence. The frequently used device in Hebrew poetry known as parallelism, in which the second line of a verse repeats the thought of the first line—sometimes in reverse order—highlights this meaning. We saw this earlier as an example in lesson 1:

Bless the Lord,   O my soul:

all that is within me,   bless his holy name.

An individual's soul is therefore *all that is within* that person. In a sense, David is talking to himself, encouraging remembrance of the Lord's goodness. Similar "soul talk" is found in Psalm 42:5, 11. A person's *name* represents that individual's character or uniqueness. God's holiness is one of His most prominent qualities (examples: Leviticus 19:2; Joshua 24:19; Psalm 99:3, 5, 9; Isaiah 6:1-3; Revelation 4:8; 15:4).

> *What Do You Think?*
> In what ways can the church keep God's name holy?
> *Digging Deeper*
> What will be your part in helping it do so?

2. Bless the LORD, O my soul, and forget not all his benefits.

One's offering of praise to God is closely linked with remembering all He has done. Thus David expresses the desire not to *forget* all the blessings the Lord provides. Moses urged the Israelites who were on the verge of entering the promised land to remember the Lord's goodness. He also warned them of the high price that would accompany forgetfulness (Deuteronomy 8:10-20). Israel's track record in this matter is hardly exemplary (see Psalm 106).

B. Remembrance of Blessings (vv. 3-5)

3. Who forgiveth all thine iniquities; who healeth all thy diseases.

Here David specifies some of the Lord's blessings. They are both spiritual (the forgiveness of *iniquities*) and physical (the healing of *diseases*) in nature. As Immanuel ("God with us"; compare Isaiah 7:14), Jesus demonstrated His power both to forgive sins and heal diseases, as in the case of the paralytic brought to Jesus (Mark 2:1-12).

4. Who redeemeth thy life from destruction; who crowneth thee with lovingkindness and tender mercies.

David describes God's power to change our circumstances from the worst to the best—to be treated as royalty as we are crowned *with lovingkindness and tender mercies*. Christians can give thanks for the redemption provided by Jesus' death and resurrection; His work has left death itself destroyed (1 Corinthians 15:26).

5a. Who satisfieth thy mouth with good things.

David focuses on the material blessings (*good things*) that only the Lord can provide. The Lord as provider is a theme repeated often in the Psalms (examples: Psalms 103:5; 104:28; 145:16).

5b. So that thy youth is renewed like the eagle's.

Compare Isaiah 40:29-31.

II. God's Character
(PSALM 103:6-17a)
A. Righteous (vv. 6, 7)

6. The LORD executeth righteousness and judgment for all that are oppressed.

David now calls attention to the Lord's compassion toward the *oppressed*. *The Lord* has always been passionate that *righteousness and judgment* (in terms of a just judgment) be carried out on behalf of those who are often mistreated or overlooked because of their powerless status. The Lord makes clear how compassionate He is toward groups such as widows and orphans (Deuteronomy 24:17-22; compare Exodus 23:3, 6, 9).

His people, however, do not always demonstrate such compassion, which is why the Scriptures (both Old and New Testament) highlight the necessity of seeing such people, or anyone in need, as God sees them (Isaiah 1:17, 23; Jeremiah 7:1-7; Matthew 25:31-46; James 1:27).

7. He made known his ways unto Moses, his acts unto the children of Israel.

Within pagan religions, the worshippers are often left groping and guessing what the deities desire. There is no concept of revealed truth. In contrast, the Lord has not left His covenant people in such uncertainty. He has revealed His will for all people through the words of Holy Scripture.

Moses told the Israelites "The secret things belong unto the Lord our God: but those things which are revealed belong unto us and to our children for ever, that we may do all the words of this law" (Deuteronomy 29:29). God's *acts* on behalf of His people cannot be duplicated by any other god, for there is no other god.

B. Gracious (vv. 8-12)

8. The LORD is merciful and gracious, slow to anger, and plenteous in mercy.

This verse proclaims one of the most important statements of faith within the Old Testament. It was first revealed to Moses when the Lord permitted him to see a portion of His glory on Mount Sinai and "proclaimed the name of the Lord" before him (Exodus 34:5-7). It is highlighted, with minor variations, at various places within the Old Testament (Numbers 14:17-19; Nehemiah 9:16, 17; Psalms 86:15; 145:8; Joel 2:13; Jonah 4:2).

9a. He will not always chide.

The word translated *chide* comes from a Hebrew word that indicates accusing or bringing a case to court (Hosea 4:1-4; Micah 6:1, 2). That happens when human sin reaches a critical point and must be confronted. But God delights most of all in showing grace, as the previous verse notes. Satan is the one who carries the reputation of being "the accuser of our brethren" (Revelation 12:10).

9b. Neither will he keep his anger for ever.

God does not let His anger smolder or allow it to control His entire perspective and temperament, as is often the case with human anger. God's anger is not like human anger, which is often uncontrolled, irrational, and guided by highly questionable motives. "The wrath of man worketh not the righteousness of God" (James 1:20). God's wrath, by contrast, is a holy, righteous response to human sin. He alone knows when and how to administer it. But it is clear to David (and to all those in Scripture who know God in an intimate way) that God's mercy and grace are what make Him worth "blessing" with all one's soul.

10. He hath not dealt with us after our sins; nor rewarded us according to our iniquities.

The clearest evidence of God's mercy is in the way He deals with human sin. If He were to treat us as we deserve, based on *our sins*, then our plight would be hopeless. "If thou, Lord, shouldest mark iniquities, O Lord, who shall stand? But there is forgiveness with thee, that thou mayest be feared" (Psalm 130:3, 4).

❧ ABUNDANT MERCY ❧

I heard a loud crash from the bedroom where my daughter was playing. It sounded like a waterfall of knickknacks, all of them breaking on their way down. I ran to the bedroom to see what had happened.

Entering the room, I saw my daughter standing in front of a pile of rubble that had once been ceramic figurines, picture frames, and handmade art projects. The shelf they had been on lay on top of them.

"I don't know what happened, Mom! It just fell off the wall!" my daughter exclaimed. We began the clean-up process and managed to salvage quite a few of the most favored objects. I told her that accidents happen, and we went back to our separate activities.

A few minutes later, my daughter emerged from her room, a penitent look on her face. "I have to tell you something. It didn't just fall off the wall," she said. "I was jumping, and I knocked it down." She looked down in embarrassment.

While I was shocked and unhappy that my daughter had lied to me earlier, her obvious shame went to my heart. She was penitent, and I could see that she regretted her lie. We talked about why lying is wrong and how it can destroy relationships. Then I forgave her.

The psalmist (David) says that God's anger does not last forever. He is "merciful and gracious, slow to anger, and plenteous in mercy," and He has not "rewarded us according to our iniquities." Do you forgive as God forgives you? See the next two verses.

—L. M. W.

11, 12. For as the heaven is high above the earth, so great is his mercy toward them that fear him. As far as the east is from the west, so far hath he removed our transgressions from us.

Our knowledge of the vastness of the heavens is far, far greater than it was in David's time. Yet his words are still true: their height cannot provide an adequate means of measuring the extent of the Lord's *mercy* to those who *fear* Him.

In measuring how far *the east is from the west*, some have observed that a person could begin at a certain point and travel south to the South Pole then north to the North Pole, then travel south again to the original starting point. However, a person could travel around the world many times going east, reaching the starting point repeatedly without ever moving in any direction but east. Thus we can speak of a North Pole and a South

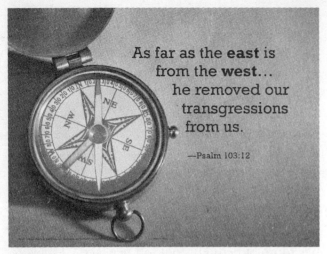

As far as the **east** is from the **west**... he removed our transgressions from us.

—Psalm 103:12

Visual for Lesson 3. *Read the commentary on Psalm 103:11, 12 aloud, and then ask, "How does what you heard help you appreciate these verses?"*

Pole but not of an East Pole or a West Pole, since there is no place at which east meets west. God's intention is that our sins be *removed* so that we never "meet" them again.

C. Compassionate (vv. 13-17a)

13. Like as a father pitieth his children, so the LORD pitieth them that fear him.

The knowledge of God as *a father* is more clearly revealed in the New Testament because of the fuller revelation of God provided by Jesus. But God as father is not totally foreign to the Old Testament (Deuteronomy 32:6; Psalm 89:26). Fathers who read a verse such as this must ask themselves how much sympathy they consistently demonstrate toward their children. Or do they "provoke" their children "to anger," which Paul warns fathers not to do (Colossians 3:21)?

14. For he knoweth our frame; he remembereth that we are dust.

As Creator, God knows how we are put together. The Hebrew verb from which *frame* comes is used in Genesis 2:7 to describe how God "formed" man from *dust*. From our perspective that fact may cause us to reflect on our unworthiness and inadequacy. God sees it as a reason for sympathy and patience.

15, 16. As for man, his days are as grass: as a flower of the field, so he flourisheth. For the wind passeth over it, and it is gone; and the place thereof shall know it no more.

These verses also comment on the transitory nature of human existence. As we age, we tend to recognize our limitations, and we sense how quickly time has passed. But even young people should acknowledge the truth of David's words and "remember now [their] Creator in the days of [their] youth" (Ecclesiastes 12:1).

17a. But the mercy of the LORD is from everlasting to everlasting upon them that fear him.

In contrast with humanity's temporary, fleeting existence, *the mercy of the Lord is from everlasting to everlasting upon them that fear him.* This echoes the previous "limitless" language of verses 11 and 12. Rather than dwell on the frailty of human beings, David finds his delight in exalting the faithfulness of God.

❧ *PRAIRIE GRASS* ❧

We moved to our new home in the Midwest in the month of June, just as the prairies surrounding our town became green and lush. Every day on my drive to work, I passed field after field of green grass dotted with yellow and purple flowers. When the wind passed over it, the grass waved in the current, resembling a green ocean tossing gently in the wind. A few times I felt compelled to stop my car and roll down the window just to watch this unique beauty.

We had lived there a few years when we heard about huge wildfires sweeping across Kansas, south of our home in Nebraska. Although the fires never came close to us, we learned that they affected more than 651,000 acres of land, destroying pastureland and killing thousands of cattle, not to mention consuming homes and taking people's lives in the process. Reports say that high winds fed the flames, spreading them quickly in grass that served as tinder after an extremely dry and warm winter.

These fires, the largest in the history of Kansas, remind us that the beautiful grasses and flowers are only temporary. Psalm 103:15-17 compares our days with that of the grass or the flowers of the field. We flourish for a time, but the wind passes over us, and we are gone. In contrast, "The mercy of the Lord is from everlasting to everlasting upon them that fear him."

—L. M. W.

III. Closing Exhortation
(PSALM 103:21, 22)
A. To the Hosts of Heaven (v. 21)

21. Bless ye the LORD, all ye his hosts; ye ministers of his, that do his pleasure.

As the psalm nears its conclusion, David returns to his original command to *bless . . . the Lord*. In so doing, David calls on *all* of God's *hosts* to do so. Angels are called on to do so in Psalm 103:20 (not in today's text). This may be another instance of parallelism, where one expression is synonymous with the other. One may think of the "multitude of the heavenly host" that assembled to praise God on the night of Jesus' birth (Luke 2:13).

On the other hand, it may be that these hosts are the starry hosts, or celestial bodies (Deuteronomy 4:19). Such were created as the Lord's *ministers*, or servants, to do His bidding, as indicated when He created them (Genesis 1:14-18).

B. To Every Place on Earth (v. 22)

22. Bless the LORD, all his works in all places of his dominion: bless the LORD, O my soul.

David concludes with a call to the entire creation to join him in his adoration of *the Lord*. Clearly he does not want to perform a solo! At the same time, praise is something intensely personal for David, and he never grows tired of expressing it. He ends the psalm with the same enthusiasm he had at the beginning.

Conclusion
A. What's Your Story?

As you think about God's blessings in your own life, what comes to mind? What's your story?

What psalm, poem, or testimony could you compose to "bless the Lord"?

No doubt every one of us could point to circumstances, whether in another country, our own nation, our city or county, or our personal lives, that reflect how badly broken by sin this world continues to be. David, the author of Psalm 103, certainly experienced much heartache and sorrow during his lifetime—much of it due to his own choices to disobey God.

It may seem hard to believe that we are in the midst of another Christmas season and approaching the end of another year. If you have a calendar on the wall somewhere in your home, flip back to January of this year. Go through each month and think about the blessings you have received. (You may want to write them down or keep a record of them electronically.) Consider, as David did, both the spiritual and material blessings given by the Lord. Thank Him for the circumstances and the people He brought into your life—even during the hard times, those situations that were not on your schedule or even in your mind when the year began. And take time to "bless the Lord."

Some of the brokenness resulting from the curse of sin will not be fully eliminated until Jesus returns and "a new heaven and a new earth" (Revelation 21:1) are established for eternity. At that time, all diseases of all varieties will be done away with for good. Until then we—like Paul, whose thorn in the flesh remained despite his prayers that it be removed—must trust God's grace to be sufficient and trust that He will use us to bear witness of His power even in the throes of our pain (2 Corinthians 12:7-10). There is no excuse not to bless the Lord!

B. Prayer

Father, may we bless and magnify Your name! We praise You for the grace You have shown to us, especially now during this season of remembering the wondrous gift placed in the manger in Bethlehem. In Jesus' name we pray. Amen.

C. Thought to Remember
Learn to speak the language
of blessing and praise.

INVOLVEMENT LEARNING

Enhance your lesson with KJV Bible Student *(from your curriculum supplier) and the reproducible activity page (at www.standardlesson.com or in the back of the* KJV Standard Lesson Commentary Deluxe Edition*).*

Into the Lesson

Distribute self-stick notes and pens. As you do, ask learners to take one minute to write down one or two blessings for which they are thankful. After you call time, have volunteers share their blessings and affix their notes onto the board or wall.

State: "Today we will be reading a psalm that David wrote in which he praises God for his blessings. Let's read David's psalm and consider his reasons for feeling blessed and the ways he praised the Lord."

Alternative. Distribute copies of the "Satisfied with Good Things" activity from the reproducible page, which you can download. Have students work in pairs to unscramble the words and solve the puzzle. Tell them the message is the main theme of today's lesson.

Into the Word

Have a volunteer read Psalm 103 aloud to the class. Allow learners to work in pairs or teams of three to read the psalm again, identifying reasons for David's thankfulness. Make sure each pair or group has paper and pen. After five to seven minutes, they should have identified the following regarding God's actions: *He forgives iniquities, heals diseases, redeems life, crowns with lovingkindness and mercies, satisfies with good things, renews youth, executes righteousness and justice, is merciful and gracious, has not dealt with us according to our sins/iniquities.* Have each reason written on a self-stick note ahead of time. Use notes of a different color from those used earlier.

Ask pairs or groups to share identified reasons for David's praise. As they do so, affix the note with that reason on the board or wall where students placed their notes earlier. Draw attention to the fact that David's praise can be divided into categories. Verses 1 and 2 address reasons to praise. Verses 3-5 are a remembrance of blessings. Verses 6-17a contain praise for God's character.

As you place each reason on the board or wall, encourage learners to share how they might be able to relate to the reason and why it is meaningful to them. Ask, "How do you think David blesses or praises God in this psalm?" To help learners to realize the importance of recognizing and remembering our blessings, explain that the very action of being thankful for our blessings is a blessing to God. Ask, "How do we know that we should all praise the Lord?" If no one else does so, point out that in verse 22, David says, "Bless the Lord, . . . bless the Lord, O my soul."

Remind learners that in Luke 19:40, Jesus told the Pharisees, when they asked Him to rebuke His disciples for praising Him that, "I tell you that, if these should hold their peace, the stones would immediately cry out."

Ask learners to look again at the reasons David praised and think about the new covenant that we have because of Jesus. Ask, "How do these reasons apply to Christians living under the new covenant?" Jot responses on the board during a time of open discussion.

Into Life

Say, "In the busyness of life, especially in the weeks between Thanksgiving and Christmas, we may fail to recognize our blessings and praise God who provides for us. Let's take the next five minutes to write a group song or prayer of praise."

Provide sheets of paper on which learners can write the lines of the prayer or praise song. After they do, ask them to read it together. Say, "Perhaps you can post your praise song on your refrigerator or mirror so you can read it again and again to bless the Lord in the coming weeks."

Alternative. Distribute copies of the "Praise Journal" activity from the reproducible page. Provide about one minute for learners to complete as indicated. Close by reading or singing "To God Be the Glory, Great Things He Has Done."

LOVE GOD FOR THE GIFT OF JESUS

DEVOTIONAL READING: Isaiah 49:1-7
BACKGROUND SCRIPTURE: Luke 1:26-31; 2:21-35

LUKE 1:26-31

26 And in the sixth month the angel Gabriel was sent from God unto a city of Galilee, named Nazareth,

27 To a virgin espoused to a man whose name was Joseph, of the house of David; and the virgin's name was Mary.

28 And the angel came in unto her, and said, Hail, thou that art highly favoured, the Lord is with thee: blessed art thou among women.

29 And when she saw him, she was troubled at his saying, and cast in her mind what manner of salutation this should be.

30 And the angel said unto her, Fear not, Mary: for thou hast found favour with God.

31 And, behold, thou shalt conceive in thy womb, and bring forth a son, and shalt call his name JESUS.

LUKE 2:22, 25-35

22 And when the days of her purification according to the law of Moses were accomplished, they brought him to Jerusalem, to present him to the Lord;

· ·

25 And, behold, there was a man in Jerusalem, whose name was Simeon; and the same man was just and devout, waiting for the consolation of Israel: and the Holy Ghost was upon him.

26 And it was revealed unto him by the Holy Ghost, that he should not see death, before he had seen the Lord's Christ.

27 And he came by the Spirit into the temple: and when the parents brought in the child Jesus, to do for him after the custom of the law,

28 Then took he him up in his arms, and blessed God, and said,

29 Lord, now lettest thou thy servant depart in peace, according to thy word:

30 For mine eyes have seen thy salvation,

31 Which thou hast prepared before the face of all people;

32 A light to lighten the Gentiles, and the glory of thy people Israel.

33 And Joseph and his mother marvelled at those things which were spoken of him.

34 And Simeon blessed them, and said unto Mary his mother, Behold, this child is set for the fall and rising again of many in Israel; and for a sign which shall be spoken against;

35 (Yea, a sword shall pierce through thy own soul also,) that the thoughts of many hearts may be revealed.

KEY VERSES

Mine eyes have seen thy salvation, which thou hast prepared before the face of all people. —**Luke 2:30, 31**

OUR LOVE FOR GOD

Unit I: God Is Worthy of Our Love

LESSONS 1–5

LESSON AIMS

After participating in this lesson, each learner will be able to:

1. Tell the story of how Mary learned of her miraculous pregnancy.

2. Explain why Simeon was emotionally moved when he encountered baby Jesus.

3. Share with another person how meeting Jesus changes lives.

LESSON OUTLINE

Introduction

A. Introduction to the Church

A church tradition from years past involved the happy fuss made over a baby's first Sunday in church. Usually a week or two after birth, the proud mother and father would carefully pack up their new child (along with a diaper bag) and present their bundle of joy to the women who staffed the church nursery department. The child might even be enrolled in the "cradle roll," with the parents receiving a certificate and a photograph to mark the event.

Later, the minister might ask the new parents to bring their infant to the main worship service where he would announce to the church that a new little person was in their midst. The biggest fuss would come after the service, when the people of the church would surround the proud parents in the foyer to get a peek at the baby and congratulate the mom and dad. For various reasons, that practice of decades gone by will not be so easy for the year 2019 in many cases!

Even so, this integration is important. While a baby may not be a "member" of the church in the sense of a regularly attending and faithfully giving adult, these little ones must find a welcome home among the people of God. They should not need to wait until their teenage or adult years to garner acceptance. Today's lesson points us to one who underwent a mixture: one who was to live his short life both accepted and rejected, in both infancy and adulthood.

B. Lesson Context: Nazareth in Galilee

First-century Palestine consisted of three provinces: Galilee, Samaria, and Judea. Jesus ministered in all these areas, but began in Galilee. This was "The land of Zabulon, and the land of Nephthalim, by the way of the sea, beyond Jordan, Galilee of the Gentiles" (Matthew 4:15). This was hill country, receiving enough rain to sustain successful farming rather than just grazing; therefore, it was primarily rural in character. Galilee was geographically separated from the main Jewish area surrounding Jerusalem by Samaritan territory.

Luke locates the home of Mary in the Galilean village of Nazareth (Luke 1:26; see Mark 1:9). The insignificance of tiny Nazareth, its distance from Jerusalem, and its location in a less-than-pure Jewish area make Nazareth an unlikely home for the woman chosen to be the mother of the promised Messiah of Israel. On the reputation of Nazareth, see John 1:46.

C. Lesson Context: Jerusalem in Judea

The Jewish people understood the need for incorporation of babies into the people of God. Backdrops for today's lesson are the things Jesus' parents did in accordance with Jewish custom. They have Him circumcised on the eighth day (Luke 2:21; see Leviticus 12:3; compare Philippians 3:5), officially marking him as a son of the covenant. This would have been a time of celebration for the little family, attended by friends and relatives as available. It was also at this time that the baby was formally named Jesus.

The circumcision and naming happened while the parents were still residing in Bethlehem, a two- or three-hour walk from the temple in Jerusalem. Luke indicates they stayed in David's city until Mary was ready to undergo purification at the temple (Luke 2:22). That was 33 days after the baby's circumcision, so 40 days after His birth (Leviticus 12:4).

I. The Angel Announces
(LUKE 1:26-31)
A. Visit from Gabriel (vv. 26, 27)

26. And in the sixth month the angel Gabriel was sent from God unto a city of Galilee, named Nazareth.

While angels are mentioned over 300 times in the Bible, only two of these servants of God are named: *Gabriel* and Michael (see Daniel 9:21; 12:1). While Michael appears in the role of a heavenly combatant (Revelation 12:7), Gabriel appears in the Bible as a messenger of the Lord sent with specific information for chosen people.

This verse introduces Gabriel in this messenger role, being *sent from God* to *Nazareth in the sixth month*. This is a reference to the two-thirds point

of the pregnancy of Mary's relative Elisabeth, the mother of John the Baptist (see Luke 1:19, 24). Nazareth, generously referred to by Luke as a *city*, is a village of perhaps 400–500 people.

27. To a virgin espoused to a man whose name was Joseph, of the house of David; and the virgin's name was Mary.

Before telling us what Gabriel's message is, Luke introduces *Mary*, the soon-to-be mother of Jesus. The fact that she is a *virgin* is entirely consistent with the fact that she is unmarried in a small Jewish village in the first century. She is young, just reaching the age where marriage would be both expected and acceptable.

Although unmarried, Mary is *espoused to a man* named *Joseph*. This is somewhat equivalent to our engagement practices leading to marriage, with some important differences. To be espoused means that Joseph has struck a deal with Mary's father, and she is his wife in every way except living and sleeping with him.

The fact that Joseph is *of the house of David* means that King David is a distant ancestor. This cherished fact undoubtedly has been preserved in his family records for many generations (see Luke 2:4; 3:23, 31). It is important for us because being an heir of David is a prophetic prerequisite for the Messiah (see 2 Samuel 7:16, 17; Psalm 132:11).

B. Favor with God (vv. 28-31)

28. And the angel came in unto her, and said, Hail, thou that art highly favoured, the Lord is with thee: blessed art thou among women.

HOW TO SAY IT

Annunciation	Uh-*nun*-see-**ay**-shun.
Gabriel	*Gay*-bree-ul.
Galilean	Gal-uh-*lee*-un.
Galilee	*Gal*-uh-lee.
medieval	mee-*dee*-vul or mee-dee-*ee*-vul.
Nazareth	*Naz*-uh-reth.
Nephthalim	*Nef*-thuh-lim.
Nunc Dimittis	Nuhnk Dih-*mit*-us.
Samaritan	Suh-*mare*-uh-tun.
Simeon	*Sim*-ee-un.
Zabulon	*Zab*-you-lon.

This event is known in church tradition as the Annunciation, the announcement of God's messenger to Mary of her status as the chosen mother of the Messiah. Luke's description of *the angel coming in* is an indication that Mary is indoors when Gabriel comes *unto her.* Artistic presentations often depict Mary in a lavish, spacious home with stone columns and carpets, but this is unlikely. Nazareth has few homes like this (if any), and later details in Luke indicate the poverty of Mary and Joseph.

The salutation in context is both simple and revealing. *Hail* is a greeting word like "hi" or "hello" or "hola." To follow this by saying that the unsuspecting young woman is *favoured* by *the Lord* is intended to be good news.

29. And when she saw him, she was troubled at his saying, and cast in her mind what manner of salutation this should be.

Rather than comforting Mary, the greeting does the opposite. It sets her mind spinning in an effort to bring meaning to the angel's words.

Mary cannot dismiss this experience as some sort of mind trick, for she sees the angel as well as hears him. Despite this inner turmoil, she waits for more information, not challenging the angel or his purpose (contrast Luke 1:18).

> **What Do You Think?**
> What will you do the next time you are "troubled" by something in God's Word?
> *Digging Deeper*
> Under what circumstances, if any, is it a good idea to keep your concerns to yourself? Why?

30, 31. And the angel said unto her, Fear not, Mary: for thou hast found favour with God. And, behold, thou shalt conceive in thy womb, and bring forth a son, and shalt call his name JESUS.

The fuller explanation comes quickly; the *favour with God* is revealed: Mary will *conceive a son* and *call his name JESUS.* But no father is mentioned. Mary is as good as married to Joseph, an honorable villager. But they have not come together in an intimate way, for Luke has made it clear she is still a virgin. Joseph will not be the father.

If we read a little further, we find that Mary's questions are answered. The baby in her womb will come from an act of the Holy Spirit (Luke 1:35). Mary's response to this troubling situation rings throughout history as an example of faith: "Behold the handmaid of the Lord; be it unto me according to thy word" (1:38).

❧ AN EXCITING ANNOUNCEMENT ❧

When my husband and I found out we were expecting our first child, we debated about waiting to tell family and friends. We decided to tell them right away; it was too exciting to keep secret.

I had been working on a family tree, so I printed out a version of it for each parent. Instead of placing my name and my husband's name as the latest generation of our families, we wrote "Baby" and the baby's anticipated due date.

We took the family tree with us to a family get-together. As we were chatting, I told my mom I'd been making a family tree and wanted her to see it. I handed her the rolled-up paper and watched her unroll it. She surveyed each generation, and then her eyes fell on the last one. She looked up in disbelief. "Does this say 'Baby'? Does that mean what I think it means?" she asked. We nodded. She jumped up and hugged us. What an announcement! Her first grandchild was on the way!

The announcement to Mary must have sparked an intense mix of emotions. Luke, the author, does not dwell on these at this point, merely summing them up with the phrase "she was troubled." We see an implication of fear in the angel's encouraging "fear not." Much more emotion is evident in Mary's Song of Luke 1:46-55. Is it even possible to consider the Christ Child anew this Christmas season and *not* share Mary's emotions on some level?
—L. M. W.

> **What Do You Think?**
> How can you make progress in learning not to fear those things you should not?
> *Digging Deeper*
> Can the discoveries and principles of secular psychology help us in this, or should we stick to Scripture as our only guide? Why?

II. The Spirit Reveals

(LUKE 2:22, 25-35)

A. Baby Is Presented (v. 22)

22. And when the days of her purification according to the law of Moses were accomplished, they brought him to Jerusalem, to present him to the Lord.

Today's lesson does not include the well-known Christmas stories of the trip to Bethlehem, the birth in a stable, and the story of the shepherds (Luke 2:1-20). Our focus is on events following Jesus' birth. The trip to the temple in *Jerusalem* serves for Mary's ritual *purification* sacrifice and for the presentation of the baby Jesus.

The purification process includes a waiting period in which the mother is considered unclean. This is likened to a woman's period of "uncleanness" for a week each month due to her menstrual cycle (Leviticus 12:1, 2). The blood involved is associated with ritual impurity (see 15:25).

The standard sacrificial animals for a mother's purification is a lamb and a bird, but the law allows for substitution of two birds in cases of hardship (Leviticus 12:6-8). The offering of two birds for Mary (Luke 2:24, not in today's text) reveals the humble financial situation of the new parents.

The fact that Joseph brings Jesus for presentation at the temple indicates he has embraced the role of father and considers Jesus to be his legitimate son.

> **What Do You Think?**
> What are ways the church can support men serving as fathers to children who are not their biological offspring?
>
> *Digging Deeper*
> What Scripture passages, if any, inform your answer?

B. Wait Is Over (vv. 25-27)

25. And, behold, there was a man in Jerusalem, whose name was Simeon; and the same man was just and devout, waiting for the consolation of Israel: and the Holy Ghost was upon him.

Public venues often have regular visitors who are well-known to the community. Luke tells us of two such characters at the Jerusalem temple: Anna the prophetess (Luke 2:36-38) and Simeon (Luke 2:25-35). Our lesson looks at the second.

Five things about *Simeon* are disclosed. First, he is a resident of *Jerusalem*. Our impression is not that he is necessarily a lifelong resident of the city, but that he has come there in his old age to await the Messiah. Second, he is *just and devout*. To be just means he cares about righteous living and justice in his community. To be devout implies he is a man of prayer and faith, and that he participates in the worship activities associated with the temple.

Third, he waits *for the consolation of Israel*. This refers to a new era, a promised time when the Lord will move to console or comfort the distressed Jewish people (see Isaiah 49:13; 57:18; 61:2, 3). Fourth, Simeon has *the Holy Ghost* resting *upon him*. The Holy Spirit is a comforting and revealing presence in human lives, and we see both elements here. The presence of the Holy Spirit is a strong theme in both Luke and Acts (also written by Luke). The power of the Holy Spirit gives Simeon both strength and understanding.

26. And it was revealed unto him by the Holy Ghost, that he should not see death, before he had seen the Lord's Christ.

Fifth, the Holy Spirit has granted Simeon supernatural insight into God's plan for comforting Israel: it centers on the coming of *the Lord's Christ*. The Greek word *Christ* and the Hebrew word *Messiah* both mean "the anointed one," the one commissioned to redeem Israel. Simeon understands his role in the unfolding of God's plans, for he has been promised that the Messiah would be born before his *death*. Further, Simeon believes he will meet this individual personally.

27. And he came by the Spirit into the temple: and when the parents brought in the child Jesus, to do for him after the custom of the law.

All of this comes together when Joseph, Mary, and Jesus enter the *temple* courtyards. Simeon is there by the guidance of the Holy Spirit. Jesus is there to fulfill the obligation of His parents as prescribed in *the law* of Moses, the consecration of the firstborn son (Exodus 13:2; Luke 2:23, 24).

C. Salvation Is Seen (vv. 28-32)

28. Then took he him up in his arms, and blessed God, and said.

Much is unsaid in this verse, including why a new mother would allow a stranger to take her baby *up in his arms.* Simeon either has a recognized role in the temple precincts or his demeanor suggests trustworthiness (perhaps encouraged by the Holy Spirit). He holds the baby for the blessing rather than simply placing a hand on his head, an intimate and beautiful act. Simeon blesses God in the sense of offering praise as it springs from his heart on this long-awaited occasion.

> *What Do You Think?*
> What more can your church do to surround infants with the love of the larger body of members of the congregation?
> *Digging Deeper*
> What reasonable (and perhaps additional) safeguards should be in place while doing so?

29. Lord, now lettest thou thy servant depart in peace, according to thy word.

The content of Simeon's praise begins here and goes through the three verses that follow. All this is presented to us as poetry, sometimes called the Song of Simeon (also known by the Latin *Nunc Dimittis*). It is likely these words were used as a praise song in the early church, so when Luke's first readers come to them, they are already familiar with the words and appreciate understanding them in their original setting.

First, Simeon acknowledges to the Lord that with the promise having been kept (*according to thy word*), he is now ready to die (*depart in peace*). The reason why is given in the next verse.

30, 31. For mine eyes have seen thy salvation, which thou hast prepared before the face of all people.

Seeing the Messiah is what Simeon has been waiting for, what he has been living for. For him to say he has *seen* the Lord's *salvation* does not mean that he believes all of God's saving activity is now accomplished. Simeon condenses this salvation to a person, a baby whom the Holy Spirit has revealed as the Savior in the sight *of all people.* To

see the baby on this day is possible for anyone in the temple courtyard. But to know this is the Savior requires supernatural insight from the Spirit.

> *What Do You Think?*
> Accomplishing what additional things of God would make you ready to finish life "in peace"?
> *Digging Deeper*
> Which individual listed in Hebrews 11 most inspires you in this regard? Why? How does 2 Timothy 4:6-8 influence your answer?

❧ THE DOCTOR AND THE BABY ❧

The doctor who delivered our youngest child spent the hours prior to her birth shuffling between the maternity floor and the floor where his mother-in-law lay dying. She had lived a long, full life. She looked forward to seeing loved ones again in Heaven. Her family gathered around her, showing their love for her and for each other.

After examining our daughter shortly after her birth, the nurse put a little knit hat on her head and wrapped her in a pink blanket. The newborn fell asleep as my husband and I took turns holding her. Then the doctor came back, fresh from a visit to his mother-in-law's bedside. He asked if he could hold the baby. My husband handed our hour-old daughter to him.

He held her quietly, looking intently at her at length. Finally he said, "It's so amazing. Upstairs one life is fading, and here one is just beginning."

The doctor was feeling the impermanence of life, the fleeting nature of our days. He realized that the infant's potential would someday be "in the books," just as his mother-in-law's now was.

We cannot see the future of an individual as Simeon was enabled. But we can see potential. What remaining potential do you see in the Lord's servant whose image you behold every time you look in a mirror?
—L. M. W.

32. A light to lighten the Gentiles, and the glory of thy people Israel.

Simeon understands at some level that God's Savior will benefit both *Gentiles* and the *people of Israel* (Jews). This is a universal application, because everyone falls into one of those two categories. Jesus will bring *light* to the nations as prophesied (Isaiah 9:1, 2; Matthew 4:13-16). The revealing of the Messiah to the world is a *glory* for Israel; it culminates their purpose to be a light to all nations (Isaiah 49:6).

D. Thoughts Are Revealed (vv. 33-35)

33. And Joseph and his mother marvelled at those things which were spoken of him.

Joseph and Mary must feel they have embarked on a journey that continues to amaze them. What they are hearing is astonishing pieces of a larger puzzle. This larger picture includes the words of the angel and the report of the shepherds (Luke 2:16-18). Luke's language may indicate an interview with Mary herself in his process of writing, for he earlier tells us that she has treasured and pondered these things (Luke 2:19).

34, 35. And Simeon blessed them, and said unto Mary his mother, Behold, this child is set for the fall and rising again of many in Israel; and for a sign which shall be spoken against; (Yea, a sword shall pierce through thy own soul also,) that the thoughts of many hearts may be revealed.

Having blessed God, *Simeon* blesses the little family. He then offers prophetic words, in four parts, concerning *this child*.

First, the child *is set for* both *the fall* and the *rising again of many* of his people. This may be a reference to prophecies of the Messiah as a "stone." This may be a stumbling block (Isaiah 8:14; Romans 9:33), or it may be a cornerstone (Psalm 118:22; Acts 4:11) upon which the new people of God will be built. Second, Jesus will be *a sign* that causes opposition (see Luke 11:30).

Third, *Mary* will suffer great sorrow on account of her son, likened unto a *sword* piercing her *soul*. She has already been through a lot (surprise pregnancy, relocation to Bethlehem away from her family, humble birth in a stable), but more pain is to come. Finally, through Jesus *the thoughts of many hearts* will *be revealed*. Hypocrisy will be unmasked as part of Jesus' ministry (see Luke 12:1, 56).

The sum of these four is that Jesus' ministry will not bring joy to all. Many will feel threatened

Visual for Lesson 4. *Have this visual on display as you ask, "In what ways can we 'see' the Christ Child anew this Christmas season?"*

by Him (John 11:48); His rejection will be particularly painful for His mother.

Conclusion
A. Encountering Jesus

Simeon's encounter with Jesus is remarkable when we consider the Messiah was still a baby. It is wrong to portray Jesus as we see Him in some medieval art: sitting on His mother's lap, back straight as a tent pole, hand in a teaching posture, and with a look of adult wisdom on His face. Simeon saw a baby. It was the Holy Spirit who revealed the significance of this infant to him, not His appearance or His words.

We encounter Jesus in different ways yet today. We may experience Him in a powerful way by reading what the Bible says about Him. We may understand Him better when we hear other believers give a testimony. We may grow in our relationship through prayer and a quiet time with Him. There is no greater thing than knowing Jesus.

B. Prayer

Father, may the Holy Spirit prod our hearts to learn more of Your Son so that we may be more like Him in word and deed. We pray this in Jesus' name. Amen.

C. Thought to Remember

Encountering Jesus changes lives.

INVOLVEMENT LEARNING

Enhance your lesson with KJV Bible Student *(from your curriculum supplier) and the reproducible activity page (at www.standardlesson.com or in the back of the* KJV Standard Lesson Commentary Deluxe Edition*).*

Into the Lesson

Ask learners to think of a time when they were truly surprised, good or bad. Then ask volunteers to briefly share their surprise with the class. After no more than three have shared (don't let this drag out), say, "Sometimes we are surprised and it is completely wonderful and welcome. At other times, we may not be sure of the value of the surprise, or we may even find the surprise to be unwelcome."

Ask those who shared their surprises to think about the final outcome. Explore disappointments and extra blessings experienced. Say, "Today we will consider the surprise of two who experienced firsthand the gift of Jesus."

Into the Word

Have learners read and discuss Luke 1:26-31 in groups of two or three. Inform groups that the goal is to be able to retell to an unbeliever the account of how Mary learned about her miraculous pregnancy. Encourage learners to discuss memorization techniques and parts of the account they need to clarify. Monitor small-group discussions for progress and misunderstandings. Clarify issues in ensuing whole-class discussion.

Option. As a test to see how well class members know the account, distribute copies of the "The Big Announcement" activity from the reproducible page, which you can download. Have learners complete as indicated individually. Assure them before the activity that you will not collect the results. After no more than one minute, discuss results.

Follow with this story: "A few years ago, a woman and her husband were heading to Tanzania to work with Bible translators. While heading through the airport, the woman sensed a strong urge to purchase an extra pair of reading glasses. When they arrived at the first meeting in Tanzania, their interpreter was wearing a pair of glasses with only one good lens—the other was cracked! Even more amazing, the glasses the woman had purchased in the airport were perfect for the interpreter! When was an occasion you have had a strong feeling that you needed to do something?"

Ask volunteers to share the event, how they did or did not act on the feeling, and what resulted. Then ask how their actions and inactions contrasted with those seen in Luke 2:22. (*Expected response:* the action of the parents was not based on feeling, but on Scripture [explained in Luke 2:23, 24, not in today's text].)

Next read Luke 2:25-32. Ask about the significance of the following facts about Simeon (hints are in *italics*): being "just and devout" *[compare Luke 1:6]*, "waiting for the consolation of Israel" *[compare Isaiah 40:1; 51:3; 57:18; 66:11]* , and having the Holy Ghost upon him *[significance is in the next seven verses, Luke 2:26-32]*. Point to the words "*salvation*" (v. 30), "*prepared*" (v. 31) and "*all people*" (v. 31) and ask how these point forward to Luke 3:4-6 (quoting Isaiah 40:3-5).

Option 1. The above can be a small-group exercise for which you have prepared handouts.

Option 2. Arrange the above Scripture references into an activity in which learners match the Scripture references with the individual verses of Luke 2:25-32.

Into Life

Make a transition by saying, "Meeting baby Jesus was the highlight of Simeon's life. Share with a partner how meeting Jesus changes lives today. Give examples." Encourage sharing in whole-class discussion.

Alternative. Distribute copies of the "The Gift of Jesus" activity from the reproducible page. Have learners complete it as indicated in study pairs.

Close the lesson in prayer, remembering to ask for the wisdom of the Holy Spirit.

Love God and Serve Others

Devotional Reading: James 2:14-26
Background Scripture: Matthew 25:31-46

Matthew 25:31-46

31 When the Son of man shall come in his glory, and all the holy angels with him, then shall he sit upon the throne of his glory:

32 And before him shall be gathered all nations: and he shall separate them one from another, as a shepherd divideth his sheep from the goats:

33 And he shall set the sheep on his right hand, but the goats on the left.

34 Then shall the King say unto them on his right hand, Come, ye blessed of my Father, inherit the kingdom prepared for you from the foundation of the world:

35 For I was an hungred, and ye gave me meat: I was thirsty, and ye gave me drink: I was a stranger, and ye took me in:

36 Naked, and ye clothed me: I was sick, and ye visited me: I was in prison, and ye came unto me.

37 Then shall the righteous answer him, saying, Lord, when saw we thee an hungred, and fed thee? or thirsty, and gave thee drink?

38 When saw we thee a stranger, and took thee in? or naked, and clothed thee?

39 Or when saw we thee sick, or in prison, and came unto thee?

40 And the King shall answer and say unto them, Verily I say unto you, Inasmuch as ye have done it unto one of the least of these my brethren, ye have done it unto me.

41 Then shall he say also unto them on the left hand, Depart from me, ye cursed, into everlasting fire, prepared for the devil and his angels:

42 For I was an hungred, and ye gave me no meat: I was thirsty, and ye gave me no drink:

43 I was a stranger, and ye took me not in: naked, and ye clothed me not: sick, and in prison, and ye visited me not.

44 Then shall they also answer him, saying, Lord, when saw we thee an hungred, or athirst, or a stranger, or naked, or sick, or in prison, and did not minister unto thee?

45 Then shall he answer them, saying, Verily I say unto you, Inasmuch as ye did it not to one of the least of these, ye did it not to me.

46 And these shall go away into everlasting punishment: but the righteous into life eternal.

Key Verse

The King shall answer and say unto them, Verily I say unto you, Inasmuch as ye have done it unto one of the least of these my brethren, ye have done it unto me. —**Matthew 25:40**

OUR LOVE FOR GOD

Unit I: God Is Worthy of Our Love

LESSONS 1–5

LESSON AIMS

After participating in this lesson, each learner will be able to:

1. Identify the setting for Jesus' sheep and goats teaching.

2. Explain what separates people into "sheep" and "goats" in Jesus' teaching.

3. Express one way to improve his or her congregation's benevolent outreach.

LESSON OUTLINE

Introduction
  A. Social Justice Rediscovered
  B. Lesson Context
I. Gathering of Nations (MATTHEW 25:31-33)
  A. Judge Is Seated (v. 31)
  B. Judged Are Separated (vv. 32, 33)
II. Sheep on the Right (MATTHEW 25:34-40)
  A. Sheeps' Blessing (vv. 34-36)
    A Drink of Cold Water
  B. Sheeps' Surprise (vv. 37-39)
  C. Sheeps' Justification (v. 40)
III. Goats on the Left (MATTHEW 25:41-45)
  A. Goats' Curse (vv. 41-43)
    God, Our Judge
  B. Goats' Challenge (vv. 44)
  C. Goats' Condemnation (v. 45)
IV. Eternal Destinies (MATTHEW 25:46)
Conclusion
  A. Justice Delayed
  B. Prayer
  C. Thought to Remember

Introduction

A. Social Justice Rediscovered

Many people have a great interest in pursuing social justice. This is a common passion within the so-called millennial generation, a group that churches desperately want to reach. Church leaders find that millennials have little interest in supporting traditional church programs (especially Sunday morning services that have not changed for decades). Millennials want to do more than talk about being Christians; they want to do Christian things, especially things they believe advance social justice.

Pursuing social justice today isn't so much about blaming those who cause injustice as it is about helping those who suffer from injustice. The church's concern for millennials and the millennials' concern for social justice have given this cause a rebirth, almost as if it has been discovered for the first time.

We are wise to remember, though, that the church has a long history of helping those in need, a history based on the teachings of Jesus and the practices of the early church. A key biblical basis for this is Jesus' illustration in Matthew 25 of the separation of sheep and goats, the text for today's lesson.

B. Lesson Context

Jesus' final week of ministry, the days leading to His crucifixion and resurrection, began with His entry into Jerusalem on Palm Sunday. This event is recorded in all four Gospels and traditionally is called the Triumphal Entry (Matthew 21:1-11; Mark 11:1-11; Luke 19:28-44; John 12:12-19). The events beginning with that entry into Jerusalem, known as Passion Week or Holy Week, comprise a disproportional percentage of the material in each Gospel account—about 36 percent of Matthew, 37 percent of Mark, 28 percent of Luke, and 44 percent of John.

These eight days, culminating with Resurrection Sunday, are huge when contrasted with the other 33 years of Jesus' life. It has been said that the Gospel authors' accounts of Passion Week are the story they dearly want to tell; everything else is prelude. This is overstatement, but we should certainly pay attention to what happens during this week!

We might think that Jesus spends these last few days preparing His disciples for His death and saying His good-byes (and He does some of this), but a significant part of the week is dedicated to teaching. The longest block of teaching comes on Tuesday. This block is known as the Olivet Discourse because of its setting on the Mount of Olives, which looms over Jerusalem to the east. In this discourse, Jesus spoke prophetically about the future destruction of Jerusalem (fulfilled in AD 70), about His return in power and glory, and about the future judgment of humankind. In Matthew, this represents two full chapters: 24 and 25.

Matthew ends this discourse with Jesus' teaching on the separation of the sheep and the goats. Sometimes this is referred to as a parable, but it is unlike the majority of Jesus' parables for several reasons. First, it is not referred to as a parable (compare Matthew 13:3). Second, it is not framed as being about the "kingdom of heaven," as are many of Jesus' parables in Matthew (see 13:24). Third, it is not a made-up story used to illustrate Jesus' teaching, but is about future events presented in a prophetic and symbolic manner.

Our lesson is from the third section of Matthew 25. The first section is the parable of the 10 virgins, a story about wedding attendants and their preparations (or lack thereof) for a delayed bridegroom. The second section, the parable of the talents, relates how servants have used resources entrusted to them during their master's absence. The general point of both parables is to be ready, because you don't know when the bridegroom/master will return (Matthew 25:13).

These lead to the final section, which begins with a picture of the return of the Messiah.

I. Gathering of Nations
(MATTHEW 25:31-33)
A. Judge Is Seated (v. 31)

31. When the Son of man shall come in his glory, and all the holy angels with him, then shall he sit upon the throne of his glory.

As Jesus speaks of *the Son of man* coming, we are to understand this as referring to himself. Matthew uses this designation for Jesus numerous times, always on the lips of Jesus (examples: Matthew 9:6; 16:13; 20:18). This title emphasizes the humanity of Jesus, but it is also a term for the Messiah drawn from Daniel 7:13.

As in Daniel, Jesus presents a dramatic vision of the future that emphasizes *glory*, the Lord's *angels*, and a *throne* designated for the Son of man. This throne is not a decorative antique, as portrayed in pictures we see. Rather, it is a seat of judgment, the throne of a judge-king (see Psalm 9:7).

B. Judged Are Separated (vv. 32, 33)

32, 33. And before him shall be gathered all nations: and he shall separate them one from another, as a shepherd divideth his sheep from the goats: and he shall set the sheep on his right hand, but the goats on the left.

The audience for the judge is *all nations*, an inclusive, worldwide term that indicates much more than the nation of Israel (see Isaiah 66:18). This is judgment of all humanity.

This scene does not depict individual trials with evidence and attorneys. Rather, the mass of people is divided into two groups. Jesus likens this to *a shepherd* separating his mixed flock into two groups based on species. *Sheep* and *goats* might be herded together for grazing, but they are of different value to the shepherd. Both animals may be slaughtered for meat, but the other products of goats are milk and cheese, whereas sheep provide wool.

HOW TO SAY IT

Micah   *My*-kuh.
Olivet   *Ol*-ih-vet.

We should not be drawn into this analogy too far, however. These are not animals but people (*all nations*) and the Son of Man (the *shepherd*) is their judge.

II. Sheep on the Right
(MATTHEW 25:34-40)
A. Sheeps' Blessing (vv. 34-36)

34. Then shall the King say unto them on his right hand, Come, ye blessed of my Father, inherit the kingdom prepared for you from the foundation of the world.

The sheep/goats analogy is dropped when the judge renders His verdicts. He is not just a judge, though, but *the King*. Kings in the ancient world are more than heads of state or military commanders. They are lawgivers and judges for their people, reigning and rendering judgments (example: 1 Kings 3:28). The dual roles are often attributed to the Lord, the ultimate king and judge (Psalm 96:10; Isaiah 33:22).

The first verdict is given to those *on his right hand*, the sheep of the analogy. They are invited to *come* and claim *the kingdom* which has been *prepared for* them as an inheritance. This is an invitation to enter Heaven, for their kingdom has been ready since *the foundation of the world*, an allusion to the truth of Genesis 1:1.

Jesus' words also help us know the identity of the judge. He is surely the "Son of man" (Matthew 25:31, above), Jesus himself in all His glory. He invites those judged favorably to enjoy the blessing of His *Father*, a proper pronouncement for this king who is the judge, who is the Son of God.

35, 36. For I was an hungred, and ye gave me meat: I was thirsty, and ye gave me drink: I was a stranger, and ye took me in: naked, and ye clothed me: I was sick, and ye visited me: I was in prison, and ye came unto me.

The king gives the basis for this favorable verdict, and it is unlike anything we would hear in a law court today. He does not cite statutes or legal precedent, but speaks in personal terms. Those the king invites to share Heaven receive this judgment because of the way they have acted toward Him. This judge lists six areas in which they have acted correctly: helping people with lack of food, lack of water, lack of housing, lack of clothes, lack of health care, and lack of visitation *in prison*. All of these are easy for us to understand except two: clothing nakedness and visiting prisoners.

First, the Bible sometimes uses *naked* in the sense of inadequate clothing to guard against weather conditions (see 2 Corinthians 11:27). In Jesus' depiction, the act of kindness is not to cover a stark-naked person to prevent social embarrassment as much as it is to give warm clothes to a shivering unfortunate who has no protection from the weather.

Second, in the ancient world (and in many countries today), jailers supply prisoners with few, if any, provisions. Food, clothing, and medical care are more likely to come from family and friends who bring such things from outside.

All six kindnesses are acts of justice. In a basic sense, righteousness is doing the right thing, as well as not being guilty of doing the wrong thing. Justice, a similar concept in the Bible to righteousness, is wanting to see the right thing done for other people. The key to understanding this is to remember that true justice is seeing the right thing done for others from God's perspective, which is not necessarily identical to our own perspective. When we do things to relieve human suffering, we are doing God's work. We are doing justice. This is social justice, one person at a time.

> *What Do You Think?*
> What are specific ways our church can address the six needs of people given in this story?
> *Digging Deeper*
> What will be your part in correcting any identified deficiencies?

❧ *A DRINK OF COLD WATER* ❧

In the 1970s I was a missionary in Liberia, an African nation plagued with a corrupt government. Police officers were both victims and perpetrators in this unjust system. They harassed motorists as a way of subsidizing their meager pay. In the reverse of the problem people of color sometimes face in the United States today, at times I found myself guilty of "driving while white." Almost all light-skinned people in Liberia were high-paid foreign nationals working for American or European corporations that were there to extract Liberia's wealth of natural resources. They were obvious targets for bribe-seeking policemen, and so were missionaries.

Here is a typical scenario: I would hear a police whistle, then look to see who wanted me to pull over. The officer would say, "It's a very hot day; I need a drink of cold water." Those were code words for "I'm looking for a bribe."

When asked what I was doing in the country, I would identify myself as a missionary. At that point the talk of a bribe would usually cease. It was common knowledge that missionaries were bringing something of great value *into* the country, and doing so on a very low salary. In this case, our bringing the gospel and Christian schooling were the "drink of cold water"!

With the knowledge that we were in the country to bless the officer's people, his sense of injustice turned into gratitude. As Jesus said, those who serve Him will be blessed! —C. R. B.

B. Sheeps' Surprise (vv. 37-39)

37. Then shall the righteous answer him, saying, Lord, when saw we thee an hungred, and fed thee? or thirsty, and gave thee drink?

This blessed group, *the righteous*, who are offered the riches of Heaven, are incredulous. Something does not make sense to them. They don't recall ever serving the king in this way. When did they relieve His hunger or thirst?

38, 39. When saw we thee a stranger, and took thee in? or naked, and clothed thee? Or when saw we thee sick, or in prison, and came unto thee?

When did they provide housing for the king? When did they bring clothes to cover His nakedness? When was the king *sick* and needed a friend to nurse Him to health? When did they ever make a visit to the *prison* to provide for the needs of the imprisoned king? This last one is the most fantastic of all. Who ever heard of a king in a prison? Obviously, something else is behind the judging words of the king.

What Do You Think?
What methodology should our church use in prioritizing its resources for local ministries of benevolence?
Digging Deeper
Which needs are best met by cooperating with secular agencies and/or other churches? Why?

C. Sheeps' Justification (v. 40)

40. And the King shall answer and say unto them, Verily I say unto you, Inasmuch as ye have done it unto one of the least of these my brethren, ye have done it unto me.

The King solves the mystery quickly by identifying the precise objects of the acts of righteousness for the blessed ones. They have been kind to *the least of these my brethren*, and the king considers such benevolence to be a service to Him personally. This judge, who might never need food, water, shelter, clothes, medical care, or prison visitation, has a heart of compassion for the unfortunate people who need such help.

We should not understand this to imply that the "sheep" have earned their blessing and salvation. Salvation cannot be earned. And even if it could, the acts have been done unwittingly, without intent to curry favor with the king. These kindnesses have been motivated by hearts of kindness, hearts in tune with the king's own heart.

What Do You Think?
Thinking of a time when you relieved, or attempted to relieve, the suffering of another, what did you learn from that experience for future application?
Digging Deeper
In what ways do you anticipate that assisting others will help you grow in your faith?

III. Goats on the Left
(MATTHEW 25:41-45)
A. Goats' Curse (vv. 41-43)

41. Then shall he say also unto them on the left hand, Depart from me, ye cursed, into everlasting fire, prepared for the devil and his angels.

In Jesus' world, to be positioned on the right hand of the king is the most favored position. To be *on the left hand* is less favored, and this is certainly true here. The judge now addresses the goats, who have been gathered there.

The king-judge's verdict to the goat group starkly contrasts His message to the sheep group. They are not blessed, but *cursed*. They are not invited to enter the kingdom, but commanded to *depart*. Their destination is not an inheritance waiting for them from the foundation of the world, but *everlasting fire*. This is a place specially *prepared for the devil and his angels* (compare Revelation 12:9).

❧ GOD, OUR JUDGE ❧

I led an early morning men's Bible study for several years. One of the regular members of the group resisted any talk of God as the judge of the world. Whenever the text we were studying declared (or even hinted at) the idea that God would judge people, the man would try to reason his way around it.

For a long time I sought to understand his objections intellectually. I would answer the issues he raised as logically as I could, citing other biblical evidence that supported the concept of a loving yet judging heavenly Father.

Then, during one morning's study, my friend broke into tears and opened his heart to the group. He told us about the family in which he had been raised. His father professed to be a Christian, but he was an angry, judgmental, violent, and abusive man. My friend and his siblings lived in constant fear of their father's sometimes vicious retribution. An act of the slightest disobedience could result in extreme punishment, either physically or psychologically. The children grew to hate their father so much that when he died none of them attended his memorial service.

Perhaps you have friends whose family experience has twisted their view of God. How can you help them overcome a distorted view of our heavenly Father?　　　　　　　—C. R. B.

42, 43. For I was an hungred, and ye gave me no meat: I was thirsty, and ye gave me no drink: I was a stranger, and ye took me not in: naked, and ye clothed me not: sick, and in prison, and ye visited me not.

The cursed group have failed in all six areas of compassion listed as part of the first verdict: hunger, thirst, housing, clothing, sickness, and visitation.

B. Goats' Challenge (vv. 44)

44. Then shall they also answer him, saying, Lord, when saw we thee an hungred, or athirst, or a stranger, or naked, or sick, or in prison, and did not minister unto thee?

The pronouncement just given seems mysterious, however, in that the goat group apparently has not heard anything said to those ones on the right a few minutes earlier. As did the righteous ones, those cursed question the king's assessment. They cannot remember any situation in which they failed to assist the *Lord*, their judge. When does a king ever need food or water? When does a mighty judge lack in housing or clothing? When does a king fail to have medical care or become imprisoned?

C. Goats' Condemnation (v. 45)

45. Then shall he answer them, saying, Verily I say unto you, Inasmuch as ye did it not to one of the least of these, ye did it not to me.

The same standard is cited for the cursed as the king used for the blessed. They are guilty of failing to serve Him because of their lack of compassion for *the least of these*. There were plenty of opportunities to help those in need, lots of people who needed assistance. Denial of compassion for people in the community is equivalent to spurning the needs of the judge himself.

> *What Do You Think?*
> ▶ What will others see in your life in terms of "sheep" characteristics as a result of today's lesson? How will you make it happen?
> *Digging Deeper*
> Considering 1 Thessalonians 5:4-11, what sorts of things need to be in your life to be considered a child "of the day"? Why?

IV. Eternal Destinies

(MATTHEW 25:46)

46. And these shall go away into everlasting punishment: but the righteous into life eternal.

Again, we should be cautioned to remember that Jesus is not teaching a system in which our works make us righteous or blessed. No one is unfailingly responsive to the needs of others. And no one is so hard-hearted as to never care about others. The point is that God, the ultimate judge, does notice what we do and don't do. If we want to serve Him, we will serve others. This is justice enacted, righteousness at work. The time for so doing is not unlimited; either *everlasting punishment* or *life eternal* await all humanity.

Conclusion

A. Justice Delayed

"Justice delayed is justice denied" is a saying in the legal world. The saying advocates timely decisions by judges. This may be compared with Jesus' parable in which a corrupt judge keeps putting off rendering a verdict to bring justice to a cheated widow (Luke 18:1-8). Jesus likens this parable to the final judgment in language similar to that of our lesson: "When the Son of Man shall come" (Matthew 25:31; also Luke 18:8), final justice will be administered.

By God's plan, then, this final justice is delayed. Does that mean it is denied? Not at all! This is the message of Jesus in our lesson. We should not worry about our destiny at the final judgment; rather, we should attend to our attitudes in serving the Lord today. Do we truly have the heart of Jesus, the one who had great compassion for the sufferers He encountered (Matthew 15:32)? He healed diseases. He fed multitudes.

We enact God's justice—His righteousness—on a small scale whenever we act compassionately to relieve suffering. This may take many forms. It can involve ministries of famine relief (food), drilling wells (water), building homes (housing), thrift stores (clothing), free medical clinics (health), and/or prison ministry (visitation). Some Christians may not have the capacity for physi-

Visual for Lesson 5. *Point to this visual and ask your learners to take a silent minute to rank-order the needs in your area. Compare and contrast results.*

cal participation, but they support such ministries financially.

Furthermore, we should understand this is not entirely an individual matter. Churches can take active roles in acts of compassion for the needy in their community and with international relief organizations.

As with the caution for individuals in these areas, churches should take care too. If social justice projects are designed to garner publicity or enhance community reputation, they will flounder. Doing justice must be motivated from a heart that loves justice (Micah 6:8). It must be motivated by the ethic of the Golden Rule: that we would treat others the ways we want to be treated.

If we were without food, wouldn't we welcome a hot meal? If we were without housing, wouldn't we welcome shelter? Benevolent acts are not self-serving, but gain the heart of the king. We don't need to wait for His judgments; we can judge ourselves by our actions and inactions now.

B. Prayer

Heavenly Father, may we never turn our backs on the hungry, the thirsty, the homeless, the poorly clothed, the sick, or the imprisoned! May our hearts be like that of Your Son. We pray this in the name of Jesus. Amen.

C. Thought to Remember

Caring for others is serving Jesus.

INVOLVEMENT LEARNING

Enhance your lesson with KJV Bible Student (from your curriculum supplier) and the reproducible activity page (at www.standardlesson.com or in the back of the KJV Standard Lesson Commentary Deluxe Edition).

Into the Lesson

Display the following on a tattered piece of cardboard:

I'm hungry. Please help.

Say, "We've all seen sad-looking people holding up signs like this. What are some reasons for being reluctant to help a person holding such a sign?" Jot responses on the board during several minutes of free discussion. Then ask, "How did things turn out when you took action to meet a need in such a situation?"

After volunteers describe two or three situations, say, "Even though we may have good reasons for not attempting to help in certain ways, that doesn't mean we should give up on helping. Let's see why and how."

Alternative. Write the following on the board:

Hungry / Sick / Homeless / Lonely

Have students pair off to discus times when one or more of these words described their lives, how it happened, and who helped (if anyone). After a few minutes of sharing, say, "After being in such situations, people tend to be more compassionate to others in similar straits. In today's lesson we'll learn the best reason for reaching out to the hurting."

Into the Word

Ask students to open their Bibles to Matthew 24. Then pose the following questions: 1–In what passage do we discover where Jesus was when He taught His disciples? (*24:3*); 2–What verse begins Jesus' teachings about the visibility of His return? (*24:30*)? Use these and questions of your own to set the context for the study passage of Matthew 25:31-46.

Next, have students form groups of three or four. Designate groups as evenly as possible to be representing either "the Sheep" or "the Goats." Distribute the following assignment to all groups on handouts you prepare. *Assignment:* Read Matthew 25:31-46. 1–Where will the Son of man **initially** place those of your group's designation? 2–What six ways to help people are mentioned? 3–Why will those whom your group represents be so surprised by what Jesus will say and do? 4–How do one's actions or inactions relate to Jesus? 5–Where will those whom your group represents end up? (*Location of answers*: 1–vv. 33,; 2–vv. 35, 36, 42, 43; 3–vv. 37-39, 44; 4–vv. 40, 45; 5–vv. 34, 41, 46.)

Allow sufficient time for students to work through the questions; then have them share their answers. Make the point of why the people will be separated into each group; use the commentary to fix misconceptions.

Make a transition by asking, "How easy or hard is it for you to have the right attitude toward people who need help?" Raise the issue of 2 Thessalonians 3:10 if no one else does.

Into Life

If your church is involved in some type of benevolence outreach in your community (food pantry, homeless shelter, etc.), ask the person heading up the program to speak to your class about it and name ways class members can help.

If your church has no such ministry, discuss how your church can start one; list ideas on the board. Then ask, "What ministries already established by others can we support?" Allow time to discuss the subject; make plans for some type of follow-up.

Option. Several days in advance, distribute copies of the "Vignettes of Kindness" scripts to class members willing to serve as actors. These scripts are on the reproducible page, which you can download.

After each vignette, ask, "In what ways did the attitude and action of one of the two people match and not match that of Jesus?"

WALK IN LOVE

DEVOTIONAL READING: John 15:12-17

BACKGROUND SCRIPTURE: 2 Thessalonians 2:13–3:5; 2 John 4-11

2 THESSALONIANS 3:1-5

1 Finally, brethren, pray for us, that the word of the Lord may have free course, and be glorified, even as it is with you:

2 And that we may be delivered from unreasonable and wicked men: for all men have not faith.

3 But the Lord is faithful, who shall stablish you, and keep you from evil.

4 And we have confidence in the Lord touching you, that ye both do and will do the things which we command you.

5 And the Lord direct your hearts into the love of God, and into the patient waiting for Christ.

2 JOHN 4-11

4 I rejoiced greatly that I found of thy children walking in truth, as we have received a commandment from the Father.

5 And now I beseech thee, lady, not as though I wrote a new commandment unto thee, but that which we had from the beginning, that we love one another.

6 And this is love, that we walk after his commandments. This is the commandment, That, as ye have heard from the beginning, ye should walk in it.

7 For many deceivers are entered into the world, who confess not that Jesus Christ is come in the flesh. This is a deceiver and an antichrist.

8 Look to yourselves, that we lose not those things which we have wrought, but that we receive a full reward.

9 Whosoever transgresseth, and abideth not in the doctrine of Christ, hath not God. He that abideth in the doctrine of Christ, he hath both the Father and the Son.

10 If there come any unto you, and bring not this doctrine, receive him not into your house, neither bid him God speed:

11 For he that biddeth him God speed is partaker of his evil deeds.

KEY VERSE

This is love, that we walk after his commandments. This is the commandment, That, as ye have heard from the beginning, ye should walk in it. —**2 John 6**

Graphic: Zoonar RF / Zoonar / Thinkstock

OUR LOVE FOR GOD

Unit II: Loving God by Trusting Christ

LESSONS 6–10

LESSON AIMS

After participating in this lesson, each learner will be able to:

1. Tell why John advised withholding hospitality from false teachers.

2. Explain what John meant by "antichrist."

3. Express how he or she will react biblically to false teaching when confronted by it personally.

LESSON OUTLINE

Introduction

A. False Teachers in the Church

False teaching in the church is a multimillion dollar enterprise. Many organizations offer research and opinions on various Christ-claiming groups that are seen to be on the edge of orthodoxy or that have strayed into heresy. Such heresy-hunting is supported by donations, publishing, conferences, etc. These organizations perform an important service, given the seemingly endless supply of false teachers. The problem is that what one church considers heresy might be normal and central to another church's doctrine!

Since the early days of the church, accusations of false teaching have been flying. Some of the first issues, such as requiring circumcision for church membership (Acts 15), may seem irrelevant to us today. Other early issues seem very contemporary, such as the role of works in salvation and the authority of Scripture.

One of the constant threats from false teachers centered on the nature of Christ. The first-century church taught that Jesus was fully human and fully divine (as hard as that might be to comprehend). Church leaders knew that an overemphasis or underemphasis on either part of this doctrine would quickly lead to heresy. So they guarded both the divinity and the humanity of Jesus as cornerstones of the faith.

The authors of today's passages, Paul and John, both needed to deal with false teachers who denied the teaching of the apostles and threatened the church's existence. From their writings we learn ways to identify false teachers and how to deal with them.

B. Lesson Context: 2 Thessalonians

Paul wrote 2 Thessalonians from the city of Corinth in AD 52. This dating makes the letters of 1 and 2 Thessalonians, likely written just a few months apart, among the earliest writings of the New Testament.

Paul had been in Thessalonica earlier, but he didn't stay long due to Jewish opposition (Acts 17:1-10). The intent of his letters was to help the infant congregation understand his teachings more accurately in his absence. The church in Thessalonica would then be more resistant to heresy.

False teachings in the first century had many faces, some more dangerous than others. One particularly dangerous heresy that threatened the church's survival was *Judaizing*. It was related to the church's emergence from Judaism and separation from the synagogue. Many early Christians were Jews, and some of them saw Christianity as the next step of the Jewish faith—a sort of super-Judaism. Such teachers believed that all aspects of the Jewish law applied to the church, even to believers of Gentile background. This included circumcision for the males and adherence to Jewish food laws for every Christian. The error of Judaizing was a belief that salvation required keeping such laws.

C. Lesson Context: 2 John

The author given in 2 John is merely "the elder." But the three letters of John have been attributed to John the apostle from the first century. Church tradition tells us that he had come to the city of Ephesus and lived there until his death, sometime before the end of the first century. We do not know the order in which the three letters of John were written.

This letter is addressed to "the elect lady and her children" (2 John 1). The elect lady may be a prominent woman in one of the churches in the Ephesus region, or this may be John's figurative way of referring to the church. The letter encourages its recipients to continue living lives of love but also to be on guard against, and reject, the false teachers who have been visiting their congregation. In so doing, it touches on a then-emerging threat to the first-century church, a threat that scholars today call *Docetism*.

This threat originated with Gentiles and their Greek philosophical traditions. The term *Docetism* comes from a Greek word that means "to seem." The primary tenet of Docetism was that Christ's sufferings were only apparent; they only seemed real, but were not. As one writer sums it up, Docetism maintained, against Christian affirmations to the contrary, that Christ's existence was "mere semblance without any true reality."

We see the apostle John explicitly declare otherwise in 1 John 4:2, 3. He knew that if this teaching prevailed, then the entire basis for the Christian message would be lost. If Jesus did not suffer, then He could not have died. As a result, there would be no death to pay for sin (contrast Philippians 2:7, 8; Hebrews 2:14; etc.). Docetism transformed into the highly destructive heresy of Gnosticism in the second century AD.

I. Direct Your Hearts
(2 Thessalonians 3:1-5)

A. Praying for Deliverance (vv. 1-3)

1. Finally, brethren, pray for us, that the word of the Lord may have free course, and be glorified, even as it is with you.

Paul ends the final section of 2 Thessalonians by asking for prayer, a request he also made in the first letter (1 Thessalonians 5:25; compare Colossians 4:3). Paul saw prayer as a shared responsibility. He prayed for his friends (2 Thessalonians 1:11), and he does not hesitate to ask them to pray for him and his companions.

In this verse and the next, Paul mentions two specific areas in which he desires prayer. His first concerns *the word of the Lord*, meaning the preaching of the gospel. Paul wants his evangelistic efforts to *have free course*, as they had with the Thessalonians themselves. This is not to add to Paul's reputation, but for the purpose of glorification that might come to the gospel itself, and therefore to the Lord. This is the language of worship, and Paul sees his ministry and efforts in this light, bringing glory to God (see Galatians 1:22-24).

HOW TO SAY IT

apostasy	uh-*pahs*-tuh-see.
Colossians	Kuh-*losh*-unz.
Docetism	Doe-*set*-iz-um or Doe-*see*-tih-zum.
Ephesus	*Ef*-uh-sus.
Gnosticism	**Nahss**-tih-*sizz*-um or **Nahss**-tuh-*sih*-zum.
Judaizing	**Joo**-duh-*ize*-ing.
Thessalonians	*Thess*-uh-*lo*-nee-unz (*th* as in *thin*).
Thessalonica	*Thess*-uh-lo-**nye**-kuh (*th* as in *thin*).

What Do You Think?

In what ways can we be more effective in prayer for one another?

Digging Deeper

Which of the following texts convicts you most in that regard: Luke 21:36; 22:40; Romans 15:30-33; Philippians 1:9-11; 4:6; Colossians 4:12; James 5:16; 3 John 2? Why?

2. And that we may be delivered from unreasonable and wicked men: for all men have not faith.

Paul's second prayer request goes to the reason his first request needs God's help: Paul knows the nature of the opposition. He had experienced it firsthand in Thessalonica (see Acts 17:5).

3. But the Lord is faithful, who shall stablish you, and keep you from evil.

Paul moves quickly from unfaithful opponents to the rock of faithfulness, *the Lord.* Whereas the opponents bedevil Paul and the Thessalonian believers, the Lord can be counted on to *keep* the readers *from evil.* Paul is absent and must give over his worries to his *faithful* master for preserving the Thessalonians from those who would destroy their faith.

B. Acting with Confidence (vv. 4, 5)

4. And we have confidence in the Lord touching you, that ye both do and will do the things which we command you.

Paul bases his *confidence in the Lord,* but he also has confidence in the Thessalonians. God's preserving and empowering of their congregation will result in current and future obedience to the godly teachings of Paul. Even the most challenging of Paul's congregations engendered confidence in him (see 2 Corinthians 2:3).

What Do You Think?

What are some ways we can overcome pessimism with "confidence in the Lord"?

Digging Deeper

What guardrails can we put in place to ensure that confidence doesn't become arrogance?

5. And the Lord direct your hearts into the love of God, and into the patient waiting for Christ.

Paul ends this section with a return to one of the main topics in the Thessalonian letters: the return of *Christ.* Paul did not have time to teach the new Christians in Thessalonica everything they needed because of his brief tenure there. One thing that seems to have been distorted was his preaching that Christ would soon return. Some of the church members took this so literally that it caused problems within the congregation. Paul offers corrective teaching in this area in 1 Thessalonians 4 and 5 and in 2 Thessalonians 2. It is good to expect the return of our Lord any day, but we must also be willing to wait for Him and His timing.

In the meantime, the Thessalonians should give their attention to *the love of God.* Paul is encouraging their devotion to the Lord, but the context would lead us to understand this as also expressing their love by service to other people. We have plenty to do while we wait for Christ to come. May He find us deeply involved in works of compassion when He does.

II. Walk in Truth
(2 John 4-6)
A. Basis (vv. 4, 5)

4. I rejoiced greatly that I found of thy children walking in truth, as we have received a commandment from the Father.

The *children* John speaks of are the children of "the lady" to whom the book is addressed (2 John 1). Whether these are a woman's physical offspring or is a figurative reference to the members of the church, they are Christians. John is joyfully encouraged because these believers have continued to walk *in truth.* John measures this by their adherence to *a commandment,* one that has its origin with *the Father,* God himself.

❧ *"True" Truth* ❧

Western culture has been sliding for a long time down a precipitous slope away from a belief in "true" truth—the idea that, at the very least, a few things are absolutely true. To illustrate this shift in perspective, one late-night television comedian has popularized the term *truthiness*—the belief that something is true based on perception apart from evidence or facts—in his satirical news report. It has become common these days to hear people say, in the heat of an argument, "Well, that may be true for *you*, but that's not *my* truth!"

That idea was illustrated anew in the 2016 presidential election campaign. The candidates, their staffs, and various political pundits had a lot to say about "fake news." Some people found it entertaining, but I suspect most of us found the argument depressing. It seemed that each campaign really believed its "news" was *truer* than the "news" being quoted by the other side! The fact that both major candidates finished the race with unfavorable ratings above 50 percent may indicate how cynical Americans have become about the possibility of knowing whether *anyone* is telling the truth.

This attitude undercuts the basis on which we may build a moral society. It raises questions about whether the Bible is really true. And it certainly ends up casting unfounded doubt that the apostle John was saying anything meaningful when he told us that God wants us to be "walking in truth" if there is no "true" truth!　　　　　—C. R. B.

5. And now I beseech thee, lady, not as though I wrote a new commandment unto thee, but that which we had from the beginning, that we love one another.

This *commandment* to *love one another* is second only to the commandment to love God (Matthew 22:35-40). It is not a *new* teaching; believers have had this command *from the beginning* of their Christian walk. John does not make it complicated. This commandment was repeated by Jesus to John and the other disciples at the last supper (John 13:34, 35; compare 15:12). The apostle has made this commandment a cornerstone of his teaching ministry, repeating or referring to it six times in 1 John 3:11, 23; 4:7, 11, 12, 21. John refers to this as a new/old commandment (2:7, 8; see also Leviticus 19:18) in his day, and it is still a new/old commandment for us, over 1,900 years later.

What Do You Think?
In what ways can our church better demonstrate the commandment to "love one another?"
Digging Deeper
What will be your part in making this happen?

B. Imperative (v. 6)

6. And this is love, that we walk after his commandments. This is the commandment, That, as ye have heard from the beginning, ye should walk in it.

Jesus taught His disciples that keeping His commandments is an expression of *love* for Him (John 15:10). John narrows this to the single *commandment*, the old one that dates from Jesus—namely, to love one another. They have *heard* this teaching *from the beginning*, now meaning from the beginning of their relationship with John. He has always taught them to love each other. This command is not an advanced teaching, but the most basic teaching of all that undergirds the Christian life.

III. Reject the Deceivers
(2 John 7-11)

A. What They Do Not Confess (vv. 7, 8)

7a. For many deceivers are entered into the world, who confess not that Jesus Christ is come in the flesh.

The mutual love that is so primary for John is sorely tested by false teachers, the *many deceivers*. This is not a hypothetical situation. These false teachers have *entered into the world,* meaning they have their origin in the church (see 1 John 2:18, 19). This is the idea of apostasy—a type of heresy that implies leaving or deserting the true faith. Therefore, John has already warned his readers to walk in the truth, because their opponents do not trade in truth.

Instead of embracing truth, these false teachers deny that Jesus has *come in the flesh.* This is a denial of the humanity of Jesus, the heresy discussed in the Lesson Context of 2 John. Denying this central teaching of the faith (the incarnation)

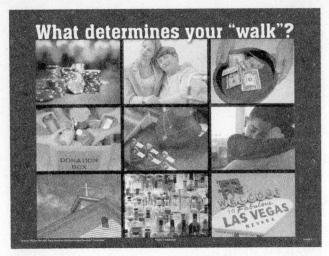

Visual for Lesson 6. *Start a discussion by pointing to each image in turn as you ask, "What does this one say about a person's 'walk'?"*

means the deceivers must be teaching a different type of salvation, because they cannot have the doctrine of the atoning death of Jesus (see 1 John 1:7; 2:2). John will not stand for this.

7b. This is a deceiver and an antichrist.

Although the term *antichrist* is often associated with an evil personage who is to appear at the end of all things, this is not its primary meaning here. The term *antichrist* in English seems to mean "one who is against Christ," but there is more to it in the original language. The word *anti* in Greek has the sense of "substitute" or "alternate" (example: Luke 11:11, where Greek *anti* is translated "for" in the sense of "instead"). So the idea is closer to "false Christ." John's idea of antichrist in this verse is something or someone in his own day who is threatening the church (see 1 John 4:3).

The "spirit of antichrist" (again, 1 John 4:3) is not confined to a single person (2:18). John seems to dub these deceivers interchangeably as "false prophets" (4:1). Jesus warned against such counterfeits (Mark 13:22). False teaching does not arise spontaneously; it comes from false teachers who have something to gain by their deception.

❧ THE LINE WE MUST NOT CROSS ❧

Christians recently observed the 500th anniversary of the Reformation. October 31, 1517, is widely held to be the day that Martin Luther nailed his *Ninety-five Theses* to the door of a church in Germany, making him a heretic in the eyes of many. His understanding of the biblical teaching on justification by faith made him unorthodox by Roman Catholic standards. Luther was a Catholic monk, but his study of the Bible had convinced him that the church had strayed from biblical truth. Luther's actions resulted in him being considered a deceiver.

The movement Luther set in motion now moves in the opposite direction in certain quarters. Recent decades have seen the creation of several denominational unions, regardless of sometimes major doctrinal differences. In some ways, this reflects culture's scorn for honest disagreement even when the issue is significant.

Yet we are still left with the apostle John's warning that we must reject deceivers. Today's lesson text places special emphasis on our teaching truth. If we stray from the Bible's teaching regarding the person and work of Christ, we have crossed a line that separates us from God's truth. Do you know where that line is?   —C. R. B.

8. Look to yourselves, that we lose not those things which we have wrought, but that we receive a full reward.

John gives a warning to the readers, but not a dire prediction. Rather, it is an encouragement for them to stay the course and finish well (compare 2 Timothy 4:7). The idea of *reward* is addressed in Matthew 10:42; 1 Corinthians 3:8; and Hebrews 10:35, but not in a sense of earning salvation by works. The idea is more in line with Luke 19:16-19 and 1 Corinthians 3:10-15. John sees his readers as partners in ministry, coworkers who are building the church through hard work. They are to take care lest they end up with less than what they or God expect.

B. What They Do Not Have (vv. 9-11)

9. Whosoever transgresseth, and abideth not in the doctrine of Christ, hath not God. He that abideth in the doctrine of Christ, he hath both the Father and the Son.

The word *transgresseth* here has the sense of "going too far" rather than the traditional sense of "sin." In warning against going too far *in the doctrine of Christ,* John may be indicating that the false teachers present their doctrines as new and better, the next step in the evolution of the Christian message. John demands that his people abide in the doctrine of Christ to which they have been faithful in the past. This, most specifically, is the teaching about the nature of Christ—His full humanity and death for our sins.

To go beyond this doctrine is to abandon the central promise of Christianity: forgiveness and reconciliation with God through the work of Christ. The ones who hold fast to the doctrines of incarnation and atonement retain their relationship with *the Father* and His *Son*, their Savior.

> ### What Do You Think?
> What are some ways our church can "contend for the faith" (Jude 3) without destroying the unity of the church in the process?
> ### Digging Deeper
> How will you determine which truths are to be contended for at the risk of offense or disunity (compare Matthew 15:10-14) and which are not (compare Matthew 17:24-27)?

10, 11. If there come any unto you, and bring not this doctrine, receive him not into your house, neither bid him God speed: for he that biddeth him God speed is partaker of his evil deeds.

John ends his discussion of false teachers with a strong command, one that almost seems a contradiction with his expectation that the readers "walk in love" and "love one another." They are not to allow the teacher who denies the incarnation even to enter one's *house*. There is likely a double sense to this in that a "house" is not only a personal home but also the location of a church. House churches are likely the norm in John's day. The leaders reading this letter are to offer no forum for this false teaching. To refute heresy is the responsibility of the elders of a church (see Titus 1:9).

This directive to deny access to teachers of falsehoods is accompanied by two specific qualifications. First, the readers should not bid *God speed*—the traditional friendly and polite greeting for John's people—to such teachers. This is not an invitation to be rude, but rather is a warning to extend no encouragement, food, or shelter to such teachers lest impressionable members of the church receive a mixed message about the danger the false teachers pose. Second, John warns that those who disregard the warning become, in effect, partners with the false teachers.

This is why it is so important, in any church, to have leaders who are trained in doctrine. They are the gatekeepers of the congregation. They cannot ignore this responsibility.

> ### What Do You Think?
> If a teacher of false doctrine knocked on your door tomorrow, what level of hospitality would you offer, if any, for the purpose of engaging in dialogue?
> ### Digging Deeper
> Does your decision depend on the nature of the false doctrine? Why, or why not? (Possible resources: Romans 12:13; 1 Corinthians 5:9-11; Hebrews 13:2.)

Conclusion

A. Doctrine and Love

There will always be those in the church who are looking for innovations and modifications to Bible doctrines that make them uncomfortable. We sometimes must walk a tightrope between loving tolerance for such people and rigid intolerance of their false teaching. As difficult as that may be, church leaders cannot neglect their responsibilities in this regard. When leaders allow the "love one another" mandate to suppress their duty to reject dangerous false teaching, they are not acting in love for church members as a whole—members who need the guidance of mature Christian leaders in their congregation.

B. Prayer

Lord, may we be motivated by love, not hate. May we love truth and reject falsehood. We pray this in the name of Jesus, who died for our sins. Amen.

C. Thought to Remember

Loving Jesus and loving truth go together.

INVOLVEMENT LEARNING

Enhance your lesson with KJV Bible Student *(from your curriculum supplier) and the reproducible activity page (at www.standardlesson.com or in the back of the* KJV Standard Lesson Commentary Deluxe Edition*).*

Into the Lesson

Divide your class into two teams and say, "Some of the most memorable characters in our favorite movies are the villains. Your teams will compete to see who can best identify the movies in which these villains appeared." Ask each team to choose a spokesperson (or you can announce a rotation format so each person has an opportunity to answer without consulting team members). Decide randomly which team will go first. Villains: 1–Norman Bates (*Psycho*); 2–The Joker (*Batman*); 3–Darth Vader (*Star Wars*); 4–Wicked Witch of the West (*Wizard of Oz*); 5–Cruella de Vil (*101 Dalmatians*).

Alternative. Distribute copies of the "Can You Spot a Liar?" activity from the reproducible page, which you can download. Give students no more than one minute to work individually, then discuss results as a class.

After either activity say, "Alfred Hitchcock said, 'The more successful the villain, the more successful the picture.' While that may be true for movies, encounters with ungodly people in real life can be very painful. Both Paul and John had experience with wicked, deceiving people, and they have words of wisdom for us on how to handle them."

Into the Word

Assign half of the class to work on 2 Thessalonians 3:1-5 (written by the apostle Paul) and the other half to examine 2 John 4-11 (written by the apostle John). If your class is large, break the halves into groups of three or four. Distribute copies of the part of the Lesson Context dealing with Judaizers to those assigned 2 Thessalonians; distribute the part dealing with Docetism to those assigned 2 John. Also give the 2 John groups copies of the commentary on both halves of verse 7. Further, distribute handouts (you prepare) that asks groups to answer the following interview questions for either Paul or John, depending on text assigned.

Paul's Interview: 1–Why were you able to stay only three weeks in Thessalonica? (See Acts 17:1-10.) 2–What are the characteristics of the "wicked" Judaizers you have encountered? 3–Why did you ask the Thessalonian Christians to pray for you? 4–What is your prayer for the Christians there?

John's Interview: 1–Why is love so important? 2–What teaching by the Docetic deceivers is especially harmful to the church? 3–What do you mean by the term *antichrist*? 4–Why is it so important for Christians not to have anything to do with false teachers?

With yourself as the interviewer, rotate your questions among the groups. Have spokespersons answer as they think Paul and John would respond. Express appreciation to your class for their willingness to research their answers.

Into Life

Say, "False teaching in the first-century church by Judaizers was causing problems for Gentile believers who were falsely told that they had to obey the law to be saved. In later years, the Gnostics caused trouble for churches by teaching that Jesus wasn't human, thereby diminishing or eliminating the importance of the incarnation and resurrection. Each era of church life has problems with false teachers. I'm going to write some topics on the board. You tell me what they might have to do with false teaching."

Write the following, pausing to discuss each before writing the next: 1–Health and Wealth Preaching; 2–Legalism; 3–Eastern Religion Practices. For each one ask, "How would you react to the false aspects of this teaching were someone to present it to you personally?"

Option. Distribute copies of the "What's Love Got to Do with It?" activity from the reproducible page. This can be either an exercise for small groups or for the class as a whole.

SUBMIT TO GOD

DEVOTIONAL READING: Proverbs 3:27-35
BACKGROUND SCRIPTURE: James 4:1-10

JAMES 4:1-10

1 From whence come wars and fightings among you? come they not hence, even of your lusts that war in your members?

2 Ye lust, and have not: ye kill, and desire to have, and cannot obtain: ye fight and war, yet ye have not, because ye ask not.

3 Ye ask, and receive not, because ye ask amiss, that ye may consume it upon your lusts.

4 Ye adulterers and adulteresses, know ye not that the friendship of the world is enmity with God? whosoever therefore will be a friend of the world is the enemy of God.

5 Do ye think that the scripture saith in vain, The spirit that dwelleth in us lusteth to envy?

6 But he giveth more grace. Wherefore he saith, God resisteth the proud, but giveth grace unto the humble.

7 Submit yourselves therefore to God. Resist the devil, and he will flee from you.

8 Draw nigh to God, and he will draw nigh to you. Cleanse your hands, ye sinners; and purify your hearts, ye double minded.

9 Be afflicted, and mourn, and weep: let your laughter be turned to mourning, and your joy to heaviness.

10 Humble yourselves in the sight of the Lord, and he shall lift you up.

KEY VERSE

Draw nigh to God, and he will draw nigh to you. Cleanse your hands, ye sinners; and purify your hearts, ye double minded. —**James 4:8**

OUR LOVE FOR GOD

Unit II: Loving God by Trusting Christ

LESSONS 6–10

LESSON AIMS

After participating in this lesson, each learner will be able to:

1. Summarize James's view on pride.

2. Explain why pride and humility are opposite realities.

3. Pray a prayer of humility and surrender that reflects his or her relationship with God.

LESSON OUTLINE

Introduction

A. Pride and Arrogance

We are told that pride is an essential element to making things better. We should have school pride, community pride, and personal pride.

In the Bible, however, pride is often seen as a corrosive personality trait, something to be avoided. What the Bible means by pride (when seen negatively) is similar to boastful arrogance (James 4:16). It can also be likened to vanity or vainglory, a distorted sense of one's value and importance in the world (Philippians 2:3). Pride can even be related to envy, covetousness, or greed —the belief that your desires are more important than those of others (Romans 1:29).

Those to whom James wrote his letter apparently had problems with pride; they lacked humility. Many Christians and churches today suffer the same malady, so James's words are timely and vital to us.

B. Lesson Context

There are at least four and possibly five men by the name of James in the New Testament. The one who wrote the book of the New Testament that bears his name was the brother of Jesus, the son of Mary and Joseph (Matthew 13:55; Mark 6:3).

James was not a disciple of Jesus during His ministry (John 7:5), but after the resurrection he became a believer (Acts 1:14) and a leader in the Jerusalem church (Acts 15:13; Galatians 1:19). Yet James humbly describes himself as a "servant of God" (James 1:1), seemingly reluctant to use his family credentials.

We do not know when the letter of James was written. The Jewish historian Josephus (AD 37–100) notes his death about AD 62 at the hands of Jewish opponents in Jerusalem. This makes it likely the book was written sometime in the AD 50s, thus reflecting an early stage in the history of the first-century church.

The recipients of the letter are evidently Jewish believers, as indicated by the reference to the scattered "twelve tribes" (James 1:1). Perhaps they were members of the original church in Jerusalem who were forced to flee due to the persecution spawned by Stephen's martyrdom and thus were no longer centered in one location (Acts 11:19). It would be natural for James, were he their former spiritual leader, to encourage them in the midst of their trials (James 1:2-4, 12; 5:7-11).

James held very high expectations for his readers. He specifically wanted them to tone down the rivalries in their communities, some of which involved conflicts between rich and poor (James 2:5-7). This fits well with the theme of humility to which James turns in chapter 4.

I. War with Covetousness
(James 4:1-3)
A. The Battle Within (vv. 1, 2a)

1. From whence come wars and fightings among you? come they not hence, even of your lusts that war in your members?

James begins this section with tough language, noting the internal disputes within his addressees' fellowships. There are *wars and fightings*. The first term implies strong adversarial relationships, a word used more often in a military sense to signify battles between armies. The second term has the sense of verbal spats, nasty exchanges between rivals (compare Titus 3:9).

James points to the root cause of these troubles: *your lusts that war in your members*. He is not referring to the membership of the church, but the parts ("members") of the human body. This battle originates internally, inside the hearts of the combatants. Church fights often result from personal, individual issues, from the strong-willed individual who has selfish motives and tolerates no other opinions. Rather than forbid fighting, James goes after the root causes behind these struggles.

2a. Ye lust, and have not: ye kill, and desire to have, and cannot obtain.

The evil, lustful desires of some adversaries are so strong that their outcome might be murder, although the use of *kill* may be figurative for hate (compare Matthew 5:21, 22; 1 John 3:15). Whether the animosity among believers has escalated to the point of murder, which is unlikely, James's warning is on target. This is a dangerous and regrettable situation.

B. The Battle of Prayer (vv. 2b, 3)

2b, 3. Ye fight and war, yet ye have not, because ye ask not. Ye ask, and receive not, because ye ask amiss, that ye may consume it upon your lusts.

James shifts his focus from the contentious and destructive desires of the adversaries to another aspect of the problem: lack of prayer. The readers' personal rivalries are not getting them what they want. So they fight over a pie without enough pieces to satisfy everyone. We can interpret this to mean that envy and greed are the root problem. This might indicate quarrels over the funds of the congregation. Such battles can be the nastiest of all church fights.

James teaches them that the underlying problem is to be found in their prayer practices. Their prayer requests are *amiss*, reflecting envy and jealousy. Their requests in prayer are for things that they can consume to satisfy their *lusts*.

God will not honor prayers made from evil desires or selfish motives. To pray correctly, effectively, means the selfishness that is fueling the fighting must be quelled. Aligning prayers with the will of God will remove the motives tearing apart their community.

> *What Do You Think?*
> What can you do to make your prayers more effective?
> *Digging Deeper*
> In what ways, if any, do Jeremiah 7:16; 11:14; 14:11; and 1 John 5:16b help inform your answer?

II. War with Pride
(James 4:4-6)
A. Friends with the World (v. 4)

4. Ye adulterers and adulteresses, know ye not that the friendship of the world is enmity with God? whosoever therefore will be a friend of the world is the enemy of God.

James moves from conflict caused by envy to another problem: pride. Just as we should not be at war with fellow church members, we must be at war with the pride in our own souls.

James begins this line of thought by introducing a stark choice: his readers must choose between *friendship* with the things *of the world* and friendship with God. They cannot have both. If they choose the world, they choose to be *the enemy of God*.

Is James calling for a radical, thoroughgoing purge of everything "worldly" from our lives? Should we withdraw into separate communities so that we have no worldly temptations to entice us? Some believers have understood the Christian life to be a call for such separation, but this does not seem to be James's intention.

James begins this verse with an epitaph for those who have fallen into conflict: they are *adulterers and adulteresses*. Although it is possible that the churches James addressed were wracked with sexual immorality, this does not seem to be the problem (although see James 2:11). Instead, James uses "adultery" in a way common for the prophets of the Old Testament. They often used adultery as a metaphor for unfaithful Israel, the bride of the Lord (see Hosea 1:2). For James, to choose the world over God is to commit spiritual adultery.

This verse is subject to misuse and misinterpretation. Christians will find it difficult to win the world for Christ if they withdraw from the world completely. Community participation and having non-Christian friends and neighbors is not spiritual adultery. The danger lies in allowing one's love for God to be eclipsed by one's love for the world. Our loyalty and commitment must be to God and to Him alone.

B. Grace for the Humble (vv. 5, 6)

5a. Do ye think that the scripture saith in vain.

James loves the Word of God and is a master of using it to add context and authority to his teaching. First, he asks the readers if they think *the scripture* speaks *in vain*. No faithful Christian of

Jewish descent would doubt the efficacy of Scripture, for it speaks with the power of God behind it (Isaiah 55:10, 11; compare John 10:35).

5b. The spirit that dwelleth in us lusteth to envy?

It is unclear what Scripture James now refers to. Some students see general references to Genesis 2:7; Exodus 20:5; and/or Proverbs 14:30. At any rate, James asks if the readers think *the spirit* God has caused to dwell within them is naturally prone *to envy*. Was God negligent or inept in creating us? As with the first question, the answer is a clear no. God did not make men and women to be driven by envy, thereby destroying the unity of the church.

6. But he giveth more grace. Wherefore he saith, God resisteth the proud, but giveth grace unto the humble.

James answers the second question and then provides a Scripture quotation. The possibility of God's misbegotten making of us as designed to be controlled by envy is countered by James's assertion that God has given us *grace*. We are vessels of grace, not envy. Our envy and pride issues do not have their source with the Lord. Our problem cannot be pinned on God, for He has shown more than enough grace and mercy to us to make our envy obsessions seem out of place.

James's choice for Scripture, Proverbs 3:34, is well known to his readers (compare 1 Peter 5:5). God's resistance to pride and prideful people is a theme in Jewish teaching. Human pride kindles the wrath of God (see 2 Chronicles 32:24-26; Job 40:11). Pride is self-exalting, but only the Lord is to be exalted (Isaiah 2:17).

The flip side of the coin is that while God brings down *the proud*, He does not ignore *the humble*. Those who lack the pride that God abhors will be given the sustaining grace of the Lord to get them through their difficult circumstances.

Thus does James condemn the most worldly thing of all: pride. Pride is warped self-love. Pride is a type of self-worship, allowing our personal selves to become idols. This is every bit as much spiritual adultery as the love of money or power. God does not call us to hate ourselves, but our sense of self-worth has limits.

HOW TO SAY IT

epitaph	*eh*-puh-*taf.*
Hosea	Ho-*zay*-uh.
Josephus	Jo-*see*-fus.

Throughout history, the church has seen numerous movements intended to help its members avoid the allure of the world. Some of these movements become cultish as they begin controlling their adherents' lives in terms of dictating employment, living arrangements, friendships, etc.

I have had friends who became part of such groups. In every case, the group started with good intentions: a desire to provide more fellowship, better (or more relevant) biblical teaching, and an escape from prior experiences in churches that were lacking in Christian love and evangelistic spirit. In each case, I observed some members exhibiting what seemed to be inappropriately high levels of satisfaction with how they were "doing church" compared with the fellowships from which they came. From what James says, we might even question whether their satisfaction bordered on pride.

How do we escape from the insidious, ever-tightening grip of pride when we are trying so hard to follow the Lord? As James reminds us, we can escape pride only by recognizing we are saved by God's grace. We are not saved by how much better we are than others at figuring out how to live the Christian life. See also Ephesians 2:8, 9.

—C. R. B.

> **What Do You Think?**
> How can we successfully control our pride without losing self-confidence in the process?
> **Digging Deeper**
> How do 2 Corinthians 7:4; 8:24; and Galatians 6:3, 4 influence your attitude about the type of pride you may have?

III. War with the Devil
(JAMES 4:7-10)
A. Submission to God (vv. 7, 8)
7a. Submit yourselves therefore to God.

James moves into a writing style that has often drawn comparisons with the book of Proverbs: short, pithy statements that stand well on their own.

He begins with a command: *Submit . . . to God.* This is the opposite of pride. Pride is self-exalting. Submission is self-lowering, self-yielding, self-denying. The word James employs has a military background, used to describe the submission of a soldier to his superior officer. It means you take orders from someone higher, and that when you receive an order, you obey it.

> **What Do You Think?**
> Considering Jesus' submission in Luke 22:42, what plan can you make to overcome the conflict between pride and submission?
> **Digging Deeper**
> What role should prayer play in overcoming this conflict?

7b. Resist the devil, and he will flee from you.

The other side of our submission to God is our resistance to *the devil.* There is another who seeks to be our master, our partner in spiritual adultery. James again uses the word *resist,* which was used in the previous verse to characterize God's actions toward the proud. Here it is the opposite of *submit.* Resistance to the devil is refusal to submit to his temptations or his influence.

This command comes with a promise. The devil can be a persistent adversary, but James promises that if we resist him, he will abandon us as a target. We must remember that while the devil is a powerful spiritual being, he is not all-powerful or in any way equal to God. As a created being, his power and influence are limited and must be employed strategically. When we keep resisting the devil, he will redeploy his evil assets to a more productive target.

> **What Do You Think?**
> What strategies you can recommend to resist the devil?
> **Digging Deeper**
> In that regard, which techniques of Jesus' resistance of the devil in Matthew 4:1-11 and Luke 4:1-13 serve as a model for you? In what ways does it not? Why?

8. Draw nigh to God, and he will draw nigh to you. Cleanse your hands, ye sinners; and purify your hearts, ye double minded.

The previous verse tells us that our lives are best lived when we are in submission to God and resist the devil. James returns to our relationship with the Lord, refining his command to submit and offering a promise for those who do so. If we *draw nigh to God,* James promises us that God will meet us. We are reminded of Jesus' words, "Seek, and ye shall find" (Matthew 7:7). God is already near to us and meets us when we seek Him (see Lamentations 3:57).

This is the opposite of the devil, who flees when we resist him. God will never flee, even if we neglect our relationship with Him.

How do we draw near to the Lord? The rest of the verse gives us these directives: we must have deeds that honor God (clean *hands*), and we must have the proper commitment to Him (pure *hearts*). These qualities define the proper worshipper of the Lord.

In Psalm 24:3, 4, the clean hands and pure heart are associated with the one who refuses to worship idols, akin to the resisting of Satan for James. Worship is to focus on God and no other. There can be no double-minded approach to worship. We must worship "in spirit and in truth" (John 4:23, 24).

❧ CLEAN HANDS ❧

I was recently in a doctor's consultation room in which a sign was prominently displayed regarding how to wash hands. It read something like this:

1. Wet hands with water
2. Apply enough soap to cover hands
3. Rub hands palm-to-palm
4. Rub hands on top of each other, interlacing fingers
5. Rub palm-to-palm with fingers interlaced
6. Interlock fingers
7. Rub with back of fingers in opposing palms
8. Twist thumbs with opposing fingers
9. Rub palms in a circle with opposing fingers
10. Rinse hands
11. Dry hands with a single-use towel
12. Use towel to turn off faucet

Whew! Aren't you glad Mom didn't go into that much detail? The medical profession treats cleanliness seriously (as the sign in the doctor's office indicates), especially in flu season. Doesn't it make even more sense to be serious about cleansing ourselves spiritually?

Given the moral pollution of our world, how should we go about getting the clean hands of which James writes? —C. R. B.

B. Lifting by God (vv. 9, 10)

9, 10a. Be afflicted, and mourn, and weep: let your laughter be turned to mourning, and your joy to heaviness. Humble yourselves in the sight of the Lord.

James presents this cleansing of the heart in terms associated with repentance. When we repent, we do not laugh and rejoice. We have a deep sorrow that brings *mourning* and a heavy heart. Times of repentance are not celebrations. They are funerals in which we put our pride to death, smother our envy, and swallow our stubbornness. To jest about sin or wink at wickedness is contrary to any sense of repentance. This is a root problem among James's readers. They have become comfortable with sin among their members and have failed to repent.

Repentance is related to self-humbling. When we repent, we do not justify our wrongs, but admit them. Admission of wrongdoing is never easy, and some people seem nearly incapable of this simple act, preferring denial or excuses instead. We should notice that James is not talking about being humbled by other people or unfortunate events. He advises us to *humble* ourselves, to lose our pride and arrogance.

> **What Do You Think?**
> What practices can you adopt to ensure you don't become comfortable with sin?
> *Digging Deeper*
> Considering Matthew 7:1-3, how can a church encourage its members to live godly lives without such encouragement becoming legalistic?

10b. And he shall lift you up.

That command comes with a promise too. Our self-humbling will not go unnoticed by God. He will *lift us up*. This has been connected by some to events in our lives, as if to say, "If you deny yourself, God will reward you with happiness, material blessings, and a better position in life." This may be, but it is not what James intends here. The "lifting up" is to rescue our souls from the mourning and weeping we have entered as an act of repentance.

When we truly repent, God lifts our hearts by forgiving us and restoring our joy (Psalm 51:12). We do not humble ourselves to be rewarded, but our humility will be blessed by the Lord—an oft-repeated principle in the Bible (Matthew 23:12; Luke 14:11; 1 Peter 5:6).

Selfish pride and arrogance risk everything if they characterize our relationship with God. Pride of comparison falls flat when applied to us versus the Lord. We can never compete with the one who created the universe. The Bible teaches that God's intolerance for human pride is consistent and unyielding (see Proverbs 8:13; Isaiah 13:11). Only by laying aside our arrogance are we fully able to be lifted up by the Lord.

Conclusion

A. Proudly Humble

Can you imagine a humility contest in your church? If we are told to practice humility, shouldn't we honor the humblest among us? This could include nominations and campaign-style speeches where candidates tout their humility credentials to garner votes from the congregation. Then we could be proud of our humbleness. We could crown the king and queen of humility, the humblest people in our church!

This is ridiculous, of course. Humility and pride are strange bedfellows indeed. Humility, by its nature, is a private act, a personal practice. Drawing attention to our humility is like a peacock strutting after its tail feathers have been plucked.

How can we practice humility? Here are some suggestions. First, meditate on the greatness of God. Realizing the vast expanse of God's creation—its beauty and intricate design—should make you feel very small by comparison.

Visual for Lesson 7. *Start a discussion by pointing to any two items and asking how they relate to each other. Repeat as appropriate for your class.*

Second, remember the undeserved love God has lavished upon you. Paul said that while we were still sinners, enemies of God, Christ died for us (Romans 5:6-11). Our love is almost always tinged with selfishness, but God's love never is. His great love outshines anything we can claim (see Ephesians 2:4, 5).

Third, let us find ways to serve that are unrecognized. I recently helped serve a meal at a homeless shelter. I made some new friends and received a hearty "Thank you," but I wasn't paid or otherwise rewarded. The people I served were often unresponsive and ungrateful, even greedy. I stayed to help clean the kitchen, and that was nasty work. I got a good dose of humility, remembering that there are those who do these jobs every day.

God is great. God is loving. I serve God by serving others. These are lessons of humility that will serve us well. May we lay down our crowns, our claims to greatness—and pick up our crosses, our submission to God's will, so that God may lift us up in His perfect timing.

B. Prayer

Lord God, may we humble ourselves with sincere love for You. Knock the pride out of us. Let us love others without guile. We pray in the name of the one who humbled himself on the cross. Amen.

C. Thought to Remember

Our job is humility. God's job is lifting us up.

INVOLVEMENT LEARNING

Enhance your lesson with KJV Bible Student (from your curriculum supplier) and the reproducible activity page (at www.standardlesson.com or in the back of the KJV Standard Lesson Commentary Deluxe Edition).

Into the Lesson

Write the following on the board:

> *It doesn't matter what people think or do,
> as long as it doesn't hurt anyone else.*

Ask learners why they agree or disagree with this statement; jot responses on the board. Explore whether it is possible to know for certain if the statement is true. Ask learners to describe outcomes on occasions when they were personally harmed by someone else's sense of freedom.

Now write this on the board:

> *"Humility is the first of virtues—for other people."*
> —*Oliver Wendell Holmes, Jr. (1841–1935)*

Ask, "In what way, if any, is this second statement a good gauge of pride and humility?" List suggestions on the board. Explore relationships learners see between the two statements. Say, "Let's see what James tells us about these issues."

Into the Word

Read James 4:1-10 aloud. Then divide the class into three groups; designate one as *Wrong Desires,* another as *Wrong Friendships,* and another as *Right Solutions.* Give each group one or more handouts (you prepare) of the below, according to designation. (Larger classes can form more groups with duplicate designations.)

Wrong Desires Group(s): Read James 4:1-3. 1– What does the text say about the source of disagreements? 2–In what ways do people try to achieve their desires? 3–What is lacking in the solutions people choose?

Wrong Friendships Group(s): Read James 4:4-6. 1–What to James must be *either/or,* not *both/and?* 2–Why is the analogy to adultery appropriate for what James has to say? 3–How does God's response differ to the proud and to the humble?

Right Solutions Group(s): Read James 4:7-10. 1– What actions are we to take? 2–What will be the results of those actions? 3–What characterizes the humble person?

When the groups have completed their questions, interrelate their summations in whole-class discussion. Pose one or more of the following questions at appropriate points:

1–Is it possible to please ourselves without affecting others? Why, or why not?

2–What blinds people to the devastating pitfalls of exalting self and selfish desires?

3–How do we rid ourselves of prideful hearts? (Expect students to give the answer James does: via humility, which includes contriteness and sorrow for sins.)

4–What Bible examples can you give of those who humbled themselves? What was the result? (Possible responses include Pharaoh [temporarily], Exodus 10:16-20; Ahab, 1 Kings 21:27-29; Josiah, 2 Kings 22:11-20; and the king of Nineveh, Jonah 3:6-10.)

Option. Take the discussion of question 4 deeper by using the "Prideful Bible Characters" activity from the reproducible page, which you can download. Assign one Bible character to each group, pair, or individual learner to summarize for the class as a whole.

Into Life

Present the following case study.

Sharing was mandatory in Mark's family while growing up. So Mark grudgingly shared his prized scuba-diving equipment with his older brother. One day the brother sold the equipment and kept the money. The resulting estrangement is now in its third decade. Convinced he is "in the right," Mark refuses to take any first step toward reconciliation.

Pose this question for whole-class discussion: What role is pride playing in this situation?

Option. Use the "Prideful Heart vs. Humble Heart" activity from the reproducible page as a closed Bible post-test.

Rejoice in All Circumstances

DEVOTIONAL READING: 1 Peter 4:12-19
BACKGROUND SCRIPTURE: Philippians 1:12-21

PHILIPPIANS 1:12-21

12 But I would ye should understand, brethren, that the things which happened unto me have fallen out rather unto the furtherance of the gospel;

13 So that my bonds in Christ are manifest in all the palace, and in all other places;

14 And many of the brethren in the Lord, waxing confident by my bonds, are much more bold to speak the word without fear.

15 Some indeed preach Christ even of envy and strife; and some also of good will:

16 The one preach Christ of contention, not sincerely, supposing to add affliction to my bonds:

17 But the other of love, knowing that I am set for the defence of the gospel.

18 What then? notwithstanding, every way, whether in pretence, or in truth, Christ is preached; and I therein do rejoice, yea, and will rejoice.

19 For I know that this shall turn to my salvation through your prayer, and the supply of the Spirit of Jesus Christ,

20 According to my earnest expectation and my hope, that in nothing I shall be ashamed, but that with all boldness, as always, so now also Christ shall be magnified in my body, whether it be by life, or by death.

21 For to me to live is Christ, and to die is gain.

KEY VERSE

I would ye should understand, brethren, that the things which happened unto me have fallen out rather unto the furtherance of the gospel. —**Philippians 1:12**

Our Love for God

Unit II: Loving God by Trusting Christ

LESSONS 6–10

LESSON AIMS

After participating in this lesson, each learner will be able to:

1. Recall the difficult circumstances in which Paul expressed his joy in Christ to the Philippian church.

2. Explain how the gospel produces persistent joy even in difficult circumstances.

3. Create a plan for expressing persistent joy in Christ through one's present circumstances.

LESSON OUTLINE

Introduction

A. Observation of Persistent Joy

Why do some people respond to hardship differently than others? That question drove Francis Collins, former head of the Human Genome Project and later director of the National Institutes of Health, to look for an answer.

Collins was in his residency as a physician when he realized how differently his patients responded to devastating illnesses. Some seemed more resilient under the stress of pain and with the knowledge that their illnesses were terminal. In time, Collins realized that many of the resilient patients were Christians with deep personal faith. He began investigating Christianity and eventually came to faith himself.

Our text is one of the great expressions of Christian faith that is resilient in the worst of conditions.

B. Lesson Context

Paul's letter to the Philippians was written to Christians in Philippi, a city in Macedonia (northern Greece). Paul founded the church there during his second missionary journey (Acts 16:11-40). Philippi was a well-established, prosperous city on a major Roman road, the Via Egnatia, which connected the east and west coasts of the Grecian peninsula.

Philippi had a rich history, of which its inhabitants were proud. In 42 BC, war between factions of the Roman ruling classes came to an end with a battle fought near Philippi. The victors rewarded their soldiers by granting them nearby lands, establishing Philippi as a Roman colony.

Paul wrote this letter while a prisoner (Philippians 1:7, 12-14). Though some scholars have suggested other possible places and times in Paul's life, it remains most likely that Paul wrote Philippians while under house arrest in Rome (Acts 28:16-31), awaiting trial before Nero. This was during Paul's first Roman imprisonment of AD 61–63, with another following in AD 67.

For the Philippian Christians, those circumstances likely prompted a crisis of faith. Accustomed to taking pride in all things Roman and to looking up to Paul, God's apostle, they had to come to terms with their hero's imprisonment at the hands of Rome.

But the church had problems in addition to this crisis. Conflict and rivalry had begun to threaten the church's unity. Paul mentions by name two who were in conflict (Philippians 4:2, 3). But the letter's contents suggest this was an example of a wider problem.

I. Gospel Advanced
(Philippians 1:12-14)
A. Unexpected Result (v. 12)

12. But I would ye should understand, brethren, that the things which happened unto me have fallen out rather unto the furtherance of the gospel.

Reports of Paul's imprisonment doubtless produce dismay among the Christians in Philippi and elsewhere who have learned of Jesus from Paul. Has God abandoned Paul? Has Paul been unfaithful to God? Or is Paul's gospel false, his God no god at all, and Paul an imposter?

Paul's answer is more than just a face-saving strategy. It is more than just making the best of a bad circumstance or looking for the silver lining in a dark cloud. Paul interprets his circumstances according to *the gospel* of Jesus. As God brought His salvation to the world in the suffering and death of Jesus, so now He extends His salvation into the world through the suffering of Paul. The good news of God goes forward by the same means that it came into existence: by faithful, lowly, self-sacrifice for others.

What Do You Think?
> What are some ways our church can better serve leaders who labor under various kinds of restrictions and hindrances?
> *Digging Deeper*
> How will it make a difference, if at all, if those restrictions and hindrances are self-inflicted?

B. Unexpected Places (v. 13)

13. So that my bonds in Christ are manifest in all the palace, and in all other places.

Paul could already point to tangible expressions of the gospel's advance. As a prisoner of the Roman emperor, Paul was guarded day and night by members of the Praetorian Guard, an elite military unit entrusted with the safety of the emperor and other high imperial officials. These highly trained, loyal soldiers were a potent expression of Rome's power and prestige. This was the last place one would expect the gospel of Jesus, the story of a man whom Rome crucified as a rebel, to spread.

Yet this was the very result of Paul's imprisonment. As the Roman centurion at the cross confessed Jesus' divine supremacy (Mark 15:39), so now Rome's most celebrated soldiery hear the same declaration from a lowly prisoner in their custody. For Christians, such a circumstance should not be an occasion of despair but a reinforcement of joy.

It is interesting that Paul says his *bonds* are known throughout *the palace*. He thereby emphasizes that the message of Christ is being made known through the life of the messenger. Paul's captivity reflects Jesus' own lowliness in arrest, trial, and death. For Paul, the messenger and the message are inseparable.

What Do You Think?
> Under what circumstances should we draw attention to our restrictions vs. downplaying or keeping quiet about them? Why?
> *Digging Deeper*
> How will your answer change, if at all, with the level of threat that is present?

C. Unexpected Means (v. 14)

14. And many of the brethren in the Lord, waxing confident by my bonds, are much more bold to speak the word without fear.

Paul explains how his testimony has affected other believers (*brethren in the Lord*) in Rome. Once fearful, they are now *much more bold to speak the word* of God despite dangers and opposition. Paul's courage renews their own, as they rediscover what it means to follow the Christ who suffered on their behalf. As Paul's *bonds* have been the means of spreading God's message to the imperial guards, so has the gospel been unbound among the Christians of Rome.

My late wife, Pat, contracted poliomyelitis when she was 11 years old. It happened during one of the last major epidemics before the Salk vaccine was developed. As a result of the disease, her weakened back became a source of severe chronic pain.

She struggled for decades as doctors prescribed various therapies and medications, but no cure ever came. Then came post-polio syndrome, which never relented. However, Pat's faith in Christ proved to be her anchor, giving her a strength of spirit many people could not comprehend.

Pat eventually died of colorectal cancer. During her decline, a score of dedicated Christian "lady-sitters" (as Pat called them) stayed with her while I was at work. Perhaps the most interesting result of these saints' gift of grace was their response to their visits with Pat. I couldn't count the times they told me, with tears of joy on their faces, "I came here to bless Pat with my presence, but she blessed me with hers instead!"

God's gifts of grace sometimes come in the removal of the problem. At other times, He strengthens us to endure our trial. Others may experience blessings vicariously as they observe our response to either situation or both. And that may be the bigger picture that we dare not miss!

—C. R. B.

II. Christ Preached
(Philippians 1:15-18a)

A. Contrasted Motives (vv. 15-17)

15, 16. Some indeed preach Christ even of envy and strife; and some also of good will: The one preach Christ of contention, not sincerely, supposing to add affliction to my bonds.

Not every Christian's boldness stems from pure motives, however. Some are motivated by selfish desires. They want Paul's prominence for themselves, or they see Paul as an obstacle to their own ambitions. So with Paul in prison, they *preach* about Jesus in hope that they will become as well-known and influential as Paul, eclipsing him as a Christian leader.

Those who preach from *envy and strife* are acting with motives that contradict the message they preach. They preach the selfless *Christ*, but for selfish reasons. Such inconsistency cannot stand for long. Paul highlights these opponents to warn the Philippian Christians. The envy and strife in their congregation stem from similar motives of selfishness.

> *What Do You Think?*
> What steps can we take to identify and disarm threats to church unity?
> *Digging Deeper*
> What Scripture texts support your conclusions?

17. But the other of love, knowing that I am set for the defence of the gospel.

In contrast, many desire for Paul the best and want to follow his bold example. Their preaching of Christ reflects Paul's sincere dedication. In them is no contradiction between motive and message. Regardless of their circumstances, the *love* they express in their preaching is the reflection of God's love. Their respect for Paul is based on Paul's own faithfulness to his message. They know that his suffering is for the sake of Christ who suffered for them, that by word and life Paul defends *the gospel,* the story of Jesus.

Paul's preaching while a prisoner of the Roman Empire demonstrates in the present the power of Christ, who gave himself in death in the past. Paul's steadfast faithfulness in hardship brings a victory that reflects the victory of Christ in His death and resurrection. True faith in the true gospel creates a love that hardship can challenge but never overcome fully.

B. Triumphant Gospel (v. 18a)

18a. What then? notwithstanding, every way, whether in pretence, or in truth, Christ is preached.

Certainly Paul has every right to condemn those who oppose him, we may think. But consider Christ's response to His own enemies. Falsely accused, He made no defense (Mark 14:60-62; 15:2-5). Subjected to torture, He prayed for His enemies (Luke 23:34). Mockingly invited to use His kingly power by which He had saved others to save himself, He stayed on the cross to the end (Mark 15:29-32). Paul's response to his rivals reflects Jesus' selfless sacrifice.

Paul is unconcerned to restore his reputation or maintain his standing. For him, Christ is everything. The fact that *Christ is preached,* even if it means shame for Paul, is evidence that the gospel is advancing. Those who preach with impure hearts will doubtlessly stand in judgment before the God who examines the heart. But until that day, the gospel will go forward even in cases of insincere preaching.

III. Results Considered
(PHILIPPIANS 1:18b-21)
A. Joy Is Experienced (v. 18b)
18b. And I therein do rejoice, yea, and will rejoice.

The word *therein* points to the reason Paul can *rejoice.* That reason is not his circumstances as such, but the fact that Christ is preached regardless. That reality makes Paul's situation tolerable to him, even as his ministry circumstances during his missionary journeys have caused him to vacillate from despair "even of life" (2 Corinthians 1:8) to being "not in despair" (4:8). Is this true of us as well?

> **What Do You Think?**
> In what ways can you be a greater source of joy to others?
> *Digging Deeper*
> Categorize your responses in terms of attitudes and actions.

B. Spirit Is Supplied (v. 19)
19. For I know that this shall turn to my salvation through your prayer, and the supply of the Spirit of Jesus Christ.

Paul now explains why his joy in Christ will continue even in the most extreme circumstances. This was no theoretical exercise for Paul. He is in Roman custody, awaiting trial before the emperor. The outcome of the trial may mean his death. As happened to the Lord Jesus previously, Paul is about to stand trial before the Roman imperium

for his very life. His readers knew this grim reality all too well.

Yet Paul speaks with complete confidence that the outcome of his trial will be *salvation.* Further, that salvation will come because of the Philippian Christians' prayers to God, and likewise through what God's Holy Spirit, *the Spirit of Jesus Christ,* will *supply.* Paul has complete confidence that the victorious power of God at work in his ministry will continue to bring victory.

Here Paul is using *salvation* in a way that may be hard for us to hear, as we are so used to the term in a Christian context. For the people of Paul's world, salvation is most often used in a military or economic sense. People were "saved" when their army triumphed, protecting them from invasion, or when a benefactor gave them needed food in a famine or managed governmental affairs effectively in a crisis. Normally one thinks that salvation for a prisoner means being found not guilty at trial and being set free without penalty.

Paul, however, is viewing salvation at this point from the perspective of the gospel. By that he does not simply mean salvation as escaping eternal punishment and experiencing life with God in Heaven at death, though that promise plays a key part in his meaning. Rather, salvation for Paul is the entirety of life as a follower of Christ. Faith in Christ means not just life with Christ after death; it means life with Christ in the present. It means restoration to the life for which God made humans, the life that reflects the very nature of God as revealed in Jesus.

The life that Paul leads as a Christian—the life of proclamation, of fellowship, of suffering, and now of imprisonment—is the saved life, the true life. God's people rely on God's power for this life as they pray continually for His provision. The Holy Spirit empowers this life, a life like the life of Jesus, God's true king. The saved life is the God-supplied, Spirit-empowered, Christ-honoring life.

C. Christ Is Glorified (vv. 20, 21)
20a. According to my earnest expectation and my hope, that in nothing I shall be ashamed.

Arrest is shameful. Imprisonment is shameful. Trial is shameful. Execution is the supreme shame.

But Paul says he cannot be made *ashamed*, even though these were his circumstances and perhaps his prospects.

Why this indomitable confidence? Paul's view of shame and honor have been transformed by the message of Jesus. Jesus willingly accepted the very shame that Paul faces: arrest, trial, and execution. Yet God vindicated Jesus through that experience, granting Him triumph by His resurrection. The same God will vindicate Paul. Nothing can take away the honor that Paul has by his identity with Jesus. In following the way of the cross of Christ, Paul has no shame.

20b. But that with all boldness, as always, so now also Christ shall be magnified in my body, whether it be by life, or by death.

In fact, Paul is bold. Before the supreme tribunal of his world, Paul can count on God's power to enable him to declare boldly that Jesus, not Caesar, is the world's true king. The one whom Rome crucified now rules at God's right hand and will return to judge His enemies and to share His victory with His people.

By this bold, faithful proclamation, Paul makes the name of Jesus great. Unlike those who preach for selfish motives, Paul's life and message are consistent. He proclaims the crucified and risen Christ, and he lives as one who understands that Christ's way is the way of true life, of salvation. Paul's *boldness* before the tribunal, not giving in to the fear of what might happen, will reflect Jesus' own determination. Paul's confession will be faithful like Jesus' own confession (1 Timothy 6:11-16).

In this way Paul will glorify *Christ*, demonstrating to the world who the world's king truly is, by shaping his life in Christ's mold. Thus he will glorify Christ whether in a *life* of continued ministry or in a *death* that reflects Christ's own selfless faithfulness. Focused on Christ, Paul can express joy in even the most extreme circumstances, and he does.

21. For to me to live is Christ, and to die is gain.

This brief verse is certainly one of the best known, best loved, and most widely memorized verses in the Bible. It brings Paul's discussion of his circumstances to a rousing climax. Its simplicity belies the challenging ideas it presents.

To think of death as *gain* defies human experience. Death marks the failure of our bodies, the end of our activity, the end of our earthly consciousness. It would seem that death can only be gain if life has become utter loss, if life has become living death.

But the gospel transforms that understanding. Because Christ died and rose for the sake of unworthy humanity, death means something very different for Christ's followers. By raising Christ from the dead, God demonstrated His unfailing faithfulness to His people. As Christ rules at God's right hand, He administers that same faithfulness to His suffering followers. Having promised that in losing their lives they will find them (Matthew 10:39), Christ assures His people that even death cannot separate them from His love (see Romans 8:34-39).

So to die is gain, as it means experiencing the triumph that Christ brings even in death. That triumph yields what Paul discusses in the following context: to die is to be with Christ, free of the suffering of this age, sharing His triumphant rule in Heaven (Philippians 1:23). That is surely a gain greater than any loss the believer can experience.

Alongside that promise is another statement: *to live is Christ.* What Paul means by that short pronouncement he goes on to explain in the following context. Paul's present life reflects Christ's life as a life of self-giving service for others. Jesus explained to His disciples this implication from His death: their purpose, like their master's, is to serve all (Mark 10:41-45). Paul describes his life as labor for bearing fruit (Philippians 1:22), serv-

HOW TO SAY IT

Caesar	*See*-zur.
Grecian	*Gree*-shun.
Macedonia	Mass-eh-*doe*-nee-uh.
Nero	*Nee*-row.
Philippi	Fih-*lip*-pie or *Fil*-ih-pie.
Philippians	Fih-*lip*-ee-unz.
poliomyelitis	*poh*-lee-*oh-my*-uh-*lie*-tuhs.
Praetorian	Pree-*tohr*-ee-uhn.
Via Egnatia	*Vee*-uh Egg-*nay*-shuh.

ing the Philippian Christians and others (1:24, 25). Living, for Paul or for any follower of Jesus, *is Christ* in that it is focused on rendering to others the joyous, selfless service that Jesus rendered to us.

❧ LIVING IN EXTREMITY ❧

The apostle Paul knew about living under extreme conditions. So did many of his converts throughout the Roman Empire. Most of us are not likely to experience the deprivations or persecutions they did.

Of course, we all have our occasional "trying times." Our experience may be getting laid off from a job during a recession, having our house destroyed by a tornado or flood, or having to replace one of our family cars because of an accident. And most of us know of a few people who really are living in extremity. But the average American lives in a state of privilege compared with the majority of the world.

A Gallup poll a few years ago showed the United States median per-capita annual income to be $15,480. Five countries in Europe ranked above the US, the highest being Norway at $19,308. The contrast with the poorest area surveyed, which was sub-Saharan Africa, is striking. Tenth from last on the list was Zambia at $287. At the very bottom in per-capita annual income was Liberia at $118. Not many of us can imagine living in such an extremity!

In some of those countries, poverty-stricken Christians also have to deal with the reality of religious persecution by anti-Christian governments and terrorist groups. What does all of this suggest to us about our attitudes and behavior?

—C. R. B.

Visual for Lesson 8. *Use this visual to introduce the question associated with Philippians 1:21, directly to the left.*

Conclusion
A. The Joy of Service

Why are some people able to express joy in every circumstance, even the painful ones? It has to do with how God made us and with how, in Christ, He has remade us. We were made not to hold on to our lives but to give them away. When we try to hold on, we run away from our divinely created purpose. We mar our divine image. We destroy our joy. When we learn to let go, we discover again the reason we exist. We find our true selves. We reflect our true king. We find true joy.

Paul found a way to serve others even as a prisoner. He knew that even in the bleakest circumstance, God provided a means for him to glorify Christ in self-giving.

How do your circumstances present opportunities for you to serve selflessly? How has the faithful God delivered that joy to you before? Are you ready to discover how He will do so again?

B. Prayer

Father, by Your Spirit we ask that You empower us to give our lives freely for others as we rejoice in Your Son who gave His life freely for us. We pray this in His name. Amen.

C. Thought to Remember

Real life and real joy come from
freely giving life and joy to others.

INVOLVEMENT LEARNING

Enhance your lesson with KJV Bible Student *(from your curriculum supplier) and the reproducible activity page (at www.standardlesson.com or in the back of the* KJV Standard Lesson Commentary Deluxe Edition*).*

Into the Lesson

Write the following phrases on the board.

To Gain Access   To Gain Approval
To Gain Money   To Gain Power
To Express Love

Ask how each might be a driving force for an individual starting a business. Jot responses on the board. When the discussion winds down, ask how those motives can be the driving force for an individual who wants to participate in church work. Again, record responses on the board.

Say, "The apostle Paul knew that some people were preaching the gospel from motives that were far less than ideal. His reaction may surprise us!"

Option. Place in chairs copies of the "God's Redemptive Work" activity from the reproducible page, which you can download, to pique learners' interest as they arrive. Do not refer to or otherwise discuss this until the Into Life segment.

Into the Word

Divide your class into three groups. Distribute instructions on handouts (you create) as follows.

Paul's Bondage Group: Read Philippians 1:12-14. 1–What did Paul want the addressees to know? 2–What had happened as a result of Paul's imprisonment? 3–How did Paul's imprisonment affect the believers who knew what had happened to him?

Paul's Challenge Group: Read Philippians 1:15-18. 1–What wrong motives did some people have for preaching the gospel? 2–What right motives did others have for doing the same? 3–Why did Paul rejoice regardless of the motivations?

Paul's Champion Group: Read Philippians 1:19-21. 1–What two things was Paul counting on to result in his rescue? 2–For what did Paul expect and hope not to happen? 3–Why did Paul expect both possible outcomes of death or continued life to be good things?

Have groups present their conclusions in whole-class discussion. Then pose this question: How has God used Paul's imprisonment to advance the gospel, even to the present day?

Several answers are possible. But make sure to stress this one if no one else does: Paul's involuntary, enforced down time from mission travels resulted in a shift to a writing ministry. The long-lasting result is that for centuries now Christians have had the magnificent letters of Ephesians, Philippians, Colossians, 2 Timothy, and Philemon—all written during imprisonments—as vital parts of the Word of God.

Into Life

After a volunteer reads Philippians 1:12-14, ask, "What stories would you like to share of seeing God's hand at work only in hindsight, after a period of difficulty was over?" After several minutes of sharing, ask, "Why is it often easier to see the hand of God at work after a trial is over than when we're in the middle of it?" Be prepared to summarize the events leading up to Joseph's declaration in Genesis 50:20 as an example. (*Option.* If you distributed "God's Redemptive Work" at the outset, discuss it at this point.)

Brainstorming. Ask participants to suggest ways to see God's hand at work during difficult times. Jot ideas on the board. Evaluate ideas only after declaring brainstorming to be ended.

Option. Reopen brainstorming in a private and personal way by distributing copies of the "What's Stopping You?" activity from the reproducible page. Allow volunteers to share responses, but don't put anyone on the spot. If no one mentions Romans 8:28, be sure to do so yourself to discuss appropriate and inappropriate ways to apply the affirmation of that passage.

Close with a prayer that includes affirmations of both your students' struggles and the same source of strength that Paul had.

IMITATE CHRIST

DEVOTIONAL READING: Psalm 119:65-72
BACKGROUND SCRIPTURE: Philippians 2:1-11

PHILIPPIANS 2:1-11

1 If there be therefore any consolation in Christ, if any comfort of love, if any fellowship of the Spirit, if any bowels and mercies,

2 Fulfil ye my joy, that ye be likeminded, having the same love, being of one accord, of one mind.

3 Let nothing be done through strife or vainglory; but in lowliness of mind let each esteem other better than themselves.

4 Look not every man on his own things, but every man also on the things of others.

5 Let this mind be in you, which was also in Christ Jesus:

6 Who, being in the form of God, thought it not robbery to be equal with God:

7 But made himself of no reputation, and took upon him the form of a servant, and was made in the likeness of men:

8 And being found in fashion as a man, he humbled himself, and became obedient unto death, even the death of the cross.

9 Wherefore God also hath highly exalted him, and given him a name which is above every name:

10 That at the name of Jesus every knee should bow, of things in heaven, and things in earth, and things under the earth;

11 And that every tongue should confess that Jesus Christ is Lord, to the glory of God the Father.

KEY VERSE

In lowliness of mind let each esteem other better than themselves. —**Philippians 2:3**

OUR LOVE FOR GOD

Unit II: Loving God by Trusting Christ

LESSONS 6–10

LESSON AIMS

After participating in this lesson, each learner will be able to:

1. Describe the incarnation, death, and resurrection of Jesus as the climax of God's self-revelation.

2. Explain how Jesus' self-sacrifice defines true human existence.

3. Express ways and conviction to imitate Christ in relationships.

LESSON OUTLINE

Introduction
    A. Which Way Is Up?
    B. Lesson Context
I. Exhortation to Selflessness
                  (PHILIPPIANS 2:1-4)
    A. Christ's Selfless Gifts (v. 1)
    B. Our Selfless Imitation (vv. 2-4)
      Look Not Every . . . Goose?
II. Revelation of Selflessness
                  (PHILIPPIANS 2:5-11)
    A. The Divine Christ (vv. 5, 6)
    B. The Lowly Christ (vv. 7, 8)
      Quite a Difference!
    C. The Exalted Christ (vv. 9-11)
Conclusion
    A. The Christian Mind-set
    B. Prayer
    C. Thought to Remember

Introduction

A. Which Way Is Up?

Experts offer a surprising conclusion about victims of drowning: they often die not because they cannot swim but because they do not know where to swim. Suddenly submerged deep underwater, victims often swim toward where they believe the surface to be, but in fact they are swimming deeper into the water.

We can compare that situation to a vital biblical idea communicated in today's text. Sinful human beings are swimming for their lives, trying to find the surface. But as they swim toward what they think is up—toward power, prestige, wealth, comfort—they are swimming deeper into what will ultimately ruin their lives. The gospel teaches us that the true way up is the way we usually think of as down.

B. Lesson Context

Under his own humble circumstances of Roman imprisonment, Paul wrote his letter to the Philippians. This situation was addressed in the Lesson Context of last week's lesson and need not be repeated here. Paul wrote, in part, to address the church's problems with interpersonal conflict (Philippians 4:2, 3). But the core of Paul's teaching is found in today's text.

Philippians 2:6-11 of our text is poetic in form in that the lines have parallel structure and build to a climax. Many scholars suggest that this is an early Christian hymn. It is easy to imagine the first generation of Jesus' followers singing or chanting these verses together as an expression of their new, revolutionary faith.

In addition to the poetic rhythm of the original text, the content of this passage closely resembles other texts that also seem to cite ancient hymns. Some possibilities in that regard are John 1:1-14; Colossians 1:15-20; and 1 Peter 3:18-22. These focus on the nature and work of Christ by highlighting His divinity and preexistence, role in creation, incarnation, painful death, resurrection, and exaltation (although not all these passages contain all these elements). The hymn in Philippians 2 includes most of these elements.

I. Exhortation to Selflessness
(Philippians 2:1-4)
A. Christ's Selfless Gifts (v. 1)

1a. If there be therefore any consolation in Christ.

Paul begins his exhortation by reminding his readers of what they have received as a result of Christ's selflessness. The beginning *if* does not cast doubt on whether the Philippians have received these gifts. Rather, this is a common way of speaking to draw attention to what speaker and listener both agree to be true. Implied at the end of each *if* clause is "and there is." The resulting list is a broad catalog of the ways that God's grace is experienced by Christ's followers.

The list begins with *consolation,* translating a common term in the New Testament. It is also translated "comfort" (example: 2 Corinthians 1:3, 4), "exhortation" (example: Hebrews 13:22), etc. The idea is encouragement to do what is right.

1b. If any comfort of love.

The second expression, *comfort,* has a broadly similar meaning. This comfort is particularly associated with *love,* God's expression of His commitment to bless His people despite their rebellion and unworthiness.

1c. If any fellowship of the Spirit.

Fellowship signifies not just a sense of connection between people, but active sharing of their resources (see Acts 2:42-47). The fellowship is *of the Spirit,* as the Holy Spirit given by Christ to His people binds them together in a way that transcends differences that exist among them (compare 2 Corinthians 13:14).

What Do You Think?
What techniques can we use to discipline ourselves in being mindful of the benefits of being connected with Christ in fellowship?

Digging Deeper
What techniques have you seen or experienced that don't work in that regard?

1d. If any bowels and mercies.

Bowels is a literal translation of a word that is used figuratively to refer to compassion (compare 1 John 3:17). It is paired with *mercies:* attitudes and actions that refrain from exacting vengeance or punishment on others, giving generous blessing in place of the negative response that is deserved (compare Luke 1:78).

Christ gives His followers a transformed perspective and experience. They receive abundantly these gifts of God that they do not deserve. And receiving them together, they are drawn into a relationship with each other in which their common gifts are more important than their individual differences.

B. Our Selfless Imitation (vv. 2-4)

2a. Fulfil ye my joy, that ye be likeminded.

Paul now describes the right response for having received Christ's gracious gifts. If we have been drawn together as one by our humble Lord, then living as one must be our aim.

Again Paul piles up terms for emphasis. This unity can be described as being *likeminded,* or thinking the same thing (also Romans 15:5; Philippians 4:2). Christian unity is expressed not as people deny their individuality but as they unite their individualities in pursuing thinking that is like Christ's—focused on humble service.

2b. Having the same love.

This is the action part of being of the same mind. The *love* that the readers have received from Christ, the *love* that comforts and encourages them continually, must dictate their actions toward one another. As Christ has loved them, they give as they have received.

2c. Being of one accord.

This is a sharing in common of attitudes and perspectives. As the readers become more Christlike, this will come naturally.

2d. Of one mind.

It is notable that Paul begins and ends this description with expressions concerning thought. Our understanding of Christ must transform every aspect of our lives, inside and out, but it starts with thought. Paul's aim in sharing the gospel is not just to bring people to initial faith but also to see them grow to reveal God's intention for their lives together. Paul's joy is seeing that connection fully realized.

3a. Let nothing be done through strife or vainglory.

Paul draws a contrast with his previous description. *Strife* is the playing out of hostile division among people, the opposite of the Christlike, humble life. It is paired with *vainglory*—that is, the selfish pursuit of empty praise for oneself at the expense of others.

3b. But in lowliness of mind let each esteem other better than themselves.

In contrast, the positive is described again, this time in terms of *lowliness of mind*. The term being translated is sometimes rendered "humility" (example: Acts 20:19). We commonly use the word *humble* to describe a person who is soft-spoken and modest about accomplishments. A humble person is not a braggart. Biblical humility goes beyond this characteristic to genuine lowliness. The biblically humble person does more than avoid the spotlight. Biblical humility takes the position of servant to others.

To do so is to *esteem other[s] better than* oneself. But our natural instinct is to take care of our own interests first. Survival dictates that we do! But the gospel turns that order of life upside down. Having received God's promise that He will always supply what we need, and receiving the fullness of His grace through Jesus' self-giving death, we are freed from the need to protect our own interests and empowered to pursue the good of others. This indeed is the very thing that Jesus did, and now we do it in imitation of Him and in response to His lowly service for us.

4. Look not every man on his own things, but every man also on the things of others.

This verse restates the second half of the previous verse, but uses more challenging terms. Paul urges readers to no longer do what seems natural: pursuing and protecting their own interests. They are to abandon that in favor of pursuing the interests *of others*. Prioritizing others must mean abandoning self-interest, or others are not our true priority.

❧ LOOK NOT EVERY . . . GOOSE? ❧

It is a common sight in an autumn sky. Geese, flying south to escape the cold Canadian winter, travel in a familiar V-formation. While we are likely well acquainted with this phenomenon, perhaps we should take a closer look. When we do, we can see an illustration of selflessness.

Bigger birds, like geese and pelicans, create a significant updraft by flapping their wings. Therefore, a bird flying behind and slightly below another receives some additional lift from the bird in front. Birds in a V-formation literally lift one another up as they fly, bearing one another's burdens on their long trip.

Another benefit of this flight pattern is increased visibility. Members of the flock can see one another, making sure that all are present. This keeps lines of communication open and ensures that all remain heading in the right direction.

Finally, birds flying in this pattern share the work and the benefits of traveling together. The bird in front is meeting the most wind resistance, while the birds farthest from the front have the easiest flight. If you watch the flock for any length of time, you will witness a graceful acrobatic maneuver. After a while the leader will drop back from the most stressful position and retire to the end of the line, while another takes the lead.

As Paul instructed the church that "nothing be done through strife or vainglory," the geese provide a clear illustration of just that. "Look not every [goose] on his own things, but every [goose] also on the things of others!" —J. E.

II. Revelation of Selflessness
(PHILIPPIANS 2:5-11)

A. The Divine Christ (vv. 5, 6)

5. Let this mind be in you, which was also in Christ Jesus.

Now Paul makes explicit the basis for this radically humble life to which Christians are called. Again he stresses *mind,* for the humble life is first a way of thinking about ourselves and others. Then he states directly that our mind must be like Christ's mind.

This mind must govern our lives together, just as it did the life of Jesus, our king. The mind of Christ must be adopted consciously and pursued vigorously.

6. Who, being in the form of God, thought it not robbery to be equal with God.

This verse begins one of the most profound and memorable biblical descriptions of Christ's actions. It needs careful attention for accurate understanding.

John 1:1 helps us understand what it means for Christ to exist *in the form of God.* We might conclude that a *form* was merely an appearance and not a reality, that Christ appeared to be God but was not truly God. This is not how this word is used, however. The form of an individual in this sense is the real status by which the being relates to other beings. To be in the form of God is to exist as God and be rightly regarded as God by other beings. From eternity, the preexistent Christ was fully divine, the one true Creator God.

As God, Christ possessed equality *with God.* That is, sharing the divine nature with God the Father, Christ experienced the fullness of divine existence. In that status He was not subject to the difficulties of a temporal creature's life. Existing eternally, Christ possessed all power. Thus He did not consider that equality *robbery.*

B. The Lowly Christ (vv. 7, 8)

7. But made himself of no reputation, and took upon him the form of a servant, and was made in the likeness of men.

Never using His divine prerogatives for His own advantage, Christ *made himself of no reputation,* or more literally translated, "emptied himself." The gospel story shows us that this self-emptying was not the loss of His divine nature or power. During His ministry, Jesus consistently said and did things that only God could truly say and do (Matthew 7:24-29; 9:1-8; 12:1-8). Rather it was the prerogatives—immunity from death, His glorious status, etc.—that He willingly surrendered.

As a result, His *form,* the status by which He related to other beings, became that *of a servant.* Paul's word literally means a "bondslave," someone who serves by compulsion. Though Christ took this role willingly, Paul uses the term to express His utter lowliness—focused on serving others. Paul's words echo the terms that the prophet Isaiah used to describe the coming servant of the Lord who would willingly give His life for others (Isaiah 53:3, 11).

The servant Christ was a fully human Christ. His humanity was that of all other humans. He experienced everything, including temptation and suffering, that humans experience. But unlike other humans who seek their own interests, He led a life completely characterized by humble service for others.

8. And being found in fashion as a man, he humbled himself, and became obedient unto death, even the death of the cross.

HOW TO SAY IT

Caesar	*See*-zer.
Philippi	Fih-*lip*-pie or *Fil*-ih-pie.
Philippians	Fih-*lip*-ee-unz.
Zeus	Zoose.

Christ's first self-lowering was in becoming human, what Christians call His incarnation. But the climax of His humbling was in accepting *death* on *the cross* for the sake of others.

Certainly all humans experience dread as they contemplate death, fearing both the pain that accompanies it and the terrible thought of leaving behind a familiar life. But Paul emphasizes that Christ's death was death by crucifixion. This act of extreme torture was especially painful and shameful. But we should also remember that it was a demonstration of power used for one's own advantage by the Roman Empire. Having all power but refusing to use it for His advantage, Christ agreed to suffer this torturous death at the hands of an evil empire that used such atrocities to express its own power for its own advantage.

The first humans, Adam and Eve, owed God their submission but rebelliously sought equality with God for their own advantage, receiving a sentence of death as the consequence (Genesis 3:2-5). Christ was equal with God the Father but willingly *humbled himself* and submitted to death, never using His equality with God for His own advantage. As Paul describes Christ, we see that in Christ God has brought human existence to something it had never before attained.

❧ QUITE A DIFFERENCE! ❧

The Greco-Roman world within which Paul ministered was familiar with Zeus, also known as Jupiter, as chief of the gods (compare Acts 14:12). All other deities served Zeus, who assigned the roles they played in his service.

Myths tell us that Zeus would leave his throne on occasion for a visit to earth. But the purpose of his trips was often to *take from* rather than *give to* humankind. Zeus would find attractive mortal women and then take a variety of forms to seduce and impregnate them. The beautiful Helen of Troy, it is told, was born of Leda after Zeus seduced her by taking the form of a beautiful swan. The stories go on and on.

The Bible records the reactions of those who believed in such deities when Paul spoke of Jesus (example: Acts 17:16-34). Unlike the fictitious Zeus, Jesus did not flaunt His authority. He came

to earth not to *take* but to *give*—a giving that included His own life. Which model will we emulate, the one that uses power to take or the one that surrenders power to give?   —J. E.

C. The Exalted Christ (vv. 9-11)

9. Wherefore God also hath highly exalted him, and given him a name which is above every name.

In response to Christ's self-emptying and selfless death, God raised Him from the dead—not just alive but victoriously alive. God then seated Christ at His own right hand, the position of supreme power (Ephesians 1:20-23).

Thus does the story of Christ demonstrate the real path of human life that bears the image of God. Exaltation comes not by pursuing one's own interests but by lowering oneself to serve others, surrendering one's own interests in submission to God. This is not just Christ's restoration to His *exalted* position. It is the elevation of the humble, incarnate, human Christ to share in God's rule.

10. That at the name of Jesus every knee should bow, of things in heaven, and things in earth, and things under the earth.

Again, Paul's words echo those of the prophet Isaiah, this time in a description of God's exaltation (Isaiah 45:23). Christ's glory is the glory that belongs to God alone, the glory of the universe's supreme king. As Paul refers to *heaven . . . earth . . . under the earth*, he names every place imaginable and so every being imaginable (compare Ephesians 1:10; Colossians 1:18-20).

Notably, it is here in the hymn-poem, which extends from Philippians 2:6 to verse 11 (see the Lesson Context), that Paul first refers to *the name of Jesus*. That human name suggests the entire story of authoritative deeds and words, humble service, willing self-sacrifice, and resurrection from the dead. The Jesus with that history is the Jesus to whom every creature *should* one day *bow* (compare Psalm 95:6; Romans 14:11). He is the true king, the one who used His authority not for His own advantage but for others.

11. And that every tongue should confess that Jesus Christ is Lord, to the glory of God the Father.

Again Paul refers to *Jesus* as the one to be confessed by all creatures (again, see Romans 14:11). But Paul elaborates on the content of the confession: this crucified and risen Jesus is *Christ*—that is, God's anointed one, God's true king. He *is Lord*, the one who rules over all.

In Paul's time Roman subjects and citizens, including the Roman citizens of Philippi, identify themselves as loyal subjects of the empire by saying "Caesar is Lord." But "Jesus Christ is Lord" is the greater and truer confession. Real lordship belongs not to the emperor who asserts power for his own advantage, but to the incarnate Son of God who gives himself for the unworthy. Soldiers of the Roman Empire die in battle on behalf of the emperor; by contrast, the Lord Jesus, king of the universe, died on behalf of humanity. He is recognized as such by some now; He will be recognized as such by all eventually.

By this *the glory of God the Father* is realized. God achieves His purpose and expresses His true nature not by destroying rebellious humanity but by sending His beloved, divine Son to become a human, experience the pangs of death for others' sake, and receive His life again by God's gift. In that story, we find the real meaning and truest direction for our lives.

Conclusion

A. The Christian Mind-set

Think of events in Jesus' life. He was tempted to turn stones to bread to satisfy His own hunger (Matthew 4:3). He refused. On other occasions, Jesus faced the opportunity to alleviate the hunger of others. He did so (Matthew 14:13-21; 15:32-38). He refused to use His divine author-

Visual for Lesson 9. *Start a discussion by pointing to this visual as you ask, "What are the most common ways that Christians fail to imitate Christ? Why?"*

ity for himself. He did not consider equality with God something to use for His own advantage. That mind of Christ has been present from all eternity.

How would you describe the direction of your life so far? In your career, family interactions, friendships—is your life about your own advantage or is it about others' needs? Do you follow the common path of modest selfishness that seems so culturally right, or the Christlike way of lowly, self-giving pursuit of others' advantage?

We are not the first or the worst to think that serving ourselves seems the right way to live. We can point in any direction and see lives governed by that common mind-set. But every part of the gospel story tells us the opposite. To experience life as God designed it, we need to put into action the mind of Christ.

B. Prayer

Heavenly Father, the scope of Your Son's self-sacrificial gift to us is beyond our comprehension! It challenges every part of our minds and hearts. May we offer ourselves daily to be used in the service of Your Son. As we do, may we serve one another in love, even at the cost of our very lives. We pray in the name of the Son, who did just that. Amen.

C. Thought to Remember

The way up is down.

INVOLVEMENT LEARNING

Enhance your lesson with KJV Bible Student *(from your curriculum supplier) and the reproducible activity page (at www.standardlesson.com or in the back of the* KJV Standard Lesson Commentary Deluxe Edition*).*

Into the Lesson

Have the following request written on the board as learners arrive.

> *Write three things that are most important to you in relationships.*

After learners finish, form them into pairs for sharing of responses. After a few minutes, ask for volunteers to summarize their partner's (but only with their partner's permission). Sum up by saying, "A thread we've just seen is that a characteristic of a healthy relationship is each person caring about what is important to the other. This is seen when each goes out of his or her way to support, in various ways, the other person's priorities."

Option. To explore what can interfere with relationships, distribute copies of the "Levels of Authority" activity from the reproducible page, which you can download. Allow students to work on this individually for no more than one minute. Then discuss the correct ranking quickly so there's more time to discuss your students' responses to the question below the ranking.

Lead into the Bible study by saying, "Relationships best flourish when, among other things, we put our own preferences on the back burner and avoid 'pulling rank' for selfish reasons. Let's see how to do both."

Into the Word

Divide your class in half and give each half a handout (you create) of one of the following assignments. (Groups should not exceed four or five in size; larger classes should form additional groups with duplicate assignments.)

The Getting Along Group. Read Philippians 2:1-4. 1–How does Paul describe the characteristics of unity toward which he wanted the Philippian believers to strive? 2–What did Paul want them to avoid and to do instead? 3–What relationship do you see between Philippians 1:4 and Romans 15:1?

The Christ's Example Group. Read Philippians 2:5-8. 1–What relationship do you see between Philippians 2:5 and John 13:34? 2–In what way(s) is Christ's servanthood evident? 3–What aspects of Jesus' servanthood are we to imitate in a general way (Philippians 2:7), but we should not (and need not) try to imitate Him by exactly repeating what He did (2:8)?

As groups work, write these on the board:

How we are to imitate Christ in relationships: ___
Why we are to imitate Christ in relationships: ___

After groups finish, draw attention to the unfinished statements. Ask, "From what you've discussed in your groups, how do we complete these statements?" Jot responses on the board. (Many responses that touch on being like-minded are possible.)

Wrap up with a discussion of Philippians 2:9-11 as you stress the end result of verses 1-8. Note the sweeping, all-inclusive language as you ask rhetorically, "Is anyone left out?"

Into Life

Divide the class into three groups and give each an index card on which you have printed one of the following three scenarios. (Note: some may be "too hot to handle" or "too hot *not* to handle"; also, names are intentionally gender-neutral.)

Group 1: Morgan wants to go to the beach for vacation, but spouse Taylor wants to visit parents.
Group 2: The seniors want to sing hymns during worship, but young adults want to sing praise choruses.
Group 3: Chris wants Chinese food, but best friend Pat wants Mexican food.

Allow groups to propose solutions during whole-class discussion.

Option. Distribute copies of the "Hidden Message" activity from the reproducible page as a take-home exercise.

Press On in Christ

DEVOTIONAL READING: 1 Corinthians 15:50-58
BACKGROUND SCRIPTURE: Philippians 3:1-16

PHILIPPIANS 3:7-14

7 But what things were gain to me, those I counted loss for Christ.

8 Yea doubtless, and I count all things but loss for the excellency of the knowledge of Christ Jesus my Lord: for whom I have suffered the loss of all things, and do count them but dung, that I may win Christ,

9 And be found in him, not having mine own righteousness, which is of the law, but that which is through the faith of Christ, the righteousness which is of God by faith:

10 That I may know him, and the power of his resurrection, and the fellowship of his sufferings, being made conformable unto his death;

11 If by any means I might attain unto the resurrection of the dead.

12 Not as though I had already attained, either were already perfect: but I follow after, if that I may apprehend that for which also I am apprehended of Christ Jesus.

13 Brethren, I count not myself to have apprehended: but this one thing I do, forgetting those things which are behind, and reaching forth unto those things which are before,

14 I press toward the mark for the prize of the high calling of God in Christ Jesus.

KEY VERSES

Forgetting those things which are behind, and reaching forth unto those things which are before, I press toward the mark for the prize of the high calling of God in Christ Jesus. —**Philippians 3:13, 14**

Photo: gabri_prato / iStock / Thinkstock

OUR LOVE FOR GOD

Unit II: Loving God by Trusting Christ

LESSONS 6–10

LESSON AIMS

After participating in this lesson, each learner will be able to:

1. Identify faith in Christ as not just the condition of belonging to God but the compulsion for becoming like Christ.

2. Contrast a life that grows in Christlikeness with a life focused on status or attainments.

3. Identify and abandon one or more things that hinder his or her growth in Christlikeness.

LESSON OUTLINE

Introduction

A. Knowing Where You Are Going

An old joke begins with the scene of a man driving his family to a certain destination, but they became lost. After a while, the wife asked the husband, "Do you know where you are going?" Choosing his words carefully, the husband paused a few seconds before replying, "No, I don't. But we're making excellent time!"

If we ever expect to arrive at our destination, we have to know where we are going. The route may need some discovery and modification. But if we know where we are going, we can adjust to get there.

This obvious truth is part of the message of today's text. When we know where God has us going, we can be confident that in every circumstance we are still moving toward that blessed destination.

B. Lesson Context

Many circumstances had come together to create disunity in the Philippian church. We can surmise that personal differences and rivalries played a role. Certainly the selfishness to which all people are vulnerable was the fertile ground in which the problem grew. But another factor was the influence of those who advocated that Jewish people have a place of preeminence in the church. As in other churches founded by Paul, the Philippian church was troubled by those whom we identify as *Judaizers*. These insisted that to belong to God's people, believers in Jesus must toe the line with regard to the Law of Moses, especially the requirement for circumcision (Philippians 3:2, 3).

Paul understood, however, that Christ had brought the fulfillment of the Law of Moses. This meant that God accepted non-Jews as they were. Paul understood that the division between Jew and Gentile had been taken away, making one body of anyone who accepted Christ (Acts 2:37-39; 15:1-31; Ephesians 2:11-22; Colossians 3:11). What faith produces is an identity marker of the people of God in Christ, not the keeping of the Law of Moses. If Christ came as the lowly servant of all (last week's lesson), then no follower of

His can look upon another Christian as a second-class citizen of the kingdom of God. In Christ, all Christians are first-class citizens of that kingdom. Christ must be the standard that the church pursues in unity, not score-keeping regarding adherence to a set of laws.

In the context preceding our text, Paul had used himself as an example of this contrast. Others may make the claim to be the true, first-class people of God because of their observance of the Law of Moses, but Paul could make a greater claim. He was in all respects highly observant of all the laws that marked Israel as a distinctive people (Philippians 3:4-6). As our text begins, Paul declares what faith in Christ demands that he say regarding his attainments as a faithful observer of the law.

I. Gain and Loss
(PHILIPPIANS 3:7-11)
A. Reevaluation of the Past (vv. 7, 8)

7. But what things were gain to me, those I counted loss for Christ.

In the verses before this one, Paul has just listed his outstanding characteristics as a Jew who meticulously observed the Law of Moses. These observances had been of supreme value to him, like profits on a balance sheet (*gain to me*). They were the things that had once defined his identity.

But Jesus has changed the basis for that identity. Paul now knows the crucified, risen Jesus as God's true king, the head of God's people. The only identity Paul has is Christ's identity.

Paul, of course, continues to identify as a Jew, or Israelite, after becoming a Christian (Acts 21:39; 22:3; Romans 11:1). He does not deny his past or his heritage. In fact, he celebrates it;

HOW TO SAY IT

Corinthians	Ko-*rin*-thee-unz (*th* as in *thin*).
Damascus	Duh-*mass*-kus.
Judaizers	*Joo*-duh-*ize*-ers.
Mosaic	Mo-*zay*-ik.
Philippians	Fih-*lip*-ee-unz.
Thessalonians	*Thess*-uh-**lo**-nee-unz (*th* as in *thin*).

for in the history of Israel, God was at work to promise and prepare for the coming of Jesus. But compared with the supreme value of *Christ*, that former identity—valuable as Paul thought it to be—can only be *counted loss*.

8. Yea doubtless, and I count all things but loss for the excellency of the knowledge of Christ Jesus my Lord: for whom I have suffered the loss of all things, and do count them but dung, that I may win Christ.

Paul amplifies his point from the previous verse. He calls attention to the strong contrast he is drawing: the phrase translated *yea doubtless* puts emphasis on the difference between his identification as a law-observant Jew and his new identification as a follower of Jesus. In fact, Paul says, all parts of his life, except for following Jesus, are now like his law-observant past: they are *loss* compared with that great gain or profit.

Paul has literally *suffered the loss of all things* as a follower of Jesus. His commitment led him into conflict with people everywhere who opposed the gospel he preached, and he suffered physically and materially as a result (2 Corinthians 11:23-33). So here he interjects not just that he counts all things as loss but that in a real sense he has lost much because of Christ.

Dung might not be a word that we would expect at this point. But Paul uses it to add to the emphasis on what he considers loss. In the original language, the word translated *dung* can refer to any waste that has a repugnant smell. Paul's expression can hardly be stronger.

This loss of all things contrasts with the prospect that Paul *may win Christ*. Here again Paul uses the language of accounting, but in a limited way. There is no idea here of somehow earning Christ as a something-for-something (quid pro quo) result of a swap. God gives us His blessing through Christ freely; it cannot be earned or purchased (Acts 8:18-20; etc.). We respond in a way that expresses that this gift is what we value most greatly.

✸ *NOT SO "NOBEL"* ✸

Since 1991, the scientific humor magazine *Annals of Improbable Research* has planned and presented a parody of the annual Nobel Prize awards. The Ig Nobel Prizes (created from a play on the word *ignoble*), presented by actual Nobel laureates each fall, bring to light various trivial, unusual, or outright silly scientific research projects. By extension, the "awards" poke fun at those who find their identity in scientific research of dubious value. The ceremony concludes with the announcement, "If you didn't win a prize—and especially if you did—better luck next year!"

Recent Ig Nobels were awarded for determining that acute appendicitis can be accurately diagnosed by the amount of pain patients experience when driven over speed bumps (diagnostic medicine), discovering why dragonflies are fatally attracted to black tombstones (physics), and asking a thousand liars how often they lie and then deciding whether to believe their answers (psychology).

At one time, Paul thought his long list of accomplishments were noble. But he learned on the road to Damascus and through the ministry experiences that followed that those were not adequate as the ultimate context of his life. Which side of that fence are you on—the one that clings to diplomas, titles, and net assets as ultimate context, or the side that surrenders what cannot be kept, having received what cannot be lost?　　　—J. E.

B. Righteousness in the Present (vv. 9, 10)

9a. And be found in him.

Still elaborating on his point, Paul switches to a different description of his new identity in Christ. To *be found in him* certainly means to be fully identified as Christ's follower. That in turn implies a life that is utterly committed to Christ, utterly trusting in Christ, but also a life that in its thoughts and actions deeply reflects Christ's own life.

9b. Not having mine own righteousness, which is of the law, but that which is through the faith of Christ, the righteousness which is of God by faith.

This identity with Christ, founded on the trusting belief that Jesus is indeed God's true king, is the source of true *righteousness*. Here Paul uses *righteousness* to refer to genuine membership in God's people, what we sometimes call "right standing with God." What makes someone God's

person, Paul says, is not what he or she does in terms of keeping the Mosaic law. Nor is it anything that anyone might do to try to make oneself the right kind of person to belong to God. Rather, *faith* is the foundation of true righteousness.

We should pause to take note of a translation difficulty. When something is said to be "of" something else, the translators often have to decide whether the right-hand side of the phrase is the subject or object of the left-hand side. For example, the phrase "love of God" may mean either "God's love" (God is the subject or producer of the love) or "love for God" (God is the object or recipient of the love). That's the issue with the phrase *the faith of Christ* here. Is Paul talking about Christ's faith(fullness), or is he talking about our faith in Christ? Scholars are divided on this.

Either way, Christ is different from the Mosaic law or other "on our own" means of belonging to God. That difference is that God has supplied the means of our salvation. So rather than putting trust in our abilities to be righteous, we put trust in Him to provide all the righteousness we need. It is not "we do our best and God does the rest." It is, rather, God does it all. When we realize that truth, we give control of our lives to Him instead of holding onto them ourselves. It is making Jesus king.

> ### What Do You Think?
> How would you counsel someone who believes that Christ's righteousness keeps the Christian out of Hell, but one's personal righteousness gets him or her into Heaven?
>
> ### Digging Deeper
> How would you counsel that same person using only logic, neither quoting nor referring to Scripture passages?

10a. That I may know him.

Faith reorients one's life away from self-righteousness, self-reliance, and self-fulfillment. In place of those, Christ becomes the focus—not only as the source of identity with God but also as the exemplar of the true life of God's people.

So to *know* Christ is not merely to know His story or even to affirm His authority, but to live a life that imitates His. In that way, one comes to know Christ by experience, consciously living to serve others as Christ did (Mark 10:43-45; Philippians 2:1-11).

10b. And the power of his resurrection.

Such a life is obviously costly. As Paul has noted, it cost him "all things." How can one live with such a deep loss? Paul says that the follower of Christ also comes to know *the power of his resurrection.* Christ literally gave "all things" by willingly surrendering His life. But God the Father answered His loss with greater gain, raising Christ from the dead.

That same power God exercises for Christ's followers, meeting their needs as they suffer loss for the sake of Christ. And God even overcomes the greatest loss, death—however it comes to them —as they share in the resurrection from the dead (1 Corinthians 15:20-28, 50-58; 2 Corinthians 5:1-10; Philippians 1:21-24; 1 Thessalonians 4:13-18). No matter the circumstances, near or far, the power of Christ's resurrection is at work in Christ's people. They come to know that power as they experience God's constant provision for their need.

10c. And the fellowship of his sufferings.

Christ's gift was given through His suffering for others. His exaltation came in response to His suffering for others. Christ's followers join Him in that suffering. This is not suffering for its own sake, suffering that hopes to impress God with one's dedication. Jesus did not die on the cross to prove how dedicated He was. Rather, Christ's suffering was suffering to bring blessing to others. Thus, Paul speaks of the *fellowship* of Christ's *sufferings*—not just sharing suffering with Christ, but sharing through suffering, as we give of our lives for the sake of others.

> **What Do You Think?**
> In what ways can a Christian expect life to change when he or she joins Paul in desiring to share in Christ's sufferings?
> **Digging Deeper**
> Which of the following texts speaks to your heart most strongly in this regard: Romans 8:17; 2 Corinthians 1:5; 4:7-10; 1 Peter 4:13?

10d. Being made conformable unto his death.

The climax of Christ's earthly ministry was His sacrificial death; and so for His followers, life takes that same shape. Relatively few Christians will die as martyrs, but all Christians are to lead lives that are shaped by Christ's self-sacrifice. The Lord in whom we put our trust is the one after whom we model life. His life, we affirm, is the best life, even if it is starkly different from that led by the majority.

> **What Do You Think?**
> What qualities will others see in us when we get serious about living by Jesus' example?
> **Digging Deeper**
> Considering Matthew 13:1-9, 18-23, what three challenges to your commitment are you most likely to encounter?

C. Resurrection in the Future (v. 11)

11. If by any means I might attain unto the resurrection of the dead.

For all writers of the New Testament, discussion of Christ's death inevitably leads to discussion of His resurrection. Having just spoken of knowing the power of Christ's resurrection, Paul now speaks of *the resurrection* as a future hope.

We should not mistake the significance of *if* and *attain.* As in Philippians 2:1, here Paul uses *if* not to cast doubt (as in "if maybe"), but with assurance ("if, and indeed it will be the case"). Similarly, *attain* does not mean "earn" or "achieve," but "arrive" or "come to" (compare translation of the same word as "came" in Acts 16:1; 18:19, 24). Paul does not see resurrection as something that he must prove worthy of but rather as something to which God will faithfully bring him by His grace.

These observations help us understand the expression *by any means.* As Paul contemplates his future, he is confident by faith in Christ that God's promise of resurrection from *the dead* will be the climax of his future. Until that day, Paul remains uncertain as to exactly what will befall him, though he remains confident of God's constant provision and of the final resurrection. Paul knows something about resurrection, having performed one himself (Acts 20:7-12). So *by any means* expresses not uncertainty about the outcome of resurrection but of the circumstances through which he will journey to that point.

II. Forgetting and Pressing
(PHILIPPIANS 3:12-14)
A. Goal to Grasp (v. 12)

12a. Not as though I had already attained, either were already perfect.

Having looked forward to the promised resurrection, Paul assesses his present situation. Make no mistake: God's full purpose for Paul is not yet achieved. The resurrection that he will one day have will be the full realization of God's purpose. This is not just for Paul but for all of God's people, as those still living are united with the risen dead, both transformed to a new existence (1 Corinthians 15:50-55; 1 Thessalonians 4:13-18).

That is the sense in which the word *perfect* is used here. In Paul's original language, the term indicates the accomplishment of a goal or purpose (compare John 4:34; 5:36; 17:4). As it is God's goal and God who accomplishes it, this future perfection is certain.

12b. But I follow after, if that I may apprehend that for which also I am apprehended of Christ Jesus.

But God's action demands Paul's response. Prompted by faith, he must participate in what God is doing. *Christ* has *apprehended* Paul—that is, taken hold of him—for a purpose. That purpose is that Paul's life should be transformed to be like Christ's life, culminating in resurrection from the dead. So Paul ministers in light of that goal with his entire being. The resurrection from the dead to come shapes his entire ministry effort.

What Do You Think?
How will the certainty of future resurrection shape your attitudes and actions from this day forward?
Digging Deeper
Knowing that attitudes shape action, in what ways have you seen the reverse—actions of yours that have modified your attitudes?

B. Race to Finish (vv. 13, 14)

13. Brethren, I count not myself to have apprehended: but this one thing I do, forgetting those things which are behind, and reaching forth unto those things which are before.

Taking hold of the future is a lifelong process. Assured of God's victory, Paul pursues that future with abandon. His past, whatever its honor or shame, he no longer values. The future is his focus. It will not merely be a never-ending life, but a fully transformed life. It will be a life brought into complete conformity with the image of God in Christ.

In the resurrection, all Christ's people will be like Him (1 John 3:2). We, like Paul, will have been transformed from the selfish behavior of this present age to reflect completely Christ the selfless servant. Until then, we are being transformed to be what we will be fully when raised from the dead (Romans 8:29; 2 Peter 1:4). It is no surprise, then, that Paul can compare baptism, which occurs at the beginning of the Christian walk, with "resurrection" (Romans 6:3-11; compare Colossians 2:12), as it initiates the transformation, the overcoming of sin and becoming more like Christ.

What Do You Think?
What is the next thing you need to be reaching for in your pursuit of becoming more like Jesus?
Digging Deeper
What things or thoughts will you need to let go of in order to reach that goal? Why?

---

14. I press toward the mark for the prize of the high calling of God in Christ Jesus.

Thus, Paul can allude to his life as being an arduous, long-distance race (compare 1 Corinthians 9:24; Galatians 2:2; Hebrews 12:1). At the end lies *the prize*, the one for which he was called to the starting line by *God in Christ Jesus*. That prize is to be like Christ in His divinely granted resurrection. The prize is given to all who finish, for the prize is the Lord's gracious gift (2 Timothy 4:7, 8). But the race is nevertheless the pursuit of the goal, in which each moment must bring one closer. If we believe in the Christ who died and rose, the pursuit of the prize becomes all that matters to us.

During a prayer service at Emanuel African Methodist Episcopal Church on June 17, 2015, 21-year-old Dylann Roof killed nine people. Roof was arrested the next morning. He later confessed that he committed the horrible act in the Charleston, South Carolina, church hoping to ignite a race war; all those killed were African-Americans.

Roof's website substantiated his racist views. It contained photos of Roof posing with symbols of white supremacy and neo-Nazism. Roof longed to widen the racial divide in the country and thwart hopes of racial unity.

But Roof's actions did not accomplish his goal. Later, at Roof's hearing, some survivors and family members of victims offered this troubled young man their forgiveness and promised to pray for him. On the following Sunday evening, a racially diverse crowd estimated at 20,000 marched peacefully through the city in a show of solidarity for those slain.

Everyone knows that the goal of racial unity cannot be achieved with a single rally. It is an ongoing process that must be accomplished with perseverance as we confront evil day after day with love and forgiveness.

Paul the apostle recognized that personal change does not happen overnight. There are many distractions along the way of "the high calling of God in Christ Jesus." But the goal toward which he strove daily is worth any sacrifice necessary to attain it. Certainly, the same is true for each of us as we anticipate resurrection while striving to correct personal and societal flaws. If there's something you are not yet willing to give up in that regard, be assured that Satan will attempt to use it as a hindrance. —J. E.

Conclusion

A. Knowing How You Are Doing

Today's text certainly prompted the Philippian Christians to reassess the direction of their lives. Remembering Christ's life, death, and resurrection, looking forward to resurrection and life with Him at His return—these meant that the readers' present lives had to be transformed into greater like-

Visual for Lesson 10. *Point to this visual as you ask, "What are some common hindrances that come our way in the race of the Christian life?"*

ness to Christ. There was no place for the division that had begun to afflict this congregation (compare Philippians 4:2). There was only room for self-giving service, empowered by the risen Lord.

We are confronted with the same need for self-assessment. What is our direction? Are we caught up in our own achievement or dragged down by our failures? Are we wrapped up in ourselves? We can begin a self-assessment by considering how Paul evaluated his own losses and gains. As a Christian, he had a difficult, miserable life (again, 2 Corinthians 11:22-33). But Christ showed him that real worth is found in trusting God's provision and giving oneself for others as Christ gave himself for us. The end result will be worth it: resurrection and eternity with Christ.

Christ calls us to continue the race, to renew our reassessment of profit and loss, to remember the one who laid hold of us so that we can lay hold of that to which He called us. How is Christ calling you to be more like Him?

B. Prayer

Father, empower us for the race ahead! As we run that race, may we reflect on Your grace anew and run with the end in view: the goal of resurrected, eternal life. We pray in the name of the one who makes this possible, Your Son. Amen.

C. Thought to Remember

Let the goal of the Christian life shape your now.

INVOLVEMENT LEARNING

Enhance your lesson with KJV Bible Student *(from your curriculum supplier) and the reproducible activity page (at www.standardlesson.com or in the back of the* KJV Standard Lesson Commentary Deluxe Edition*).*

Into the Lesson

Before class, write the following or similar on separate index cards: $5 coffee gift card; porcelain angel; fidget spinner; new laptop; all-expense paid trip to Israel; old bus; log cabin; $450,000 house. You will need as many cards as you have participants, so add to or subtract from these as needed. Put cards in separate envelopes, which you number from 1 upwards.

Shuffle the envelopes, then give each learner one. As you do, say, "We are going to play a version of the white-elephant game. Please don't open your envelope yet." After each person has one, ask the learner with envelope #1 to open it and read the card. That person can then either keep the card or trade for someone else's, all other cards being unknown at this point. (*Option.* Stipulate that each card can change hands only once.) Proceed until everyone has had a turn. (*Option.* Allow more than one turn each, depending on class size.) Then ask, "Generally speaking, how do we assign value to things?"

Alternative. Distribute copies of the "Ultimate Prizes?" activity from the reproducible page, which you can download. Announce a one-minute time limit. After announcing correct answers, ask, "Which of these prizes would you most want to win and why?"

After either activity, make a transition by saying, "If we were to repeat this activity years from now, our choices and desires may be very different. That's because the values we assign change as new alternatives come along. The reasoning behind the apostle Paul's change in what he valued has much to teach us in this regard."

Into the Word

Read Philippians 3:7 (only). Then divide the class into *The Before Group* and *The After Group*. Give each group a handout (you prepare) with instructions as follows. *The Before Group:* Begin-ning with Paul's statement about gain and loss, work backward two verses and forward two verses to discover specific things Paul previously considered gain but ultimately decided were loss. *The After Group:* Read Philippians 3:8-14 and find specific things Paul considered to be gain after being called to the service of Christ.

Have groups summarize findings in whole-class discussion. (*Expected responses—The Before Group:* things Paul ultimately decided were loss are listed in verses 5, 6, and 9. Things he had counted on to get him into Heaven he concluded to be worthless in and of themselves. *The After Group:* things Paul ultimately decided were gain are listed throughout verses 8-14. He realized that the most valuable prize he could pursue was a relationship with Jesus.) Refer to the commentary to fill in gaps.

Option. Have groups summarize as if describing Paul's experience to someone who is not familiar with Christian terminology.

Into Life

Draw the following scale on the board:

⟵————————————————⟶

Clinging to the past   Pressing toward the prize

Ask one or more of the following questions, pausing for responses between each: 1–Where do you see yourself on this scale and why? 2–What are you clinging to that may be hindering your spiritual growth? 3–In what way do you want to be more like Christ?

Since responses may be very personal, you as the teacher should be prepared to go first. Participants may need some time for self-evaluation, so don't rush to fill silence with talk.

Alternative. Distribute copies of the "Losses and Gains" activity from the reproducible page. Have students work in pairs to complete as indicated. Ask for volunteers to share answers. Be prepared to refer to Mark 10:28-31 as appropriate.

OUR LOVING GOD

DEVOTIONAL READING: Psalm 93
BACKGROUND SCRIPTURE: Psalm 48:1-3, 9-14

PSALM 48:1-3, 9-14

1 Great is the LORD, and greatly to be praised in the city of our God, in the mountain of his holiness.

2 Beautiful for situation, the joy of the whole earth, is mount Zion, on the sides of the north, the city of the great King.

3 God is known in her palaces for a refuge.

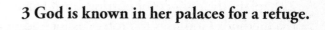

9 We have thought of thy lovingkindness, O God, in the midst of thy temple.

10 According to thy name, O God, so is thy praise unto the ends of the earth: thy right hand is full of righteousness.

11 Let mount Zion rejoice, let the daughters of Judah be glad, because of thy judgments.

12 Walk about Zion, and go round about her: tell the towers thereof.

13 Mark ye well her bulwarks, consider her palaces; that ye may tell it to the generation following.

14 For this God is our God for ever and ever: he will be our guide even unto death.

KEY VERSE

This God is our God for ever and ever. —**Psalm 48:14**

OUR LOVE FOR GOD

Unit 3: Songs That Glorify the God of Love

LESSONS 11–13

LESSON AIMS

After participating in this lesson, each learner will be able to:

1. Summarize the concept of God's covenantal love.

2. Explain the dangers of putting confidence in the methods God uses to protect us instead of trusting directly in Him.

3. Write a prayer thanking God for His love and protection.

LESSON OUTLINE

Introduction
A. "Do You Love Me?"
B. Lesson Context
I. God Glorifies Zion (PSALM 48:1-3)
A. With His Greatness (v. 1)
B. With His Presence (v. 2)
C. With His Protection (v. 3)
II. Celebrate God's Leadership
(PSALM 48:9-11)
A. Because of His Loyalty (v. 9)
Love Letters
B. Because of His Righteousness (v. 10)
C. Because of His Judgments (v. 11)
III. Teach Future Generations (PSALM 48:12-14)
A. Based on God's Protection (vv. 12, 13)
Home Church Memories
B. Based on God's Presence (v. 14)
Conclusion
A. Our Loving God Leads and Protects Us
B. Prayer
C. Thought to Remember

Introduction

A. "Do You Love Me?"

In the musical *Fiddler on the Roof*, we encounter a poor dairy farmer, Tevye, who values highly the traditions of his people. But the rapidly changing times in which he lives finds him stretched when each of his three daughters defies tradition. Tevye's role as family patriarch is to find a suitable match for each daughter. His tradition values finding a financially stable partner from within the ancient faith.

A hired matchmaker arranges for the oldest daughter to be wed to an elderly, widowed butcher. But she is secretly in love with a poor tailor. Those two beg Tevye to call off the arranged marriage so they can marry. Tevye is conflicted, but he sees how deeply his daughter cares for the tailor, so he relents out of love for her.

Tevye's middle daughter reveals disregard for tradition by marrying a university student with a head full of revolutionary ideas. Tevye feels he has no choice but to accept the marriage. Then his third daughter does the unthinkable by marrying a Christian. Tevye reaches his breaking point and disowns her. No more!

In the middle of his turmoil, he finds himself insecure. Each of his daughters married for love, a choice not afforded Tevye and his wife when their marriage was arranged 25 years earlier. So Tevye turns to his wife and asks her if she loves him. They have never spoken of their feelings for each other, so she gives an indirect answer by offering evidence of her love: she has washed his clothes, cooked meals, cleaned house, and starved with him. Her loyalty is all the proof needed of her love for him.

Does God love us? The author of today's psalm would reply, "Just look at the evidence!"

B. Lesson Context

Psalm 48 is often categorized as one of the Zion Songs. This category also includes Psalms 46, 76, 84, 87, and 122 (some students also include 126, 129, and 137). These celebrate the glory of Mount Zion, the hill on which the temple in Jerusalem stood. They are concerned with the theme of God's kingship, having been written against a backdrop of competing gods and warring nations. Nationalism and religion were inseparable in biblical times, and each nation was thought to have a dominant deity who was responsible for the protection of its people. When nations warred, their gods warred as well. We see this in Exodus 12:12, where God, preparing Israel for the tenth and most devastating plague, says,

> For I will pass through the land of Egypt this night, and will smite all the firstborn in the land of Egypt, both man and beast; and against all the gods of Egypt I will execute judgment: I am the LORD.

Thematically, these songs celebrate God as Israel's king, who chose to rest His presence in Jerusalem and, in it, the temple (Psalm 46:5; 76:2; 84:1; 87:1-3; 122:1-3; plus today's text). From a perspective of comparative religion, a deity choosing to rest his presence on a strong mountain was not unique. For example, the pagan deity El was said to reside on Mount Zaphon (see more on Psalm 48:2, below). What is exceptional is the theme that God's reign doesn't stop at Israel's borders. He is "a great King over all the earth" (Psalm 47:2, plus today's text; compare 1 Kings 20:23, 28).

I. God Glorifies Zion
(PSALM 48:1-3)
A. With His Greatness (v. 1)

1. Great is the LORD, and greatly to be praised in the city of our God, in the mountain of his holiness.

When King David set out to unify the tribes of Israel, he strategically chose Jerusalem to be his capital. Jerusalem was centrally located between the upper and lower tribes; and as a Jebusite stronghold, it wasn't associated with either region. A walled city set on a *mountain* or hill was the perfect spot from which to reign.

However, the song doesn't open with a description of the height of the walls or the strength and numbers of the army stationed inside. Instead, attention is given to God's greatness and *holiness*.

Interestingly, Jerusalem is referred to as "the city of David" more than three dozen times in the Old Testament, but never that way in any psalm. Instead, the Psalms refer to Jerusalem (or Zion; see 1 Kings 8:1) as, among other designations, *city of God* or *city of our God* four times. All Old Testament instances of those are in the Zion Songs (here and in Psalms 46:4; 48:8; and 87:3).

The mountain of [God's] holiness is Mount Zion (Psalm 48:2, next). This is not the first time that God is associated with a mountain in His developing relationship with His people. Moses had stated that God would bring His people to live on "the mountain of thine inheritance" (Exodus 15:17). Chapters later, God has the nation camp at the base of Mount Sinai, where He revealed His power and gave the Ten Commandments (20:1-17).

Now, here on Mount Zion, the people are reminded of the greatness of Yahweh (God's name in Hebrew, rendered *Lord* in translation). This greatness must result in praise.

B. With His Presence (v. 2)

2. Beautiful for situation, the joy of the whole earth, is mount Zion, on the sides of the north, the city of the great King.

Having established the emphasis on Yahweh, the psalmist briefly diverts his attention to the renown and setting of *mount Zion*. With the designation *on the sides of the north*, the translators have made a difficult choice. The Hebrew word that means "north" is *Zaphon*, a word that appears untranslated in Joshua 13:27 to designate a specific place rather than a compass direction.

If a specific place is intended, then the psalmist is making a reference to a location where a pagan deity is imagined to dwell (see the Lesson Context). The psalmist leaves no doubt that the

HOW TO SAY IT

Babylonian	Bab-ih-*low*-nee-un.
Jebusite	*Jeb*-yuh-site.
Nebuchadnezzar	*Neb*-yuh-kud-**nez**-er.
patriarch	*pay*-tree-ark.
Sinai	*Sigh*-nye or *Sigh*-nay-eye.
Tevye	*Tev*-yuh.
Yahweh *(Hebrew)*	*Yah*-weh.
Zaphon	*Za*-fon.
Zion	*Zi*-un.

God of Mount Zion is superior. On the other hand, if the psalmist intends a geographical direction, then this is further commentary on Jerusalem's geography (compare Isaiah 14:13).

Either way, the exuberant conviction of the psalmist is obvious: Mount Zion, *the city of the great King*—designated this way only here and in Matthew 5:35—is (or should be) *the joy of the whole earth* and not of Israel alone. The close connection between God and Mount Zion is further seen in the Zion Songs at Psalms 76:2; 84:7; 87:2, 5.

C. With His Protection (v. 3)

3. God is known in her palaces for a refuge.

The psalmist turns his attention from Mount Zion back to *God*. The designation of God as Israel's *refuge* continues a thought from an earlier Zion Song (Psalm 46:1, 11). By calling God their refuge, the psalmist reminds the people that God is their ultimate source of protection.

Strong walls are important for cities (see Nehemiah 1:1–6:15). Government, religion, and life itself are protected by such stone and mortar barriers. But the God who brought down the walls of Jericho (Joshua 6) can also bring down the walls of Jerusalem. The people must never lose sight of the fact that God, not walls of stone, is their ultimate refuge.

He will be their refuge as long as they do not forget Him (compare Psalm 94:22). The psalmist seems to be creating an analogy, given that the word translated *refuge* is also the Hebrew word for physical, material defenses (Isaiah 25:12; 33:16).

In Psalm 48:4-8, not in today's text, we see the consequences for those who dare threaten Zion's security: God rightfully receives credit for destroying the enemy's military strength.

II. Celebrate God's Leadership
(PSALM 48:9-11)
A. Because of His Loyalty (v. 9)

9. We have thought of thy lovingkindness, O God, in the midst of thy temple.

This is the only occurrence of the word *temple* in the Zion Songs (see the Lesson Context), although the alternative designation "house" occurs several times (Psalm 84:4, 10; 122:1, 9). Up until now, the reader's imagination has been directed to the geography and defenses of Jerusalem. As the psalmist shifts attention to the temple, he again reminds the people that the true strength of Israel is to be found in God's presence among them.

When King Solomon prayed his prayer of dedication for the newly built temple, he was aware that even though God chose to make the temple His meeting place with Israel, God was in no way constrained by the structure. Solomon marveled at the fact that the vast heavens couldn't contain God, let alone the temple (2 Chronicles 6:18). Even so, God revealed that He had chosen the temple as His dwelling place as He sent His glory to fill it (7:1-3) and communicated to Solomon at night (7:12-22).

The temple is the ideal place to contemplate God's *lovingkindness*. The Hebrew behind this translation is very common in the Old Testament, occurring over 130 times, but in the Zion Songs it occurs only here. Elsewhere it is often translated "mercy" (example: Psalm 5:7). This disposition assumes a hierarchy in which one in a higher position is merciful to one in a lower. In biblical times, kings would enter into treaties with their subjects. These treaties outline the relationship between the two parties. The loyalty that is expected between the two parties may be expressed in terms of love. The king would love his people by protecting them and by ruling them with just laws. The people, in turn, would express their love for the king through their loyal obedience.

So *lovingkindness* in this context refers primarily to King Yahweh's fierce and unwavering loyalty to His people. As the people meditate on God's track record as their king, they will find Him to be nothing less than a perfect ruler. He has never failed them. He has provided for the Israelites throughout their history.

✤ LOVE LETTERS ✤

Valentine's Day is nearly here. It is love-letter time.

How long has it been since you received a love letter or sent one? I have an old Whitman's chocolates box that my father gave to my mother in the late 1940s. Though the chocolates are long gone, the box is full of memories of their love. It contains 30 letters my dad sent to my mom while he was stationed away in the Army. They were newlyweds at the time.

Even though those letters have been in my possession for more than 25 years, I haven't read any of them. Why? I am fearful of invading my mother's privacy. I realize that there might be something intimate in those letters. My homesick father could have written something meant for my mother's eyes only. I don't want to intrude on that, so those letters will never be read by me.

I have no hesitation when it comes to reading the love letters of my heavenly Father, though. He wrote those letters specifically for me. He wants to maintain a deep relationship with me. He loves me and doesn't care who knows it.

Our heavenly Father knows we need to hear from Him. His love compelled Him to send us valuable letters. Are you meditating as deeply on the Psalms as you should?　　　　—C. T.

B. Because of His Righteousness (v. 10)

10a. According to thy name, O God, so is thy praise unto the ends of the earth.

The psalmist returns to a predominant theme of the Zion Songs. Yahweh's rule knows no lim-

its. God's praises don't end at Israel's borders. When His people consider His faithfulness to them, their worshipful response should be so great that it extends to *the ends of the earth*. (In other Zion Songs, compare "unto the end of the earth" in Psalm 46:9; plus "praise" and "praising" in Psalms 76:10; 84:4, respectively.) The half-verse before us therefore scoffs at the notion that any of the countless deities of the ancient Near East can challenge God's reign.

10b. Thy right hand is full of righteousness.

Interestingly, God's might is not mentioned as proof of His singular existence. Instead, the proof of His superiority over any so-called gods is depicted here in terms of His *righteousness*. This is a straightforward concept: it means that God always does the right thing.

This is the only place in the psalms known as Zion Songs where this word occurs (see the Lesson Context). But other psalms speak to God's righteousness, with contexts often pointing to God's righteous acts rather than only to God's righteous nature per se (compare Psalm 5:8; 9:8; 65:5; 103:6). So important is the concept of righteousness that in Psalm 89:14 it is paired with "justice" as "the habitation" (foundational pillars) of God's throne.

> *What Do You Think?*
> How will you answer someone who asks, "If God is righteous, then why is there so much injustice in the world?"
> *Digging Deeper*
> Consider how Paul interacted with audiences that accepted the authority of Scripture (example: Acts 13:13-43) and those that did not (examples: Acts 17:16-34; 24:24, 25).

C. Because of His Judgments (v. 11)

11. Let mount Zion rejoice, let the daughters of Judah be glad, because of thy judgments.

Here we have another rarity: as "righteousness" in Psalm 48:10, above, occurs only there in the Zion Songs, the paired concepts of *rejoice* and *be glad* also occur only this one time in these psalms, although found frequently elsewhere (examples:

Psalms 31:7; 32:11; 40:16). Indeed, the two concepts are found to be interchangeable as an author uses the typical Hebrew style of parallelism in poetic writing. Parallelism is where one line of text says virtually the same thing as the line that follows by use of synonyms or near synonyms.

An example of such parallelism involving joy and gladness is Psalm 53:6: "Jacob shall rejoice, and Israel shall be glad." Jacob was the name of the patriarch who had his name changed to Israel (Genesis 32:28), thus the two terms describe the same people group that are named after that man. The parallelism extends to what this people group is predicted to do: rejoice/be glad. Although not precise synonyms, they are very close in meaning.

And so it is in the verse at hand. *Mount Zion* refers to the city of Jerusalem and *daughters of Judah* is figurative for the rural hamlets nearby. Thus they both describe locations of people. God's protective *judgments* cover both (compare Psalm 97:8).

III. Teach Future Generations
(Psalm 48:12-14)

A. Based on God's Protection (vv. 12, 13)

12. Walk about Zion, and go round about her: tell the towers thereof.

After being explicit that the source of Jerusalem's security doesn't lie in her defense systems, the psalmist startles us with his encouragement that the people take stock in their man-made *towers*! The fall of Jericho affirmed that God's power is greater than brick and mortar protection (Joshua 6:1-25). That said, the psalmist seems to acknowledge that God uses walls (and armies) as methods of fulfilling His covenant loyalty toward His people. (Deuteronomy 28:52 indicates the exact opposite should the people fail to honor their part of the covenant.)

13. Mark ye well her bulwarks, consider her palaces; that ye may tell it to the generation following.

The inspection of structures continues, with a purpose now revealed: to inform *the generation following* (compare Psalms 34:11; 78:4-6). The worshippers are to become so familiar with the defenses of Jerusalem that they will be able to tell

their children about the city's might. At first blush that may seem like an exercise in putting stock in human strength. But in this case, Jerusalem's strength is a figurative representation of God's protection and care.

> **What Do You Think?**
> How can we ensure that our support for, say, an antimissile defense system is not a failure to trust God for protection? What, if anything, does Deuteronomy 28:15, 52 add to the discussion?
>
> **Digging Deeper**
> Conversely, how can we ensure that our opposition to that same system is not out of line with the attitude expressed in Psalm 48:12, 13?

Ultimately, Israel fails to communicate to the next generation the importance of keeping its side of the covenant. Kings lead the people into idolatry, with injustice marring the nation. This results in a period of captivity, when God allowed foreign armies to conquer the land of the 12 tribes. The army of King Nebuchadnezzar will besiege Jerusalem, destroy its walls, and carry its people into exile (2 Chronicles 36:15-20).

> **What Do You Think?**
> What creative ways can you imagine for telling the generation that follows yours about how God has provided for and sustained you?
>
> **Digging Deeper**
> Consider the relative values of direct, personal testimony and indirect (social media, etc.) testimony.

❧ HOME CHURCH MEMORIES ❧

I get a little misty-eyed when I walk through the door of my boyhood church. Going home causes you to remember. I think back to my Sunday school classroom—filled with active, inquisitive children. Oh, how our hearts thrilled at the character-building stories of the Bible! We memorized our Bible verses, and still can quote them after these many years. We made craft projects that brightened the day of a parent or grandparent.

Small things? Mere entertainment? Not on your life! Through such methods we were taught God's Word. I can still see the faces of those who came up out of the water, grinning from ear to ear, after being baptized into Christ.

God showed himself to us, alive and active, in every gathering. He still does today, and He tends to do so through human vessels. What should be your role in this? —C. T.

B. Based on God's Presence (v. 14)

14. For this God is our God for ever and ever: he will be our guide even unto death.

The psalm resolves on a final note of confidence regarding *our God* (compare Psalms 48:1, 8; and 122:9). In verse 13, the readers are instructed to pass their knowledge of God and His ways to their offspring. But the knowledge of God is not the only thing moving in the future. God, himself, goes with His people. The one who *will be our guide* is the one who leads or brings (same Hebrew word in Psalms 78:26, 52; 80:1). Our source of protection and safety will lead us throughout our entire lives, if we let Him. We have the assurance that when we reach the end of our days (*unto death*), God will be right there.

Conclusion

A. Our Loving God Leads and Protects Us

A song celebrating the city walls might seem out of place to the modern reader. For the Israelites, however, the structure was a tangible indication of God's rule and presence. He was their king, the one who promised to lead and protect them.

This psalm would have presented a challenge to the worshipper during the time of the Babylonian exile. The reality of Jerusalem's destruction in 586 BC starkly contrasted with the message of Psalm 48.

The tension is relieved as we consider again King Solomon's prayer of dedication of the newly built temple. He anticipated the possibility that Israel would rebel against God and be cast into exile as a result. Solomon implored God that if His people would deeply repent of their sins and turn their hearts back to Him, then He would hear

Visual for Lessons 11 & 12. *During discussion of the question for Psalm 48:13b, ask how music can be part of the "telling" process.*

them, forgive them, and restore them (2 Chronicles 6:36-39). The irony is palpable, since wise Solomon himself ended up much less than wise as he allowed foreign wives to lead him into idolatry within Jerusalem's walls (see 1 Kings 11:7-10).

God continued to be their king and their fortress, even after the city walls were demolished by a foreign army. The subsequent exile challenged Israel's confidence in their God, but He proved His sovereign loyalty to them time and again. And He displayed His loyalty even as their disloyalty resulted in their own demise.

Today, we serve our Lord Jesus, who expressed His loyalty to us through His death and resurrection. We can be confident in His good rule and love for us. Our task is to pass that love and message to others (Matthew 28:19, 20). That's the greatest show of loyalty to Him we can offer!

B. Prayer

Lord God, You are our strong and mighty king. We thank You for the tangible ways that You've protected us throughout the years. We thank You for governing us with Your holiness and righteousness. May everything we do, think, and say be an expression of our love for You. We pray in the name of King Jesus. Amen.

C. Thought to Remember

God's protection is
an expression of His love.

INVOLVEMENT LEARNING

Enhance your lesson with KJV Bible Student *(from your curriculum supplier) and the reproducible activity page (at www.standardlesson.com or in the back of the* KJV Standard Lesson Commentary Deluxe Edition*).*

Into the Lesson

Form learners into pairs. Then say, "I am going to name a location, and you and your partner have 15 seconds to come up with the name of a famous wall there. The wall can be from the past or present. But here's the tough part: you cannot talk to your partner. You must share thoughts in writing back and forth until you agree on an answer. We'll go over correct answers after I've given you seven locations. Remember, you will work in silence the entire time."

As you read off the following locations, pause for 15 seconds after each for pairs to reach consensus: China, Germany, Croatia, England, Turkey, Iraq, Jerusalem. (*Expected responses, respectively:* the Great Wall, the Berlin Wall, the Walls of Ston, Hadrian's Wall, the Walls of Troy, the Walls of Babylon, the Western or Wailing Wall.)

Alternative. Distribute copies of the "Follow the Leader?" activity from the reproducible page, which you can download, for learners to complete as indicated. (*Option.* Make this exercise harder by removing the rightmost column, thereby turning a challenge of matching into fill-in-the-blank.) As you discuss answers, ask learners which leader they would most and least liked to have lived under.

After either activity, make a transition by saying: "Let's take a look at how the psalmist uses his praise of Mount Zion (the city of Jerusalem) and elements of its wall to express his praise for God, the ultimate leader worthy of following."

Into the Word

Have volunteers take turns reading the eight verses of Psalm 48:1-3, 9-14. Give a mini-lecture on why Mount Zion was God's holy mountain, the focal point of honoring His unmatched character and power.

Give each participant a handout (you prepare) on which is printed the lesson text. Then form learners into groups of two or three; give each group three fine-tip markers or ballpoint pens in the colors of green, red, and black. Write these three categories on the board:

> *Praise for God*
> *Praise for Mount Zion (Jerusalem)*
> *Praise for the City's Defensive Structures*

In addition to featuring the lesson text, the handouts should instruct groups to underline in green those phrases in the text that correspond with the first category, red for phrases that correspond with the second, and black for phrases that correspond with the third.

In the discussion that ensues after groups finish, explore how the psalmist intertwines the three categories. Make sure to bring this "what's so" discussion to its ideal conclusion of application by asking "So what?" That will serve as your transition to the Into Life segment.

Into Life

Write on the board, or distribute on handouts (you prepare) the following descriptions of God:

> **P**RINCE OF PEACE
> **R**IGHTEOUS
> **A**LL-POWERFUL
> **I**NFINITE
> **S**AVIOR
> **E**VERLASTING FATHER

Challenge learners to write a brief prayer of praise that uses each description of God at least once. (*Option.* Explore the what from, why, and how of praise distractions by having learners complete the "Be an Overcomer" activity from the reproducible page.) Close with this prayer: "Lord, may we be ever grateful for your steadfast love and protection! As we reflect on Your provisions, we are especially thankful for these things. *[Pause to allow learners to list things silently.]* In the matchless name of Jesus, we pray. Amen."

OUR MIGHTY GOD

DEVOTIONAL READING: Psalm 114
BACKGROUND SCRIPTURE: Psalm 66

PSALM 66:1-9, 16-20

1 Make a joyful noise unto God, all ye lands:

2 Sing forth the honour of his name: make his praise glorious.

3 Say unto God, How terrible art thou in thy works! through the greatness of thy power shall thine enemies submit themselves unto thee.

4 All the earth shall worship thee, and shall sing unto thee; they shall sing to thy name. Selah.

5 Come and see the works of God: he is terrible in his doing toward the children of men.

6 He turned the sea into dry land: they went through the flood on foot: there did we rejoice in him.

7 He ruleth by his power for ever; his eyes behold the nations: let not the rebellious exalt themselves. Selah.

8 O bless our God, ye people, and make the voice of his praise to be heard:

9 Which holdeth our soul in life, and suffereth not our feet to be moved.

. . . .

16 Come and hear, all ye that fear God, and I will declare what he hath done for my soul.

17 I cried unto him with my mouth, and he was extolled with my tongue.

18 If I regard iniquity in my heart, the Lord will not hear me:

19 But verily God hath heard me; he hath attended to the voice of my prayer.

20 Blessed be God, which hath not turned away my prayer, nor his mercy from me.

KEY VERSE

Make a joyful noise unto God, all ye lands. —**Psalm 66:1**

OUR LOVE FOR GOD

Unit 3: Songs That Glorify the God of Love

LESSONS 11–13

LESSON AIMS

After participating in this lesson, each learner will be able to:

1. Identify the allusions in Psalm 66 to God's rescue of Israel at the crossing of the Red Sea.

2. Discuss the impact that sharing one's personal testimony can have on other believers.

3. Write a prayer of gratitude to God for one way that He has shown His power in his or her life.

LESSON OUTLINE

Introduction

A. The Mother of All Bombs

As I sat down to write the draft for this commentary, the radio informed me that the US military had just dropped a MOAB (Massive Ordnance Air Blast) bomb in a strike in Afghanistan. Nicknamed the "Mother of All Bombs," MOAB is the largest nonnuclear bomb in the US arsenal. Due to its massive size—21,000 pounds and 30 feet long—it can't be delivered like other conventional bombs. It is transported within range of its target by a specially modified cargo plane, released, and then remotely guided to its target. One MOAB yields an explosive force equivalent to 11 tons of TNT.

The power of the bomb wasn't limited to the battlefield. The MOAB also took over the news cycle. Whatever else the commentators planned on discussing that day fell by the wayside. Pundits debated whether such a show of force was justified and speculated on the political implications of the event. Others wondered if there was justification for such a weapon to exist at all. Throughout the day, world governments weighed in with messages of support or condemnation regarding the use of the bomb. The entire world took notice when a weapon of that magnitude was unleashed.

Psalm 66 explores a different type of might—God's power. God's mighty acts toward Israel were so great that every nation had to take notice and react.

B. Lesson Context

Traditionally, the Psalms are seen as a collection of five books. These five are Psalms 1–41, 42–72, 73–89, 90–106, and 107–150. Our texts for today and last week fall in the second of these five books. As overall characteristics, the psalms of this second book feature relatively many songs of trust and/or complaint plus some praise hymns.

The five books that compose the Psalms are seen to consist of subcollections that share similar themes. In that light, today's text from Psalm 66 fits with the short collection Psalms 65–68. These four songs focus on the entire earth and all her nations. The nations are depicted as confessing (or needing to confess) God's power and praising (or needing to praise) Him for His just rule.

This concern in Psalm 66 with other nations' worship of God has led scholars to wonder if an international crisis was the background for its writing. Two possibilities are usually suggested. One is the Assyrian crisis of 701 BC (see 2 Kings 18:13–19:36); the other is after the release from Babylonian captivity. The date of the psalm's writing under the latter proposal would be after the rebuilding of the temple in 515 BC, since Psalm 66:13 refers to that structure (compare Ezra 6:15).

No one knows which theory (if either) is correct. Yet this uncertainty does not rob the psalm of its dynamic power. It can be applied to any deliverance the people of God experience.

Remembering that psalms are ancient Israel's worship songs, Psalm 66 presents itself as five stanzas. These five consist of verses 1-4, 5-7, 8-12, 13-15, and 16-20. Three of the stanza transitions are marked by the word *Selah*, occurring at the ends of verses 4, 7, and 15. One stanza transition is marked by the psalmist's shift to writing in the first person in verse 13. Today's lesson explores the first two stanzas in full, part of the third stanza, and the entirety of the fifth.

I. Come and Praise
(PSALM 66:1-4)

A. Appeal Made to Everyone (vv. 1, 2)

1. Make a joyful noise unto God, all ye lands.

The hymn opens with a roar as *all . . . lands* of the world are charged to make *a joyful noise* in acknowledgement of the one true *God*. Since His works are not constrained within the borders of Israel, every nation everywhere is challenged to join Israel in worshipping Him. The same challenge concludes the stanza (see below). The imperative *make a joyful noise* suggests to some the idea of a triumphant army celebrating a victory (see also Psalms 81:1; 95:1; 98:4; 100:1).

2. Sing forth the honour of his name: make his praise glorious.

The nature of the joyful noise is now refined in terms of *the honour* that God is due. The challenge for the crowd to sing in such a manner as to *make his praise glorious* allows no half-hearted or insincere praise! The word *glorious* captures the idea of an individual's reputation in the community and how others regard that person (compare Psalms 79:9; 86:9; Isaiah 42:8, 12).

The Hebrew words for *glory* and *glorious* are based on a root that means "heavy" in various contexts. Some students propose, therefore, that to glorify someone is to add weight to his or her reputation. But conclusions regarding such added meanings are best avoided unless the author makes it clear that it is intended. One example of such an intention seems to be 2 Corinthians 4:17, where Paul—writing in Greek while having an expert knowledge of Hebrew—speaks of a "weight of glory." A play on the common Hebrew root for the words *heavy* and *glory* is obvious in this case, given the construction of the sentence. But the same is not obvious in Psalm 66:2.

We may wonder how our singing glorifies God's *name*. Is it through the skill of our voices, the level of our sincerity, the volume that results, or the nature of the lyrics? The psalmist doesn't specify, but undoubtedly the level of our sincerity is the starting point for honoring the name of God.

> **What Do You Think?**
> Other than congregational singing, what are some other ways we can bring honor to God's name and reputation?
> *Digging Deeper*
> Conversely, what are some ways that we may inadvertently detract from God's reputation?

❧ *THOSE ANNOYING SONGS* ❧

It's happened to all of us: we get a song stuck in our head—one that goes around and around without end. That can be so annoying!

I've found that a short stint in children's church can do just that. "Father Abraham had many sons. Many sons had Father Abraham. I am one of them, and so are you. So let's just praise the Lord. Right arm! . . ."

There—I've planted the seed. "Father Abraham" will run through your mind all day long!

Though a song stuck in one's head may be annoying, it is not damaging. But some thoughts that stick in our heads can indeed do great damage to us, thoughts like these: *No one loves me. I always blow it. There's no hope for me. I never do anything right.*

Where do such thoughts originate? They are planted in our minds by our enemy. Satan keeps singing the same choruses over and over to us. It is a song with the title "God Does Not Care for You."

How do you get rid of the devil's songs that get stuck in your head? The wrong approach is to try to force those songs out of your head by strength of will; even if you succeed, they will merely return later (compare Luke 11:24-26). The right approach is to replace those songs with better ones. The Psalms, the hymnbook of ancient Israel, is a good place to find some great songs. They are life-giving and faith-building.

Genuine worship will renew your heart. Sing songs of praise like you mean it.

By the way, Father Abraham *did* have many sons. I am one of them, and so are you. So let's just praise the Lord!
—C. T.

B. Acclaim Given to God (vv. 3, 4)

3. Say unto God, How terrible art thou in thy works! through the greatness of thy power shall thine enemies submit themselves unto thee.

Having addressed the peoples of all lands in the first two verses, the psalmist now instructs them in a proper way to address *God*. The word *terrible* is not used here in the modern sense of "awful,"

HOW TO SAY IT

Assyrian	Uh-*sear*-e-un.
Babylonian	Bab-ih-*low*-nee-un.
Canaanites	*Kay*-nun-ites.
Edomites	*Ee*-dum-ites.
Moabites	*Mo*-ub-ites.
Philippians	Fih-*lip*-ee-unz.
Philistines	Fuh-*liss*-teenz or *Fill*-us-teenz.
Selah (Hebrew)	*See*-luh.
Zechariah	Zek-uh-*rye*-uh.

but in the older sense of "terrifying"; the idea of "inspiring awe" conveys the sense.

So great are God's *works* of power that His *enemies* have no choice but to *submit themselves* to Him. The word translated *submit* doesn't imply that the submission springs from heartfelt adoration! (Compare David's use of this word in 2 Samuel 22:44-46 and its parallel Psalm 18:43-45.) God's enemies are so overwhelmed by Him that it's necessary for them to put on an outward show of deference to God, even if their hearts are not in it.

4. All the earth shall worship thee, and shall sing unto thee; they shall sing to thy name. Selah.

We should be careful in understanding the sense of *all the earth shall worship thee*. In both the psalmist's day and ours, most peoples of the earth do not worship the one true God. Thus this phrase should be understood as prophetic; this conclusion is supported by the future nature of the word *shall*. The Scriptures foretell a time when the entire world will worship Jesus (see Romans 14:11; Philippians 2:10).

From the very beginning, God's plan has been to use Israel as the beachhead from which He brings salvation to all the nations (Genesis 12:1-3; 22:17, 18). We know this is accomplished through Jesus and the spread of the gospel (Isaiah 49:6; Matthew 28:19, 20; Acts 13:47).

When Jesus returns, He will come not as a suffering servant but as a conqueror. Then all the nations of the world will submit either out of heartfelt worship or begrudging obligation. Revelation 15:3, 4 predicts that those in Christ will sing the Song of Moses: "Great and marvellous are thy works, Lord God Almighty; just and true are thy ways, thou King of saints."

Regarding the word *Selah,* see the Lesson Context.

II. Come and See
(PSALM 66:5-9)

A. Recalling God's Deliverance (vv. 5, 6)

5. Come and see the works of God: he is terrible in his doing toward the children of men.

Echoing his own words in Psalm 66:3, above, the psalmist stresses anew why everyone should worship the Lord: His *works* toward humanity are *terrible*, again in the sense of inspiring terror or awe. What the psalmist implores the reader to *come and see* is the topic of the next verse.

6. He turned the sea into dry land: they went through the flood on foot: there did we rejoice in him.

Specifically, the psalmist invites his audience to ponder anew what God did in the exodus. By the time God *turned the sea into dry land* to allow the Israelites to pass *through the flood on foot* (Exodus 14:21, 22), He had already worked 10 miracles in the form of plagues (Exodus 7–11). When the people saw the bodies of the Egyptian soldiers washed up on the beaches, they "feared . . . and believed the Lord" (14:31). Next came rejoicing (15:1-21). Every subsequent generation of Israelites should *rejoice in him*, as well, in remembering these facts (compare 1 Corinthians 10:1).

Psalm 66:2 refers to God's glory or reputation. Here we are given a tangible way that God established His reputation among "the children of men" (66:5). The Song of Moses describes the fear that would fall over the Philistines, Edomites, Moabites, and Canaanites—all peoples that Israel would eventually face in their conquest of the promised land—when they learned how God mightily delivered His people (Exodus 15:14-16).

> **What Do You Think?**
> What steps can we take to remind each other of our victorious history with God?
> **Digging Deeper**
> Which biblical figure in Hebrews 11 convinces you most of the importance of this question? Why?

B. Rejoicing in God's Reign (vv. 7-9)

7. He ruleth by his power for ever; his eyes behold the nations: let not the rebellious exalt themselves. Selah.

The readers cannot be reminded too often of God's eternal rule in power. The Song of Moses ends with this declaration: "The Lord shall reign for ever and ever" (Exodus 15:18). It is God who is the king of all the earth. In that capacity, He rules with great *power* and His accomplishments are awesome (compare Psalm 145:13).

As He rules, He sees everything. Nothing escapes His notice. He is able to *behold the nations* easily because He is sovereign over them as well as over Israel (compare Exodus 3:16; Psalm 11:4).

Any nation can suffer the consequences of being an enemy of God. Rebellion is always characterized by defiance of a higher authority. In effect, those who do so justify their actions by switching allegiance to a different authority. Often that different authority is merely the rebels themselves as they attempt to become autonomous; thus do *the rebellious exalt themselves.*

But no rebellion against God ever results in good. Before a nation, society, or person dares try to exalt self above God, the lessons of history should be consulted!

Again, see the Lesson Context regarding the word *Selah.*

❧ POWER WITHOUT ELECTRICITY ❧

A thunderstorm rolled through, and the power went out. Our praise team was unplugged. No electric guitars, no electric keyboard, no microphones, and no overhead projectors. Our power for worship was gone.

No electricity also meant no lights and no air conditioning. Our sanctuary has no windows that can be opened, and it was cloudy outside; so the room was very dimly lit.

But as the service started, a cool breeze began to blow through the open doors. The aroma of fresh-fallen rain was exhilarating. The room brightened a bit as the clouds rolled back. We began praising Jesus to the accompaniment of a piano. It turned into a morning blessed by God.

Before we started the service, the elders and I prayed that God would get the power turned on . . . and He did! It was a powerful worship service. We praised God. We fed on the Word of God and the bread of life. We still didn't have any electricity, but there was no shortage of power.

By the time we dismissed, the clouds were gone. I was locking up, a little past noon, when the lights came back on. "Go figure," I said to myself.

But then I said, "Thank You, Lord, for turning on the power before the power came on."

What a great day in the Lord it turned out to be! Thinking about it makes me want to flip off all the circuit breakers this coming Sunday. Or perhaps I should leave to the Lord what level, type, and source of power we should experience. How often do you let earthly types of power—electrical or otherwise—pull your gaze away from the ultimate source of power? See Zechariah 4:6.

—C. T.

What Do You Think?

What Scriptures will you memorize to remind yourself during times of crisis that the sovereign God is the ultimate source of power?

Digging Deeper

How can you ensure that your recall of such Scriptures during crisis doesn't end up being an empty mantra?

---

8. O bless our God, ye people, and make the voice of his praise to be heard.

As we read the psalmist's exhortation to the Israelites here, we remind ourselves that Christians inherit this mandate. It is both a privilege and a responsibility to *make the voice of his praise to be heard*. The recipients of God's generosity need to take the lead in worshipping Him. How much more this is true for Christians today, who are aware of the great salvation provided by Jesus Christ (compare 1 Corinthians 10:11)!

9. Which holdeth our soul in life, and suffereth not our feet to be moved.

The reason for this renewed praise is God's continuing care for His people. The God who rescued an entire nation in the exodus is more than capable of preserving every individual *soul* (compare Psalm 30:3).

The psalmist's generation may have experienced a life-threatening event (see the Lesson Context). Yet God sustains those who remain loyal to Him (compare 1 Kings 19:18; Romans 11:4). Life is always precarious and precious. Without God's constant care, we are dead. The fact that He *suffereth not our feet to be moved* should assure us that we need not rely on our own power. That is what

the wicked do, and they ultimately lose (compare Deuteronomy 32:35; Job 12:5).

III. Come and Hear
(Psalm 66:16-20)
A. Give Heed to My Testimony (vv. 16-19)

16. Come and hear, all ye that fear God, and I will declare what he hath done for my soul.

As we rejoin the psalm in the final stanza, the scene has changed again. In the first stanza (Psalm 66:1-4), all the nations are challenged to praise God. In the second stanza (66:5-7), Israel is to lead the praise before the nations by recounting God's mighty rescue of His people from Egypt. The third stanza (66:8-12) recalls either the exodus or a more recent time of trouble and rescue. In the fourth stanza (66:13-15), the psalmist personally vows to offer sacrifices extravagantly to God as a response to His recent rescue.

Now, in the fifth and final stanza (66:16-20), the psalmist begins a personal testimony regarding God's work in his life. His personal experience is about to become one of public declaration.

What Do You Think?

What preparations can you make to ensure that the story of what God has done in your life endures as a witness to the next generation?

Digging Deeper

Should drafting your own eulogy be part of this effort? Why, or why not?

---

17. I cried unto him with my mouth, and he was extolled with my tongue.

This is another instance of parallelism that so often characterizes Hebrew poetry, with the words *cried*, *him*, and *my mouth* in the first statement reflecting *extolled*, *he*, and *my tongue* in the second expression, respectively. Thus it would be a mistake to think the psalmist is saying two different things. He is actually offering one thought, which he repeats with similar words.

This singular thought is important: instead of immediately asking for help or complaining about something, the psalmist *extolled* God. (The original word behind the translation "extolled" is rendered "high praises" in Psalm 149:6.) This reminds us that our praise of God should come first, no matter the circumstances of life.

18. If I regard iniquity in my heart, the Lord will not hear me.

This acknowledgment is also reflected by David in Psalm 32:3-5. The psalmist knows that the condition of his *heart* matters to God. There are certain conditions that hinder the effectiveness of prayers (examples: Lamentations 3:40-44; 1 Peter 3:7), and unconfessed sin is certainly one of them.

> *What Do You Think?*
> What plan can you enact to ensure that you take inventory on the condition of your heart on a regular basis?
>
> *Digging Deeper*
> Is this something that others can assist with, or is it strictly personal? Why?

19. But verily God hath heard me; he hath attended to the voice of my prayer.

The psalmist recognizes that *God* has, in fact, *heard* him. Given this successful outcome, the reader may be tempted to draw up a checklist of the various points of the previous verses that lead up to here. That may be useful in terms of the broad contours that prayer should take. But we should always caution ourselves that God is not like a fictional genie who grants our wishes as long as we follow a certain procedure.

B. Give Praise to God (v. 20)

20. Blessed be God, which hath not turned away my prayer, nor his mercy from me.

In closing, the psalmist voices a praise blessing to God for attending to the psalmist's prayer. Prayers to fictional gods are never heard (Psalm 115:4-6), and praying to the one true God is no guarantee that He will listen (compare Jeremiah 11:11; 14:12).

Going hand in hand with the psalmist's prayer being heard is God's continuing *mercy*. The word being translated occurs about 250 times in the Old Testament, with varying translations such as "lovingkindness" (Psalm 17:7).

How Great Thou Art

And when I think, that God,
His Son not sparing;
Sent Him to die,
I scarce can take it in;
That on the Cross,
my burden gladly bearing,
He bled and died
to take away my sin.
Then sings my soul,
My Saviour God, to Thee,
How great Thou art,
How great Thou art.
Then sings my soul,
My Saviour God, to Thee,
How great Thou art,
How great Thou art!

Visual for Lessons 11 & 12. *Associate this with the question to the left as you ask, "What role does singing play in indicating the condition of the heart?"*

Conclusion

A. Remembering Our History with God

Despite the circumstances in the psalmist's day, God was still sovereign and all-powerful. He was still worthy of praise. He was still the judge who ruled all nations and knew the true condition of every individual human heart.

All the above remains true today. Although we are surrounded by those who do not fear God, we can do so nonetheless. Although we are surrounded by those who do not praise God, we can do so nonetheless. We can make a commitment to remind ourselves continually of His history with us. We can also encourage each other by sharing our personal testimonies of how He has demonstrated His strength in our lives.

As we do (or, perhaps, because we do), we will find ourselves submitting to His ways, regardless of whether those around us do so as well.

B. Prayer

God, we know that You are always good and always strong, regardless of our circumstances. We praise You for the times when you have been our mighty deliverer. We pray this in the name of Jesus, who delivers us from sin. Amen.

C. Thought to Remember

Praise reminds us of God's might,
and God's might reminds us to praise.

INVOLVEMENT LEARNING

Enhance your lesson with KJV Bible Student *(from your curriculum supplier) and the reproducible activity page (at www.standardlesson.com or in the back of the* KJV Standard Lesson Commentary Deluxe Edition*).*

Into the Lesson

As the class settles in, announce, "We are going to play a little 'Name That Tune.' As I hum the tunes, just shout out the title if you know it." Choose tunes from secular culture that are familiar to your learners—show tunes, kid songs, classic rock, country, etc. If you are not musical, ask someone with musical talent to do this for you.

Option 1. Place in chairs copies of the "Sing and Shout" crossword puzzle from the reproducible page, which you can download, for learners to begin working on as they arrive. *Option 2.* Distribute the crossword puzzle as a take-home activity at the conclusion of class.

After either activity, introduce Bible study by saying, "Secular culture uses music in ways that do not honor God. But when we lift up voices in praise to God, it is music to His ears. Let's explore reasons to shout for joy to our Creator."

Into the Word

Have students take turns reading the eight verses of Psalm 66:1-9, 16-20. Then form students into three smaller groups, each to come up with a two-minute radio-commercial jingle that praises God for His mighty works. Announce that groups are free to choose whatever music genre they desire for their commercials: soul, country, jazz, Christian rap.

Option 1. If groups find it too difficult to come up with both lyrics and tune, suggest they start with a familiar jingle and rewrite the words while keeping the tune. Be ready to suggest some jingles as examples for groups that are still stuck.

Option 2. You can flip the above option and suggest groups use the words of the lesson text as lyrics they will put to a tune of their own creation.

Allow groups several minutes to complete the assignment. Offer the chance do a live performance before the class to any group open to doing so. Discuss why this task was hard (or easy).

Option. Distribute handouts (you create) that are headed this way:

God's mighty deeds of
Creation / Deliverance from Egypt / Salvation

Form small groups and assign each group one of the three topics in the second line. Say, "Psalm 66 leads us to praise God joyfully for His mighty deeds. Use the next few minutes to list from the text specific actions by God in your assigned category that make Him worthy of praise." Allow time for groups to share their resulting lists.

Into Life

Make a transition by saying, "We live in a noisy world, but so many of the sounds we hear involve arrogant boasting. 'I did this. I am incredible. Look at me!' But the psalmist reminds us to put the spotlight on God."

Have students pair off to discuss something great that God has done in their lives. After allowing time for volunteers to share their stories, ask, "Don't you feel encouraged by hearing these stories? How can we do a better job of telling others about how God has blessed us?" Encourage free discussion and brainstorming.

Wrap up by asking each person to write a prayer of gratitude to God for one way He has shown His greatness and power to him or her. Offer volunteers the chance to read their prayers aloud. Time permitting, discuss reasons (excuses) people fool themselves with for not praising God. (*Option.* Use the "Boasting about God" activity from the reproducible page to explore another angle regarding praise of God.)

Close with this prayer: "We praise you mightily on Sundays, O Lord! But during the week we often fall short in doing so. Forgive us when we fail. *[Pause to allow learners a time for personal confession and reflection.]* With hearts lifted in gratitude, we pray in Jesus' name. Amen."

Our Rescuing God

Devotional Reading: Romans 8:31-39
Background Scripture: Psalm 91:1-16

Psalm 91:1-8, 11-16

1 He that dwelleth in the secret place of the most High shall abide under the shadow of the Almighty.

2 I will say of the Lord, He is my refuge and my fortress: my God; in him will I trust.

3 Surely he shall deliver thee from the snare of the fowler, and from the noisome pestilence.

4 He shall cover thee with his feathers, and under his wings shalt thou trust: his truth shall be thy shield and buckler.

5 Thou shalt not be afraid for the terror by night; nor for the arrow that flieth by day;

6 Nor for the pestilence that walketh in darkness; nor for the destruction that wasteth at noonday.

7 A thousand shall fall at thy side, and ten thousand at thy right hand; but it shall not come nigh thee.

8 Only with thine eyes shalt thou behold and see the reward of the wicked.

. . . .

11 For he shall give his angels charge over thee, to keep thee in all thy ways.

12 They shall bear thee up in their hands, lest thou dash thy foot against a stone.

13 Thou shalt tread upon the lion and adder: the young lion and the dragon shalt thou trample under feet.

14 Because he hath set his love upon me, therefore will I deliver him: I will set him on high, because he hath known my name.

15 He shall call upon me, and I will answer him: I will be with him in trouble; I will deliver him, and honour him.

16 With long life will I satisfy him, and shew him my salvation.

Key Verse

He shall call upon me, and I will answer him: I will be with him in trouble; I will deliver him, and honour him. —**Psalm 91:15**

OUR LOVE FOR GOD

Unit 3: Songs That Glorify the God of Love

LESSONS 11–13

LESSON AIMS

After participating in this lesson, each learner will be able to:

1. Outline God's promises to protect.

2. Identify dangers from which Christians need God's protection.

3. Propose one way his or her church can extend the Lord's rescuing protection to those in need.

LESSON OUTLINE

Introduction

A. Our Protection and Salvation

People understand protection and security in different ways. Children often feel most secure when in the strong and trusting arms of their parents, possibly holding a threadbare blanket or teddy bear. Parents might feel most secure in a safe neighborhood, with doors that lock and money in their savings account. A backpacker seeks protection from a storm under a rock overhang that can block the elements.

As Christians, however, we know that our ultimate protection and security come from God. It is no wonder that the Bible uses images of strength to describe Him: rock, refuge, fortress. No blanket or padlock can compare with the strong protection available from God.

Elisabeth Elliot (1926–2015) was well known for sharing the gospel with an indigenous tribe in Ecuador some 60 years ago. The title of her book *Shadow of the Almighty* alludes to the description of God in Psalm 91:1. As such, it highlights her belief in God's protective grace, even in dangerous circumstances. Elliot understood that God was not distant, but very close—a steadfast refuge. And she lived out her trust in radical ways. Psalm 91 can teach us to live the same way.

B. Lesson Context

The historical setting of Psalm 91 is unclear, but the literary context sheds light on its meaning. The preceding psalm, Psalm 90 (which begins Book IV of the Psalter), is a lament. As such, it reflects mournfully about the fleeting nature of life, which withers under the wrath of God because of sin. That psalm ends with a petition for renewal from God. Psalm 91 seems to be a response to the lament of Psalm 90.

Psalm 91 is comprised of four stanzas, which are distinguished by shifts in speaker. These four are verses 1, 2; 3-8; 9-13; and 14-16. Analyzed in a more technical way, the structure of Psalm 91 has as its touchstone a certain Hebrew conjunction that can be translated in various ways. Depending on context, some possibilities for translating this word are "for," "that," "if," and "when." This word also can be an emphatic "indeed," "truly," or "surely," again depending on context. In Psalm 91 this conjunction is translated "surely," "because," and "because" in verses 3, 9, and 14, respectively.

We should also keep in mind that the psalms are poetry, and one of the defining features of Hebrew poetry is *parallelism*. As discussed in previous lessons, this is often seen where one line corresponds in some way with the line that follows, as the second line repeats the thought(s) of the first line in different ways. Parallelism can also feature contrasting ideas or even show how one event or action leads to a certain consequence. While English poetry is often identified by the rhyming of words, Hebrew poetry has been described as the "rhyming of ideas"—that's parallelism.

I. Safe Place
(PSALM 91:1-8)
A. Basis of Protection (vv. 1, 2)

1. He that dwelleth in the secret place of the most High shall abide under the shadow of the Almighty.

These first lines of Psalm 91 "rhyme" (see above) with the shared imagery of the Lord's protection for those who seek refuge in Him. This echoes Psalm 90:1, which describes the Lord as Israel's "dwelling place" from generation to generation.

The idea that God himself is a *secret place* for His people answers the burning questions of Psalms 88:14 and 89:46, which ask why God is hiding. As the unidentified psalmist declares that God is the secret place, he implies that God is not hiding. In that regard, the opening *he* generalizes this psalm for each of God's people. Everyone who seeks the protective *shadow of the Almighty* will find it (compare Psalms 27:5; 31:20).

Notice that the one protected must actively seek the protection of the Lord. The one who is the subject of the verbs *dwelleth* and *abide* is the individual seeking the Lord. God's people are not passive participants in relationship with Him, but active covenant-keepers. Throughout this psalm, the author alternates between the actions of the worshipper and the actions of God, thus highlighting the dynamic covenant relationship. On

the idea of *shadow*, see also Psalm 63:7; Isaiah 49:2; and Lamentations 4:20.

2. I will say of the LORD, He is my refuge and my fortress: my God; in him will I trust.

This, the final part of the psalm's first stanza (see the Lesson Context), distills the previous metaphors into the simple, though sometimes difficult, idea of *trust*. The psalmist seeks *refuge* in the Lord specifically by trusting *in him*.

Notice the transition of imagery from the previous verse, with those of *refuge* and *fortress* being more military in nature (compare 2 Samuel 22:2, 3). The Lord's steadfast strength is highlighted.

These images bring to mind the confidence that the people of Judah once had in the protection and surety of Jerusalem and the temple. Before the destruction of Jerusalem and the exile to Babylon, God's people mistakenly saw the holy city and the temple as their security and as proof of God's presence and protection (Jeremiah 7:4). After the exile, however, the Israelites come to understand that God himself is their true protection and security.

B. Forms of Protection (vv. 3-8)

3a. Surely he shall deliver thee from the snare of the fowler.

The psalmist now expands on the protective imagery introduced in the first stanza. In so doing, he likens the reader to a bird delivered from *the snare of the fowler* (compare Psalm 124:7; Hosea 9:8). The Lord is able to deliver His people from the trap of human enemies.

3b. And from the noisome pestilence.

Pestilence, by contrast, is not something we normally think of as being inflicted on one person by another (although we know of "biological warfare" in the modern era). Rather, pestilence or plague is seen as being inflicted by God (see Exodus 5:3; 9:3, 15; Psalm 78:50; Habakkuk 3:5). It can be deadly (*noisome*). Just as birds are helpless before a well-constructed trap set by enemies, so human beings are helpless before destructive pestilence. This is particularly true in a time before antibiotics and vaccines, which is most of human history.

4a. He shall cover thee with his feathers, and under his wings shalt thou trust.

God is now likened to a mother bird protecting her young in the shelter of her *wings* (compare Psalms 17:8; 36:7; 57:1; 63:7; and Ruth 2:12). Jesus uses this same imagery to describe His desire to protect the people of Jerusalem, though their hearts are too hardened to seek Him (Matthew 23:37; Luke 13:34). In so doing, Jesus echoes God's desire that people actively trust in Him for protection.

❧ PROTECTION FOR THE LOWLY ❧

Recently, a robin flew out of the tall shrubbery sheltering my front porch, causing me to notice a hidden nest. In it were two tiny birds slouched down, with their open beaks waiting for a meal to drop in. When I again passed the nest later, I heard bird noises coming from a nearby bush. And there was a robin perched, worm in mouth, on a branch. It seemed to be calling to its young to lie still until danger passed. Sure enough, as soon as I was a safe distance away, the adult bird glided into the nest and fed the waiting offspring.

This is not an unusual scene; researchers and various other observers often catch glimpses of the various species of the animal world in unusual and unexpected places. We laugh and are amazed at the way adult animals guard and protect their young in the face of potential predators.

Think about it: if animals instinctively know how to protect their young, how much more does God know how to do so for those created in His image! Even when (or especially when) we are feeling helpless, He is the one who remembers us "in our low estate" (Psalm 136:23).   —C. M. W.

4b. His truth shall be thy shield and buckler.

Returning to military terms, *shield* is the perfect symbol for protection. Regarding *buckler,* the Hebrew word being translated appears only here in the Old Testament, which makes its meaning difficult to determine. Perhaps the idea is that of a wall or bulwark that protects a city.

Notice that it is specifically God's *truth* that is described in terms of these defensive armaments. God is true to His promises. His faithfulness to these is seen nowhere more clearly than when He sends His own Son to take on human flesh, die for the sins of humanity, and rise again in triumph over sin, Satan, and death.

5, 6. Thou shalt not be afraid for the terror by night; nor for the arrow that flieth by day; nor for the pestilence that walketh in darkness; nor for the destruction that wasteth at noonday.

In addition to being strong and sure, God's protection is constant; this is the idea behind the images of *by night, by day, darkness,* and *noonday.* The *terror* is a general image of something dreadful.

At first thought, we may conclude that *the arrow* describes a threat from a human enemy, but the Bible sometimes uses that word figuratively to refer to flashes of lightning in storms (see Psalm 18:14; 77:17, 18; 144:6). Thus it may not be far off to suggest that the expression *the arrow that flieth* refers to what we call "the storms of life." *The pestilence* is the same just discussed in Psalm 91:3. *The destruction that wasteth* seems to be a parallel way of saying pestilence.

What Do You Think?
> What are some steps you can take to transform fear to trust the next time you feel threatened?

Digging Deeper
Which of those steps apply to everyone, and which may apply only to you? Why?

When we find ourselves in dangerous situations, fear is a God-given emotion that helps protect us. So fear in and of itself is not sinful. The point is that we need not fear enemies of any kind. God is greater than all enemies.

7. A thousand shall fall at thy side, and ten thousand at thy right hand; but it shall not come nigh thee.

The deaths of those *thousand . . . and ten thousand* who might perish at the *side . . . right hand* (that is, in close proximity) of God's protected ones can be the result of military actions, a plague of some sort, or a natural disaster. It doesn't matter. God is present for His people in all crises.

Salvation of the faithful and punishment of the unfaithful are two sides of the same coin. When enemies are punished, God's people are protected from them (Psalm 37:37-40).

8. Only with thine eyes shalt thou behold and see the reward of the wicked.

When we see the word *reward*, we are accustomed to thinking in positive terms: compensation for doing something well. A mason's hard work is rewarded with a paycheck. A nursery volunteer's hard work is rewarded with baby snuggles and the gratitude of the church. The main issue here is that the Hebrew behind the word *reward* is difficult to translate because this is the only place it occurs in the Old Testament. But the meaning is clear enough from context: *reward* is to be understood in the sense of "recompense." Sooner or later, the wicked will indeed get what's coming to them.

Unfortunately, God's people are sometimes distracted by the fact that those who do wicked works are often prosperous. That fact is noted in the Bible (examples: Job 21:7; Psalm 73:12; Jeremiah 12:1, 2). We can rest assured that God

HOW TO SAY IT

Babylon	*Bab*-uh-lun.
Constantine	**Kawn**-stun-*teen*.
Habakkuk	Huh-*back*-kuk.
Lamentations	Lam-en-*tay*-shunz.
Maxentius	Mak-*sen*-tee-us.
Psalter	*Saul*-tur.

Visual for Lesson 13. *Start a discussion by pointing to this visual as you ask, "Which of this quarter's lessons taught you the most about love? Why?"*

knows this and has plans to deal with it in His time (example: Habakkuk 1:1–2:20). The important thing is not to question God's justice in the meantime, lest He turn our questions back on us, as in Job 38–42!

❧ *A Fateful Day* ❧

October 28, 312 was a bad day for Emperor Maxentius. While games celebrating the anniversary of his accession to the throne were being held, the crowds could not fail to see the challenging army of Constantine bearing down upon Rome. Though Maxentius had twice survived a siege, he made the surprising choice to confront Constantine's forces.

The place where Maxentius made his stand was the Milvian Bridge outside Rome. Constantine, a skillful tactician, sent into battle his cavalry followed by his infantry. Maxentius's forces retreated toward the city, but the bridge collapsed. Maxentius drowned in the muddy waters of the Tiber River, by some accounts pulled under by the weight of his own armor. Maxentius's bad day became a victory march into Rome for Constantine. He ended up being uncontested as emperor, reigning until AD 337.

Armies throughout history have used assorted weaponry to guard strongholds, plunder riches, and gain territory. But even the battle plans and equipment cannot guarantee success. Emperor Maxentius's protective armor may have hastened his death, ironically doing the opposite of its intended purpose.

When news of accidents, catastrophes, and crime reach our ears, it is easy to drift into a state of perpetual uncertainty or unease. Worry becomes self-reinforcing, a vicious circle, unless we turn over our anxieties to God (see Psalm 2:1-6; Daniel 2:21). God's protection surpasses all human efforts at security in this world. Of course, that's easy to say when threats seem distant. Whether we actually can rest on that assurance is proven only in the crucible of danger.

—C. M. W.

II. Trustworthy Protector
(PSALM 91:11-13)

A. With the Help of Angels (vv. 11, 12)

11. For he shall give his angels charge over thee, to keep thee in all thy ways.

Moving to the middle of the third stanza takes us to observations regarding the role of *angels* in our protection. These are created, heavenly beings who can take visible forms to do God's work. In addition to delivering messages (Luke 1:19; etc.), they are depicted as strong protectors and warriors (Daniel 6:22; etc.) In the verse before us is assurance that God's protection includes angelic resources.

12. They shall bear thee up in their hands, lest thou dash thy foot against a stone.

It is tempting to test God's promises of protection to verify them. Satan tempted Jesus that way by quoting Psalm 91:11, 12 to Him in Matthew 4:6. Jesus responded with Deuteronomy 6:16: "It is written again, Thou shalt not tempt the Lord thy God" (Matthew 4:7).

Now if Jesus had jumped from the top of the temple, God's angels most certainly could have caught Him. (He could have caught himself for that matter!) God's angels were apparently nearby throughout the whole ordeal, and they ministered to Jesus' needs afterward (Matthew 4:11). Jesus was proving to Satan that God called the shots. Jesus chose to trust God rather than test Him. God invites certain tests (Malachi 3:10) but not others. We must know the difference.

B. Against Nature's Predators (v. 13)

13. Thou shalt tread upon the lion and adder: the young lion and the dragon shalt thou trample under feet.

The previous two verses tell us that God will defend His people even to the extent of sending His heavenly agents to protect us. In the verse before us, God's protection moves from the defensive to the offensive: not only will God keep His people from harm, but He will empower us to defeat the fiercest of foes!

No one doubts that *the lion* is "king of the beasts." The *adder* or cobra is an extremely poisonous snake (see Job 20:14, 16; Psalm 58:4; Isaiah 11:8). *The young lion* is one that is at the beginning of its strength. *The dragon* is a large snake or serpent in this context (see Deuteronomy 32:33; Jeremiah 51:34). These creatures are used figuratively to represent any and all persons and powers that threaten God's people.

III. Sure Promises
(PSALM 91:14-16)

A. Basis of Blessing (v. 14)

14. Because he hath set his love upon me, therefore will I deliver him: I will set him on high, because he hath known my name.

Here begins the final stanza of the psalm (see the Lesson Context). This marks a transition of speakers from the psalmist to God himself.

This verse elaborates on the result of trusting in the Lord, in parallel thoughts. The larger context is that of something being conditional. The condition for receiving the promised deliverance from evil is to have placed full devotion in the

Lord. The expression *he hath known my name* denotes intimacy of knowing about someone. In other contexts, variations of this expression carry the ideas of trust, reverence, or covenant faithfulness (examples: Psalm 9:10; Isaiah 52:6; Jeremiah 16:21).

God knows His true followers by their love for Him and by their understanding of who He is. Those who actively trust, love, and serve Him will find refuge in His protective salvation (compare Jesus' strong words in Matthew 7:21-23).

What Do You Think?
How will you express your love for the Lord in the month ahead?
Digging Deeper
How do Mark 12:30; John 14:15; and 1 John 5:3 inform your answer?

B. Forms of Blessing (vv. 15, 16)

15, 16. He shall call upon me, and I will answer him: I will be with him in trouble; I will deliver him, and honour him. With long life will I satisfy him, and shew him my salvation.

These verses climax the psalm. They should be read together in order to appreciate the intensification of the Lord's promises.

The two opening phrases establish the relationship that is the focus of Psalm 91:14: when God's people *call upon* Him, He is faithful to *answer*. God is not aloof or disinterested. He initiated the relationship with His people and established a means of communication. The lines of communication of prayer, worship, and reading God's Word remain open today.

Several promises follow the opening phrases. These can be seen broadly as two categories: blessings for the present life and certainty of ultimate salvation. Notice that God does not promise that His faithful people will never experience *trouble*, but that He will be with them in the midst of it.

God has already secured our salvation in Christ, but He has not yet eradicated evil and suffering from His creation. That is why we can trust Him in the midst of suffering. He is with us, He will deliver us, and He will honor us.

Conclusion

A. God Is Our Protection and Salvation

In this fallen world, God's people are surrounded by evil, danger, and suffering. Psalm 91 is an emphatic reminder that God is trustworthy and mighty to save. Christians should expect to share in Christ's suffering, even unto death (Matthew 16:24, 25; 1 Peter 2:19-21). But we should also expect God's protective blessings. Rather than contradictory realities of the Christian life, the existence of persistent sin in the world alongside the victory of Christ is a dynamic tension.

Elisabeth Elliot understood this tension and fiercely trusted in God as her refuge. She knew firsthand that God's protection did not preclude suffering and death in this life. Her book mentioned in the Introduction is a biography of her late first husband, Jim Elliot, who was killed by the very people with whom he tried to share the gospel. After his death, Elisabeth Elliot returned to her husband's murderers. She was frightened, but she was faithful. She knew of the dangers, but she also knew of God's trustworthy protection and salvation.

For twenty-first century Christians, it is all too easy to seek protection in something other than God himself. It is tempting to trust in financial security, military defenses, reputation, or even in church membership. Service to the church is an important responsibility of all Christians; but as we give of our time, talent, and treasure, we take care that our trust is in God himself and not in what we think our works earn.

B. Prayer

Almighty God, You are our true protection and salvation. Please strengthen our trust and protect us against the evil and danger that surrounds us. Equip us to be agents of Your protection and bold proclaimers of Your salvation to the ends of the earth. For all that You have done for us and for all You promise to do, we give You thanks and praise. We pray in the name of Jesus. Amen.

C. Thought to Remember

God is greater than all circumstances.

INVOLVEMENT LEARNING

Enhance your lesson with KJV Bible Student *(from your curriculum supplier) and the reproducible activity page (at www.standardlesson.com or in the back of the* KJV Standard Lesson Commentary Deluxe Edition*).*

Into the Lesson

Say, "Our homes and various other structures protect us from many dangerous things—protection that is so commonplace that we may take it for granted. What are some of those dangerous things, great and small?" Jot responses on the board. (*Possible responses*: weather, animals, criminals, disease, etc.)

Alternative. Distribute copies of the "Methods of Protection" activity from the reproducible page, which you can download. Have students work on the seven matches individually for no more than one minute. Then invite volunteers to share their responses to the question below the matches.

After either activity, lead into the Bible study by saying, "The writer of Psalm 91 uses metaphors to depict God's sheltering influence against physical and spiritual dangers that surround us. Let's see how that works."

Into the Word

Have students take turns reading aloud the verses of today's lesson text, Psalm 91:1-8, 11-16. Then divide the class into three groups of three or four learners each. Distribute handouts (you prepare) with the following instructions for three groups. (Larger classes can form more groups and give duplicate assignments.)

The Protected-By Group: What poetic images in Psalm 91:1, 2, 4 describe the various ways God protects us? How do these metaphors help us understand God's protective influence?

The Protected-From Group: What poetic images in Psalm 91:3, 5, 6 indicate the things God protects us from? How do these metaphors help us understand the physical and spiritual dangers from which God ultimately protects us?

The Promise Group: What promises from God are included in Psalm 91:7-16? How do they help us understand the protection of God, even when disaster and evil seem to be winning?

Launch the exercise by pointing out that each set of instructions has two questions: a "what's so?" question followed by a "so what?" question. Allow several minutes for intra-group research and discussion, then ask groups to share findings in whole-class discussion.

Answers to the "what's so?" questions. Protected-By Group: a secret place, shadow, refuge, fortress, feathery wings, shield, buckler; Protected-From Group: fowler's snare, pestilence, terror, arrow, destruction; Promise Group: protection despite the odds, seeing justice done, angelic guardian; deliverance from dangers, love, honor, long life, salvation. *Responses to the "so what?" questions* may vary widely.

Into Life

Have the following on display from the beginning of class: five pennies, five aspirins, five matches, and five puzzle pieces. (You may need more or fewer of each, depending on class size.)

Say, "Let's close the class in prayer, asking the Lord for protection and rescue in a particular area of life. If you need God's protection and rescue from a financial problem, come up and take a penny; for a health concern, come up to get an aspirin; for a relational issue, pick up a match; for any other problem, take a puzzle piece. Hold these while praying silently for God's protection and rescue in your areas of difficulty." Allow enough time for participants to do so before closing the class in prayer yourself.

Option. Time allowing, distribute copies of the "In Need of Protection" activity from the reproducible page. Have students work in pairs to see who can finish the quickest. Conclude by challenging learners to pick one of the words in the puzzle as a prompt for praying for God's protection in the area of life that word indicates. (If time does not permit using the activity this way, give each learner a copy as a take-home.)

DISCIPLESHIP
AND MISSION

Special Features

Lessons
Unit 1: Call to Discipleship

Unit 2: Call to Ministry

Unit 3: Call to Life in Christ

QUARTERLY QUIZ

Use these questions as a pretest or as a review. The answers are on page iv of This Quarter in the Word.

Lesson 1

1. Jesus taught that the person who humbles himself will be _____. *Luke 14:11*

2. When is recompense for helping the poor received? (at the resurrection, never, when we are in need?) *Luke 14:14*

Lesson 2

1. What was the occupation of Peter and Andrew? (carpenters, brickmakers, fishermen?) *Mark 1:16*

2. To be disciples of Jesus, we must each bear our _____. *Luke 14:27*

Lesson 3

1. The prodigal son was so hungry he wanted to eat what? (pig food, garbage, grass?) *Luke 15:16*

2. Before restoring the prodigal son, his father scolded him for leaving. T/F. *Luke 15:22-24*

Lesson 4

1. Jesus encountered Zacchaeus in what city? (Jerusalem, Bethany, Jericho?) *Luke 19:1, 2*

2. Because he was short, Zacchaeus climbed a tree in order to see Jesus. T/F. *Luke 19:4*

Lesson 5

1. Jesus left Capernaum to live in Nazareth. T/F. *Matthew 4:12, 13*

2. Jesus preached that because the kingdom of Heaven was near, all should do what? (repent, obey, forgive?). *Matthew 4:17*

Lesson 6

1. Two of the 12 disciples chosen by Jesus were named Simon. T/F. *Matthew 10:2-4*

2. When the disciples went out to preach in the villages, what were they not to take? (belt, gold, a companion?) *Matthew 10:9*

3. If unwelcome in a village, the disciples were to shake the _____ off their feet. *Matthew 10:14*

Lesson 7

1. When in Bethany, Jesus was anointed at the house of Simon the _____. *Matthew 26:6*

2. Jesus told His disciples they would not always have poor people. T/F. *Matthew 26:11*

Lesson 8

1. The first witnesses of the resurrected Christ were two women named _____. *Matthew 28:1, 9*

2. Guards were paid to keep quiet about the empty tomb. T/F. *Matthew 28:11-13*

Lesson 9

1. What directive did Jesus *not* give in the Great Commission? (go, baptize, pray?) *Matthew 28:19*

2. Before ascending, Jesus told His disciples they would be His _____ in various places. *Acts 1:8*

Lesson 10

1. Because we have sinned, we fall short of the _____ of God. *Romans 3:23*

2. Both circumcised and uncircumcised are justified by or through faith. T/F. *Romans 3:30*

Lesson 11

1. Paul says the law was made weak because of human _____. *Romans 8:3*

2. Even if not walking according to the Spirit, we can sometimes please God. T/F. *Romans 8:8*

Lesson 12

1. Jewish unbelief opened the door for salvation to come to the _____. *Romans 11:11*

2. Paul acknowledged himself as apostle of the _____. *Romans 11:13*

Lesson 13

1. What are we to present to God as a living sacrifice? (bodies, souls, offerings?) *Romans 12:1*

2. Paul says the church has many members but a single _____. *Romans 12:4*

QUARTER AT A GLANCE

by Jim Eichenberger

"So, WHAT DO you do?" Within moments of meeting a stranger, this question is likely to be asked. Our culture makes one's job tantamount to identity. What you *do* is what you *are*.

The words *vocation* and *avocation* describe activities that shape individualities. Typically, the former refers to career, the way one earns a living. The latter usually describes side interests— activities that are enjoyed but are not central.

This unit turns this usage on its head. For the believer, one's true calling has nothing to do with earning a living. Careers are avocations while our true vocation is following Jesus.

Whom We Study

Our true vocation begins when we heed the call of Jesus to be a disciple, the issue of our first unit this quarter. A disciple is a learner. To be successful in our ultimate calling, we must be shaped, trained, and changed in the College of Christ.

Education sometimes breeds conceit. Those who know a little bit more become know-it-alls! But the more we study from our master, the less we feed our egos and dismiss others. The longer we follow the less we look to climbing the corporate ladder or placing our security in money alone.

As we progress toward Graduation Day when we are in our teacher's presence for eternity, we pass Humility 101, learn the advanced economics of the kingdom of Heaven, and invite others into His classroom and into the life He offers.

How We Serve

In putting our study into practice, our discipleship goes through stages. We move from on-the-job-training to accepting the master's values and vision before venturing out on missions to advance the master's interests. The second unit in this quarter moves from education to practice this way.

We continue to learn from Jesus as we venture forth for Him. There will always be various reasons and excuses to delay venturing. Yet we must venture out of our cloister and begin making a difference in the real world.

Like the fishermen on the shores of Galilee, we learn to venture where the master's voice leads. We pledge to count the cost of our choices and give up our lives to Him. Our values continue to be shaped as we do Jesus' work, until our voice is His voice and the song of His resurrection is the sound track of our lives. We don't work on commission —we *are commissioned*, placing everything of our own into the cause of Christ.

Who Will Carry On

At some point, someone will take the job we perform. Great companies build continuity. They stay directed and driven toward success as they plan for a new generation to take the helm. The third unit in this quarter is a case study of how the apostle Paul moved toward such a transition.

Paul had not founded the church at Rome as he had founded churches throughout Asia and Europe. He knew just a few believers there, yet he wrote his most doctrinally heavy training manual for them! The book of Romans allows successive generations to keep the church doctrinally pure so

> *Careers are avocations while our true vocation is following Jesus.*

it could continue to accomplish the work to which Paul himself had dedicated his life.

Paul taught others to deal with the big issues of the Christian vocation: How to play good defense as well as good offense. How to fit all the pieces of the puzzle together. How to do right, etc.

This quarter encourages true life change. When someone asks, "What do you do?" may all vocational believers—all disciples—be prepared to give the right answer!

GET THE SETTING

MAKING PHONE CALLS is effortless and cheap these days. We touch "Contacts" on our smartphones, then touch the "Phone" icon. We use a calling plan that involves little or no cost. We take it all for granted. But sending a message in ancient times was anything but effortless and cheap!

The 12 disciples called to deliver the message of the Messiah likely had heard the legendary story of Phidippides. He was the courier who, in 490 BC, is said to have run from the battlefield at Marathon to the city of Athens—about 26 miles—to bring a report of a Greek victory over the Persians. This legend illustrates, in certain ways, the task of fulfilling the Great Commission.

Mission and Method

Speed is often of the essence in delivering a message. To send someone on foot rather than a rider on horseback in such cases seems wrongheaded. But horses are expensive and riding skill is required. Such skill is especially needed in rugged terrain. In those cases, a horse may be no faster than a person on foot. Beasts of burden are useful, even necessary, in many contexts. But the cost of upkeep must be weighed against benefit of speed and cargo capacity (compare Genesis 24:19, 20, 32; Judges 19:19-21; 1 Kings 4:27, 28).

The Roman Empire had excellent roads, suitable for horses and wheeled conveyances (compare Acts 8:28; 23:23). But Galilee was a backwater province on the fringe of the empire. The priority of ancient road building, as today, was to connect major urban centers and ports. That pretty much left Galilee out! That fact and others worked against the use of horses and the speed they might otherwise provide. So, for example, necessary speed for the mission of the 12 disciples in lesson 6 is found in Jesus' instructions that they had to travel light (Matthew 10:9, 10a) and be prepared to move on quickly (10:14).

Jesus recognized the value and necessity of choosing the proper method for a given mission. He himself seemed to have walked everywhere (Matthew 4:18; 14:25; Luke 24:13-17; one notable exception is Matthew 21:1-7). So did Paul when traveling overland. His missionary travels included several transits across water (2 Corinthians 11:25; etc.). To buy or sell mounts at ports when debarking or embarking would have distracted from the mission in terms of both time and cost. The method he used fit the mission.

Message and Martyrdom

Couriers from battles often carried messages of defeat or victory. An example of the former is found in 1 Samuel 4:12-22; the message was one of fear. An example of the other is Phidippides, noted above. His message was one of good news, or *euangelion* in Greek. A form of this word is transliterated *evangelist* in Acts 21:8; Ephesians 4:11; and 2 Timothy 4:5. Another form is translated *gospel* (meaning "good news") dozens of times in the New Testament. This good news was founded on the death and resurrection of Jesus (1 Corinthians 15:1-8). God had transformed the fear produced by the apparent defeat of Jesus' death (John 20:19) into the best news possible!

The role of courier was a dangerous one, however. Phidippides collapsed and died after delivering his good news (compare 2 Samuel 1:1-16). The pages of history are stained with the blood of Christian martyrs.

Wisdom is called for in all these areas (Colossians 4:5). Do we use proper methods, given the nature of our (com)mission? For example, does the speed of posting our witness on social media lure us into self-deceptive thinking that we are thereby fulfilling our obligation of lesson 9? In personal encounters, do we water down the message to lessen chances of hostile reactions, or do we pray for the boldness of Acts 4:29?

CHART FEATURE

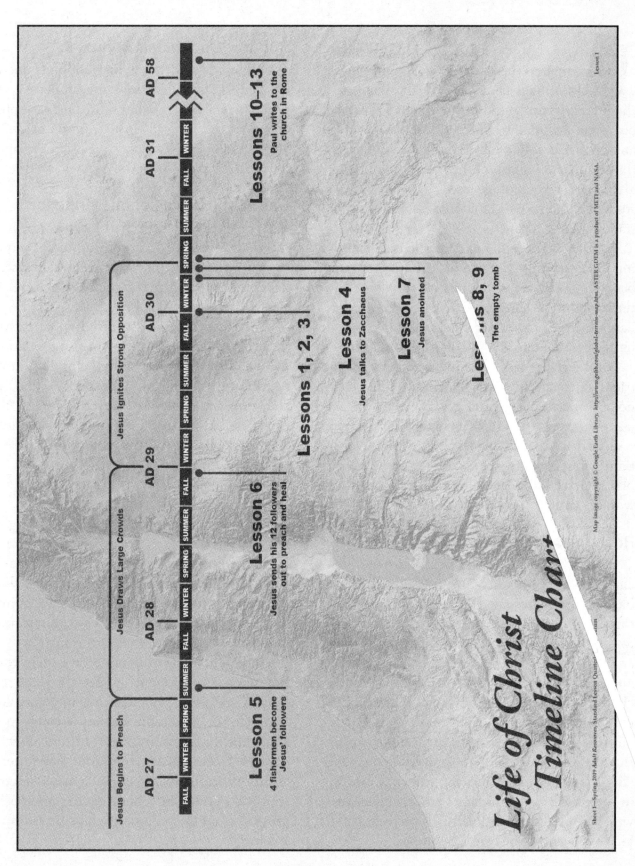

Life of Christ Timeline Chart

Jesus Begins to Preach

Jesus Draws Large Crowds

Jesus Ignites Strong Opposition

AD 27 · AD 28 · AD 29 · AD 30 · AD 31 · AD 58

Lesson 5
4 fishermen become Jesus' followers

Lesson 6
Jesus sends his 12 followers out to preach and heal

Lessons 1, 2, 3

Lesson 4
Jesus talks to Zacchaeus

Lesson 7
Jesus anointed

Lessons 8, 9
The empty tomb

Lessons 10–13
Paul writes to the church in Rome

Map image copyright © Google Earth Library. http://www.gelib.com/global-terrain-map.htm. ASTER GDEM is a product of METI and NASA.

Sheet 1—Spring 2019 Adult Resources, Standard Lesson Quarterly

Lesson 1

· 231 ·

THE FLOOR PLAN

Part 3 of Building Bible Literacy   *Teacher Tips by Jim Eichenberger*

IN THE PRECEDING two articles in this series, we compared the story arc of Scripture with the blueprint of a house. We further compared the literary types found in the Bible to different but essential building materials. Just as a blueprint and quality building materials allow a builder to frame a house, a grasp of the historical and literary contexts of a passage from the Bible allows a student of God's Word to frame his or her understanding of Scripture.

Another vital step in building a house is reviewing the floor plan. The various materials of lumber, wiring, etc., are merely parts of the whole. But the rooms of the house are where we live. In a similar fashion, Christian doctrines make up our "living space," shaping our daily faith and practice.

Before we begin to construct and defend doctrinal statements, we must understand Bible chronology and properly interpret the literary types (also known as *genres*) in Scripture. Failure here will lead to anemic teaching at best and outright heresy at worst. Let's consider some principles and pitfalls in defending Christian doctrines with Scripture.

Recognize Progression

A human father relates to his children in different ways as they mature. So also God the Father has acted and revealed His will progressively throughout history. Keeping this in mind is a key to evaluating Bible doctrine. For example, some argue that Old Testament holy days, dietary laws, and other ordinances must be observed by the church today. A good Bible teacher is prepared to note that the old law is nailed to the cross (Colossians 2:14); a better teacher is prepared to explain the relationship of Christ to the covenants, and why the old covenant needed to be superseded in the course of time. Many Old Testament laws were given for the Jews only, being preparatory for God's full plan to be revealed in Jesus.

Support Doctrines Adequately

Warn your students about building a doctrine on a single, difficult verse. For example, a certain group that claims to follow Christ uses the phrase "baptized for the dead" in 1 Corinthians 15:29 as a basis for an elaborate doctrine of proxy baptism for the deceased. Not good!

Use Proper Rules of Interpretation

Each literary type in the Bible must be recognized and interpreted according to the requirements of that type. For example, much research has come to recognize that the book of Revelation is of the type known as *apocalyptic*.

This type is defined (partially) as featuring "a narrative framework in which a revelation is mediated by an otherworldy being to a human recipient, disclosing a transcendent reality." That transcendent reality is Heaven, and one must expect figurative language will occur as the author tries to fit what he sees within his normal, earthly frame of reference.

Beware the Novel

When someone proposes an intriguing new interpretation of a Scripture that for centuries has been interpreted differently—beware! The axiom "the newer, the truer" is a falsehood. You should occasionally review key Bible doctrines, pointing out how widely accepted they have been throughout church history.

Good Bible teaching is never a mere recitation of creeds, of course—especially since sinful human reasoning has a tendency to negate God's truth (Mark 7:7, 8). But helping learners understand and support the proper, historic doctrines of Christ's church is essential to Bible literacy. When we teach established, Bible-based doctrine, we teach nothing new, but what the apostles have given us from the beginning (compare 1 John 2:7; 2 John 5).

CALLED TO SERVE

DEVOTIONAL READING: Luke 14:15-24
BACKGROUND SCRIPTURE: Luke 14:7-14

LUKE 14:7-14

7 And he put forth a parable to those which were bidden, when he marked how they chose out the chief rooms; saying unto them,

8 When thou art bidden of any man to a wedding, sit not down in the highest room; lest a more honourable man than thou be bidden of him;

9 And he that bade thee and him come and say to thee, Give this man place; and thou begin with shame to take the lowest room.

10 But when thou art bidden, go and sit down in the lowest room; that when he that bade thee cometh, he may say unto thee, Friend, go up higher: then shalt thou have worship in the presence of them that sit at meat with thee.

11 For whosoever exalteth himself shall be abased; and he that humbleth himself shall be exalted.

12 Then said he also to him that bade him, When thou makest a dinner or a supper, call not thy friends, nor thy brethren, neither thy kinsmen, nor thy rich neighbours; lest they also bid thee again, and a recompence be made thee.

13 But when thou makest a feast, call the poor, the maimed, the lame, the blind:

14 And thou shalt be blessed; for they cannot recompense thee: for thou shalt be recompensed at the resurrection of the just.

KEY VERSE

Whosoever exalteth himself shall be abased; and he that humbleth himself shall be exalted. —**Luke 14:11**

DISCIPLESHIP AND MISSION

Unit 1: Call to Discipleship

LESSONS 1–4

LESSON AIMS

After participating in this lesson, each learner will be able to:

1. Describe Jesus' view of humility.

2. Distinguish between behaviors that indicate humility and those that don't.

3. Demonstrate humility in one choice in the week ahead.

LESSON OUTLINE

Introduction

A. God's Way Up Is Down

Some drivers hate to make turns against heavy traffic. Faced with the need to turn at an intersection across several busy lanes, they will drive out of their way to avoid the turn. In countries where people drive on the right side of the road, they will make three right turns to avoid one left turn. For them, the way left is right, and right, and right again.

Jesus expressed a similar idea throughout His teaching. He taught that under God's reign, the way up, the way of honor and exaltation, is actually down, in lowly, self-giving service to others. Those who seek prestige, power, wealth, and status will be brought low. But those who lower themselves, who seek nothing for themselves and instead minister to others in humility, God will exalt. Jesus, the divine Lord who gave himself in death for undeserving sinners, taught and demonstrated that humility is the way to exaltation. This is the theme of today's text.

B. Lesson Context

Today's text is part of the account of Jesus' final journey to Jerusalem; the account extends from Luke 9:51 to 19:28. Jesus was approaching Israel's sacred city, having warned His disciples before the trip began that there He would be handed over to His enemies. They would put Him to death, but He would be raised again to life by God the Father (Luke 9:22). Although Jesus stressed, "Let these sayings sink down into your ears," it didn't (9:44).

The immediate backdrop of our lesson is an occasion on which Jesus was invited to a Sabbath day meal at the home of a powerful religious leader. At this grand meal was a man afflicted with dropsy, a malady characterized by painful swelling of the limbs (Luke 14:1, 2). Jesus confronted the other guests about their objections to His healing the afflicted man on the Sabbath. Receiving only silence as a response, Jesus proceeded to heal the man, pointing out their hypocrisy in the process (14:3-6). Our text is divided into two parts: advice given to guests at a banquet and advice given to the host.

I. The Humble Guest

(LUKE 14:7-11)

A. Unpretentious (vv. 7-9)

7. And he put forth a parable to those which were bidden, when he marked how they chose out the chief rooms; saying unto them.

Our text today begins with a teaching of Jesus identified as *a parable*. The noun being translated occurs 50 times in the New Testament, and 48 of those are in the Gospels of Matthew, Mark, and Luke.

Speaking in parables is a key characteristic of Jesus' teaching. Parables range from brief comparisons ("Unto what is the kingdom of God like? . . . It is like a grain of mustard seed," Luke 13:18, 19), to elaborate stories ("A certain man had two sons," 15:11-32). Parables are designed to provoke the listeners' thought processes and challenge the listeners' assumptions.

Jesus delivers this parable at a grand meal. Shared meals in Jesus' culture are occasions for the display of social status. The wealthy could display their abundance on such occasions, and places at the table closest to the host are regarded as carrying the greatest honor. Those not invited to such banquets can observe the proceedings from outside, and the ostentatious display of wealth is often the host's objective. These factors all play a role in our understanding of Jesus' teaching in this text, though His focus is on far more than correcting the customs of His day.

Jesus obviously speaks to those present with Him at the meal. But by calling them *those which were bidden* (invited), the writer Luke emphasizes that Jesus speaks to people who are in a position of privilege. Their important host has invited them as his peers to his sumptuous table. None of them are in positions of weakness like the seriously ill man whom Jesus has just healed.

HOW TO SAY IT

Abraham	*Ay*-bruh-ham.
Deuteronomy	Due-ter-*ahn*-uh-me.
Jerusalem	Juh-*roo*-suh-lem.
Moses	*Mo*-zes or *Mo*-zez.

In response to the invitation, and as people generally do, these seek the most prominent places at the table (*the chief rooms*). We might think of how people at a crowded event featuring open seating rush to get the best seats with good views.

8. When thou art bidden of any man to a wedding, sit not down in the highest room; lest a more honourable man than thou be bidden of him.

Weddings are common occasions for large meals to which many people are invited. Thus they provide a fitting backdrop for Jesus' example. His counsel is to avoid the typical behavior of assuming the best position (*the highest room*) that one can get at the table. To do so is to risk embarrassment. Someone worthy of more honor than oneself might also be in attendance, and that person's presence might result in a socially awkward outcome!

> **What Do You Think?**
> In what ways can your congregation challenge common secular ideas about who deserves honor?
> *Digging Deeper*
> How does the parable in Matthew 20:1-16 inform your conclusions, if at all?

As Jesus speaks of those *more honourable*, we hear an echo of His description of himself on other occasions. In the upper room at the last supper, He will admonish His disciples for the argument about who is greatest, noting that He, clearly the greatest of their company, lives among them as one who serves (Luke 22:24-27). Jesus' own nature as a servant, not their habitual desire for prominence, is what must determine the position that His followers seek.

9. And he that bade thee and him come and say to thee, Give this man place; and thou begin with shame to take the lowest room.

The end result of seeking the highest, most honored place may well be the opposite: *shame*. The host of the banquet, the one to whom guests are beholden for the privilege of attending the meal, may tell the honor-seeking guest to give up the place of prominence to allow the more honored person to have the proper seat. But isn't that just common sense? Don't those listening to Jesus know this (and perhaps have experienced it) already? Most likely! But there's a point here that must not be missed: it's not the guests who determine who takes which seats; that privilege belongs to the host of the banquet.

Just before telling this story, Jesus had honored an uninvited guest, the man with dropsy who humbly sought healing, by acknowledging his suffering and restoring him to wholeness. In doing so, He accepted the scorn of religious leaders who saw His actions as a Sabbath violation. Like the host in His story, Jesus exalted the one who took a low position. Like the wise guest in His story, Jesus willingly takes the lowest place, serving others instead of himself. His permanent move to the seat of highest honor becomes certain (Luke 22:69; Ephesians 1:20; Colossians 3:1).

> **What Do You Think?**
> What are some situations in which you should do better at humbling yourself?
> *Digging Deeper*
> What Scripture passage, other than today's text, challenges you the most in this regard? Why?

❧ *Donut Do That!* ❧

It seemed like a good idea at the time: impersonate a police officer to get a discount on donuts. So Charles Barry pulled up to the pickup window of a donut shop, flashed a sheriff's badge, and asked for the discount for law-enforcement officers.

The plan worked so well that the fake cop returned multiple times! But eventually an employee got suspicious. When he balked during one of Barry's visits, Barry again displayed his badge and pointed to a holstered firearm. The clerk took down Barry's license plate number and reported the incident to the police.

Barry was caught and charged with impersonating a law-enforcement officer and improper exhibition of a firearm. The police shield and weapon in Barry's possession were real, belonging to his father, a retired police officer.

Posturing catches up with the pretender sooner or later. Pretending we are entitled to something ends up fooling only ourselves. The eventual unmasking and humiliation are quite costly! Most of us know this either from observation or personal experience. So, why do we still do it?   —J. E.

B. Exalted (vv. 10, 11)

10. But when thou art bidden, go and sit down in the lowest room; that when he that bade thee cometh, he may say unto thee, Friend, go up higher: then shalt thou have worship in the presence of them that sit at meat with thee.

Jesus' counsel is to do the opposite: to seek *the lowest room* rather than the highest. Doing so not only avoids the potential shame of being moved to a lower place—indeed, there is no lower place—but also makes possible the honor that the host will exalt the humble guest. Jesus adds to this image by having the host address the humble guest as *Friend*. At this banquet, the true friend of the host is not the person who seeks status but the one who acts in lowliness.

From this new position the humble guest will receive due recognition from the other guests. (The word translated *worship* is elsewhere translated "honour" [John 5:41, 44]; thus there is no implication of the kind of worship bestowed only on God.) The host reverses the guests' situations so that the humble guest receives the honor that the self-seeking guest had sought.

Jesus' words mirror Proverbs 25:6, 7:

> Put not forth thyself in the presence of the king, and stand not in the place of great men: For better it is that it be said unto thee, Come up hither; than that thou shouldest be put lower in the presence of the prince whom thine eyes have seen.

The context of Jesus' teaching shows, however, that He goes beyond that well-known wisdom. The person who seeks status ignores not just the threat of humiliation, but also the revelation of God in Christ. The person who humbly puts others above self follows Christ as Lord and example. The wisdom of the banquet is not simply about how to conduct oneself in public but how to live as God's humble servant. Like Jesus, such a servant gives up status for the sake of others.

11. For whosoever exalteth himself shall be abased; and he that humbleth himself shall be exalted.

Jesus ends the first of the two parables with a summary statement, one that He repeats on other occasions (Matthew 23:12; Luke 18:14; compare James 4:10). God does not grant glory to those who exalt themselves, but to those who humbly take the lowly position, sacrificing themselves for the sake of others as Jesus did.

History begins with humans who, given an ideal world in which to live, abandon God's provision for the offer of self-exaltation (Genesis 3:5). In the story that unfolds, God grants His promises and does His work through those in lowly circumstances: Abraham, an elderly, childless man; Moses, a speech-impaired fugitive; David, an immature shepherd boy; even all Israel, a weak nation formed in slavery. Meanwhile, the great nations and people of the world, seeking status and power for themselves, come to nothing at God's hand.

In Jesus that story comes to its climax. He has status that belongs only to God, but He willingly takes the lowly position, even to the point of death, for the sake of those in need. His actions reveal the nature of God and of true humanity made in God's image. Jesus' story of guests at the banquet illustrates this larger biblical story and revelation of God. God always turns upside down our ideas of strength and status.

II. The Humble Host
(LUKE 14:12-14)
A. Wrong Action (v. 12)

12. Then said he also to him that bade him, When thou makest a dinner or a supper, call not thy friends, nor thy brethren, neither thy kinsmen, nor thy rich neighbours; lest they also bid thee again, and a recompence be made thee.

Jesus' teaching on humility is for all, host as well as guest. Thus a second story focuses on the host, encouraging similar selfless lowliness in the service of others.

Invitations to meals in Jesus' time are part of a culture of what might be called "returning the favor," the idea of *recompence*. Receiving an invitation, whether to the customary late morning meal (translated *dinner*) or the second meal in late afternoon (*supper*), carries the unspoken obligation to offer an invitation in return. The savvy host therefore invites those from whom he can expect a similar invitation. Friends and family are natural to invite as guests and can be counted on to return the favor. Invitations to the rich in one's community promise even greater return on investment. Jesus' audience is familiar with the customs of inviting such people to a meal with the expectation of receiving an invitation in return.

Jesus, however, rejects all such expectation. Obviously, He seeks and accepts friendship with all kinds of people. But giving in order to receive is the opposite of Jesus' teaching of gracious generosity (Luke 6:27-30, 37, 38). For Jesus, such behavior betrays a lack of understanding of and trust in God.

> **What Do You Think?**
> What challenges must you overcome in order to practice hospitality toward those who are not part of your demographic or cultural comfort zone?
> *Digging Deeper*
> How can your fellow believers assist you in this?

B. Right Action (vv. 13, 14)

13. But when thou makest a feast, call the poor, the maimed, the lame, the blind.

In place of friends, relatives, and the rich, Jesus' recommended guest list features those unable to provide anything in return. Their poverty and disability indicate that they cannot provide adequately for themselves, let alone hosting a meal for others. An invitation to such people would be completely gracious, made with no consideration for returning the favor. It is a gift without strings attached.

The poor, the maimed, the lame, the blind are the same as "the poor, and the maimed, and the halt, and the blind" in the story that follows this one (Luke 14:21, same Greek words). There a wealthy man whose dinner invitations are refused instructs

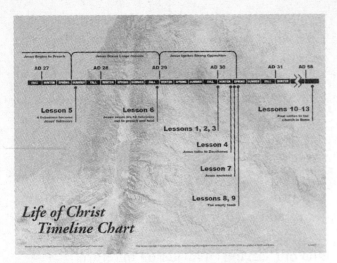

Life of Christ Timeline Chart

Visual for Lesson 1. *Keep this timeline posted throughout the quarter to give your learners a chronological perspective.*

his servants to find such people. It is the weak, not the strong, whom the Lord comes to bless (Luke 5:31; etc.). Jesus had announced as much at the beginning of His ministry in Luke's Gospel, quoting from the prophet Isaiah (Luke 4:18). But this is really nothing new: long before Jesus' day, God had instructed Israel to use its tithes every three years to be generous with those who had no means of paying back (Deuteronomy 14:28, 29).

The basis for such generosity is no less than God's own graciousness (compare Matthew 5:45). Though humans may think of themselves as strong and well supplied, we are all weak, poor, and vulnerable in the eyes of God. Our strength is nothing; our wealth cannot last. Yet God gives freely to us, as He gave freely to Israel enslaved in Egypt. For all weak, poor, helpless, unworthy humans, Christ came to die, providing an incomparable gift that can never be repaid in any part.

Only when we understand that we are weak like those whom Jesus describes can we rightly receive God's gracious gift. And when we do, then we cannot help but respond with similar generosity. As we do, we will take no thought of our own position or expectation of repayment.

❧ THE NIGHT GRACE SHONE ❧

Several years ago, sports celebrity Tim Tebow revealed an idea he had in an interview in *People* magazine: his foundation would create "Night to Shine." This would be a worldwide prom for peo-ple with special needs. Tebow said that he wanted to redefine Valentine's Day by encouraging people to show love to the least among us.

The first Night to Shine in 2015 featured 44 simultaneous prom events with more than 7,000 people with special needs. Attendees walked the red carpet while dressed in formal wear. Special hair, makeup, and shoeshine stations helped them look their best as they headed to the dance floor.

Later, on a talk show while reflecting on the successes of his special-needs proms, Tebow revealed that he had never attended his own prom. The talk-show host then presented Tebow with a corsage, which he in turn presented to a special needs girl in the audience. The band struck up a tune, and the two danced on national television.

Although those with celebrity status can host parties for the rich and famous, Tebow took the command and promise of Jesus seriously. Will you?
—J. E.

> **What Do You Think?**
> What are some ways your church can model gracious humility as a whole?
> **Digging Deeper**
> How does whole-church humility differ in appearance and action from humility exhibited by individual Christians?

14. And thou shalt be blessed; for they cannot recompense thee: for thou shalt be recompensed at the resurrection of the just.

Like guests who deliberately take the low position, hosts who invite those who *cannot recompense* them look to someone of higher standing still. God promises to bless the openhandedly generous, as they follow the pattern of His own generosity. The generous person trusts Him in the act of generosity, knowing that only God can repay or reward when the recipient cannot.

That reward, however, does not take the form of immediate compensation. Rather, Jesus speaks of repayment to occur *at the resurrection of the just*, when God raises from the dead His faith-filled, generous people. This will vindicate our openhandedness. Our generosity will be rewarded with even greater gifts of His grace (Luke 19:10-19).

The promise of resurrection at the end of this age is the assurance that God will make things right. This assurance also points us again to Jesus' own generosity and reliance on God. Jesus delivers this teaching while on His way to His crucifixion in Jerusalem, a death about which He knows and has warned His disciples (Luke 9:22).

> **What Do You Think?**
> How can we keep our service motives selfless and pure as we consider the restitution that awaits us at the resurrection?
> **Digging Deeper**
> Consider the self-contradictory situation of attempting to develop a sense of humility of which one can be proud.

Confident in God's faithfulness, Jesus has also promised His disciples that God will raise Him from the dead. Jesus' death will not be a random event beyond His control; rather, it will be an act of lowly, humble, self-giving service on behalf of others. Jesus is about to give His life for those who have no means of repaying Him, trusting that God will restore Him to victorious life in response to His generous self-sacrifice.

As the disciples act generously and humbly with no consideration for status or repayment, they follow in their Lord's footsteps. By faith they (and we) commit themselves to God's care. As God the Father will raise Jesus from the dead, so will He do for them (and us).

Conclusion

A. What Is Biblical Humility?

The twin teachings of Jesus in this lesson focus on proper behavior at a grand dinner. But we mistake His intent if we think that the two teachings are merely about such behavior. They combine to reveal that a person genuinely knows God only as He is revealed in the cross of Christ. Such knowledge of God leads to a radical reordering of one's life, from selfish status-seeking to self-sacrificial generosity and service.

The term *humility* is often attached to the point Jesus makes, and that term too is often misunderstood. It is more than modesty about one's accomplishments or sensitivity about displaying one's status. Biblical humility is the lowly spirit that puts others before oneself. As such, it combines Jesus' counsel in these two teachings: we are to seek the lowly position first and seek always to serve others generously.

As we embrace Jesus' teaching, we take no thought of what we think we are entitled to receive in return. Biblical humility is not just social reserve. It is following a lowly Master who willingly surrendered His life for the weak and undeserving. It is Christlike love put into action, with no thought of having earned the right to receive anything in return. It faithfully trusts God's promise of victorious resurrection.

How might Jesus offer these teachings if He were addressing them to our time and place? How might He describe the humble servant-disciple in the workplace, in the neighborhood, in the family, in the school or church? How would those stories challenge our deeply held assumptions and cherished attitudes? How can you live out stories like that in the places where you find yourself? How can you live as one who is called to serve, who understands that God's way up is down?

B. Prayer

Heavenly Father, we are overwhelmed as we contemplate Your Son's humility. Your gift to us of His life is worth far more than we could ever repay. May we respond not with an attitude of repayment, but as humble servants who take the lowly position. As we give no thought of receiving earthly reward, may we trust Your promise of resurrection. We pray in Jesus' name. Amen.

C. Thought to Remember

God's way up is down.

VISUALS FOR THESE LESSONS

The visual pictured in each lesson (example: page 238) is a small reproduction of a large, full-color poster included in the *Adult Resources* packet for the Spring Quarter. That packet also contains the very useful *Presentation Tools* CD for teacher use. Order No. 3629119 from your supplier.

INVOLVEMENT LEARNING

Enhance your lesson with KJV Bible Student (from your curriculum supplier) and the reproducible activity page (at www.standardlesson.com or in the back of the KJV Standard Lesson Commentary Deluxe Edition).

Into the Lesson

Challenge learners to name the title of the movie as you describe this scene:

Evelyn was about to pull into a parking spot when two women in a red sports car zipped into it first. When she complained to them, they said, "Face it, lady. We're younger and faster!" As they walked off, they heard a crash as Evelyn rammed their car. Before Evelyn drove off she said, "Face it, ladies. I'm older and I've got more insurance."

After you reveal (if no one else does) the movie to be *Fried Green Tomatoes,* say, "I'm sure we've all been in similar situations where someone acted selfishly." After a brief time for responses, continue: "Today's lesson has something to say about humility that we may find surprising."

Alternative. Distribute copies of the "Defining Humility" activity from the reproducible page, which you can download. Give students no more than a minute to complete it, then reveal the answers. Say, "All of the quotes except for the last one contain at least one element of what it means to be humble. As we study what Jesus has to say, we'll learn His viewpoint on humility."

Into the Word

Recruit a student in advance to be interviewed as the healed man of Luke 14:1-6. Provide the following questions to your actor as part of that preparation:

1–Where was Jesus when you came to Him?
2–What was your medical condition?
3–What did Jesus say before He healed you?
4–What example did Jesus use from everyday life to justify healing on the Sabbath?

After the interview, give each learner an 8½" x 11" sheet of paper upon which you have printed a large arrow. Form learners into small groups of three or four, then designate each group as either a *Banquet Guest Group* or a *Banquet Host Group.* Inform your groups that as you read aloud the text

that is relevant to their designation, group members are to hold up their arrow cards as they use them to indicate how the position of the guest or host changes position.

Proceed to read Luke 14:7-11 slowly for the *Banquet Guests Group(s).* Expected arrow responses as you read: *the guest puts himself **up** at the wedding feast, but he is forced to go **down***; *it's better to go **down** to a low spot and then be raised **up** by the host.*

Then read Luke 14:12-14 slowly for the *Banquet Host Group(s).* Expected arrow responses as you read: *the host had put himself **up** by inviting only family and wealthy friends. Jesus said he should invite those **down** in society. He would be lifted **up** and blessed at the final resurrection.*

Option. Add one or more *Healed Man Group(s).* Start the activity by reading Luke 14:1-6 slowly, expecting the following responses from group(s) of this designation: *the man was **down** because of his disease and position in society; he went **up** when Jesus noticed him; he was **down** because the Pharisees didn't think he should be healed on the Sabbath; he was **up** when Jesus healed him anyway.*

Into Life

Give each group a sheet of paper that features a giant V, the word *Heaven* printed at the top of the V, the word *earth* at the bottom of the V, and the text of Philippians 2:5-11 (you create). Ask groups to write each of the seven verse designations on one of the three points of the V to describe Jesus' position as a given verse indicates. Groups should consider the passage of time from left to right across the V. After a few minutes, lead a discussion regarding proper placement of the references, which are obvious from the text. Wrap up by posing this question: How will you demonstrate the humility of Jesus this week?

Alternate. Distribute copies of "Could You Do It?" from the reproducible page. Have students pair off and discuss.

CALLED TO SACRIFICE

DEVOTIONAL READING: Philippians 3:7-16
BACKGROUND SCRIPTURE: Mark 1:16-20; Luke 14:25-33

MARK 1:16-20

16 Now as he walked by the sea of Galilee, he saw Simon and Andrew his brother casting a net into the sea: for they were fishers.

17 And Jesus said unto them, Come ye after me, and I will make you to become fishers of men.

18 And straightway they forsook their nets, and followed him.

19 And when he had gone a little further thence, he saw James the son of Zebedee, and John his brother, who also were in the ship mending their nets.

20 And straightway he called them: and they left their father Zebedee in the ship with the hired servants, and went after him.

LUKE 14:25-33

25 And there went great multitudes with him: and he turned, and said unto them,

26 If any man come to me, and hate not his father, and mother, and wife, and children, and brethren, and sisters, yea, and his own life also, he cannot be my disciple.

27 And whosoever doth not bear his cross, and come after me, cannot be my disciple.

28 For which of you, intending to build a tower, sitteth not down first, and counteth the cost, whether he have sufficient to finish it?

29 Lest haply, after he hath laid the foundation, and is not able to finish it, all that behold it begin to mock him,

30 Saying, This man began to build, and was not able to finish.

31 Or what king, going to make war against another king, sitteth not down first, and consulteth whether he be able with ten thousand to meet him that cometh against him with twenty thousand?

32 Or else, while the other is yet a great way off, he sendeth an ambassage, and desireth conditions of peace.

33 So likewise, whosoever he be of you that forsaketh not all that he hath, he cannot be my disciple.

KEY VERSE

Whosoever doth not bear his cross, and come after me, cannot be my disciple. —**Luke 14:27**

Photo: Design Pics / Thinkstock

DISCIPLESHIP AND MISSION

Unit 1: Call to Discipleship

LESSONS 1–4

LESSON AIMS

After participating in this lesson, each learner will be able to:

1. Restate Jesus' concept of discipleship.

2. Explain how a Christian is to evaluate commitments in light of the call of discipleship.

3. Identify a problem area in his or her discipleship to Christ and implement a plan to correct it.

LESSON OUTLINE

Introduction

A. No Nominal Christians

Perhaps you have heard or read news stories about the percentage of people who are Christians in various parts of the world. Social scientists commonly survey populations to discover people's religious affiliation, noting trends over time.

To be identified as a Christian in most such surveys usually requires only a claim to be Christian. Few surveys ask about behaviors and practices as evidence of Christian commitment; the foundations of prayer, Bible reading, and worship attendance are ignored. Thus many people are counted as Christians merely through their self-identification as such. A term often applied to such people is *nominal Christians*. They are Christians in name only.

Before we form an opinion regarding the validity of that designation, we should consider what Jesus has to say about it in today's lesson.

B. Lesson Context: Jesus' Ministry Begins

The first of today's two texts comes from the beginning of Mark's Gospel. His storyline begins with John the Baptist's preaching that all must repent and be cleansed by God to prepare for the imminent arrival of God's king (Mark 1:2-8). Jesus then appears in the storyline for His baptism. At that time, He is identified by a voice from Heaven as God's kingly Son (1:9-11). After His triumph over the devil's tests (1:12, 13), Jesus repeats John's message of repentance, announcing that God's promised reign is very near (1:14, 15).

The coming of God's promised reign, His "kingdom," is central to Jesus' teaching. God's kingdom is the reestablishment of His rule over all creation, especially over rebellious humanity. The well-known words of the Lord's Prayer express this idea: "Thy kingdom come. Thy will be done in earth, as it is in heaven" (Matthew 6:10). Jesus links His coming and ministry to the inauguration of God's kingdom. This is a movement that will one day extend the rule of God to the ends of the earth (Acts 1:8), reaching complete fulfillment as Jesus returns as king (1:11). It is in this light that Jesus calls the first of His disciples.

C. Lesson Context: Jesus' Death Looms

Our second text, from Luke's Gospel, occurs in the period of Jesus' ministry when He was on His final trip to Jerusalem. He knew He was to die there, and He had warned His disciple of that fact (Luke 9:22, 44). But they failed to understand (9:45). The crowds that joined Him had high expectations of His kingly triumph. He would indeed triumph as king, but not in a way anybody expected!

I. Heed the Call
(MARK 1:16-20)

Against the background noted earlier, Jesus began to call Galilean fishermen to be His disciples. Fishing was a major industry on the Sea of Galilee in Jesus' time. Fishing operations were organized into a large guild, and many fish were processed into a tasty paste—an early version of MSG—that was sealed in jars and shipped all over the Roman Empire.

Fishing was hard work, and profits were constrained by taxes and guild regulations. But fishing provided a reliable income for hundreds of families in a place and time where life was an overwhelming struggle for most. To simply walk away from the fishing profession was unheard of.

A. Gathering (vv. 16-18)

16. Now as he walked by the sea of Galilee, he saw Simon and Andrew his brother casting a net into the sea: for they were fishers.

Jesus' ministry begins and largely focuses on Galilee. This is the northern region of Israel's homeland that features as its geographical focus *the sea of Galilee*, which is a large freshwater lake.

HOW TO SAY IT

Corinthians	Ko-*rin*-thee-unz (*th* as in *thin*).
Ezra	*Ez*-ruh.
Galatians	Guh-*lay*-shunz.
Galilee	*Gal*-uh-lee.
Haggai	*Hag*-eye or *Hag*-ay-eye.
Nehemiah	Nee-huh-**my**-uh.
Zebedee	*Zeb*-eh-dee.

Along that lake Jesus sees two brothers working as fishermen. We can picture them standing in a wooden boat about 20 feet long, skillfully throwing a heavy net into the water to gather some of the abundant fish that the lake supplies.

> *What Do You Think?*
> In what ways might the Lord call you to minister for Him in the week ahead?
> *Digging Deeper*
> What techniques might Satan use to get you to disregard that call? How can you resist these?

These two will become members of the 12 disciples, or followers, whom Jesus will later designate to be "apostles" (lesson 6, page 275, discusses definition per Matthew 10:2; also see Luke 6:13). Listings of the apostles occur in Matthew 10:2-4 [lesson 6]; Mark 3:16-19; Luke 6:13-16; and Acts 1:13.

Simon (also known as Peter) will become the most prominent member of those 12. That's probably why his name occurs first in all four lists. Indeed, he is called "first" in Matthew 10:2. The name of his brother *Andrew* occurs in the top third of all four lists, also indicating prominence (compare John 6:8; 12:22; see also page 276).

The paths of the 12, especially that of Peter, will be complicated, marked as much by failure as by faithfulness. But here we see simply two ordinary, hardworking fishermen with nothing to commend them as exceptional.

17. And Jesus said unto them, Come ye after me, and I will make you to become fishers of men.

Jesus' invitation is blunt and brief. His challenge is to follow Him as disciples as learners follow their teacher. The custom of Jesus' time is that students of Jewish religious teachers actually live side by side with their teachers. That allows observance of actions as part of the teaching process. Jesus' invitation is to that kind of life.

But the outcome *to become fishers of men* sets Jesus apart from other teachers. Since these fishermen used nets (not rods) and fishing lines with hooks, we can see Jesus' image is one of gathering. It echoes the words of the prophet Jeremiah, who used the image of fishermen to promise that

God would regather His scattered people after Judah's exile (Jeremiah 16:16). God's kingdom, Jesus has announced, is about to appear (see the Lesson Context). These two men will join Jesus in gathering a people who are ready to live as loyal subjects under God's rule.

Thus the invitation to become disciples of Jesus is an invitation to work to extend God's kingdom. This is the most consequential work that one can undertake. It is a work that ultimately will extend to all nations.

18. And straightway they forsook their nets, and followed him.

Peter and Andrew's response is as abrupt as is Jesus' invitation: they abandon their trade, their way of life and means of survival, and follow Jesus. Their lives will never be the same. But their lives will be not less but much more than before.

❧ *LEAVING NETS . . . AND NETWORKS* ❧

As a child star of the sitcom *Growing Pains* (1985–1992), Kirk Cameron eventually rejected atheism and turned to Christ. Cameron would ask that lines be removed from the script for his TV character that went against his faith. His more recent roles have been in faith-based films.

Those who become followers of Jesus may struggle with conflicts between the demands of their careers and the commands of their Savior. Many find ways to survive and even thrive in their careers after becoming Christians. Others choose

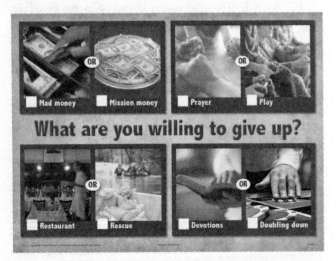

Visual for Lesson 2. *Keep this visual hidden until the lesson's conclusion. Then pose its choices for discussion.*

to leave their current employment to avoid these conflicts. Cameron is just one example of Hollywood stars of the recent past to have done so.

A growing relationship with Jesus caused some Galilean fishermen to revisit their career choices. That fact should cause us to ponder the next question here.   —J. E.

> **What Do You Think?**
> Under what circumstances, if any, should one not take immediate action on a perceived call to serve? Why?
> **Digging Deeper**
> Consider Nehemiah 1:1-4, 11; 2:11-16; Haggai 1:9; Luke 9:59-62; 14:31; Romans 10:2; Galatians 1:15-18; and 1 John 4:1 in your response.

B. Forsaking (vv. 19, 20)

19, 20. And when he had gone a little further thence, he saw James the son of Zebedee, and John his brother, who also were in the ship mending their nets. And straightway he called them: and they left their father Zebedee in the ship with the hired servants, and went after him.

Jesus issues a similar call, and two more brother-fishermen respond. These two, *James the son of Zebedee, and John,* will always be listed in the top third of the four lists mentioned above.

Mark emphasizes the cost of their decision as he notes that they leave behind a father as well as *hired servants.* The brothers' roots in their business are deep, and the work is apparently successful enough. But forsaking all is for them not too high a price when the "pay" is to take part in fulfilling the work of God in the world.

Looking across the gospel story, we can better understand these men's response to Jesus. Though this invitation is abrupt, other Gospel writers show us that the fishermen are prepared for it. John the Baptist has already identified Jesus to them as "the Lamb of God" (John 1:29, 35-42). Luke shows us that Jesus' call is accompanied by an impressive miracle (Luke 5:1-11).

Neither are these men chosen because they are choice. Mark will emphasize that Peter will argue with Jesus (Mark 8:31-33) and even deny Him (14:66-72). James and John will presumptuously ask to sit in the places of power when Jesus is enthroned, failing to understand that Jesus is going to His death (10:35-45). All members of the 12 will fail Jesus at His arrest, abandoning Him to His enemies (14:43-50).

Even so, Jesus will invite them back into His company at His resurrection (Mark 14:27, 28; 16:7). He will commission them as His messengers (Matthew 28:18-20). Impressive as their response is in the moment, the Lord's persistent grace is even more powerful.

II. Count the Cost
(Luke 14:25-33)

Our next passage is one of several in which Jesus redirects expectation from easy glory to costly suffering. The shadow of the cross falls across this passage, but the light of Easter morning shines on it as well.

A. Greatest Commitment (vv. 25-27)

25. And there went great multitudes with him: and he turned, and said unto them.

Crowds have grown as Jesus continued teaching and performing miracles on His way to Jerusalem (see the Lesson Context). Expectation that Jesus is God's promised king spread. His presence must mean political freedom and economic prosperity for Israel. So Jesus begins to address the crowds to confront them with the real nature of His kingdom.

26. If any man come to me, and hate not his father, and mother, and wife, and children, and brethren, and sisters, yea, and his own life also, he cannot be my disciple.

Jesus begins with a list of family relationships that people cherish most. These are not merely valued by His audience. They were regarded rightly as sacred. Faithfulness as a child, spouse, parent, or sibling is demanded by God's law. Added to this list is one's *own life,* one's very existence. Yet Jesus says that to be His *disciple*—one who follows Him and learns from Him how to live the godly life—one must *hate* all these!

This is how Jesus makes His point. Important as such relationships are, following Jesus is even more important. Those who follow Him must do so with the understanding that nothing else can be allowed to interfere. To be a disciple is greater than any other value or relationship.

Disciples learn that following Him does not diminish love for others. Rather, it increases it. The irony of Jesus' instruction is that only by putting Him in unchallenged first place does one learn to love faithfully those most cherished. But make no mistake: relationships with those for whom one would give one's own life are still of less value than following Jesus as a disciple.

> *What Do You Think?*
>   What struggles might you have to undergo in order to "hate" your family in the way Jesus intends that word to be taken?
> *Digging Deeper*
>   What insights, if any, do Ezra 10:1-17; Job 2:7-10; Luke 8:19-21; and 1 Corinthians 7:12-16 offer in this regard?

❧ A Revered Second Place ❧

After being sworn in as vice president in 2017, Mike Pence's personal priorities came under intense scrutiny by the press. Those priorities were driven by his and his wife's professed commitment to Jesus. That commitment included certain rules they held in their marriage. One such was the husband's promise not to go to dinner with a woman unless his wife accompanied him.

When a reporter asked wife Karen about the couple's commitment to put each other first, she quickly corrected the misunderstanding: although the Pences valued family above fame, power, and politics, they were not first place in each other's lives. She went on to tell of a time when they were dating. When she referred to Mike as her "number one," her husband-to-be warned that she would be disappointed if he were number one to her. The first-place position had to go to someone who truly deserved it—the Lord Jesus.

This is consistent with the warning Jesus gave to those who would follow Him. Compared with the love of Jesus, one's love of family members should seem like "hate!" In what ways is Jesus still not first in your life? —J. E.

27. And whosoever doth not bear his cross, and come after me, cannot be my disciple.

The *cross* is so familiar in Christianity that we often forget its significance for Jesus' audience. The Roman Empire uses death by crucifixion as a way of asserting its absolute power over subject peoples. Crucifixions are public spectacles of torture and terror, making examples of those who dare to defy Roman authority. Anyone who carries a cross is marked as a defeated enemy of Rome, about to feel the full effect of Rome's wrath.

Jesus uses the image of cross-bearing because of His own impending death by crucifixion. But His cross will not mean defeat. By giving His life willingly, surrendering to His enemies and letting them do their worst, Jesus will pay sin's price. In what is known today as *the substitutionary atonement*, Jesus will give His worthy life on behalf of the unworthy.

Those who follow Jesus as disciples do so to join Him in the work of God's kingdom, establishing God's reign in the world. As they do, they must carry out that work as Jesus has modeled: by giving themselves sacrificially in service to others (Luke 9:23). They, like Jesus, must trust God to provide and vindicate. They must bear in mind that they will see the full fruit of their labor only at the resurrection from the dead.

Perhaps you have heard someone say, "I guess that is my cross to bear" in response to a tragedy or loss. But the cross we bear does not refer to issues of inconvenience or painful circumstances that normally come our way in this fallen world. Rather, the cross we bear is what characterizes the life of one who follows Jesus. We live not to serve self but to serve others as the Lord did, holding nothing back (Luke 22:24-30).

B. Calculated Commitment (vv. 28-30)

28. For which of you, intending to build a tower, sitteth not down first, and counteth the cost, whether he have sufficient to finish it?

Jesus now uses a comparison to impress on His followers the nature of such a commitment. Though buildings in the ancient world are simpler than those today, they are still very expensive relative to one's resources. *A tower*, which might be used to guard a plot of agricultural land or even a town or city, is especially costly. It requires careful accounting to be sure that one has the resources to finish it. So Jesus urges His followers to listen carefully to His teaching, to understand the cost that He will pay and that they in turn will pay as well.

29, 30. Lest haply, after he hath laid the foundation, and is not able to finish it, all that behold it begin to mock him, saying, This man began to build, and was not able to finish.

An incomplete tower is not just a material failure. It is also a cause for public shame and mockery. The failed project becomes the basis for cruel jokes and ridicule. A tower in Jesus' time is a means of protection, a projection of power. By contrast, a failed tower is an expression of shame and weakness.

> **What Do You Think?**
> How will you know when a pause to count cost reaches the point of being mere procrastination and lack of faith?
> **Digging Deeper**
> Is that point the same for everyone? Why, or why not?

There is seeming shame in taking up one's cross (Hebrews 12:2). But there is glory in following the enthroned king who was crucified. The real shame is in failing to recognize Jesus as God's king, failing to surrender the price to follow Him. That opportunity is not to be missed at any price.

C. Absolute Commitment (vv. 31-33)

31. Or what king, going to make war against another king, sitteth not down first, and consulteth whether he be able with ten thousand to meet him that cometh against him with twenty thousand?

Jesus now provides a second comparison, also about assessing costs. Here a king faces a battle against an adversary with an army double the size of his own. Can the king with the smaller army prevail?

In this comparison, the answer seems clear: only under the exceptional circumstances can an army defeat an adversary twice its size. A proper assessment of the situation suggests only one possible course of action (next verse).

32. Or else, while the other is yet a great way off, he sendeth an ambassage, and desireth conditions of peace.

The outnumbered king has only one choice. He cannot take the risk of battle. He can only send his representatives to meet his adversary *a great way off*, long before their armies meet, to sue for peace on unfavorable terms. That choice is humiliating, but it is far better than defeat and death. This illustration includes the challenge of facing reality.

33. So likewise, whosoever he be of you that forsaketh not all that he hath, he cannot be my disciple.

This statement brings Jesus' comparisons to bear on the audience. Like a person building a tower, they must understand the true cost of following Jesus. Like a king facing an army of overwhelming force, they must be prepared to pay a cost that seems like defeat but is in fact the way to life.

That cost is all that a person has. No possession, no status, no relationship, no home, no identity, no dream can measure up to following and serving the ruler of God's kingdom. Nothing or no one else can give the life that He gives. Nothing else can restore us to our true selves as He does. It is a hard choice, the supreme choice—a choice that comes at great cost. But it is the only choice, no matter the cost.

What Do You Think?
How will a person know when he or she has given up everything to follow Christ?

Digging Deeper
How is your response informed by Bible examples of those who gave up much status (Moses, Paul, etc.) vs. those who gained status (Joseph, Daniel, etc.) in God's service?

Conclusion

A. Giving Our All

In our study of today's two lesson texts, we have seen how two seemingly incompatible ideas belong together. Jesus indeed brings God's promised rule, but He warns us that God's victory is achieved in weakness, lowliness, and suffering.

We cannot expect to receive a calling from the Lord as dramatic as the one that Peter, Andrew, James, and John received. None of us are called to be eyewitnesses of Jesus' ministry on earth as those four were. Yet like them, we share in His mission of advancing the promised reign of God. Jesus calls us to be His instruments so that God's will can be done on earth as it is in Heaven.

That calling makes us more than people who give lip service to a vaguely Christian identity. Rather, Jesus' call demands of us our all. That call challenges our fundamental relationships, even as it compels us to love our family and friends more than we ever have before. The call demands that all our possessions and time be put at God's disposal as we invest earthly resources for eternal return: the harvest of souls. The call means leaving many treasures behind but receiving countless more in return (Luke 18:29, 30).

Some think of the word *Christian* to be a term for those who confess Christ, while the word *disciple* is reserved for those seriously committed to following Him. The New Testament knows no such distinction. To confess Christ as Lord demands a counting of the cost of that confession. The cost is everything, but the payoff (if that's the best term) is participation in the eternal, victorious rule of God Almighty.

B. Prayer

Almighty God, may we acknowledge Your rule in our lives to the extent that we submit fully to Your Son. Strengthen us in the way of the cross, even as we thank You for eternal life that awaits. We pray this in Jesus' name. Amen.

C. Thought to Remember

"He is no fool who gives what he cannot keep to gain what he cannot lose." —Jim Elliot

INVOLVEMENT LEARNING

Enhance your lesson with KJV Bible Student (from your curriculum supplier) and the reproducible activity page (at www.standardlesson.com or in the back of the KJV Standard Lesson Commentary Deluxe Edition).

Into the Lesson

Form students into pairs to discuss these questions: 1–Who has had high expectations for you? 2–How have you responded to that?

After a few minutes of discussion, ask volunteers to share insights. Then say, "Studies show that the higher the expectations a parent, teacher, or coach has for a child, the more likely the child is to try to meet those expectations. In today's lesson we'll see how Jesus' high expectations of four men become His expectations for us as well."

Alternative. Distribute copies of the "Highest Percentage" quiz from the reproducible page, which you can download. After no more than one minute, reveal answers and ask learners which answers surprise them most and why. Make the point that the results come from surveys to which people merely self-report their religion. Then say, "There's no way of knowing how many of these respondents are Christians in name only. Today we'll see the very high standards that Jesus sets for those who are His disciples in the fullest sense."

Into the Word

Form students into two groups of no more than five each. (If your class is larger, form more groups and give duplicate assignments of those below.) Distribute the following on handouts (you prepare) to the group you designate *Responding to the Call Group:* Use Mark 1:16-20 as a launching point to answer the following questions: 1–When Jesus called Simon and Andrew to come and follow him, what did the two understand Him to mean? 2–In what way different from the call of traditional Jewish teachers did Jesus call the two to follow? 3–When Simon and Andrew chose to follow Jesus, what did they leave behind—not only in terms of what the text says, but by implication?

Also distribute the following on handouts (you prepare) to the group you designate *Counting the Cost Group:* Use Luke 14:25-33 as a launching point to discuss the following questions: 1–What did Jesus imply in speaking of hating family members? 2–What did Jesus' illustrations of a tower and a king with an undersized army signify? 3–When James and John followed Jesus, what did they leave behind—not only in terms of what the text says, but by implication?

In the ensuing whole-class discussion, first go over answers to the first two questions of the *Responding* group(s), skip the third, then go over responses to the first two questions of the *Counting* group(s), followed by simultaneous discussion of the third question of both groups.

Expect the following responses from the *Responding* group(s): *1–Become disciples as you live alongside me, learning how best to serve God. 2–They would be catching men, not fish.* Expect the following responses from the *Counting* group(s): *1–Devotion must be to Jesus above all else. 2–One needs to think carefully about what a commitment to discipleship entails.*

For the simultaneous third questions: *to abandon what the text says they abandoned was to give up their means of livelihood.*

Into Life

Write the following list on the board: 1–Love Jesus more than family; 2–Be willing to lose your life in service to Him; 3–Give up everything you own. Have students pair off and choose one category. Ask them to discuss how they are doing in meeting Jesus' expectations for discipleship in that area and propose how to improve.

Alternative. Distribute copies of the "Which Would You Choose?" activity from the reproducible page. Allow one minute to complete it, then pair students off to discuss the choices they made. As a class discuss the final choice and why so many people choose to live as Christians in name only rather than as committed disciples. Close with a prayer to be more committed.

CALLED TO RETURN

DEVOTIONAL READING: Ezekiel 34:11-16
BACKGROUND SCRIPTURE: Luke 15

LUKE 15:11-24

11 And he said, A certain man had two sons:

12 And the younger of them said to his father, Father, give me the portion of goods that falleth to me. And he divided unto them his living.

13 And not many days after the younger son gathered all together, and took his journey into a far country, and there wasted his substance with riotous living.

14 And when he had spent all, there arose a mighty famine in that land; and he began to be in want.

15 And he went and joined himself to a citizen of that country; and he sent him into his fields to feed swine.

16 And he would fain have filled his belly with the husks that the swine did eat: and no man gave unto him.

17 And when he came to himself, he said, How many hired servants of my father's have bread enough and to spare, and I perish with hunger!

18 I will arise and go to my father, and will say unto him, Father, I have sinned against heaven, and before thee,

19 And am no more worthy to be called thy son: make me as one of thy hired servants.

20 And he arose, and came to his father. But when he was yet a great way off, his father saw him, and had compassion, and ran, and fell on his neck, and kissed him.

21 And the son said unto him, Father, I have sinned against heaven, and in thy sight, and am no more worthy to be called thy son.

22 But the father said to his servants, Bring forth the best robe, and put it on him; and put a ring on his hand, and shoes on his feet:

23 And bring hither the fatted calf, and kill it; and let us eat, and be merry:

24 For this my son was dead, and is alive again; he was lost, and is found. And they began to be merry.

KEY VERSES

The father said to his servants, Bring forth the best robe, and put it on him; and put a ring on his hand, and shoes on his feet. . . . For this my son was dead, and is alive again; he was lost, and is found. And they began to be merry. —**Luke 15:22, 24**

Graphic: YuriyVlasenko / iStock / Thinkstock

DISCIPLESHIP AND MISSION

Unit 1: Call to Discipleship

LESSONS 1–4

LESSON AIMS

After participating in this lesson, each learner will be able to:

1. Recall the details of the parable of the prodigal son.

2. Interpret the parable as illustrating God's response to the repentant sinner.

3. Reflect on ways to have the outlook of Jesus toward those who seek redemption.

LESSON OUTLINE

Introduction

A. The Scandal of Forgiveness

"That is just unforgiveable."

Have you ever said something like that, or heard someone say it? We all believe in the importance and necessity of forgiveness. We all rely on forgiveness, from other people and from Almighty God.

But some wrongs seem impossible to forgive. They are too heinous, too painful. We can hardly imagine forgiving those who committed history's great crimes against humanity. But more practically, we struggle to forgive those whose deeds have deeply hurt us personally.

Likewise, we may struggle to believe we can be forgiven. Our wrongs go with us every moment. We cannot escape the deep regret we have for the harm we have done to others. Forgiveness is as hard to receive as it is to give.

Forgiveness is a scandal. We question those who offer it, question whether we can receive it, doubt whether it can really happen, doubt whether it should happen. The opponents of Jesus questioned both His ability to forgive sin (Luke 5:20, 21) and His association with those most in need of it (15:2). How Jesus responded is highly instructive yet today.

B. Lesson Context

Today's text, one of the most beloved (and misapplied) of Jesus' parables, is one of a series that He spoke in response to His opponents. Jesus was surrounded by publicans (tax collectors), hated in His time as collaborators with the oppressive Roman Empire. Sinners of various stripes flocked to Him. None of this sat well with religious leaders opposed to Jesus. They grumbled about His associating with such people, and especially about His eating with them.

With Luke 15:1, 2 noting the above, Luke 15:3 marks the beginning of Jesus' response. That response consists of three parables, each about the recovery of something: a lost sheep (15:4-7), a lost coin (15:8-10), and an errant son (15:11-32).

When Jesus used parables to address Jewish leaders, the stories were often meant to be "in your face" tweaks aimed at their hypocrisy. In the parable told at his house, Simon the Pharisee was to understand that he was the debtor who "loveth little" (Luke 7:47). "The chief priests, and the scribes, and the elders" were to know that the parable of the tenants was directed at them (Mark 11:27; 12:1-12). The three parables in Luke 15 are similar: they were meant to be rebukes of pious leaders who disdained Jesus because He "receiveth sinners" (Luke 15:2).

> *What Do You Think?*
> What guardrails can you adopt to avoid misapplying parables to today's situations?
> *Digging Deeper*
> Consider Jesus' original intent for using parables (Matthew 13:10-17), the original audience of a given parable, and the general difficult in interpreting figurative language (Matthew 15:15, 16; 16:5-12).

I. Desire
(LUKE 15:11, 12)
A. Description (v. 11)

11. And he said, A certain man had two sons.

Parables begin with images from common experience. This family depicted is no different in that regard—so far.

B. Request (v. 12a)

12a. And the younger of them said to his father, Father, give me the portion of goods that falleth to me.

Jesus' audience knows that the oldest son in a family has privileges and responsibilities that other sons do not (Genesis 25:31). One privilege is to receive a double share of the estate (Deuteronomy 21:15-17). This is computed by adding up the number of sons, adding one, then dividing the estate equally by the result. Each son except the oldest then receives a single share; the oldest son receives two shares as his birthright.

Since the father in the story has only two sons, this means that *the younger of them* is requesting one-third of the father's estate right now—this son

wants to "cash out." Of course, such distribution is always made at the father's death. To ask for one's inheritance before that is to say to one's father, "I want you to treat me as if you were dead."

C. Response (v. 12b)

12b. And he divided unto them his living.

An angry response would be understandable. But the father in the story accedes to the request! Is he being simply naïve in doing so? (See Proverbs 20:21.)

Our sanctified imaginations can see this as not only generous but also devastating. We may wonder how the family can thrive as a third of the assets suddenly vanish. This grant is bound to bring consequences on the father that may never be undone. But financial ruin of the father and the rest of the family is not part of the illustration, so we should not get sidetracked by it.

> *What Do You Think?*
> Without giving advice, how would you counsel someone who is about to use this verse as a basis for granting a similar request to a restless offspring?
> *Digging Deeper*
> Consider what the story as originally told was designed to illustrate.

II. Consequences
(LUKE 15:13-16)
A. Abandoning Covenant (v. 13)

13. And not many days after the younger son gathered all together, and took his journey into a far country, and there wasted his substance with riotous living.

The younger son seems to take as little time as possible to turn his share of the estate into cash. As he does, he puts his plan into action. For the audience of Jesus' day, this is much more than a long-distance move in a modern sense. The son is abandoning not only his family, but also the promised land and God's covenant. Having been born into an Israelite family, he now abandons that identity in favor of—something else.

As he lives wildly in the *far country*, the man has no concern for moral boundaries or prudence. As a result, he wastes the father's legacy. The accumulated wealth that could have given the son a start on an independent life later is now dissipated even while his father lives.

> ### What Do You Think?
> What guardrails can a church put in place to help members who are in danger of becoming spiritual prodigals and rejecting Christianity? What will be your part in this?
>
> ### Digging Deeper
> What are some warning signs that a rejection of Christianity is about to happen?

This verse also gives the story its familiar name: the parable of the prodigal son. While the word *prodigal* is often associated with the son's decision to rebel against parental oversight and leave home prematurely, the word actually means "recklessly wasteful of one's property or means." This definition therefore points to the son's poor stewardship more than his desire to cut ties with his family, although the two concepts are related here.

B. Experiencing Hunger (vv. 14-16)

14. And when he had spent all, there arose a mighty famine in that land; and he began to be in want.

Food shortages brought on by drought, pests, or social upheaval are common in the ancient world. Because a majority of people make a subsistence living in the best of times, death by starvation always looms. The younger brother has grown up in a prosperous household. Now he is estranged from family and far from his homeland by his own foolhardy actions. He is hungry and without anyone to call on for help.

❧ THE LURE OF WEALTH ❧

It's a common fantasy: *If only I could win the lottery. Then my life would be perfect!* The evidence demonstrates otherwise, however.

After winning $16.2 million in the Pennsylvania lottery in 1988, the winner had the worst year of his life. His own brother hired a hit man to kill him, hoping to inherit a share of the winnings. The winner invested his gain in business ventures that failed and put him $1 million in debt.

Another man thought it the best Christmas gift ever when he won a $315 million Powerball jackpot in December 2002. But his marriage disintegrated as he spent money on alcohol and adultery.

A woman who won a $5 million lottery in 1991 gave $2 million of it to an illegitimate child her husband knew nothing about. When he discovered his wife's deception, he poisoned her.

Those fascinated with wealth do well to heed Solomon's warning: "The abundance of the rich will not suffer him to sleep" (Ecclesiastes 5:12).   —J. E.

15. And he went and joined himself to a citizen of that country; and he sent him into his fields to feed swine.

To underscore the prodigal's plight, Jesus introduces an element that is particularly troubling to Jewish people: the destitute man is hired *to feed swine*—unclean animals (Leviticus 11:7; Deuteronomy 14:8). This indicates that the *citizen of that country* who hires the prodigal is Gentile. It is virtually impossible to honor the Law of Moses in such a context. Though the prodigal has forsaken family and country, the pigs remind the readers how far he has fallen (or jumped).

16. And he would fain have filled his belly with the husks that the swine did eat: and no man gave unto him.

Pigs are valued as livestock because of their ability to eat nearly anything and produce meat. But there is no indication that the prodigal is allowed to eat any such meat; the fact that *no man gave unto him* would seem to indicate the opposite. Instead, he must rely on *the husks that the swine did eat*—probably seed pods from carob plants.

We sometimes speak of those who experience consequences of bad decisions as "hitting rock bottom." That's where the prodigal is.

HOW TO SAY IT

Gentiles	*Jen*-tiles.
Pharisees	*Fair*-ih-seez.
prodigal	*praw*-dih-gul.

III. Reflection
(LUKE 15:17-19)
A. Reckoning with Reality (v. 17)

17. And when he came to himself, he said, How many hired servants of my father's have bread enough and to spare, and I perish with hunger!

At the bottom, the prodigal is forced to reevaluate his situation and the solution. His previous abundance had clouded his judgment. His destitute situation makes things crystal clear. Gone is the self-deception that created chaos for him and others.

B. Planning to Repent (vv. 18, 19)

18. I will arise and go to my father, and will say unto him, Father, I have sinned against heaven, and before thee.

Reality prompts the man to a new course of action. Having acted with high-handed selfishness, he now recognizes that sin for what it was. So he plans to take responsibility for his actions by openly affirming that he has done wrong.

To sin *against heaven* is to sin against God, to violate God's law and will. God is Father to His people, a generous, loving, forgiving Father who commands His people to show honor to their parents on earth (Exodus 20:12). The young man's actions were terribly dishonoring.

Likewise, abandonment of the covenant people to live as a pagan among idolaters is an affront. Jesus' Jewish audience is undoubtedly recognizing that the prodigal's spiritual poverty is more serious than his physical one. Does that audience think the man's sins to be beyond forgiveness?

19. And am no more worthy to be called thy son: make me as one of thy hired servants.

The man continues to rehearse his repentance speech as he assesses his responsibility for his situation. A legal reality is in view: because he has already spent his share of the inheritance, his father's obligation to recognize him as his *son* no longer exists. This fact is underlined by the son's callous disrespect for his father. The son has treated the father as if dead. Further, the son cannot return the inheritance because it is gone. The only hope is that repentance can result in being hired as a servant.

We may pause to ask ourselves what life would be like for an estranged but repentant son to be brought back into the household as a servant. Would the father make extra demands of him? Would the son sense a constant obligation to seek his father's approval? Some Christians today may sense they have the relationship of a hired servant with God more than that of a beloved son or daughter. If we see ourselves as such, we have much to consider in this story.

IV. Restoration
(LUKE 15:20-24)
A. Father's Welcome (v. 20)

20. And he arose, and came to his father. But when he was yet a great way off, his father saw him, and had compassion, and ran, and fell on his neck, and kissed him.

Having reached the point of repentance, the son returns to face *his father*. The son's repentance and return are necessary to be restored to his family, but will not be sufficient. It will be the father's action that accomplishes the restoration. In the preceding parables of the lost sheep and the lost coin, everything else is put on hold until what is missing is recovered through active searching. But that is not the case in the parable at hand. No searching for the errant son is said to be done. There is no indication that the family business is put on hold until the son is recovered.

When he sees the son, the father does not wait for him to arrive at the front door. The father did not run after the son when he left, but he runs toward him now! The driving force to do so is the father's *compassion*, deep feelings of love and mercy, for his estranged son, and so he runs despite the indignity.

When the two draw near each other, the father does not halt abruptly to wait to hear what the son has to say. Rather, the father's reaction indicates that the son's repentant presence is more than acceptable. Without having spoken, the prodigal son has already received more than he hoped for, and certainly more than he deserved.

B. Son's Confession (v. 21)

21. And the son said unto him, Father, I have sinned against heaven, and in thy sight, and am no more worthy to be called thy son.

The son begins his prepared speech of repentance. But the son seems to be interrupted (next verse) before he can get to the part where he plans to say "make me as one of thy hired servants" (Luke 15:19).

C. Relationship's Renewal (vv. 22-24)

22. But the father said to his servants, Bring forth the best robe, and put it on him; and put a ring on his hand, and shoes on his feet.

The father interrupts with the instructions we see here. *The best robe*, likely very costly, is a sign of sonship. Such clothing is very costly in the ancient world. The *ring* is not just ornamental jewelry, but likely bears a seal for identifying legal documents in the family's affairs. *Servants* commonly do not wear shoes, but family members do.

23. And bring hither the fatted calf, and kill it; and let us eat, and be merry.

In each of the two preceding parables, the finding of the lost object prompted owners to gather friends and relatives for a celebration (Luke 15:6, 9). The same happens in this story.

In biblical times, the slaughter of an animal is always a special occasion. Ordinary, everyday family meals often do not feature meat. The reason is that the lack of refrigeration means that all meat of a slaughtered animal must be cooked and eaten immediately. That won't happen unless a lot of people are present.

A calf is an especially extravagant animal for slaughter, as the owner is foregoing the growth that the animal might attain and the offspring it might bear. This is provision for the most festive of celebrations. The father is holding back nothing to welcome his lost son back to the family.

We might have expected the father to make some provision for the son to repay what he had taken. But he offers not a word in that direction. Instead, the father gives generously. His forgiveness for the repentant son is graciously full and complete.

24a. For this my son was dead, and is alive again; he was lost, and is found.

The father's final statement to the younger son summarizes the story. The son's original desire effectively treated his father as dead to the son. But in fact it was the son who ended up effectively dead to the father! The father had had no realistic expectation of ever seeing his son again, let alone of enjoying a loving relationship with him. But the son's restoration is as if he has been raised from the dead. Like the sheep and the coin in the preceding stories, what was lost no longer is.

24b. And they began to be merry.

And so the celebration begins. Friends and family gather to share the joy. Their presence honors and affirms the grace the father is showing to his son. How unlike the religious leaders who criticize Jesus for His eating with sinners!

❧ *A Famous Prodigal?* ❧

He was given a job as an apprentice in the family print shop. All he needed to do was learn the trade, and he would be guaranteed a rewarding career. But things did not work out that way.

Soon conflicts arose with his boss, who happened to be his stepbrother James. Not content with merely setting type, the apprentice wanted to write and have his words read by everyone in Boston. James was not impressed with his writing and refused to publish it.

But the apprentice began to submit essays under a pen name. These were accepted by James for publication, and soon readers in Boston eagerly awaited the next letter from "Mrs. Silence Dogood."

The deception angered James when it was discovered. So the rebellious 17-year-old apprentice left without his brother's permission.

He went to Philadelphia for a new start. Work in several printer shops there was unsatisfying, so he headed to London. Lured by an empty promise of help in starting a newspaper, he ended up working again as a typesetter.

Returning to Philadelphia, he found work as a store clerk and bookkeeper. That return was fateful because that young man was Benjamin Franklin, who went on to become one of America's founding fathers!

A popular but loose, extended definition would describe him as an American prodigal. We can let that stand as long as we don't lose sight of Jesus' original intent in our text. See below. —J. E.

Conclusion

A. The Essence of Repentance

We must stress what should be obvious: Jesus was not using a heartwarming story to illustrate how a family reconciliation should occur. Rather, Jesus was telling the story of every person who has ever turned away from God and squandered the blessings of His love and grace. This observation explains the father's startling behavior at the outset: God might not stop a person from turning to a sinful lifestyle.

Even so, He is ready to take back the repentant. He may watch in silence as we depart, but He leaves the door open for our return. The older brother's complaint (Luke 15:25-32) is not considered in this lesson so this point is not overshadowed.

> *What Do You Think?*
> What should churches do, if anything, regarding unrepentant backsliders whose sins are separating them from the heavenly Father?
> *Digging Deeper*
> How should those actions differ, if at all, regarding the nature of the sin?

Jesus celebrated repentant sinners whom He had restored to fellowship with God. For the publicans and sinners, that meant admitting that what others said about them was true: they had ostracized themselves from God's people. That meant

Visual for Lesson 3. *Use this visual as a backdrop to the discussion question that is associated with the lesson's conclusion, below.*

they needed God's mercy. They found that mercy in Jesus. The religious leaders of the day saw no relevance for Jesus in obtaining that mercy. But in fact, He was (and is) the only relevance in that regard. The fact that Jesus spoke this parable to stress the available mercy of the Father has another teaching point: we dare not think of anyone as "too far gone" to be eligible for God's mercy.

While the parable can be viewed on a personal level in illustrating God's acceptance of repentant individuals, many students see a larger theme here: the prodigal son as representing the Gentiles. Surely the religious experts of Jesus' day had read Isaiah 49:6, where God promised that His servant would not only "raise up the tribes of Jacob" and "restore the preserved of Israel," but also was to be "a light to the Gentiles, that thou mayest be my salvation unto the end of the earth" (quoted in Acts 13:47). This speaks to how we are to view people-groups today (Matthew 28:19, 20).

B. Prayer

Father, we thank You for Your mercy! May we join in Your joyous celebration as others become reconciled to You. Teach us to express that joy as we treat others with the grace and mercy You granted to us. We pray in Jesus' name. Amen.

C. Thought to Remember

God's banquet celebrates the forgiveness of self-aware failures.

INVOLVEMENT LEARNING

Enhance your lesson with KJV Bible Student *(from your curriculum supplier) and the reproducible activity page (at www.standardlesson.com or in the back of the* KJV Standard Lesson Commentary Deluxe Edition).

Into the Lesson

Write the following words on the board: *keys, purse or wallet, cell phone, credit card, pet.* Ask what these items have in common. After a few guesses, propose (if no one else does) that these are things that cause panic when lost. As a whole-class or in small groups, have students discuss the emotions of having lost something important and having that item turn up later, with or without a search.

Alternative. Distribute copies of the "Helpful Directions?" activity from the reproducible page, which you can download. Have students pair off to discuss how they like to give and receive directions. Ask students to share experiences of, and reactions to, following someone's directions only to end up hopelessly lost.

Follow either activity by saying, "In today's lesson Jesus tells a parable about someone who was lost, yet found his way home. This parable has often been misapplied, but today we'll consider it as Jesus originally intended."

Into the Word

Ask two of your best readers to take turns reading aloud the verses of Luke 15:11-24. (This will work best if both are reading from the same version of the Bible.)

Have students close their Bibles or student books so that they cannot see the text. Divide the class in half and ask each group to select a spokesperson. Tell the groups that they are going to take turns telling the story of the prodigal son. The first group will begin telling the story until you say "Switch." Then the other group will continue the parable. Others in the group are encouraged to make suggestions to the spokesperson.

Start them off by saying, "A certain man had two sons," and then point to one of the groups. Every 10 to 15 seconds as appropriate, say "Switch." Commend groups for the retelling.

Alternative. Distribute copies of the "Mixed-up Parable" from the reproducible page. Have learners work in pairs or threes.

After either activity, discuss the parable by posing the following questions. Pause for discussion after each before asking the next.

1–In what way did the son reject his family? 2–In what way did the son reject his homeland? 3–In what way did the son reject his religion? 4–What caused him to have a change of heart? 5–How did the father's actions at the son's return demonstrate acceptance and forgiveness? 6–What point was Jesus trying to get across?

Anticipated responses: *(1) in asking for his inheritance, he treated the father as if dead; (2) moving a long distance meant leaving the promised land; (3) to live among idolatrous people, engage in wild living, and work among unclean animals (pigs) implied rejecting God's covenant; (4) being hungry and destitute; (5) runs to meet and kiss him, has the servants bring a robe, a ring, and shoes for the son, then declares a great feast; (6) we should not despise those who seem beyond redemption because they are the very ones Jesus came to save and welcome back.*

Into Life

Say, "When the religious leaders grumbled because Jesus was being gracious to sinners and eating with them, He told parables about a lost sheep, coin, and son. In each case, rejoicing resulted when that which was lost was found."

Pose these questions: 1–How does the fact that "there is joy in the presence of the angels of God over one sinner that repenteth" (Luke 15:10) contrast with the Pharisees' outlook (15:2)? [Pause to discuss.] 2–How well are we doing in having Jesus' attitude? [Pause to discuss.] 3–In what ways can we do better? [Pause to discuss.] 4–How can we improve our celebrations when a sinner comes to Christ? Allow a time of prayer for learners to reflect on how he or she can improve in these areas.

CALLED TO REPENT

DEVOTIONAL READING: 1 Chronicles 16:8-13, 23-27
BACKGROUND SCRIPTURE: Luke 19:1-10

LUKE 19:1-10

1 And Jesus entered and passed through Jericho.

2 And, behold, there was a man named Zacchaeus, which was the chief among the publicans, and he was rich.

3 And he sought to see Jesus who he was; and could not for the press, because he was little of stature.

4 And he ran before, and climbed up into a sycomore tree to see him: for he was to pass that way.

5 And when Jesus came to the place, he looked up, and saw him, and said unto him, Zacchaeus, make haste, and come down; for to day I must abide at thy house.

6 And he made haste, and came down, and received him joyfully.

7 And when they saw it, they all murmured, saying, That he was gone to be guest with a man that is a sinner.

8 And Zacchaeus stood, and said unto the Lord; Behold, Lord, the half of my goods I give to the poor; and if I have taken any thing from any man by false accusation, I restore him fourfold.

9 And Jesus said unto him, This day is salvation come to this house, forsomuch as he also is a son of Abraham.

10 For the Son of man is come to seek and to save that which was lost.

KEY VERSE

The Son of man is come to seek and to save that which was lost. —Luke 19:10

DISCIPLESHIP AND MISSION

Unit 1: Call to Discipleship

LESSONS 1–4

LESSON AIMS

After participating in this lesson, each learner will be able to:

1. Recall details of the story of Jesus' encounter with Zacchaeus.

2. Illustrate the transforming effect of God's grace through the example of Zacchaeus.

3. Commit to a change in attitude toward money and compassion for others.

LESSON OUTLINE

Introduction

A. From All to Nothing and Back Again

What is the measure of your life? An accountant can calculate your wealth. Your boss can state your contribution to the organization. Your family and friends can tell you how much you mean to them. Internet sites can tell you the impact of your social media posts. A physician can assess your health. Your résumé can detail your professional accomplishments. Which of these, if any, is the best measure?

We may also ask how the choice of measuring instrument has changed for you over the years. Were you once concerned with wealth, power, and/or popularity, but now you reject those touchstones in favor of assessing your life differently?

Such a change in assessment is central to what the Bible calls "repentance." Repentant people revalue their lives, and with renovated values they embark on renovated behavior, the subject of today's lesson.

B. Lesson Context

Our text is part of Luke's narrative of Jesus' journey to Jerusalem. Jesus had warned His disciples that He would be put to death but raised to life again (Luke 18:31-34; see also 9:22, 44; 13:31-33). Having arrived in Jericho, the setting of today's lesson, Jesus was only about 15 miles from Jerusalem and its momentous events.

This lesson's account is the last of three in close succession in which Jesus interacted with individuals who sought Him out. The first was a conversation with the man we call the rich young ruler (Luke 18:18-30); the second involved a blind beggar (18:35-43). The first man seemingly had every advantage and had followed every law of God; the second had nothing except the audacity to cry out persistently for Jesus' mercy.

The surprising outcomes were that the advantaged man departed disappointed, while the disadvantaged one received his request and followed Jesus on the way. The reason we say surprising is because of commonly held viewpoints on privileged wealth and disadvantaged poverty (compare Matthew 19:23-25; John 9:2; James 2:1-4).

Those outcomes set the stage for the third and final encounter of the sequence. This encounter is with a publican (a tax collector). People in every time and place grumble about taxes and tax collectors. But tax collectors in first-century Israel were especially despised. The Roman Empire had a practice of contracting for the collection of certain taxes. The process involved an auction for the authority to collect taxes in a particular location.

Recognizing an opportunity to make a profit, people would estimate the taxes that could be collected and bid accordingly. The winning bidder would then do everything possible to maximize taxes collected in order to maximize personal profit.

Tax collectors were therefore despised for two reasons. One was the unfair and burdensome taxes they charged to enrich themselves. The other was the fact that such Jews were collaborators with the occupying force of pagan, oppressive Romans.

I. Determined Glimpse
(Luke 19:1-4)
A. Challenging Setting (vv. 1-3)
1. And Jesus entered and passed through Jericho.

Jericho is a prosperous settlement in an oasis in the desert of the Jordan River valley. Though only about 15 miles from Jerusalem, it is more than 3,000 feet lower in elevation and thus a demanding, uphill journey. *Jesus* is approaching the place of His predicted death and resurrection. The shadow of the cross and the light of the empty tomb fall across this episode.

2. And, behold, there was a man named Zacchaeus, which was the chief among the publicans, and he was rich.

We now meet the man with whom Jesus will interact. *Zacchaeus* is described first as *the chief among the publicans*—those who collect taxes for the Romans (see the Lesson Context). Mentioned in the Bible only here, his description likely means that Zacchaeus is responsible for a region and supervises other tax collectors. This intensifies our sense that Zacchaeus is powerful and

despised. The added note that Zacchaeus is *rich* confirms his status and reminds us of the rich young ruler (Luke 18:23).

> **What Do You Think?**
> As we seek to make disciples (Matthew 28:19, 20), under what circumstances, if any, will it be helpful to categorize people in terms of their wealth or lack thereof? Why?
>
> **Digging Deeper**
> In what ways, if any, do the multiple ways of defining "wealthy" have a bearing on the question above?

3. And he sought to see Jesus who he was; and could not for the press, because he was little of stature.

Luke has noted the crowds that surround *Jesus* as he travels to Jerusalem (Luke 12:1; 14:25). The growing multitude fills the narrow streets of Jericho and prevents Zacchaeus from seeing Jesus. Luke implies that Zacchaeus desires to learn about this well-known prophet so that he may evaluate Him. Zacchaeus's short stature prohibits him from looking over the crowd, and his outcast status makes it unlikely that anyone will make space for him.

> **What Do You Think?**
> What safeguards can we adopt to ensure that we don't block others' view of Jesus as He should be seen today?
>
> **Digging Deeper**
> Think in terms of acts of both omission and commission in behavior and speech.

B. Humiliating Solution (v. 4)
4. And he ran before, and climbed up into a sycomore tree to see him: for he was to pass that way.

Zacchaeus solves his problem with actions that do not comport with his powerful status. In biblical times, powerful men do not run. They have people do that for them. But Zacchaeus accepts the humiliation of running to get ahead of the crowd following Jesus. That expedience

Visual for Lesson 4. *As you reach Luke 19:7, call for silent discussion by challenging learners to create a hand sign that reflects the opposite of the above.*

accomplishes little, though, when the crowd catches up as Jesus passes by.

So Zacchaeus takes another exceptional action: climbing into *a sycomore tree.* This is one of the fig trees that flourishes in Jericho, with its hot climate and abundant spring water. Grown men—especially powerful men—do not climb trees in Jesus' time. For the moment, Zacchaeus has humbled himself in hopes of seeing Jesus (Luke 18:14).

❧ NAPOLEON COMPLEX ❧

It's called "Napoleon complex" or "short-man syndrome." The theory is that short men may exhibit overly aggressive social behavior to compensate for below-average height. Napoleon Bonaparte was thought to compensate for his 5′2″ frame by seeking power and conquest.

The existence of such a complex has long been disputed, but recent research seems to strengthen arguments for it. A study conducted by the Centers for Disease Control and Prevention found that men who struggle with their masculinity are more than three times as likely to commit violent assault.

Though Zacchaeus of Jericho lived long before Napoleon, one wonders if we could classify him as having short-man syndrome. While the Bible does not mention any physically aggressive behavior on his part, his rise to be a top-dog tax collector may have been a way of compensating for self-perceived deficiencies. That's just speculation, but this is a

fact: the only deficiency that counts in the long run is sin. Until we realize that, we focus on the wrong thing.   —J. E.

II. Surprise Announcement
(LUKE 19:5, 6)
A. Invitation by Guest (v. 5)

5a. And when Jesus came to the place, he looked up, and saw him, and said unto him, Zacchaeus.

We are not surprised when *Jesus* sees the curious sight of a grown man in a tree. But Jesus' reaction is in every way exceptional.

To address *Zacchaeus* by name is a remarkable personal note, for minor characters in the gospel story are seldom addressed by name. In any event, it is astonishing that Jesus recognizes and calls by name a man He has never met. This is one of many examples in the gospel story in which Jesus exhibits supernatural knowledge, knowledge that can be rightly expected of God alone (see Luke 5:22; 6:8; 7:36-50; 8:46; 19:29-34; 22:7-13).

5b. Make haste, and come down; for to day I must abide at thy house.

Here Jesus' divine knowledge is applied to expressing a personal, urgent invitation to the man in the tree. Zacchaeus is to *make haste*: that is, to do all in his power to accomplish what Jesus commands. Zacchaeus had climbed the tree to see Jesus; but now, having humbled himself, he will need no such undignified posture. Jesus will come to be a guest at Zacchaeus's *house.*

Jesus of course will be Zacchaeus's guest, yet Jesus initiates the invitation! It is as if He were the host. Jesus takes the role of authority in the exchanges, yet in so doing He dignifies Zacchaeus by designating the man's home as the place where Jesus will receive refreshment. The added note of time (*to day*) stresses the urgency of the invitation.

Further, Jesus uses a telling expression translated *must.* In Luke's Gospel, which features 12 of the four Gospel's 30 occurrences in Greek, this word often signifies something that has to take place to fulfill God's purpose. Despite Zacchaeus's being despised by his contemporaries as a traitor, Jesus' visit to the man's home is a divine necessity.

B. Response of Host (v. 6)

6. And he made haste, and came down, and received him joyfully.

Luke describes Zacchaeus's reaction with words that precisely replicate Jesus' instructions. The wealthy tax collector readily submits to Jesus' greater authority; he does not submit fearfully or grudgingly, but joyfully. He has hoped only to catch a glimpse of Jesus, but now he has been chosen to be Jesus' host. Zacchaeus seems to recognize the invitation as one of divine grace, representing a new opportunity of some sort.

> **What Do You Think?**
> What are some practical ways your church can demonstrate the joy of encountering Christ?
> *Digging Deeper*
> How might these practical ways differ from church to church due to the nature of their surrounding communities?

❧ RECIPEACE ❧

The International Day of Peace has been observed in some form on September 21 every year since 1982. It is dedicated to world peace and envisions the absence of violence. In 2013, the day was dedicated by the Secretary-General of the United Nations to peace education.

Peace Day is celebrated in a variety of ways by various organizations. Of these, perhaps none is as intriguing as the efforts of a social movement known as "Recipeace." Partnering with professional chefs, Recipeace strives to bring people together over food.

Recipeace offers recipes based on historical "peace meals." For example, a plum pudding recipe recalls a Christmas Eve during World War I. Weary soldiers from Germany, Britain, Scotland, and France laid down weapons and left trenches to celebrate with carols and sweet treats. A three-meat mock-turtle soup recalls a dinner meeting between President Theodore Roosevelt and Booker T. Washington in 1901. This first-ever meal shared by a sitting president and an African-American in the White House featured discussions on ways to ease racial tensions.

Recipeace also gives directions for Underground Railroad jerky (hidden in tree stumps for escaping slaves) and Amish friendship bread. Eating meals together has long been part of recipes for peace.

Jesus understood the goals of Recipeace. He broke bread with the chief tax collector Zacchaeus. He promised the lukewarm Laodiceans that He would come and eat with them (Revelation 3:20). He even accepted dinner invitations from Pharisees bent on trapping Him (Luke 14).

As you follow our Savior's footsteps, who can you invite to share dinner, coffee, or dessert?

—J. E.

III. Varied Attitudes
(LUKE 19:7-10)

A. Crowd's Complaint (v. 7)

7. And when they saw it, they all murmured, saying, That he was gone to be guest with a man that is a sinner.

Not everyone is joyous, however. The crowds that accompany Jesus include many who recognize Zacchaeus as a notorious tax collector. They express the common opinion that such people are, by definition, evil. Disloyal to God and His people, publicans opportunistically link their fortunes with the pagan oppressors.

Jesus frequently receives such criticism in this Gospel (Luke 5:30; 7:34; 15:1, 2). Only here do we see the hostility directed against a specific individual. And historical sources show us that this is unlikely to be the first time Zacchaeus has faced such hostility. He is of a despised class, and those who despise the class do so for what they believe are godly reasons. It's likely that Zacchaeus has never gotten used to such treatment, even though it is painfully familiar.

HOW TO SAY IT

Jericho	*Jair*-ih-co.
Laodiceans	Lay-*odd*-uh-**see**-unz.
Mosaic	Mo-*zay*-ik.
Pharisees	*Fair*-ih-seez.
Zacchaeus	Zack-*key*-us.

B. Zacchaeus's Promises (v. 8)

8a. And Zacchaeus stood, and said unto the Lord; Behold, Lord, the half of my goods I give to the poor.

It is not clear where and when *Zacchaeus* speaks these words. Bible translations and commentators propose one of three scenarios: (1) immediately, on the spot, (2) while walking to his home with Jesus, or (3) when the two are inside the man's house. Time and place are not nearly as important as the content of the declaration, however.

Luke draws our attention to the importance of the pronouncement by indicating that Zacchaeus stands to speak and begins with the word *behold*. This expression draws attention to what is to follow (compare Luke 21:29). Further, Zacchaeus addresses Jesus as *Lord*. This indicates at least high respect (as in "sir"), if not Jesus' divine, supreme authority.

For Zacchaeus to pledge to give *half* his wealth *to the poor* is an exorbitant gift! This act of generosity reflects the generosity that God is now showing him through Jesus.

8b. And if I have taken any thing from any man by false accusation, I restore him fourfold.

Next, Zacchaeus responds to his prior life. *If I have taken any thing from any man* might sound as if Zacchaeus is waffling on responsibility for his actions. But in the original language text, it is clear that he is confessing openly that he has done such things and is ready to make restitution. This will be to any and all, not just to some, whom he has wronged. The Mosaic Law called for restitution between two and five times when theft or fraud is committed (Exodus 22:1-14). Zacchaeus does not debate the proper number. Rather, he openly promises a high level of restitution.

What Do You Think?

What challenges should we anticipate when a person with a notorious reputation comes to Christ?

Digging Deeper

Under what conditions, if any, should conversion of such a person be accompanied by expectations of restitution?

We wonder if Zacchaeus's promise is foolhardy. Since he begins by promising half his wealth as a gift to the poor, does he not run the risk of exhausting his resources before fulfilling all the restitutions? This very extravagance seems to be Luke's point. Zacchaeus is no longer the profit-minded opportunist. He is now the recipient of the extravagant grace of God, so he responds with similar extravagance.

Zacchaeus displays the full ideal of repentance. Repentance is a change of mind, heart, and life in response to God's gracious gift. Its fullness is measured not in how guilty the individual feels, not in how emotional is the transition, not even in how immediate the change is. Rather, repentance is genuine when an individual's life increasingly reflects God's goodness and grace. Zacchaeus is now on the right track in that regard.

C. Jesus' Declarations (vv. 9, 10)

9a. And Jesus said unto him, This day is salvation come to this house.

Jesus celebrates and affirms Zacchaeus's repentance. This is a momentous occasion, one that reflects fulfillment of God's promises and Jesus' mission.

Salvation in the New Testament reflects all that we typically associate with it and more than we sometimes realize. To be saved by the Lord is to be graciously granted life with the Lord beyond death. It is to guarantee resurrection to eternal life in God's recreated heavens and earth. It is also to be restored to God's blessed life in the present, to begin to experience the authentic life for which humans were made.

The latter does not imply an easy or materially wealthy life, of course. Salvation comes by the cross and calls the saved to take up their crosses (Luke 9:22-26). But salvation also transforms our perspectives to realize that the life of humble service in the Lord's name is the divinely blessed life for which God has created us. For Zacchaeus, the salvation that comes to his *house . . . this day* is more than the assurance that death will not have the final word. It is also his restoration to the authentic life of God's people.

9b. Forsomuch as he also is a son of Abraham.

Zacchaeus's contemporaries consider him a traitor who has forfeited citizenship in Israel, God's people. Jesus now pronounces the opposite: Zacchaeus *is a son of Abraham*.

It is no accident that Jesus refers to Abraham instead of Jacob, Abraham's grandson who became father of the 12 tribes. God's promise is to bless all nations through Abraham's seed (Genesis 12:3; 22:18). Having been considered by his neighbors to be part of the pagan nations, Zacchaeus is now reclaimed for God's people according to God's promise. Ironically, those devout Jews who are hostile to Zacchaeus run the risk of missing out on God's promise if they fail to respond to God's generosity in Jesus as Zacchaeus has just done.

10. For the Son of man is come to seek and to save that which was lost.

In the New Testament, the expression *Son of man*, with one exception (John 12:34), is used only by Jesus to refer to himself. Though its significance is widely debated, most scholars today affirm that Jesus is alluding to Daniel 7:13, 14. There "one like the Son of man" is a figure who reigns over God's kingdom as God defeats the beastly empires that have oppressed His people in the past. In other words, Jesus' referring to himself as *the Son of man* is a veiled claim to be God's triumphant king.

How does that king rule? This episode of today's text illustrates Jesus' rule as one who seeks and saves *that which was lost*. Jesus called Zacchaeus down to Him as that man looked down from a tree. Jesus invited himself to Zacchaeus's home as an expression of grace. Jesus has pronounced salvation as coming to Zacchaeus's house; that affirmation is of Jesus' authority alone, apart from temple and sacrifice. Whatever opinion of Zacchaeus his neighbors hold, Zacchaeus is now surely identified as having been lost but now found and saved. He is a success story of the divine search-and-rescue mission.

When Jesus encountered criticism for eating with tax collectors previously in this Gospel, He restated His mission in similar terms (see Luke 5:32). The result was celebration for the lost as having been found (15:7, 10, 32).

Conclusion

A. Two Different Responses

Considering Zacchaeus's pledge to give half his wealth to the poor, we may wonder why Jesus celebrated that promise when He had challenged the rich young ruler to give it all (Luke 18:22). The difference is in how each man viewed himself and how that view directed the response of each.

The ruler came to Jesus in self-assurance. He intended to do some great deed that would earn God's favor (Luke 18:18). He was quite sure that he was blameless before God's law (18:21). Zacchaeus, on the other hand, responded with repentant generosity. He recognized his real need—his weakness in what seemed like strength—and was ready to accept indignity in order to catch a glimpse of Jesus.

God's grace in Jesus seemed to be far more than Zacchaeus had hoped for. His generous pledge was not a means of earning God's gift. Rather, it was a grateful response to the gift he had received in his weakness. His generosity reflected that of the Christ who stood before him on the way to the cross.

Which man are you more like? Are you trying to offer something to God as a gift? Or having received His gift without merit, are you reflecting it with a life of Christlike generosity?

B. Prayer

Father, we are helpless on our own. Grateful for Your incomparable gift, we ask that Your Spirit empower us to reflect Your grace in every part of our lives. We pray this in Jesus' name. Amen!

C. Thought to Remember

God grants His grace to those
who know they need it.

INVOLVEMENT LEARNING

Enhance your lesson with KJV Bible Student *(from your curriculum supplier) and the reproducible activity page (at www.standardlesson.com or in the back of the* KJV Standard Lesson Commentary Deluxe Edition*).*

Into the Lesson

Prepare slips of paper on which are printed these job descriptions, one per slip: I work from home; my job involves accounting; I am on the computer four or more hours a day; I checked my work e-mail this weekend; my work involves transportation; I work in sales; I can wear jeans to work. Have everyone stand (or hold a hand up).

Say, "If the slip I read applies to your current (or if retired or unemployed, previous) work situation, please sit down (or drop your hand)." Draw a slip from a container and read it aloud. Repeat until only one person is left. Give the winner a token prize, such as a box of paper clips.

Say, "The work situations mentioned may be stressful personally, but they don't necessarily cause others to hate you. But what would it be like if everyone treated you as an outcast because of your profession? Zacchaeus met a man one day who did not hate him. Let's see why."

Alternative. On the board, draw blanks for a seven-letter word. Announce that you're going to play a game of Snowman to guess a word. Divide the class in half and ask one side to begin guessing letters. For every wrong guess, write that letter on the board and draw one of the parts of a snowman so that nine mistakes results in a complete snowman and loss of game. Once the correct answer of *Jericho* is revealed, say, "This is the city in which today's lesson takes place."

Then erase that game and do the same for the name *Zacchaeus,* for the other team. Afterward, say, "Jesus was passing through Jericho on His way to Jerusalem to die. Zacchaeus was headed toward eternal death until he encountered Jesus. Let's see how much you know about the story."

Into the Word

Test learners' familiarity with the account of Zacchaeus by reading the following statements and inviting answers of either true or false as to whether it applies to Zacchaeus. 1–Well-respected *(F)*; 2–A tax collector *(T)*; 3–Rich *(T)*; 4–Tall *(F)*; 5–Climbed a tree *(T)*; 6–Had met Jesus before *(F)*; 7–Jesus addressed him by name *(T)*; 8–He invited Jesus to his home *(F)*; 9–The crowd was happy for Zacchaeus *(F)*; 10–He offered to give half of his goods to the poor *(T)*; 11–He denied ever having cheated anyone *(F)*; 12–Jesus said salvation had come to his house *(T)*. (*Option.* Put the statements [without answers] on handouts for learners to take individually, then score their own.)

Distribute handouts of the following assignment (you prepare) to groups of four or five: "Interview Zacchaeus to find out why his life changed so dramatically. Select someone from your group to be the interviewer and another to be Zacchaeus. Then work together to write searching questions and appropriate responses. Be sure to explore what he was like before and after he met Jesus."

Ask each group to present its best question and answer to the rest of the class.

Option. Distribute copies of the "Transformed!" activity from the reproducible page, which you can download. Have learners work in pairs to complete it. Ask volunteers to share their answers.

Into Life

List the following categories on the board:

*Attitude Toward Money / Hope of Heaven
Compassion for Others / Quality of Work*

Say, "After he encountered Jesus' loving acceptance, Zacchaeus's life was dramatically changed in each of these areas." Have students pair off and discuss how their own lives have been changed as a result of their encounter with Jesus in one or more of those areas.

Option. Distribute copies of the "Big Announcement" activity from the reproducible page. Encourage completion either in class or during devotional time in the week ahead.

CALLED TO FOLLOW

DEVOTIONAL READING: Psalm 91
BACKGROUND SCRIPTURE: Matthew 4:12-22

MATTHEW 4:12-22

12 Now when Jesus had heard that John was cast into prison, he departed into Galilee;

13 And leaving Nazareth, he came and dwelt in Capernaum, which is upon the sea coast, in the borders of Zabulon and Nephthalim:

14 That it might be fulfilled which was spoken by Esaias the prophet, saying,

15 The land of Zabulon, and the land of Nephthalim, by the way of the sea, beyond Jordan, Galilee of the Gentiles;

16 The people which sat in darkness saw great light; and to them which sat in the region and shadow of death light is sprung up.

17 From that time Jesus began to preach, and to say, Repent: for the kingdom of heaven is at hand.

18 And Jesus, walking by the sea of Galilee, saw two brethren, Simon called Peter, and Andrew his brother, casting a net into the sea: for they were fishers.

19 And he saith unto them, Follow me, and I will make you fishers of men.

20 And they straightway left their nets, and followed him.

21 And going on from thence, he saw other two brethren, James the son of Zebedee, and John his brother, in a ship with Zebedee their father, mending their nets; and he called them.

22 And they immediately left the ship and their father, and followed him.

KEY VERSE

He saith unto them, Follow me, and I will make you fishers of men. —**Matthew 4:19**

Discipleship and Mission

Unit 2: Call to Ministry

LESSONS 5–9

LESSON AIMS

After participating in this lesson, each learner will be able to:

1. Recall the reason for the need to repent.

2. Explain the relationship between repentance and the kingdom of heaven.

3. Make a plan to identify a sacrifice to make for better discipleship.

LESSON OUTLINE

Introduction

A. Be Reasonable?

In the spring of 2014, Dr. Kent Brantley went to Liberia to serve as a medical missionary. One day he woke up with the realization that he himself was about to become a patient—he had contracted the Ebola virus. His goal transitioned from saving lives for the glory of God to being a Christian example of faith whether he lived or died. "We didn't believe that because we were going there as medical missionaries we would automatically be divinely protected from getting Ebola."

Indeed, he was right. Far from being protected from a dread disease because he was a follower of Christ, it was the fact that he was a dedicated follower of Christ that put him in the position of contracting Ebola!

Christians are reasonable people. We are solid citizens and reliable employees and mates. We try to avoid excess in all areas of our lives. But what about the radical demands of following Jesus? Is moderation a virtue there? Have we placed "reasonable" restrictions on discipleship?

B. Lesson Context

The book of Matthew is commonly recognized as being "the most Jewish" of the four Gospels. This is evident from the outset in Matthew's use of the numeric value of King David's name as a memory device in Jesus' genealogy (Matthew 1:17). Using more than 60 quotes from the Old Testament, Matthew explains the life of Jesus from birth to resurrection. The flight to and from Egypt is reminiscent of the nation of Israel's enslavement in and delivery from Egypt. Herod's opposition to Jesus mirrors that of Pharaoh to Moses. The parallels are many! Matthew notes that John the Baptist's preaching is also according to Scripture, preparing the way for Jesus.

Matthew's Jewishness is also evident in his use of the phrase "kingdom of heaven" rather than "kingdom of God." The former expression occurs more than 30 times in the New Testament, and all of them are in the book of Matthew. "Kingdom of heaven" is a respectful Jewish way of saying "kingdom of God," since God's name was not spoken by devout Jews of the day. Other words would be substituted for the divine name so clarity would be maintained. Thus the use of the word *heaven*.

This is not a universal rule, since Matthew himself has at least four instances of "kingdom of God." (There may be five, depending on how a textual variant is counted.) Even given these exceptions, the difference is striking.

Another point regarding the Jewishness of Matthew's Gospel is Jesus' time in a wilderness, which immediately leads into today's lesson text. The parallel is with the nation of Israel's experience in the wilderness after leaving Egypt. The 40 years of Israel's stay is mirrored in Jesus' stay of 40 days (Numbers 14:33, 34; Matthew 4:2). But unlike that case, Jesus did not suffer defeat as a result (compare Numbers 14:39-45). Instead, He faced Satan's temptations victoriously, defeating him with the faithful and proper use of Scripture three times. Today's text comes next.

I. Two Transitions
(Matthew 4:12, 13)
A. John in Prison (v. 12a)

12a. Now when Jesus had heard that John was cast into prison.

John the Baptist began his ministry "in the fifteenth year of the reign of Tiberius Caesar" (Luke 3:1-3). The issues involved in pinning down this exact year by modern reckoning are complicated. But we can say with a reasonable degree of certainty that this was AD 28. The Gospel accounts imply that Jesus' ministry begins shortly after John's when the fact of Jesus' age of "about 30 years of age" is taken into account (Luke 3:23).

John's imprisonment is also noted in Matthew 11:2; 14:3; Mark 6:17; Luke 3:19, 20; John 3:24. We take care, of course, not to confuse John the Baptist with John the Evangelist, the latter being the one who writes the Gospel that bears his name.

B. Jesus to Capernaum (vv. 12b, 13)
12b. He departed into Galilee.

All four Gospels report that Jesus begins His public ministry by preaching in Galilee (Mark 1:14; Luke 4:14; John 4:3). These accounts portray Jesus as resolute. We can be sure He does not react without prayerful consideration, given the 40 days just spent in the wilderness (see the Lesson Context).

At first glance, it may appear that Jesus travels *into Galilee* for safety concerns. But He is not running scared. He did not run from the devil in the wilderness experience just completed (see the Lesson Context), and He doesn't need to run from earthly authorities. In instances where He escapes danger (see Luke 4:28-30; John 8:59; 10:39), the issue is one of timing: "They sought to take him: but no man laid hands on him, because his hour was not yet come" (John 7:30). In this regard, the danger posed in John 10:39 presents itself anew when Jesus returns to that scene in the account beginning in John 11:7 because the time is right.

Furthermore, Galilee at this time is ruled by Herod Antipas, who will later behead John the Baptist (Matthew 14:1-11). So there is no safety there. To put it another way, if Jesus is running for His safety, He does not run far enough! The real reason for the retrograde movement to Galilee will be seen shortly.

13a. And leaving Nazareth.

There seems to be a lot left unspoken in this simple phrase. *Nazareth* does not have a good reputation (John 1:46). But that doesn't seem to be the reason Jesus leaves His hometown of some three decades (Luke 2:4, 39, 51).

Perhaps divine insight causes Him to realize in advance that He will have no credibility there

HOW TO SAY IT

Capernaum	Kuh-*per*-nay-um.
Esaias	E-*zay*-us.
Herod Antipas	*Hair*-ud *An*-tih-pus.
Naphtali	*Naf*-tuh-lye.
Nazareth	*Naz*-uh-reth.
Nephthalim	*Nef*-thuh-lim (*th* as in *thin*).
Sepphoris	*Sef*-uh-ris.
synagogue	*sin*-uh-gog.
Tiberius Caesar	Tie-*beer*-ee-us *See*-zer.
Zabulon	*Zab*-you-lon.
Zebedee	*Zeb*-eh-dee.
Zebulun	*Zeb*-you-lun.

(compare Luke 4:16-30; John 4:44). Because of their hard-hearted rejection of the man who grew up among them, the people of Nazareth will not see their town become the center of His ministry (see Matthew 13:53-58). Even so, "of Nazareth" becomes part of Jesus' identity (Matthew 26:71; etc.).

13b. He came and dwelt in Capernaum, which is upon the sea coast, in the borders of Zabulon and Nephthalim.

Capernaum is a typical working-class village of the era. One estimate puts its population at about 1,500. Sited *in the borders of Zabulon and Nephthalim,* it is about 20 miles northeast of Nazareth. Zabulon and Nephthalim are regions named for two of the sons of Jacob (see Genesis 30:8; 35:23, where the names are spelled Zebulun and Naphtali). The borders of their land grant go back to the days of Joshua (Joshua 19:10-16, 32-39).

If there ever was a backwater place in the Roman Empire, this is it! It is possible that many first-century readers of Matthew are not even aware of this little fishing village. Although mentioned by name 16 times in the four Gospels (and nowhere else), it is not nearly as significant as Jerusalem, Sepphoris, Tiberius, or, of course, Rome.

Yet Jesus chooses insignificant Capernaum as the base of operations from which to launch His public ministry. John 2:12 notes that after the miracle of turning water into wine at the wedding in Cana, Jesus returns to Capernaum, not Nazareth, with "his mother, and his brethren, and his disciples."

Our expanded look at Capernaum serves at least two purposes. First, the role the village is about to play is witnessed by an intertextual bond with the book of Isaiah (see below). Second, the early mention of Capernaum creates context for first-century readers who may not know anything about the village.

Regarding Jesus himself, He is a nobody by outward appearance (Isaiah 53:2). He was not born in a palace, but in a shelter for livestock (Luke 2:7). His hometown is not magnificent Jerusalem, but the middle-of-nowhere village of Nazareth—a village with a less than sterling reputation (John 1:46). He was born to poor parents (compare Luke 2:22-24; Leviticus 12:1-8). His early experience was as a refugee in Egypt (Matthew 2:13-15). When His parents returned with Him to Nazareth, He experienced life as a carpenter (Mark 6:3). His life has been one shared by common humanity.

II. One Light
(Matthew 4:14-17)
A. Prophecy's Fulfillment (v. 14)

14. That it might be fulfilled which was spoken by Esaias the prophet, saying

Esaias the prophet is probably more familiar to us as Isaiah. His prophetic ministry lasted from roughly 740 to 680 BC. The four Gospels quote from the book of Isaiah more than 20 times. The book's vital prophecies of the coming Messiah has earned it the designation "the fifth Gospel" to many Bible students. Regarding Matthew's respect for and use of the Hebrew Scriptures, see the Lesson Context.

B. Fulfillment's Result (vv. 15, 16)

15. The land of Zabulon, and the land of Nephthalim, by the way of the sea, beyond Jordan, Galilee of the Gentiles; the people which sat in darkness saw great light; and to them which sat in the region and shadow of death light is sprung up.

The quotation is from Isaiah 9:1, 2. The phrase *Galilee of the Gentiles* recognizes that that region had been conquered by foreigners as the 10 northern tribes were taken into exile in 722 BC. To see and hear the ancient tribal names *Zabulon* and *Nephthalim* is to revive hope in the promises of God. What may at first glance look like a retreat to a supposedly safer territory is actually a full-throated rally with language rooted deeply in the narrative of a just and merciful God. He is the one who rescues!

❧ *Light in a Dark Place* ❧

Richard Wurmbrand (1909–2001) is remembered as the twentieth century's voice of the persecuted church. He began an underground church movement in Romania as part of protest against the government's control of churches. His subsequent imprisonment totaled 14 years.

He spent several of those years in solitary confinement. His dark, windowless cell, 12 feet underground, was designed to cut him off completely from the outside world. But Wurmbrand refused to let himself be overcome by that darkness.

After his release, Wurmbrand dedicated his life to exposing the brutal persecution of believers in Communist countries. He wrote 18 books in English, testified before the Internal Security Subcommittee of the U.S. Senate, and began the organization now known as Voice of the Martyrs. The imprisonment meant to silence Wurmbrand only increased his influence.

This same irony is true in the life of John the Baptist. Herod's attempt to silence John only served to signal the beginning of Jesus' ministry. His earthly ministry has now passed to us. What darkness are you helping overcome today? —J. E.

> *What Do You Think?*
> How will you use Isaiah 9:1, 2, if at all, when witnessing for Jesus to someone who has never even heard of Isaiah?
> *Digging Deeper*
> Consider which parts of Paul's evangelistic approach in Acts 17:22-32 are relevant in a modern context in this regard.

C. What Must Happen (v. 17a)

17a. From that time Jesus began to preach, and to say, Repent.

The exact amount of *time* that passes between when Jesus settles into Capernaum and when He begins *to preach* is unspecified. Furthermore, Matthew is quite succinct in reviewing the content of Jesus' preaching.

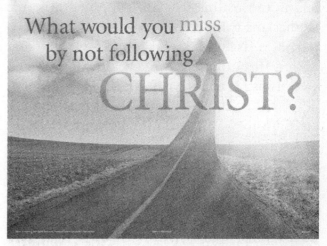

Visual for Lesson 5. *This question can be posed for discussion at various points in the lesson. It is particularly well suited for the lesson's conclusion.*

What Jesus expects as a result of His preaching is summed up in the single word *repent*. When we see that word, our first thought (which is not wrong) may be to think in terms of leaving a life of sin (John 8:11; etc.) and embracing righteousness (Matthew 3:8; etc.). More foundationally, repentance is grounded in a change of thought and heart (compare 1 Kings 8:47-50; Matthew 3:9; Acts 8:20-22; etc.). Sincere changes in behavior result from changes in heart.

D. Why It Must Happen (v. 17b)

17b. For the kingdom of heaven is at hand.

The requirement to repent is immediately backed up with the reason we see here. But this raises three questions: (1) What exactly is *the kingdom of heaven*? (2) What does the phrase *at hand* mean? and (3) What does each phrase signify in relation to the other?

The kingdom of heaven refers to the fulfillment of God's promise to reverse the course of history, a history tainted by sin. That reversal involves establishing His reign in place of the tyrannous, selfish reign of sin and death (Romans 5:14, 21). It is a kingdom, as Jesus later told Pilate, that "is not of this world" (John 18:36).

God, of course, has never ceased to reign over the entire universe since its creation. Therefore His rule has always included planet Earth and its kingdoms (Isaiah 37:16; Romans 13:1). Forces both physical and spiritual in nature have set up reigns and realms that have opposed His rule (Ephesians 6:12; etc.). God uses these for His purposes (Isaiah 7:18-25; John 19:11; etc.) and assigns them to the garbage heap of history and eternity as He wills (Isaiah 10:5-19; Daniel 2:40-43; 4:35; 7:7, 20-25; Luke 10:18; Revelation 21:8; etc.). History as it has unfolded since the days of Jesus reveals that the kingdom He announces supplants all others, but not in the way anyone in the first century AD supposes.

For Jesus' audience, God's promise of a kingdom to come includes a strong nationalistic focus on Israel. Devout Jews expect God's promised kingdom to result in the defeat of Israel's enemies, with the Roman Empire especially in the cross hairs (compare Acts 1:6). God's kingdom, in other words, is commonly expected to be political and military in nature like any other, with the exception that it is to be ruled righteously by, and in submission to, God.

A primary way Jesus will challenge this expectation as His ministry unfolds is through parables (see, for example, lesson 1 of this quarter). These project a very different vision of God's promised kingdom than commonly anticipated.

> *What Do You Think?*
> What steps can your church take to help its members avoid equating allegiance to any particular nation with allegiance to the kingdom of Heaven?
> *Digging Deeper*
> Consider nationalistic errors such as the phrase *Gott mit uns* ("God with us") as inscribed on German equipment during World War II.

The exact meaning of the verb that is translated *at hand* (along with its closely related adverb form) is the subject of much debate. One clear way it is used in the New Testament is to specify that something is physically near, or getting nearer to, something else (examples: Matthew 21:1; Luke 24:28; John 6:19). This is known as a *spatial sense*. Another unmistakable way the word is used is in referring to something that is near, or getting nearer, in time (examples: Matthew 21:34; 26:18; John 6:4). This is known as a *temporal sense*. A possible third meaning-usage speaks of closeness of a relationship (examples: Romans 10:8; Ephesians 2:13, 17; James 4:8). This may be called a *relational sense*.

All may be true for the case at hand. Wherever Jesus is, the kingdom is. Those standing near Jesus are standing next to the perfect embodiment (incarnation) of the kingdom of Heaven. He has come in "the fulness of the time" (Galatians 4:4) to put right our relationship with God (4:5). Thus the spatial, the temporal, and the relational senses all have support. We also may discern the idea of spiritual proximity in Luke 17:20, 21.

In the person of Jesus, the kingdom of Heaven is nearer than it ever has been. It is coming in a power that does not reflect the power of human kingdoms that wax and wane. Rather, the kingdom of Heaven will redefine what power means.

❧ HOME TRANSITIONS ❧

As baby boomers (those born between 1946 and 1964) reach retirement age, they face the realization of necessary change. Never fear, however: companies such as Close at Hand Home Transitions are dedicated to helping make the necessary adjustments as boomers embrace the next phase of life.

For those choosing to downsize their living arrangements, Close at Hand helps draw up a new floor plan, determines what furniture will fit, oversees movers, sets up new utility and subscription services, etc. The service only works, however, for folks who are not in denial regarding their changing needs.

As Jesus began His ministry, He challenged those who would listen that a new living arrangement was at hand: residency in the kingdom of Heaven. Listeners were free either to accept or deny the reality of that statement. Those who accepted it had did so by repenting. Making the transition to become a resident of the kingdom of Heaven is only preparatory to another transition, however. That further and final transition is set forth in John 14:2, 3. We might say that Jesus is the original and ultimate "close at hand home transition" company. And He charges nothing for His services!

—J. E.

III. Four Responses

(MATTHEW 4:18-22)

A. Simon Peter and Andrew (vv. 18-20)

18-20. And Jesus, walking by the sea of Galilee, saw two brethren, Simon called Peter, and Andrew his brother, casting a net into the sea: for they were fishers. And he saith unto them, Follow me, and I will make you fishers of men. And they straightway left their nets, and followed him.

See the commentary on Mark 1:16-18 in lesson 2, pages 243, 244. To that we may add that *Simon called Peter, and Andrew* and the two mentioned next are models of discipleship as they set the positive example of responding to Jesus' call *straightway* (contrast Matthew 8:21, 22). Another way to translate the Greek word behind *straightway* is "immediately," which is exactly what verse 22, below, does.

B. James and John (vv. 21, 22)

21, 22. And going on from thence, he saw other two brethren, James the son of Zebedee, and John his brother, in a ship with Zebedee their father, mending their nets; and he called them. And they immediately left the ship and their father, and followed him.

See the commentary on Mark 1:19, 20 in lesson 2, page 244.

> *What Do You Think?*
> Were you to perceive a call from Christ to a certain ministry tomorrow, how would you test the validity of that call?
>
> *Digging Deeper*
> How will you know whether God is calling you to immediate action vs. to a ministry that involves a degree of delay? Consider in your response the urgencies (or lack thereof) in Luke 9:59-62 and John 11:6.

Conclusion

A. Boat Time, Dock Time

When Jesus invited Peter, Andrew, James, and John to join His ministry, He was inviting men who knew the importance of both the boat-time activity of casting nets (Matthew 4:18) and the dock-time activity of preparing those nets to be cast (4:21). Effective ministry today must recognize the same distinction. What Christians see and hear in half-hour sermons is boat time, when their minister is casting a net. Undergirding that boat time is (or should be) a lot of dock time—time spent preparing. Sermons that lack adequate dock time of preparation will be ineffective.

We can expand this analogy to the life of any Christian. When the opportunity to speak a word for Jesus presents itself, will we have put in the necessary dock time so that word will be persuasive (see 1 Peter 3:15)?

The analogy applies also to vocation changes. Would you consider leaving one career for another in order to follow Jesus more closely? Or will you hurriedly think *I have to provide for my family, or I'm worse than an infidel!* to dismiss such a possibility immediately (1 Timothy 5:8).

Consider how today's world might look if the four disciples of today's lesson had said no. They received no assurance that their families would be adequately provided for, but they had no higher priority than Jesus' call on their lives (compare Matthew 19:27; Luke 5:28; 9:59-62). What about you?

> *What Do You Think?*
> What is one transition you need to make (and perhaps have been putting off) in order to serve Christ better?
>
> *Digging Deeper*
> In addition to the transitions made by the first four disciples, consider how the transitions in these passages influence your response: Genesis 12:4; 31:3; Exodus 3; Nehemiah 1, 2; Acts 8:26; 9:15; 26:15, 16.

B. Prayer

Father, strengthen us to follow Your Son without reserve. Give us ears to hear His call and a willingness to follow Him no matter the cost. We pray this in Jesus' name. Amen.

C. Thought to Remember

Following Jesus is our highest priority.

INVOLVEMENT LEARNING

Enhance your lesson with KJV Bible Student *(from your curriculum supplier) and the reproducible activity page (at www.standardlesson.com or in the back of the* KJV Standard Lesson Commentary Deluxe Edition*).*

Into the Lesson

Have participants use their smartphones to perform an Internet search for the phrase *new directions*. Ask learners to call out (1) the names of businesses that use that phrase in their names and (2) the product or service of the businesses. Continue until four or five responses are voiced. Possible results will include companies that treat mental health issues, publish cutting-edge books, produce alternative medicines, and arrange travel for those with physical disabilities. (If fewer than half your class members have smartphones, do the Internet search yourself beforehand. Distribute one-page handouts that list four or five companies as above.)

In discussing use of the phrase *new directions* in the business names, ask for possible reasons the companies did so. Ask learners about times they sensed a need for a new direction in life.

Alternative. Distribute copies of the "Going My Way?" activity from the reproducible page, which you can download. After no more than one minute, reveal the answer and discuss the quote. Ask learners about times they sensed a need for a new direction in life.

After either activity say, "At times, we encounter people and ideas that challenge us to take a radical new direction in life. When Jesus called His first disciples with a new direction, they accepted."

Into the Word

Divide the class in half. Designate one of the halves as *The Seeing Group.* Give members this assignment on a handout (you prepare): Read Matthew 4:12-17. Write three questions that summarize how seeing the light of Jesus can give us a new direction. Designate the other half as *The Following Group.* Give members this assignment on a handout (you prepare): Read Matthew 4:18-22. Write three commands that summarize how agreeing to follow Jesus results in a new direction.

Possible results for *The Seeing Group:* Do you see a path forward? (v. 16a) / Do you want a life worth living? (v. 16b) / Can you see changes you need to make in your life? (v. 17). *Possible results* for *The Following Group:* Change your career! (v. 19) / Leave the past behind! (v. 20) / Love me more than anyone else in your life! (v. 22). Encourage creative thinking; many responses are possible.

Allow groups a few moments to summarize their texts and what they have written.

Alternative. Distribute copies of the "Complete the Outline" activity from the reproducible page. Have students work in small groups to complete it.

After either activity say, "Like the fishermen of Galilee, we cannot see Jesus for who He truly is and remain the same. How will knowing Jesus alter your behavior this week?"

Into Life

Write these statements on the board:

Jesus' teaching helps me understand
what my future can hold.
Jesus' call to repentance points out
how my life should change.
Jesus' challenge to follow Him
must rearrange my priorities.

Allow class members to consider these statements silently as they ask themselves, "What commitment can I make in response to each one?" *Possible responses*: Since the light of Jesus lights our paths, we do not have to fear what might jump out of the shadows to harm us. Because we see His perfect example, we can change the way we have been treating someone. Because He wants us to do His work, we can decide to invest time in His kingdom.

After a few moments, lead in a closing prayer, promising to answer Jesus' call to discipleship.

Option. If you did not use the "Going My Way" activity earlier, use it here as part of a closing prayer of commitment.

CALLED TO MISSION

DEVOTIONAL READING: Matthew 15:21-28
BACKGROUND SCRIPTURE: Matthew 10

MATTHEW 10:1-15

1 And when he had called unto him his twelve disciples, he gave them power against unclean spirits, to cast them out, and to heal all manner of sickness and all manner of disease.

2 Now the names of the twelve apostles are these; The first, Simon, who is called Peter, and Andrew his brother; James the son of Zebedee, and John his brother;

3 Philip, and Bartholomew; Thomas, and Matthew the publican; James the son of Alphaeus, and Lebbaeus, whose surname was Thaddaeus;

4 Simon the Canaanite, and Judas Iscariot, who also betrayed him.

5 These twelve Jesus sent forth, and commanded them, saying, Go not into the way of the Gentiles, and into any city of the Samaritans enter ye not:

6 But go rather to the lost sheep of the house of Israel.

7 And as ye go, preach, saying, The kingdom of heaven is at hand.

8 Heal the sick, cleanse the lepers, raise the dead, cast out devils: freely ye have received, freely give.

9 Provide neither gold, nor silver, nor brass in your purses,

10 Nor scrip for your journey, neither two coats, neither shoes, nor yet staves: for the workman is worthy of his meat.

11 And into whatsoever city or town ye shall enter, enquire who in it is worthy; and there abide till ye go thence.

12 And when ye come into an house, salute it.

13 And if the house be worthy, let your peace come upon it: but if it be not worthy, let your peace return to you.

14 And whosoever shall not receive you, nor hear your words, when ye depart out of that house or city, shake off the dust of your feet.

15 Verily I say unto you, It shall be more tolerable for the land of Sodom and Gomorrha in the day of judgment, than for that city.

KEY VERSE

When he had called unto him his twelve disciples, he gave them power against unclean spirits, to cast them out, and to heal all manner of sickness and all manner of disease. —**Matthew 10:1**

DISCIPLESHIP AND MISSION

Unit 2: Call to Ministry

LESSONS 5–9

LESSON AIMS

After participating in this lesson, each learner will be able to:

1. Describe the backgrounds of the 12 apostles.
2. Explain Jesus' mission instructions to the 12.
3. Determine one way to participate in Jesus' calling to continue His work.

LESSON OUTLINE

Introduction

A. On Having a Commission

The word *commission* is well known, and the dictionary offers no less than seven definitions, with several sub-definitions, depending on context. Two definitions in Merriam-Webster's that should catch our attention are these: "a formal written warrant granting the power to perform various acts or duties" and "authority to act for, in behalf of, or in place of another." Those definitions are hard to tell apart; it seems like if one definition applies to you, then the other would as well, right?

Some might point out that the difference lies in distinguishing between *power* (the ability to do something) and *authority* (the right to do something). Others might suggest that the difference is in the part about a commission being written. This kind of commission is well known to Christians, since Matthew 28:19, 20 is our formal written charge to make disciples (contrast Acts 26:12).

Commission more in the sense of "authority to act . . . in place of another" without the element of being written is also in the Bible, but less well known. That's our topic for this lesson.

B. Lesson Context

Matthew and Luke locate the events of our passage after the 12 disciples had had significant exposure to Jesus' message and work. Another account notes that several disciples mentioned in Matthew 10 met Jesus shortly after His baptism and witnessed His first miracle (John 1:35–2:11).

Jesus later encountered Peter, Andrew, James, and John in Capernaum and famously called them from their nets to become "fishers of men" (see lessons 2 and 5). In so doing, He was challenging them to leave their careers and travel with Him full-time. From that vantage point, they witnessed Jesus' teachings and healings across the region. Somewhere during this campaign, Matthew the publican (tax collector) accepted the call to itinerant discipleship as well (Matthew 9:9-13).

As Jesus' mission grew, He urged prayer that God would raise up more people to help with the work (Matthew 9:35-38). Our lesson text today immediately follows this call to prayer.

I. Called to Imitate

(MATTHEW 10:1-4)

A. Empowered (v. 1)

1a. And when he had called unto him his twelve disciples.

This verse seems to represent fulfillment of the immediately preceding prayer for workers. This is the first time in Matthew that those followers closest to Jesus are designated by the expression *twelve disciples*. We may be surprised to learn that that expression is relatively rare in the New Testament. It occurs only here and in Matthew 11:1; 20:17; and Luke 9:1—and the word *disciples* doesn't occur in some Greek texts in the latter two. (Compare "eleven disciples" in Matthew 28:16.)

More common is the shorthand designation "the twelve," which occurs almost two dozen times in the New Testament. These 12 (named below) are the ones Jesus chooses to extend His ministry, which includes spiritual and physical healing. The word translated *disciples* occurs more than 250 times in the Gospels and Acts (only). It refers to those who subscribe to the lessons and lifestyle of a great teacher (compare Matthew 10:24, 25; Luke 6:40). The common practice is to live alongside one's teacher or master in order to imitate the master's behavior.

HOW TO SAY IT

Alphaeus	Al-*fee*-us.
Assyria	Uh-*sear*-ee-uh.
Bethsaida	Beth-*say*-uh-duh.
Canaanite	*Kay*-nun-ite.
Capernaum	Kuh-*per*-nay-um.
Gomorrha	Guh-*more*-uh.
Herod Agrippa	*Hair*-ud Uh-*grip*-puh.
Herod Antipas	*Hair*-ud *An*-tih-pus.
Judas Iscariot	*Joo*-dus Iss-*care*-ee-ut.
Lebbaeus	Leh-*bee*-us.
Messianic	Mess-ee-*an*-ick.
Samaritans	Suh-*mare*-uh-tunz.
Thaddaeus	Tha-*dee*-us.
Zebedee	*Zeb*-eh-dee.
Zechariah	Zek-uh-*rye*-uh.
Zelotes	Zeh-*low*-teez.

1b. He gave them power against unclean spirits, to cast them out, and to heal all manner of sickness and all manner of disease.

The action verb "called" of the previous phrase is now followed by the action verb *gave*. Before sending the Twelve on their mission, Jesus empowers them to do the miracles they have seen Him do (Matthew 4:23, 24; 8:1-16, 28-34; 9:18-33). If God's will is to be done on earth as in Heaven (Matthew 6:10)—and it shall indeed be done in fullness on earth when Christ returns—then there should be no *unclean spirits*, *sickness*, or *disease*. The message that is to accompany the exercise of power over these is described in Matthew 10:7, below.

B. Identified (vv. 2-4)

2a. Now the names of the twelve apostles are these.

Alongside the rare designation "twelve disciples" (above) is the equally rare phrase *twelve apostles* (compare only Luke 22:14 and Revelation 21:14). The meaning of the noun is "he that is sent," which is how the word is translated in John 13:16. The fact that this is the first time the Twelve are called *apostles* is quite appropriate, since this is the first instance of Jesus sending them to proclaim His message. The verb form of the noun *apostle* is regularly translated as some form of "send" (examples: Matthew 2:16; 8:31; 10:5 [below]). Regarding the significance of the number 12, see on Matthew 10:5, 6, below.

2b. The first, Simon, who is called Peter, and Andrew his brother; James the son of Zebedee, and John his brother.

There are four listings of the Twelve in the Bible: Matthew 10:2-4; Mark 3:16-19; Luke 6:13-16; and (lacking Judas the betrayer) Acts 1:13. The names in the verse before are always the top four in those lists, which seems to indicate their importance relative to the other eight.

Simon . . . Peter is always listed first. This probably acknowledges his leadership among the Twelve (compare his frequent outspokenness in Matthew 16:16-23; 17:1-8, 24-27; 18:21; 19:27; 26:33; Acts 1:15-26; 2:14-41). The order of the other three names here varies from list to list. Peter, *James*, and *John* are sometimes referred to as Jesus' inner circle, being privileged to witness things the others are not (see Matthew 17:1-9; Mark 5:37-42; 14:32-36).

The pattern repeats as the fifth and ninth names are the same across all lists, while names in the sixth through eighth and tenth through twelfth positions swap places from list to list, but always within those boundaries. Judas the betrayer is listed last in three cases and not at all in the fourth. With the minor exception of the latter, all listings of the Twelve thus fall into thirds of four names each.

Peter had been introduced to Jesus by *Andrew his brother* (John 1:40-42). Andrew was apparently Jesus' very first follower (1:40) and is one of two apostles who have Greek names. This speaks to Greek influence in the area. See further commentary in lessons 2 and 5 (pages 243, 270).

3a. Philip, and Bartholomew; Thomas, and Matthew the publican.

Philip is the other apostle who has a Greek name. He is from Bethsaida, the hometown of other apostles as well (see John 1:44). His name always appears fifth in the listings just discussed; the names of the other three apostles noted here vary in appearing in the sixth through eighth positions. *Bartholomew* is generally identified as the Nathanael in John 1:45-51. He is otherwise not mentioned in the New Testament.

Thomas is the one whom many Christians today refer to as "doubting Thomas" because of his refusal to believe testimony of Jesus' resurrection (John 20:24, 25). This designation overlooks the courage he shows as the events surrounding his declaration in John 11:16 come to pass.

It's interesting that this is the only list of the four in which *Matthew* is designated *the publican*, a despised tax collector. And Matthew is the one who writes this particular list!

3b., 4. James the son of Alphaeus, and Lebbaeus, whose surname was Thaddaeus; Simon the Canaanite, and Judas Iscariot, who also betrayed him.

The name *James the son of Alphaeus* occurs in the ninth position in all four listings of the Twelve. The name *James* occurs more than 40 times in the New Testament to refer to as many as five men by that name, so it's easy to get confused. Some think this James is the same as "James the less" (Mark 15:40).

The only thing we know of *Lebbaeus . . . Thaddaeus* is the question he asks in John 14:22. He is the same as "Judas . . . of James" in Luke 6:16 and Acts 1:13. Likewise, *Simon the Canaanite* is referred to differently in those two texts, where "Zelotes" (zealot—a zealous revolutionary) replaces the word *Canaanite. Judas Iscariot* is, of course, infamous for betraying Jesus (Matthew 26:14-16, 47-50).

The collective identity of the 12 apostles is perhaps more significant than their individual biographies. All are close associates of Jesus. They are familiar with His lifestyle, teaching, and methods of ministry. They are therefore well-prepared to continue and expand His work.

II. Commissioned to Do
(MATTHEW 10:5-12)
A. Directing the Mission (vv. 5, 6)

5, 6. These twelve Jesus sent forth, and commanded them, saying, Go not into the way of the Gentiles, and into any city of the Samaritans enter ye not; but go rather to the lost sheep of the house of Israel.

The Gentiles are people who are not Jews. Free trade, travel, and colonization have resulted in a diverse population, even here on the edge of the Roman Empire. Even so, devout Jews associate with neither them (Acts 10:28) nor *Samaritans* (John 4:9). The latter are scorned for their mixed-blood heritage that resulted from the Assyrian conquest of 722 BC (see 2 Kings 17; compare Ezra 4:1-5).

The instruction Jesus gives is not ethnic or racial discrimination. Jesus has a plan that includes an offer of the gospel to everyone. But the plan must unfold in an orderly, focused way. The plan's progression is later laid out for the apostles as witnessing "in Jerusalem, and in all Judaea, and in Samaria, and unto the uttermost part of the earth" (Acts 1:8; compare Romans 1:16; 2:9, 10).

Jesus' previous visits in areas with heavy concentrations of Gentiles (Matthew 8:28a) and Samaritans (John 4) are not inconsistent with this plan. To preach the gospel does not seem to have been Jesus' reason for entering those areas (compare John 4:1-4). Belief resulted when residents of those areas sought Him out rather than the reverse (Matthew 8:28b; John 4:39-42). The focus for now is on restoring and renewing the Israelite people.

The number 12, for its part, corresponds symbolically to the 12 tribes of Israel (compare Matthew 19:28a; Revelation 21:12, 14). Since the forthcoming mission focuses on calling Israel to return to God, it is fitting that Jesus chooses 12 envoys to extend His ministry.

Jesus' description of the target audience as *lost sheep* (compare Jeremiah 50:6) is consistent with His Messianic identity and mission as prophesied in Ezekiel 34:11-25 and Micah 5:2-5 (compare Matthew 2:3-6). Similar language will be reflected later in Jesus' self-description in John 10:7-18.

> *What Do You Think?*
> Under what circumstances, if any, will it be a good idea to use a "targeted demographic" approach when planting a new church? Explain.
>
> *Digging Deeper*
> Consider this from several angles: targets of age group, economic status, etc.

B. Describing the Ministry (vv. 7, 8)

7. And as ye go, preach, saying, The kingdom of heaven is at hand.

The message the Twelve are to preach is identical to that preached so far by John the Baptist and Jesus (Matthew 3:1, 2; 4:17). The message doesn't change, only the messengers. On the meaning and significance of the phrases *kingdom of heaven* and *at hand*, see lesson 5, pages 269, 270.

Text messaging, like it or not, has changed the way we communicate. The use of abbreviations such as *LOL* for *laughing out loud* or *IMO* for *in my opinion* are widely used. But we wonder what the long-term effect will be.

In recent years, the New Zealand department of education ordered that students should not be penalized for answering questions on tests by using such text-speak. While still encouraging students to use standard English, authorities instructed teachers to give credit when an answer shows the required understanding. These educators argue that text-speak is just another way to communicate. While many support the policy, others responded "R U c RE us!" (translation: "Are you serious!"). They are concerned that such abbreviated language will lead to misunderstandings and degradation of the language.

The apostles were given a short message: just five words consisting of 26 letters in Greek. But they were to take no shortcuts in communicating it. Neither must we.   —J. E.

> *What Do You Think?*
> Which will be more important in presenting the gospel, the accuracy of the presentation or the perception that we are acting in the other person's best interest? Explain your answer.
>
> *Digging Deeper*
> Identify the strengths and weaknesses of both answers. What are the dangers of too much emphasis on one at the expense of the other?

8. Heal the sick, cleanse the lepers, raise the dead, cast out devils: freely ye have received, freely give.

The works the disciples are enabled to perform are tied to Jesus' proclamation of the coming of God's kingdom. The miracles Jesus performed to establish the truth of His message will be the same for the Twelve (compare in Matthew 9:35).

The instructions parallel Jesus' later reply to John the Baptist's question in Matthew 11:4, 5. God's kingdom is indeed coming powerfully! It comes not in the form of a military revolution but rather in terms of physical and spiritual healing.

Notably, the disciples are not to accept payment. Their works are to proclaim God's rule, not to enrich themselves (compare Acts 8:18-20; contrast 2 Kings 5:15-27).

C. Defining the Method (vv. 9-12)

9, 10a. Provide neither gold, nor silver, nor brass in your purses, nor scrip for your journey, neither two coats, neither shoes, nor yet staves.

The disciples are to travel light. The antique English word *scrip* is related to the modern word *scrap* and refers to a bag that would be used for holding scraps—miscellaneous items. *Staves* are walking sticks. The disciples are to travel with only the clothes on their backs.

10b. For the workman is worthy of his meat.

The logic behind the instructions to travel light appears in the form of a proverb (see also 1 Timothy 5:18). How Jesus expects this to work practically comes next.

11. And into whatsoever city or town ye shall enter, enquire who in it is worthy; and there abide till ye go thence.

While the Twelve are not to solicit money for their preaching and healing ministry (Matthew 10:8, above), they are allowed to accept room and board. They should expect to receive this from those to whom they minister (compare Numbers 18:31; Luke 10:7; 1 Corinthians 9:14). *Worthy* does not refer to people who are unusually spiritual, but rather to those who are receptive to the disciples' message and willing to provide hospitality (compare 3 John 5-8).

While moving around might give the disciples more opportunities to preach to more families, Jesus' instruction here is consistent with those of the previous three verses. Once it becomes known that the disciples can "heal the sick, cleanse the lepers, raise the dead, [and] cast out devils" (Matthew 10:8, above), they will quickly receive many invitations to stay at the finest houses in town. Various temptations would come from doing so, not to mention the time that would be wasted. The disciples are instead to lodge with the first person who welcomes them in a given town, even if it means living with less (again, see Luke 10:7).

12. And when ye come into an house, salute it.

This verse envisions that the disciples will take their message from door to door in each new village. When they come to a new town and begin preaching, they should offer a friendly greeting and blessing on any home they enter. Their approach should be a positive one, offering peace and healing and assuming that people will receive the message.

III. Counseled to Expect
(Matthew 10:13-15)

13, 14. And if the house be worthy, let your peace come upon it: but if it be not worthy, let your peace return to you. And whosoever shall not receive you, nor hear your words, when ye depart out of that house or city, shake off the dust of your feet.

In Jesus' mind, there are only two ways to respond to His message: accept it wholeheartedly or reject it. Since the disciples will preach Jesus' message and use His methods, they should expect exactly the same outcomes.

Notably, the success of the disciples' mission is not measured in terms of how many people accept the message. The apostles are not instructed to stay in town until 75 percent of the population have heard or 20 percent of the sick have been healed; they have fulfilled their mission as soon as they have proclaimed the kingdom and demonstrated its power.

The symbolism of shaking *off the dust* graphically communicates that the disciples are not responsible for other people's choices. While they are permitted to take shelter and food from those who accept them (Matthew 10:10, above), they are to take nothing from those who reject the message—not even loose dirt from the road (compare Acts 13:51).

It seemed like an offer too good to refuse—until it was refused! The Chamber of Commerce of Murcia, Spain, sponsored a contest called "Shopping Against the Clock." The winner was to be awarded a shopping spree worth a little over $7,000. The only catch was that the winner had to spend the money in less than three hours.

About 600 businesses were involved, hoping that the promotion would boost interest in the local economy. More than 60,000 contestants entered. But when the winner was notified, she replied that she would have to think about accepting it. In the end, she declined, saying that she was just too busy to waste a morning shopping!

By contrast, the runner-up gladly accepted. Taking three hours out of her day, she ended up with jewelry, clothing, shoes, home décor, sunglasses, presents for her family, and a whole ham!

We may be surprised that Jesus would caution His apostles regarding those who would refuse something as valuable as they had to offer. But then as today, some do refuse. That leads us to ask the question that comes next.   —J. E.

What Do You Think?
How will we know when it is time, if ever, to "move on" from a person who consistently resists the gospel message?

Digging Deeper
Consider how these Scriptures do or do not inform your answer: Matthew 7:6; 13:52-58; Acts 13:44-52; 1 Timothy 1:18-20; Titus 3:9-14.

---

15. Verily I say unto you, It shall be more tolerable for the land of Sodom and Gomorrha in the day of judgment, than for that city.

We come to an analogy between the disciples' mission and the mission of angels to rescue Lot and family from *Sodom* (Genesis 19). Like the angels, the disciples bring a message of salvation. Those to whom the disciples preach will have more time than did Lot as well as much more evidence of the truth. If the healings, exorcisms, and lifestyle of the disciples do not convince them, they will have no excuse come *the day of judgment.*

Visual for Lesson 6. *Start a discussion by posing the question on this visual. Dig deeper by asking, "Does God ever call us from a ministry or only to one?"*

Conclusion
A. Get with the Program

In some respects, the mission of the 12 apostles was a test run for the later work of the 70 in Luke 10:1-12, 17. Both missions were pilots for the imperatives of Matthew 28:18-20. These verses have become widely known as the Great Commission, often cited as a convenient summary of Jesus' instructions to all future followers. The church's missionary efforts have long been grounded in that final teaching of Matthew's Gospel.

While the Great Commission extends far beyond the area of Jesus' earthly ministry, close inspection reveals that Jesus simply instructs His followers to do what He himself has done. He made disciples; now His disciples are to do the same. In many respects, the Great Commission is a nutshell version of Jesus' own program. The question now is, will you get with the program?

B. Prayer

Father, help us to be wise and courageous as we seek to fulfill Your Son's calling on us. Give us the strength and abilities we need to proclaim Your kingdom whenever and wherever You need us to do so. We pray in Jesus' name. Amen.

C. Thought to Remember

The "all nations" of Matthew 28:19 still await the gospel.

INVOLVEMENT LEARNING

Enhance your lesson with KJV Bible Student *(from your curriculum supplier) and the reproducible activity page (at www.standardlesson.com or in the back of the* KJV Standard Lesson Commentary Deluxe Edition*).*

Into the Lesson

For about a dollar, purchase and download the *Mission Impossible* theme from a music website. On the board write, "What are some 'impossible missions' people have attempted in history?" Play the theme song and direct class members' attention to the question on the board to begin class.

After the music ends, help the class list some missions that came to mind (military missions, exploratory missions, scientific and commercial ventures, etc.) Discuss by asking, 1–Why were these ventures difficult? 2–What potential costs were involved? 3–What potential rewards would have come with success?

Alternative. Distribute copies of the "Military Missions" activity from the reproducible page, which you can download. Have students work individually for no more than one minute. Reveal the answers and discuss the missions by posing the questions above.

After either activity say, "At times people are challenged to accept a mission that will change their lives and even influence the course of history. When Jesus called His first disciples, they became a part of just such a challenging operation."

Into the Word

Before class, use a Bible dictionary to research and summarize on 12 sheets of paper all biblical background information on each of the 12 apostles, one apostle's information per sheet. (Research background only, not what they did after Matthew 10. About some, little or nothing will be known.)

Divide students into three groups, giving each group one of these identities: 1–Peter, Andrew, James, John; 2–Philip, Bartholomew, Thomas, Matthew; 3–James of Alphaeus, Thaddaeus, Simon the Canaanite, Judas Iscariot.

Have each group choose an actor or actors to portray their characters and dramatize backgrounds. The dramatizations should include also how life has changed because of Jesus (up through Matthew 10 only), what has Jesus called them to do during the upcoming mission, and how Jesus has prepared them for the mission.

For example, Group 1 should talk about family fishing businesses. Answering Jesus' call required that they give up their livelihood and settled lives in order to travel through the countryside with Jesus, etc.

Allow preparation time first. As groups work, move among them to help as necessary. Your advance research will have added to information that is available in the commentary. Have the class act out the skit(s).

Alternative. Distribute copies of the "Operation Lost Sheep" activity, from the reproducible page. Have students work in groups to paraphrase the cited portions of the Bible text to complete the dossier for the mission.

After either activity say, "Jesus trained His apostles so that they would be prepared for this first mission on their own. We have received hours of training by way of sermons and Bible studies. Let's think about how we can use what we have learned to fulfill a mission Jesus has for us."

Into Life

Before class, gather information about the missions supported by your congregation. If your congregation has a missions committee, invite a member of that committee to explain the work and needs of these missions. Be sure to have him or her mention needs for volunteers in these mission endeavors.

After the presentation, distribute handouts (you prepare) that list all the missions just discussed. Select a task force from your class to plan a way to participate in a project of one of the mission programs. Ask the task force to report back in two weeks. (*Alternative.* Distribute the handout for class members' participation as individuals.)

CALLED TO REMEMBER

DEVOTIONAL READING: Acts 2:29-39
BACKGROUND SCRIPTURE: Matthew 26:1-13

MATTHEW 26:1-13

1 And it came to pass, when Jesus had finished all these sayings, he said unto his disciples,

2 Ye know that after two days is the feast of the passover, and the Son of man is betrayed to be crucified.

3 Then assembled together the chief priests, and the scribes, and the elders of the people, unto the palace of the high priest, who was called Caiaphas,

4 And consulted that they might take Jesus by subtilty, and kill him.

5 But they said, Not on the feast day, lest there be an uproar among the people.

6 Now when Jesus was in Bethany, in the house of Simon the leper,

7 There came unto him a woman having an alabaster box of very precious ointment, and poured it on his head, as he sat at meat.

8 But when his disciples saw it, they had indignation, saying, To what purpose is this waste?

9 For this ointment might have been sold for much, and given to the poor.

10 When Jesus understood it, he said unto them, Why trouble ye the woman? for she hath wrought a good work upon me.

11 For ye have the poor always with you; but me ye have not always.

12 For in that she hath poured this ointment on my body, she did it for my burial.

13 Verily I say unto you, Wheresoever this gospel shall be preached in the whole world, there shall also this, that this woman hath done, be told for a memorial of her.

KEY VERSE

Verily I say unto you, Wheresoever this gospel shall be preached in the whole world, there shall also this, that this woman hath done, be told for a memorial of her. —**Matthew 26:13**

Discipleship and Mission

Unit 2: Call to Ministry
Lessons 5–9

Lesson Aims

After participating in this lesson, each learner will be able to:

1. Locate events within Jesus' final week.

2. Contrast the religious leaders' hostility toward Jesus with Mary's expression of love for Him.

3. Send a message of thanks to someone for his or her courageous service to Jesus.

Lesson Outline

Introduction

A. Unintended Result

Back in 1912 (so an oft-told story goes), President William Howard Taft was attending a Washington Senators baseball game. After the top of the seventh inning was completed, Taft (a rather large man) was feeling a bit tired, so he stood up to stretch. On seeing the President of the United States stand, those nearby did the same. Soon everyone in the ball park was standing. Thus began a tradition still observed at baseball games yet today: the seventh-inning stretch.

President Taft had no intention of creating a tradition. All he wanted to do was take a break from sitting. Yet his simple act had enduring consequences. The same is true of the woman in today's lesson. She did not intend her act to "go down in history," but it did.

B. Lesson Context: Passover

Today is Palm Sunday, the day we remember Jesus' triumphal entry into Jerusalem (John 12:13). That event occurred early in the time frame of what has come to be called passion week or Jesus' final week. So important are the teachings and events of this week that more than a third of Matthew's Gospel focuses on just these few days.

Our lesson today takes us about midway into this week, after Jesus and many others have arrived in Jerusalem for the Feast of the Passover. On the origin of this single-day observance and the week-long Feast of Unleavened Bread that accompanies it, see Exodus 12:6, 15-20, 43-49; Leviticus 23:5, 6; Numbers 28:16, 17; Deuteronomy 16:1-4.

C. Lesson Context: Jesus' Opponents

Part of our lesson considers the attitudes and actions of the Jewish ruling council, which was based in Jerusalem. Some students trace the beginnings of this council to the body of elders who returned from exile in about 536 BC per Ezra 5:5, 9; 6:7, 8, 14. The line is then said to be traceable to the priests, nobles, and officials of Nehemiah 2:16; 5:7. A key figure among the nobles was Zerubbabel (Ezra 4:3; 5:2). He was of David's royal line

(1 Chronicles 3:1-19), but Zerubbabel's authority was certainly not that of a king.

As the royal authority of the house of David faded, the priesthood gained more and more power. The high priest became, in effect, the head of state in the time between the Old and New Testaments. Serving with him was a council of elders. A record of Jewish history of about 187 to 162 BC notes the recognition of this council by a certain king (see nonbiblical 2 Maccabees 11:27). The power of the high priest continued to increase with time (see nonbiblical 1 Maccabees 12:6; 14:24-49).

The council's power was sharply curtailed by Herod when he began to rule from Jerusalem in 37 BC as a client-king of Rome. When the Romans changed their governing system after Herod's death, the council again increased in power.

Council membership numbered 70 plus the high priest, for a total of 71. Support for this 70+1 arrangement was drawn from Numbers 11:16 after the fact. The power of the council and the limits of that power are seen by comparing Mark 10:33; 14:55; Luke 24:20; John 9:22; 18:31; Acts 4:1-22; 5:17-42.

Many Bible commentaries refer to this council as *the Sanhedrin*. That designation is just a transliteration of the underlying Greek word; it is translated "council" in 22 occurrences in the New Testament (example: Acts 5:21). Transliteration is a process whereby the letters of a Greek or Hebrew word are merely swapped with English letters that sound the same. There are many transliterations in the Bible (examples: *apostle*, *baptism*, and *Christ*).

I. Jesus Is Hated
(MATTHEW 26:1-5)
A. Awareness (vv. 1, 2)

1. And it came to pass, when Jesus had finished all these sayings, he said unto his disciples.

All these sayings refers to teachings recorded in Matthew 24, 25. There Jesus has just discoursed at length on events in the distant future.

2a. Ye know that after two days is the feast of the passover.

Switching gears, Jesus turns the attention to what will take place *after two days*. There are many time indicators in Scripture that have been used to construct timelines of Jesus' final week. We list these below:

Matthew 12:40; 16:21; 17:23; 26:2, 17-20; 27:62; 28:1
  Mark 14:1, 4, 12, 16, 17; 15:42; 16:2
    Luke 3:2; 9:22; 18:33; 22:1, 7, 8, 13-15; 23:54; 24:1, 21
    John 11:55; 12:1; 13:2; 18:13, 28, 39; 19:14, 31, 42
  Acts 10:40   1 Corinthians 11:23; 15:4

Given all this information, one might think that a timeline would be relatively easy to construct. But it's not as easy as it may seem. One hurdle centers on the intent of the word *day(s)*. Jews of the time use that word to refer both to part of a day and to a whole day. Thus the word *day* does not necessarily indicate a precise 24-hour period.

Another problem with properly interpreting the word *day* is that the Gospels of Matthew, Mark, and Luke seem to consider the passage of days as being from sunrise to sunrise; Galilean Jews and Pharisees are said to use this method. The Gospel of John, however, seems to follow the method of Judean Jews and Sadducees, who are said to measure days from sunset to sunset.

Thus it is with a bit of uncertainty that we propose that Jesus is speaking these words on Tuesday evening of His final week, which not a few might consider to be Wednesday, depending on the two issues above. In any case, Jesus' fateful and final Passover observance is drawing very near.

2b. And the Son of man is betrayed to be crucified.

Jesus has spoken to His disciples of His coming death at least three times to this point (see Matthew 16:21; 17:22, 23; 20:17-19). Two of those three previous occasions included, as here, predictions of betrayal and crucifixion.

The phrase *Son of man* is the most used designation for Jesus in the Gospels (about 80 times)

HOW TO SAY IT

Annas	*An*-nus.
Bethany	*Beth*-uh-nee.
Caiaphas	*Kay*-uh-fus or *Kye*-uh-fus.
Maccabees	*Mack*-uh-bees.
Sanhedrin	*San*-huh-drun or San-*heed*-run.
Zerubbabel	Zeh-*rub*-uh-bul.

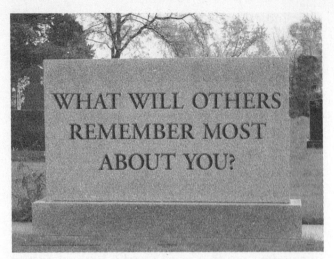

Visual for Lesson 7. *Pose the question on this visual for application of Matthew 26:13 or at the lesson's conclusion.*

other than the name *Jesus* itself (occurs more than 900 times).

B. Animosity (vv. 3-5)

3a. Then assembled together the chief priests, and the scribes, and the elders of the people.

The scene now changes to those plotting to carry out their murderous intentions against Jesus. *The chief priests, and the scribes, and the elders* are members of the Jewish ruling council (compare Matthew 26:59; Mark 15:1; John 11:47; see also the Lesson Context: Jesus' Opponents).

3b. Unto the palace of the high priest, who was called Caiaphas.

Caiaphas is the son-in-law of Annas, who had served as high priest AD 6–15 (compare Luke 3:2; John 18:13, 24). Annas has managed to keep the office of high priest in his family and is influential enough to be regarded as high priest while Caiaphas carries out the official duties of the position (compare Acts 4:6).

To meet where *the high priest* resides rather than in the temple area where the council normally convenes may be attributed to the secretive nature of what is being discussed. One theory is that the meeting is held here in the event that it lasts well into the night, since night meetings are not allowed in the temple area.

4. And consulted that they might take Jesus by subtilty, and kill him.

Some of these men were present when Jesus spoke the parable of the wicked husbandmen (Matthew 21:33-44), and they recognized that the husbandmen referred to them. They bear responsibility for killing the servants and the son of the vineyard owner (21:23, 45). The religious officials had wanted to arrest Jesus right then and there, but they feared the reaction of the crowds (21:46).

Now, gathered at the residence of the high priest, they conclude that they will have to arrest Jesus not openly, but *by subtilty*. The word in the original language is also translated "deceit" in Mark 7:22 and "guile" in 1 Peter 2:1. The phrase *and kill him* indicates they have already decided the outcome of a trial before a trial even begins!

❧ ASSASSINATION PLOTS ❧

History tells us of more than 30 attempts to kill sitting and former presidents and presidents-elect of the U.S. Four such attempts have succeeded.

Some assassination attempts are attributable to mental instability. But historians generally agree that most such attempts have been politically motivated. Such motivations may include a perception that the target is a threat to vested interests.

The Bible is clear about the mental state and motivation of the religious leaders who plotted against Jesus. They were methodical, weighing the best way to carry out the plan. John 11:48 gives the motive: eliminate a threat to vested interests.

We rightly recoil in horror that such a motive led to the crucifixion of the innocent Son of God. Our horror should give way to a resolve not to do that which would "crucify . . . the Son of God afresh, and put him to an open shame" (Hebrews 6:6).

—J. E.

> *What Do You Think?*
> What steps can you take to protect yourself from being influenced by the wrong motives of a larger group?
> *Digging Deeper*
> Consider these passages as you form your plan: Exodus 23:2; Jeremiah 9:2; Matthew 27:17-25. Also research the psychological phenomenon known as *groupthink*.

5. But they said, Not on the feast day, lest there be an uproar among the people.

The feast day is the day of the Passover observance (see the Lesson Context: Passover). Studies of population densities of ancient cities lead some to estimate that the population of Jerusalem can be upwards of 80,000. This number temporarily swells greatly during Passover. The plan of the ruling council takes into account the danger that this fact poses.

II. Jesus Is Honored
(MATTHEW 26:6-13)
A. Action (vv. 6, 7)

6. Now when Jesus was in Bethany, in the house of Simon the leper.

Matthew proceeds to record an incident that happened "six days before the passover" (John 12:1). The village of *Bethany* is the one noted in Matthew 21:17; Mark 11:1; and Luke 19:29. Its distance of "about fifteen furlongs" from Jerusalem (John 11:18) converts to a bit less than two miles. The town is the location of the home of Mary, Martha, and Lazarus (John 12:1-3; compare 11:1, 2).

The designation *Simon the leper* is not to be taken that this man still has leprosy. Rather, it is likely that he is one of the many lepers already healed (compare Matthew 8:2, 3; 10:8; 11:4, 5).

7. There came unto him a woman having an alabaster box of very precious ointment, and poured it on his head, as he sat at meat.

The *woman*, not named in Matthew's account, is Mary, the sister of Martha and Lazarus (John 12:3). She is mentioned elsewhere as possessing a singular devotion to hearing what Jesus had to say (Luke 10:38-42).

The *very precious ointment* Mary brings is further specified as "spikenard" in Mark 14:3 and John 12:3. This designates a plant that is imported from northern India, thus very costly (see further below). The older weight designation of "pound" in John 12:3 converts roughly to 12 fluid ounces—about a cup and a half. This is more than enough to anoint Jesus' *head*, so Mary anoints his feet as well, again per John 12:3.

B. Angst (vv. 8, 9)

8. But when his disciples saw it, they had indignation, saying, To what purpose is this waste?

Ten of the *disciples* had previously expressed *indignation* with the other two (Mark 10:41; same Greek word). Now this reaction is directed at Mary for her seeming *waste*.

9. For this ointment might have been sold for much, and given to the poor.

John's account tells us that it is Judas Iscariot who is the most vocal in objecting. He even provides an estimate of the ointment's value: "three hundred pence" (John 12:5). That's about the same as an entire year's wages of a day laborer (see Matthew 20:2). But Judas has his own sinful motive for voicing his objection (see John 12:6).

> **What Do You Think?**
> Under what conditions, if any, would we be justified in declaring something or some act in the church to be "waste"?
>
> *Digging Deeper*
> Under what conditions, if any, would the good intentions of the one who is seen to be wasteful influence our answer?

❧ *AN EXTRAVAGANT AROMA* ❧

For centuries, women have known that the scent of the perfume they wear can enter a room before they themselves make their appearance. Thus, good perfumes always fetch a high price. But how much is perfume really worth in that regard?

The cost of the world's most expensive colognes will shock most people. Poivre by Caron is costly for its wonderful fragrance but also for its jewel-encrusted bottle with gold trim. The bottle contains two ounces of perfume and costs $2,000. Notorious by Ralph Lauren is available only from Harrods in London. It is said that the "beautiful people" believe it to be the perfect scent for the Christmas holidays. The price tag affirms the notoriety of its name: $3,540 per bottle! Topping the list is Imperial Majesty Perfume by Clive Christian. In its dazzling bottle that is embedded with white diamonds, it commands a price of $215,000! Do we wonder why only 20 bottles were ever produced?

When we think of such expensive perfumes, we begin to sympathize with the disciples' objection. Given that the average salary for a blue-collar worker is about $43,000, the cost of any of these perfumes seems like a waste. Isn't there a better use for the money? While caring for others is essential, the recognition of God's extravagant gift is the greatest of all necessities. Thus we may have different answers depending on whom the expensive perfume is for. See the next verse.   —J. E.

C. Approval (vv. 10-13)

10. When Jesus understood it, he said unto them, Why trouble ye the woman? for she hath wrought a good work upon me.

Undergirding the disciples' objection and Jesus' rebuttal is an important fact: Mary has recognized something about Jesus that the disciples have not. Thus Jesus' approval of her *good work*. Were the disciples to recognize that the king of the universe sits among them, would any expenditure on His behalf be too much? The pettiness evident back in Mark 10:35-45 in the request of James and John—two of Jesus' inner circle!—indicates a lack of awareness, among other things. Their spiritual discernment seems not to have progressed much since a similar "who's greatest" incident in Luke 9:46-48.

> *What Do You Think?*
>   What guardrails can we put in place to avoid making the same mistake that Jesus' disciples made?
> *Digging Deeper*
>   What should we do, if anything, if we see others making the same mistake that Jesus' disciples made? Why?

11. For ye have the poor always with you; but me ye have not always.

Jesus' statement echoes words found in the Law of Moses: "the poor shall never cease out of the land" (Deuteronomy 15:11). Poverty is a consequence of living in a broken, fallen world. The

world still reels from the impact of sin's curse (see Romans 8:22). The Scriptures are filled with many expressions of compassion for the poor and exhortations to God's people (under both old and new covenants) to demonstrate compassion tangibly. Deuteronomy 15:11, for example, is preceded by commands to God's people not to harden their hearts against the poor (15:7-10).

Similar is 1 John 3:17. But just because the poor will always be among us does not mean that we should make no effort to address their condition. As Jesus has already indicated in His teaching, helping such individuals is the same as ministering to Him (Matthew 25:40).

Jesus' point in saying what He does about the poor in the context at hand is that there will be many opportunities in the future to demonstrate care for the poverty stricken. He, on the other hand, knows that His time on earth is short. (At this point, the crucifixion is less than a week away.) If someone such as Mary desires to express her devotion to Him in a personal though unconventional way, now is the time to do so.

> *What Do You Think?*
>   What are some extravagant gifts that can demonstrate our love for Jesus openly?
> *Digging Deeper*
>   In what contexts might extravagant gifts *not* result in demonstrating love for Jesus? Why?

12. For in that she hath poured this ointment on my body, she did it for my burial.

Jesus states a significance to Mary's act that the critical onlookers have not recognized. The *ointment* Mary has *poured* on Jesus is similar to the kinds of spices that accompany a burial in that day, in order to offset the effects of decomposition (compare John 11:39; 19:39).

Does Mary herself possess this understanding of what she has done? It is hard to know for certain. Perhaps Mary, whose heart for the words of Jesus has already been noted, senses that Jesus' death is imminent. Therefore, if she is going to demonstrate awareness of Jesus' approaching death, she must do it now—as unorthodox as her actions may appear to be. Her critics have had their say; all that matters to Mary is what Jesus thinks. And He has judged Mary's action to be a "good work." Mark 14:8 records this commendation from Jesus: "She hath done what she could."

13. Verily I say unto you, Wheresoever this gospel shall be preached in the whole world, there shall also this, that this woman hath done, be told for a memorial of her.

Regardless of what Mary may or may not understand of Jesus' impending burial, she cannot foresee what Jesus now says about her action. Her demonstration of her devotion to Jesus, though scorned by most who witness it, will be cited as exemplary and praiseworthy.

Certainly her public action is to be contrasted with the private hatred and scheming of the religious leaders noted earlier. They too want to prepare for Jesus' burial. But their motives and methods are far different from humble Mary's.

(Note: This account should not be confused with the similar but different one in Luke 7:36-50.)

What Do You Think?

What can you do to help honor the unsung servants in your church?

Digging Deeper

In that process, how can you prevent the honoring or memorializing of faithful Christians from robbing honor that is due Christ? How does the memorializing of the faithful in Hebrews 11 help you answer this question?

Conclusion

A. Know Any Marys or Her Critics?

Many followers of Jesus choose to serve Him in dangerous or primitive settings, thousands of miles from home. They have exercised their devotion to the cause of Christ and His kingdom in what appears to be a radical manner.

Because of their decision to do so, some of their family members and friends may look upon them as "wasting" their talents and education. As family and friends think and talk that way, they echo the criticisms of the disciples who viewed Mary's action toward Jesus as a waste.

Sometimes the labor of those who invest their lives for Christ may not seem to be bearing much fruit. That can give skeptics even more cause to question what others have chosen to do with their lives. And let's face it: sometimes critics are right. But in those frequent cases where they're wrong, they can cause doubt. That's why people who invest their lives in kingdom work need encouragement. They need affirmation that what they are doing is the right thing.

Think about it: What if Jesus had merely remained silent as the disciples voiced their criticism? What would that have done to Mary? As we ponder that question, we may also examine whether our own extravagant giving is being held back by what we imagine critics might say were we to make that potential gift a reality.

To receive words of encouragement from others can be a great source of blessing to those who serve in difficult mission fields. Perhaps your class or your congregation is aware of an individual or family who has such a need. What can you do to keep in touch with them? How about keeping track of their birthdays or anniversaries? How about communicating with them on holidays? What gifts can the class or congregation provide to assist in the work being done?

One great blessing can be to ask them what specific prayer needs exist. To know that others are praying for you can be one of the best sources of encouragement there is!

Expressions of kindness and gratitude will lift the spirits of both those who offer them and those who receive them. And Jesus, who sees such acts, will certainly not view them as "waste."

C. Prayer

Father, help us to examine our motives lest we become scornful toward people whose expressions of devotion to You may seem wasteful to us. Help us be as generous as Mary was in our service to You. We pray this in Jesus' name. Amen.

D. Thought to Remember

Nothing done for Jesus is wasted.

INVOLVEMENT LEARNING

Enhance your lesson with KJV Bible Student *(from your curriculum supplier) and the reproducible activity page (at www.standardlesson.com or in the back of the* KJV Standard Lesson Commentary Deluxe Edition*).*

Into the Lesson

Begin class by reading this true story:

Thomas Archibald Brown (1889–1959) was known as "Big Tom," the tough police chief of St. Paul, Minnesota, in the 1930s. To the public Tom Brown was a tough lawman who killed an escaped murderer. He was an important member of the city's "Purity Squad," a task force that fought corruption.

But there was a hidden side to Big Tom. This public crime fighter was actually a criminal himself! He worked hand-in-hand with mob boss Leon Gleckman. Brown secretly assisted infamous criminals such as John Dillinger and the Barker gang. Big Tom's double life was suspected, but he was never prosecuted.

Over the years, many people thought they knew Big Tom the lawman, but they did not know the real Big Tom the criminal.

Pose the following questions for discussion: 1–What other stories do you know about people who led double lives? 2–How did they get away with it for as long as they did? 3–What percentage of ourselves is hidden from others?

Alternative. Distribute copies of the "The Real Me" activity from the reproducible page, which you can download. Have students work individually for no more than one minute to complete as indicated. Allow volunteers to share parts of their lists. Ask why we allow only those closest to us to know personal details about us.

After either activity say, "People who are merely acquainted may not really understand one another. Let's see why Jesus commended a woman whose action demonstrated that she 'got' Him."

Into the Word

Write this at the top of the board: "How does what we believe about Jesus affect the way we spend money?" Under that create three columns headed this way: To attack Jesus and the gospel (Matthew 26:3-5, 15) / To do good works in the name of Jesus (Matthew 26:8, 9) / To honor Jesus as Savior (Matthew 26:7, 12).

Have the class fill in the chart as you ask these questions: 1–Who in today's account go in each column? 2–What motivated each person or group? 3–What are some present-day examples of people spending money in each of these ways? 4–What criticism can be leveled at each group?

During discussion point out that those hostile to Jesus tried to silence the message of the gospel. The woman (Mary of Bethany) was criticized by other Jesus followers for an act that recognized the saving work of His sacrifice—the very crux of the gospel!

Alternative. Distribute copies of the "Who Is Jesus?" activity from the reproducible page. Have students work in pairs to analyze how the main characters in today's text understood Jesus.

After either activity, make a transition by saying, "People hostile to the gospel still seek to silence Jesus. This happens through ridicule, dismissiveness, and even persecution. The real Jesus is also marginalized when people reduce Him to being no more than a good, moral teacher. How can we support those we know who live lives to lift up Jesus as Savior?"

Into Life

Help the group think of those they know personally who live sacrificially in a way to honor Jesus as Savior. Distribute blank thank-you cards. Encourage each learner to write a brief thank-you note to someone who has faithfully served Jesus with little recognition. Suggest that learners structure their thanks by writing, *Your understanding of who Jesus is can be seen in all you do. This is what I have learned about Jesus from watching you:* _____

Allow them to finish and deliver their notes from home. Close in prayer, asking for courage to live in a way that reveals the real Jesus to the world.

CALLED TO BELIEVE THE RESURRECTION

DEVOTIONAL READING: 1 Corinthians 15:12-22
BACKGROUND SCRIPTURE: Matthew 28:1-15

MATTHEW 28:1-15

1 In the end of the sabbath, as it began to dawn toward the first day of the week, came Mary Magdalene and the other Mary to see the sepulchre.

2 And, behold, there was a great earthquake: for the angel of the Lord descended from heaven, and came and rolled back the stone from the door, and sat upon it.

3 His countenance was like lightning, and his raiment white as snow:

4 And for fear of him the keepers did shake, and became as dead men.

5 And the angel answered and said unto the women, Fear not ye: for I know that ye seek Jesus, which was crucified.

6 He is not here: for he is risen, as he said. Come, see the place where the Lord lay.

7 And go quickly, and tell his disciples that he is risen from the dead; and, behold, he goeth before you into Galilee; there shall ye see him: lo, I have told you.

8 And they departed quickly from the sepulchre with fear and great joy; and did run to bring his disciples word.

9 And as they went to tell his disciples, behold, Jesus met them, saying, All hail. And they came and held him by the feet, and worshipped him.

10 Then said Jesus unto them, Be not afraid: go tell my brethren that they go into Galilee, and there shall they see me.

11 Now when they were going, behold, some of the watch came into the city, and shewed unto the chief priests all the things that were done.

12 And when they were assembled with the elders, and had taken counsel, they gave large money unto the soldiers,

13 Saying, Say ye, His disciples came by night, and stole him away while we slept.

14 And if this come to the governor's ears, we will persuade him, and secure you.

15 So they took the money, and did as they were taught: and this saying is commonly reported among the Jews until this day.

KEY VERSE

Then said Jesus unto them, Be not afraid: go tell my brethren that they go into Galilee, and there shall they see me. —**Matthew 28:10**

DISCIPLESHIP AND MISSION

Unit 2: Call to Ministry

LESSONS 5–9

LESSON AIMS

After participating in this lesson, each learner will be able to:

1. Retell Matthew's record of the discovery of the empty tomb.

2. Compare and contrast the reactions of those who became aware that Jesus' body was missing.

3. Prepare a testimony based on the truth of the resurrected Jesus.

LESSON OUTLINE

Introduction

A. The Greatest Discovery

An online search for the 10 most significant discoveries in history reveals many lists. Most include breakthroughs in the field of medicine—development of antibiotics such as penicillin, etc. Eventually, however, death comes to everyone (Hebrews 9:27). That is why the greatest discovery of all time happened on the day we celebrate as Easter Sunday.

The great discovery that was made by those who came to Jesus' tomb after His crucifixion was the absence of something: Jesus' body. Never before and not since that morning has the absence of something conveyed such a profound message. Today's lesson introduces us to that message.

B. Lesson Context

The events in last week's text from Matthew occurred at a point when the Jewish religious leaders were plotting to arrest Jesus. But they did not want to create a public disturbance by doing so (Matthew 26:3-5). To their delight, the leaders found among Jesus' disciples an ally for the scheme: Judas Iscariot (26:14-16).

After the Passover meal, Jesus led His disciples from the upper room to the Garden of Gethsemane. That was a place to which He had brought them often. Therefore the location was known to Judas, who guided those who arrested Jesus there (Matthew 26:47; John 18:1-3). There followed the series of appearances before the Jewish ruling council (the Sanhedrin; see last week's Lesson Context) and Pilate that resulted in Jesus' crucifixion.

Of the four Gospel writers, only Matthew records the concern of the chief priests and Pharisees that Jesus' disciples might attempt to steal His corpse. Their concern was based on being aware of the claim of "that deceiver" that He would rise from the dead. A missing body meant that a resurrection could be claimed. Therefore the chief priests and Pharisees recommended to Pilate that steps be taken to ensure against such a hoax (Matthew 27:62-66). Pilate agreed. The results of that effort are considered in today's lesson.

All four Gospels record the actions of devoted women who returned to Jesus' tomb to honor Him after His death. We say "returned" because they had been there when Jesus' body was interred (Matthew 27:61; Mark 15:47; Luke 23:55). Their intent was to finish the hurried job started by two others (John 19:38-41) in anointing His body with various preparations (Mark 16:1; Luke 23:55, 56; compare 2 Chronicles 16:14).

I. Amazing Sight
(MATTHEW 28:1-4)
A. Women's Arrival (v. 1)

1. In the end of the sabbath, as it began to dawn toward the first day of the week, came Mary Magdalene and the other Mary to see the sepulchre.

In the end of the sabbath means that the Sabbath had passed (compare Mark 16:1). *The first day of the week* is what we call Sunday.

There are several women named Mary in the New Testament, and it's easy to get them mixed up. The designation *Magdalene* is not a last name, but indicates a village she comes from that is located on the shore of the Sea of Galilee (compare Mark 16:9; Luke 8:2).

The other Mary is likely "the mother of James and Joses" (Matthew 27:56). The parallel accounts designate "the mother of James" (Mark 16:1 and Luke 24:10). If we combine Matthew 13:55; 27:56; and Mark 15:40, 47, then this Mary may be the mother of Jesus, but this is not certain. For the

HOW TO SAY IT

Bethlehem	*Beth*-lih-hem.
Caesar	*See*-zer.
Galilee	*Gal*-uh-lee.
Gethsemane	Geth-*sem*-uh-nee (*G* as in *get*).
Judas Iscariot	*Joo*-dus Iss-*care*-ee-ut.
Magdalene	*Mag*-duh-leen or Mag-duh-*lee*-nee.
Pharisees	*Fair*-ih-seez.
Pilate	*Pie*-lut.
Sadducees	*Sad*-you-seez.
Sanhedrin	San-huh-drun or San-*heed*-run.
sepulchre	*sep*-ul-kur.

women's intention in coming *to see the sepulchre*, see the Lesson Context.

B. Angel's Actions (vv. 2, 3)

2. And, behold, there was a great earthquake: for the angel of the Lord descended from heaven, and came and rolled back the stone from the door, and sat upon it.

An *earthquake* occurred at the moment of Jesus' death (Matthew 27:50, 51); now one takes place as part of the unfolding drama here. Matthew is the only Gospel writer to record them. These are supernatural temblors, a sign of the activity and presence of God (compare Isaiah 29:6).

Angels have already appeared at crucial occasions during the life and ministry of Jesus: His birth (Luke 2:8-14), His temptation (Matthew 4:11), and at Gethsemane (Luke 22:43). The heavy *stone* that *the angel of the Lord* moves indicates that the tomb has been carved out of a rocky hillside (Matthew 27:57, 60). Such stones seal the entrances to tombs.

3. His countenance was like lightning, and his raiment white as snow.

Such a description as this is fitting for a being whom the previous verse says has "descended from heaven"! The brightness of both the angel's *countenance* (face) and *raiment* (clothing) is reminiscent of how Jesus appeared at His transfiguration (Matthew 17:1, 2).

C. Guards' Alarm (v. 4)

4. And for fear of him the keepers did shake, and became as dead men.

The keepers (guards) stationed at the tomb experience both the sight of the angel of the Lord and the sudden terror of the earthquake. They *shake* as much as the earth does! The overall shock of what they witness leaves them paralyzed with fear or unconscious. The phrase *they became as dead men* does not mean they actually died, because some of them report the stunning series of events to the religious leaders in Jerusalem (Matthew 28:11, below).

II. Assuring Words
(MATTHEW 28:5-7)
A. News to Hear (vv. 5, 6)

5. And the angel answered and said unto the women, Fear not ye: for I know that ye seek Jesus, which was crucified.

This is not the only place in the Bible where those to whom an angel appears are encouraged to *fear not* (compare: Genesis 21:17; Luke 1:13, 30; 2:10). Since angelic appearances are sudden and unexpected, this greeting is certainly appropriate.

We can note, however, that there was no message of "fear not" to the guards of Matthew 27:65, 66; the angel's intention for them is the opposite. By contrast, *the angel* carries out a ministry of comforting assurance to the bewildered women by affirming awareness of their mission to *Jesus, which was crucified* and buried.

Luke 24:4 records the appearance of "two men . . . in shining garments," later described as "angels" (24:23). Matthew chooses to include only the angel who speaks to the women.

6a. He is not here: for he is risen, as he said.

This is the grand announcement. The reminder *as he said* refers to Matthew 16:21; 17:22, 23; 20:17-19. The fact of Jesus' resurrection fulfills the promise of a sign to the skeptics who demanded one (see 12:38-40).

❧ *No Doubt About the Tomb* ❧

Several years ago, I went with about a dozen friends on a guided tour of the Middle East. We visited the usual tourist sites, both secular and sacred. We saw Jewish sites such as the Wailing Wall. We visited Islam's Dome of the Rock, the golden-domed seventh-century edifice on the site of Solomon's temple.

I was more drawn to places that reminded me of Jesus' time among us. The olive groves of Gethsemane held special meaning for me, as did the area surrounding the Sea of Galilee. As significant as those places were to me, it was my reaction to the Garden Tomb that caught me by surprise.

I knew before seeing the tomb that is usually shown to tourists that it was likely not the one briefly occupied by Jesus' body. But seeing a place where His body conceivably could have lain triggered my imagination: my mind's eye pictured the moment when the Lord's followers first realized that He had risen.

We may not know into which tomb Jesus' body was placed, but the eyewitnesses did! As I stood in front of a tomb in Jerusalem, I was moved by the knowledge that the angel's words were and are true. If you're not convinced, what evidence would you have to have to change your mind?—C. R. B.

6b. Come, see the place where the Lord lay.

The women had seen a dead body lain in this rock-hewn grave (Matthew 27:60, 61). Now they are invited to witness the absence of that body. Can we really understand how dumbfounded the women must be as they hear the angel speak? Jesus was dead, but now He is not. The women's quest for a dead Jesus has become pointless.

> **What Do You Think?**
> How can you better prepare yourself to offer evidence for the fact that Christ rose from the dead? Why is it important to do so?
>
> *Digging Deeper*
> Watch an online video by J. Warner Wallace to learn how a homicide detective approaches these questions. Compare and contrast your approach with his.

B. News to Tell (v. 7)

7a. And go quickly, and tell his disciples that he is risen from the dead.

The "come, see" of the previous verse gives way to the *go . . . tell* we see here. The women had arrived as seekers (Matthew 28:1-5, above). They then transitioned from seekers to finders (28:6, above)—but finding something better than expected. Now they must make the transition from finders to tellers. When it comes to knowledge of Jesus, there's no such thing as God's being content with those who never progress out of the seeker stage.

Time will tell whether the disciples will believe the women's testimony. According to the Jewish historian Josephus (AD 37–100), women of that time are not allowed to testify in court (*Antiquities,* 4.8.15). The affirmation by angels of the women's role thus flies in the face of a first-century practice. The first witnesses to the evidence of Jesus' resurrection are indeed women.

While the women seek the tomb as soon as enough daylight allows, the 11 disciples are still cowering in fear behind locked doors. They fear retribution at the hands of the same men who crucified Jesus (John 20:19).

7b. And, behold, he goeth before you into Galilee; there shall ye see him: lo, I have told you.

These phrases repeat and reinforce Jesus' promise in Matthew 26:32 and Mark 14:28 that He is to go before the disciples *into Galilee.*

III. Astonishing Appearance
(MATTHEW 28:8-10)
A. Moving Quickly (v. 8)

8. And they departed quickly from the sepulchre with fear and great joy; and did run to bring his disciples word.

Both the *fear* and the *great joy* of the women are easy to imagine. It is no wonder that they run to tell the disciples (also John 20:2). Mark 16:8 puts this in even stronger terms: "They went out quickly, and fled from the sepulchre." Such a mixture of emotions is only fitting for the astounding news the women now bear.

What Do You Think?
Who among your acquaintances is ready to hear the message that Jesus is risen? What will cause them to be receptive?

Digging Deeper
How do you know when a slower, more measured approach in sharing this message is better than a faster, more exuberant approach?

B. Meeting Jesus (vv. 9, 10)

9. And as they went to tell his disciples, behold, Jesus met them, saying, All hail. And they came and held him by the feet, and worshipped him.

The women's surprises are not finished. Before they can complete the task of telling Jesus' *disciples*, they meet Jesus himself. We are told nothing about Jesus' appearance, but we can see that the women recognize Him. Their worshipful response is understandable.

To grasp Jesus *by the feet* means that the women are on their knees. As speculation, perhaps they are trying to convince themselves that they are not hallucinating. Can this be the same Jesus whom they had known and worshipped prior to His death? Yes, He is the same Jesus: once crucified, now alive.

An ironic touch lies in Jesus' greeting *All hail*. The Greek word behind this translation is the same word translated "hail" of the soldiers' mocking worship (Matthew 27:29) and of Judas betraying Jesus before that (26:49).

10. Then said Jesus unto them, Be not afraid: go tell my brethren that they go into Galilee, and there shall they see me.

Jesus' words of comfort and instruction mirror those of the angel. A distinction is noted in Jesus' referring to the disciples as *my brethren*. This indicates the special closeness that still exists despite their recent desertion (compare Matthew 26:56; John 20:17).

Naturally, these men plan to return home to Galilee anyway. But now there is incentive for speed: the promise of seeing Jesus back there. Even so, the trip back to Galilee does not begin for several days (John 20:26).

IV. Arranged Cover-up
(MATTHEW 28:11-15)
A. Guards' Concern (v. 11)

11. Now when they were going, behold, some of the watch came into the city, and shewed unto the chief priests all the things that were done.

Only Matthew records the report of *the watch* (soldiers) who were charged with guarding the

Visual for Lesson 8. *When you reach Matthew 28:7a, start a discussion by asking, "In what ways is the angel's command ours too? In what ways is it not?"*

tomb to keep the body in it (Matthew 27:66). They have failed. It may seem odd that the Roman guards do not report to Pilate, the Roman governor. But there are two reasons for reporting to *the chief priests* instead. First, the religious authorities were the ones given the authority by Pilate to post the guard and seal the tomb. The second is seen in verse 14, below.

B. Leaders' Conspiracy (vv. 12-15)

12, 13. And when they were assembled with the elders, and had taken counsel, they gave large money unto the soldiers, saying, Say ye, His disciples came by night, and stole him away while we slept.

This is a meeting of the Jewish ruling council (compare Matthew 27:1). "The chief priests" of verse 11 are Sadducees, while *the elders* are Pharisees. Their successful plot to kill Jesus has not ended their "problem." Now another problem has developed. As with Judas Iscariot (Matthew 26:15), they use money as the "solution." As with previous miracles of Jesus, the religious leaders cannot deny that something supernatural has occurred. So they resort to a paid-for lie to calm the aftershocks of the resurrection earthquake.

14. And if this come to the governor's ears, we will persuade him, and secure you.

The first reason the soldiers report back to the council instead of Pilate is noted in verse 11, above. The verse before us gives us the second rea-

son. Guards who fall asleep on duty or otherwise fail in their task are subject to execution (compare Acts 12:1-19). But the religious leaders assure the soldiers no negative consequences will befall them. Should Pilate hear of what has occurred, the leaders promise that they can and will protect the soldiers from suffering consequences. The religious leaders' confidence that they can do so reflects the high degree of influence they have. Their influence was previously seen in successfully pressuring Pilate to crucify Jesus (John 19:12-16).

15a. So they took the money, and did as they were taught.

No voice of protest is recorded; the guards simply accept the payoff and do as told. Money now has been used to purchase both the betrayal of Jesus for His death (Matthew 26:15) and a lie about Jesus regarding His resurrection.

15b. And this saying is commonly reported among the Jews until this day.

Matthew's Gospel is generally considered to be the earliest of the four Gospels. Scholars date its writing to about AD 50 (or perhaps even earlier). Thus the phrase *until this day* indicates that the lie has been circulating for some 20 years as Matthew writes.

This lie, *this saying,* falls apart immediately when we consider the eventual martyrdoms of the apostles. People are known to be willing to die the deaths of martyrs for two things: (1) for truth and (2) for a lie believed to be true. But people are not willing to die for a lie that they know is a lie. But that doesn't stop twenty-first century skeptics from creating other theories to explain away the account of Jesus' resurrection.

> ### What Do You Think?
> How should responses to common misunderstandings of the gospel message differ from responses to biased misrepresentations?
> #### Digging Deeper
> Distinguish between situations that call for *no response* (example: Mark 14:60, 61a) vs. an *explanatory response* (example: John 4:19-26) vs. a *pushback response* (example: Mark 12:18-27).

Richard Nixon was the first president to resign from office. But many observers believe others should have done so as well. Innumerable politicians have seen their proverbial "skeletons in their closets" dangled in public view. Still they persist in secretive underhanded dealings and liaisons.

The Old Testament prophets often called Israel's leaders to task for their sins. One of the most memorable of these rebukes is Nathan's confrontation with David for the king's involvement with Bathsheba and subsequent attempt at a cover-up via murder of her husband (2 Samuel 12:1-14).

The Jewish leaders of Jesus' day failed to learn from history. Their conspiratorial cover-up was rooted in their vested interests as noted in John 11:48: "If we let [Jesus] thus alone, all men will believe on him: and the Romans shall come and take away both our place and nation." In the end, the efforts at killing Jesus and covering up His resurrection did not negate the threat of John 11:48. In AD 70, the Romans did indeed come. The ensuing siege and destruction of Jerusalem marked the end of "place and nation" of the Jewish leadership. The ruling council's attempt to solve its problem by using falsehood in various ways (see Matthew 26:59; compare Acts 6:13) ultimately failed. Today, the truth is available for all to see.

The church's explosive early growth suggests the liars ultimately end up fooling mainly themselves. Learn from the ruling council's sinful errors! Truth still has a way of getting out. Stay alert for your chance to reveal the grace and truth of Jesus (see John 1:14, 17) to those who are under the spell of the world's lies.   —C. R. B.

What Do You Think?
Regarding the *explanatory response* in the previous question, how will you avoid shifting from "defending the faith" to being "defensive about the faith"?

Digging Deeper
How do passages such as Daniel 3; Acts 24–26; 1 Corinthians 9:1-23; and 2 Corinthians 10–12 inform your answer?

Conclusion
A. No "Fake News"

The phrase "fake news" became a part of the vocabulary during the 2016 American presidential campaign. Certain news outlets were accused of creating stories that had no basis in fact in order to further an agenda. Christians may similarly be accused of propagating "fake news" regarding the resurrection of Jesus. The idea is that Christians accept on faith something that cannot be proven to be an actual event of history.

But the resurrection can be proven true, as this lesson has demonstrated. Yet getting people to see the truth can be a slow process. This calls for prayer and patience. Even Jesus' own disciples were not convinced at first. When the women reported to the disciples what they had found and not found at Jesus' tomb, "Their words seemed to them as idle tales, and they believed them not" (Luke 24:11). The apostle Thomas (in)famously declared, "Except I shall see in his hands the print of the nails, and put my finger into the print of the nails, and thrust my hand into his side, I will not believe" (John 20:25).

Why would men who were slow to believe news of a resurrection end up trying to make it appear as though one had happened if it had not? No one, neither the women nor the disciples, was anticipating that Jesus would arise. They were not spending the days following His death planning how they could perpetrate a hoax on the public.

Paul's declaration in 1 Corinthians 15:20 is the one that followers of Jesus gladly embrace and proclaim: "But now is Christ risen from the dead, and become the firstfruits of them that slept." Fake news—no; actual news—absolutely!

B. Prayer

Father, how thankful we are that on this Easter Sunday and every day we can celebrate the triumph of Jesus over death. Use us to change hearts and minds with this good news of a risen Savior. We pray this in His name. Amen.

C. Thought to Remember
We serve a risen Savior!

INVOLVEMENT LEARNING

Enhance your lesson with KJV Bible Student *(from your curriculum supplier) and the reproducible activity page (at www.standardlesson.com or in the back of the* KJV Standard Lesson Commentary Deluxe Edition*).*

Into the Lesson

Begin a "create-a-story" activity by saying, "It seems too good to be true! I just got a message that when I go home today I will find . . ." Ask class members to add to the story. Keep going, expecting the unbelievable story to become more and more outrageous!

Alternative Distribute copies of the "Gone Phishing" activity from the reproducible page, which you can download. Have students read examples of e-mails designed to steal personal information. Have them point out reasons why they would be too good to be true and how they would react.

After either activity say, "In a world that often seems cruel and pointless, really good news might seem too good to be true! Let's see how those witnessing the events of Jesus' resurrection reacted."

Into the Word

Divide students into three groups. Assign each group one of these Scripture passages: Matthew 28:1-5; Matthew 28:6-10; Matthew 28:11-15.

After reading their passage, group members should summarize it by writing two or three headlines in supermarket-tabloid style. *For example*: Graveyard Fright!—Women Report Divine Encounter / Spiritual Experience or Too Much Spirits?—Guards Struggle to Explain Why They Were Found Unconscious / Dead Man Walking!—Crucified Prophet Reported Meeting with His Followers / Military Cover-up!—Guards Reportedly Bribed to Give False Testimony.

Option. If time allows, you may wish to assign groups to write a paragraph or two summarizing the content of their assigned Scripture passage in the tabloid style. Point out that tabloids tend to exaggerate and sensationalize reports to attract readers.

After groups finish, allow them to share and explain their headlines to the class.

Allow for discussion and then say, "The account of the resurrection may sound like a tabloid tale, but it was established by eyewitnesses, became the message of the church, and has changed lives over centuries. Let's examine our personal reactions to this incredible—but credibly true—Easter message."

Into Life

Divide the class into pairs. Have each person prepare an "elevator speech," a talk of 30 seconds, which is the time it takes an elevator to move one floor. The talk is to begin this way: "I once thought the idea of a resurrected Savior was too good to be true. But that truth has changed my life this way . . ." Ask members of pairs to practice their talks with each other.

Examples:

• Having new friends due to church fellowship has made it easier to cut ties with old friends that were negative influences.

• Trusting Jesus for daily needs has helped conquer financial issues.

• Daily prayer and dependence on the Holy Spirit has resulted in the strength to conquer bad habits and even addictions.

In any of these cases, expect class member to point out that his or her human strength alone was unable to make a difference. If learners do not do so, stress that relying on the power of God, as displayed in the resurrection, is what makes these life changes possible. Request volunteers to share their speeches with the class.

Alternative: Distribute copies of the "Reassemble!" activity from the reproducible page to complete as indicated. Briefly discuss the quote by asking, "Can you name one or two of God's promises that might seem too good to be true?" Follow responses by asking why we can believe them. This can be done just before prayer or as a take-home activity.

CALLED TO MAKE DISCIPLES

DEVOTIONAL READING: Colossians 3:12-17
BACKGROUND SCRIPTURE: Matthew 28:16-20; Acts 1:6-8

MATTHEW 28:16-20

16 Then the eleven disciples went away into Galilee, into a mountain where Jesus had appointed them.

17 And when they saw him, they worshipped him: but some doubted.

18 And Jesus came and spake unto them, saying, All power is given unto me in heaven and in earth.

19 Go ye therefore, and teach all nations, baptizing them in the name of the Father, and of the Son, and of the Holy Ghost:

20 Teaching them to observe all things whatsoever I have commanded you: and, lo, I am with you alway, even unto the end of the world. Amen.

ACTS 1:6-8

6 When they therefore were come together, they asked of him, saying, Lord, wilt thou at this time restore again the kingdom to Israel?

7 And he said unto them, It is not for you to know the times or the seasons, which the Father hath put in his own power.

8 But ye shall receive power, after that the Holy Ghost is come upon you: and ye shall be witnesses unto me both in Jerusalem, and in all Judaea, and in Samaria, and unto the uttermost part of the earth.

KEY VERSES

Go ye therefore, and teach all nations, baptizing them in the name of the Father, and of the Son, and of the Holy Ghost: teaching them to observe all things whatsoever I have commanded you: and, lo, I am with you alway, even unto the end of the world. Amen. —**Matthew 28:19, 20**

DISCIPLESHIP AND MISSION

Unit 2: Call to Ministry

LESSON AIMS

After participating in this lesson, each learner will be able to:

1. Give the content of Jesus' commissions.

2. Describe challenges to keeping the Great Commission as the church's top priority.

3. Create a series of steps to improve his or her church's efforts at fulfilling the Great Commission.

LESSON OUTLINE

Introduction

A. "This Changes Everything"

The slogan "This changes everything" has been used at length in advertising. The claim has been attached to a flavoring for water, an allergy relief medication, a truck, and a brand of mayonnaise. Even a book bears that slogan as a title!

Obviously, the overuse of any slogan can rob it of its original appeal. But when we consider the impact of Jesus' resurrection, we can say beyond a shadow of a doubt that "this changes everything." Today's lesson tells us why.

B. Lesson Context: Matthew

Today's lesson text presents two accounts of Jesus' giving His disciples instructions for continuing His ministry in His absence. The first, from Matthew 28, comes immediately after the passage from last week's study. That passage recounted events surrounding the resurrection of Jesus and the resurrection itself.

All that took place in and near Jerusalem. A change in geographical context is introduced, however, by the transition noted in Matthew 28:16, which opens today's lesson.

C. Lesson Context: Acts

The second account comes from the book of Acts. This book is Luke's record of the history of the first-century church. A vital part of what preceded the founding of the church (Acts 2) was a commission or charge given to the apostles before Jesus' ascension near Bethany (Luke 24:50, 51).

At first glance, the author Luke seems to record two locations for that event: Bethany, as above, and the Mount of Olives, per Acts 1:12. But no contradiction exists when we realize that Bethany was so close to the Mount of Olives that the village is said to be "at" the mount (Mark 11:1; Luke 19:29). This location was at least 60 miles south of Galilee, but less than two miles from Jerusalem. The tiny village of Bethany is mentioned 11 times in the New Testament, all occurrences being in the four Gospels.

The geographical contexts of our two lesson-segments are different, but the time frame is the same. Both occur during the 40 days of Acts 1:3. This period begins at Jesus resurrection and ends before Pentecost, when the church is established.

I. Commission in Matthew

(MATTHEW 28:16-20)

The location of our first lesson-segment is in accordance with the instructions from both the angel at the tomb and the resurrected Jesus himself (Matthew 28:7, 10).

A. Disciples Gather (vv. 16, 17)

16. Then the eleven disciples went away into Galilee, into a mountain where Jesus had appointed them.

With Judas no longer among their number, *the eleven disciples* make the multi-day trip back to *Galilee*. The text does not tell us which specific *mountain* this is.

17a. And when they saw him, they worshipped him.

Exactly how long after Jesus' resurrection this appearance takes place is also not clear. The first-day appearances are recorded in Matthew 28:9, 10; Mark 16:9-14; Luke 24:13-32; and John 20:19-25. The next recorded appearance was "after eight days" (John 20:26-29). Following that was an appearance to 7 of the 11 by the Sea of Galilee (John 21:1-23). The appearance to over 500 believers recorded in 1 Corinthians 15:6 may

HOW TO SAY IT

ascension	uh-*sen(t)*-shun.
Corinthians	Ko-*rin*-thee-unz (*th* as in *thin*).
Cornelius	Cor-*neel*-yus.
Emmanuel	Ee-*man*-you-el.
Galatians	Guh-*lay*-shunz.
Galilee	*Gal*-uh-lee.
Gentile	*Jen*-tile.
Judaea	Joo-*dee*-uh.
Pentecost	*Pent*-ih-kost.
Philippians	Fih-*lip*-ee-unz.
Pilate	*Pie*-lut.
Samaria	Suh-*mare*-ee-uh.
synecdoche	suh-***neck***-duh-*kee*.

occur between that of John 21 and the one in the text before us—much uncertainty exists.

17b. But some doubted.

Despite the previous appearances of Jesus, doubts persist. It would seem by this point that the 11 disciples are fully convinced that Jesus has risen from the dead. Therefore the group gathered here in Galilee may include other followers of Jesus, some of whom have not yet seen Him since His resurrection. One theory is that this occasion is also that of 1 Corinthians 15:6, just noted.

What Do You Think?
> What's the best way to react the next time doubts interfere with your worship? Why?

Digging Deeper
> Which of the following passages helps you most in this regard: Matthew 14:28-33; 21:21; Mark 9:24; John 20:24-29, James 1:6-8; Jude 20-25? Why?

B. Jesus Commands (vv. 18-20)

18. And Jesus came and spake unto them, saying, All power is given unto me in heaven and in earth.

Such a sweeping statement reflects Jesus' conquest of death (compare Revelation 1:18). The word in the original language behind the translation *power* is also translated "authority" in other contexts (examples: Matthew 7:29; 8:9). We may think of power as the ability to do something, while authority is the right to do something. Thus the two ideas are closely related, and Jesus has both in an absolute sense. Indeed, the word *all* dominates this section of three verses. There is nothing partial or halfway about anything here!

This has been clearly implied on many occasions throughout His ministry. His teaching in the Sermon on the Mount, for example, overturned commonly held views with the declaration, "But I say unto you . . ." (Matthew 5:22, 28, 32, 34, 39, 44). He had exercised power over disease, nature, and death. Now His own resurrection proves the claim beyond a shadow of a doubt. And what He claims is what He possessed in the beginning (John 1:1-3).

The fact that this power *is given* to Jesus implies that the heavenly Father, having sent the Son (Galatians 4:4), is the one who has given the Son all power and authority. What is implied here is unmistakable in Matthew 11:27; John 3:35; 13:3; 17:2; Ephesians 1:20-22; and Philippians 2:9-11.

> **What Do You Think?**
> In what ways can and will your choices in the coming week show that Christ is the ultimate authority and power in your life?
> *Digging Deeper*
> How can you make those choice also speak against popular alternative "authorities"?

19a. Go ye therefore, and teach all nations.

Jesus can do many things with the power and authority He has. He can take immediate vengeance on those who crucified Him. He can destroy the Roman occupiers and restore Israel's self-governing status. Jesus does indeed desire that *all nations* recognize and honor Him. But the method here is not that of brute force. Instead, He desires it to happen by means of teaching. The Greek verb translated *teach* is also translated as the English noun "disciple" in Matthew 27:57. Thus the task is one of disciple-making.

It is interesting to consider occasions during Jesus' ministry when He told someone who had been blessed by a miracle not to tell anyone (Matthew 8:3, 4; 9:29, 30; 12:15, 16; 17:9; etc.). The reason for this directive is seen in what happened when it was disobeyed: "Jesus could no more openly enter into the city, but was without in desert places" (Mark 1:45).

Now, however, the time for silence is over! The good news about Jesus is to be made known to everyone everywhere. Jesus had focused His three-year ministry on Israel (Matthew 10:5, 6; 15:21-24). But He has also indicated that His kingdom will be inclusive of all peoples (Matthew 8:11; Luke 13:29). This is nothing new, since Old Testament prophets predicted this (Isaiah 42:6; 49:6; Jeremiah 3:17; Daniel 7:14; Micah 4:2; etc.). This is how the promise to Abraham that "in thee shall all families of the earth be blessed" will be fulfilled (Genesis 12:3; compare Galatians 3:8).

> **What Do You Think?**
> What one thing extra can you do in the week ahead to help take the gospel to a nation other than your own?
> *Digging Deeper*
> What distractions might Satan offer to divert your attention from doing so?

19b. Baptizing them in the name of the Father, and of the Son, and of the Holy Ghost.

Making disciples is characterized, in part, by *baptizing* those being taught. The meaning and significance of baptism are addressed elsewhere (Acts 2:38; 19:4, 5; Romans 6:3, 4; Galatians 3:27; Colossians 2:12; 1 Peter 3:21; etc.). The stress here is submission and allegiance to *the Father, . . . the Son, and . . . the Holy Ghost.*

Obedience to this command is seen in Acts 8:36-38; 9:18; 16:33; 18:8; etc. But some students wonder why Peter will command baptism only "in the name of Jesus Christ" on the Day of Pentecost (Acts 2:38) and later (10:48). The fact that Peter does so indicates that he does not see a contradiction. It is clear from Jesus' teaching that Father, Son, and Holy Spirit are in complete unity with one another (John 16:12-15; compare 1 Peter 1:2). To baptize in the name of Jesus must include the other two.

❧ Figurative, Literal, Literalistic? ❧

I've spent much of my life as a teacher in Christian colleges. During those decades, my students have included some who doubted their faith, others who were solid Christians, and yet others who were so "solid" that they could not be swayed from an overly rigid approach to biblical truth.

For example, one student in the latter category said she believed that everything in the Bible should be "interpreted literally." In an attempt to help her see that figurative language such as hyperbole was in the Bible, I asked if she still had both eyes and both hands—in spite of what Jesus said in Matthew 5:29, 30.

She began to catch the idea, but still found it hard to give up her insistence on unbending literalism. Finally, she said, "OK, I literally believe some of the things in the Bible are figurative!" I suggested to her that what she was really trying to say was that she always approached the Bible seriously.

Some Christian fellowships struggle over the flexibility (or inflexibility) of Bible language. How can baptism administered "in Jesus' name" be as valid as baptism done "in the name of the Father, Son, and Holy Ghost"? The answer may lie in the category of figurative language known as *synecdoche*. That is a figure of speech where mention of a part is intended to refer to the whole or vice versa.

A serious acceptance of biblical truth must not require us to exercise a "one size fits all" method of interpretation to every verse in the Bible. When Jesus says "I am the door" in John 10:7, He is literally a door in the sense of being a portal or barrier between two areas. He is not a door in a literalistic sense of being made from wood and swinging on iron hinges!　　　　—C. R. B.

20a. Teaching them to observe all things whatsoever I have commanded you.

Teaching does not end once someone becomes a disciple of Jesus. Discipleship is in truth a school of lifelong learning from which one does not graduate while on this earth. Every follower of Jesus must continue to learn how to be Christ's person anew through the various stages of life—teenager, adult, spouse, parent, grandparent, widow(er), etc. Being a disciple of Jesus informs each transition, providing the disciple with additional opportunities to present the good news of Jesus to others.

20b. And, lo, I am with you alway, even unto the end of the world. Amen.

Jesus concludes what we call the Great Commission with the assurance of His presence at all times. Matthew mentions toward the beginning of his Gospel how Jesus' birth fulfilled the prophecy of Isaiah 7:14, that a virgin will give birth to a son who will be called Emmanuel (Matthew 1:22, 23), meaning "God with us." Now Matthew concludes his record with Jesus' assurance that He will be with His followers as they carry out the task He gives them.

II. Commission in Acts
(Acts 1:6-8)

In the first recorded words of Jesus in the book of Acts, He tells His apostles not to leave Jerusalem until the promised baptism of the Holy Spirit (Acts 1:4, 5). Our lesson picks up at this point. The 40-day period of Acts 1:3 is coming to a close.

A. Flawed Question (v. 6)

6. When they therefore were come together, they asked of him, saying, Lord, wilt thou at this time restore again the kingdom to Israel?

The word *therefore* connects the apostles' question with Jesus' teachings concerning "the kingdom of God" (Acts 1:3) and His promise that they will be "baptized with the Holy Ghost" (1:5). The very nature of the question reveals that the apostles just don't get it! Jesus has taught repeatedly, through both parable and direct teaching, that His kingdom is spiritual in nature. But these men are still thinking in terms of a political kingdom. They are anticipating a conqueror who will overthrow Rome and vanquish all enemies of Israel. They are expecting that the "glory days" experienced under King David will be restored.

B. First Priority (vv. 7, 8)

7. And he said unto them, It is not for you to know the times or the seasons, which the Father hath put in his own power.

Jesus had previously warned His disciples not to let themselves be distracted by a fascination with setting dates for His return (Matthew 24:36-44; 25:13). Here the issue is the establishment of His kingdom, but the warning remains the same: God is the ultimate timekeeper. Information such as this has been withheld from humanity.

> *What Do You Think?*
> What tactics might Satan use to get Christians distracted with end-times speculation?
> *Digging Deeper*
> Propose a defense to each tactic you imagine Satan might use.

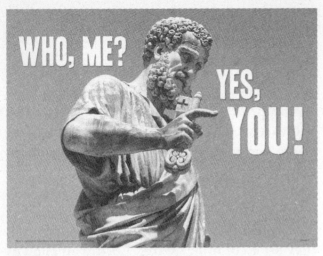

Visual for Lesson 9. *Have this visual clearly visible as you pose the discussion question associated with either Matthew 28:19a or Acts 1:8b.*

❧ SECRETS BEST KEPT THAT WAY ❧

"I'll tell you a secret, but you have to promise you won't tell anyone" is a guaranteed conversation starter. Who can resist the chance to learn a secret, especially if it's really juicy? Perhaps you've heard about the person who said, "I never say anything about anybody unless it's good, and let me tell you, this is really good!"

Jesus' parting words to His disciples included recognition of a secret: there are certain things regarding time lines that humans are not privileged (or burdened!) to know. That fact has troubled Christians ever since (compare 2 Thessalonians 2:1, 2). It seems that many of the first-century Christians understood Jesus to be saying He would return within their lifetimes (compare 2 Peter 3:3, 4). But when the last of the apostles had died, that perspective was proven false.

Even so, some modern Christians have asserted that Christ "returned" in a spiritual sense at the destruction of Jerusalem in AD 70. Various movements have been founded on the premise that Christ's return would be within the founders' lifetimes. Yet the secret remains a secret.

When the disciples asked Jesus to reveal the full secret, He told them, in effect, not to bother themselves with this issue. Instead, they were to focus on the task ahead and the supernatural help He was sending (see the next verse). Task or speculation—which do we focus on? —C. R. B.

8a. But ye shall receive power, after that the Holy Ghost is come upon you.

Jesus has a far more significant work for His followers to engage in than date-fixation. Their priority must be to *receive power* of the *Holy Ghost* (which happens on the Day of Pentecost; Acts 2). Thus Jesus makes sure that the distraction question of verse 6 hasn't caused them to miss His statement of verse 5.

8b. And ye shall be witnesses unto me both in Jerusalem, and in all Judaea, and in Samaria, and unto the uttermost part of the earth.

Many students of the Bible have noted that this sequence of places provides an outline of the gospel's progress as recorded by Luke in the book of Acts. The gospel is first preached by Peter *in Jerusalem* on the Day of Pentecost. The impact of that message is immediate as 3,000 are led to become followers of Jesus (Acts 2:41).

Later the movement expands into *Judaea* (the region in which Jerusalem is located) and *Samaria*. This is spurred by the persecution initiated by Saul, which forces the believers out of Jerusalem (Acts 8:1).

Taking the message *unto the uttermost part of the earth* begins with the conversion of Cornelius and his household (the first Gentile converts). It is furthered by the missionary journeys of Paul. On one such journey, He too will speak of the futility of being concerned with "the times and the seasons" (1 Thessalonians 5:1).

At the conclusion of Acts, Paul is in Rome—a location which at that time represents "the uttermost part." It marked a goal that Paul had been keenly intent on reaching (Acts 19:21; 23:11). The gospel was already there before Paul came. Of course, Paul was always thinking of new frontiers, such as Spain (Romans 15:23, 24) to which the gospel might be taken (compare 2 Corinthians 10:15, 16).

While the commissions of Jesus in Matthew and Acts differ in certain details, they have one crucial item in common: Jesus wants His followers to take His message of salvation to the entire world. That is to be the top priority for the apostles as the Day of Pentecost approaches. It must still be the church's top priority today.

Jesus' commission here is immediately followed by His ascension into Heaven. Luke records this both in his Gospel (Luke 24:51) and in the first chapter of Acts.

> *What Do You Think?*
> What practical steps can and will you take in the week ahead to become a more effective witness for the Lord?
> *Digging Deeper*
> In what ways can nonbiblical resources help you in this, if at all? Why?

Conclusion

A. What Only the Church Can Do

Dr. Joe Ellis was a highly respected and innovative authority on church growth. His books include *The Church on Purpose* and *The Church on Target,* both of which are intended to provide encouragement and practical guidelines for growth to congregations and their leadership.

One of Dr. Ellis's most insightful statements comes from another book he wrote entitled *The Personal Evangelist.* It is this: "The most important tasks the church can do are those that only the church can do."

What is it that the church, and only the church, can do? What makes the church unique?

The answer is that the church alone possesses and can pass along the message of salvation from sin. This message is founded on the facts of the death, burial, and resurrection of Jesus Christ. That is the good news, the gospel, as defined by Paul in 1 Corinthians 15:1-4.

No other organization or institution in the world declares, or is charged with declaring, such a message. And that is only fitting since Jesus' kingdom is "not of this world" (John 18:36). His final recorded words before ascending, as we have seen in this study, were that the gospel be taken to the entire world.

Today, however, the church is pulled in different directions by a host of causes and issues. Many of these causes and issues involve societal ills, a number of which most certainly should be addressed. The Bible is highly concerned with issues of social justice. Even so, the church must not compromise or forsake its primary mission: to take to a lost and dying world the good news of eternal life available through Jesus.

Acts 6:1-4 is a brilliant example of the tension. Two important social issues loomed: (1) providing food for widows in need and (2) ensuring fairness in the distribution of that food. The Jerusalem church took those issues seriously. But when the apostles said, "It is not reason that we should leave the word of God, and serve tables" (6:2), the primary mission remained unchanged. As the church makes disciples who in turn make disciples, then the church is accomplishing its primary mission.

The locations mentioned in Acts 1:8 can provide a model for any church's evangelistic strategy. A congregation must first seek to reach its own surroundings, but it must not be satisfied with that. The people must be challenged to expand the church's outreach. That involves thinking globally. Support through prayer, financial resources, and personal involvement will be the result.

A book title from several years ago stated an important truth: *Disciples Are Made, Not Born.* For a church to present itself as an attractive place to put one's membership is relatively easy. For a church to commit to making disciples is an entirely different matter. A church must strive always and consciously to keep the main thing the main thing. The head of the church, Jesus Christ, has given the church its marching orders. Those orders have never been amended. The issue is whether the church needs to amend its priorities. Thus it bears repeating: *the most important tasks the church can do are those that only the church can do.*

B. Prayer

Father, may we give the words of Jesus, the head of the church, the attention they (and He) deserve. We pray Your help to keep us focused on the Great Commission we have. We pray in Jesus' name. Amen.

C. Thought to Remember

Jesus' last words before ascending must be the church's first priority always.

INVOLVEMENT LEARNING

Enhance your lesson with KJV Bible Student *(from your curriculum supplier) and the reproducible activity page (at www.standardlesson.com or in the back of the* KJV Standard Lesson Commentary Deluxe Edition*).*

Into the Lesson

To every pair of participants, give one index card on which you have printed a story of personal tragedy or crisis. (Examples of tragedies: loss of job, cancer diagnosis, runaway child, loss of home, bankruptcy, divorce). Be sensitive to any recent tragedies a class member has experienced and avoid using that category.

Ask one member of each pair of learners to imagine going to a friend who has experienced the tragedy on the card. Ask, "How would you counsel without giving advice?" After a few minutes, reassemble the class for reactions. Possible discussion starters:

1–How confident were you in offering counsel?

2–What is most difficult for you to do when comforting a friend who has experienced a tragedy or crisis?

Alternative. Distribute copies of the "Now What?" activity from the reproducible page, which you can download. Have students work together to complete as indicated.

After either activity say, "Some events are so overwhelming that we are not sure what to do next! After the resurrection, Jesus gave the disciples clear directions about their next steps."

Into the Word

Divide students into groups of three to five. Give each group copies of the lesson's Scripture text. Also give each group a handout (you create) with these instructions for all groups: "Read the text and write the table of contents to a book called *What to Do and Not Do Until Jesus Returns*. Your table of contents should reflect a book of at least three chapters, depending on how you think the texts of Matthew 28:16-20 and Acts 1:6-8 should be approached. The entries for your table of contents will be the chapter titles in the book. Typically, such titles summarize a chapter's contents with just a few words."

Give as few hints as possible, but as many as necessary using elements of the following possible outline:

Chapter 1
The Authority's Identity, Clearly Established
(Matthew 28:16-18)

Chapter 2
The Authority's Directive, Clearly Defined
(Matthew 28:19, 20)

Chapter 3
The Authority's Plan, Clearly Stated
(Acts 1:6-8)

Have groups summarize their work in whole-class discussion. Ask these questions to probe deeper: 1–If we were to ask unbelievers what they think the task(s) of the church should be, how might they respond? 2–Why is that question important or unimportant?

Option. Follow the above by distributing copies of the "Translation, Please!" activity from the reproducible page to study pairs to be completed as indicated.

Make a transition to the Into Life segment by saying, "In leaving earth, Jesus gave His followers a clear commission—commands for the next steps to take until He returns. Let's look to see how well we are doing in keeping the main thing the main thing."

Into Life

Put these two phrases on the board as column headers: *What the Church Preaches / What the Church Does.* Brainstorm entries for the two columns. After two lists are compiled, ask the class to evaluate which items on the list should be marked **P**rimary, **S**econdary, and **N**onessential. Continue brainstorming steps to take to keep the main thing the main thing.

CALLED TO RIGHTEOUSNESS

DEVOTIONAL READING: John 10:1-11
BACKGROUND SCRIPTURE: Romans 3

ROMANS 3:21-31

21 But now the righteousness of God without the law is manifested, being witnessed by the law and the prophets;

22 Even the righteousness of God which is by faith of Jesus Christ unto all and upon all them that believe: for there is no difference:

23 For all have sinned, and come short of the glory of God;

24 Being justified freely by his grace through the redemption that is in Christ Jesus:

25 Whom God hath set forth to be a propitiation through faith in his blood, to declare his righteousness for the remission of sins that are past, through the forbearance of God;

26 To declare, I say, at this time his righteousness: that he might be just, and the justifier of him which believeth in Jesus.

27 Where is boasting then? It is excluded. By what law? of works? Nay: but by the law of faith.

28 Therefore we conclude that a man is justified by faith without the deeds of the law.

29 Is he the God of the Jews only? is he not also of the Gentiles? Yes, of the Gentiles also:

30 Seeing it is one God, which shall justify the circumcision by faith, and uncircumcision through faith.

31 Do we then make void the law through faith? God forbid: yea, we establish the law.

KEY VERSES

Being justified freely by his grace through the redemption that is in Christ Jesus: whom God hath set forth to be a propitiation through faith in his blood. —**Romans 3:24, 25**

DISCIPLESHIP AND MISSION

Unit 3: Call to Life in Christ

LESSONS 10–13

LESSON AIMS

After participating in this lesson, each learner will be able to:

1. Cite evidence that all have sinned.

2. Explain how God maintains His just nature while providing a way for sinful humans to be justified.

3. Sing with personal conviction a hymn that accurately summarizes God's grace as salvation.

LESSON OUTLINE

Introduction

    A. Universal Sinfulness

    B. Lesson Context

I. Just and Justifier (ROMANS 3:21-26)

    A. God's Righteousness (vv. 21-23)

        Past Tense Only?

    B. God's Grace (vv. 24-26)

II. Faith and Law (ROMANS 3:27-31)

    A. Boasting Excluded (vv. 27, 28)

    B. Jew and Gentile Included (vv. 29-31)

        Spiritual Elitism

Conclusion

    A. God's Dilemma

    B. Prayer

    C. Thought to Remember

Introduction

A. Universal Sinfulness

The theologian Reinhold Niebuhr (1892–1971) has often been quoted as saying, "The sad duty of politics is to establish justice in a sinful world," a maxim based in an article he wrote in 1937. Niebuhr, a keen student of the writings of the apostle Paul, insisted that political considerations, no matter how noble, would always be influenced by human sinfulness. He saw the tension between our desire for justice (serviced by politics) and our human tendencies toward pride, self-assertion, and conflict. With both Paul and Niebuhr, sin and justice were not partners but enemies.

In Romans 3, Paul looks at this tension between sin and justice from God's perspective.

B. Lesson Context

Paul wrote to the church in Rome in about AD 58, during his third missionary journey. He had not planted that church, but expressed a desire to visit. He envisioned Rome to be a future stop on his way to Spain for missionary work (Romans 15:24, 28). Paul did indeed come to Rome a couple of years later, but not as part of a missionary trip. Instead, He arrived under Roman guard due to his appeal to Caesar (Acts 25:9–28:16).

Rome was the center of an empire that encompassed most of the territories bordering the Mediterranean Sea, among others. Rome was a colossal city, the largest in the ancient world. Considerations of water, sanitation, and food supply limited the practical size of ancient cities, with just a handful being over 100,000 in population. Rome, however, was 10 times this size or more. Jews made up a significant minority of Rome's residents, perhaps as many as 10,000–20,000.

The church in Rome had a mixed membership of Jews and Gentiles. We can only guess at the church's size. Paul's greetings in Romans 16 list more than two dozen people by name, implying many more. It's reasonable to think of a church of several hundred—still a tiny fraction of the city's total population.

Paul wrote to prepare the church in Rome for his intended future visit. He was aware of issues between the Jews and Gentiles in the church and had words for both groups. In the process, Paul gave a thorough presentation of the gospel that he had been preaching. It was a message that had already influenced the Roman church through people such as Aquila and Priscilla (Romans 16:3; see Acts 18:2).

A central doctrinal concern for Paul was to demonstrate the universal sinfulness of humanity and the magnificent scope of God's plan for redemption of men and women from the consequences of this sin. Paul based his conclusions on both the historical facts of Jesus' life and proper interpretation of Jewish Scriptures. Today's lesson assumes the case for universal sinfulness has been made in Romans 1:18–3:20. With that foundation in place, the question that arises is how the sinless, holy God can rescue sinners from the wrath that divine justice requires. This weighty matter is the subject of this week's lesson.

I. Just and Justifier
(ROMANS 3:21-26)
A. God's Righteousness (vv. 21-23)

21. But now the righteousness of God without the law is manifested, being witnessed by the law and the prophets.

The two words *But now* mark an important transition. God had revealed part of His nature in the old covenant's system of *law*. But now, in the new covenant inaugurated by Christ's death (see below), God has revealed (*manifested*) more of His nature in a different way.

The now-revealed part of God's nature is called *the righteousness of God*. The meaning of this and closely related phrases shifts depending on context (see Romans 3:25, below). For the verse before us, Paul continues the sense of *the righteousness of God* that he used in Romans 1:17: God has now revealed the method by which people can be made permanently right with Him.

Although the plan Paul is about to describe is not based in the old law, that does not mean it is a new insight. It has indeed been *witnessed by* earlier Scripture, *the law and the prophets* (compare Acts 10:43).

22a. Even the righteousness of God which is by faith of Jesus Christ unto all and upon all them that believe.

Paul moves to the key element of his discourse concerning *the righteousness of God*, and that key element is *Jesus Christ*. Paul's description *faith of Jesus Christ* is vital, although it also presents an issue of proper interpretation: Does the phrase *faith of Jesus Christ* mean "the faith we put in Christ," or does it mean "the faithfulness Christ exhibited"?

Either is possible, but the former is supported by the same Greek phrasing in Galatians 2:16. There "faith" is contrasted with "works" as a means of being justified. But either way, Jesus is the point of interaction between God and humans.

We gain access to God through belief in Jesus. There are not multiple ways to make up for the fact of sin and be admitted into Heaven. There is not one system through the Law of Moses for the Jews along with a parallel system through faith in Christ. The reason why is given next.

22b, 23. For there is no difference: for all have sinned, and come short of the glory of God.

Just as there is *no difference* in the problem (*all have sinned*) and no difference in consequence (*come short of the glory of God*), so also there is no difference between Jews and Gentiles regarding the remedy.

❧ *PAST TENSE ONLY?* ❧

Many years ago, I was a guest preacher in a Midwest church when the church's minister was on vacation. After the service, one of the church's elders invited me to dinner. The meal was fine and the conversation was pleasant until the elder got on his doctrinal hobbyhorse. The topic he wanted to discuss was his belief that, since he was a mature Christian, he no longer sinned!

I had recently finished graduate school and was therefore studied up on my doctrine. I was also youthfully confident of its correctness, so I accepted the challenge to set him straight. When I quoted Romans 3:23, he pointed out that Paul's statement was in the past tense,* thus not applying to him on the day of our discussion.

We argued on, well past the point at which either of us was willing to give in. The battle of mind and will had hardened our positions. Looking back on that day, I can see that we both were so proud of our perspectives that we were proving Paul's point in coming short of the glory of God: Even our attempts to glorify God by being faithful to Scripture were being tainted by the sin of pride!

By the way, do you know the difference between a hobbyhorse and a real horse? You can get off a real horse! —C. R. B.

[*Note: the English translation "have sinned" is actually the present perfect tense. The Greek being translated is in the aorist tense, which is not always equivalent to the English past tense.]

> *What Do You Think?*
> What techniques can we use to help people understand the consequences of their sin?
> *Digging Deeper*
> Consider the varying techniques Paul used given the nature of his audience in different contexts.

We tend to think of God's glory in terms of brilliant, supernatural light or radiance (see Luke 2:9). Glory also has the sense of being worthy of praise, which God certainly is (Revelation 5:12). When we gain right standing with God through Christ, we also gain a measure of glory (2 Corinthians 3:18; 4:17). That fact comes full circle: when we are justified through faith in Christ, we bring glory to God; He alone is the proper object of worship (Romans 11:36).

> *What Do You Think?*
> In what ways can you bring glory to God as you serve others?
> *Digging Deeper*
> Will your answer change based on whether you are ministering to believers or unbelievers? Why, or why not?

B. God's Grace (vv. 24-26)
24a. Being justified freely by his grace.
Paul does not want his readers to forget the chasm of sin that is bridged by Christ. So in verses 24 and 25, Paul uses three weighty words to define our sin status and how it is overcome.

The first word is *justified,* a legal term of Paul's day. Although we are indeed guilty sinners, to be *justified freely by his grace* means to hear the great judge pronounce "guilty, but no penalty." We will not suffer the eternal consequences of our sin. The reason why comes next.

24b. Through the redemption that is in Christ Jesus.
Paul's second weighty word is *redemption.* This introduces the basis for the "no penalty" part of the great judge's pronouncement above. Part of the Old Testament usage background of the equivalent word in Hebrew occurs in contexts of being set free from bondage by intervention by a third party (examples: Leviticus 25:25; Deuteronomy 9:26).

As the meaning of the word shifts over the centuries, it comes to include the idea of paying a ransom to release the one who is in bondage (compare Mark 10:45; 1 Timothy 2:6; contrast Psalm 49:7-9). All this is building to Paul's conclusion regarding how exactly this redemption *is in Christ Jesus,* next.

25a. Whom God hath set forth to be a propitiation through faith in his blood.
Our salvation is possible because of *a propitiation,* Paul's third of three weighty words. This word is drawn from the system of sacrificing animals to atone for sins (example: Numbers 29:11). Such atonement was for the purpose of turning aside God's wrath. But that system was temporary.

If God's holy wrath comes down on us because of our sin, then we will pay the price in the eternal lake of fire (Revelation 20:13, 14). There is an alternative, but only one: Christ. He serves as the final and perfect atoning sacrifice for sins; His death satisfies any penalty our sins require (see 1 John 2:2; 4:10; compare Hebrews 9:11–10:18). But it's not automatic; rather, it becomes effective *through faith in his blood.* That thought is incomplete, however, without what Paul says next.

> *What Do You Think?*
> How will the reality of Christ's sacrifice influence your thoughts and actions in the week ahead?
> *Digging Deeper*
> Which Scriptures help you most in understanding the idea of propitiation or atonement? Why?

25b, 26. To declare his righteousness for the remission of sins that are past, through the forbearance of God; to declare, I say, at this time his righteousness: that he might be just, and the justifier of him which believeth in Jesus.

The two instances of *to declare* plus the two calendar references of *are past* and *at this time* lock these lines together. This helps us understand that the two instances of the phrase *his righteousness* refer to God's consistency. Whether past, present, or future, God's actions are always consistent with His character or nature.

Part of that consistency is God's merciful *forbearance,* a word related to "longsuffering" (see Romans 2:4). With rare exceptions (Acts 12:23; etc.), God does not punish sin immediately. His delay allows us a chance to repent (2 Peter 3:9, 15). But He does not postpone punishment indefinitely either. We have a choice to make: suffer eternal punishment for our sins or accept Christ's death on our behalf.

Paul caps his presentation of God's remedy for sin by giving us an ironic and wonderful truth. For God to be *just* means that the penalty for sin must be paid. For sin to go unpunished would mean that God is unjust. And indeed, sin's penalty has been paid—by Christ on the cross. Through the work of Christ, God retains His perfectly just nature while being *the justifier* of sinners.

A way of illustrating this is to imagine yourself before a judge who rightly imposes the death penalty on you for an offense you have committed. With your guilt beyond question, the only outcome is death so that the demands of justice will be satisfied. But as things turn out, the just judge is also a compassionate judge. So he decides to

HOW TO SAY IT

Aquila	*Ack*-wih-luh.
Caesar	*See*-zer.
Corinthians	Ko-*rin*-thee-unz (*th* as in *thin*).
Galatians	Guh-*lay*-shunz.
Gentiles	*Jen*-tiles.
Mediterranean	*Med*-uh-tuh-**ray**-nee-un.
Priscilla	Prih-*sil*-uh.
propitiation	pro-*pih*-she-**ay**-shun.

come down from the bench and die in your place. As a result, you go free. Justice is not lost, for the penalty is paid and God's holiness is upheld. We can be admitted into Heaven, thus demonstrating the triumph of God's love. In Christ, God pays for our sins through His Son's willing sacrifice for our sins. Thus God is both *just, and the justifier of him which believeth in Jesus.*

At this point, some will say, "But it's not fair for an innocent person to die in the place of a guilty person!" That's exactly right—it's *not* fair. What it is is *grace,* especially when we remember that Christ died voluntarily on our behalf. He didn't have to, but He did anyway.

II. Faith and Law
(ROMANS 3:27-31)
A. Boasting Excluded (vv. 27, 28)

27. Where is boasting then? It is excluded. By what law? of works? Nay: but by the law of faith.

Paul lays out practical implications for all he has just said, for both Jews and Gentiles. Some Jews may be clinging to a sense of religious superiority over their Gentile neighbors because they have the Law of Moses. Paul, a Jew himself, realizes that any law *of works* cannot possibly be a way to be justified. If anyone can and does keep the law perfectly, that person would have reason for boasting. But no one keeps the law perfectly; "all have sinned" (Romans 3:23).

But there is a law that does applies: *the law of faith.* Paul's language here drips with irony. We cannot be saved by keeping all the commands in the Law of Moses, thought to be 613 in number by Jewish scholars of the day. Instead, we have a law based on faith. Faith is not a work whereby we earn salvation. Rather, faith is putting trust and confidence in Jesus Christ as having secured our salvation on the cross (Romans 10:9, 10; Colossians 2:12-14).

28. Therefore we conclude that a man is justified by faith without the deeds of the law.

Paul does not believe the Jewish law is valueless. Its great value is in defining sin (Romans 7:7). Even so, lasting justification must come from some other quarter, and Paul has shown this to be faith in the person and atoning work of Jesus Christ. Therefore, Paul's inescapable conclusion is that justification and salvation are possible without reference to *deeds of the law*. This must be true whether the word *law* refers to the Law of Moses or any other religious or secular system based on law-keeping.

B. Jew and Gentile Included (vv. 29-31)

29. Is he the God of the Jews only? is he not also of the Gentiles? Yes, of the Gentiles also.

The status *of the Gentiles* (that is, everyone who is not a Jew) is clear. There is only one God, and He cannot be the God of only some people. The Gentiles have plenty of false gods in Paul's day (see Acts 14:12), but they are only fictitious substitutes for *the God of the Jews*. The one, supreme God, revealed in creation and in Jewish Scripture, is the only God. He is the Lord of both Jew and Gentile, for there is no alternative.

❧ SPIRITUAL ELITISM ❧

When I was a boy, my father served for many years as president of a Bible college. The small college's facilities were located adjacent to the campus of a state university. Dad was a friend of an administrator at the university, and one day they were discussing the church affiliations of the Bible college faculty and their counterparts at the university.

The university administrator said that, among Protestants, administrators tended to be affiliated with Denomination A, full professors were likely to be members of Denomination B, associate professors might be part of Denomination C or D. In other words, the church mirrored the social structure of the world to some extent. A form of elitism based on one's place in the educational hierarchy was at work in a person's choice of denominational affiliation.

The General Social Survey of 2016 notes that Americans' affiliation with mainline denominational Christianity fell from 28 percent to 10 percent between 1972 and 2016. Given that fact, the situation at that university may be very different now. However, we still face the problem the first-century church faced: some Christians consider themselves better than others. Such spiritual elitism may be based on one's income, education, social class, race, preference for a certain style of worship, etc. Regardless, it's all irrelevant to God. Since He looks at us without regard for where we fit in the world's pecking order, shouldn't we do so as well?
—C. R. B.

> **What Do You Think?**
> What steps can we take to stay alert to distinctions among people that in some way mirror the Jew/Gentile tension of Paul's day?
> **Digging Deeper**
> Distinguish between cultural viewpoints that are most likely to infect and divide the church vs. those less likely to do so.

30. Seeing it is one God, which shall justify the circumcision by faith, and uncircumcision through faith.

Paul draws on another common way of categorizing Jews and Gentiles: *circumcision . . . and uncircumcision*. This refers to the old covenant act for Jewish males that distinguished them physically from non-Jews. This verse is not about circumcision, however. It is about justification—being counted as righteous in the eyes of God. His plan is the same for both groups: *faith* (compare Romans 4:11, 12; Galatians 3:8).

Some have seen a distinction here in Paul's terms *by faith* and *through faith*. In the second instance, the original language has a definite article (a "the") that has not been translated. This could be understood to mean "through [that same] faith," referring back to the first instance of the word *faith* in this verse. Paul is not drawing a distinction, but an equivalence.

> **What Do You Think?**
> How might your perceptions of others change were you to remind yourself daily that God justifies in the same way all who are willing?
> **Digging Deeper**
> What Scripture passages or biblical principles help you think through how God's grace should affect our view of others?

31. Do we then make void the law through faith? God forbid: yea, we establish the law.

We are wrong to think that Paul is trashing the Jewish law so that it is to be jettisoned from the church altogether. His intention has never been to sever the church from its foundation in Jewish Scripture. Were he alive today, Paul would insist that the Old Testament has an indispensable place in the church. Without it, the concepts of sin, sacrifice, atonement, righteousness, and divine justice would have no anchor point. The doctrinal truths of Christianity would drift into chaos.

Therefore, the apostle reminds his readers in his closing comments of this section that his arguments do not *make void the law.* Indeed, Paul believes he has established the true purpose of the law: to define sin and the necessity for a remedy for human sinfulness.

Paul's treatment of the law is consistent with Jesus' claim that He came not to do away with the law, but to fulfill it (Matthew 5:17). The Jews of Paul's day undoubtedly contend that God gave them the law, and God's gifts are good, not evil. Paul agrees, but still insists that faith is the way to justification, not the keeping of the commands of the law.

Conclusion

A. God's Dilemma

Responsible parents know that children must sometimes be disciplined. Healthy discipline is not a release of a parent's anger. Rather it is an enforcement of family standards that allow a household to function harmoniously and a child to learn self-discipline.

This does not make disciplining children easy, however. A loving parent may struggle with imposing loss of privilege on a child. Some parents may think they are letting love win out when they avoid imposing punishment, believing that natural consequences for bad decisions will be adequate without parental consequences. From a biblical perspective, the parent who does not punish may be loving but is not being just. If lack of parental-imposed consequences stems from a parent's desire to avoid conflict, it is not even loving.

Visual for Lesson 10 & 11. *Use this visual as a backdrop as you discuss the distinction between 'guilty, but no penalty' and 'not guilty.'*

Our Lord God is both loving and just. Both are essential to His nature. Humans, through their sin, create a dilemma for God. How can God maintain both His love and justice in the face of that sin? Sin leads to eternal death according to God's just and holy nature, but how can a loving God consign those created in His image to eternal punishment?

The solution is God's Son. Jesus' death on the cross allows both God's justice and love to be preserved. The wrath of God, called forth by the necessity for justice, is satisfied by the sacrifice of Jesus, the gift of God's love. Our sin debt is paid.

Perhaps you are familiar with the old hymn titled "I Am So Glad That Salvation's Free," by James Rowe. Salvation is indeed free—to us. But it was not free to God. The cost to Him was enormous. There is no truth of which we should remind ourselves of more often!

B. Prayer

Heavenly Father, so often we let our days pass without concern for our eternal destiny. Keep us mindful that a day of judgment is coming. May we be counted righteous on that day by grace made possible by Your Son. We pray this in His glorious name. Amen.

C. Thought to Remember

Let us leave guilt, embrace forgiveness, and live in God's grace.

INVOLVEMENT LEARNING

Enhance your lesson with KJV Bible Student (from your curriculum supplier) and the reproducible activity page (at www.standardlesson.com or in the back of the KJV Standard Lesson Commentary Deluxe Edition).

Into the Lesson

Write the following on the board:

Authoritarian Parent: "Do it because I say so!"

Permissive Parent: "Do whatever you want; it will be OK."

Authoritative Parent: "Haven't we discussed the rules and the consequences for breaking them?"

Ask class members to give examples of times they have seen each in action, without mentioning names. After a few examples are offered, ask, "Under what conditions might a situation call for an authoritarian or permissive parent to shift to an authoritative style?"

Possible responses—An authoritarian parent who sets strict curfews without exception and a permissive parent who never set curfews should shift to an authoritative style when certain factors call for case-by-case exceptions. The authoritative style engages the child in dialogue, considering carefully the plea for an extended curfew, but requiring that the child assure the parent that adequate adult supervision exists for activities that exceed the normal curfew.

Alternative. Distribute copies of the "Justice Without Pity" activity from the reproducible page, which you can download. Allow students no more than one minute to complete the activity individually.

After either activity, say, "We understand that behavior has to have consequences. We also want to show mercy to those who do wrong, because we know that we all make mistakes. Today we take a look at how the tension between God's justice and love toward sinners are resolved by a perfect plan."

Into the Word

Have students read the text as it is segmented in the commentary. Then test their understanding by having them summarize each segment regarding God's plan of salvation. (*Option.* You can refer to these summaries as paraphrases.) Write the paraphrases sequentially on the board. You will want your final list to look something like this:

21: God makes known a new process
22a: Jesus is our point of interaction with God
22b, 23: Everyone has the same problem: sin
24a: Everyone is offered the same solution: grace
24b: Pardon for sin is in Jesus
25a: Jesus' death turns away God's wrath
25b, 26: God is consistent in His actions toward sin
27: No room for human self-congratulation
28: Faith, not works, is the key
29: There is only one God and plan for everyone
30: Faith is the key for everyone
31: Faith does not mean that the law is out

Option. Follow the above by distributing copies of the "Sort 'em Out" activity from the reproducible page. Use this as a whole-class activity if your class is small; larger classes can use small groups. Introduce the activity by saying, "This activity will help determine if you can distinguish between permissive, legalistic, and biblical views of sin."

After the ensuing discussion, say, "Today's lesson text sets forth the Bible's view of righteousness, sin, and justification by grace. This has allowed us to see how we get in right standing before God, the seriousness of sin, and the depth of God's love. So how do we respond?"

Into Life

From a hymnal or online source, find the lyrics to a few hymns that speak of God's plan of salvation through Jesus. Some possibilities are "Blessed Assurance," "Heaven Came Down [and Glory Filled My Soul]," "There Is a Fountain," "Rock of Ages," and "Victory in Jesus."

Close the class by singing a verse from a few of these salvation-focused hymns. Pause between hymns to evaluate the accuracy of the lyrics against the Bible text.

Called to Life in the Spirit

DEVOTIONAL READING: Romans 6:1-14
BACKGROUND SCRIPTURE: Romans 8

Romans 8:1-14

1 There is therefore now no condemnation to them which are in Christ Jesus, who walk not after the flesh, but after the Spirit.

2 For the law of the Spirit of life in Christ Jesus hath made me free from the law of sin and death.

3 For what the law could not do, in that it was weak through the flesh, God sending his own Son in the likeness of sinful flesh, and for sin, condemned sin in the flesh:

4 That the righteousness of the law might be fulfilled in us, who walk not after the flesh, but after the Spirit.

5 For they that are after the flesh do mind the things of the flesh; but they that are after the Spirit the things of the Spirit.

6 For to be carnally minded is death; but to be spiritually minded is life and peace.

7 Because the carnal mind is enmity against God: for it is not subject to the law of God, neither indeed can be.

8 So then they that are in the flesh cannot please God.

9 But ye are not in the flesh, but in the Spirit, if so be that the Spirit of God dwell in you. Now if any man have not the Spirit of Christ, he is none of his.

10 And if Christ be in you, the body is dead because of sin; but the Spirit is life because of righteousness.

11 But if the Spirit of him that raised up Jesus from the dead dwell in you, he that raised up Christ from the dead shall also quicken your mortal bodies by his Spirit that dwelleth in you.

12 Therefore, brethren, we are debtors, not to the flesh, to live after the flesh.

13 For if ye live after the flesh, ye shall die: but if ye through the Spirit do mortify the deeds of the body, ye shall live.

14 For as many as are led by the Spirit of God, they are the sons of God.

Key Verse

There is therefore now no condemnation to them which are in Christ Jesus. —**Romans 8:1**

DISCIPLESHIP AND MISSION

Unit 3: Call to Life in Christ

LESSON AIMS

After participating in this lesson, each learner will be able to:

1. State two benefits for those who live by the Spirit.

2. Explain Paul's distinction between living by the Spirit and living by the flesh.

3. Identify a specific area where he or she is not living according to God's Spirit and make a plan to change.

LESSON OUTLINE

Introduction
    A. Spiritual but Not Religious
    B. Lesson Context
I. Law of the Spirit (ROMANS 8:1-4)
    A. Freedom from Sin (vv. 1, 2)
       Guilt Without Condemnation
    B. Weakness of the Law (vv. 3, 4)
II. Indwelling of the Spirit (ROMANS 8:5-11)
    A. Life and Peace (vv. 5-8)
    B. Four Facts (vv. 9-11)
III. Leading of the Spirit (ROMANS 8:12-14)
    A. The Good Kind of Debt (vv. 12, 13)
    B. The Right Kind of Status (v. 14)
       Led by the Spirit?
Conclusion
    A. Flesh and Spirit
    B. Prayer
    C. Thought to Remember

Introduction

A. Spiritual but Not Religious

For the last couple of decades, researchers have detected an increase in spiritual interest among people, but little or no increase in church affiliation or attendance. Some identify themselves as "spiritual but not religious" (SBNR). This usually means they have personal beliefs and practices that could be understood as "spiritual," but have no desire to participate with what they see as "institutional religion."

Some SBNR folks desire their own religious world apart from a church. This desire is not necessarily Christian in orientation, however. It often borrows spiritual practices from Eastern religions, Native American traditional religions, or ancient pagan sources. The good news: a spiritual thirst exists out there. The bad news: the church is not being seen as the source for quenching that thirst. The insights of the apostle Paul are decisive in overturning this outlook—today's lesson.

B. Lesson Context

The baseline for last week's lesson from Romans 3 was that all men and women are sinners. Even so, God has made a way for us to be counted righteous in His eyes.

In the texts that intervene between that lesson and this week's, Paul went on to examine the life of the great ancestor of the Jews: Abraham. The key verse in that regard is that "Abraham believed God, and it was counted unto him for righteousness" (Romans 4:3, quoting Genesis 15:6; compare Romans 4:22). Abraham's righteousness came through his faith. And that was before he was circumcised (Genesis 17:24) and long before the law was given through Moses.

Paul thereby concludes that faith (as opposed to works) is the God-established pathway to right standing with Him. This pathway predates both circumcision and the law. Abraham was essentially a Gentile when God reckoned him as righteous, since Israel did not exist at the time. This fact undercuts any argument that proposes keeping the Law of Moses is the way to earn God's favor and attain right standing with Him.

In the chapters from Romans that follow, Paul discusses the three terrifying tyrants of humanity: sin, the law, and death. Sin had dominion over us, but we are freed by the grace of God (Romans 6:14). Sin held out the terror of death as its consequences (6:16, 23). The law enslaved us, but we have been freed to a new life (7:6).

Paul ends Romans 7 with an expression of sincere gratitude for his deliverance from the bondage of sin and the law (Romans 7:25). As he does so, he prepares to address further the issue of the three tyrants.

I. Law of the Spirit
(ROMANS 8:1-4)
A. Freedom from Sin (vv. 1, 2)

1a. There is therefore now no condemnation to them which are in Christ Jesus.

The opening *therefore* connects what follows with the now-powerless tyrants noted in the Lesson Context. The fact stated by this verse means, among other things, that the law no longer has power to judge us as requiring punishment. The punishment we have escaped *in Christ Jesus* is the sentence of eternal death due to our sin (see last week's lesson; compare Romans 5:21).

❧ *GUILT WITHOUT CONDEMNATION* ❧

An article in the online edition of *The Washington Post* of August 26, 2017, carried this intriguing title: "Is accepting a pardon an admission of guilt?" The short answer: it's complicated.

On the one hand, the U.S. Supreme Court declared in 1915 that acceptance of a pardon carries with it a confession of guilt. A pardon therefore releases a person from penalty for a crime, but it does not change a "guilty" verdict to "not guilty."

On the other hand is the case of Keith Cooper, sentenced in 1997 to 40 years in prison for robbery. As the years passed, mounting evidence prompted the governor of Indiana to pardon Cooper in 2017 for being "innocent of that crime."

A dictionary definition of pardon is "release from the legal penalties of an offense." Consider also Numbers 14:19: "Pardon . . . the iniquity of this people . . . as thou hast forgiven this people, from Egypt even until now." Pardon and forgiveness are the same; wrongdoing is admitted, but relief from penalty is requested nevertheless. What the factually innocent Mr. Cooper should have received was not a pardon but full exoneration.

Sinners who stand before the judge of the universe, however, cannot expect exoneration for the simple fact that we *are* guilty of sin. But Christians have the next best thing: no condemnation despite our guilt. How often does realization of this fact shake you to your core?   —R. L. N.

> *What Do You Think?*
> In what ways will you live differently in the week ahead given the realization that there is "now no condemnation" for you?
> *Digging Deeper*
> Frame your response in terms of one pattern each of behavior, speech, and thought.

1b. Who walk not after the flesh, but after the Spirit.

Many early manuscripts do not have this half verse. But we know that its content is original with Paul since its thought is reflected again in Romans 8:4, below; see commentary there.

2. For the law of the Spirit of life in Christ Jesus hath made me free from the law of sin and death.

The opening *for* introduces Paul's reasoning for the claim he makes in the previous verse. That claim is based in a contrast of two laws we see here.

Paul has used this approach before, and Bible students naturally have attempted to match them

HOW TO SAY IT

Corinthians	Ko-*rin*-thee-unz (*th* as in *thin*).
Ephesians	Ee-*fee*-zhunz.
Galatians	Guh-*lay*-shunz.
Lamentations	Lam-en-*tay*-shunz.
Pentecost	*Pent*-ih-kost.
Philippians	Fih-*lip*-ee-unz.
shalom (*Hebrew*)	shah-*lome*.
Thessalonians	*Thess*-uh-**lo**-nee-unz (*th* as in *thin*).

up. For example, is *the law of the Spirit of life in Christ Jesus* here the same as "the law of faith" in Romans 3:27a? Is *the law of sin and death* here the same as the "law . . . of works" in 3:27b and/or "the law of sin which is in my members" in 7:23?

Both *yes* and *no* conclusions are based on complicated analyses of the Greek text, and good arguments can be made in both directions. But perhaps more to Paul's point is what we might call "dominion transfer." This idea (1) recognizes our new status as having been transferred from the dominion of sin and death to the dominion of life in Christ and (2) the agent of that liberation is *the Spirit*.

Some may object to this idea on the basis of seeming contradiction with the observation that Christ is the one who is the agent of liberation. To clarify, we look again at the beginning of the verse and the New Testament as a whole: the Spirit is indeed the one who gives life (see Romans 8:10, 13, below; compare Galatians 6:8; Titus 3:5, 6). But that work happens only within the context of the sin-penalty having been paid by Christ. So that there's no mistaking the foundational work of Christ, Paul is quick to stress it again (next verse).

> *What Do You Think?*
> How will you witness to someone who doesn't accept the Bible's categories of sin and freedom from it?
> *Digging Deeper*
> How does Paul's change of tactics between Acts 17:2, 3 and 17:22-31 inform your response?

B. Weakness of the Law (vv. 3, 4)

3. For what the law could not do, in that it was weak through the flesh, God sending his own Son in the likeness of sinful flesh, and for sin, condemned sin in the flesh.

Paul has no argument with the integrity of the Jewish law. He has said it is good and holy (Romans 7:12). The weak link is in our keeping of *the law*. Our fleshly nature presents a problem not because it is inherently evil, but because it is weak. Our weakness negates any sort of saving power the law might represent (compare 7:18, 19).

God's remedy for this weakness was to send *his own Son*. Our situation was dire and hopeless. The law can only condemn. No human being can overcome sin. So God provided one who *condemned sin in the flesh,* one who could live a victorious, sinless life. This is the act of the incarnation, the Son of God assuming human form according to God's plan (see Galatians 4:4, 5).

Paul chooses his words carefully. Jesus came *in the likeness of sinful flesh*—He appeared, physically, like any other man of His day. Had we seen Him, we would have wrongly assumed Him to be a sinner just like us. He was truly human, but without sin (2 Corinthians 5:21).

Jesus had full awareness that His mission included His death as a sacrifice for sin, paying the price for our salvation (Mark 10:45; 1 Timothy 2:6). This price could not be paid unless Jesus died as a human (compare Hebrews 2:14, 17).

4. That the righteousness of the law might be fulfilled in us, who walk not after the flesh, but after the Spirit.

The righteous requirements of *the law* are not discarded but *fulfilled* through Christ. This fulfillment finds its expression *in us* because we are the beneficiaries of being justified (counted as righteous). The law maintains its righteousness without compromise while losing its power to condemn. The differences between those *who walk . . . after the Spirit* and those who do not come next.

> *What Do You Think?*
> What are some ways we can make ourselves more open to the Spirit's influence?
> *Digging Deeper*
> How do John 14:15-18; Galatians 5:16-26; Ephesians 4:29-32; 1 Thessalonians 5:19; and 1 John 4:1 inform your response?

II. Indwelling of the Spirit
(ROMANS 8:5-11)
A. Life and Peace (vv. 5-8)

5a. For they that are after the flesh do mind the things of the flesh.

Paul gives examples of *the things of the flesh* in Galatians 5:19-21. Those "whose God is their belly" are focused on "earthly things" (Philippians 3:19). Such people existed in the Old Testament era (example: Isaiah 56:11, 12), and, as we know all too well, they still exist today.

5b. But they that are after the Spirit the things of the Spirit.

The word *they* does not refer to people who are so spiritual as to ignore bodily needs such as food, sleep, and clothing. It refers, rather, to those who are not controlled by such desires. Their primary focus is achieving spiritual intimacy with God. They find ways to do His will rather than their own. Paul gives examples in Galatians 5:22-25.

6a. For to be carnally minded is death.

To be carnally minded is to focus on the bodily impulses of the moment. Paul has previously noted that "the end" (that is, result of) of such shameful behavior "is death" (Romans 6:21). The wording in the text before us is even stronger: it equates carnal mindedness with *death* itself.

6b. But to be spiritually minded is life and peace.

By contrast, those who are *spiritually minded* have a certain kind of *life and peace* that the carnally minded do not. Paul expands on what he means by life in Galatians 6:8: "He that soweth to the Spirit shall of the Spirit reap life everlasting" (compare Romans 8:13, below). This kind of life removes our fear of death. That, in turn, results in us having peace about our future.

The way Paul uses the Greek word translated *peace* carries a significant difference from how the pagan world of his day uses it. For pagans, the word points primarily to outward peace, as in the absence of war or civil unrest. But Paul uses the word in terms of how the Greek Old Testament translates *shalom,* from the Hebrew Old Testament. In this sense, peace is more than the absence of strife. One who has the *shalom* kind of peace has inner contentment that results from having the blessings of God (Isaiah 48:18; etc.). Those who live by the Spirit have such peace.

7a. Because the carnal mind is enmity against God: for it is not subject to the law of God.

Visual for Lesson 10 & 11. *Use this visual as a backdrop to comparing and contrasting the words* condemn, pardon, forgiveness, *and* exoneration.

With the opening *because,* Paul moves from describing *what is so* to explaining *why it is so.* As we examine the two phrases *the carnal mind* and *enmity against God,* we notice that Paul does not say that one results in the other (contrast Romans 6:21, 22). Rather, he simply equates the two; to be one is to be the other. James 4:4 is quite similar in equating "friendship of the world" with "enmity with God."

The law of God plays a defining role in all this. For the law to have been nailed to the cross (Colossians 2:14) means for Christians that our penalty for breaking the law has already been paid. But the law doesn't disappear as a standard of conduct. For example, the sin of partiality or favoritism under the old covenant (Exodus 23:3; Leviticus 19:15) is still sinful law-breaking under the new covenant (James 2:1, 9).

To live by the principles of the world is to live as if God's law and the sin it defines do not exist. To live in such a way is to attempt to be a law unto oneself (compare Romans 10:3; 2 Corinthians 10:2, 12). And a focus on self is idolatry.

7b, 8. Neither indeed can be. So then they that are in the flesh cannot please God.

The phrase *neither indeed can be* concludes an inability to relate to the law as just discussed. Pleasing God is the only reasonable choice we can make (compare Galatians 1:10; 1 Thessalonians 2:4; 4:1). If we reject the way of faith, we will never *please God* (see Hebrews 11:6). What we do with this freewill choice is the most critical decision one can make (Matthew 23:37; John 3:16; etc.).

B. Four Facts (vv. 9-11)

9. But ye are not in the flesh, but in the Spirit, if so be that the Spirit of God dwell in you. Now if any man have not the Spirit of Christ, he is none of his.

The phrases *ye are not in the flesh, but in the Spirit* reflects Paul's assumption that those to whom he writes have "crucified the flesh with the affections and lusts" (Galatians 5:24). The dominion concept in commentary to Romans 8:2, above, presents itself again. A person is either within the dominion of the flesh or that of the Spirit. There is no in between, and four facts are important.

Fact 1 is that *the Spirit of God* indwells the Christian. This is spiritual language, but that does not take away from its reality. The Holy Spirit cannot be detectable by scientific instruments, but is present nonetheless as a constant influence. While we may be able to quench the Spirit and dull its influence (1 Thessalonians 5:19), our faith guarantees the Spirit's presence (see 2 Corinthians 1:22; 5:5). Paul also calls God's Spirit *the Spirit of Christ.* This is not a different person. The Holy Spirit is God's Spirit and Christ's Spirit.

Fact 2 is that the lack of the Holy Spirit's presence means a person *is none of his.* The Holy Spirit is God's mark of His chosen (Ephesians 1:14). There is no such thing as a Christian believer without the indwelling presence of the Holy Spirit; that would be a contradiction in terms.

10. And if Christ be in you, the body is dead because of sin; but the Spirit is life because of righteousness.

Fact 3 is that we can have a living, vibrant relationship with God in the here and now. This is possible despite the fact that our bodies are *dead because of sin* (Romans 5:12). What makes such a relationship possible is the imputed righteousness Christians have by means of Christ's death (3:21-26). *The Spirit is life!*

Interestingly, Paul makes no difference between the Holy Spirit's indwelling a believer and *Christ be in you.* To have the constant presence of the

Holy Spirit is to have the presence of Christ in a real way. There is one God in three persons (see Matthew 28:19).

11. But if the Spirit of him that raised up Jesus from the dead dwell in you, he that raised up Christ from the dead shall also quicken your mortal bodies by his Spirit that dwelleth in you.

Fact 4 is that the presence of God's Spirit assures Christians of resurrection life, life beyond the day our current *mortal bodies* expire. The only way this happens is through *the Spirit of him that raised up Jesus from the dead* (compare John 5:21). Eternal life is not mentioned here as such, but it is implied. After all, what point would there be in being raised from the dead only to die yet again later?

III. Leading of the Spirit
(Romans 8:12-14)

A. The Good Kind of Debt (vv. 12, 13)

12, 13. Therefore, brethren, we are debtors, not to the flesh, to live after the flesh. For if ye live after the flesh, ye shall die: but if ye through the Spirit do mortify the deeds of the body, ye shall live.

Paul stresses a choice, a choice sharpened by his use of *debtors* terminology. This word can refer to financial obligations (as in Matthew 18:24). But Paul uses it in the sense of moral obligations (compare Romans 1:14; 15:27; Galatians 5:3). His readers, *brethren* in Christ, indeed have such an obligation. Since that obligation is *not to the flesh, to live after the flesh,* then it must be to the only other choice: *the Spirit.* That obligation is to kill *the deeds of the body.* This is Paul's great plea. Life in *the Spirit* must include rejecting self-centered impulses approved by the world (compare Colossians 2:20-23). Those who do fail to do so are aptly described by Paul's list in 2 Timothy 3:1-8.

This self-mortification is not easy. It is a complete reorientation of our priorities with God as the focus. We could never do this by our own willpower. It must happen *through the Spirit.* God does not expect us to live the spiritually pleasing life without giving us the resource we need to be successful. Through the leadership of the Holy Spirit, we are able truly to live and produce the deeds of a godly life (Galatians 5:22-25).

> **What Do You Think?**
>   What warning signs should we be alert to that indicate a fellow believer is slipping back into the deadness of life before the Spirit?
>
> **Digging Deeper**
>   Under what circumstances should a church's intervention to help reverse the problem give way to disfellowshipping to protect the congregation as a whole? Consider in your response Matthew 7:1-5, 15-20; 18:15-17; Romans 2:1-4; 14:1–15:2; 16:17, 18; 1 Corinthians 5:11-13; 2 Thessalonians 3:14, 15; 1 Timothy 6:3, 4; and Titus 3:10.

B. The Right Kind of Status (v. 14)

14. For as many as are led by the Spirit of God, they are the sons of God.

To "live by the Spirit" or "walk in the Spirit" is to be *led by the Spirit of God.* We live to serve God according to His direction, not according to our own desires. Then we are *sons of God,* with all the privileges a child of the king may expect. We are heirs (Romans 8:17; Galatians 4:7).

We remind ourselves that by the phrase "the flesh" Paul is referring not just to self-centered lusts, etc. He is also referring more broadly to the "world" as he uses that word in Colossians 2:8.

⁂ LED BY THE SPIRIT? ⁂

My cousin, a minister himself, tells of a preacher friend who was invited to speak at a church that had no fixed order of worship. Instead, what happened in a worship service depended on when and how the participants "felt the Spirit moving."

The service began with everyone sitting quietly. Eventually, someone began to sing a hymn, and the congregation joined in. More silence followed. Then someone prayed. More silence. Another hymn. Then came a very long silence followed by a prayer offered by the man who had issued the invitation to the guest speaker. It was obvious that this prayer was a benediction.

After the "amen," the congregation filed out. The would-be speaker approached the man who had invited him to speak and said, "I thought I was supposed to speak." The response: "I thought so too. But finally I decided you didn't feel the Spirit leading you to speak!"

There is a lot more to being "led by the Spirit" than whether one is moved to pray or sing or speak in a worship service. In fact, if our Sunday morning conduct doesn't match that of our daily conduct, something is wrong. Here's a hint: it's not the Holy Spirit who is leading you to live a double life!   —C. R. B.

> **What Do You Think?**
>   What guardrails can we erect to ensure that our living by the Spirit doesn't become a "holier than thou" hindrance to our witness?
>
> **Digging Deeper**
>   How should Paul's stance of being "all things to all men" in order to "save some" (1 Corinthians 9:22) inform your response, if at all?

Conclusion

A. Flesh or Spirit?

Living above the principles of the world is not easy. A media-saturated society surrounds us with opportunities to gratify the flesh. Hungry? Gluttons are welcome at the all-you-can-eat buffet. Sexually anxious? Check out the Internet with your private web browser turned on. Need money for a luxury car? Play the lottery.

Some enticements may not be sinful in and of themselves. But they all can appeal to a persuadable (weak?) part of our nature. They tempt us to take our eyes off God. They have no view of eternity. Let us walk by the Spirit, not the flesh.

B. Prayer

Father, strengthen us this day to live by Your Spirit and nothing else. We pray this in the name of Jesus, the one who died for us. Amen.

C. Thought to Remember

Yield control to God's Spirit.

INVOLVEMENT LEARNING

Enhance your lesson with KJV Bible Student (from your curriculum supplier) and the reproducible activity page (at www.standardlesson.com or in the back of the KJV Standard Lesson Commentary Deluxe Edition).

Into the Lesson

Write the following on the board for learners to consider as they arrive:

Guilt—the gift that keeps on giving.

Discuss the quip as you ask how class members have experienced its truth; jot responses on the board. (*Possible responses among many*: sleep disturbance; indigestion; damaged relationships.)

At appropriate points, pose the following questions individually, allowing for responses before asking the next one:

1–What are some things that someone might feel guilty about but should not?

2–What are some things that *should* inspire a degree of guilt?

3–What happens when we do not deal with guilt?

Alternative. Distribute copies of the "Syllables" activity from the reproducible page, which you can download. Have students work in pairs or groups to piece together the answers to the clues and discover the possible cause of the maladies found there.

After either activity say, "Feelings of guilt can haunt us, destroy relationships, and even compromise our health! Paul describes a life free of guilt and condemnation."

Into the Word

Divide the class into three groups (larger classes can form six or nine groups). Designate these as *Flesh Group, Mind Group,* and *Spirit Group.* Give each group handouts (you create) that reproduce the text of the lesson. Instruct groups to read the lesson text and underline every instance of the word for which their group is named. Each group should then summarize in one or more rhyming couplets how the text uses its key word. Some examples follow. Reveal these only as learners seem stuck.

Flesh Group
Flesh is too weak to keep God's law.
    Making one's efforts worth nothing at all.

Mind Group
A carnal mind will cause life to cease,
    But a mind set on Jesus brings eternal peace.

Spirit Group
Since the Holy Spirit lives always in me,
    From law's condemnation I'm forever free.

As groups work, move among them to offer help as necessary. When group work is complete, allow groups to share and explain their couplets.

Alternative. Distribute copies of the "Just Because" activity from the reproducible page. Have students work in groups to paraphrase key ideas from Paul's arguments.

After either activity say, "It is possible to live a life free of guilt and condemnation. But it is something done by divine power, not by human effort. Our life can be transformed, putting our flesh-controlled life to death and allowing God's Spirit to direct our path. We no longer must earn God's approval, but rather accept His leading. Could there be a step you can take this week to give the Spirit more control of your life? Let's see."

Into Life

Write *Step Forward / Step Back* as two column headings on the board. Ask the class to complete these columns by naming things a person can do to "step forward" in his or her walk in the Spirit and things a person can do to "step back" from a flesh-driven habit. When columns have several answers each, ask the class to consider silently which steps would be appropriate for them to take personally in the coming week.

Option. As learners depart, give each a novelty item that will be a tangible reminder to walk in the Spirit daily. Ideal would be a pendant or sticker of a shoe or footprint. These can be purchased inexpensively from "dollar stores," etc.

CALLED TO
MUTUAL ACCEPTANCE

DEVOTIONAL READING: Romans 10:5-13
BACKGROUND SCRIPTURE: Romans 11

ROMANS 11:11-24

11 I say then, Have they stumbled that they should fall? God forbid: but rather through their fall salvation is come unto the Gentiles, for to provoke them to jealousy.

12 Now if the fall of them be the riches of the world, and the diminishing of them the riches of the Gentiles; how much more their fulness?

13 For I speak to you Gentiles, inasmuch as I am the apostle of the Gentiles, I magnify mine office:

14 If by any means I may provoke to emulation them which are my flesh, and might save some of them.

15 For if the casting away of them be the reconciling of the world, what shall the receiving of them be, but life from the dead?

16 For if the firstfruit be holy, the lump is also holy: and if the root be holy, so are the branches.

17 And if some of the branches be broken off, and thou, being a wild olive tree, wert graffed in among them, and with them partakest of the root and fatness of the olive tree;

18 Boast not against the branches. But if thou boast, thou bearest not the root, but the root thee.

19 Thou wilt say then, The branches were broken off, that I might be graffed in.

20 Well; because of unbelief they were broken off, and thou standest by faith. Be not highminded, but fear:

21 For if God spared not the natural branches, take heed lest he also spare not thee.

22 Behold therefore the goodness and severity of God: on them which fell, severity; but toward thee, goodness, if thou continue in his goodness: otherwise thou also shalt be cut off.

23 And they also, if they abide not still in unbelief, shall be graffed in: for God is able to graff them in again.

24 For if thou wert cut out of the olive tree which is wild by nature, and wert graffed contrary to nature into a good olive tree: how much more shall these, which be the natural branches, be graffed into their own olive tree?

KEY VERSE

Boast not against the branches. But if thou boast, thou bearest not the root, but the root thee.

—**Romans 11:18**

DISCIPLESHIP AND MISSION

Unit 3: Call to Life in Christ
LESSONS 10–13

LESSON AIMS

After participating in this lesson, each learner will be able to:

1. Describe the components of Paul's analogy of the olive trees.

2. Explain the inclusive nature of God's grace.

3. Repent of self-congratulatory pride.

LESSON OUTLINE

Introduction

A. "It's Complicated"

A Bible-knowledge quiz might ask this seemingly straightforward question: "How many apostles were there?" Many would quickly respond "12." That familiar answer is based on Gospel texts such as Matthew 10:2; Mark 3:14; and Luke 6:13.

A better answer is "it's complicated." After Matthias replaces Judas (Acts 1:25, 26), Barnabas and Paul are called apostles (14:14). Paul himself then may have designated Andronicus and Junia as apostles, depending on how the sentence structure of Romans 16:7 is understood. Then there are the cases of the Lord's brother James (Galatians 1:19), Silas (Acts 17:4; 1 Thessalonians 2:6), and even Jesus himself (Hebrews 3:1)! Were we to take the time to sort through the issues of the designation *apostle*, we may find the answer "it's complicated" to be less and less flippant and more and more appealing as we go along!

We don't have to dig very far, however, before we reach the ironclad conclusion that Paul was an apostle under any definition of that word excepting that he was not of the original 12. His commission and authority to that office came directly from Jesus himself (Acts 9:1-6, 15; Galatians 1:1).

His approach to the problem addressed in today's text is similar. At one level, it's a complicated issue. Complications fall away and conclusions become ironclad as Paul uses an analogy from everyday life to focus on the main issue that then serves as a touchstone for all "but what about . . ." complications.

B. Lesson Context: Paul, Jews, and Gentiles

The observations in the Lesson Contexts of the previous two lessons still apply, so that information need not be repeated here. But as Paul's letter to the church in Rome crosses into chapter 9, a new issue occupies his thoughts: the problem of Israel.

Fewer than 1 percent of Christians today come from a background of Judaism. But that was not the case in Paul's day. Initially, the majority of Christian believers were of that background. The church in Rome had a mix of Jews and Gentiles. There were apparently significant numbers of both, with evidence suggesting that those of Gentile background were in the majority (compare Romans 1:5, 6, 13; 11:13; 15:11).

This put Paul in a unique position to address the church in Rome, a congregation he had never visited. His educational background was that of a learned Jewish rabbi. He had earned this distinction from having studied under Gamaliel, one of the best Jewish teachers of the day (Acts 22:3; compare 5:34). This gave Paul great credibility with any informed Jew.

Yet Paul had devoted much of his efforts to evangelizing Gentiles (Romans 15:15, 16; Galatians 2:8, 9; Ephesians 3:8). He even defended their legitimacy as believers before the gathering of "apostles and elders" known as the Council at Jerusalem (Acts 15:1-4). These actions resulted in Paul's having great standing among believers of Gentile background.

Both groups in the church in Rome would therefore listen to Paul. And it was important that they did so as he continued to address the issue of relationship between Christians of different backgrounds.

In Romans 9:1, Paul began to work through a heartbreaking reality: great numbers of his own Jewish people had rejected the Jewish Jesus as the Jewish Messiah. Paul's missionary travels had resulted in not just disinterest, but ferocious rejection (see Acts 14:19; 17:5; 18:6). Why?

HOW TO SAY IT

Andronicus	*An*-dro-**nye**-kus.
Antioch	*An*-tee-ock.
Barnabas	*Bar*-nuh-bus.
Corinthians	Ko-*rin*-thee-unz (*th* as in *thin*).
Ephesians	Ee-*fee*-zhunz.
Galatians	Guh-*lay*-shunz.
Gamaliel	Guh-*may*-lih-ul or Guh-*may*-lee-al.
Gentiles	*Jen*-tiles.
Jotham	*Jo*-thum.
Junia	*Joo*-ni-uh.
Leviticus	Leh-*vit*-ih-kus.
Matthias	Muh-*thigh*-us (*th* as in *thin*).
synagogue	*sin*-uh-gog.

Paul turned to Scripture to find the explanation. From Romans 9:1 to 11:10 he quotes from (what we call) the Old Testament 25 times. Given that there are only 64 verses in this section, that's about one Old Testament quote every two and a half verses! Those texts reveal, among other things, Israel's long history as a "disobedient and gainsaying people" (Romans 10:21; quoting Isaiah 65:2).

Romans 11:7-10 summarizes 9:1–11:6 by concluding that the proclamation of the gospel has resulted in two camps among the people of Israel: those who accept the gospel are "the election," while those who do not are "the rest . . . blinded." The significance of all this is the subject of today's study.

C. Lesson Context: Olive Trees

Today's lesson text features an analogy involving olive trees. In the Mediterranean world of Paul's day, olive trees were found all over: from Jerusalem to Antioch to Corinth to Rome. The produce of these trees had several uses. Olives themselves were food. Olive oil had value for cooking and as fuel for lamps. It had ceremonial and medicinal value.

The value of olive trees is attested in Jotham's parable where—in an obvious ranking of most valuable to least—an olive tree, a fig tree, a vine, and a bramble are asked in turn to reign over the trees. The olive tree's answer is, "Should I leave my fatness, wherewith by me they honour God and man, and go to be promoted over the trees?" (Judges 9:9). Olive tending was serious and profitable business.

I. Result of Stumble
(Romans 11:11-15)
A. Provoking to Jealousy (vv. 11, 12)
11a. I say then, Have they stumbled that they should fall?

The phrase *I say then* introduces implications of Romans 11:7-10 regarding Israel's division (see the Lesson Context, above). In so doing, Paul acknowledges that the widespread unbelief of his fellow Jews is indeed a stumble. But he does not see this trespass as unrecoverable. When we combine the words *stumbled* and *fall* with the "spirit of slumber" ascribed to Jewish unbelievers in Romans 11:8, we have a picture something like that of a person sleepwalking. He is oblivious to hazards in such a state. A family member screams a warning of a hazard the sleepwalker does not see. The sleepwalker, not yet fully awake, pays no heed and trips. He is on his way to the ground, with no hope of regaining his balance in time. Right?

11b. God forbid: but rather through their fall salvation is come unto the Gentiles, for to provoke them to jealousy.

God forbid, says Paul. Recovery is possible because of two connected results of Jewish unbelief. First, as the Jews have rejected the great salvation message of the gospel, it has impelled Paul to offer this message *unto the Gentiles* (see Acts 13:46; 18:6; 28:28). Paul has found many Gentiles gladly receptive of the gospel (13:48).

Contrasting the use of the word *fall* here with that word in the first half of the verse is important. The Greek noun behind the second instance of *fall* is elsewhere translated "offence(s)," "sin(s)," and "trespass(es)," and those inform the sense here (examples: Romans 5:15-17). To be sure, Israel's lack of faith is sinful. But repentance and forgiveness are still possible, as Paul goes on to establish.

Second, the Gentiles' receptivity to the gospel can serve as an incentive for Jews to believe as well. When we see someone receive a benefit, our

Visual for Lesson 12. *Start a discussion by pointing to this visual as you ask, "How do we overcome hurdles to Christianity that nationalism may pose?"*

impulse is to want that benefit too! Jewish unbelievers, seeing Gentile lives radically changed by Christ, will want this change and joy in their own lives (compare Deuteronomy 32:21, quoted in Romans 10:19).

> *What Do You Think?*
> What boundaries or limits should we observe regarding techniques used to win people to Christ?
> *Digging Deeper*
> Evaluate the phrase "the end justifies the means" in relation to this question.

12. Now if the fall of them be the riches of the world, and the diminishing of them the riches of the Gentiles; how much more their fulness?

Paul often characterizes the benefits of Christian faith as *riches* (compare Romans 2:4; Ephesians 1:7; 3:8). The gospel's gracious offer of salvation through faith represents the greatest spiritual treasure in the universe! But most Jews are leaving this offer on the table. Their *diminishing* is accompanied by the "unspeakable gift" (2 Corinthians 9:15) being offered to *the Gentiles*.

Since that's the as-is case, then would it not be better still were Jews to accept the offer as well? Paul's vision is grand here. Imagine if all Gentiles and Jews accept the salvation made possible through Christ! This would include every single person on earth. We gain a glimpse of what motivated Paul with such extraordinary passion as to suffer as he did for the sake of the gospel.

B. Pushing for Emulation (vv. 13-15)

13, 14. For I speak to you Gentiles, inasmuch as I am the apostle of the Gentiles, I magnify mine office: if by any means I may provoke to emulation them which are my flesh, and might save some of them.

Paul addresses the Gentiles in his readership with a direct appeal: he intends to do everything in his power to *provoke to emulation them which are [his] flesh* for the sole purpose of saving *some of them*. His technique will be to use his *office* as *the apostle of the Gentiles* in any way possible to win as many Gentiles to Christ as possible. By implication, the Gentiles' part is to live in such a way that Jewish unbelievers will want to have what they have.

What Do You Think?
> Under what circumstances, if any, should Paul's ministry to Gentiles be a precedent for sending missionaries to other cultures rather than training evangelists from within those cultures? Why?

Digging Deeper
How do Acts 13:46; 18:6; Galatians 2:7-9; and Philippians 3:5 inform your viewpoint, if at all?

15. For if the casting away of them be the reconciling of the world, what shall the receiving of them be, but life from the dead?

By *casting away of them* Paul refers to the Jewish refusal to believe in Christ. As he has already shown, the Jewish unbelievers are culpable for this, but it also fits into God's plan for the reconciling of the world, the inclusion of Gentiles into the people of God (see Romans 5:11; 2 Corinthians 5:19). What a great marvel would it be if, as a result, Jews come to faith! It would seem miraculous, like *life from the dead.*

II. Outcome of Brokenness
(Romans 11:16-21)

A. Partaking of Fatness (vv. 16-18)

16. For if the firstfruit be holy, the lump is also holy: and if the root be holy, so are the branches.

Paul now reasons with two examples tied to Jewish history. First, breadmaking is considered. *The lump* in his illustration is the final dough ball that is ready to be baked. This process begins with grinding grain to make flour. Moses had commanded the people of Israel to take *the firstfruit*, a portion of this flour and make a loaf that was to be offered to the Lord (Numbers 15:17-21; compare Nehemiah 10:37; Ezekiel 44:30). Paul considers this act of offering to be making the firstfruit loaf *holy*, and, by extension, this holiness can be applied to the whole batch of flour and its resultant bread loaves.

The second illustration has to do with a tree, its *root* and its *branches*. Branches are dependent upon the health of a tree's root system. If the root dies, so will the branches. Branches detached from the main tree and its root will die (compare John 15:4-6). Paul has in mind here a family tree, the tree of the nation of Israel. In a sense, Israel is continually blessed and made holy by the covenant God made with its great patriarchs: Abraham, Isaac, and Jacob (see Exodus 2:24; Leviticus 26:42). If the essential root of the tree (the patriarchs) is considered holy, this holiness extends to any branches attached to the tree.

What Do You Think?
> Considering Christianity's roots in Judaism, how should this text influence our view of the value of the Old Testament?

Digging Deeper
Consider also Romans 15:4; 1 Corinthians 10:11; Colossians 2:14

17, 18. And if some of the branches be broken off, and thou, being a wild olive tree, wert graffed in among them, and with them partakest of the root and fatness of the olive tree; boast not against the branches. But if thou boast, thou bearest not the root, but the root thee.

Paul expands this analogy of a holy tree and its branches to imagine some of the branches being *broken off*. This may be from pruning or wind damage, but branches removed from a tree are usually unhealthy or unproductive. Such branches are fit only to be firewood (John 15:6). If an olive farmer cuts off some unproductive branches, it could be for the purpose of grafting on new, healthy branches from *a wild olive tree*. This description fits the Gentiles well, for they have been growing wild, apart from the supervision and care of God given to Israel for hundreds of years.

These new, grafted branches will be productive only if they tap *the root and fatness of the olive tree*. The new branches must receive water and the nourishment of the soil from their new host. They have been given a huge upgrade from their scrubby wild tree origins. They flourish because of the new tree, not the other way around. Paul's word to the Gentile believers is to remember that their inclusion in the church allows them to be recipients of the great blessings the Lord has lavished on Israel for centuries. They, with faithful Jews, are now fellow heirs of God's promises (Ephesians 3:6). There is no justification for boasting about status (compare John 4:22).

B. Grafting by Faith (vv. 19-21)

19, 20. Thou wilt say then, The branches were broken off, that I might be graffed in. Well; because of unbelief they were broken off, and thou standest by faith. Be not highminded, but fear.

Paul continues to warn his Gentile readers to consider God's purpose in all of this. The word *Well* indicates that those who make the argument *the branches were broken off, that I might be graffed in* are correct up to point. What they miss is the reason those Jews were broken off: it was *because of unbelief.* This is not a cause for being *highminded* (proud), as if the Jews have been humiliated by God so Gentiles can feel superior. Instead, this is a cause for *fear*, realizing how dire their situation was and how gracious God has been to them.

✢ GRAFTING TODAY ✢

In 2001, I moved to Fallbrook, California, the self-proclaimed "Avocado Capitol of the World." Avocado groves cover the hillsides surrounding the quaint village. However, as the population has grown, many of the groves have been subdivided for housing. The good news for avocado lovers is that the developers left an avocado tree or two on many of the building lots. I was pleased to buy one such. But I was disappointed with both the quantity and quality of the fruit.

Research revealed the tree was not the Hass variety, the fruit of which most consumers prefer. So I hired a specialist to graft six Hass shoots onto my tree. The grafts thrived, and I had an abundance of excellent avocados the next season.

This experience caused me to reflect anew on how people come to Christ and His church. Gentiles turned to Christ in such great numbers that within a few decades—and to the very present day—Christians of non-Jewish background far outnumber Christians of Jewish background. What does this suggest about whom God might choose to graft into the church today?—C. R. B.

21. For if God spared not the natural branches, take heed lest he also spare not thee.

Arrogance that displeases God can result in more pruning! What has been grafted in (the Gentiles) can just as easily be removed.

III. Possibility of Restoration
(ROMANS 11:22-24)

A. Continuing in Goodness (vv. 22, 23)

22. Behold therefore the goodness and severity of God: on them which fell, severity; but toward thee, goodness, if thou continue in his goodness: otherwise thou also shalt be cut off.

Paul reflects that this situation reveals a paradox: God is good and severe at the same time. While the analogy of the olive tree is still in view here, this is more akin to presenting God as a parent. Parents know there is a time to show great love and kindness to a child, but also a time when discipline is necessary. Severe discipline does not negate the love of a good parent. To receive the kindness, the child must be obedient. Continuing in God's goodness is a matter of continuing in the faith. As with the unbelieving Jews, unfaithfulness risks being cut off for the ingrafted Gentiles.

✢ REBELLION AND RESTORATION ✢

I work with a ministry that provides a setting in which at-risk, rebellious youth may be rescued from damaging lifestyles. The vast majority of these young people have struggled with alcohol and drugs. Nearly half have been abused. Almost all are unable to graduate from high school with their age cohort.

These youth encounter Christ in this ministry through biblical teaching, counseling, mentoring, physical work, and schooling adapted to individual needs. Distractions such as cell phones and social media are removed—action considered "severe" by some students. The youth see God's goodness in the unconditional Christian love they receive and in the life-structure this love provides. Eventually, the majority come to see God beginning to work in their lives.

Regardless of age, most of us tend to resist God's discipline, thinking it to be too severe. But there's a big difference between restorative discipline that is temporary and retributive punishment, which is eternal. Will you accept the former so you can avoid the latter? —C. R. B.

> **What Do You Think?**
> What steps can you take to help your fellow believers better understand both God's kindness and severity?
> *Digging Deeper*
> What will happen in cases where one is stressed to the exclusion of the other.

23. And they also, if they abide not still in unbelief, shall be graffed in: for God is able to graff them in again.

Unbelieving Jews have been cut off, a display of God's harshness. But they can be grafted back in, included anew, if they change unbelief to belief. God's kindness is ready and waiting for them. There is still time and hope.

B. Regrafting onto God's Tree (v. 24)

24. For if thou wert cut out of the olive tree which is wild by nature, and wert graffed contrary to nature into a good olive tree: how much more shall these, which be the natural branches, be graffed into their own olive tree?

For Paul, there is an unnatural sense to bringing the Gentile believers into the people of God, perhaps like mixing metric and standard tools. It works, but doesn't always seem to fit right. The churches of Paul's day struggle with things like

food forbidden to Jews being served at church functions (Galatians 2:11, 12). Basic understandings of things such as one God, personal holiness, and respect for Scripture are assumed by Jews but are foreign to Gentiles. Their religion and behavior is *wild by nature* in contrast.

Paul's vision is not just Gentile inclusion, but a return of fellow Jews. The tree would then thrive as never before. What a magnificent tree it would be! What a glorious church we would see!

Conclusion

A. Grace Is Always Prior to Salvation

Romans is consistent in always presenting faith, not works, as the way to be justified in God's reckoning. Paul insists this is nothing new. In the history of Israel, the Jewish remnant is saved, as always, by grace not works (Romans 11:5, 6). Grace is always prior to salvation, and salvation cannot be earned. Salvation begins with God's response of grace to our situation and our response of faith in return.

Paul maintains a certain pecking order in all of this: God's salvation through faith comes first to the Jews, then to the Gentiles (Romans 1:16). The punishment of God for unbelief also comes first to Jews, then to Gentiles (2:9). This is validated by history, by God's choice of Israel to be His holy nation and vehicle for bringing salvation to the world. Jews first, then Gentiles—both in terms of privilege as well as accountability.

But as true as that is, isn't it just hypothetical today? Here in the year 2019, the details of relations between Jews and Gentiles in the church have faded. But foundational lessons still stand. One is that it's easy to become prideful, to focus on self rather than God and His plan. As Paul opposed that, so must we.

B. Prayer

Father, help us stay grafted in! May our faith replace pride as we trust in You for all things. We pray in the name of Jesus, our Savior. Amen.

C. Thought to Remember

God is still able.

INVOLVEMENT LEARNING

Enhance your lesson with KJV Bible Student (from your curriculum supplier) and the reproducible activity page (at www.standardlesson.com or in the back of the KJV Standard Lesson Commentary Deluxe Edition).

Into the Lesson

Distribute to each student a sheet of paper and a pen. Hold up a can or jar of olives and say, "Olive trees are some of the oldest known plants. Here's a fun fact: An olive is actually a fruit, not a vegetable! In one minute, see how many foods you can list that might have olives in them. Ready, set, go!" *(Responses may include pizza, Greek salad, hummus, pasta salad, stuffed olives, baked cheese olives, and green olive dip.)* Ask volunteers to share their lists.

Say, "Hold up your hand for one of three choices: Do you prefer green olives, black olives, or no olives? [Allow responses.] No matter which category you fall into, none of us is superior because of it. The apostle Paul used an analogy involving olive trees to point out something important about our faith. Let's see what it is."

Alternative. If there is an expert gardener in your congregation who can give a short talk on grafting (or a person who is willing to research it and share the information), ask him or her to share the knowledge with the class. Then say, "Paul uses the analogy of grafting a new branch into an older tree to point out something important about our faith. Let's see what it is."

Into the Word

Have volunteers take turns reading aloud three or four verses from Romans 11:11-24.

Divide the class into three groups, and distribute to each group a sheet of paper and a pen. Tell each group to choose a well-known tune and rewrite the lyrics incorporating the words *God, graft,* and *branches.* Encourage full use of today's lesson text.

If students need help getting started, suggest tunes from hymns such as "Amazing Grace" or "Blessed Assurance" or from contemporary worship music such as "What a Beautiful Name" or "Good Good Father." Or the groups could use tunes such as "Home on the Range" or "This Land Is Your Land." For a fun challenge, suggest that groups rhyme their lyric lines.

Allow about 10 minutes for groups to compose their songs. Have group representatives take turns reading or singing their groups' creations. Discuss as appropriate.

Option. Distribute copies of the "Spiritual Heritage" activity from the reproducible page, which you can download. Allow students about five minutes to work in pairs to complete and discuss. Encourage learners to share ways their spiritual walk has been strengthened by godly people. Use this as a transition to the Into Life segment.

Into Life

Say, "Some of us may bristle when newcomers to church offer a different approach to a solution, one that brushes against 'this is the way we've always done things' approach." Initiate a discussion on how a sense of "better than" can drift into the church. Ask, "In what ways might Christians today boast about spiritual status?" After each response ask, "What Bible verses can help us gain a proper view of our grafting into God's eternal family in this regard?" Jot answers on the board.

Alternative. Distribute copies of the "Spiritual Superiority" activity from the reproducible page. Have students complete the checklist individually, then discuss the questions together.

Conclude your time together with this prayer: "Thank You, God, that You do not love us more or love us less because of our backgrounds or how long we've walked with You. We confess any prideful thoughts or actions we have toward others in the church [*pause for a moment of silent reflection*]. We are truly grateful that we are like olive trees, rooted and grounded in a relationship with You. In Jesus' victorious name we pray. Amen."

CALLED TO
BE TRANSFORMED

DEVOTIONAL READING: Psalm 34:1-14
BACKGROUND SCRIPTURE: Romans 12

ROMANS 12:1-8

1 I beseech you therefore, brethren, by the mercies of God, that ye present your bodies a living sacrifice, holy, acceptable unto God, which is your reasonable service.

2 And be not conformed to this world: but be ye transformed by the renewing of your mind, that ye may prove what is that good, and acceptable, and perfect, will of God.

3 For I say, through the grace given unto me, to every man that is among you, not to think of himself more highly than he ought to think; but to think soberly, according as God hath dealt to every man the measure of faith.

4 For as we have many members in one body, and all members have not the same office:

5 So we, being many, are one body in Christ, and every one members one of another.

6 Having then gifts differing according to the grace that is given to us, whether prophecy, let us prophesy according to the proportion of faith;

7 Or ministry, let us wait on our ministering: or he that teacheth, on teaching;

8 Or he that exhorteth, on exhortation: he that giveth, let him do it with simplicity; he that ruleth, with diligence; he that sheweth mercy, with cheerfulness.

KEY VERSE

I beseech you therefore, brethren, by the mercies of God, that ye present your bodies a living sacrifice, holy, acceptable unto God, which is your reasonable service. —**Romans 12:1**

DISCIPLESHIP AND MISSION

Unit 3: Call to Life in Christ

LESSON AIMS

After participating in this lesson, each learner will be able to:

1. List several spiritual gifts.

2. Explain why "living sacrifice" seems paradoxical.

3. Make a plan to use a spiritual gift more effectively.

LESSON OUTLINE

Introduction

A. Asking the Right Question

Church leaders often decry the so-called 80/20 rule in church operations: 80 percent of the members account for only 20 percent of the giving and volunteer service. Many areas of business and economics are viewed through the lens of the 80/20 rule, also known as "the Pareto principle." Businesses, for example, may expect 80 percent of its customers to yield only 20 percent of the company's sales revenue.

Whether the formula is actually more like 85/15, 90/10, etc., is not the primary issue. The bigger picture is that a source of input can be expected to yield results far out of proportion to its size. Church leaders lament this. Many are the preachers and elders who have thought *What if we could fully mobilize 100 percent of our membership? We could increase our ministry impact enormously!*

In turn, these musings lead one to wonder how to know when members were fully mobilized. How much volunteer time should a church expect from each of its members?

Or are these even the right questions to be asking? Today's lesson may surprise us in that regard. Make no mistake: this is a vitally important issue. Acceptance of Jesus as Lord (Romans 10:9) must be followed by service to Him as Master.

B. Lesson Context

The Lesson Contexts of the previous three lessons apply, so that information need not be repeated here. Even so, a bigger picture needs to be kept in mind: Paul always understood (1) the church had its roots in the synagogue, (2) the gospel had its basis in the Jewish Scriptures, and (3) Jesus was the Messiah the Jews had long awaited. These three facts could not be ignored. The issue Paul confronted was how the Christians of Jewish background could welcome Christians of Gentile background as full-fledged members of the body of Christ.

We see the members of the famous council of Jerusalem wrestling with this issue in Acts 15, perhaps around AD 51. Roman history mentions a dispute among the Jews in Rome about this same time. We surmise from comments made by the Roman historian Suetonius (lived about AD 69–122) that this was a nasty fight between Jews who had converted to Christianity and those who had not.

The result was that Emperor Claudius (reigned AD 41–54) expelled all Jews from Rome, including a husband and wife by the names Aquila and Priscilla. Paul met these two Christians in Corinth afterward (Acts 18:2). It was likely therefore that Christians of Gentile background, who were not subject to the edict, remained in Rome as leaders of the church in the city.

The death of Claudius in AD 54 opened the door for Jews to return to Rome after a few years of absence (including Aquila and Priscilla, per Romans 16:3). With Paul writing to the church in Rome in about AD 58, issues of reintegration there still needed to be sorted out. Paul was aware of these issues, given the content of the letter we now study.

I. Transformed Person
(Romans 12:1, 2)
A. Sacrificed Body (v. 1)

1a. I beseech you therefore, brethren, by the mercies of God.

Paul has just completed three chapters of discussion regarding the disappointing lack of faith in Jesus Christ among most of his fellow Jews. With the striking phrase *I beseech you therefore, brethren*, he connects what is about to follow with the doctrinal truths of those prior chapters. The word in

HOW TO SAY IT

Aquila	*Ack*-wih-luh.
Claudius	*Claw*-dee-us.
Colossians	Kuh-*losh*-unz.
Corinthians	Ko-*rin*-thee-unz (*th* as in *thin*).
Ephesians	Ee-*fee*-zhunz.
exhortation	eks-or-*tay*-shun.
Gentiles	*Jen*-tiles.
Messiah	Meh-*sigh*-uh.
Priscilla	Prih-*sil*-uh.
Suetonius	Soo-*toe*-nee-us.

the original language translated *beseech* points to a desire that is stronger than a mere request but not as strong as an outright command (see also 1 Corinthians 4:16; Ephesians 4:1; and 1 Timothy 2:1). Compliance with the desire Paul is about to express should be motivated *by the mercies of God* (previously described) rather than by obligation to obey a command of one in greater authority.

1b. That ye present your bodies a living sacrifice, holy, acceptable unto God.

Here is Paul's desire. But without doubt, *a living sacrifice* is a contradiction in terms for both Jews and Gentiles. Each group is familiar with the distinctives of the sacrificial system of its own past, of course. But one thing those systems have in common is the slaughter of animals. A sacrifice isn't a sacrifice if it's still living!

Having caught his readers' attention with this seeming paradox, Paul proceeds to stress the nature of such a sacrifice. The concepts of *justification* and *sanctification* are important to consider. To be justified is to be pronounced in right standing before God; Jesus' death in payment of sin's penalty makes this possible (compare Romans 3:21-26; 4:25; etc.). To be sanctified speaks to holiness, consecration, being set apart for sacred use. The work of Christ sanctifies us initially; the Holy Spirit works to separate us from sin for the rest of our earthly lives (Romans 8:13; 15:16; 1 Corinthians 6:11; 1 Peter 1:2). A *holy* sacrifice is an *acceptable* sacrifice.

> *What Do You Think?*
> How will you know when you have become a living sacrifice? What will you do to be this?
> *Digging Deeper*
> What Scriptures support your conclusion?

1c. Which is your reasonable service.

This summary phrase is rich with significance. The two Greek terms behind the translation have a range of meanings, depending on context.

The first term, which is translated *reasonable*, is the basis for the English word *logic*. Thus it speaks to something that is reasonable and rational. The use of the second term, translated *service*, can be compared with its use in John 16:2; Romans 9:4;

and Hebrews 9:1, 6. These contexts connect the ideas of service and worship. The sense is that of serving God with worship in an ordered and well-thought-out manner. We serve God when we worship (think of the phrase "a worship service"), but we also worship God when we properly serve Him. These are inseparable for Paul.

B. Renewed Mind (v. 2)

2. And be not conformed to this world: but be ye transformed by the renewing of your mind, that ye may prove what is that good, and acceptable, and perfect, will of God.

Paul's admonition for self-sacrifice resulting in worshipful service is accomplished in two ways. First, is the *renewing of your mind*. For Paul, this is a departure from conformity to the world. We are called to be renewed by being *transformed*. The word being translated is the basis for our word *metamorphosis*. It points to a complete, radical change, a change contrasted with the patterns and desires of the world (see 1 Peter 1:14).

This is not wholly of our doing, for Paul does not command us to transform ourselves. We are changed through the work of the Holy Spirit, the great sanctifier and transformer of men and women (2 Corinthians 3:18). As we find sinful ways more repugnant and God's ways more appealing, we are being transformed.

II. Transformed Congregation
(Romans 12:3-8)

A. Checked Egos (vv. 3-5)

3. For I say, through the grace given unto me, to every man that is among you, not to think of himself more highly than he ought to think; but to think soberly, according as God hath dealt to every man the measure of faith.

Keeping in mind the Roman church may have had some recent leadership turmoil (see the Lesson Context), Paul lays down some ways for that church to conquer their strife. First must come individual self-examination. For someone to *think of himself more highly than he ought to think* is a key ingredient of a recipe for disaster. Dueling personalities are often at the root of church conflict. We don't just have to be right; we must win. Whether this resulted in a crisis when leaders of Jewish background returned to the church (see the Lesson Context) and desired to regain the upper hand, we don't know. But the story is far too familiar for many church leaders.

Paul knows this is touchy, so he speaks *through the grace given* to him. He is plenty blunt, though, in asking for sober thinking. His readers must sober up from their ego binge.

This gives us some questions for today. Can you evaluate your motives in conflict objectively and *soberly*? Are you acting in the best interests of the church or according to your own desires? Paul reminds us that everyone is on an equal footing here, for whatever *measure of faith* one has has been given by God. No one in the church has a relationship with God that is more important or privileged than anyone else.

> *What Do You Think?*
>   On a scale from 1 to 10, from "a worm" (Psalm 22:6) to "a god" (Acts 12:22), where should you see yourself? Why?
> *Digging Deeper*
>   In what contexts, if any, should this fluctuate? Why?

4, 5. For as we have many members in one body, and all members have not the same office: so we, being many, are one body in Christ, and every one members one of another.

Equality in God's eyes does not mean uniformity in service, however. Paul echoes the language of 1 Corinthians 12, a text that some Christians in Rome may be familiar with. His point in that text is the same here: we have both unity and variety in the body of Christ. We are united as *one body in Christ,* and *all members* are in this one body. Even so, there is variety of *office.* The word being translated that way is elsewhere rendered as "works" (Matthew 16:27) and "deeds" (Luke 23:51; Acts 19:18; Romans 8:13; Colossians 3:9). Thus the idea is not one of position or rank, but of differing abilities of service.

When Paul speaks of *members,* he is using an analogy to refer to body parts such as arms, legs, etc. In English we see this idea when we say a body has been dismembered, meaning its parts have been divided. Here there is no splitting of parts, for they are *members one of another*. It is one body made up of very different parts. It is one Christ, one church, with many members.

❧ IT'S (NOT) ALL ABOUT ME! ❧

I was in a fast-food restaurant one day when screams filled the place. Startled, I and other patrons turned to see the source: a 3-year-old boy standing on a seat, protesting his mother's choice of food.

The embarrassed woman plaintively tried to reason her son into silence, but in vain. A few moments later, the young manager came from behind the counter and walked briskly over to the boy. The man bent down close to the child and looked him in the eye. With a loud, assertive voice, the manager said, "Sir! We cannot have you acting this way in our restaurant!" The shocked child sank into his seat in cowed silence while his mother tried to regain her dignity.

We reluctantly accept this "it's all about me" attitude in small children who are still learning the rules of conduct. Yet society fawns over celebrities, and, in so doing, encourages their self-centeredness. We are tempted to follow their bad examples, glorying in our own imagined importance.

This is a sign of emotional and/or spiritual immaturity. Paul warns us against such attitudes. He reminds us that, as members of the body of Christ, we each have a gift or gifts from God. Since the glory is God's, then not one of us is more important than any other. You see, it's not all about me . . . or you either!   —C. R. B.

> **What Do You Think?**
> What are some ways your church can affirm differences among individual members while maintaining an overall spirit of unity?
>
> **Digging Deeper**
> What would indicate that unity was being stressed at the expense of individual differences or vice versa?

B. Activated Gifts (vv. 6-8)

6. Having then gifts differing according to the grace that is given to us, whether prophecy, let us prophesy according to the proportion of faith.

Paul now addresses the difference in offices as *gifts* from God. Given *according to* God's *grace*, they are true gifts, not payment or reward for work. Therefore, the nature of each person's gift is determined by God. The differences are intentional, provided for the body of Christ according to the church's needs and God's plans.

The first gift Paul mentions is the ability to *prophesy*, an esteemed gift in the first-century church. Prophesying is done by prophets, individuals entrusted by God to speak publicly on His behalf, even in (or especially in) the face of opposition (1 Corinthians 12:28).

To exercise the gift of prophecy *according to* the prophet's *proportion of faith* surely means that both the giving and receiving of a prophetic word is an act of faith. But some commentators suggest that there is more to it here. They propose that the phrase *according to the proportion of faith* is best understood as "according to the analogy of faith."

Traditionally, the analogy of faith has described and used the tenets of faith that unite Christian doctrine and Scripture in a comprehensive way. These are things like the oneness of God, the divinity of Christ, and the authority of Scripture for faith and practice.

Those proposing this understanding of the phrase point out that the analogy of faith helps us clarify less clear teachings and doctrines with those that are clearer and explained more fully in Scripture. Thus, Paul is thought to be giving a subtle warning to aspiring prophets in the church: their prophetic words should be measured against the well-understood doctrines of the church.

In this "analogy of faith" sense, prophecy in the church is not for the purpose of innovation but for reinforcement. That is, it clarifies and applies previous teachings. Under this theory, Paul is seen as having no fear of encouraging any prophets in the church in Rome. The reason is because he believes they will reinforce rather than contradict his teachings.

7a. Or ministry, let us wait on our ministering.

Ministry is focused on helping others, whereas the service/worship mentioned of Romans 12:1 focuses more on God. Church volunteers who are given tasks involving serving others often burn out quickly. To be a person with a lifelong passion for helping others is truly a gift of God.

This does not excuse any member from refusing to care about others, for we are members of the same body (Romans 12:5). But this gift does recognize that some Christians are tireless servants who are called to relieve the suffering of others.

7b. Or he that teacheth, on teaching.

Teaching is explaining the Scriptures. Christian teaching helps people better understand God, their duty to Him, and the nature of their salvation. Jesus saw teaching as an important element to His earthly ministry (see Mark 14:49; Luke 21:37), and so does Paul (Acts 18:11).

To be "apt to teach" (1 Timothy 3:2) is a gift (1 Corinthians 12:28; Ephesians 4:11), but effective teaching requires preparation and study. The gift is in the passion to teach others more about God through an exposition of Scripture. In addition, many experienced teachers can relate instances where their effectiveness in teaching seemed to go beyond their preparation, experiences of spiritual insight sometimes called serendipity. A church without capable teachers is somehow missing out on a vital gift God intentionally gives to the church.

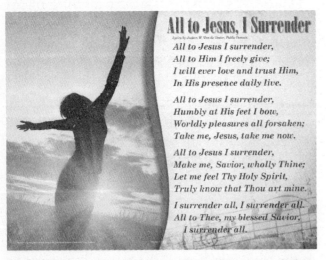

All to Jesus, I Surrender

Lyrics by Judson W. Van de Venter, Public Domain

All to Jesus I surrender,
All to Him I freely give;
I will ever love and trust Him,
In His presence daily live.

All to Jesus I surrender,
Humbly at His feet I bow,
Worldly pleasures all forsaken;
Take me, Jesus, take me now.

All to Jesus I surrender,
Make me, Savior, wholly Thine;
Let me feel Thy Holy Spirit,
Truly know that Thou art mine.

I surrender all, I surrender all.
All to Thee, my blessed Savior,
I surrender all.

Visual for Lesson 13. *Start a discussion by pointing to this visual as you ask, "How does having a transformed mind relate with being fully surrendered?"*

8a. Or he that exhorteth, on exhortation.

Paul rounds out his list by moving to four more gifts for the church. The word translated *exhortation* is elsewhere translated "consolation" (example: Luke 2:25) and "comfort" (example: 2 Corinthians 1:3). But Paul is not speaking merely in the sense of one who empathizes with and comforts those who are suffering. The sense here is more like the coach who pushes an athlete to increase performance to the maximum level.

Most churches need voices that prod complacent members to higher levels of commitment. This can be a discouraging and thankless task. The gift is not just the ability to motivate others. It is also the diligence encouragers need to offer a persistent word of higher expectations.

8b. He that giveth, let him do it with simplicity.

A spiritually gifted giver is not always the person with the most money. Rather, these are the ones who understand the self-sacrifice Paul speaks of in Romans 12:1. Some of the best givers in churches may be persons of modest means, yet the amount of money given over their lifetimes may be staggering. "Liberality" (2 Corinthians 8:2) and "bountifulness" (9:11) are additional ways to translate the word behind *simplicity*.

8c. He that ruleth, with diligence.

One who *ruleth* is a church leader in the fullest sense. The word implies direction of others, a leader of men and women (compare how the same word is translated in 1 Timothy 3:4, 12; 5:17). Church leadership may take on a variety of specific responsibilities, but Paul insists this must be done *with diligence*. As with all of these gifts, this requires ego-suppression and self-sacrifice. For example, coordination of volunteers can be discouraging, for the coordinator's commitment often exceeds that of some workers. *Diligence* implies patience and attention to details.

8d. He that sheweth mercy, with cheerfulness.

The gift of *mercy* is somewhat related to the gift of giving or the gift of service. The members of a church should well understand the great mercy shown to them through the work of Jesus Christ. All should be merciful, but some are called to shower this mercy on others.

We understand this better when we see Paul expecting mercy to be shown *with cheerfulness*. Showing mercy is not to be done grudgingly. Bringing cheer into the life of a discouraged or downtrodden individual may be an expression of mercy all by itself.

As with all these gifts, showing mercy requires a degree of self-sacrifice and self-denial. Paul himself is something of an expert on the subject of mercy, having received it himself in abundance (1 Timothy 1:13, 16).

❦ *What Gift(s) Do You Have?* ❦

"What is your spiritual gift?" Asking that of your friends will elicit varying opinions, both on- and off-target.

Take, for example, a friend of mine who has a PhD in history. He recently retired from a long teaching career at a prestigious California university, where his specialty was early Christian history. That was an unusual discipline in a secular university! He consistently got rave reviews from students and administrators for his courses. Would you say he had the gift of teaching?

One particular individual did not think so. This person, a member in a church a friend attended, claimed to have special insights into the spiritual gifts of others. He (let's call him John) was not impressed by the unique opportunity my professor friend had to be a witness to the historical validity of the Christian faith in a hostile setting. John advised the professor to quit his job at the university and take a position in a community agency teaching English to Hispanic children. My judgment was that John's spiritual gift was definitely not that of discernment!

How does one discover his or her spiritual gift(s)? A web search will bring up numerous tests claiming to help you determine just that, some in as little time as five minutes! A better approach might be to (1) ask for God's guidance in evaluating your potential spiritual gifts, (2) start using them, (3) see if you end up being passionate about them, and (4) see if others are blessed by what you do. You may be surprised at how God has equipped you to serve! —C. R. B.

What Do You Think?
What procedure should your church use to energize the members to recognize and use their spiritual gifts?
Digging Deeper
How will you know whether the procedure you propose is the best one?

Conclusion

A. Drawing the Right Conclusion

Two principles seem to present themselves in today's lesson. First, all the gifts Paul has listed call for sacrifice. How do we become a "living sacrifice"? Paul implies that it happens by the exercise of our spiritual gifts. As we do, we will find ourselves transformed. But let us not fool ourselves into thinking that we are transformed by our own efforts. We are transformed into a living sacrifice through the work of the Holy Spirit, the same Spirit that gives us the passion and skills for a specific gift or gifts within the church.

This leads to a second great principle: spiritual gifts are all for the unity and benefit of the church. We are not called to prophesy to ourselves, give to ourselves, or show mercy to ourselves. The gifts Paul lists are necessary for the church to be all that Christ intended her to be.

B. Prayer

Father, help us both to discern and employ the gifts given to us! As we do, transform and renew us through Your Spirit. We pray this in the name of Jesus, our great example of sacrifice. Amen.

C. Thought to Remember

Be transformed as you serve.

INVOLVEMENT LEARNING

Enhance your lesson with KJV Bible Student *(from your curriculum supplier) and the reproducible activity page (at www.standardlesson.com or in the back of the* KJV Standard Lesson Commentary Deluxe Edition*).*

Into the Lesson

Form students into groups of three or four. Distribute a sheet of paper to each student. Say, "Working with your group, you can do anything you like with your papers until I say that time is up. You might tear or fold the papers into a shape, make or draw something, or anything you want to do. Be creative. Go!"

After a few minutes, let the groups show what they did with their papers.

Alternative. Distribute copies of the "Survey Says" activity from the reproducible page, which you can download. Allow students 60 seconds to write one answer for each survey statement. After you call time, have students share their answers. Commend those who voice especially creative ones.

After either activity say, "God gave us our bodies and our unique talents so that we can work together to serve Him."

Into the Word

Ask two students to alternate reading the eight verses from today's text aloud. Then have the first verse read again. Lead a brief discussion of the verse with these questions:

1–When the Roman Christians—whether Jewish or Gentile in background—heard the word *sacrifice,* what mental picture popped into their heads? *(Expected response: an animal being killed as an offering to God or a god.)*

2–Why is the image of being "a living sacrifice" so unusual? *(Expected response: those who see themselves as such remain alive while sacrificing themselves in service—thus a paradox.)*

Form learners into groups of three or four. Distribute index cards printed with the following statements (you prepare), one per card:

1–I have so much going on with work, family, and things that I just don't have much time for church activities.

2–I'm so glad that I'm not like some of the people who come to church here who don't lift a finger to help.

3–Why can't more people be part of the hospitality team and help greet people?

4–The lady in charge of the nursery was upset with me when I said I could no longer work there, but I cannot lift babies because of my back.

5–I don't really know for sure what my gift is.

6–I think my spiritual gift is mercy, but I wish I had one that was more significant and useful.

As you distribute the cards, say, "Find a verse from today's text, and use it to help you come up with a response to someone who might make the statement on the card." When students are finished, allow time for each group to share and defend its responses.

Into Life

Record the spiritual gifts listed in Romans 12:6-8 on the board. Ask students to voice which they think they have and how to use it/them better. Jot ideas on the board as they are voiced. Ask students also to share real-life examples of how others are using those same spiritual gifts in service to God.

Option. Distribute copies of the "May I Serve You?" activity from the reproducible page. Invite students to select the correct multiple-choice answers in less than a minute. The first one to do so can shout *Serve!* Have that learner share his or her answers. Discuss. Give an inexpensive token prize to match the nature of the activity.

Conclude the lesson in prayer: "Lord, give us strength and courage to not conform to the world, but to live transformed lives for You. We know that You are delighted when we use the spiritual gifts You've given us to make the body of Christ stronger. Help us do our best to work with others to accomplish the work of Your kingdom. We praise You in Jesus' name. Amen."

COVENANT
IN GOD

Special Features

Lessons

Unit 1: A Fulfilled Covenant

Unit 2: A Heartfelt Covenant

Unit 3: Covenant: A Personal Perspective

QUARTERLY QUIZ

Use these questions as a pretest or as a review. The answers are on page iv of This Quarter in the Word.

Lesson 1

1. Jesus' prediction of His betrayal saddened the apostles at the last supper. T/F. *Mark 14:19*

2. The new covenant is established on _____ promises. *Hebrews 8:6*

Lesson 2

1. Pontius Pilate was willing to release Jesus, finding Him innocent. T/F. *Mark 15:9, 10*

2. Moments after Jesus died, the temple veil was torn from _____ to _____. *Mark 15:38*

Lesson 3

1. Christ is the high priest and the _____ of the new covenant. *Hebrews 9:15*

2. God's forgiveness of sin can be accomplished without the shedding of blood. T/F. *Hebrews 9:22*

Lesson 4

1. What other town of believers did Paul mention in Colossians? (Thessalonica, Laodicea, Ephesus?) *Colossians 2:1*

2. In Jesus Christ, all the _____ of the Godhead dwells in human form. *Colossians 2:9*

Lesson 5

1. According to Jesus, to whom belongs the kingdom of Heaven? (the poor in spirit, the meek, the pure in heart?) *Matthew 5:3.*

2. The meek shall inherit the earth; the merciful shall receive _____ *Matthew 5:7.*

Lesson 6

1. Jesus compared His disciples to what? (pick two: heat, salt, gold, ice, light?) *Matthew 5:13, 14*

2. Jesus did not come to _____ the Law and the Prophets, but to _____ them. *Matthew 5:17*

Lesson 7

1. We are to make our offerings to God before pursuing reconciliation. T/F. *Matthew 5:24*

2. One should act quickly in trying to reach an out of court settlement. T/F. *Matthew 5:25*

Lesson 8

1. Jesus tells us not to _____ an evil person. (challenge, resist, join?) *Matthew 5:39*

2. We are to only love those who reciprocate our affection. T/F. *Matthew 5:46*

Lesson 9

1. You will be judged by the same _____ by which you judge others. *Matthew 7:2*

2. Sometimes bad trees can bear good fruit. T/F. *Matthew 7:18*

Lesson 10

1. After David became a permanent fixture of Saul's court, what did Jonathan give to David? (garments, a boat, a curse?) *1 Samuel 18:4*

2. After listening to his son plead for David's life, Saul swore that he was going to kill David anyway. T/F. *1 Samuel 19:6*

Lesson 11

1. Both of Naomi's daughters-in-law were willing to go to Judah with her. T/F. *Ruth 1:10*

2. Ruth was _____ to go with Naomi to Judah. (hesitant, determined, reluctant?) *Ruth 1:18*

Lesson 12

1. The name of Naomi's relative who allowed Ruth to glean in his field was _____. *Ruth 3:2*

2. The man in the previous question was "first in line" as Ruth's family redeemer. T/F. *Ruth 3:12*

Lesson 13

1. Christ's relationship with the _____ is analogous to the relationship of marriage. *Ephesians 5:23*

2. Husbands are to love their wives as much as they love what? (sports, their own bodies, their jobs?) *Ephesians 5:28*

QUARTER AT A GLANCE

by Jim Eichenberger

HUMAN RELATIONSHIPS are built on interpersonal agreements. We formalize these agreements as contracts or covenants. Covenants promise that debts will be paid or services will be performed regardless of the situations in which the parties may find themselves after the contract is finalized.

At times, a party to a contract may be deemed a poor risk. That person may have a history that does not provide adequate assurance that he or she will be able to meet the obligations of a covenant. Situations such as these may require a guarantor or cosigner. The guarantor assumes the responsibility for terms of the covenant when a party defaults on the agreement.

During this quarter, we will develop a clearer understanding as to why our relationship with God through Christ is expressed as a covenant.

Guarantee of Payment

Let's face it: human beings have a dismal "credit rating" with God! Old Testament history illustrates that God's people defaulted on promises to their Creator time after time. How can a working relationship ever be forged between God and such unreliable signatories?

The first unit of this quarter focuses on the role of Jesus as our guarantor. We come before God with a massive debt to Him. A fair look at our "spiritual finances" would yield the inevitable conclusion that we have liabilities that we can never repay. But enter the guarantor!

Gathering with His disciples on the last Passover they shared, Jesus used that reminder of the past to institute a covenant for the future. His very body and blood was to clear our sin-debt, making a relationship with God possible. While we must never assume that our duty to God is trivial or nonexistent, we can know that our guarantor has done what animal sacrifices and ritual actions can never accomplish.

Power to Perform

The guarantee of a contract is not the end, but the beginning. The second quarter in this unit moves from debt to performance. Jesus paid our sin debt. But how can we now live as responsible citizens of God's kingdom?

Jesus' Sermon on the Mount addresses that very issue. Christ's followers are called to display a superior, imputed righteousness. Empowered by the Holy Spirit, believers have transformed attitudes, world-changing influence, and a discernment to view the world from the perspective of their king.

Help in Difficult Times

Life is filled with challenges. Sometimes those trials make it difficult to live as a forgiven, reborn child of God. The third unit in this quarter is a series of case studies of God-followers overcoming those difficulties and living as faithful children of the Father.

David (King Saul's anointed successor) and Jonathan (a bloodline heir to Saul's throne) maintained a friendship despite the conflict inherent in their respective positions. What could have been an adversarial relationship between Ruth and

> *Covenants promise that debts will be paid or services will be performed.*

Naomi became one of mutual support because of their relationship with the God of Israel. The joining of Boaz and Ruth with a marriage covenant was preparatory to an immeasurably greater covenant to come.

May this quarter cause us to rejoice in the remarkable covenant we have with God. Through Jesus, our guarantor, our sin-debt to God is paid, our behavior is empowered by the Spirit, and the most difficult, faith-shaking tests can be overcome!

GET THE SETTING

by Lloyd M. Pelfrey

COVENANTS COME with consequences. The people of the biblical world knew these consequences as blessings or curses. The curses employed graphic language to express dire retribution for anyone who would dare not keep a covenant. The Mosaic covenant between the Lord and Israel also promised forms of retribution. Who witnessed the covenant and who would carry out its terms, however, was unique.

Covenants of Conquerors and Kings

Covenants were usually made after military victories, with the terms being dictated by the conquering nation. Future generations were often included as active participants. These national treaties routinely expressed what various gods would do to any vassal or subservient nation that dared to break a covenant.

One such covenant, dated about 1350 BC, listed over 70 witnessing gods and goddesses. They included storm gods, warrior gods, and gods of regions as well as gods and goddesses of mountains, rivers, winds, and clouds. The implications were clear: it would be very foolish for anyone to break a covenant because these gods or goddesses would retaliate if any participant chose to break the covenant.

It was also a custom to express lengthy lists of curses for the covenant breakers. The penalties pronounced for a disobedient king included general misery, poverty, loss of the throne, being exterminated from the country, being childless, and being hated by a thousand gods. The threats were expressed so strongly that no one would want to experience the wrath of so many gods. Sooner or later one or more of these things would happen, and the lawbreakers would assume that the gods were punishing them.

A king of the seventh century BC listed similar curses, preceding them with ways that someone might try to void a covenant or oath. The preliminary phrases try to exhaust the possibilities and use these terms: changes, neglects, transgresses, erases, removes, burns, throws into water, buries, destroys, annihilates, or turns it face down. Such a list tried to cover the possibilities to prevent anyone from negating a covenant.

Punishments were often violent. In about 750 BC, a covenant between a king of Assyria (the sovereign) and a ruler of Arpad (the vassal) stated that the disobedient king, his children, his officials, and his people would be treated like a sacrificial animal; as the head of the lamb was torn off, so the heads of others will be removed. In other treaties the gods were summoned to enact terrible punishment: pronounce evil; bring disease, worry, poor health, leprosy, and blindness; feed them to birds; cause floods, locust invasion, and famine; infest with animal predators; give perpetual sores; cause thirst; make them watch atrocities to their family; and other vicious descriptions.

The Mosaic Covenant

The Mosaic covenant between the Lord and Israel was different. It stated that God himself would inflict the penalties if other gods were served. A listing of such curses is found in Deuteronomy 28:15-68. (See also Leviticus 26:14-39.) In Deuteronomy it is repeatedly affirmed that "the Lord shall" bring about the curses.

The subsequent history of Israel shows that the Lord was patient and forgiving time after time. The nations of Israel and Judah finally learned that to swear allegiance to the Lord and then worship other gods would change privilege into punishment—and exile.

The lessons that are about to be studied accent positive aspects of different types of covenants. The astute person, however, knows that there are unpleasant consequences when any covenant is broken—in marriage, in business, or in the new covenant provided by the Messiah.

Answers to the Quarterly Quiz on page 338

Lesson 1—1. true. 2. better. **Lesson 2**—1. true. 2. top, bottom. **Lesson 3**—1. mediator. 2. false. **Lesson 4**—1. Laodicea. 2. fullness. **Lesson 5**—1. the poor in spirit. 2. mercy. **Lesson 6**—1. salt, light. 2. destroy, fulfill. **Lesson 7**—1. false. 2. true. **Lesson 8**—1. resist. 2. false. **Lesson 9**—1. judgment. 2. false. **Lesson 10**—1. garments. 2. false. **Lesson 11**—1. true. 2. determined. **Lesson 12**—1. Boaz. 2. false. **Lesson 13**—1. church. 2. their own bodies.

CHART FEATURE

Chronological Outline of Selected Events in Matthew

EARLY PERIOD

Genealogy (1:1-17)
The Birth of Jesus (1:18–2:12) ———————————————— **4 BC**
The Flight to Egypt and Return to Nazareth (2:13-23)

BEGINNING OF JESUS' MINISTRY ———————————————— **AD 26**

John's Ministry (3:1-12)
The Baptism of Jesus (3:13-17)
The Temptation (4:1-11)

THE GALILEAN MINISTRY ———————————————— **AD 27**

The Calling of four Fishermen (4:18-22)
Teaching and Miracles in Capernaum (8:14-17)
The Call of Matthew (9:9-13)
Teaching and Healing the Multitudes (12:15-21) ———————— **AD 28**
The Sermon on the Mount (5:1–8:1)
Opposition to Jesus (12:22-45)
The Great Sermon in Parables (13:1-35)
Miracles of Compassion (9:18-38) ———————————————— **AD 29**
The Twelve Apostles named (10:1-4)
The Feeding of 5000 (14:13-21)
Walking on Water (14:22-33)
Peter's Great Confession (16:13-20)
The Transfiguration (17:1-8)

JOURNEY TO JUDEA ———————————————— **AD 30**

Jesus in Perea (19:1-12)
The Rich Young Ruler (16:16-22)
The Blind Men at Jericho (20:29-34)

THE FINAL DAYS

The Triumphal Entry (21:1-17)
The Day of Questions (22:1-46)
Prediction of the Second Coming (24:45-51)
The Parable of the Ten Virgins (25:1-13)
The Passover Meal and the Lord's Supper (26:17-29)
Agony in the Garden (26:36-46)
The Arrest and Trials of Jesus (26:47–27:26)
The Death of Jesus (27:27-66)
The Resurrection (28:1-15)
The Great Commission (28:16-20)

CHOOSING THE DECOR

Part 4 of Building Bible Literacy   *Teacher Tips by Jim Eichenberger*

IN THE PRECEDING three articles in this series, we compared the story arc of Scripture to the blueprint of a house, the literary types found in the Bible to different but essential building materials, and the rooms in the floor plan to key doctrines of the faith. But after the building is complete, one step remains. It must be properly decorated and equipped to suit its occupants.

A Bible student may gain a mastery of the content of God's Word and yet lack Bible literacy. A Bible teacher must both tell how the Scriptures inform our beliefs and how God's Word guides our actions.

Some Cautions

A house needs walls before the owner can hang pictures. Likewise, in building Bible literacy, it is essential to give your group members an understanding of Bible chronology, literary types, and basic Christian doctrine before looking to the Bible for specific life direction.

There is a thin line between application *of* Scripture and justifying one's stances *from* Scripture. Application involves a fair reading of the Bible to discern principles for living. Justification will pick and choose from God's Word. It is the difference between "What would Jesus do?" and "What will I tell Jesus when He asks why I did it?"

Guiding Principles

The maxim, "In Essentials Unity, In Nonessentials Liberty, In All Things Charity," is a worthy compass to consult as we seek to apply Scripture to our lives. There are universal norms that should guide all believers. But the very nature of humankind tempts us to go beyond those essentials to insist that others keep a much more complex moral code. When Jesus himself was asked to prioritize God's commands, He reduced the laundry list of Jewish laws to two essentials—love of God and love of neighbor (Matthew 22:36-40).

As the Bible teacher helps students apply Scriptures, he or she must help them understand how the same universal norms can be fulfilled in different ways at different times and in different cultures. The Bible both commands that Christians meet together (Hebrews 10:25) and gives examples of them doing so (Acts 4:31; 11:26; 15:25). But that command may be met in many different circumstances.

Areas to Explore

Studies that help believers apply God's Word to contemporary life fall into several categories. Here are a few to consider:

Christian Living. The Bible gives general principles for life that a skilled Bible teacher, with an understanding of a class and current situations, can use as a basis for practical "how-to" lessons. Parenting, marriage and dating, money management, and many more are topics on which God's Word can be consulted to have the abundant life we are meant to have.

Church Practices. There is no one way to "do church." Churches have always employed different worship styles, distributed their shared wealth in a variety of ways, and chosen specific leaders that suited their ministry goals. Mature believers can consult Scripture to look for guiding principles, even when there are no direct commands.

Social Issues. Matters such as abortion, pornography, poverty, and even war are much more complex than they first appear. While divisive, believers may study them to look for common ground. Refusing to make decisions based on self-interest, Christians can look for God's perspective on these troubling issues.

It is tempting to make practical studies a priority of Christian education. It is wise, however, to build a solid foundation for Bible literacy before dealing with topics that may be much more ambiguous.

JESUS INSTITUTES THE NEW COVENANT

DEVOTIONAL READING: Jeremiah 31:31-34
BACKGROUND SCRIPTURE: Mark 14:12-31; Hebrews 8

MARK 14:17-25

17 And in the evening he cometh with the twelve.

18 And as they sat and did eat, Jesus said, Verily I say unto you, One of you which eateth with me shall betray me.

19 And they began to be sorrowful, and to say unto him one by one, Is it I? and another said, Is it I?

20 And he answered and said unto them, It is one of the twelve, that dippeth with me in the dish.

21 The Son of man indeed goeth, as it is written of him: but woe to that man by whom the Son of man is betrayed! good were it for that man if he had never been born.

22 And as they did eat, Jesus took bread, and blessed, and brake it, and gave to them, and said, Take, eat: this is my body.

23 And he took the cup, and when he had given thanks, he gave it to them: and they all drank of it.

24 And he said unto them, This is my blood of the new testament, which is shed for many.

25 Verily I say unto you, I will drink no more of the fruit of the vine, until that day that I drink it new in the kingdom of God.

HEBREWS 8:6, 7, 10-12

6 But now hath he obtained a more excellent ministry, by how much also he is the mediator of a better covenant, which was established upon better promises.

7 For if that first covenant had been faultless, then should no place have been sought for the second.

· ·

10 For this is the covenant that I will make with the house of Israel after those days, saith the Lord; I will put my laws into their mind, and write them in their hearts: and I will be to them a God, and they shall be to me a people:

11 And they shall not teach every man his neighbour, and every man his brother, saying, Know the Lord: for all shall know me, from the least to the greatest.

12 For I will be merciful to their unrighteousness, and their sins and their iniquities will I remember no more.

KEY VERSE

Now hath he obtained a more excellent ministry, by how much also he is the mediator of a better covenant, which was established upon better promises. —**Hebrews 8:6**

COVENANT IN GOD

Unit 1: A Fulfilled Covenant

LESSONS 1–4

LESSON AIMS

After participating in this lesson, each learner will be able to:

1. Quote from memory Jesus' words regarding the bread and cup of the last supper.

2. Explain how the lesson texts from Mark and Hebrews interrelate.

3. Develop a plan to make observance of the Lord's Supper more meaningful.

LESSON OUTLINE

Introduction
  A. A Monumental Explanation
  B. Lesson Context
I. Covenant Anticipated (MARK 14:17-25)
  A. Enacted Through a Betrayal (vv. 17-21)
  B. Celebrated as a Passover (vv. 22-25)
    Food for the Holidays
II. Covenant Described (HEBREWS 8:6, 7, 10-12)
  A. Fulfilling Israel's Covenant (vv. 6, 7)
  B. Making a New People (vv. 10-12)
    Carry It with You
Conclusion
  A. How the Lord's Supper Defines Us
  B. Prayer
  C. Thought to Remember

Introduction

A. A Monumental Explanation

Monuments need explanations. Sometimes a monument has a plaque or inscription that tells us what it commemorates. Always, though, a monument means that an important event took place, one to be remembered in joy or in sorrow. Customs can serve as monuments, reminding people who observe them of great events. Annual holidays, birthdays, and anniversaries include special ceremonies or meals to commemorate events that are important to us. We celebrate these together as families, communities, and nations to share the events' importance.

> *What Do You Think?*
> What are some ways to use secular "monuments" to enhance our commitment to Christ? Or is that even possible? Explain.
> *Digging Deeper*
> Consider physical monuments (example: tombstone of a famous national leader) as well as those of a nonphysical nature (example: days on the calendar).

Israel's greatest monuments were its annual feasts, celebrating God's mighty acts of salvation (Leviticus 23:2-43). Passover was especially notable, commemorating God's bringing Israel out of slavery in Egypt (Exodus 12:1–13:16; Deuteronomy 16:1-8). As time went on, it became customary to begin that feast with a question to introduce the epic story of Israel's deliverance: "Why is this night different from all other nights?" The head of the family would then explain, telling the story of Israel's deliverance.

B. Lesson Context

The story of Jesus eating the Passover meal with His disciples before His death is a turning point in the gospel story. After Peter's confession of Jesus as the Christ in Mark 8:29, Jesus began warning His disciples of His coming death and resurrection (8:31; 9:31; 10:33, 34). Yet they did not understand these warnings (9:32). For them, the Christ must triumph over His foes militarily, replacing the rule of the Gentile nations with the rule of God (Acts 1:6). Jesus' triumphal entry into Jerusalem, when He was given the welcome of a king before the Passover, must have been a high mark of that expectation. Surely Jesus was to be the one to renew David's kingdom (Mark 11:7-10)!

The Passover that followed a few days later must have been tinged with this expectation. But Passover observances were always both joyous and solemn. Each of its elements was intended to remind participants of God's triumph over Egypt. For example, bread made without leaven (yeast) was a reminder of the haste with which the meal was prepared in anticipation of leaving the land of slavery (Exodus 12:15, 17-20, 33, 34). The annual celebration of Passover affirmed for Israel that God had liberated them and made them His people (12:42).

The resulting covenant was the expression of God's actions, promises, and expectations for His people. God's covenant with Israel had begun with Abraham (then known as Abram; see Genesis 15:18-21) and was affirmed for the entire nation at Sinai (Exodus 24:1-8). But that covenant ended up being broken time and again. A new one was needed.

I. Covenant Anticipated

(MARK 14:17-25)

Jewish leadership schemed to arrest Jesus while He was out of the public eye. As our text opens, they have enlisted Judas to help find Jesus at such a time (Mark 14:1, 2, 10, 11).

A. Enacted Through a Betrayal (vv. 17-21)

17. And in the evening he cometh with the twelve.

The twelve disciples have accompanied Jesus from early days (Mark 3:13-19). It appears likely that Jesus deliberately chose 12 disciples to evoke the regathering of the scattered 12 tribes of Israel, a symbol of God's bringing the promised new covenant. These 12 show themselves faithful but are often slow to understand or believe Jesus' words (4:40; 8:31-33; 10:35-45). Yet Jesus intends to eat His final meal with these men, and only them, during Passover.

18. And as they sat and did eat, Jesus said, Verily I say unto you, One of you which eateth with me shall betray me.

The disciples' failure now approaches a climax in one of their own. Jesus begins solemnly with *verily* (a translation of the Greek word *amen*), an expression He uses when announcing warnings or promises (Mark 10:15, 29).

Jesus' words reveal that the secret plot against His life is no secret to Him. Throughout the story of His arrest, trials, and death, Jesus is in control of events, willingly submitting and never taken by surprise (Mark 14:35-38; John 19:11). Repeatedly He has warned of His death (Mark 8:31; 9:30-32; 10:32-34). Now He anticipates a betrayal that is all too common in Israel's history (compare Genesis 4:1-12; 37:12-36; Judges 16:18; 2 Samuel 15; 1 Kings 21:8-10; etc.). In this way, He again enters into the fullness of human experience, sparing himself no pain that can be experienced by a person (Philippians 2:8).

19. And they began to be sorrowful, and to say unto him one by one, Is it I? and another said, Is it I?

The disciples perceive themselves to be faithful to Jesus regardless of their prior lapses. Their repeated question reflects bewilderment. It is asked in a way that indicates the disciples expect the answer to be "no."

20. And he answered and said unto them, It is one of the twelve, that dippeth with me in the dish.

In Mark's Gospel, Jesus' answer to the disciples' question leaves all uncertain. Sharing the Passover meal at a common table, they all dip pieces of unleavened bread in the common bowls. John 13:26-30 makes clear who the traitor is, but Mark's account seems to underline the idea that all of them are potential betrayers.

VISUALS FOR THESE LESSONS

The visual pictured in each lesson (example: page 348) is a small reproduction of a large, full-color poster included in the *Adult Resources* packet for the Summer Quarter. That packet also contains the very useful *Presentation Tools* CD for teacher use. Order No. 4629119 from your supplier.

Visual for Lesson 1. *Start a discussion by pointing to this as you ask, "What connection do you see between these transitions and the Lord's Supper?"*

21a. The Son of man indeed goeth, as it is written of him.

Jesus refers to himself as *the Son of man* more than 80 times in the Gospels. It appears that He uses the phrase to connect His work to the figure in the vision of the prophet Daniel. There "one like the Son of man" establishes God's rule and destroys the evil kingdoms that have dominated His people (Daniel 7:13, 14).

The phrase emphasizes Jesus' authority and power as well as His humanity and humility (compare Philippians 2:6-11). Nearer the beginning of His ministry, Jesus used the phrase primarily when asserting His authority as the divine king (Mark 2:10, 11, 28). But after Peter confessed Him to be the Christ, Jesus began to use the phrase to warn of His coming suffering and death (8:31; 9:12, 31; 10:33, 34, 45).

Those predictions are about to be realized. This is in keeping with the prophets who spoke of one who was to be rejected and suffer as God's servant (Isaiah 52:13–53:12; Zechariah 13:7). This, says Jesus repeatedly, is the climax and fulfillment of God's plan.

21b. But woe to that man by whom the Son of man is betrayed! good were it for that man if he had never been born.

God's purpose does not absolve the betrayer of guilt (see Acts 1:15-25). Judas is not compelled by God to do what God's plan requires. Even so, the all-knowing, all-powerful God can use Judas's

evil act for good (compare Genesis 50:20). The betrayer, like all humans, remains fully responsible for his actions and so fully subject to God's judgment.

But that holy judgment stands alongside God's loving mercy. One disciple will betray Jesus, but all will abandon Him (Mark 14:27-31, 50). Those willing to receive His mercy can be welcomed back—and will be after the resurrection (16:7). The faithful are those who seek and receive Christ's forgiveness, not those who never need it, as if such people even exist (2:17).

B. Celebrated as a Passover (vv. 22-25)

22. And as they did eat, Jesus took bread, and blessed, and brake it, and gave to them, and said, Take, eat: this is my body.

In Jesus' time, the host customarily takes the *bread* and distributes it to the others at the table. But Jesus does so with an unexpected declaration: *this is my body.* The dividing of a body suggests the cutting up of an animal offered as a sacrifice on the altar of the tabernacle or temple (see Leviticus 1:6, 12). Jesus is thus identifying himself as the supreme sacrificial offering for sins. He takes the place of the sacrificial lamb (compare Exodus 12:3-10, 21-23).

Jesus' actions also echo His miraculous feeding of great crowds in the wilderness. As at this Passover meal, Jesus had taken the loaves and fish to bless or give thanks before feeding the people (Mark 6:41; 8:6). Those events in sparsely populated areas served as reminders of God's provision for Israel when He sent manna to feed them in the wilderness (Exodus 16). Jesus' actions also recall Israel's expectation of a great feast that celebrates God's reclaiming the world for himself (Isaiah 25:6-9; compare Matthew 8:11). Now all these events are tied together in Jesus' impending death and resurrection.

23. And he took the cup, and when he had given thanks, he gave it to them: and they all drank of it.

Jesus repeats His actions, this time with *the cup,* the content of which is "the fruit of the vine" (see Mark 14:25, below). At Passover, the host invokes God's blessing on the guests' drinking of this in celebration of Israel's deliverance from Egypt. Previously, Jesus had used the word *cup* as a figure of speech for His impending death. In so doing, He asked the disciples if they were ready to drink of the same cup (Mark 10:38). Now He offers them a literal cup, and the imagery is that they will receive the benefit of His death and follow Him in self-sacrificial service (8:34-38; 10:43-45).

> *What Do You Think?*
> What are some ways your church can help people better understand and appreciate the significance of the Lord's Supper?
>
> *Digging Deeper*
> As you consider historical and doctrinal points to emphasize, think also of how to spot false analogies.

---

24. And he said unto them, This is my blood of the new testament, which is shed for many.

We easily imagine the disciples are startled as Jesus identifies the contents of the cup with His own *blood*. Hindsight tells us that *shed for many* indicates blood to be poured out as that of a sacrificial animal (compare Leviticus 4:7; 1 Peter 1:18, 19). This represents the animal's life being given to make atonement (Leviticus 17:11). Thus does Jesus frame His looming death in terms that remind us of God's promise in Isaiah 53:11, 12.

Blood is associated with the covenant that God made with Israel at Mount Sinai. Moses took a basin of blood from a sacrificial animal and sprinkled it on the assembled people of Israel as a sign of God's covenant (Exodus 24:8). Now Jesus announces a *testament* (elsewhere translated *cov-*

HOW TO SAY IT

Abraham	*Ay*-bruh-ham.
Corinthians	Ko-*rin*-thee-unz (*th* as in *thin*).
Deuteronomy	Due-ter-*ahn*-uh-me.
Gentile	*Jen*-tile.
Isaiah	Eye-*zay*-uh.
Jeremiah	Jair-uh-*my*-uh.
Leviticus	Leh-*vit*-ih-kus.
Sinai	*Sigh*-nye or *Sigh*-nay-eye.
Zechariah	*Zek*-uh-*rye*-uh.

enant; see Luke 1:72) that fulfills the intent and promises of the earlier covenants God made with Israel (compare 2 Samuel 7:5-16; Ezekiel 37:24-25). This intent concerns, above all, the forgiveness of sin (Jeremiah 31:34). That forgiveness results in the promised restoration of God's blessing and the establishment of His rule. All God's promises converge here (compare Isaiah 2:2; 42:6; 49:6; etc.).

❧ FOOD FOR THE HOLIDAYS ❧

Holiday celebrations often include specific foods as a part of the observance. For instance, in Great Britain on Guy Fawkes Night, British citizens light bonfires and snack on bonfire toffee. Americans eat pumpkin pie almost exclusively at Thanksgiving. In the Philippines, a traditional Christmas dinner includes a whole roasted pig. Some Christians celebrate Shrove Tuesday, the day before the fasting associated with Lent. Depending on where one is celebrating, pancakes, omelets, and various soups might be part of the local culinary tradition.

The Passover meal in first-century Judaism also required specific foods. These included lamb, bitter herbs, fruit of the vine, and unleavened bread. Jesus and His disciples certainly knew the meaning of the food eaten at His final Passover meal. But when Jesus took the bread and the cup, He replaced old significance with new. Are we sure we grasp the full import of that change?   —J. E.

25. Verily I say unto you, I will drink no more of the fruit of the vine, until that day that I drink it new in the kingdom of God.

Jesus again summarizes the significance of His actions with the solemn invocation *verily* (see commentary on Mark 14:18, above). To forego *the fruit of the vine* suggests a significant interruption. What seems hidden from the disciples is clear enough to us in hindsight: Jesus is pointing to His impending death.

Further, Jesus is pointing beyond His death to the establishment of God's promised rule of justice and peace over the world. Only then will He celebrate again: *in the kingdom of God,* with all His disciples. Jesus' actions at Passover are pointing to the celebration in the future when God's victory is complete and all His people are gathered in celebration (compare Isaiah 2:1-5; Micah 4:1-5).

> What Do You Think?
> What are some ways we can deepen our awareness of God's present and future reign while we participate in the Lord's Supper?
> Digging Deeper
> Consider further how that deepened awareness should influence your walk with Christ daily.

II. Covenant Described

(HEBREWS 8:6, 7, 10-12)

The book of Hebrews was written to urge Jewish Christians not to abandon their faith in Jesus as God's promised king. The book demonstrates how the new covenant in Jesus does greater things than God's covenant with Israel could do.

A. Fulfilling Israel's Covenant (vv. 6, 7)

6. But now hath he obtained a more excellent ministry, by how much also he is the mediator of a better covenant, which was established upon better promises.

To say that Jesus has *a more excellent ministry* is to compare Him favorably with those who ministered before. He is the true *mediator* between God and humanity, a priest who is free from sin and so able to make an effective sacrifice of His own life for others (Hebrews 9:11-14).

Therefore, Jesus establishes *a better covenant* than what had come before. He does not merely point forward to God's salvation; Jesus' covenant actually accomplishes salvation (Hebrews 9:15). The *promises* fulfilled are thus greater as well. God's people are led not just by God's king or prophet but by God's own Son (2 Samuel 7:11-14; Hebrews 7:17-25).

Lasting rest is now possible (see Revelation 14:13; 21:1-4). Such rest is not possible in earthly cities such as Jerusalem. But it is guaranteed in the heavenly Jerusalem, a city built by God. There God will dwell with His people forever (Revelation 21:9-27).

> What Do You Think?
> How will your understanding of the benefits of God's covenant promises help you overcome temptations to abandon the Christian faith?
> Digging Deeper
> Consider various contexts in which that temptation might occur (examples: relationship crisis; health crisis; church conflict).

7. For if that first covenant had been faultless, then should no place have been sought for the second.

God did not make a mistake in giving the *first covenant*. Neither did Moses or the other prophets who delivered and affirmed it. Rather, the old covenant's problem was that by design it could not rescue people permanently from sin (compare Ezekiel 11:17-20). It was partial, pointing to something greater.

Israel's failure to keep the old covenant demonstrates that it could not prevent the people from sinning and falling away from faithfulness. Because of their wayward hearts, the Israelites found themselves not blessed by the covenant but instead under the curse of exile (Deuteronomy 11:26-28). The greater covenant to come, brought by Jesus, carries the perfect fulfillment of God's blessings. It provides the power by which people can genuinely fulfill His purposes in the world (John 14:12-17; 17:1-5).

B. Making a New People (vv. 10-12)

10. For this is the covenant that I will make with the house of Israel after those days, saith the Lord; I will put my laws into their mind, and write them in their hearts: and I will be to them a God, and they shall be to me a people.

Having introduced the concept of a greater covenant, the author of Hebrews quotes from Jeremiah 31:31-34. This text promised Israel that after its exile, God would establish a better covenant. By it we can experience the fulfillment of His purposes.

Jeremiah prophesied of laws written not on stone like the Ten Commandments but on hearts, internalized by covenant members. The lives of

His *people* under the new covenant demonstrate that God is fulfilling His will in them. Christians are a people who show God's light in a dark world that does not know Him (compare John 1:9-13).

❧ CARRY IT WITH YOU ❧

The early 1990s saw the release of a pocket-size resource titled *The U.S. Constitution & Fascinating Facts About It*. This booklet became a best-seller. In the weeks preceding the 2016 U.S. election, the demand for pocket-size copies of the Constitution was so great that over 100,000 free copies were distributed by a nonprofit organization. A college went a step further, offering not only free pocket editions but also a free online class on the U.S. Constitution.

As vital as the U.S. Constitution is to American citizens, words of greater importance exist: those of the new covenant. In the new covenant, God did more than make a small version of His laws available for us to carry in our pockets. He promised to write them on our hearts. How do you remember that you carry His covenant with you?

—J. E.

11. And they shall not teach every man his neighbour, and every man his brother, saying, Know the Lord: for all shall know me, from the least to the greatest.

Membership in Old Testament Israel was primarily, though not exclusively, a matter of family (Numbers 15:14-16). One was born into the covenant people, and the sign of the covenant, circumcision, was applied to male children eight days after their birth (Genesis 17:10-14). Though they were made covenant members by birth and especially by male circumcision, Israelites still required instruction in their faith (Deuteronomy 6:6-9).

In Jesus, by contrast, the gospel message is the means of incorporation. Those who belong to the covenant belong by faith in the Jesus who is proclaimed in the gospel (Romans 3:21-24; Galatians 2:15, 16). All covenant members are those who already know the Lord. The book of Hebrews of course does not rule out additional instruction for Christ's followers. The letter itself is additional instruction! But the covenant prom-

ised through Jeremiah now has its fulfillment in the community of those who believe the gospel message. (Another viewpoint proposes that the phrase *all shall know me* points to an ultimate future in Heaven.)

> *What Do You Think?*
> Which should be more important to our walk with Christ: knowing God's laws in our mind, or feeling them in our hearts? Why?
> *Digging Deeper*
> In what ways, if any, should your response take into account personality differences and/or spiritual maturity? Why?

12. For I will be merciful to their unrighteousness, and their sins and their iniquities will I remember no more.

The grace that God has always exercised comes to full fruit in this new covenant (Isaiah 43:25). The sin of all humanity has its answer here. By God's mercy, made available through Christ's sacrifice, all people can find forgiveness in this new covenant (Matthew 28:18-20; Acts 26:18).

Conclusion

A. How the Lord's Supper Defines Us

As Passover defined Old Testament Israel as God's covenant people, so the Lord's Supper defines Christians. This feast is a way of remembering how God covered our imperfect lives with His perfect mercy by Jesus' sacrificial death. It represents the connections of mercy, love, and service we have with one another as God's people. It reminds us of the greater covenant by which we serve as God's light in the world.

B. Prayer

Lord God, we are filled with thanksgiving to be called Your people! By Your Spirit, empower us to live and serve as those who have been forgiven by the blood of our Lord Jesus. In Jesus' name, amen.

C. Thought to Remember

God's fulfilled promises call us
to lives filled with Christlikeness.

INVOLVEMENT LEARNING

Enhance your lesson with KJV Bible Student *(from your curriculum supplier) and the reproducible activity page (at www.standardlesson.com or in the back of the* KJV Standard Lesson Commentary Deluxe Edition*).*

Into the Lesson

Ask the class to name special observances and holidays that are important to them. Jot responses on the board. Then go through that list and ask the following of each one named: 1–What does this commemorate? 2–What elements of this holiday or observance are joyful and which are sorrowful? 3–Is this something celebrated with families, specific communities, or as a nation?

Alternative. Place copies of "A Jewish Holiday" activity from the reproducible page, which you can download, in students' chairs before they arrive. Have students work individually to match the list of Jewish traditions to the list of Jewish holidays with which they belong. After a minute, have students share their answers with the class, including their knowledge of the significance of the holidays or traditions listed.

After either activity, lead into the Bible study by saying, "The Israelites themselves had greatly revered commemorations. But there was one in particular that Jesus took time to teach His disciples a new way to celebrate. To fully understand this new celebration, we must first look at the Passover feast as originally instituted."

Into the Word

Form learners into pairs and give each a handout (you create) of a blank Venn diagram. Explain that a Venn diagram consists of two large circles that overlap, with the overlapping area representing what the two circles have in common.

Ask one person of each pair to look up Mark 14:17-25 and the other to look up Hebrews 8:6, 7, 10-12. Ask learners to examine assigned texts closely as they fill in the Venn diagram. Instruct them to label the left circle "Passover" and the right circle "Lord's Supper." Explain that the Passover section that does not overlap should include elements that are unique to the Passover; likewise, the Lord's Supper section that does not overlap should include elements that are unique to the Lord's Supper. Stress that the overlapping middle section should include elements common to both.

Possible responses: Passover–celebrated annually, usually observed at home with the full family, includes bitter herbs and a retelling of the story of the exodus from Egypt; *Lord's Supper*–observed regularly throughout the year, usually observed in a church setting, expresses the foundation of the new covenant; *Overlapping*–joyful yet solemn, unites those who experience it together, the use of unleavened bread and fruit of the vine.

After pairs finish, create a larger Venn diagram on the board. Fill in each section as a class. Use the lesson text, commentary, and other passages to resolve misunderstandings.

Into Life

Close the class by having the students take a personal look at the Lord's Supper. Do this by encouraging students to finish this sentence: "The Lord's Supper is significant to me because _____." Then ask students to finish this sentence: "Practical ways to add more significance to partaking of communion include _____." (*Possible responses:* recalling that this act reaffirms the new covenant; when taking the bread, remembering why the bread is without yeast; etc.)

Then say, "Be sure to implement the practical plans that promote the most biblical meaning the next time you partake of the Lord's Supper." Read 1 Corinthians 11:23-26 and allow a minute of reflection on the passage.

Alternative. Distribute the "The Lord's Supper" activity from the reproducible page. Have students take one minute to reflect individually on how the elements of the Lord's Supper are significant. Then ask for volunteers to share their thoughts.

Close in prayer: "Lord, thank You so much for Jesus' sacrificial death. May our lives be defined by His sacrifice. We pray in Jesus' name. Amen."

JESUS SEALS THE NEW COVENANT

DEVOTIONAL READING: Psalm 22:1-8, 21b-28
BACKGROUND SCRIPTURE: Mark 14:32-50; 15

MARK 15:6-15, 25, 26, 33-39

6 Now at that feast he released unto them one prisoner, whomsoever they desired.

7 And there was one named Barabbas, which lay bound with them that had made insurrection with him, who had committed murder in the insurrection.

8 And the multitude crying aloud began to desire him to do as he had ever done unto them.

9 But Pilate answered them, saying, Will ye that I release unto you the King of the Jews?

10 For he knew that the chief priests had delivered him for envy.

11 But the chief priests moved the people, that he should rather release Barabbas unto them.

12 And Pilate answered and said again unto them, What will ye then that I shall do unto him whom ye call the King of the Jews?

13 And they cried out again, Crucify him.

14 Then Pilate said unto them, Why, what evil hath he done? And they cried out the more exceedingly, Crucify him.

15 And so Pilate, willing to content the people, released Barabbas unto them, and delivered Jesus, when he had scourged him, to be crucified.

. . . .

25 And it was the third hour, and they crucified him.

26 And the superscription of his accusation was written over, THE KING OF THE JEWS.

. . . .

33 And when the sixth hour was come, there was darkness over the whole land until the ninth hour.

34 And at the ninth hour Jesus cried with a loud voice, saying, Eloi, Eloi, lama sabachthani? which is, being interpreted, My God, my God, why hast thou forsaken me?

35 And some of them that stood by, when they heard it, said, Behold, he calleth Elias.

36 And one ran and filled a spunge full of vinegar, and put it on a reed, and gave him to drink, saying, Let alone; let us see whether Elias will come to take him down.

37 And Jesus cried with a loud voice, and gave up the ghost.

38 And the veil of the temple was rent in twain from the top to the bottom.

39 And when the centurion, which stood over against him, saw that he so cried out, and gave up the ghost, he said, Truly this man was the Son of God.

KEY VERSE

When the centurion, which stood over against him, saw that he so cried out, and gave up the ghost, he said, Truly this man was the Son of God. —**Mark 15:39**

COVENANT IN GOD

Unit 1: A Fulfilled Covenant

LESSON AIMS

After participating in this lesson, each learner will be able to:

1. List the salient events that occurred on Good Friday.

2. Explain how Mark's narrative identifies Jesus' crucifixion as His suffering in place of sinful humanity.

3. State one way he or she will live out in the week ahead the reality that the suffering Christ is the world's true king.

LESSON OUTLINE

Introduction

A. The Struggle to Rule

Accounts of rulers coming to power often make for fascinating storytelling. Whether historical like the American Revolution or fictional like the *Lord of the Rings* trilogy, we are captivated by *The* struggle to gain and maintain rule. We follow the alliances, the plotting, the intrigue, the betrayals. We weigh the characters in the balance of good and evil. Who will have the resources, the cleverness, the luck to come out on top? Once that person reaches power, how will it be used? Who benefits under the rule of this new leader?

B. Lesson Context

The Roman Empire was one of a series of powerful empires that the Bible cites as having dominated Israel. It followed Egypt, Assyria, Babylon, and Persia in that regard (see Exodus 1; 2 Kings 15:29; 16:7-9, 18; 24:15-17; 25:8-12; 2 Chronicles 36:22, 23; Ezra 1; Esther 1:1-4; 10:1-3). Roman rule was not simply a *political* problem for Israel; it was a religious difficulty. The Romans claimed absolute authority for Rome, not for Israel's God. Many of Jesus' contemporaries hoped for a mighty military leader who, with God's power, would rally Israel to overthrow their Roman oppressors. This leader was expected to establish God's rule over the entire world, beginning with Jerusalem. Revolt always seemed to be in the air (compare Acts 5:36, 37).

One way Rome demonstrated its determination to squelch such movements was crucifixion. This style of execution involved hanging or nailing a victim on a wooden frame and allowing the victim to die slowly from shock, exposure, dehydration, and loss of blood. Crucifixion was reserved for those whom Rome wanted to make a public example.

At the point where today's text begins, Jesus has repeatedly told His disciples of His forthcoming death and resurrection (Mark 8:31; 9:31; 10:33, 34). Knowing full well that He could avoid that death, Jesus submitted to the Father's will nonetheless. He felt all the fear that any person would have when facing execution (14:35, 36). He knew His death was to be a sacrifice for many (10:45; 14:22-25).

I. Exchanged for a Rebel

(Mark 15:6-15)

Having appeared before "the high priest . . . and . . . all the chief priests and the elders and the scribes" (Mark 14:53), Jesus has been convicted of blasphemy (14:64). This ruling council—which many commentators refer to by the transliteration "the Sanhedrin"—need the Roman governor to authorize Jesus' execution.

A. Pilate's Proposal (vv. 6-10)

6. Now at that feast he released unto them one prisoner, whomsoever they desired.

Rome wants peace in its provinces. To that end, Roman governors such as Pilate have established a practice at Passover of granting a pardon to *one prisoner* who awaits capital punishment for crimes against Rome (see John 18:39). The practice is intended to establish goodwill between Rome and the Jewish people during their most sacred annual feast.

7. And there was one named Barabbas, which lay bound with them that had made insurrection with him, who had committed murder in the insurrection.

Violent movements to overthrow Roman power occurred repeatedly in Judea of the first century AD (see the Lesson Context). *Barabbas* has participated murderously in one such *insurrection*, though he is unknown outside of Gospel accounts.

HOW TO SAY IT

Antonia	An-*toe*-nee-uh or An-*toe*-nyuh.
Assyria	Uh-*sear*-ee-uh.
Babylon	*Bab*-uh-lun.
Barabbas	Buh-*rab*-us.
Caesar	*See*-zer.
Elias	Ee-*lye*-us.
Eloi, Eloi, lama sabachthani *(Aramaic)*	
	Ee-*lo*-eye, Ee-*lo*-eye, *lah*-mah suh-*back*-thuh-nee.
Herod	*Hair*-ud.
Pilate	*Pie*-lut.
Praetorium	Pree-*tor*-ee-um.
Sanhedrin	San-huh-drun or San-*heed*-run.
Zephaniah	Zef-uh-*nye*-uh.

The contrast with Jesus could hardly be greater! For guilty Barabbas to be executed is understandable (see also Matthew 27:16; Luke 23:19).

8. And the multitude crying aloud began to desire him to do as he had ever done unto them.

Jesus is appearing before Pilate in or near a place called the "Praetorium" (Mark 15:16). There are two theories regarding its location. The first puts it at Herod's palace, where Pilate resides when in Jerusalem. The second is the Fortress of Antonia, a Roman military building next to the temple. Both locations have courtyards where a crowd can gather (compare John 18:28, 33; 19:9).

Many people hostile to Jesus do indeed gather. To call on Pilate *to do as he had ever done unto them* is to request him to act on the custom of releasing a prisoner for Passover (see commentary on Mark 15:6, above; also see Luke 23:17).

9. But Pilate answered them, saying, Will ye that I release unto you the King of the Jews?

At this point, Pilate has already declared Jesus to be innocent (Luke 23:4, 13-16; John 19:12). Perhaps knowing that Jesus is popular with many who are visiting Jerusalem, Pilate offers to release Jesus according to custom.

The governor's sarcasm in referring to Jesus as *King of the Jews* reflects Pilate's own questions of John 18:33, 37; Jesus' response affirmed His role as king but also affirmed that His "kingdom is not of this world" (John 18:36, 37; compare Matthew 27:11; Mark 15:2; Luke 23:3). Pilate ignores that part and sticks with *King of the Jews.*

Pilate's use of that title for the abused man standing before him (see Mark 14:65; Luke 23:11) seems designed to tweak the noses of those who brought Jesus to him. The council clearly despises Jesus, so calling Him their king is a way for Pilate to show his disregard for their nationalistic concerns.

10. For he knew that the chief priests had delivered him for envy.

Pilate was interested in justice earlier (again see Luke 23:4, 13-16; John 19:12). But now his aim is to one-up *the chief priests.* Their aim isn't justice either; rather, they're trying to protect vested interests (see John 11:48) by retaining the loyalty of the Jewish people. Jesus is a pawn in a sordid power play.

B. People's Demand (vv. 11-15)

11. But the chief priests moved the people, that he should rather release Barabbas unto them.

A crowd of several hundred would be sizeable. But that would represent only a fraction of the thousands of religious pilgrims present for Passover. Encouraged by *the chief priests* to gather at the early morning hearing (see also Matthew 27:20; John 18:28), these people appear quite willing to do as their religious leaders desire.

The ugly mood of the crowd is often contrasted with that of the crowd who greeted Jesus enthusiastically at His entry into Jerusalem days before (Mark 11:8-10). Has that crowd changed its view of Jesus? Or is this a different segment of the populace, a group with sympathies for the chief priests? The Gospels sometimes depict the people as fickle (Luke 7:31-35) and other times as divided (John 7:43). Mark does not make clear which of these scenarios is correct. Indeed, the people can be both fickle *and* divided.

❧ Prisoner Exchange ❧

In 1960, U.S. pilot Francis Gary Powers (1929–1977) was shot down while flying a spy mission in Soviet airspace. A few years earlier, the FBI had captured Rudolf Abel (1903–1971), who was then convicted of espionage and imprisoned. The Soviets similarly convicted Powers of espionage and sentenced him to 10 years of incarceration. The incident further cooled already chilly U.S. and Soviet relations.

Negotiations among the U.S., the Soviet Union, and East Germany resulted in a prisoner swap. On February 10, 1962, Powers was exchanged for Abel at the Glienicke Bridge in Ber-

lin. Both men were guilty of espionage. Theirs was a fair exchange.

Almost 2,000 years earlier, however, an unfair exchange took place: Jesus for Barabbas. Barabbas was guilty, yet he went free; Jesus, though innocent, went to His death. Even more shocking was the death of Jesus in taking our sin-penalty upon himself. We can call it unfair—and it was. But Jesus experienced death voluntarily so we wouldn't have to. And there's a special word for that; it is grace.   —J. E.

12. And Pilate answered and said again unto them, What will ye then that I shall do unto him whom ye call the King of the Jews?

Pilate is reluctant to do what the people ask (compare Matthew 27:19; Luke 23:22). Perhaps hoping to put them in a dilemma about the fate of another of their countrymen, Pilate asks what the people want done with *the King of the Jews*. The air is supercharged with a mixture of mockery, challenges to conscience, and high emotion.

13, 14. And they cried out again, Crucify him. Then Pilate said unto them, Why, what evil hath he done? And they cried out the more exceedingly, Crucify him.

The response is not what Pilate expects. But it is just what the religious leaders have urged. To be crucified is to be marked as an enemy of the Roman Empire. What Jesus had told His disciples in advance is happening.

Challenging the people to name Jesus' crime is an attempt to thwart the council's wishes and uphold the rule of law. But Pilate's reasonable and logical question is met with the raw emotion of hatred: an intensified call for Jesus' crucifixion. If there ever was a "rush to judgment," this is it.

15. And so Pilate, willing to content the people, released Barabbas unto them, and delivered Jesus, when he had scourged him, to be crucified.

Pilate now believes that he has no choice. Should he fail to keep the peace, he can at minimum lose his position. Worse yet, the people's unrest may spread through the city, overwhelming the Roman forces stationed therein. Pilate seeks to maintain power over the Jewish council, but his greater interest is keeping the peace. So with a "the end justifies the means" mentality, he hands Jesus over to a detachment of soldiers for crucifixion. *Barabbas*, on the other hand, goes free.

What Do You Think?
How should you respond, if at all, to those who use emotional appeals to arouse opposition to Christ and the gospel?
Digging Deeper
Consider different contexts: at work/school, in the family, etc.

II. Enthroned on a Cross
(MARK 15:25, 26)

Jesus is severely abused in the intervening verses that are not part of our lesson text. Though there is no standard procedure for Roman crucifixion, it is not out of the ordinary that Jesus is severely beaten (Matthew 27:26; Mark 15:15; John 19:1) and stripped (Matthew 27:35; Luke 23:34) before being nailed to His cross. Eventually, Jesus is brought to the place of crucifixion, which is outside the city walls (Hebrews 13:12).

A. Act of Crucifixion (v. 25)

25. And it was the third hour, and they crucified him.

Jesus' crucifixion likely takes place where roads converge just to the north of Jerusalem. The Romans make crucifixions as visible as possible to serve as a deterrent to insurrection; thus a crossroads is a logical place. *The third hour* is counted from sunrise, so Jesus' crucifixion begins at midmorning.

B. Identity of the Crucified (v. 26)

26. And the superscription of his accusation was written over, THE KING OF THE JEWS.

The same mocking words that Pilate used at Jesus' trial are affixed over Jesus' head. John 19:19-22 shows the full import of Pilate's action in this regard: it's one further snipe at the religious authorities whom Pilate believes have forced his hand. But this pettiness obscures the fact that Pilate speaks and writes better than he knows:

Jesus is indeed *The King of the Jews* (2 Samuel 7:12-16; Zechariah 9:9). But He is even more than that: He is the world's king (Isaiah 9:6, 7; 11:1-9; Romans 15:7-12). Jesus' crucifiers are involved in something far greater than they realize (Luke 24:44-49; Acts 10:43; 2 Corinthians 1:20; etc.). He is enthroned as king in His crucifixion (Acts 2:36).

What Do You Think?
What are some "everyday" ways to emulate Jesus' sacrifice in putting others' interests ahead of our own?
Digging Deeper
What limits, if any, are there to doing so? Why?

III. Suffering in Affirmation
(MARK 15:33-39)

Our next segment of lesson text takes us forward in time by three hours. During that period the dying Jesus is mocked by the religious authorities, various onlookers, and by two criminals also suffering crucifixion.

A. Cry of the Righteous (vv. 33, 34)

33. And when the sixth hour was come, there was darkness over the whole land until the ninth hour.

The *darkness* that comes *over the whole land* is further described in Luke 23:45 as "the sun was darkened." This cannot be a solar eclipse for two reasons. First, solar eclipses do not last anywhere close to three hours, which is the length of the time of the darkness. Second, the crucifixion takes place in conjunction with Passover, which occurs at the time of a full moon; by contrast, a solar eclipse requires the opposite—a new moon.

Darkness is sometimes an image of God's judgment (Joel 2:2, 31; Amos 8:9; Zephaniah 1:15). It is also an expression of despair (Psalms 88:12, 18; 143:3). Certainly all who witness this darkness are compelled to acknowledge that something extraordinary is occurring.

34. And at the ninth hour Jesus cried with a loud voice, saying, Eloi, Eloi, lama sabachthani?

which is, being interpreted, My God, my God, why hast thou forsaken me?

Jesus cries out with the words of Psalm 22:1. The psalm laments the suffering of a righteous person being mocked and tortured by enemies. The righteous one's situation appears hopeless; God seems distant. These words from the beginning of the psalm express the deep anguish of a person in such a situation. Jesus has now entered fully into that experience of rejection, mockery, torture, and seeming abandonment.

But like many psalms of lament, Psalm 22 turns from anguish to expressions of hope. In verse 19 the psalmist cries out for God's help, and in verse 22 begins a declaration that the psalmist will praise God for His sure and faithful deliverance of His people. Jesus' words express anguish yet are deliberately not without hope. His earlier declarations that God would raise Him from the dead (Mark 8:31, 32; 9:9, 31; 10:33, 34; 14:28) remain true even though Mark chooses not to restate them in the moments of Jesus' suffering.

Thus the hopeful ending notes of confidence from Psalm 22 remain in the background. But they offer the one who is familiar with that psalm a hint: all is not as it seems while Jesus dies. God will be present to deliver the true king whom He has enthroned.

> ### What Do You Think?
> What are some ways we can encourage people in seasons when they feel God has abandoned them?
>
> ### Digging Deeper
> Consider how your approach may differ in situations when the suffering is due to one's own poor choices vs. suffering undeserved.

B. Response of Mockers (vv. 35, 36)

35. And some of them that stood by, when they heard it, said, Behold, he calleth Elias.

The ignorance of Jesus' opponents is revealed: they mistake the Aramaic word *eloi* as being a cry to the ancient prophet *Elias* (Elijah). In so doing, they are depending on a tradition that Elijah helps those in need rather than recalling Jesus' words as a quote from their own psalms.

36. And one ran and filled a spunge full of vinegar, and put it on a reed, and gave him to drink, saying, Let alone; let us see whether Elias will come to take him down.

Vinegar, though unpleasant, is an acceptable drink in Old Testament Israel (Numbers 6:3). But offering vinegar to someone suffering shock and dehydration could be but another form of mocking torture. It may also be a way to try to prolong Jesus' suffering by giving Him some sustenance but no relief. It seems that Jesus' cry has gone unanswered. The torturers and mockers seem to have prevailed. Psalm 69:21 is fulfilled.

C. Death of the King (v. 37)

37. And Jesus cried with a loud voice, and gave up the ghost.

Jesus' death comes at last, as He had so many times predicted.

D. Rending of a Curtain (v. 38)

38. And the veil of the temple was rent in twain from the top to the bottom.

The veil of the temple is a curtain separating the holy place from the most holy place (Exodus 26:33). The latter may be entered only once a year, on the Day of Atonement, when the high priest symbolically presented to God the blood of a sacrifice offered for the sin of all Israel (Leviticus 16; 23:26-32). Clearly the rending of this curtain demonstrates God's involvement in Jesus' death! Some understand that the tearing shows that Jesus has offered the sacrifice that fulfills what the temple's sacrifices pointed to. The implication is that the way is now open for all to enter God's presence freely (Hebrews 9:6-8; 10:19, 20). Others look to Jesus' warnings that the temple will be destroyed as a sign of judgment against the temple leadership who plotted Jesus' death (Mark 12:9-12; 13:2). Indeed, the temple will be destroyed in AD 70. Both understandings are consistent with New Testament teaching regarding fulfillment of God's plan.

❧ RESCUED! ❧

In August 2010, a cave-in at a mine in Chile trapped 33 miners 2,300 feet below the surface. In attempting to locate survivors, the mining company began drilling holes. Seventeen days after the accident, a note was found taped to a drill bit pulled back to the surface. It read, "We are well in the shelter, the 33 of us."

This sparked a massive rescue effort. On October 13, an estimated 1 billion people worldwide witnessed the dramatic rescue. One by one, all 33 miners were pulled safely to the surface.

An even greater rescue happened when the barrier of sin that trapped humankind from the presence of God was penetrated. Jesus' death made it possible to be reunited with God. How do you bear witness to your miraculous rescue?   —J. E.

E. Testimony of a Soldier (v. 39)

39. And when the centurion, which stood over against him, saw that he so cried out, and gave up the ghost, he said, Truly this man was the Son of God.

A *centurion* holds a highly responsible position in the Roman army. Seeing all that has happened, this particular centurion recognizes that this is no ordinary crucifixion and no ordinary *man*. In Jewish usage, to be *the Son of God* often means to be God's king (2 Samuel 7:14; Psalms 2:7; 89:26-28). But on the lips of a Roman soldier, is this a confession of faith or no more than a cry of fear?

It's easy to get cynical and write it off as no more than fear on the part of a pagan Roman soldier, one who is worried more about his own skin than anything else. But we must pause to remember that it was of a centurion that Jesus declared, "Verily I say unto you, I have not found so great faith, no, not in Israel" (Matthew 8:10; compare Luke 7:9). And, looking forward, it will be a centurion through whom the gospel will be opened to Gentiles (Acts 10:1–11:18).

What Do You Think?
How can our church help people move from a basic comprehension of Christ to a fuller understanding of His identity?

Digging Deeper
Consider how your answer will differ for those who have no prior experience with church vs. those who have been in church for a while.

Visual for Lessons 2 & 3. *Point to the paradox between image and declaration as you pose the discussion question associated with Mark 15:39.*

Conclusion
A. The King's Way of Life

The story of Jesus' death prompts us to ask ourselves important questions. One is, "Who is my king?" Am I ruled by selfish impulses, others' opinions, culture's conformity, the past's burdens? Or is the crucified Christ my king?

Another way to ask that question is, "What do I see as power?" Is it following my dreams, getting my way, having it all, impressing others? Or is it giving myself for the benefit of others, as King Jesus did?

Jesus came to power not through a bloody insurrection or other worldly means. He humbled himself and was crucified. In this way, Jesus demonstrated that He is the Son of God. Are you following in the way of the king? In the end, the gospel calls all people to repentance and submission to the crucified and risen king, Jesus. Everyone needs His mercy, and no one is beyond the reach of it.

B. Prayer

Father, awestruck before Your Son's cross, we honor Him as our true king. Empower us to serve others. We pray this in Jesus' name. Amen.

C. Thought to Remember

In Christ's kingdom,
the way up is down.

INVOLVEMENT LEARNING

Enhance your lesson with KJV Bible Student *(from your curriculum supplier) and the reproducible activity page (at www.standardlesson.com or in the back of the* KJV Standard Lesson Commentary Deluxe Edition*).*

Into the Lesson

Place index cards and pencils in each seat. Have the following sentences written on the board and displayed as learners enter: "Think of a time you were at odds with someone you loved. How did that make you feel? Write those feelings on your index card." Ask learners to call out those feelings as you record them on the board.

Then say, "If you were able to reconcile the relationship, how did that happen?" Record responses next to the feelings. Say, "We will return to these lists at the end of the lesson."

Alternative. Have a copy of the hymn "And Can It Be That I Should Gain?" by Charles Wesley on seats as learners enter. Have them identify words that refer to our condition before salvation and words that refer to God's redemptive action. As they call them out, write them on the board.

After either activity state, "Today we will spend time looking at how God reconciled us and what our response is to that gift of redemption."

Into the Word

Write the following Scripture references from Mark 15 down the left side of the board: verses 6-8 / verses 9-11 / verses 12-15 / verses 25, 26 / verses 33, 34 / verses 35, 36 / verses 37-39.

Have one volunteer read Mark 15:6-15 aloud. Discuss the thought processes, evident or implied, per the verse segments as noted. Ensure coverage of the following:

• Barabbas was imprisoned for insurrection (vv. 6-8).

• Pilate tried to release Jesus, but the Jewish leaders stirred up the crowd to ask for Barabbas (vv. 9-11).

• Pilate allowed the innocent one to be killed and the guilty one set free as the crowd's cries of "crucify" stood in stark contrast with those that had greeted Jesus with "Hosanna" just days before (vv. 12-15).

Have another volunteer read Mark 15:25, 26, 33-39 aloud. Discuss the following concepts:

• Jesus' crucifixion can be seen as a king's enthronement as He exerts His kingly power by giving himself for others (vv. 25, 26).

• Anyone can see Jesus' use of Psalm 22:1, but only the discerning will detect Psalm 22:19-22 as well (vv. 33, 34).

• Some reveal their ignorance when they think Jesus is calling for Elijah (vv. 35, 36).

• Jesus' death results in two testimonies (vv. 37-39).

Alternative. Have students present the reader's theater activity titled "Various Viewpoints" from the reproducible page, which you can download. Give each student a copy. Compare the various perspectives of the events that took place in the lesson text.

Follow either activity by (1) identifying those involved in the events leading up to the crucifixion and (2) comparing what their actions revealed about their character. *Anticipated identity responses:* those of the Jewish leadership, the Roman leader Pilate, Barabbas, the crowd, a centurion, Jesus himself. *Possible character responses:* a mentality of "the end justifies the means" among the Jewish leaders as well as Pilate; people in the crowd swayed by the emotion of the moment; the revealing of either fear or confession of faith in the centurion's cry. (Note: expect some disagreement on the question of character!)

Into Life

Return to the lists of words from the Into the Lesson segment. Connect the first list of words to our condition before we became Christians and the second list to what Jesus did for us on the cross. (If you used the Alternative activity, review those lists and connect them to the lesson text.) Open the floor for discussion.

Alternative. Distribute copies of the "My Response" activity from the reproducible page. Allow no more than one minute to record answers. Discuss as time allows.

The New Covenant's Sacrifice

DEVOTIONAL READING: Psalm 50:1-15
BACKGROUND SCRIPTURE: Hebrews 9:11-28

Hebrews 9:11-22

11 But Christ being come an high priest of good things to come, by a greater and more perfect tabernacle, not made with hands, that is to say, not of this building;

12 Neither by the blood of goats and calves, but by his own blood he entered in once into the holy place, having obtained eternal redemption for us.

13 For if the blood of bulls and of goats, and the ashes of an heifer sprinkling the unclean, sanctifieth to the purifying of the flesh:

14 How much more shall the blood of Christ, who through the eternal Spirit offered himself without spot to God, purge your conscience from dead works to serve the living God?

15 And for this cause he is the mediator of the new testament, that by means of death, for the redemption of the transgressions that were under the first testament, they which are called might receive the promise of eternal inheritance.

16 For where a testament is, there must also of necessity be the death of the testator.

17 For a testament is of force after men are dead: otherwise it is of no strength at all while the testator liveth.

18 Whereupon neither the first testament was dedicated without blood.

19 For when Moses had spoken every precept to all the people according to the law, he took the blood of calves and of goats, with water, and scarlet wool, and hyssop, and sprinkled both the book, and all the people,

20 Saying, This is the blood of the testament which God hath enjoined unto you.

21 Moreover he sprinkled with blood both the tabernacle, and all the vessels of the ministry.

22 And almost all things are by the law purged with blood; and without shedding of blood is no remission.

Key Verse

Almost all things are by the law purged with blood; and without shedding of blood is no remission.

—**Hebrews 9:22**

COVENANT IN GOD

Unit 1: A Fulfilled Covenant
LESSONS 1–4

LESSON AIMS

After participating in this lesson, each learner will be able to:

1. Define Christ's roles as high priest and mediator.

2. Explain the significance of the death of Christ.

3. Write a prayer of gratitude for Christ's sacrifice.

LESSON OUTLINE

Introduction

A. Nothing but the Blood of Jesus

The simple melody line of Robert Lowry's gospel song "Nothing but the Blood" uses only a five-note range and two chords. The song's lyrics likewise are straightforward, punctuated by the simple declaration, "Nothing but the blood of Jesus." In its simplicity, this song celebrates the majestic theme found within Hebrews 9:11-22: our high priest Jesus Christ has offered His blood to make perfect reconciliation for sinners. By that blood, we enter into God's new covenant. This concept is unfamiliar to many.

B. Lesson Context

Undergirding today's study are three concepts that are vitally important in the book of Hebrews. Those three are high priest, covenant, and blood. Their importance is revealed in the fact that, in each case, the book of Hebrews features more uses of those words than any other New Testament book by proportion of size.

A priest is a go-between; another word we could use is *mediator*. That position in Old Testament times involved interceding with God on behalf of unclean people (see Leviticus 14, 15). The founding of the Old Testament priesthood is recorded in Exodus 28, 29 and Leviticus 8. The high priest is the one "upon whose head the anointing oil was poured" (Leviticus 21:10). The death of the high priest resulted in relief from prosecution in specific instances (Numbers 35:25, 28; Joshua 20:6).

The original word that is translated variously as "covenant" and "testament" occurs 33 times in the New Testament. The book of Hebrews has 17 of those 33 instances, demonstrating its importance. The opening verses of Hebrews 8 pronounce that Jesus has obtained a more excellent ministry than the priestly ministry of the first covenant. In so doing, He has become the mediator of a better covenant—a covenant that is based on better promises (Hebrews 8:1, 2, 6).

When the writer quotes Jeremiah 31:31-34 regarding God's offer of a new covenant (Hebrews 8:8-12), the implication is that there was a flaw in the old covenant. Any flaw, however, was not on God's side. Humanity proved unable and/or unwilling to honor the provisions of that covenant (Hebrews 8:7, 8, 13).

The early part of Hebrews 9 then describes the old covenant sanctuary, the tabernacle. This structure and its successor (the temple) provided Israel only limited access to God. Barriers still existed between the worshipper and God (compare Exodus 29:9; Hebrews 9:7, 8). The mention of blood in Hebrews 9:7 prepares the reader for the frequent use of that word throughout our lesson text for today. As with the word translated "covenant" and "testament," the word translated "blood" occurs more often proportionally in Hebrews than any other New Testament book.

Scripture treats blood as the life force of a creature (Genesis 9:4; Leviticus 17:10-14; Deuteronomy 12:23). The use of blood of sacrificed animals to save Israel is seen explicitly in the blood of lambs smeared on doorposts in Egypt (Exodus 12:7). The mention of blood is connected with violent death (see Genesis 4:10; Matthew 27:4, 24, 25).

Hebrews 9:1-10 describes the worship and sacrificial practices under the old covenant as temporary and inadequate for cleansing worshippers' sins. In God's redemptive plan, they merely anticipated "the time of reformation" that would come through the ministry of Christ (9:10). That ministry is tightly connected with the concepts of high priest, covenant, and blood.

I. Better Solution
(Hebrews 9:11-14)
A. In Heaven's Sanctuary (v. 11)

11a. But Christ being come an high priest of good things to come.

The title *Christ* is the Greek translation of the Hebrew title *Messiah* (compare John 1:41; 4:25). Both words are transliterations to speakers of English, not translations. A translation would be "Anointed One" (compare the anointing language in Hebrews 1:9).

In the Old Testament, this title can refer to anyone anointed for God's purposes. This includes priests, kings, prophets, and even the people (examples: Leviticus 4:3, 5, 16; 2 Samuel

1:14, 16; 23:1; Psalm 105:15; Lamentations 4:20). But the writer of Hebrews uses the anointing concept inherent in the title *Christ* to refer to Jesus exclusively. Jesus fulfills the tasks that all those who had been anointed before Him were meant to accomplish.

To earlier descriptions of Jesus as "a merciful and faithful high priest" (Hebrews 2:17) and as "a great high priest" (4:14), the writer now adds *an high priest of good things to come.* Those good things are the better promises and better covenant mentioned previously in Hebrews 8:6.

> ### What Do You Think?
> Should Christ's function as the new covenant's high priest be taught as a foundational doctrine, or should teaching on this subject be reserved for "advanced" classes? Why?
> ### Digging Deeper
> After completing your response, compare and contrast it with the categories in 1 Corinthians 3:1, 2 and Hebrews 5:11–6:3.

But the phrase *to come* introduces a question: Is this from the point of view of someone living before Christ or after? If it's from a perspective of people living before Christ, then what were future blessings to them—the *good things to come*—are those blessings that are now present realities to us. On the other hand, if *to come* is written from the perspective of Christians, then the focus would seem to be on blessings we do not yet experience, but will in the future.

Either way, good things have already happened under the new covenant, and even more good things await us. Our sin-debt has been paid, and Christians have a renewed relationship with God right now. As we serve Him now, we look forward to the day when we receive our eternal inheritance in full (Hebrews 9:14, 15).

11b. By a greater and more perfect tabernacle, not made with hands, that is to say, not of this building.

The reference here is that of the heavenly sanctuary that served as the pattern for the old covenant's tabernacle (Exodus 25:40; 26:30; Hebrews 8:1, 2, 5). The phrase *not made with hands* emphasizes this sanctuary's divine origin and celestial location. Because it was not made by humans, it cannot be destroyed (compare Matthew 6:19-21; 2 Corinthians 5:1; see also Acts 7:48; 17:24).

B. For Eternal Redemption (v. 12)

12a. Neither by the blood of goats and calves, but by his own blood he entered in once into the holy place.

The writer sharpens the contrast between the old covenant's Aaronic priesthood (see Exodus 28:1, 41; 29:44; etc.) and the new-covenant priestly work of Christ. God had graciously provided Israel with the sacrificial system as a means to deal with sin. The animal's life was to be given in exchange for the lives of the worshippers whose sins placed them under the penalty of death (compare Romans 3:23; 6:23).

The sacrificial animals were to be without blemish (Leviticus 4:3, 23, 28, 32; Malachi 1:8). But even if they were, their blood was ultimately inadequate to take away sin (Hebrews 10:1, 4). So, in contrast with the levitical priests who offer *the blood of goats and calves*, Christ has come into the heavenly *holy place* with *his own blood*. His blood is the perfect sacrifice because He was without sin (2 Corinthians 5:21; Hebrews 4:15). He came as the Lamb of God to take away the world's sins (John 1:29), and He offered himself willingly in that regard (John 10:14-18). The fact that *he entered in once into the holy place* underscores the total sufficiency of His sacrifice (Hebrews 7:27; 9:28; 10:10).

The writer uses the word *blood* more than 20 times in this book, but this is only the third instance so far. (The first two are Hebrews 2:14; 9:7). He will have much more to say about blood below.

HOW TO SAY IT

Aaronic	Air-*ahn*-ik.
Corinthians	Ko-*rin*-thee-unz (*th* as in *thin*).
Levitical	Leh-*vit*-ih-kul.
Leviticus	Leh-*vit*-ih-kus.
Messiah	Meh-*sigh*-uh.
Mosaic	Mo-*zay*-ik.
tabernacle	*tah*-burr-*nah*-kul.

12b. Having obtained eternal redemption for us.

This half-verse gives the result of Christ's work as superior priest and superior sacrifice. The word translated *redemption* can be used to describe the procedure by which a slave is bought out of bondage and granted freedom (see also Luke 1:68; 2:38; 24:21; Titus 2:14; 1 Peter 1:18, 19; compare Deuteronomy 7:8; Leviticus 25:25-27; etc.).

That the redemption secured by Christ is *eternal* is significant on two counts. First, redemption is one of six things described as eternal or everlasting in Hebrews. The other five are salvation (Hebrews 5:9), judgment (6:2), God's Spirit (9:14, below), inheritance (9:15, below), and covenant (13:20; same Greek word translated "everlasting"). The word *redemption* is in some powerful company indeed!

Second, and closely related, is the fact that the word *eternal* connotes a permanence associated with Heaven (Psalm 119:89, 90; 2 Corinthians 5:1) in contrast with the temporary nature of those things associated with the old covenant.

> **What Do You Think?**
> What steps can you take to allow the facts in Hebrews 9:12 to help you in future struggles against temptation?
> **Digging Deeper**
> Consider Matthew 5:48; Romans 6:1, 2, 12, 13; 8:12, 13; 10:9-11; Ephesians 4:22-24; Philippians 2:12; James 2:14-17; 1 Peter 1:15, 16; and 1 John 3:3 as you ponder the division of duties between you, Christ, and the Holy Spirit in this regard.

C. For Full Cleansing (vv. 13, 14)

13, 14. For if the blood of bulls and of goats, and the ashes of an heifer sprinkling the unclean, sanctifieth to the purifying of the flesh: how much more shall the blood of Christ, who through the eternal Spirit offered himself without spot to God, purge your conscience from dead works to serve the living God?

The thrust of these verses is made in an argument from lesser to greater. This harkens back to a purification ritual described in Numbers 19:1-10,

17-19. People could become unclean by touching dead bodies or coming into contact with things considered unclean under the Mosaic law (Leviticus 11–15; notice that being unclean is not necessarily the same as committing sin). Those in such an unclean state would profane objects with which they came in contact.

For that reason, unclean people were disqualified from participating in tabernacle or temple worship lest they profane the sanctuary. Nevertheless, the law provided sanctification rituals whereby persons could be ritually purified. If the blood of animals could provide external, ritual cleaning, then think of *how much more* effective is the cleansing provided by Christ's blood!

The cleansing Christ provides is greater than any other purification for three reasons. First, it came about *through the eternal Spirit,* by whom He *offered himself.* Matthew 4:1; 12:28; Luke 4:1; and Acts 1:2 each portray the Holy Spirit's empowering Jesus for ministry. Second, He was *without spot,* the importance of which is discussed in our commentary above. Third, He offered himself voluntarily *to God* (see Hebrews 9:26-28 and comments above). A theory from years ago is that Jesus paid the ransom (Mark 10:45) to Satan, but that's not true.

Whereas the Old Testament sacrifice would sanctify *to the purifying of the flesh,* the blood of Christ purges one's *conscience . . . to serve the living God.* A proper conscience is aware of the sins that separate a person from the Lord. This is the second of five instances of the writer using the word *conscience.* To get a better sense of the intent, compare the usage here with that of the other four: Hebrews 9:9; 10:2, 22; 13:18.

The blood of Christ is qualitatively superior to the blood of bulls and goats. Therefore, the cleansing it has effected is also qualitatively superior. The old covenant dealt with an external problem of humankind and could not cleanse the interior. But Christ has brought the sacrificial system to its fulfillment, having dealt with the whole person as he or she stands before God. "Having obtained eternal redemption" (Hebrews 9:12, above) and having had his or her conscience purged, the believer is now free *to serve the living God.*

II. Better Mediator
(Hebrews 9:15-17)
A. Through Jesus' Mediation (v. 15)

15. And for this cause he is the mediator of the new testament, that by means of death, for the redemption of the transgressions that were under the first testament, they which are called might receive the promise of eternal inheritance.

A mediator is one who intervenes between conflicting parties to remove the disagreement. In His death Christ dealt decisively with the sins to which the old covenant law had called attention. This being so, *they which are called*—that is, believers in Christ—may *receive the promise of eternal inheritance.*

The expression *they which are called* reminds readers of the author's designation of them as "partakers of the heavenly calling" (Hebrews 3:1). Whereas possession of the land of Canaan was Israel's inheritance under the old covenant (Leviticus 20:24; Numbers 26:52-56), those called into the new covenant now have the promise of entering into eternal fellowship with God (Hebrews 4:1-11). What an inheritance!

B. Through Jesus' Death (vv. 16, 17)

16, 17. For where a testament is, there must also of necessity be the death of the testator. For a testament is of force after men are dead: otherwise it is of no strength at all while the testator liveth.

It's easy to get confused at this point, because the Greek word rightly translated "covenant"/"testament" is the same word those native speakers use for a will. Think of someone's "last will and testament." Things were the same back in the first century as they are today: a will *is of no strength at all while the testator liveth.* A will may be valid while the maker of the will lives, but the will is not operative, effective, or functional until its maker dies.

So also Christ had to die in order for the new covenant to be put into effect. The Israelites had pledged their obedience to the first covenant (Exodus 19:8; 24:7), and the penalty for breaking the covenant was death (Jeremiah 34:18-20). Under the old covenant, the blood of bulls and goats was offered in place of the death the Israelites deserved. Now, in offering His righteous blood, Christ has suffered the death penalty that rightly is ours.

❧ WHERE THERE'S A WILL... ❧

History tells some surprising stories from the wills of the rich and famous. Napoleon Bonaparte's will stipulated that his head be shaved and the hair be divided among his inheritors. Clara Mae Ruth, widow of baseball great Babe Ruth, was left all his property, excepting only "souvenirs, mementoes, pictures, scrap-books, manuscripts, letters, athletic equipment, and other personal property pertaining to baseball." Finnish businessman Onni Nurmi's 780 shares of a rubber boot company didn't seem like much at first to residents of the nursing home who received them. But that company became cell phone giant Nokia, making all the heirs millionaires!

A person's share of the estate of these famous individuals varied in worth. But the wealth left by the mediator of the new covenant is of unimaginable value. Of all the inheritances real and imagined, which do you most desire to receive? Why?　　　　　　　—J. E.

III. Necessary Death
(HEBREWS 9:18-22)
A. Dedicated in Blood (vv. 18-20)

18, 19. Whereupon neither the first testament was dedicated without blood. For when Moses had spoken every precept to all the people according to the law, he took the blood of calves and of goats, with water, and scarlet wool, and hyssop, and sprinkled both the book, and all the people.

Having linked Christ's death with the activation of the new covenant, the author returns to the role that *blood* played in establishing *the first* one. He finds proof in Exodus 24:3-8. The ceremony depicted there describes the act by which Moses consecrated the people to bring them under the old covenant. With Hebrews 9:7-14, 23-25 echoing the Day of Atonement (see Leviticus 16) to help explain Christ's work, the allusion here—the ratification of the Mosaic covenant—offers another precedent for doing so. Moses had *sprinkled both the book* of the covenant and *all* Israelite *people* with the blood in order to consecrate them as God's holy nation. Now it is Christ's blood that sets apart His followers.

20. Saying, This is the blood of the testament which God hath enjoined unto you.

The writer's noting of Moses' words here recalls what Jesus said as He instituted the Lord's Supper: "This is my blood of the new testament" (Matthew 26:28; Mark 14:24; compare Luke 22:20). That connection is all the more powerful given the original audience's familiarity with Jesus' words during the last supper. The original readers have recited these words numerous times during their own communion observances.

B. Remission by Blood (vv. 21, 22)

21, 22. Moreover he sprinkled with blood both the tabernacle, and all the vessels of the ministry. And almost all things are by the law purged with blood; and without shedding of blood is no remission.

After the events of Exodus 24 to which Hebrews 9:19 alludes, Moses did indeed anoint with oil *the tabernacle* and its *vessels* (Exodus 40:9). But Scripture makes no direct statement that

Moses sprinkled blood on them during their dedication. Nevertheless, one may assume that he did so, since those things were to be consecrated (40:9; compare 24:6), and consecration of the priests had involved both oil and blood (29:21).

The recounting of this act of consecration constitutes the first half of "lesser to greater" argument, of which Hebrews 9:23-28 (not in today's text) comprises the second part. This argument essentially repeats and expands upon the content of Hebrews 9:12-14.

> ### What Do You Think?
> Which will be more important in demonstrating the cleansing power of Christ's blood: our ability to explain the gospel or our example of living as empowered people? Why?
>
> ### Digging Deeper
> Compare and contrast Romans 10:17; 1 Corinthians 9:19-22; 1 Timothy 3:7; 1 Peter 3:1, 2, 15.

❧ THE UNIVERSAL DONOR ❧

The first half of the twentieth century witnessed great strides in the medical use of blood. A pioneer in that regard was Dr. Bernard Fantus, an immigrant Hungarian. He became curious about how the blood of one could be donated to save the life of another.

His studies yielded practical application when he established the world's first blood bank in 1937. Soon blood banks were everywhere. This made surgery more accessible—and saved lives.

But in a more important sense, God beat him to it over 3,000 years before when He declared that "the life of all flesh is the blood thereof" (Leviticus 17:14). This was profoundly realized when the lifeblood of Jesus was substituted for the lives of sinners. That "transfusion" brought those dead in sin back to life. In what specific way will you witness this fact to others this week? —J. E.

Conclusion

A. The Power of the Blood of Jesus

Under the old covenant, almost all things were purged by use of blood. But the new cov-

Visual for Lessons 2 & 3. *Ask your learners to rate this visual on a scale from 1 ("means nothing to me") to 10 ("really convicts me"). Discuss.*

enant features a deeper, further reaching, once-for-all cleansing through the blood of Christ. The blood of bulls and goats could never fully atone for past, present, and future sin. Ultimate salvation required the lifeblood of the Son of God.

An incident centuries ago caused someone to notice that certain people were sinning against the Lord, in that they were eating meat with the blood still in it (1 Samuel 14:33). But in a figurative sense, Jesus invites us to do just that! The invitation came when He said, "This cup is the new testament in my blood: this do ye, as oft as ye drink it, in remembrance of me" (1 Corinthians 11:25).

We do just that when we gather around the Lord's table. Through Christ's sacrifice, we have entered into a new covenant relationship with God. We have been given full access to the Father through Christ. Hallelujah, what a Savior!

B. Prayer

Our Father, we are both saddened and grateful for Your Son's death on the cross. Saddened because it was our sins that put Him there, but grateful that He was willing to suffer in our place. Empower us to serve Him, our high priest, faithfully. We pray this in His name. Amen.

C. Thought to Remember

Christ's perfect sacrifice gives us access to God in the new covenant.

INVOLVEMENT LEARNING

Enhance your lesson with KJV Bible Student *(from your curriculum supplier) and the reproducible activity page (at www.standardlesson.com or in the back of the* KJV Standard Lesson Commentary Deluxe Edition*).*

Into the Lesson

Ask learners to help you create a list of tasks they have to repeat. Jot responses on the board. (*Possible responses:* taking out the trash, doing laundry, paying taxes, etc.). Then ask, "Which of these tasks would you most like never to have to do again?" After three or four responses, say, "Our lesson today focuses on a task Jesus completed once for all, never to be repeated."

Option. Place on chairs copies of the "Day of Atonement Match" activity from the reproducible page, which you can download, for learners to begin working on as they arrive. Assure your learners that they will score their own results later during class. Use this activity as a reference as you aid the class in working through the lesson.

Into the Word

Distribute handouts (you prepare) with the following terms listed down the left side: *high priest / tabernacle / holy place / covenant / testament / testator.* Have printed at the top an instruction to write a definition for each term. Leave sufficient space between the terms for learners to do so.

Form your learners into study pairs. Introduce the activity by saying, "Let's look at some vocabulary to review the significance of words used in Hebrews to create the imagery in today's lesson text." After the study pairs finish, ask learners to volunteer definitions.

After a brief discussion of learners' conclusions, compare and contrast with these: *high priest:* descendant of Aaron who was the religious leader of Israel; *tabernacle:* the tent that served as the center of worship for the Israelites; *holy place:* the part of the tabernacle that represented the presence of God; *covenant:* a contract; *testament:* possibly either a covenant or a will; *testator:* person who makes the will.

Have a volunteer read Hebrews 9:11-14. During discussion, emphasize the following contrasts and salient points: verse 11—Jesus is superior to all other high priests because He is both Messiah and high priest; verse 12—Jesus' blood superseded animal sacrifices; priests were obligated to offer frequent blood sacrifices, but Jesus' self-sacrifice needed to be a once-only event; verses 13, 14—The old covenant provided for impermanent cleansing, whereas the blood of Christ under the new covenant provides eternal salvation.

Have a volunteer read Hebrews 9:15-17. During discussion, emphasize the following contrasts and salient points: verse 15—Christ's death on the cross made Him a much superior mediator between mankind and God than were the old covenant priests; verses 16, 17—Jesus had to die for the new covenant (will, testament) to take effect.

Have a volunteer read Hebrews 9:18-22 and state the following comparison: under both old and new covenants, use of blood was necessary. Follow that declaration with this question to check comprehension: "Since that statement is true, then what difference does it make where the blood came from?"

If learners have been using the "Day of Atonement Match" activity as a reference, go over the answers together. Discuss any changes learners need to make to ensure they understand the significance of Christ as our sin offering.

Into Life

During whole-class discussion, have learners identify main themes of the lesson text (see the Lesson Context). Work together to create a prayer of thanksgiving to God for Christ's sacrifice. Pray it together to conclude. E-mail copies to learners so they can pray it in the week ahead.

Alternative. Distribute copies of the "Hebrew Parallelism" activity from the reproducible page. Have learners work in groups to construct prayer poems about Christ's sacrifice as indicated. Have groups share their completed prayer poems. Collect for e-mailing as above.

HEARTS UNITED IN LOVE

DEVOTIONAL READING: 1 Corinthians 3:10-17
BACKGROUND SCRIPTURE: Colossians 2:1-15

COLOSSIANS 2:1-15

1 For I would that ye knew what great conflict I have for you, and for them at Laodicea, and for as many as have not seen my face in the flesh;

2 That their hearts might be comforted, being knit together in love, and unto all riches of the full assurance of understanding, to the acknowledgement of the mystery of God, and of the Father, and of Christ;

3 In whom are hid all the treasures of wisdom and knowledge.

4 And this I say, lest any man should beguile you with enticing words.

5 For though I be absent in the flesh, yet am I with you in the spirit, joying and beholding your order, and the stedfastness of your faith in Christ.

6 As ye have therefore received Christ Jesus the Lord, so walk ye in him:

7 Rooted and built up in him, and stablished in the faith, as ye have been taught, abounding therein with thanksgiving.

8 Beware lest any man spoil you through philosophy and vain deceit, after the tradition of men, after the rudiments of the world, and not after Christ.

9 For in him dwelleth all the fulness of the Godhead bodily.

10 And ye are complete in him, which is the head of all principality and power:

11 In whom also ye are circumcised with the circumcision made without hands, in putting off the body of the sins of the flesh by the circumcision of Christ:

12 Buried with him in baptism, wherein also ye are risen with him through the faith of the operation of God, who hath raised him from the dead.

13 And you, being dead in your sins and the uncircumcision of your flesh, hath he quickened together with him, having forgiven you all trespasses;

14 Blotting out the handwriting of ordinances that was against us, which was contrary to us, and took it out of the way, nailing it to his cross;

15 And having spoiled principalities and powers, he made a shew of them openly, triumphing over them in it.

KEY VERSES

As ye have therefore received Christ Jesus the Lord, so walk ye in him: rooted and built up in him, and stablished in the faith, as ye have been taught, abounding therein with thanksgiving. —**Colossians 2:6, 7**

COVENANT IN GOD

Unit 1: A Fulfilled Covenant
LESSONS 1–4

LESSON AIMS

After participating in this lesson, each learner will be able to:

1. List three things that believers have in Christ.

2. Compare and contrast the meaning and significance of circumcision and baptism.

3. Identify one area to grow or mature in his or her walk with Christ and make a plan to do so.

LESSON OUTLINE

Introduction

A. Pursuit of Completeness

For many today, the promise of everlasting romantic love is the height of personal wellness. Tom Cruise's oft-parodied line "You complete me" from the film *Jerry Maguire* points to humanity's constant pursuit of completeness and our sense that we do not possess it on our own. Others do not seek wholeness through romance but instead through other relationships, through work, or even through hobbies. Where can we look to find true completeness?

B. Lesson Context

Members of the Colossian church came from backgrounds featuring a myriad of religious and philosophical options. On this buffet were Judaism and pagan religions from across the Roman Empire. There were mystery religions that promised spiritual enlightenment through secret knowledge. There were sophisticated systems of philosophical thought and groups that practiced black magic. Each group made its own claims about truth. Some believers at Colosse attempted to augment the gospel with a mixture of elements from this religious-philosophical buffet. The temptation to trust in humanity's knowledge rather than in faith through Christ and knowledge of Him was irresistible to some.

I. Love's Concern
(COLOSSIANS 2:1-5)
A. Paul's Intensity (v. 1)

1. For I would that ye knew what great conflict I have for you, and for them at Laodicea, and for as many as have not seen my face in the flesh.

Paul desires that his readers know of his ministry of prayer on their behalf (see Colossians 1:9-12). The word translated *conflict* is a form of the same word translated "striving" in 1:29 (speaking of Paul's own labor) and "fervently" in 4:12 (speaking of Epaphras's laboring for them in prayer).

Paul greets Archippus by name in Colossians 4:17 and knows other Christians in Colosse (Philemon and Apphia; compare Philemon 1, 2 with Colossians 4:10-17). Even so, the phrase *for as many as have not seen my face in the flesh* is widely accepted to mean that Paul has not actually been to Colosse. *Laodicea* is another city in the Lycus River valley, approximately 10 miles from Colosse. Although many within this letter's audience are strangers to Paul, they are still objects of Paul's concern that arises from the unity believers have in Christ (Ephesians 4:4; 1 Corinthians 1:2).

> **What Do You Think?**
> What plan can you create for expressing concerns for people in ways they will receive and appreciate?
> *Digging Deeper*
> Consider nonverbal expressions of concern in addition to verbal, and when it might be best to use one type over the other.

B. Paul's Purpose (vv. 2, 3)

2a. That their hearts might be comforted.

Scripture often uses the term *heart* to designate the person, especially one's center of moral and ethical deliberation, will, and attitudes (Genesis 6:5; Exodus 4:21; Matthew 9:4; 12:34; etc.). The verb translated *comforted* communicates more than offering solace; one is encouraged and strengthened in this comfort. The same root word yields a title for the Holy Spirit: Comforter (see John 14:16, 26; 15:26; 16:7); this gives depth and nuance to the ways he ministers to believers.

2b. Being knit together in love.

This suggests a unity of purpose and thought.

HOW TO SAY IT

Apphia	*Af*-ee-uh-or *Ap*-fee-uh.
Archippus	Ar-*kip*-us.
Colosse	Ko-*lahss*-ee.
Epaphras	*Ep*-uh-frass.
Ephesians	Ee-*fee*-zhunz.
Ezekiel	Ee-*zeek*-ee-ul or Ee-*zeek*-yul.
Laodicea	Lay-*odd*-uh-**see**-uh.
Messiah	Meh-*sigh*-uh.
Philemon	Fih-*lee*-mun or Fye-*lee*-mun.

The same term appears in Ephesians 4:15, 16 and Colossians 2:19 to speak of a unity derived from the church's attachment to its head, Christ. The love that unites believers has its source in their devotion to Christ, who empowers them to love each other (Ephesians 3:19; 4:1, 2; 1 John 4:11). Only a love built on the knowledge of what Christ has done and a desire to serve others can unite the church (John 13:34, 35).

> **What Do You Think?**
> In what ways can your church promote a stronger sense of unity and common purpose?
> *Digging Deeper*
> Consider how this might be done corporately (through the church's formal communication and programming channels) as well as by individual believers.

2c. And unto all riches of the full assurance of understanding, to the acknowledgement of the mystery of God, and of the Father, and of Christ.

Paul desires the saints to have the confidence and power that comes from an ability to distinguish between true and false teaching (see Acts 9:22). The focus of this understanding is to be *the acknowledgement of the mystery of God.* Paul uses *mystery,* a term found earlier in Colossians 1:26, 27, to refer to formerly hidden things now revealed by God to His people through apostolic preaching and writing concerning the gospel (see Romans 11:25). The identification of the mystery as being of God, both *of the Father* and *of Christ,* exalts Christ by pointing to the unity and equality of the Father and Son in the Trinity together with the Spirit.

3. In whom are hid all the treasures of wisdom and knowledge.

The false teachers in Colosse claim they possess hidden truth to which only the spiritual elite have access. In contrast with them, the verse before us identifies Christ as the one *in whom are hid all the treasures of wisdom and knowledge.* Though related, wisdom and knowledge are not the same. Knowledge is the mental apprehension of truth; wisdom is the ability to use knowledge appropriately. Believers can access the hidden wisdom and knowledge revealed now in Christ and can possess full understanding through the mystery of God.

❧ BURIED TREASURE ❧

In 1934, Theodore Jones and Henry Grob made a discovery most children only dream about. Jones and Grob had started a secret club and were burying the box that would hold the club's treasury and secrets. Digging in the dirt floor of Jones's cellar, the teens discovered the Holy Grail of childhood fantasy—real buried treasure! They first came across a shiny $20 gold coin. When their excavation was complete, the boys had unearthed 3,558 century-old gold coins, a fortune that would be worth more than $10 million today.

After months of legal proceedings, the coins were sold at auction. The money was then placed in two trusts that the boys could access after they turned 21.

For the most part, finding hidden treasure is a childhood fantasy. But for Jesus' followers, it is a spiritual reality. What treasures have you discovered through your friendship with Jesus? —J. E.

C. Paul's Presence (vv. 4, 5)

4. And this I say, lest any man should beguile you with enticing words.

Paul knows Christ is the full repository of wisdom and knowledge (Colossians 1:9, 10; 2:2). False teachers could dazzle and impress an audience, especially if they were not already convinced of the truth they found in Christ.

5. For though I be absent in the flesh, yet am I with you in the spirit, joying and beholding your order, and the stedfastness of your faith in Christ.

Though Paul is in prison in Rome (Acts 28:16-31; Colossians 4:10, 18), through his letter he expresses intimate knowledge of the church in Colosse and great love for them (see also 1 Corinthians 5:3). He expresses the delight he has known from hearing positive reports about the Colossian believers from Epaphras (Colossians 1:7, 8; 4:12, 13). Order and steadfastness result from *faith in Christ*. Biblical faith is more than intellectual assent to truth claims; it is a commitment to action resulting from one's trust in Jesus Christ (1 Thessalonians 1:3; James 2:14-22). A fundamental defense against deceptive and crippling doctrine is a deepened commitment to Christ.

> **What Do You Think?**
> In what situations could you provide encouragement by expressing your pride in someone else's accomplishments?
> **Digging Deeper**
> Think especially of situations and people where encouragement would not normally be expected.

II. Love's Growth
(COLOSSIANS 2:6, 7)
A. Walking in Christ (v. 6)

6. As ye have therefore received Christ Jesus the Lord, so walk ye in him.

Paul calls his audience back to what was originally preached and taught among them in contrast to the error that has arisen in their midst. He also summons them back to the exalted Savior he describes earlier in Colossians 1:15-20. By using the full title *Christ Jesus the Lord*, Paul reminds his readers that Jesus, the one who walked humbly among humanity as a man, is also the Messiah (Greek "Christ" = Hebrew "Messiah"), the anointed king, and the Lord God in flesh. He is the exalted one who is above all (Philippians 2:9-11; Colossians 1:15-20; 2:3, 9, 10).

So walk ye in him essentially summarizes the specific commands and warnings that follow: believers are to act out the lordship of Jesus Christ in their thought and deeds (James 2:14-26). Walking, a frequent biblical image for life (Genesis 48:15; Psalm 86:11; 2 Corinthians 5:7; etc.), evokes notions of being on the way toward a destination. Moreover, believers are to walk *in* Christ, not simply *with* Christ (Colossians 1:28; 2:20; 3:1-3). He is not a travel companion we call alongside us as we travel where we have already determined we want to go. As our Lord, Jesus determines our path and empowers us to walk the path to which we are called (Matthew 11:28-30; Luke 9:23).

B. Strengthened in Christ (v. 7)

7. Rooted and built up in him, and stablished in the faith, as ye have been taught, abounding therein with thanksgiving.

Paul uses a horticultural metaphor (see Colossians 1:10-12) and a reference to *thanksgiving* to expound on a command to walk in Christ. Having been *rooted . . . in him*, believers are to grow as a plant grows out of the soil in which it is planted (compare 1 Corinthians 3:10-14; Ephesians 2:20).

Stablished has the notion of confirmation or strengthening (Romans 15:8; 1 Corinthians 1:6, 8). By sticking to their roots and being built up, the saints in Colosse will be established in faith. The passive verbs *rooted, built up,* and *stablished* reveal that it is God who grounds them in faith. *Abounding therein with thanksgiving* is the believers' main task throughout this process (Philippians 4:6; Colossians 4:2). Thanksgiving will abound in the saints' lives as they (we) are attentive to what God has done in Christ and to what He is currently doing.

III. Love's Object
(COLOSSIANS 2:8-12)
A. Reject Thoughts (v. 8)

8. Beware lest any man spoil you through philosophy and vain deceit, after the tradition of men, after the rudiments of the world, and not after Christ.

Philosophy refers to systems of thought characterized by human origin. The word *rudiments* translates a Greek word that has two meanings. Though the word can refer to astrological concepts, in this verse it refers to an organized series of things, such as the letters of the alphabet. The word came to connote the basic elements necessary for a rudimentary knowledge of a subject (compare Hebrews 5:12).

World refers to the transitory systems of humanity that can and/or do stand between a person and God. *World* in this sense combined with the word *rudiments* thus refers to human ideas considered necessary to supplement or even to replace the work of Christ (Galatians 4:3, 9).

To understand more clearly the significance of philosophy and worldly rudiments, one must observe their contrast with things of *Christ*. In his address to the men of Athens, Paul repeatedly alludes to ideas discussed among Greek philosophers (Acts 17:22-31). Such thought, which depends on human tradition, is deceptive in comparison with the fullness of understanding and life available in Christ (Colossians 1:9; 2:2, 3).

Then and now, the rudiments of the world are ultimately powerless. They are the "–isms" of human tradition, culture, and pagan religion that seek or profess understanding through natural human insight alone. They do not seek to understand Christ in the light of Scripture nor do they exalt God and Christ to their proper place.

❧ POWER OF TRUTH ❧

In the novel *1984*, George Orwell envisioned a society in which truth was determined by the government for its own ends. In Oceania, the populace knew that "war is peace," "freedom is slavery," and "ignorance is strength." This knowledge was made possible through "doublethink," the ability to accept two mutually exclusive concepts as true. The government ruled in paradox: The Ministry of Love inflicted torture. The Ministry of Peace waged perpetual war. The Ministry of Plenty rationed resources.

Orwell understood that saying something is true does not make it so. In this, he would have found agreement with the apostle Paul. Paul did not see truth as relative or infinitely flexible. In fact, Paul believed truth has an author who offers us a firm foundation when we trust Him. What "truths" do you need to reevaluate in light of the truth that Christ reveals?   —J. E.

B. Embrace Fullness (vv. 9, 10)

9, 10. For in him dwelleth all the fulness of the Godhead bodily. And ye are complete in him, which is the head of all principality and power.

Paul emphasizes the magnitude of the incarnation of Jesus Christ by speaking of *all the fulness*. His use of the present tense verb *dwelleth* highlights that the incarnation is not simply a historical event but also a present reality with

Visual for Lesson 4. *Have this visual on display as you pose the discussion question that is associated with Colossians 2:2.*

contemporary significance. The power and completeness of Christ exhibited in His incarnation is available to all believers.

Colossians 1:16 earlier asserts that Christ created all things, including *all principality and power*, and that they exist for His purposes. This tandem often refers to evil powers, whether terrestrial or celestial, real or imagined. Christ thus is preeminent above them all (Philippians 2:9-11).

Sandwiched between this section's two central claims about Christ is the affirmation that believers are *complete in him*. The repetition of the concepts filling, fullness, and completeness in this letter (Colossians 1:9, 19, 24; 2:2, 9; 4:12) suggests that false teachers in the Colossian church asserted that Christians need something in addition to Christ to be complete. Paul, however, affirms that because Christ supersedes the powers, believers need not fear them as a barrier to all that is available in Christ. Neither do they possess any power to provide the fullness God offers in Christ. To seek fullness in any other person or power than Jesus Christ is futile and foolhardy.

C. Accept Cleansing (v. 11)

11. In whom also ye are circumcised with the circumcision made without hands, in putting off the body of the sins of the flesh by the circumcision of Christ.

Paul evokes the imagery of *circumcision* to describe the believer's incorporation into God's new covenant community (see Genesis 17). The Old Testament Scriptures also intimated that physical circumcision alone did not validate one's covenant relationship with God (Deuteronomy 10:16; 30:6; Jeremiah 4:4). A greater circumcision, one of the heart, was needed (Romans 2:28, 29).

Christ followers of both genders from among all people groups have now received this greater circumcision, here called the *circumcision of Christ*. Old covenant circumcision was a physical act, but Christ performs the new circumcision in the spiritual realm; it is *made without hands*. Old covenant circumcision was performed on male Israelite infants. Christ's circumcision is performed on men and women who exercise faith. Circumcision under the law involved the removal of a piece of skin; new covenant circumcision involves the removal of a whole way of life, *the body of the sins of the flesh.*

D. Rise to Full Life (v. 12)

12. Buried with him in baptism, wherein also ye are risen with him through the faith of the operation of God, who hath raised him from the dead.

As in Romans 6:1-14, *baptism* is linked with burial, and that burial imagery illustrates the completeness of death to sin. The rising out of water then pantomimes our resurrection. Paul describes the believer's resurrection life as having already begun. Believers can now access a full life through the transforming power God manifested in raising Jesus *from the dead.*

No power to destroy the old life and to raise the Christ follower to new life resides in the water itself. Rather, baptism is made effective by its connection with *the faith of the operation of God* (see also Acts 2:38; Titus 3:5; and 1 Peter 3:21).

> *What Do You Think?*
> Which Scripture passages or biblical themes have you personally found helpful in connecting faith, baptism, and daily Christian experience?
> *Digging Deeper*
> In what ways can you help others make the same connection?

IV. Love's Triumph
(COLOSSIANS 2:13-15)

A. Christ Conquers Sin (v. 13)

13. And you, being dead in your sins and the uncircumcision of your flesh, hath he quickened together with him, having forgiven you all trespasses.

The Colossians had been *dead in [their] sins* (see Ephesians 2:1). The Greek word first translated *sins* and then *trespasses* emphasizes deliberate disobedience and unfaithfulness to God. The phrase *uncircumcision of your flesh* then points to the hearers' identity as Gentiles outside the old covenant (Ephesians 2:11-13) and describes a continuing state of spiritual rebellion (Ezekiel 44:7, 9).

They are now alive with Christ (Colossians 2:12; Ephesians 2:5). *All* their *trespasses* have been *forgiven*. God's act of pardoning sins demonstrates the grace of God's forgiveness. God's forgiving *all trespasses* shows the extent of God's grace that completely removes sin.

> *What Do You Think?*
> What are some ways to help fellow believers overcome the burden of guilt associated with past sins?
> *Digging Deeper*
> How might your answer differ depending on the specific type of sin with which a person feels burdened?

B. Christ Fulfills the Law (v. 14)

14. Blotting out the handwriting of ordinances that was against us, which was contrary to us, and took it out of the way, nailing it to his cross.

In Matthew 5:17, Jesus said that He had come to fulfill the law, not eliminate it. The text before us provides a vital clue regarding how that has now happened. The phrase *handwriting of ordinances* portrays the Old Testament law as an invoice or IOU indicating we owed something to God. Elsewhere, Paul affirms that the law is "holy" and "good" (Romans 7:12). It was a righteous standard that accused the ancient Israelites and against which they could not argue.

However, Christ has blotted out this debt. By sending His own Son to suffer the penalty for our sin, God both upheld the holiness of His own law and rescued us from its accusation. Just as Pilate literally nailed words of accusation ("The King of the Jews") to the cross (John 19:19), God figuratively nailed the law and its penalty there as well.

C. Christ Gives the Victory (v. 15)

15. And having spoiled principalities and powers, he made a shew of them openly, triumphing over them in it.

Victorious imperial armies displayed their captives and their spoils of war as they marched through the streets of Rome. Christ is the conquering king who has triumphed over Satan, demonic forces, and all the powers of evil. In His death, Jesus stripped them of their power, atoned for our sins, and won a decisive victory over evil, a victory that His resurrection confirms. The open show made of them harkens back to the language of mystery (Colossians 2:2) and reminds the audience that no additional knowledge or wisdom is needed because God has accomplished His plan fully in Jesus Christ (see 2 Corinthians 2:2-5).

We are freed to live a resurrection kind of life now in Christ (Colossians 2:13). Christ's death canceled and made irrelevant all the old things that once cluttered life and opposed us (v. 14). Believers are united with Him and with each other.

Conclusion

A. Possession of Completeness

Because Christ is supreme above all and we are complete in Him, we have all we need. Rather than being led astray by other teachings, we trustingly keep our feet on the path Jesus sets for us to walk.

B. Prayer

Our Father, grant that we may be rooted and built up in Christ and strengthened in our faith. We pray in Jesus' name. Amen.

C. Thought to Remember

Mine the treasures hidden in Christ;
look nowhere else.

INVOLVEMENT LEARNING

Enhance your lesson with KJV Bible Student *(from your curriculum supplier) and the reproducible activity page (at www.standardlesson.com or in the back of the* KJV Standard Lesson Commentary Deluxe Edition*).*

Into the Lesson

Before class, prepare a time line of the history of your congregation on a large sheet of chart or butcher paper. Include milestones such as the founding date, building completions, dates for each minister, etc.

Display the time line at the front of the room, and have colored markers available for learners to use to place themselves on the time line according to when they began to attend. When everyone has done so, say, "Today we will be reading a portion of the letter Paul sent to the church at Colosse. Let's see what Paul had to say to the Colossians about their spiritual community."

Option. Place in chairs copies of the "Christian Perks" puzzle from the reproducible page, which you can download, for students to work on as they arrive.

Into the Word

Use the Lesson Context to prepare a brief summary of the religious and philosophical influences at work in the Colossian church or assign this task to a student. After the talk ask, "What were the Colossian Christians doing wrong in their presentation of the gospel?" (*Expected response*: they used false teaching to make the gospel more "acceptable" to the people in their community.)

Divide learners into four groups (or multiples of four for larger classes). Ask each group to search the lesson text of Colossians 2:1-15 to find answers to their assigned question. Ask them to include a verse reference for each answer.

- *False Teachers Group:* How did the false teachers communicate their message?
- *Gospel Defense Group:* What defense did Paul give in support of the supremacy of the gospel message?
- *Evidence Group:* What evidence did Paul give to support his defense of the gospel?
- *Results Group:* What result can Christians expect if they accept Paul's message?

Write the four group headings at the top of four columns on the board. As each group reads its question and shares its answers, write those under the appropriate heading. *Expected responses*:

False Teachers—they would "beguile" by using "enticing words" (v. 4); they would use "philosophy and vain deceit," relying on the "tradition of men, after the rudiments of the world" (v. 8).

Gospel Defense— by staying steadfast in their "faith in Christ" (v. 5), they will walk in Him (v. 6) and become "rooted and built up" and established in Him (v. 7); they will teach the superiority of Christ, in whom all the "fulness of the Godhead" dwells bodily (v. 9); they will emphasize that Christ is the "head of all principality and power" (v. 10).

Evidence—Christians experience the "circumcision of Christ" (v. 11) when they are "buried with him in baptism," and they know the power of Christ's resurrection since they "are risen with him through" faith (v. 12).

Results—Christians experience new life and the forgiveness of all their trespasses (v. 13); sins have been "blotted out" and nailed to the cross (v. 14); because of this believers can triumph over the principalities and powers of darkness. (v. 15).

Allow leeway for other verses to be used.

Into Life

Say, "Paul instructed the Colossians that their faith was rooted, built up, and established in Christ. This is also a call for us to have the same kind of faith. Let's brainstorm some ways that we can develop steadfast faith." Write learners' suggestions on the board (*possibilities*: starting daily devotions, pursuing a deeper prayer life, participating in Bible study within a small group, etc.). Challenge learners to create a plan for the coming month.

Option. Distribute copies of the "Growth Symbols" activity from the reproducible page as a take-home.

RIGHT ATTITUDES

DEVOTIONAL READING: Isaiah 61:1-8
BACKGROUND SCRIPTURE: Matthew 5:1-12

MATTHEW 5:1-12

1 And seeing the multitudes, he went up into a mountain: and when he was set, his disciples came unto him:

2 And he opened his mouth, and taught them, saying,

3 Blessed are the poor in spirit: for theirs is the kingdom of heaven.

4 Blessed are they that mourn: for they shall be comforted.

5 Blessed are the meek: for they shall inherit the earth.

6 Blessed are they which do hunger and thirst after righteousness: for they shall be filled.

7 Blessed are the merciful: for they shall obtain mercy.

8 Blessed are the pure in heart: for they shall see God.

9 Blessed are the peacemakers: for they shall be called the children of God.

10 Blessed are they which are persecuted for righteousness' sake: for theirs is the kingdom of heaven.

11 Blessed are ye, when men shall revile you, and persecute you, and shall say all manner of evil against you falsely, for my sake.

12 Rejoice, and be exceeding glad: for great is your reward in heaven: for so persecuted they the prophets which were before you.

KEY VERSE

Rejoice, and be exceeding glad: for great is your reward in heaven: for so persecuted they the prophets which were before you. —**Matthew 5:12**

COVENANT IN GOD

Unit 2: A Heartfelt Covenant
LESSONS 5–9

LESSON AIMS

After participating in this lesson, each learner will be able to:

1. List characteristics that mark a blessed life.

2. Give examples of how Jesus' teachings go against the standard practices of the world.

3. Express gratitude to a fellow believer for living "beatitude attitudes."

LESSON OUTLINE

Introduction

A. Blessed Awareness

As someone who has traveled extensively, I am acutely aware every time I come home how convenient my life is in big and little ways: clean water in my home for daily showers; refrigeration to keep food fresh and safe to eat; fast internet and dependable cell phone coverage. I come home feeling more satisfied about the accessibility of education for myself and my loved ones and less frustrated with participatory government. For a while, I do not take for granted being able to attend church without fear.

In our age of dissatisfaction, unhappiness, and continual complaining, even these comforts at home aren't always enough to convince us that we are blessed. We want something even bigger, even better, and we certainly don't hope for hardships. How can we become people who wake up counting our blessings in all circumstances?

B. Lesson Context

The word *beatitude* does not occur in the Greek New Testament; it comes into English through Latin and means "a blessing." Beatitudes in the Bible begin with the word *blessed*. A rich source for such beatitudes is the book of Psalms, which even begins with a blessing (Psalm 1:1). Jesus spoke many blessings that New Testament writers preserved in Gospels and letters.

The basis for God's blessing is His love. The person whom God blesses receives an expression of His love, whether the person knows it or not (Matthew 5:45). Some whom God blesses are further singled out for finding favor with God (Luke 1:30, 42).

Blessings often have both a present and a future fulfillment. If one is blessed, the benefits are evident now or will come soon. Unlike a curse, a blessing is never earned but is granted by God according to His good pleasure (see Psalm 8). Furthermore, a righteous action itself can be considered a blessing, because virtue is part of its own reward. When Jesus says "Blessed are they that have not seen, and yet have believed" (John 20:29), He is not advising us to believe so that we can receive a blessing. He is saying that the state of being a believer is a blessing in and of itself.

Both Matthew and Luke include the Beatitudes of Jesus in their accounts of one of His sermons (compare Luke 6:20-23). It's quite possible that those two writers recorded different teaching occasions. But if that is the case, there is at least a significant overlap in what Jesus said at both times.

The general form of the Beatitudes is (1) to pronounce a certain group of people "blessed" and then (2) give a reason for or result of that blessing. However, some key differences exist between the two writers' accounts regarding how the Beatitudes are worded (see commentary below for examples). Beyond the differences in the Beatitudes themselves, Matthew does not include woes to various groups of people who seem to be enjoying good things in this life (compare and contrast Luke 6:24-26).

I. Prelude
(MATTHEW 5:1, 2)
A. The Mountain (v. 1)

1a. And seeing the multitudes, he went up into a mountain.

Great *multitudes* had begun to follow Jesus from all the regions of Palestine (Matthew 4:25). Jesus chooses *a mountain* as a venue to address and teach these followers. In such a location, He is above them and the crowds can spread below (see Luke 6:17 regarding an alternative sermon location on a plain).

Preaching from a mountain is symbolically important for Israel because Moses received God's law for the first time at Mount Sinai (Exodus 19:2, 3). Because of Matthew's description of the location, we call this the Sermon on the Mount. The traditional site for Jesus' sermon is a mountain overlooking the Sea of Galilee from the northwest, but this is uncertain.

1b. And when he was set, his disciples came unto him.

Once Jesus has chosen his teaching platform on the mountain, *his disciples* come closer *unto him*. Matthew presents this teaching occasion as both intimate and public. It is as if Jesus is teaching a small group on the stage of an auditorium while a large crowd listens from the seats.

The full complement of 12 disciples has not yet been announced in this Gospel (see Matthew 10:1-4); only Peter, Andrew, James, and John are named thus far (4:18-22). According to the Gospel of Luke, however, the 12 were designated before the Sermon on the Plain (Luke 6:12-16).

B. The Words of Jesus (v. 2)

2. And he opened his mouth, and taught them, saying.

Jesus' teaching is always oral in the New Testament, not written. Matthew presents a situation in which the curious followers of this wonder-worker simply cannot get enough of Him. They want to hear everything He has to say, just as they want to witness His healings and exorcisms (Matthew 4:23-25).

> *What Do You Think?*
> Under what circumstances should the church give preference to oral vs. written teaching? When should it be the other way around? Why?
>
> *Digging Deeper*
> To what degree does combining the oral with the written (such as with a PowerPoint presentation) improve teaching, if at all? Why?

II. Blessings
(MATTHEW 5:3-9)
A. On the Desperate (vv. 3-6)

3a. Blessed are the poor in spirit.

This is the first of eight total beatitudes. The first four beatitudes give promises to those living tough and unfulfilling lives who need God's blessings desperately. The first group Jesus blesses is *the poor in spirit*. Both spiritual and material poverty are indicated, though in the third Gospel Jesus' words are explicitly about the materially impoverished (Luke 6:20). Poverty grinds on the human spirit, and often the poor have no hope of relief except from the Lord (1 Samuel 2:8; Psalms 72:12; 140:12; Luke 1:52, 53; 4:18, 19). Those who recognize their spiritual poverty are humble and lowly (Proverbs 16:19; see also Job 42:1-6).

3b. For theirs is the kingdom of heaven.

Jesus understands His ministry as bringing good news to the poor (see Luke 4:18, 19, quoting Isaiah 61:1, 2). Indeed, Jesus later says that it is difficult for a rich person to enter the *kingdom of heaven* (Matthew 19:23). The blessing here is that there is no entrance fee, whether in money or spiritual riches, to be welcomed into the kingdom of Heaven. The kingdom is a major theme in Matthew, mentioned over 30 times by this writer. This kingdom is anticipated as being very near because Jesus has brought it near in His ministry (4:17; 10:7). He makes this explicit in His teaching (5:10, 19, 20; 13:24, 31, 33; etc.) and gives signs of its truth with His healing ministry (see especially Matthew 8, 9).

> **What Do You Think?**
> Should ministry to those who are poor in spirit be combined with ministry to those who are poor in material things? Why, or why not?
> *Digging Deeper*
> How, if at all, does John 6:26 cause you to modify your answer? What about Romans 15:27?

4a. Blessed are they that mourn.

To *mourn* is more than tearful behavior, for the New Testament has another word for weeping (see Mark 16:10; Luke 6:25). Jesus speaks to those who are grieving, who have a deep sense of sorrow and loss. This may be for personal sins, for life's tragedies, for community loss, etc.; Jesus does not say.

4b. For they shall be comforted.

Many Jewish people of Jesus' day carry constant sorrow about their national situation and history. They are humiliated and oppressed by the Romans who occupy their land. Yet for Jesus' hearers, the promise is not of national renewal or even of improvement in their personal situations. Jesus promises they will *be comforted*. They will find relief from their sorrow (Revelation 7:17; 21:4; compare Psalm 34:18). True and lasting comfort comes from God (2 Corinthians 1:4; 7:6).

> **What Do You Think?**
> What are some practical ways for Christians to be a blessing of comfort to those who mourn?
> *Digging Deeper*
> Are there times when we should not attempt to comfort someone who mourns? Why, or why not?

5a. Blessed are the meek.

Some equate *meek* with *weak*. Better synonyms for biblical meekness are *gentleness* or *humility*. The opposite of meekness is aggression, especially self-serving aggression.

5b. For they shall inherit the earth.

Jesus is not encouraging His hearers to be meek, for such is not His purpose here. Rather, He is offering hope and a promise to those who know their meekness: they will *inherit the earth*. In so doing, Jesus recalls Psalm 37:11, where David declared the same thing. Jesus and David both use *earth* in the sense of land. Ancient Israel inherited the promised land according to God's promise (Genesis 12:1, 7; Joshua 1:1-6). In the same way, David anticipated the meek in Israel receiving their inheritance from God, and Jesus promises that the meek are not forgotten (compare Romans 4:13).

6a. Blessed are they which do hunger and thirst after righteousness.

The pangs of physical *hunger and thirst* are reminders that no one survives without food and water. But Jesus is describing those who are consumed by their pursuit of righteousness, by the pursuit of justice. Theirs is not a whim or short-term goal, but a daily obsession.

We often understand the word *righteousness* more narrowly than the original text intends, because of its religious overtones. Righteousness, at its base, is knowing and doing the right thing. Since this knowledge comes only from the Lord, it is a religious word. But its applications apply to every corner of human existence. Righteousness is for living in every facet of one's life.

Righteousness is tightly paired with judgment, what we often refer to today as justice. Justice is the desire to see the right thing done, especially for others who cannot ensure that they are treated correctly. While justice can mean punishing a wrongdoer, it is also a proactive stance. Righteousness and justice do not wait for something to go wrong so that it can be made right. Injustice should be prevented as often as possible.

These terms and concepts are ultimately defined by God (Job 29:14; Psalms 33:5; 36:6; 50:6). A human perspective might allow the exploitation of the poor in order to gain riches or simply to take care of oneself before thinking of others' needs (Isaiah 5:7). From God's perspective, however, the poor should be protected and assisted, not victimized and oppressed (Job 37:23; Psalm 103:6).

6b. For they shall be filled.

Jesus' promise is that spiritual hunger and thirst will be satisfied in the kingdom of Heaven (compare and contrast the beatitude on hunger in Luke 6:21). A trusting relationship with the Lord is the only antidote for those who yearn for spiritual food and drink (Psalm 107:9). The kingdom of Heaven is the place where everyone may eat without need of purchasing food (Isaiah 55:1, 2; see also Revelation 22:17). The kingdom of Heaven that Jesus represents fulfills all our godly desires for both personal righteousness and community justice (Isaiah 9:7; 11:4).

B. On the Hopeful (vv. 7-12)

7a. Blessed are the merciful.

The second set of four beatitudes offers promises to people who live in godly ways. Some people seem always to "err on the side of mercy." They give of themselves and their possessions selflessly. They truly feel the pain of their friends and family who are suffering and seek to bring comfort to those situations.

> **What Do You Think?**
> What safeguards can we adopt to avoid making things worse while extending mercy?
> **Digging Deeper**
> Give examples, without mentioning names, of failure to do so.

7b. For they shall obtain mercy.

Jesus promises the merciful the *mercy* of God himself. God's deep desire to be merciful will rest on them as they show mercy themselves and wait for Him (Isaiah 30:18). Jews of the first century view mercy as a primary attribute of the Lord, repeated throughout their Scriptures (2 Samuel 24:14; Nehemiah 9:31; Psalm 25:6; etc.). But God's mercy is not blind. Elsewhere, Jesus teaches that unmerciful, unforgiving people should not expect mercy or forgiveness from the Lord (Matthew 6:14, 15; 18:23-35; see also James 2:13).

8a. Blessed are the pure in heart.

The group addressed by the sixth beatitude is most perplexing. Who deserves to be identified as *pure in heart*? The Bible often speaks of evil in the human heart in a universal manner (see Genesis 8:21; Ecclesiastes 8:11; Romans 3:10), a trait that excludes purity in the same heart. Yet elsewhere the pure in heart meet God (Psalm 24:3, 4).

Jesus is not addressing a select group of people who are without sin, for no one in His audience or elsewhere meets that standard. The *heart* for Jesus' hearers is more than the seat of emotions such as love or hate. It is, rather, the source of the human will or motives. While no one is without sin, some habitually act with pure motives. For children, it is the parent who always makes decisions for the best interests of the family. For citizens, it is the official who puts the interests of the people being served above personal benefits. For church members, it is the leader who prioritizes the good of the church even if it may be painful or costly for that leader. Their primary motivation is to please God. Such are the pure in heart.

> **What Do You Think?**
> In what ways can a Christian be an example of one having a pure heart while not coming across as "holier than thou"?
> **Digging Deeper**
> Fine-tune your conclusion by considering the Bible's numerous "conscience" passages (example: 1 Corinthians 10:23-32).

8b. For they shall see God.

This promise may also seem unusual, but in the ancient world to be allowed to see the monarch is an enormous privilege (see Esther 4:11). For Jesus, the purehearted will gain this great blessing

Visual for Lesson 5

Keep this chart posted throughout the study of Unit 2 to establish a chronological perspective.

(Psalm 42:2; Hebrews 12:14; Revelation 22:4). They will experience intimate fellowship with the Lord himself; they will ascend His holy hill and enjoy His presence (Psalm 24:3, 4).

❧ POWER IN PRAISE ❧

On the night of March 31, 2014, 9-year-old Willie Myrick was playing in his driveway in Atlanta. A would-be kidnapper approached Willie and lured him until he was close enough to be forced into the car.

For three hours, the assailant drove the boy away from his home to an uncertain fate. Willie Myrick did not respond with a struggle or with tears. Instead, he began to sing his favorite gospel song, "Every Praise," repeatedly. The song visibly enraged the driver. "He was cursing at me, telling me to shut up," Willie told a reporter later. Finally, the kidnapper kicked the boy out of the car. Obviously shaken but not hurt, Willie ran to a nearby house and called his godmother.

Willie's pure heart motivated him to sing his favorite song in the face of danger, and he was delivered by God from his trial. How is the purity of your heart affecting your experience of God?

—J. E.

9a. Blessed are the peacemakers.

The seventh beatitude can call to mind diplomats brokering treaties between nations to avoid war. Such people may deserve a blessing, but they are not the target group for Jesus here. Instead He addresses those *peacemakers* in His audience who are bold to resolve conflicts, restore relationships, and avoid strife (Romans 12:18; James 3:18).

Biblical peace is not simply an absence of violence. Rather, it is a full experience of well-being and harmony (Isaiah 26:3; John 14:27; Philippians 4:7). The greatest need for peace is in our relationship with the Lord, what Paul refers to as "reconciliation" (2 Corinthians 5:18-20). Peacemakers in the kingdom of God bring about reconciliation between people and God and then between individuals as based on the shared restored relationship with the Lord (Ephesians 2:16).

9b. For they shall be called the children of God.

The promise for peacemakers to be called *the children of God* is not just as a label but as a reality (1 John 3:1). To be a child of God makes us heirs of His riches (Romans 8:17). Third-party reconciliation work can be thankless and frustrating. Jesus promises hope to such workers, namely full inclusion in God's family.

10a. Blessed are they which are persecuted for righteousness' sake.

The eighth beatitude is the other side of the coin of the seventh, just considered. Those who bring peace are not always honored and encouraged. Here, those who stand for God's *righteousness* (see comments on Matthew 5:6, above) are seeking peace, but there are many for whom injustice and unrighteousness have benefits. These are not exclusively criminals but, instead, anyone who is comfortable living in the midst of injustice and sinful behavior. Challenging this status quo will receive a strong response. Rather than heeding the message and repenting, the guilty will target the messengers for punishment (1 Peter 3:14).

10b. For theirs is the kingdom of heaven.

The promise for the persecuted comes back to the first beatitude. As with spiritual poverty, the ones persecuted for righteousness will receive *the kingdom of heaven.* Their rewards are not found in the world of sin, injustice, and corruption, but in the realm of the Lord, the sphere where God reigns as king. He will be their protector and rewarder (Genesis 15:1; Psalm 12:7, 8; Nahum 1:7).

11. Blessed are ye, when men shall revile

you, and persecute you, and shall say all manner of evil against you falsely, for my sake.

Jesus expands the simple description of persecution from verse 10 to include reviling and having *all manner of evil* said *falsely* (1 Peter 4:14). The corresponding beatitude in the third Gospel includes "when men shall hate you" (Luke 6:22). This further strengthens the magnitude of *evil* that is directed at believers. The reason for persecution is quite focused: *for my sake.* Followers of Jesus are hated and persecuted for no more complicated reason than that they are followers of Jesus (John 15:21; Acts 5:41). Even today, those who stand for Jesus and His teachings are hatefully labeled as religious bigots or dismissed as hopelessly naïve.

12. Rejoice, and be exceeding glad: for great is your reward in heaven: for so persecuted they the prophets which were before you.

Jesus has a twofold promise for His persecuted followers. First, they have a *great . . . reward in heaven.* This is sometimes called the "great reversal," that the oppressed righteous in this life will be blessed and honored in the next life (compare Luke 16:19-31).

But there is more at stake than reward in the hereafter. Jesus is ushering in the kingdom of Heaven in His lifetime (Matthew 4:17). Persecuted saints do not simply suffer now for a reward later. Despite real or threatened persecution, the Christ-following life is rich and satisfying, a reward in and of itself (2 Corinthians 6:10; 12:10; Colossians 1:24).

Second, Jesus promises that those who suffer as His disciples join an august group that has gone before: the *persecuted . . . prophets* (2 Chronicles 36:16; Matthew 23:31, 37). This is the "cloud of witnesses" spoken of in Hebrews 12:1, the honored body of God's servants. Standing for righteousness and justice is a prophetic voice not subject to human approval. It is to stand and speak for God himself.

❧ IMPRISONED BUT FREE ❧

Palani was known as the village drunk in his Laotian community. But that changed after a visit to his brother, a minister. Desperate because of his alcoholism, Palani allowed his brother to pray for him. According to his testimony, the change in his life was immediate. Palani returned to his village and began to help a local minister preach and distribute Bibles.

Only days after accepting Christ, a village leader told Palani he could no longer talk about God or distribute Bibles. Days later, police came to Palani's house and arrested him. Having then been shackled, beaten, ruthlessly interrogated, and witnessing fellow prisoners die of malnutrition, Palani surprisingly was released two months later.

Persecuted believers recognize that the freedom Christ gives cannot be taken away. What about you: Are you experiencing freedom in Christ in all circumstances?　　　　　—J. E.

Conclusion
A. Blessed Attitudes

Taken together, the Beatitudes describe characteristics of people who are earnestly seeking the Lord. Living the God-honoring life can often go unrecognized and unrewarded by society in general, leaving the godly person to wonder, "Is it worth it?" Jesus promises, "Yes, it is worth it!" and gives hope for God's blessing.

B. Prayer

God of blessings, we take comfort in the promises You give to us through the Beatitudes. As these words of encouragement have strengthened the souls of many Christians through the centuries, may they lift our hearts today. In Jesus' name we pray. Amen.

C. Thought to Remember
The Christian life is full of blessings
we don't always appreciate.

HOW TO SAY IT

beatitude	bee-*a*-tuh-tood (*a* as in *mat*).
Corinthians	Ko-*rin*-thee-unz (*th* as in *thin*).
Ecclesiastes	Ik-*leez*-ee-*as*-teez.
Ephesians	Ee-*fee*-zhunz.
Nahum	*Nay*-hum.
Palestine	***Pah***-luh-*stin* (*i* as in *eye*).

INVOLVEMENT LEARNING

Enhance your lesson with KJV Bible Student *(from your curriculum supplier) and the reproducible activity page (at www.standardlesson.com or in the back of the* KJV Standard Lesson Commentary Deluxe Edition*).*

Into the Lesson

Distribute 10 index cards to 10 students, one each. On the 10 cards have a single statement each (you prepare) of the following: 1–The founder of Alcoholics Anonymous asked for a shot of whiskey on his deathbed. 2–Tammy "Stand by Your Man" Wynette was married five times. 3–Most tobacco company executives don't smoke. 4–The inventor of the stop sign, the crosswalk, and one-way streets never learned to drive. 5–Hitler's grandmother was Jewish. 6–The world's largest ice cream cone is made by Tiny Dairies. 7–Alexander Graham Bell refused to have a telephone in his study. 8–The most shoplifted book in America is the Bible. 9–Hippopotomonstrosesquippedaliophobia means "fear of long words." 10–The inventor of basketball is the only basketball coach in University of Kansas history to have a losing record.

Ask each student to read his or her card. Then poll the class as to whether the statement is true or false. After all 10 statements have been read, reveal that all are true.

Alternative. Distribute copies of the "What's in a Name?" activity from the reproducible page, which you can download. Have students work to match the ironic names with their identities.

After either activity, ask for a definition of the word *irony.* (*Expected response:* the use of words to express something other than and especially the opposite of the literal meaning.)

Lead into Bible study by saying, "The world's tallest man is nicknamed Tiny. Drug abuse educators meet for a wine and cheese reception. A fitness guru has a heart attack while jogging . . . We see examples of irony daily. Jesus told His disciples that their lifestyle would seem just as contradictory to the world."

Into the Word

Divide the class into three groups, giving each group paper and one of the following Scriptures:

Matthew 5:1-5; Matthew 5:6-8; Matthew 5:9-12. Ask each group to rewrite each of their beatitudes to make it reflect popular wisdom. *Examples*:

Verse 3 Blessed are the confident; they conquer the world!

Verse 4 Blessed are those who laugh; the whole world laughs with them!

Verse 5 Blessed are the aggressive; everyone needs to get out of their way!

Verse 6 Blessed are those who like the way things are; change is inconvenient!

Verse 7 Blessed are the tough; they are nobody's fool!

Verse 8 Blessed are the streetwise; they know how the real world works!

Verse 9 Blessed are those who keep people riled up; people will let them have their way!

Verse 10 Blessed are those who go along to get along; life is easier when that happens!

Verse 11 Blessed are those with good reputations; no one trusts a troublemaker!

Allow the groups to share and explain their rewrites, contrasting their "commonsense" rewrites with Jesus' counterintuitive commands.

Alternative. Distribute copies of the "Unexpected Words" activity from the reproducible page. Allow no more than a minute for students to fill in the grid. Discuss why Jesus' teaching on being blessed is countercultural.

After either activity, lead into the closing activity with these words: "It goes against common thinking to say that a person can be filled when empty, powerful when peaceful, and happy when hurting. But we have known believers who exhibit those characteristics. Let's recognize someone who displays beatitude attitudes."

Into Life

Distribute blank thank-you cards. Have students review the list of beatitude attitudes and think of a believer who exhibits one or more of them. Ask each learner to write a note to the person that comes to mind, thanking him or her for being an example of a truly blessed person.

Fulfilling the Law

Devotional Reading: Psalm 119:105-112
Background Scripture: Matthew 5:13-20

Matthew 5:13-20

13 Ye are the salt of the earth: but if the salt have lost his savour, wherewith shall it be salted? it is thenceforth good for nothing, but to be cast out, and to be trodden under foot of men.

14 Ye are the light of the world. A city that is set on an hill cannot be hid.

15 Neither do men light a candle, and put it under a bushel, but on a candlestick; and it giveth light unto all that are in the house.

16 Let your light so shine before men, that they may see your good works, and glorify your Father which is in heaven.

17 Think not that I am come to destroy the law, or the prophets: I am not come to destroy, but to fulfil.

18 For verily I say unto you, Till heaven and earth pass, one jot or one tittle shall in no wise pass from the law, till all be fulfilled.

19 Whosoever therefore shall break one of these least commandments, and shall teach men so, he shall be called the least in the kingdom of heaven: but whosoever shall do and teach them, the same shall be called great in the kingdom of heaven.

20 For I say unto you, That except your righteousness shall exceed the righteousness of the scribes and Pharisees, ye shall in no case enter into the kingdom of heaven.

Key Verse

Let your light so shine before men, that they may see your good works, and glorify your Father which is in heaven. —**Matthew 5:16**

COVENANT IN GOD

Unit 2: A Heartfelt Covenant
LESSONS 5–9

LESSON AIMS

After participating in this lesson, each learner will be able to:

1. Identify the dos and don'ts of being a follower of Jesus.

2. Contrast the righteousness Jesus described with the righteousness of the scribes and Pharisees.

3. Evaluate for improvement his or her "saltiness" and/or "luminosity" as a Christian.

LESSON OUTLINE

Introduction
    A. Deadly Darkness
    B. Lesson Context
I. Who Disciples Are (MATTHEW 5:13-16)
    A. Earthy Salt (v. 13)
    B. Bright Light (vv. 14-16)
      More to "Tel"
II. Who Jesus Is (MATTHEW 5:17-20)
    A. Fulfillment of the Law (vv. 17, 18)
      The Heroic Outlaw
    B. Teacher of Righteousness (vv. 19, 20)
Conclusion
    A. I'm Gonna Let It Shine
    B. Prayer
    C. Thought to Remember

Introduction

A. Deadly Darkness

When I was growing up, my father, older brother, and I enjoyed a yearly hunting week in the back country of Idaho. We went in October when the snow had just begun to fall and the deer had descended from the high mountains. We didn't always bag this elusive game, but we had great times of bonding and excitement. We partnered with another family who had two sons the same age as my brother and me, so there were two fathers and four sons.

The year I was 12, the other father, his older son, and my older brother decided to try something new since we had not seen any deer in two days. They studied the forest service maps and thought there was a trail winding down an isolated creek near our camp. There was road access at the head of this stream and at a bridge about five miles below. The plan was for my father to dump the three out at dawn at the creek's head and let them hunt down the isolated stream while we drove down to pick them up at the bridge in the early afternoon.

My team hunted near our camp that morning, then headed down to the bridge. We built a huge fire and began to cook a meal for the other team, sure that they would be cold and hungry when they arrived. But they did not come. It began to get dark, and the below-freezing night was near. We drove as far up the creek as we could, but the other team was not found. Finally, we stopped and fired a series of three shots from a rifle, the hunter's universal signal. No response; the roar of the creek drowned out the sound of these shots. We worried. We doubted the three could survive the night. It hit me hard: my beloved brother and my friends might die if we couldn't find them!

Finally, my father decided to turn his Jeep around on the narrow road and go back to the bridge, thinking we might have missed them somehow. The vehicle turning was tricky, but we managed, and were just ready to drive away when we heard shots. We waited as the other three came bounding out of the trees. They had not heard our earlier shots, but they saw the headlights of the

Jeep. What happened? The trail down the creek had failed them, and they had waded through the icy water for several hundred yards where the stream went through an area with sheer rock walls. They were soaked and nearly frozen. They would not have survived the night alone, but they saw the lights and were saved.

B. Lesson Context

Matthew's record of Jesus' Sermon on the Mount extends the length of chapters 5–7 in his Gospel. The opening feature is the section known familiarly to many as the Beatitudes (last week's lesson). There Jesus spoke eight beatitudes in third person, seemingly as general statements of truth (Matthew 5:3-9). But in the two verses that follow, Jesus switched from third person to second person. This seemed to aim His thoughts there directly at His disciples. It was they who could expect to be insulted, persecuted, and generally bad-mouthed. But those eventualities were not to deter them from carrying out the role He had for them—the subject of today's lesson.

I. Who Disciples Are
(MATTHEW 5:13-16)
A. Earthy Salt (v. 13)

13. Ye are the salt of the earth: but if the salt have lost his savour, wherewith shall it be salted? it is thenceforth good for nothing, but to be cast out, and to be trodden under foot of men.

There are two popular ways of understanding what it means for Jesus' followers to be *the salt of the earth*. One focuses on the preservative quality of salt. Salt, if applied to fresh meat or fish, will keep it from rotting and allow such to be used as food months after the animal is butchered. Similarly, Jesus' disciples, the members of the kingdom of Heaven, preserve the earth by keeping a check on sin. The influence of the righteous may not always win the day, but it tamps down dangerous sin enough to allow communities to function in semi-lawful ways (Romans 8:12, 13; Titus 3:8).

If this influence is lost (salt losing its *savour*), then this preservative function is also lost. If the

people of God neither practice righteous behavior as examples nor stand against injustice in their communities, they become worthless. They must provide a contrast to *the earth*, those people who live according to the laws of the world (1 Corinthians 15:48-50). Should Christians fail to do so, they might as well be joined with the dirt and walked on without respect.

This interpretation finds parallels from the days of Noah, when the Lord found humanity to be so wicked that He decided to destroy the great majority of people with a flood (Genesis 6:5-7, 10-13). God recognized the righteous behavior of Noah (6:8), but that man's influence was not enough to preserve society.

A second interpretation of *salt of the earth* relies on the property of salt to cause thirst. Earlier, Jesus spoke of those who "thirst after righteousness" (Matthew 5:6). A purpose of the disciples is to cause the general population to be "thirsty" for the righteousness that Jesus brings. The right relationship with the Lord will satisfy those with spiritual thirst (Isaiah 55:1-3; John 4:10-14). If the witness of Jesus' disciples becomes tainted and compromised and no longer causes society to desire what Jesus offers, then the church's role as salt has failed. Its people are no different than the unsaved masses; they might as well join them as ordinary dirt.

Both interpretations have merit, and it is difficult to dismiss either of them. The first ("salt as preservative") has a long history and many advocates. The second ("salt as thirst-causer") fits the context in Matthew 5 well and offers parallels to the next metaphor (Matthew 5:14-16). Considering parallel passages in Mark 9:49, 50 and Luke 14:34, 35 does not clarify which interpretation Matthew intends to be the primary reading.

What Do You Think?
Where will you place your saltiness emphasis: on being a preservative or being a thirst-causer? Why?
Digging Deeper
Which is better: to be really good at one of those two, or to strive for a balance? Why?

B. Bright Light (vv. 14-16)

14. Ye are the light of the world. A city that is set on an hill cannot be hid.

Nighttime is very dark in Jesus' time because artificial lights are relatively rare. Such light comes from something being burned: a candle, an oil lamp, a pitch-soaked torch, or a wood fire. Lighting in a home after sundown is expensive and mostly unnecessary. Galilee, where Jesus is speaking, is close enough to the equator that it averages about 12 hours of daylight year-round (see John 11:9). For both fiscal and solar reasons, people rise to work at sunrise and retire for the night at sundown. The typical home is lighted artificially as little as possible.

This situation means that there is rarely light pollution after sundown. Darkness after sunset ensures that even small lights can be seen at a considerable distance. Cities with many lamps and torches are easily visible for many miles. *A city that is set on a hill* certainly *cannot be hid*! Like Jesus, His followers are to shine in the darkness, showing the way to life (John 8:12).

❧ MORE TO "TEL" ❧

When visiting Israel, a tourist may notice that many historic sites begin with the same three-letter word *tel*: Tel Aviv (compare Ezekiel 3:15), Tel Afek, Tel Kinrot, Tel Hazor, Tel Achziv, Tel Avdon, and many, many more. In a modern sense, the word *tel* is an archeological term. It refers to a man-made hill or mound under which are the ruins of a city or cities.

Each time the city was destroyed, the next city built on that site had a higher elevation. A city on a natural hill would be reinforced by raising the slopes of the hill. This cycle would repeat again and again. For this reason, a tel has several layers of accumulated construction. War and disaster would not cause a city on a hill to be wiped away. On the contrary, destruction of a city on a hill would only ensure that the next layer would be more visible!

The church of our Lord Jesus is truly a city on a hill in this ancient sense. Time after time, tyrants have attempted to extinguish her light. They only succeeded in putting that light on an even higher tel! How has your past elevated the reach of your light?

—J. E.

15. Neither do men light a candle, and put it under a bushel, but on a candlestick; and it giveth light unto all that are in the house.

Jesus also appeals to His hearers' practical use of light in a household setting. Because of the expense of burning candles or lamps, most homes limit their use. It is foolish, then, to squander the resource of light by covering a candle with a *bushel* (Mark 4:21; Luke 11:33). Instead, the wise homeowner places the light *on a candlestick* to maximize its usefulness for the entire room (8:16).

> *What Do You Think?*
> What are some ways to ensure the visibility of your light for Christ?
> *Digging Deeper*
> Which is better to focus on: making the light itself brighter, or clearing away the things that are blocking others from seeing our light?

16. Let your light so shine before men, that they may see your good works, and glorify your Father which is in heaven.

Jesus applies both of His lessons about lights (visibility in darkness, fiscal irresponsibility of limiting their shining) to His disciples in a spiritual way. The shining light represents *good works*, the righteous lives He expects of His followers (1 Corinthians 10:31; Philippians 1:11; Titus 2:14). As the saltiness of their witness points to the quenching of their spiritual thirst with God, so their blazing good works also point to God.

Their lighted lives cause those who see them to *glorify* the *Father* (Matthew 9:8). That the Father *is in heaven* emphasizes that His ways are above

HOW TO SAY IT

Beatitudes	Bee-*a*-tuh-toods (*a* as in *mat*).
Galilee	*Gal*-uh-lee.
Mosaic	Mo-*zay*-ik.
Pharisees	*Fair*-ih-seez.
Philippians	Fih-*lip*-ee-unz.

the ways of the world and cannot be achieved by earthly means. His ways are to be desired and followed (6:9-13).

> **What Do You Think?**
> What guardrails can we erect to ensure that we are not fooling ourselves regarding how much our lights are shining?
>
> **Digging Deeper**
> Under what circumstances would a Christian benefit from having a light-shining accountability partner? Why?

II. Who Jesus Is
(MATTHEW 5:17-20)

A. Fulfillment of the Law (vv. 17, 18)

17. Think not that I am come to destroy the law, or the prophets: I am not come to destroy, but to fulfil.

Jesus moves to speak of the relationship of His teachings to the lifestyle of good deeds that are practiced per *the law* and *the prophets*, the Jewish Scriptures. Jesus does not minimize the simple requirements of the law, but instead He takes the law's principles and emphasizes them for His followers (Matthew 5:21; Romans 3:31).

Jesus explains His relationship to the Law of Moses in two ways. First, He has no intention of destroying the law (compare John 10:34, 35). The word used here is not from the legal world, but from the builder's world, having the sense of "demolish." He is no wrecking ball for the Mosaic code that Israel has followed for hundreds of years.

If Jesus has no plans to knock down the law, then what is His relationship to it? Maybe He should be a law-strengthener, a law-builder, or the giver of a new and better law. Jesus does not go that direction, but says that He has come neither to establish nor build the law. Jesus' second point is not the opposite of His first. Instead He has come *to fulfil* the law.

18. For verily I say unto you, Till heaven and earth pass, one jot or one tittle shall in no wise pass from the law, till all be fulfilled.

Jesus reinforces that He is fulfilling the law, not destroying it, by emphasizing the lasting nature of the law (Psalm 119:89; Isaiah 40:8; 55:11). It will continue until *heaven and earth pass away* at the end of time (Matthew 24:35; Mark 13:31; Luke 21:33).

The law is not modified by Jesus. Not *one jot or one tittle* is changed in the law (Luke 16:17). A jot refers to the smallest letter of the Hebrew alphabet. A tittle is even smaller, just one part of a stroke that differentiates one letter from another, like a horn or dot. Jesus has no interest in modifying the law or getting into technical discussions with the scribes as to its interpretation. Jesus is certainly aware of the influence of the scribes, with their reputation for accuracy in copying Scriptures. Yet even the most careful scribe can make a mistake, a misplaced tittle or two. In exaggerated language (hyperbole), Jesus emphasizes that the law will not change by His hand.

At first glance, one might think Jesus is treating the law like a prophecy that must be fulfilled. Fulfillment of prophecy is important in this Gospel (see Matthew 1:23; 2:6, 15, 18, 23; etc.), but that does not seem to be what Jesus means here. A text with the specific wording is necessary to fulfill prophecy in this way. Jesus does not fulfill isolated pieces of the law but the entire law. Jesus and His ministry are that to which the law points. One author, Robert Banks, has pointed out that this is not about Jesus' relationship to the law, but about the law's relationship to Jesus.

God did not give the law intending that it would last forever. Ultimately it points to Christ, who makes perfect what the law could not perfect (Romans 3:20-31; Hebrews 7:16-19). It has an end time when it will *be fulfilled*. This fulfillment begins with Jesus himself, and we understand this to mean that we, as Christians, follow Jesus and not the law of the Old Testament.

❧ *THE HEROIC OUTLAW* ❧

Few literary characters are as well known as Robin Hood. He is portrayed as a supporter of the late twelfth-century King Richard the Lionheart. Richard's younger brother, John, mismanaged the kingdom while Richard was participating in the Crusades. John's excessive taxation led Robin Hood and his men to wage a shadow war against him by stealing taxes from collectors and returning them to the peasants.

Robin Hood of legend was an outlaw but stood for a higher law of compassion and justice. His purpose was not to be lawless. He desired to do what Richard, the true king, would have wanted.

A real person existed of whom Robin Hood is a mere shadow. Jesus was unfairly portrayed as a lawbreaker (Matthew 11:19). Yet He did not come to declare anarchy, but to fulfill the law of the true king of Heaven. How does Jesus' fulfillment of the law lead you to greater righteousness?

—J. E.

B. Teacher of Righteousness (vv. 19, 20)

19. Whosoever therefore shall break one of these least commandments, and shall teach men so, he shall be called the least in the kingdom of heaven: but whosoever shall do and teach them, the same shall be called great in the kingdom of heaven.

Having declared the law's fulfillment in His person and ministry, Jesus now issues a dire warning for those who continue to follow the law. It is not for them to pick and choose what *commandments* to keep, and they should not honor teachers who disregard the full impact of the law. The law must be taken as a whole, and those who break even a small commandment are guilty of breaching the entire law (see James 2:10). Jesus teaches that reward and recognition from God *in the kingdom of heaven* depend on this consistency. This kingdom is present in Jesus' ministry and is a contrast to the powers of the world that function on the basis of their own desires rather than following God's laws (Ephesians 6:12).

Since the law is fulfilled in Jesus and His teachings, this verse must point to Him. He does not offer an immoral, amoral, or careless approach to living a God-pleasing life. The law reveals the moral obligations of God's people, and we must pay attention to its principles in light of our faith in Jesus. Later, Jesus teaches that the entirety of the Law of Moses and the Prophets is summed up in two principles: love

God and love people (Matthew 22:36-40). When we live this way, we honor every jot and tittle of the law, even as we realize that certain aspects of it applied only to Old Testament Israel (example: animal sacrifices).

20. For I say unto you, That except your righteousness shall exceed the righteousness of the scribes and Pharisees, ye shall in no case enter into the kingdom of heaven.

Jesus' final statement in this section is a shock to his original hearers. He advises them that they must have a *righteousness* that is superior to that *of the scribes and Pharisees,* or else they will not be participants in *the kingdom of heaven.* The hearers assume that righteousness is determined by adherence to the Law of Moses. The religious leaders are prime examples of men who keep the law.

This verse features the second of 22 occurrences of the word *scribe* in this Gospel (see Matthew 2:4). A scribe is someone who is trained to write on a readable medium such as parchment. In the book of Matthew, scribes are more than copyists or stenographers. To be sure, they make copies of the law with great accuracy and care, but they also read the law and give interpretations as to its implications (7:29; 17:10). They specialize in studying the Law of Moses and serve as the law's expert interpreters. They miss nothing that should be obeyed (23:23-26).

The Pharisees also figure prominently in this Gospel (Matthew 3:7; 9:34; 12:14; 22:15; etc.). They are a group of Jewish men who attempt to keep the Law of Moses down to the tiniest detail. They are not paid for their efforts, but their law-keeping is done publicly and gains them great respect among fellow Jews (23:2-7).

Paul himself was a Pharisee, as was his father (Acts 23:6; Philippians 3:5). He describes the

Pharisees as "the most straitest sect" of Judaism (Acts 26:5) and claims that in his life as a Pharisee he was without fault when it came to keeping the law. He was righteous within its limits (Philippians 3:6). Paul would not be alone among the Pharisees in this boast.

There is surely some overlap between these two groups (some scribes are Pharisees), and the synergy of their relationship is strong. The Pharisees need the scribes to give them strict interpretations of the law so that they can follow it in every aspect. The scribes write the regulations, and the Pharisees enforce them in their own lives. This situation results in a legalistic understanding of righteousness and one's relationship with God.

Jesus proclaims a new type of relationship with God, one honoring the law but not based on keeping the law. This relationship is much bigger, much deeper, and results in a righteousness far superior to that of the greatest Pharisee who ever lived. Those who hunger and thirst for this ultimate righteousness will find it as Jesus' followers (Matthew 5:6). Their righteousness in God's eyes will be far superior than the self-made righteousness of the Pharisees, for it depends on faith rather than works (Isaiah 26:2; John 3:5).

> *What Do You Think?*
> In what ways will your light-shining be the same as demonstrating righteousness? In what ways will it differ?
> *Digging Deeper*
> Think in terms both of what you will do and what you will not do.

Conclusion

A. I'm Gonna Let It Shine

Visiting the famous Jewel Cave in the Black Hills of South Dakota, one is taken into the bowels of the cavern using an elevator, walkways, and electric lights. At a very deep point, the guide will halt the group and turn off all the lights. The darkness is so profound that you can wave your hand an inch from your nose and not see it. After letting everyone's eyes adjust to the darkness, the

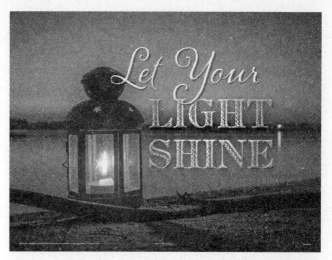

Visual for Lesson 6. *Use this visual to introduce the discussion question associated either with Matthew 5:15 or 5:20.*

guide will light a single match. The tiny flame seems like a blazing torch at first, breaking the darkness in a startling manner.

For many, life is like living in a very dark cave with no light. The darkness in the world refuses to acknowledge God as king or live in obedience to Him. The only "righteousness" suggested by the darkness is self-determined and self-made. How, then, in this world of darkness do we let our lights shine for Jesus?

It seems like an impossible task. The old spiritual says, "This little light of mine, I'm gonna let it shine." The song puts forth no time limit, no expected results, and no real strategy. It just tells us to let our lights—our lives—shine for Jesus. What if no one seems to notice? "I'm gonna let it shine." May our lives and our churches be the cities on hills that become beacons of hope in our dark and lost world.

B. Prayer

Lord God, we are stunned and transfixed by the brilliant light You offer through Your Son, Jesus. May we never depend on our feeble efforts without You, but through Your grace and Your Spirit, may our lights blaze in this dark world and cause people to give all glory to You and You alone. We pray in the name of Jesus. Amen.

C. Thought to Remember

Live in a way that draws others to Jesus.

INVOLVEMENT LEARNING

Enhance your lesson with KJV Bible Student *(from your curriculum supplier) and the reproducible activity page (at www.standardlesson.com or in the back of the* KJV Standard Lesson Commentary Deluxe Edition*).*

Into the Lesson

Before class, find examples of each type of ad below. Begin class by writing the following advertising strategies on the board:

Pathos—an attempt to make the customer feel something, an emotional appeal.

Logos—an attempt to convince the customer that buying the product makes sense, a logical appeal.

Ethos—an attempt to convince the customer that the company is trustworthy, an ethical appeal.

As you display the ads, ask the class to identify the techniques used. For example, a *pathos* ad might show happy people using the product. *Logos* appeals might show statistics to demonstrate the value of a product. *Ethos* ads might feature celebrity endorsements or customers being told that more people trust this product than another brand.

Discuss whether the advertising is factually true or whether the claims made can be proven. Do people really believe these ads? If not, why do they seem to have an effect?

Alternative. Distribute copies of the "Big Claims, Outrageous Promises" activity from the reproducible page, which you can download. Have students work in groups to unscramble brand names associated with advertising slogans.

After either activity say, "Some ads fairly represent their products. Yet many ads use words to manipulate emotions, create false images, and imply impossible promises. Jesus demanded that those who follow Him be real. He taught His disciples how to live as authentic children of God."

Into the Word

Divide students into two groups. Give each group a poster, markers, and one of these assignments (you prepare): *World-Changer Group*—Create an ad for a "world-changing believer," based on Matthew 5:13-16. Include a drawing and characteristics of such a person based on the descriptions in the lesson text. *Different Church Group*—Create an ad for a "different kind of church," based on Matthew 5:17-20. Include a drawing and characteristics of such a church, drawn from the descriptions in the lesson text.

Encourage learners to paraphrase characteristics from the text rather than simply repeating the wording. *Examples*: the *World-Changer Group* might describe a believer with phrases such as "creator of spiritual thirst," "reflection of the Father," "a beacon of hope in a dark world." The *Different Church Group* might describe the church as "what you have been looking for," "doing what you know is right," "passing values to the next generation," "humble service," "more action and less talk."

Have the groups share and explain their posters after finishing. Use the commentary to point out any missed characteristics.

Alternative. Turn this art project into a brainstorming/discussion activity. Read sections of the text as divided above and have the class look for the characteristics of a believer and of a church found there.

Lead into the final segment of the lesson by saying, "In the Sermon on the Mount, Jesus taught what an authentic follower of His would look like. Let's look within to see what we need to do to follow Jesus' teaching more closely."

Into Life

To end class, hand a salt packet and a small candle to each class member. As they hold these objects, have them reflect on their own behavior: "Do I truly 'salt' my world, preserving goodness and making people thirst for God? Am I a visible light for God wherever I go?"

Alternative. Distribute copies of the "Pass the Salt, Turn on the Light" activity from the reproducible page. Have students evaluate their "saltiness" or "luminosity" with the metaphors found there.

LOVE
ONE ANOTHER

DEVOTIONAL READING: Genesis 2:18-24
BACKGROUND SCRIPTURE: Matthew 5:21-32

MATTHEW 5:21-32

21 Ye have heard that it was said by them of old time, Thou shalt not kill; and whosoever shall kill shall be in danger of the judgment:

22 But I say unto you, That whosoever is angry with his brother without a cause shall be in danger of the judgment: and whosoever shall say to his brother, Raca, shall be in danger of the council: but whosoever shall say, Thou fool, shall be in danger of hell fire.

23 Therefore if thou bring thy gift to the altar, and there rememberest that thy brother hath ought against thee;

24 Leave there thy gift before the altar, and go thy way; first be reconciled to thy brother, and then come and offer thy gift.

25 Agree with thine adversary quickly, whiles thou art in the way with him; lest at any time the adversary deliver thee to the judge, and the judge deliver thee to the officer, and thou be cast into prison.

26 Verily I say unto thee, Thou shalt by no means come out thence, till thou hast paid the uttermost farthing.

27 Ye have heard that it was said by them of old time, Thou shalt not commit adultery:

28 But I say unto you, That whosoever looketh on a woman to lust after her hath committed adultery with her already in his heart.

29 And if thy right eye offend thee, pluck it out, and cast it from thee: for it is profitable for thee that one of thy members should perish, and not that thy whole body should be cast into hell.

30 And if thy right hand offend thee, cut it off, and cast it from thee: for it is profitable for thee that one of thy members should perish, and not that thy whole body should be cast into hell.

31 It hath been said, Whosoever shall put away his wife, let him give her a writing of divorcement:

32 But I say unto you, That whosoever shall put away his wife, saving for the cause of fornication, causeth her to commit adultery: and whosoever shall marry her that is divorced committeth adultery.

KEY VERSES

If thou bring thy gift to the altar, and there rememberest that thy brother hath ought against thee; leave there thy gift before the altar, and go thy way; first be reconciled to thy brother, and then come and offer thy gift.
—**Matthew 5:23, 24**

COVENANT IN GOD

Unit 2: A Heartfelt Covenant
LESSONS 5–9

LESSON AIMS

After participating in this lesson, each learner will be able to:

1. Recall the two *they said, but I* contrasts of Jesus regarding murder and adultery.

2. Explain the relationship between sinful thoughts and sinful actions.

3. Develop a strategy by which to monitor his or her thought life better.

LESSON OUTLINE

Introduction

A. A Crime of Passion

Is extreme anger a valid defense for murder? Called the "provocation defense," this line of thinking has two associated components. First, there is a widely held assumption that when people are in a rage, such persons are less responsible for their actions. The anger blinds them from rational response and unleashes violent behavior. Second, the provocation defense maintains that the rage that resulted in murder was provoked by the one murdered. This places some (or all) of the blame on the victim, implying the person deserved to die. A classic situation for this might be the husband who catches his spouse in an adulterous situation and his rage results in the death of the wife and her lover. Sometimes called a "crime of passion," such a person may elicit sympathy from the community despite the death of two people.

Courts generally consider provoked rage only a partial defense for murder in terms of lack of premeditation. The charge in such a case may therefore be limited to voluntary manslaughter. Attempts have been made to equate blind rage with temporary insanity. But this line of defense rarely results in exoneration.

B. Lesson Context

Matthew likely wrote his Gospel account after the destruction of the Jerusalem temple in AD 70. This outcome marked the end of the Judaism's being focused on the sacrificial system as practiced by the priesthood in the temple in Jerusalem. What survived the temple's destruction was a Judaism focused on the law and its interpreters, a shift that began in the Babylonian exile.

Any Jewish reader of Matthew's Gospel would have been particularly interested in what Jesus had to say about the law. Jesus had no intention of demolishing the Law of Moses, which included prohibitions against murder and adultery. Jesus' approach to the law was one of great respect; but it also held that simply following the law in a public manner was futile because of hypocritical hearts.

Jesus' teaching was not the simple righteousness of the Jewish scribes and Pharisees of His day

(Matthew 5:20), which would prohibit the physical acts of murder and adultery but say nothing to the heart of the matter. The scribes and Pharisees were educated men, held in esteem by common folks for their knowledge and exemplary public lives (23:5-7). However, Jesus knew the hearts of the scribes and Pharisees (see John 2:24) and repeatedly called them hypocrites (Matthew 23:13, 15, 23, 25, 29, etc.), ones who purposefully hid their sinfulness. He likened them to "whited sepulchres," looking clean on the outside but holding the uncleanness of dead bodies on the inside (23:27).

There is a basic three-part pattern to the following sayings of Jesus. First, He gives a statement of a commandment from the Law of Moses, framed as something taught from ancient times. Second, He presents an expansion of this law as given by later teachers and interpreters. Third, Jesus announces a more rigorous version of this teaching, looking to root out the cause of the sin in the heart, not just the action itself.

I. Murder
(Matthew 5:21-26)
A. Judgment Follows (v. 21)

21. Ye have heard that it was said by them of old time, Thou shalt not kill; and whosoever shall kill shall be in danger of the judgment.

Jesus begins with the sixth commandment from the Ten Commandments, the prohibition against killing (Exodus 20:13; Deuteronomy 5:17). The Greek word used by Matthew refers primarily and specifically to murder (also Matthew 19:18; 23:31, 35), not a more general sense of killing (as in Luke 15:23, 27, 30). This commandment was spoken to *them of old time* and passed down *by* them as well.

HOW TO SAY IT

Corinthians	Ko-*rin*-thee-unz (*th* as in *thin*).
Deuteronomy	Due-ter-*ahn*-uh-me.
Ephesians	Ee-*fee*-zhunz.
Judaism	*Joo*-duh-izz-um or *Joo*-day-izz-um.
Pharisees	*Fair*-ih-seez.
Raca	*Ray*-kuh or Ray-*kah*.
sepulchres	*sep*-ul-kurs.

Thus it does not originate with the scribes or Pharisees but has its roots in the law God gave to Israel through Moses (Exodus 19).

Jesus does not quote just the sixth commandment itself. He adds part two—the consequence for breaking the law. A killer is *in danger of the judgment*. This means going before a judge in a local court and being executed for the killing crime (Exodus 21:12).

B. Anger Fuels (v. 22)

22. But I say unto you, That whosoever is angry with his brother without a cause shall be in danger of the judgment: and whosoever shall say to his brother, Raca, shall be in danger of the council: but whosoever shall say, Thou fool, shall be in danger of hell fire.

Jesus has no quarrel with the sixth commandment or its enforcement. He intensifies it, however, by elevating murder's frequent cause, anger, to a status where the *angry* person is also *in danger of the judgment* like a killer (see Ephesians 4:26; James 1:19, 20; 1 John 3:15).

Jesus is not presenting three categories of angry persons, just three ways to identify such people. The first is the one who rages against fellow disciple *without a cause*. Does this mean that anger that has a cause is justified? In a limited way, perhaps. But we should hear what Jesus says in the next two descriptions, because these three are a package.

The second is a person who utters *Raca* against another, while the third labels another as a *fool*. *Raca* is the ultimate angry insult in Jesus' Jewish world, very much like the derogatory "fool" of Psalms 14:1; 53:1; 107:17; etc. There is not a tight distinction between the words. Both are nasty things to call another person, but neither carries jail time or even a fine.

The punishments here do not seem to fit the crimes. Being angry in itself is not reason to go before a judge; neither is name-calling. Yet the person who calls another *Raca* is in danger of judgment from *the council*, another way to speak of going before a judge and being sentenced. The results of these minor infractions should thus be taken together. Not only is the angry person in danger of judgment and standing before the council, ultimately the angry are *in danger of hell fire*, the final judgment of God.

❧ THE TERRIBLE POWER OF ANGER ❧

In this decade, America has exploded with anger. The seemingly sudden, overwhelming change in public acceptance of the self-styled "lesbian, gay, bisexual, transgender, and queer" agenda aroused the passions of many. A series of shootings *by* police and *of* police brought riots and demonstrations to many American cities. Polarizing presidents were elected, making many Americans of varying political persuasions angry and fearful. Advocates of the "old South" reacted strongly when a movement gained momentum to remove Confederate flags and statues. In some cases, rallies over the issue turned violent.

When passionately held values and opinions are called into question, Christians often feel moved to anger, but Jesus warns us of the dangers of allowing anger to gain control in our hearts. Murder and judgment can be the result. In fact, in Jesus' words, anger and murder are equivalent in terms of the spirit involved. How do *you* avoid God's judgment on your anger?   —C. R. B.

C. Reconciliation Prevents (vv. 23-26)

23, 24. Therefore if thou bring thy gift to the altar, and there rememberest that thy brother hath ought against thee; leave there thy gift before the altar, and go thy way; first be reconciled to thy brother, and then come and offer thy gift.

Jesus holds His disciples to a much higher standard than the scribes and Pharisees hold for the people. He calls for not only our actions to be righteous but also our motivations to be governed by love (compare 1 Corinthians 13:3, 5). Jesus' first key to dealing with anger is that we must *be reconciled* to those with whom we have conflicts. He illustrates this in a striking situational way. A person is at *the altar*, ready to offer a *gift*, or offering. This is an act of worship, a time between the person and God. When the worshipper's mind remembers an unresolved conflict with a *brother* or sister, the gift should be left behind and the worship postponed until reconciliation is accomplished. Unreconciled relationships damage not only human interactions but also relationship with God. Jesus advises that we put our anger aside and take the initiative in restoring an broken relationship in order to be able to approach God.

We do not diminish the force and difficulty of Jesus' teaching by recognizing that He is using hyperbole in these verses (exaggeration for the purpose of emphasis; examples include Matthew 18:6, 8, 9; Romans 14:21; 1 Corinthians 8:13; etc.). An analogy in churches today might be interrupting observance of the Lord's Supper or postponing the offering in order to be reconciled to other believers. As God acts in love to reconcile us to himself (John 3:16, 17; 2 Corinthians 5:18-20; Hebrews 2:17), so we are to act in love to be reconciled with others.

25, 26. Agree with thine adversary quickly, whiles thou art in the way with him; lest at any time the adversary deliver thee to the judge, and the judge deliver thee to the officer, and thou be cast into prison. Verily I say unto thee, Thou shalt by no means come out thence, till thou hast paid the uttermost farthing.

When an *adversary* has been created, such a person may seek legal actions against you. This example likely involves an unpaid debt of some kind and the simmering anger that such a situation can create. Jesus' context implies what we would call "debtor's prison," incarceration ordered by a judge until a debt is paid. This is not a matter of breaking a law, but a legal remedy employed in Jesus' world to force repayment of a loan.

The debtor remain jailed until there is payment by friends or family. A *farthing* is an old English coin equal to a fourth of a penny—a tiny amount of money. This example is appropriate given that the Roman coin indicated is also the least valuable unit of currency available. Such a judgment results in great hardship for the debtor's family that is called on to satisfy the debt. With this example, Jesus demonstrates that maintaining an angry relationship is dangerous and self-defeating. We are wise to lay anger aside and be reconciled.

> **What Do You Think?**
> What are some specific ways to deal redemptively with an adversary?
> *Digging Deeper*
> How will your response differ, if at all, regarding civil vs. criminal situations and cases?

II. Adultery
(MATTHEW 5:27-30)
A. Condemnation Follows (v. 27)

27. Ye have heard that it was said by them of old time, Thou shalt not commit adultery.

Jesus' second example is the seventh commandment, the prohibition against *adultery* (Exodus 20:14; Deuteronomy 5:18). Adultery is defined specifically as being when a married person has sexual relations with someone other than his or her spouse. Jewish tradition both upholds this prohibition and includes examples of the damage adultery causes (see 2 Samuel 11, 12; Psalm 51).

B. Lust Fuels (v. 28)

28. But I say unto you, That whosoever looketh on a woman to lust after her hath committed adultery with her already in his heart.

Jesus assumes the antiquity and validity of this commandment and then expands it to serve for a greater variety of sexual sins (compare 2 Peter 2:14). His concern is to go behind the sin to the underlying cause, human *lust*.

Adultery does not begin with physical contact. It originates in the *heart*, the seat of imagination and will. The one who imagines a sexual encounter with a non-spouse has already begun to sin. Adultery is the fulfillment of lustful desire (Proverbs 6:25-29). The need to control how one looks at others exceeds the righteousness of the scribes and Pharisees. Jesus wants us to give God more than obedient actions. True righteousness begins with giving God our hearts and abandoning an unrighteous, lustful thought life (1 Corinthians 13:5).

C. Resistance Prevents (vv. 29, 30)

29, 30. And if thy right eye offend thee, pluck it out, and cast it from thee: for it is profitable for thee that one of thy members should perish, and not that thy whole body should be cast into hell. And if thy right hand offend thee, cut it off, and cast it from thee: for it is profitable for thee that one of thy members should perish, and not that thy whole body should be cast into hell.

Jesus again uses hyperbole to drive His point home (see commentary on Matthew 5:23, 24, above). His examples here are two body parts typically involved in sexual sin. Rather than risk *hell* because of sexual sin, it is better to enter Heaven with one missing *eye* and one missing *hand* (Mark 9:42-47), isn't it?

The value of these body parts is extreme. Blindness is understood in Jesus' day to be a punishment for sin, a curse from God (see John 9:2, 3). Even partial blindness is debilitating. The disfigurement of a missing eye is socially unacceptable. For its part, the *right hand* is the social hand, used for greetings and eating from a common dish at mealtime. The left hand is the unclean hand, used for bathroom duties. Missing a right hand is as socially debilitating as an empty eye socket.

There is no command for eye-gouging or hand-chopping. Jesus' point is that we should do all we can to eliminate from our lives those things that lead to sexual sin. Because adultery begins in the heart, we should keep away from those things that result in lustful, impure thoughts. Extreme, aggressive measures are sometimes required to keep us from such temptations. Refusing to engage not only in adultery but also lust demonstrates love for a spouse and faithfulness to right relationships with others (Ephesians 5:21-33).

> *What Do You Think?*
> What are some common things Christians need to cut from their lives to keep sin at bay?
>
> *Digging Deeper*
> Which of those common things—things not necessarily sinful in and of themselves—do you see as the greatest danger?

III. Divorce
(Matthew 5:31, 32)
A. Document Finalizes (v. 31)

31. It hath been said, Whosoever shall put away his wife, let him give her a writing of divorcement.

Jesus' third example moves beyond the Ten Commandments to a contentious issue in His day: divorce. He cites Deuteronomy 24:1-4, which intends to limit the harm of a divorce that has already happened. Even though this is not one of the Ten Commandments, it is seen as a word from Moses and therefore binding on the Jewish people.

Deuteronomy does not justify divorce but regulates it to prevent the worst abuses at the hands of divorcing husbands. (Wives could not divorce their husbands.) Moses' command to give a written bill of *divorcement* provides the ex-wife a modicum of protection against divorces, given the overall thrust of Deuteronomy 24:1-4 (compare also Matthew 19:8, 9).

Since she can prove she is legally divorced, then perhaps she can remarry for her own well-being. The divorce procedure gives her some protection. For a divorced woman in Jesus' day, remarriage is the most financially stable option. Employment opportunities are few for women, and there are no government programs to offer even limited assistance. In the ancient world, a woman needs the protection by and provision from a man. This begins in her father's house and continues with her husband.

B. Sin Energizes (v. 32)

32. But I say unto you, That whosoever shall put away his wife, saving for the cause of fornication, causeth her to commit adultery: and whosoever shall marry her that is divorced committeth adultery.

Jesus offers no absolute prohibition against divorce at this point (compare Matthew 19:8, 9; Luke 16:18). Instead, He returns to a root cause of divorce: sexual sin. If a wife has committed *fornication*, which encompasses many sexual sins and includes *adultery*, the husband has just cause to divorce her. This is the only justified cause for divorce that Jesus ever teaches in the Gospels. (The apostle Paul will later set forth another situation that allows for a Christian to divorce; see 1 Corinthians 7:10-15.)

The vagueness of the phrase "he hath found some uncleanness in her" that allows divorce in Deuteronomy 24:1 is ripe for abuse. A husband might interpret "some uncleanness" any way he wishes and therefore *put away his wife* and remarry the other woman without technically violating the seventh commandment. Misuse of Deuteronomy 24:1-4 allows the husband to maintain his social standing and the appearance of righteousness while still wronging his wife.

But outward appearances aside, the husband's motives are not thereby justified. Simple lust for another woman, fulfilled through the divorce process to allow a second marriage, is no better justified than adultery itself.

Furthermore, a husband's selfish justification of his problematic motives and his callous behavior creates ongoing problems for his ex-wife. If she is unable to find another husband, she may see her only choices to be either a life of abject poverty or a life of prostitution. Jesus' purpose is not to condemn the woman who remarries, but the man who causes her dilemma in the first place.

Using an overly broad interpretation of Deuteronomy 24:1-4 as a way to avoid being seen as having violated the seventh commandment is deeply flawed. It ignores God's intentions for marriage (Genesis 2:24; Matthew 19:4-6).

What Do You Think?
How should church leaders handle a situation of previously divorced people desiring to be married, but their divorces do not meet Jesus' criterion in today's text?

Digging Deeper
How, if at all, is your conclusion modified by considering Jeremiah 3:1; Malachi 2:16; Matthew 19:3-9; and 1 Corinthians 7:10-15?

❧ WAS MY COUNSEL WRONG? ❧

As a young Bible college graduate, I was called to my first ministry. When a young woman in the congregation asked my opinion about a possible divorce from her husband, I didn't hesitate to offer the requested opinion in no uncertain terms. I was sure I knew the answer.

Many times over the years, I have regretted my self-righteous confidence in giving the answer that I did. Time and experience have taught me that I was reading Jesus' words but not hearing the spirit that prompted them.

I've come to see that I was more like a Pharisee at that point in life—mouthing what my religious culture accepted—than I care to admit. I've reconsidered, and I believe I've come to a fuller understanding of Jesus' teaching. What conviction might Jesus be calling you to reconsider? —C. R. B.

Conclusion

A. Transforming Inner Hypocrisy

Anger and murder, lust and adultery: these are not feel-good issues. But they resonate in many lives. Our hearts can harbor unrighteous thoughts, attitudes, and motivations. Jesus calls for genuine righteousness, a life-changing orientation that does not excuse anger or lust, even if they don't result in murder or adultery. To Jesus, such matters of the heart cannot be ignored.

Responding to Jesus' call to righteousness is not possible with simple rule-keeping; it requires the love of God and love for one another (Matthew 22:34-40; Mark 12:28-34; Luke 10:25-28; 1 John 4:7-12). Jesus' approach cuts through all veneers of right behavior that mask deeply ungodly attitudes and motivations. Jesus' approach also makes us aware of how unrighteous we actually are, how much we need God's grace.

The church today must maintain this insight as taught by Jesus. Keeping rules can never be seen as a pathway to being saved, for salvation is a free gift that cannot be earned (Ephesians 2:8). Yet despising or ignoring God's commands is not the way of the Christian either. The New Testament speaks with one voice that says we should strive to live godly lives, to walk in God's light rather than the darkness of sin. This call demonstrates God's concern that His people live lives of righteousness. Our good deeds, however, have a hollow ring if they come from dark hearts. Only when our hearts are fully devoted to our Lord will our acts of mercy and justice be pleasing to God, the acceptable service of a transformed life (Romans 12:1, 2).

B. Prayer

Lord, cleanse our hearts from evil thoughts and attitudes. Keep us from the sin that entices us. We pray in the name of Jesus. Amen.

C. Thought to Remember

Righteous living demands more than keeping laws.

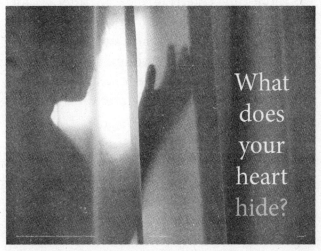

What does your heart hide?

Visual for Lesson 7. *As the lesson concludes, point to this silently for 10 or 15 seconds. Then, without commentary, offer the closing prayer.*

INVOLVEMENT LEARNING

Enhance your lesson with KJV Bible Student *(from your curriculum supplier) and the reproducible activity page (at www.standardlesson.com or in the back of the* KJV Standard Lesson Commentary Deluxe Edition*).*

Into the Lesson

Before class, attach a 10-foot length of painter's tape at eye level on a wall of the classroom. Mark the tape at one-foot increments from 1 to 10. Then write each of these actions on a separate self-stick note: *adultery, smoking, cheating on taxes, lying to a spouse, lying to a boss, abortion, homosexual activity, dancing, working on Sunday, taking a pen from work, pedophilia, swearing, shoplifting a $100 item, shoplifting a $1 item.*

Randomly distribute the self-stick notes to class members. Have them affix the notes to your tape scale at a place that reflects the moral wrongness of the activity. On your scale, 0=Not immoral at all, 5=Moderately immoral, 10=Extremely immoral. Allow class members to place the notes without comment from you or other class members. Briefly review how each activity was ranked.

Alternative. Distribute copies of the "Crime Classification" activity from the reproducible page, which you can download. Have students work in pairs to identify each of the crimes as a felony or a misdemeanor.

After either activity ask, "What are some criteria used to rate the seriousness of specific actions? Are those same criteria used decade after decade, or can the ratings change over time?" Lead into Bible study by saying, "Human systems of law and morality differentiate between major and minor infractions. But where does one draw the line? Jesus draws the line much closer to us than we might find comfortable!"

Into the Word

Divide students into two groups. Give each group one of the following assignments on handouts (you prepare). Have both groups read Jesus' words from the Sermon on the Mount as well as their case study. Then allow them to discuss in their groups how Jesus' teaching applied to the Old Testament case.

Murder Group. Jesus' words on murder and anger (Matthew 5:21-26). Jesus taught that anger can lead to hatred and even murder. He commanded that we not hold on to anger but seek to reconcile with the person with whom we are angry. He warned that there would be consequences for not resisting anger. *Case study:* Cain's murderous anger (Genesis 4:3-12). The Lord warned Cain that his anger would destroy him. Yet Cain held on to his anger. The result was Abel's murder and Cain's separation from his family.

Adultery Group. Jesus' words on adultery and lust (Matthew 5:27-32). Jesus taught that lust is the source of adultery. He commanded that we do whatever we can to resist the temptation of lust. He warned that divorce was not the cure for lust and adultery; it only hurts one's spouse and causes a continuing cycle of serial adultery. *Case study:* Men returning from exile find young pagan women more attractive than their own wives (Malachi 2:11-16). The lust for younger pagan women compromised both the faith and future of Israel. By giving in to their lust, the men betrayed their long-time spouses and fathered children to be reared by pagan mothers.

Alternative. Distribute copies of the "Dissecting the Text" activity from the reproducible page. Have students work in small groups to complete as indicated.

After either activity, make a transition by saying, "Attitudes of anger and lust are not harmless. Unchecked, they lead to disaster. Let's develop strategies to monitor our thoughts."

Into Life

Have class members write "appreciation" and "separation" on masking tape strips, then press those onto their left and right hands. Have them think how appreciation of a person's good points can alleviate anger. Have them think how separating from situations can defuse sexual temptation.

Transforming Love

DEVOTIONAL READING: Romans 12:9-21
BACKGROUND SCRIPTURE: Matthew 5:38-48

MATTHEW 5:38-48

38 Ye have heard that it hath been said, An eye for an eye, and a tooth for a tooth:

39 But I say unto you, That ye resist not evil: but whosoever shall smite thee on thy right cheek, turn to him the other also.

40 And if any man will sue thee at the law, and take away thy coat, let him have thy cloke also.

41 And whosoever shall compel thee to go a mile, go with him twain.

42 Give to him that asketh thee, and from him that would borrow of thee turn not thou away.

43 Ye have heard that it hath been said, Thou shalt love thy neighbour, and hate thine enemy.

44 But I say unto you, Love your enemies, bless them that curse you, do good to them that hate you, and pray for them which despitefully use you, and persecute you;

45 That ye may be the children of your Father which is in heaven: for he maketh his sun to rise on the evil and on the good, and sendeth rain on the just and on the unjust.

46 For if ye love them which love you, what reward have ye? do not even the publicans the same?

47 And if ye salute your brethren only, what do ye more than others? do not even the publicans so?

48 Be ye therefore perfect, even as your Father which is in heaven is perfect.

KEY VERSES

Ye have heard that it hath been said, Thou shalt love thy neighbour, and hate thine enemy. But I say unto you, Love your enemies, bless them that curse you, do good to them that hate you, and pray for them which despitefully use you, and persecute you. —**Matthew 5:43, 44**

Graphic: pialhovik / iStock / Thinkstock

COVENANT IN GOD

Unit 2: A Heartfelt Covenant
LESSONS 5–9

LESSON AIMS

After participating in this lesson, each learner will be able to:

1. Summarize Jesus' teaching about how to treat friends and enemies.

2. Explain the differences between human and divine displays of love.

3. State a way he or she will show love to an "enemy" in the week ahead.

LESSON OUTLINE

Introduction

A. The Code of Hammurabi

What limits should there be to retaliation against a person who has wronged you? Imagine a situation of two rival villages. One villager insults the chief of the other village. The result? The insulted chief takes a war party to the other town, kills all the people, and burns it to the ground. Rather than return the insult in kind, or even escalate violence only against the insulter, the retaliation is without limits, as bad as it could be.

Several centuries before Moses gave the law to the people of Israel, a Babylonian king named Hammurabi developed a set of laws to regulate the government and the behavior of citizens in business and other situations. Some of the Code of Hammurabi seems quaint and primitive now, but it represented advances in legal protections not seen before.

One of those was Hammurabi's edict, "Only one eye for one eye." This embodies the principle of limited retaliation, that punishment or compensation for an injury should be equivalent to the originally inflicted injury. Moses gave similar instruction to Israel, "As he hath done, so shall it be done to him; . . . eye for eye, tooth for tooth" (Leviticus 24:19, 20). In legal tradition, this is known as the *lex talionis*, the law of legal, limited retaliation. Punishment for a crime should be in proportion to the offense. A jaywalker should not be executed. A premeditated murder should receive more than a small fine. A person who makes a snide comment should not be beaten senseless.

B. Lesson Context

Matthew 5–7, the Sermon on the Mount, makes up the largest uninterrupted block of Jesus' teaching found in the Gospels (over 100 verses). His teachings in these three chapters are seen by some as defining the essence of what it means to be a Christian and a citizen of the kingdom of Heaven. The kingdom of Heaven is the establishment of God's promised rule over the world. Sin has made us God's enemies. But in God's kingdom, God reestablishes His reign over all. He overcomes sin and invites sinners—His enemies—to become His friends.

In Matthew 5, Jesus challenged His disciples to move beyond the righteousness they saw in the religious leaders— the scribes and Pharisees. Jesus did this to push His followers to go beyond the behavioral righteousness of the Pharisees to a broken and contrite heart yielded fully to God (compare Psalm 51:17).

Jesus' followers don't just avoid murder; they eliminate murderous anger (Matthew 5:21-26). They don't just avoid adultery or divorce; they control their lustful thoughts (5:27-32). They don't just avoid breaking oaths; they make oaths unnecessary by always telling the truth (5:33-37). The ethics that Jesus teaches are the way of the kingdom of Heaven. As such, they often run counter to popular thinking and earthly wisdom. This lesson continues Jesus' teaching on righteousness in two more areas: retaliation and love for others.

I. Turning the Cheek
(MATTHEW 5:38-42)

A. Limited Retaliation (v. 38)

38. Ye have heard that it hath been said, An eye for an eye, and a tooth for a tooth.

Jesus introduces an ancient teaching as words that *hath been said*, a formula He has already used in this sermon (Matthew 5:21, 27, 33). In this case Jesus cites a teaching found several times in the Law of Moses, the principle of limited retaliation (*lex talionis*). In its fullest expression, this allows for one to be repaid an eye for eye, tooth for tooth, hand for hand, foot for foot, and life for life for crimes committed (Exodus 21:23, 24;

HOW TO SAY IT

Babylonian	Bab-ih-*low*-nee-un.
Deuteronomy	Due-ter-*ahn*-uh-me.
Hammurabi	*Ham*-muh-**rah**-bee.
Leviticus	Leh-*vit*-ih-kus.
lex talionis	leks-*taw*-lee-**oh**-nis.
Mahatma Gandhi	Muh-*hot*-muh *Gawn*-dee.
Pharisees	*Fair*-ih-seez.
Samaritan	Suh-*mare*-uh-tun.

Leviticus 24:20; Deuteronomy 19:21). The law saw this as justice. To go beyond was to seek vengeance, and that is limited to the Lord (Leviticus 19:18; Deuteronomy 32:41-43; Romans 12:19).

As time went on, however, some understood this law to mean that people are authorized to seek personal revenge whenever they have been harmed. Rather than understanding these words as a limitation on what punishment the community could exact for a crime, the law was taken as permission to get even. Jesus does not take issue with the law in and of itself. Instead, He takes issue with people's abuse of the law.

❧ *ROAD RAGE* ❧

Tales of road rage are legion, and they follow a familiar, escalating formula. One particularly terrifying incident near Santa Clarita, California, illustrates the formula taken to extremes. An offended motorcyclist pulled alongside a car and kicked the driver's door. The driver swerved into the motorcycle, sending it toward the median barrier.

The car then lost control, crashed into the barrier, ricocheted across two lanes, and hit an SUV. The SUV flipped over and went spinning down the road on its top, the car was disabled on the shoulder, and the motorcycle sped away.

Sadly, the accepted behaviors of society can lure even Christians into committing acts of rage and even hate. This should not be true of citizens of the kingdom of Heaven. In what other areas of life besides our driving should we be modeling Jesus' "turn the other cheek" attitude?   —C. R. B.

B. No Retaliation (vv. 39-42)

39. But I say unto you, That ye resist not evil: but whosoever shall smite thee on thy right cheek, turn to him the other also.

Jesus redefines the situation of personal injury in extreme, hyperbolic ways. He cautions His disciples not to *resist . . . evil*, not to fight an evil person with evil of your own (compare Romans 12:17, 19; 1 Peter 3:9). He illustrates this in three ways. First is the insulting person. Among Jesus' hearers, to slap a person's face is more than an attempt to injure. It is a stinging, physical insult. In His example, the insulter slaps the *right cheek*. Instead of retaliating in kind and thereby getting even, Jesus' answer is to present *the other*, left cheek for a slap. Thus the one being insulted becomes vulnerable to receive yet another insult (Luke 6:29).

This text is not intended to teach absolute pacifism. Jesus' concern here is not self-defense. He is speaking about insults that take the form of minor blows, not threats of death. The context here speaks specifically about the disciples who will be insulted and persecuted for being followers of Jesus (Matthew 5:11, 12). Jesus' followers must focus on their mission to preach His message, not on retaliation for inevitable insults.

> *What Do You Think?*
> What are some guardrails you can put in place to ensure you do not strike back when insulted?
>
> *Digging Deeper*
> How would those guardrails differ, if at all, between being wronged by a friend, a family member, and a stranger? Why?

40. And if any man will sue thee at the law, and take away thy coat, let him have thy cloke also.

In His second illustration, Jesus speaks of two common garments for men of His day. The *coat* is the inner garment, worn next to the skin; the *cloke* is the outer garment. Clothes are costly in both material and production time in Jesus' day, not mass-produced inexpensively in factories. Each article is worn as long as possible. Their sturdiness makes even a well-used piece of clothing valuable. In the Law of Moses, the outer garment is not subject to being seized for debt or other reasons (Deuteronomy 24:13).

In Jesus' extreme example, the person who loses an inner garment should be willing to give up the outer garment as well. This is much more than passive nonretaliation! God does not immediately retaliate against sinners as they (we) deserve (exceptions: Daniel 4:28-33; Acts 12:21-23). Instead, He sacrifices His very Son for us. If God's people have been given such a generous gift, then we are compelled to act similarly toward others.

We can do this in the confidence that the God who gives His Son for us will also supply all our needs (Matthew 6:25-34).

41. And whosoever shall compel thee to go a mile, go with him twain.

The third illustration involves a practice of the Roman military. By law, a Roman soldier can compel a person to carry his gear, but only for one *mile*. The Romans furnish their roads with mile markers, so keeping to this limit is not difficult. The Jews hate this practice: it is an affront to their dignity to be used as menial servants or slaves; it is an arduous task to carry 40 or 50 pounds of gear for a mile; and, worst of all, it requires them to assist Roman soldiers who occupy their homeland.

Rather than seek retaliation for this indignity, Jesus' followers are commanded to carry the luggage not just one mile but two (*twain*). No one in Jesus' day offers to go an additional mile! This is a sacrifice for the kingdom of Heaven. As with the insulting slap or lawsuit, the follower of Jesus accepts insults for His sake and as His representative.

The message is clear. God's kingdom does not come about by resisting the Romans. God's kingdom does not manifest itself through military or political force. Rather, it comes through the radical gift of God given for rebellious sinners. Because God is so generous as to give His Son to die on the cross for the sake of His enemies, then His people need to show similar generosity toward those who are their enemies.

> *What Do You Think?*
> What are some ways you can go the extra mile for others?
>
> *Digging Deeper*
> Under what circumstances, if any, would going the extra mile be ill-advised?

42. Give to him that asketh thee, and from him that would borrow of thee turn not thou away.

This statement summarizes what Jesus previously said. Loans in Jesus' day are not as common as in our modern economy. They are emergency measures that allow someone without any means to continue to eat. To have surplus goods or food to the point that a poor person would seek to borrow from you would put you in a position to humiliate the needy one. Jesus instead commands that they not be turned away (Luke 6:30) or treated with disrespect (Deuteronomy 15:8).

It is not just the person's desperate circumstances that matter here. For those who know the gracious generosity of God, the only right response to need is one of generosity, like our Lord's response to our need. Because God has been generous to us, we citizens of the kingdom of Heaven are also generous to others.

> **What Do You Think?**
> Under what circumstances should we be open or not open to lending to someone who wants to borrow?
> *Digging Deeper*
> Under what circumstances will it be preferable to give, without expecting repayment, rather than to lend? How, if at all, do Psalms 37:21; 112:5; Proverbs 11:15; 22:7, 26; and Romans 13:8 influence your conclusion?

II. Confronting the Enemy
(MATTHEW 5:43-45)
A. Limited Love (v. 43)

43a. Ye have heard that it hath been said, Thou shalt love thy neighbour.

The last of Jesus' examples of righteousness that exceeds that of the scribes and Pharisees concerns love for others. Leviticus 19:18 and its injunction to "Love thy neighbour as thyself" is well known in Jesus' day. In fact, it is taught by Jesus as well (see Matthew 19:19; 22:39; Mark 12:31; Luke 10:27).

What exactly this love requires is debated by teachers of the day, as reflected in Jesus' interaction with a scribe (Luke 10:29). In that case, Jesus responds by telling a parable. He presents the most unlikely of persons—a despised Samaritan —as the one who understands that his neighbor is the person who needs his help.

43b. And hate thine enemy.

Jesus goes on to note a popular misapplication of the command wherein the logically opposite has been added: *hate thine enemy*. The command to love one's neighbor is very clear in Leviticus 19:18. But nowhere does the biblical law command one to hate an enemy. That is the idea that Jesus challenges.

It is easy for the people of God to conclude that their enemies are also God's enemies and to justify hating them on that basis. For many in Jesus' time, this outlook justifies hatred for the Roman occupiers. Yet as far as Jesus is concerned, God's people must do something very different from hating their personal enemies. Whether they are truly God's enemies or not isn't the main issue.

B. Limitless Love (vv. 44, 45)

44. But I say unto you, Love your enemies, bless them that curse you, do good to them that hate you, and pray for them which despitefully use you, and persecute you.

Jesus does not merely acknowledge the appropriateness of love for neighbors and then leave the question of love for everyone else open. Instead He demands love, active love, for *enemies* (Luke 6:27, 28).

Jesus' disciples are not to return evil for evil, nor are they merely to ignore enemies completely. Instead, they are to return *good* for evil—just as He does (Luke 23:34; John 15:20; 1 Peter 2:23). They *bless, do good to*, and *pray for* malicious opponents (see Acts 7:60; Romans 12:14; 1 Corinthians 4:12). This is not what their enemies deserve, especially in light of the "eye for an eye" provisions from the Law of Moses and the teachings of the Pharisees.

We note in passing that early manuscripts of the book of Matthew do not have the phrasing *bless them that curse you, do good to them that hate you, . . . which despitefully use you*. But its inclusion in Luke 6:27, 28 is certain, so we are utterly confident the thoughts are original to Jesus.

❧ HONEY, NOT VINEGAR ❧

It's been said that you catch more flies with honey than with vinegar. In 2012 the chief operating officer (COO) of Chick-fil-A put this axiom to the test. The man is committed to Christ, and his company reflects Christian values. As the battle over same-sex marriage was heating up, Chick-fil-A publicly announced support for traditional marriage. A group that rates colleges on friendliness to self-styled "lesbian, gay, bisexual, trans, and queer" (LGBTQ) students subsequently launched a boycott of the company.

As the public story unfolded, the COO privately sought out the founder of a nationwide LGBTQ organization. The two talked on the phone and in person many times. Though neither changed his view on same-sex marriage, the founder of the LGBTQ organization came away with a new respect for the company executive. The executive's Christlike willingness to speak openly and honestly with the founder of the LGBTQ organization was a graceful example of Jesus' call to love one's enemies. How can we also follow Jesus' example of grace and love toward those who consider us their enemies?   —C. R. B.

45a. That ye may be the children of your Father which is in heaven.

Jesus tells His disciples to look on their enemies with God's eyes, from a divine perspective. All people, friends and foes, are *children of* the *Father* for all are His creatures (see Acts 17:28). If we genuinely belong to God as children belong to their father, then we will show the family resemblance in the way we treat our enemies. Jesus pronounces blessing on "peacemakers" as God's children for this very reason (Matthew 5:9).

45b. For he maketh his sun to rise on the evil and on the good, and sendeth rain on the just and on the unjust.

Jesus uses the natural cycles of the earth as an example of how God shows mercy to all people, regardless of whether they are *good* or *evil, just* or *unjust.* From Jesus' perspective, God is the loving Father of all human beings, even those who are disobedient and do not return His love (compare Luke 6:35). Just as a parent continues to love a disobedient child, so God the Father loves all His children.

We should be careful not to push this too far. Lack of rain may be part of creation's cycles, even though it results in crop failure. But drought and famine will hit the just and the unjust too, just like rain blesses both groups. Jesus is warning that our acts of kindness, our humility, and our lack of retaliation are not reserved for those we love. These blessings must be given to all who need them.

III. Becoming Like the Father
(Matthew 5:46-48)
A. Self-Serving Love (vv. 46, 47)

46. For if ye love them which love you, what reward have ye? do not even the publicans the same?

There is no lasting merit in lavishing love or respect on those we know will return it in kind (compare Luke 14:12). This is not the type of love Jesus advocates. He teaches unselfish love that gives and expects nothing in return. If we love this way, we give our other cheek, our second mile, and our outer coat without expecting anything back.

Jesus points out that *even the publicans* show favor to those who might show favor to them (compare Luke 6:32). The publicans are the despised revenue gatherers of the Romans, Jews who had sold out to the enemy to become rich at the expense of other Jews.

These tax collectors are notoriously wicked and self-seeking. They are regularly held up as examples of immorality, living on the fringes of Jewish society (see 19:1-7). If blatantly greedy, sinful publicans manage to love their neighbors when it serves their interests, can it be counted as righteous? Jesus expects far more than self-serving love from His disciples.

47. And if ye salute your brethren only, what do ye more than others? do not even the publicans so?

In Jesus' culture, to offer greetings to people in public is an important and elaborate duty. But there are those who are excluded from the social circle. A person indicates who is a friend and who is an enemy by offering or not offering greetings.

Again, Jesus points out that such behavior does not mark one out as God's person but as someone who does not know God. God invites all to come to Him, no matter how they have rejected Him in the past. His people have to do the same.

B. Perfect Love (v. 48)

48. Be ye therefore perfect, even as your Father which is in heaven is perfect.

If the original readers wonder what Jesus' standard is for perfection, He tells them: as *perfect . . . as your Father which is in heaven* (see Leviticus 19:2; 1 Peter 1:16). This is more than "being better" than most other people. We don't compare our righteousness with even the paragons of our community. God is the measure.

What Do You Think?
How will you keep the standard of God as your own without falling prey to despair as you realize perfection cannot be attained in this life?
Digging Deeper
What roles do you see for prayer and the Holy Spirit in your answer?

Jesus wants disciples who desire deeply to be like God. He knows our hearts and knows what we need to be perfect like God. For the rich young man Jesus encounters later in Matthew, the path to perfection and life is about giving up his love for money and possessions and then following Jesus. He needs a change of heart, and in this he fails (Matthew 19:16-22). Jesus does not want us to fail. He wants to free us from the trap of earning God's favor by keeping the law. But remember, unless our self-righteousness is superior to that of the greatest law-keepers in history, the Pharisees, we have no place in the kingdom of Heaven.

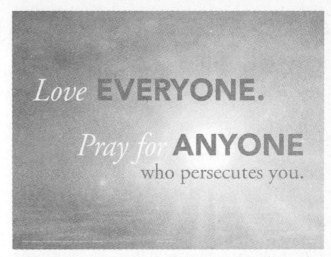

Love EVERYONE.
Pray for ANYONE
who persecutes you.

Visual for Lesson 8. *Point to this visual as you ask your learners to describe, without using names, the type of person they have the most trouble loving.*

Conclusion

A. The Code of Jesus

Mahatma Gandhi, the Hindu teacher and leader, was famously a student and admirer of Jesus' teachings. Gandhi is often attributed as saying, "An eye for an eye only ends up making the whole world blind." Gandhi understood Jesus exactly at this point. In the kingdom of Heaven that Jesus introduced, equalizing violent responses is no answer. It leaves two injured parties.

The *lex talionis* principles of Hammurabi, Moses, and others continue to guide legal systems today. Fair courts the world over still seek to limit punishment to fit the crime. Jesus, however, exhorts His followers to go beyond limited and equal retaliation to have hearts that don't desire it. Are you willing to endure insults without getting even? Are you willing to love people who will never love you back? God's love transforms us so we can learn to love others in the same way, even those who have hurt us deeply. Let us follow His example and find ways to love our enemies.

B. Prayer

Father, may we not avoid "two-mile situations," but embrace them as your Son did. We pray in his precious name. Amen.

C. Thought to Remember

Love helps heal broken relationships.

INVOLVEMENT LEARNING

Enhance your lesson with KJV Bible Student (from your curriculum supplier) and the reproducible activity page (at www.standardlesson.com or in the back of the KJV Standard Lesson Commentary Deluxe Edition).

Into the Lesson

Write these clauses on separate name tags: *he who pays the piper / calls the tune / lie with dogs / and rise with fleas / what goes around / comes around / you've made your bed / now lie in it / sow the wind / reap the whirlwind.* Shuffle the tags. To begin class, hand the name tags to 10 volunteers to wear. Have each one find the classmate that completes the proverb of his or her tag.

Alternative. Distribute copies of the "Consequential Quote" activity from the reproducible page, which you can download. Have students work to piece together a quote about vengeance, jigsaw style.

After either activity, ask, "Is it always good that someone gets what he or she deserves? Are there times when it is better if people do *not* get their 'just deserts'"? Lead into Bible study by saying, "'What goes around comes around.' 'You made your bed; now lie in it.' 'Your just deserts.' These common expressions say that people should get what they deserve. Jesus taught something different. Let's examine why His way works best."

Into the Word

Copy this page and cut apart the following three case studies. Divide the class into three groups to discuss one case each.

Case Study 1—Pool Problems

The John Smith family has a swimming pool surrounded by an 8-foot fence. While they were away on vacation, Bryan Jones scaled the fence to go swimming, slipped on the wet surface, and broke his leg. Jones sued the Smiths, and the judge ordered the Smiths to pay Jones's medical bills.

What might be the Smith's human reaction to this situation? How might the Smiths respond after studying Matthew 5:38-42?

Case Study 2—Goodbye and Good Luck

Wendy Johnson had always gotten along with her superiors at work. That is, until Michael Morgan was promoted to be her supervisor. From the start, Morgan openly criticized Wendy's work and ridiculed her publicly. This went on for almost a year. When another company offered Morgan a higher paying job, he gave his notice. Wendy's coworkers plan a going-away party for him and ask Wendy to help.

What might be Wendy's human reaction to this situation? How might Wendy respond after studying Matthew 5:43, 44?

Case Study 3—Hey, Pal!

The ladies' group at First Church assigns each other secret prayer pals every year. Over the course of the year, the women are asked to send notes of encouragement and small gifts to their secret pal. Last year, Marge Owens received nothing. She later found out that Viola Banks, who had a long-standing feud with Marge's mother, was Marge's partner. Viola had even told other women that she had no intention of giving anything to Marge. As the luck of the draw would have it, Marge was assigned to be Viola's pal the following year.

What might be Marge's human reaction to this situation? How might Marge respond after studying Matthew 5:45-48?

Gather the class together and have groups report. Point out that Jesus commands us not to be vindictive, to demand payback, or even to ask for basic fairness. We emulate God's perfect love that offers His most precious gifts to those who live in enmity with Him.

Into Life

Have class members think of people in their lives who probably consider them to be enemies. Close with silent prayers for those who live as enemies to us.

Alternative: Distribute copies of the "Persecution Map" activity from the reproducible page. Have class members take the map home and pray for leaders in the countries throughout the week.

SPIRITUAL DISCERNMENT

DEVOTIONAL READING: Galatians 5:16-26
BACKGROUND SCRIPTURE: Matthew 7

MATTHEW 7:1-6, 15-23

1 Judge not, that ye be not judged.

2 For with what judgment ye judge, ye shall be judged: and with what measure ye mete, it shall be measured to you again.

3 And why beholdest thou the mote that is in thy brother's eye, but considerest not the beam that is in thine own eye?

4 Or how wilt thou say to thy brother, Let me pull out the mote out of thine eye; and, behold, a beam is in thine own eye?

5 Thou hypocrite, first cast out the beam out of thine own eye; and then shalt thou see clearly to cast out the mote out of thy brother's eye.

6 Give not that which is holy unto the dogs, neither cast ye your pearls before swine, lest they trample them under their feet, and turn again and rend you.

· ·

15 Beware of false prophets, which come to you in sheep's clothing, but inwardly they are ravening wolves.

16 Ye shall know them by their fruits. Do men gather grapes of thorns, or figs of thistles?

17 Even so every good tree bringeth forth good fruit; but a corrupt tree bringeth forth evil fruit.

18 A good tree cannot bring forth evil fruit, neither can a corrupt tree bring forth good fruit.

19 Every tree that bringeth not forth good fruit is hewn down, and cast into the fire.

20 Wherefore by their fruits ye shall know them.

21 Not every one that saith unto me, Lord, Lord, shall enter into the kingdom of heaven; but he that doeth the will of my Father which is in heaven.

22 Many will say to me in that day, Lord, Lord, have we not prophesied in thy name? and in thy name have cast out devils? and in thy name done many wonderful works?

23 And then will I profess unto them, I never knew you: depart from me, ye that work iniquity.

KEY VERSES

Beware of false prophets, which come to you in sheep's clothing, but inwardly they are ravening wolves. Ye shall know them by their fruits. —Matthew 7:15, 16

COVENANT IN GOD

Unit 2: A Heartfelt Covenant

LESSONS 5–9

LESSON AIMS

After participating in this lesson, each learner will be able to:

1. List principles Jesus gives for evaluating godly behavior.

2. Explain how Jesus' command not to judge applies and does not apply in various situations.

3. Evaluate whether his or her attitude toward a specific person is one of condemnation, godly love, or acceptance of godless behavior.

LESSON OUTLINE

Introduction

A. Legalism vs. Liberty

In 1997, Dean Merrill published his provocative book, *Sinners in the Hands of an Angry Church*. The book expresses what many millennials (those born between approximately 1982 and 2004) believed about the church of their parents. Merrill describes a church acting like a moral bully. From its moral high ground of self-righteousness, it bludgeoned the changes occurring in culture. Though sin was running rampant outside the church, the feeling was that sin was absent within. Woe, then, to the member who admitted to moral failure or weakness, for he or she would feel the full wrath of the church. For some, this is the great debate of the church: *legalism or liberty?* Do we draw lines restricting fellowship, or do we open the doors for all to come in without enforcing moral guidelines? (And the debate takes on a different tone when framed as being one of *legalism or liberty or license?*)

No one I know willingly admits to being a legalist, for this is always a negative label, always to be avoided. Legalism does exist, however. At its core it is an orientation that treats rules as more important than people. Legalists often occupy themselves with controlling the behavior of others. Legalism can be an attempt to rally a whole community against sinful behavior. Sadly, in its obsession to crush sin, it may crush sinners instead.

Wouldn't the church be a happier place if we ran off all the legalists? Not so fast. In this lesson, Jesus tells His disciples not to judge, then advises them to judge. Where do we find the balance? Can we love the law and love people too?

B. Lesson Context

An ordered society (like the nation of Israel in Old Testament times) needs judges to be third-party deciders over human disputes (see Exodus 18:13-27; Ezra 7:25). Deuteronomy 25:1 defines the role of a judge in Israel as one who makes decisions that "justify the righteous, and condemn the wicked." To do the opposite—condemn the righteous and justify the wicked—is an abomination to the Lord (Proverbs 17:15). As shown throughout the book of Judges, these leaders were meant to remain faithful to the Lord; only then would the people be led in His ways and enjoy His protection in Israel (see Judges 2:16-19).

The Lord himself is the final and infallible judge of all the earth (Psalms 82:8; 105:7). In several places, the Bible portrays God as judge over all humanity (Exodus 12:12; 1 Chronicles 16:14; Romans 14:10; etc.). God does not consult a legal code for His judgments, because He is the author of the law. Human judges depend on laws and function best when they are enforcing clear and fair laws in an impartial way. People, though, are fallible, and even judges can be corrupt or unrighteous (Luke 18:6).

Jesus did not embrace the role of judge in human affairs during His ministry (see Luke 12:14; in contrast see Acts 17:31; 2 Corinthians 5:10). Yet His teachings are filled with moral distinctions that identify unrighteous behavior. Jesus does not hesitate to expose hypocrites, identify their dishonesty, and thus pass a type of judgment. What we see is Jesus moving beyond mere application of laws in a courtroom setting to a discernment of human behavior based on motives and higher standards such as love for others.

I. Poor Judgment
(Matthew 7:1-6)
A. Warning to Would-Be Judges (vv. 1, 2)
1. Judge not, that ye be not judged.

Jesus previously taught His disciples to trust God rather than worry (Matthew 6:34). One way to do this is not to be consumed with judging others (compare Luke 6:37; Romans 14:13; 1 Corinthians 4:5). A benefit of honoring this instruction is that others will be less likely to judge you in return.

HOW TO SAY IT

Corinthians	Ko-*rin*-thee-unz (*th* as in *thin*).
Deuteronomy	Due-ter-*ahn*-uh-me.
Ezra	*Ez*-ruh.
Galatians	Guh-*lay*-shunz.
Hosea	Ho-*zay*-uh.
Pharisees	*Fair*-ih-seez.

This verse, taken out of context, is often tossed in the face of Christians by nonbelievers. If Christians offer opinions about any sort of sinful, antisocial, or aberrant behavior, the cynical response is likely to be "I thought Jesus told you not to judge." Does this mean that Christians have no moral authority to identify sinful behavior based on biblical standards? While the answer is complicated, Paul later suggests that judgment is reserved for those within the church because they have agreed to be held to the same standards of righteousness (1 Corinthians 5:12; compare James 4:11).

2. For with what judgment ye judge, ye shall be judged: and with what measure ye mete, it shall be measured to you again.

Jesus moves to define His biggest concern: hypocritical judging (see comments on Matthew 7:5). He warns that when we judge others with our high moral standards, we should beware and be ready: the same high standards and the same judgments will be applied to us in return (compare Ezekiel 35:11; Mark 4:24; Romans 2:1). The television evangelist who rails against sexual sins from the pulpit and is found to have adulterous liaisons will be shown no mercy by his critics. The church leader who insists on tithing and giving back to God in a sacrificial way will be pilloried if found to be skimming money from his ministry for his own enrichment.

Jesus illustrates this with an economic practice. It concerns a standard for buying and selling produce such as wheat or barley. Fairness demands that the same *measure* (such as a calibrated basket) be used for both buying and selling (see Luke 6:38). If someone uses a smaller basket to sell wheat and a bigger basket to buy wheat, that dishonesty will be uncovered and the merchant's credibility will suffer. The first and most basic step for demanding high moral standards is to hold yourself to them.

✵ A Gracious Response ✵

My grandfather was raised in a church that condemned other Christians for using musical instruments in worship. On our cross-country visits, my father and grandfather always argued over the music issue and other differences in practice among Christians.

Later, I became a close friend of a leader in my grandparents' fellowship. In his early years, he had participated in narrowly defining "the faithful" as those who practiced as he did. But as the leader grew in understanding God's grace, his heart opened to others whose desired to follow Jesus, even though they disagreed on the particulars.

Some brothers in Christ condemned him with the same spirit in which he had once judged others. On one occasion, I heard this man respond softly, "Christianity began . . . with a baby." Focusing on Jesus led him to let some disagreements go. In what ways does following God incarnate call us to more than judgmental legalism?

—C. R. B.

B. Advice to Obvious Hypocrites (vv. 3-5)

3, 4. And why beholdest thou the mote that is in thy brother's eye, but considerest not the beam that is in thine own eye? Or how wilt thou say to thy brother, Let me pull out the mote out of thine eye; and, behold, a beam is in thine own eye?

As He often does in the Sermon on the Mount, Jesus uses hyperbole (exaggeration for emphasis) to make His point (see Matthew 5:29, 30, 38-42; etc.). A man can never have a *beam* in his eye while offering to remove a *mote* (a tiny particle) from another's eye. The absurd picture is of a man with a two-by-four piece of lumber protruding from his face offering to remove a piece of sawdust from another's eye.

First, the beam would get in the way and make the speck removal impossible; he would be more likely to injure the second person than to help. Second, and more to the point, it is ludicrous for

the first person to even think about offering this service when he has such grave personal matters to attend to himself. He has no credibility.

5. Thou hypocrite, first cast out the beam out of thine own eye; and then shalt thou see clearly to cast out the mote out of thy brother's eye.

Jesus' declaring the man with a plank in his eye to be a *hypocrite* is instructive. The word *hypocrite* has a background in Greek drama and refers to an actor, one who plays a role. By implication, this person hides his true identity. What the public sees in the theater does not reveal the actor's true personal life.

With Jesus' example, any pretense at hiding is demolished. The hypocrite attempting to extract a tiny mote from his friend's eye is not concealing a few little specks in his own eyes that no one detects; rather, he has a beam protruding that is easily observed by anyone! Jesus unmasks the judgmental moralists of His day, declaring that all too often their own moral failures are showing.

Jesus advises the obvious: take *the beam out of your eye*. Then, with unimpaired vision and better mobility to do close work, you can help get the tiny mote out of the other's eye (see Galatians 6:1).

> **What Do You Think?**
> Under what circumstances will direct confrontation of hypocrisy (example: Matthew 23:13-15) be better than an indirect approach (example: Matthew 21:45)?
> *Digging Deeper*
> What other choices might there be, if any? Why?

C. Plea to Undiscerning Teachers (v. 6)

6. Give not that which is holy unto the dogs, neither cast ye your pearls before swine, lest they trample them under their feet, and turn again and rend you.

Jesus circles back to His disciples, the ones He advises not to judge lest they be judged themselves. He does not want them to be hypocrites like the scribes and Pharisees (Matthew 6:2, 5, 16), yet Jesus also knows the potential for misuse of His exhortation not to judge. Neglecting to judge wisely allows evil to be called good and good to be called evil (Isaiah 5:20). In the hands of unrepentant sinners, the directive to avoid judging becomes a license to sin (compare Jude 4). Reserving judgment is often appropriate and comes with benefits, but Jesus clearly acknowledges that judgment cannot and should not always be avoided.

Jesus uses two vivid metaphors for those against whom He is warning, likely false prophets (see following section). First, He calls them *dogs*. These feral animals will turn and devour one of their own if it falls with a mortal injury. Second, they are called *swine*, the archetypical unclean animal for Jews, often associated with the worst characteristics of the Gentiles. Jesus' imagery is striking: don't throw beautiful and valuable *pearls* into the mud of the pigpen. Pigs will stomp the pearls into the dirt because they have no concept of their worth.

Many characteristics of Jesus' disciples can be exploited mercilessly by unprincipled opponents of the church. Disciples must find the correct balance and the correct time and place to judge others' motives and character. Jesus tells His disciples they must be as "wise as serpents, and harmless as doves" (Matthew 10:16). Failure to discern is disastrous in the presence of such dogs and pigs.

II. Telltale Fruits
(MATTHEW 7:15-23)

A. Fruits of False Prophets (vv. 15-20)

15. Beware of false prophets, which come to you in sheep's clothing, but inwardly they are ravening wolves.

Jesus issues a warning about *false prophets*, those who would lead His disciples astray by denying Jesus and His teachings (see Matthew 24:11, 24; Luke 6:26). The image of a wolf wearing a sheepskin to blend in with genuine sheep invites ridicule just as does a person with a plank in his eye performing eye surgery (see Ezekiel 22:27; Acts 20:29). No wolf should get away with this, especially with the shepherd watching over the flock (see John 10:5, 11, 14-16). Still, infiltration of the community of God's people by false disciples is all too common. It must be

guarded against (see Jeremiah 23:16; Galatians 2:4; 2 Peter 2:1; 1 John 4:1).

❧ DISGUISES, HELPFUL AND OTHERWISE ❧

My brother Dave and his wife lived for many years on the shore of a lake in Minnesota. The area between them and their neighbors was covered with oval rocks, brownish-gray in color. Once while I was visiting, Dave and I walked across the rocks to talk to his neighbor. That's when a killdeer, a shorebird, suddenly jumped up from the rocks, ran a few feet, stopped, then ran a few more feet. Dave warned me, "Don't step on her nest." I looked down but didn't see any sign of a nest. Then my brother pointed out the eggs, disguised by their color and shape to blend in with the rocks.

Jesus spoke of false teachers who disguise themselves to hide their true nature. They are hypocrites who only teach what benefits them. How can we distinguish between the "eggs" in our paths and the "rocks" they imitate?   —C. R. B.

> **What Do You Think?**
> How will you know when a context of spiritual wolves calls for a redemptive response, a response of maintaining the church's purity, or no response at all?
> **Digging Deeper**
> How do the following passages inform your answer: Romans 16:17; 1 Corinthians 5; 2 Corinthians 2:5-11; 1 Timothy 1:13; 2 Timothy 2:14–3:9; Titus 3:10; Jude 22, 23.

16. Ye shall know them by their fruits. Do men gather grapes of thorns, or figs of thistles?

How do we detect these false prophets, these fake disciples? These are not inconsistent disciples who struggle to live exemplary lives (a category into which most of us fit). Rather, these are non-disciples who infiltrate the church with allegiance only to themselves, not loyalty to Jesus in any way. We cannot know their hearts like God does, but we can look at their lives. What is the "fruit" of their conduct (compare Luke 6:44; James 3:12)? If they are not fruits born of the Spirit (Galatians 5:22, 23), we must suspect false prophets in our midst.

Jesus appeals to the agricultural knowledge of His hearers. No one looks for clusters of *grapes* among *thorns.* Grapes grow on grapevines. Likewise, no farmer seeks *figs* among *thistles,* a variety of weed. Figs grow on fig trees. Good works come from a heart devoted to serving God and loving other people.

17, 18. Even so every good tree bringeth forth good fruit; but a corrupt tree bringeth forth evil fruit. A good tree cannot bring forth evil fruit, neither can a corrupt tree bring forth good fruit.

Jesus knows that recognizing false prophets is not always as simple as discerning between a fig tree and a thistle plant. A *good tree* with *good fruit* might look nearly identical to a *corrupt tree* with *evil fruit.* This is like the difference between a crab apple that produces tiny, ill-tasting apples and an apple tree that yields healthy apples of good size and taste. Although the trees may look similar, they are easily distinguished by the fruit they produce.

Some false disciples are masters at hiding their inner identity. They know the community, and they blend in well. The personal lives of those who have influence in the church should be scrutinized. Do they work primarily to enrich themselves? Do they seek to make disciples of Christ into their own disciples? Are their teachings in conflict with Jesus' teachings? These and other questions must be asked when evaluating the fruit of teachers and leaders (Matthew 12:33; Luke 6:43).

What Do You Think?
How will you display good spiritual fruit in such a way that neither Matthew 5:16 nor Matthew 6:1-4 is violated?
Digging Deeper
Under what contexts would an anonymous display of good spiritual fruit be called for? Why?

19. Every tree that bringeth not forth good fruit is hewn down, and cast into the fire.

The wise farmer has no desire to care for an unproductive fruit *tree.* Instead it will be *hewn down* and used for firewood (Luke 13:7-9). Being thrown *into the fire* is a consistent symbol for God's judgment in this Gospel (Matthew 3:10,

12; 13:40, 42; 18:8, 9; etc.). That is the ultimate fate of the hypocritical false prophets. God knows their hearts and will not be fooled. Their judgment is sure. The bad tree will be replaced by another that will produce *good fruit.*

20. Wherefore by their fruits ye shall know them.

Jesus ends this section by predicting that false disciples will be revealed. They will be known. They cannot hide their false, unloving, and selfish hearts forever. Such a prediction is sad when is comes true. We take no joy in witnessing the exposure and fall of false-hearted church members. But when unveiling comes, Christians must not hesitate to remove such people from positions of authority and influence.

What Do You Think?
Under what circumstances would it be a good idea for Christians to hold one another accountable for the good fruit they are not producing, but should be, for the kingdom?
Digging Deeper
How could such a program be implemented without it becoming controlling in a cult-like sense?

B. Wonders of False Workers (vv. 21-23)

21. Not every one that saith unto me, Lord, Lord, shall enter into the kingdom of heaven; but he that doeth the will of my Father which is in heaven.

The fruit Jesus desires is to see disciples doing *the will of* Jesus' *Father which is in heaven.* This tests the sincerity or dishonesty of one's discipleship to Christ. No one can be a follower of Jesus if he or she constantly resists yielding to the will of God. The affirmation *Lord, Lord* does not take the place of actions (Hosea 8:2, 3; Matthew 25:11, 12; John 13:13, 14; contrast 1 Corinthians 12:3).

Earlier in His sermon, Jesus said that a righteousness that exceeds that of the scribes and Pharisees is required to *enter the kingdom of heaven* (Matthew 5:20). Who will be allowed to enter the kingdom? This is promised to "the poor in spirit" (5:3) and to those who suffer persecution for their loyalty to

Jesus (5:10). True members of the kingdom recognize their spiritual dependency on the Lord. They endure suffering for following Jesus and align their hearts and their actions to the will of God (Romans 2:13; James 1:22; 1 John 3:18). These are proper and rightful kingdom members (Matthew 12:50).

22, 23. Many will say to me in that day, Lord, Lord, have we not prophesied in thy name? and in thy name have cast out devils? and in thy name done many wonderful works? And then will I profess unto them, I never knew you: depart from me, ye that work iniquity.

Jesus finishes with a dramatic flourish. Imagine people who have dynamically spoken for the Lord in public (*prophesied*; see 1 Corinthians 13:2), performed exorcisms (*cast out devils*; see Luke 10:20; Acts 19:13), and performed miracles (*wonderful works*). This three-part list contains some of the most dramatic displays of Christian work we can imagine. But God is well aware that these people *work iniquity*. Jesus' verdict is that He *never knew* them as His disciples because they never knew Him (see Psalm 6:8; Matthew 25:12; Luke 13:25-27). There is no faith relationship. Even fantastic works can cover a selfish and unrepentant heart for only so long.

Conclusion

A. Confessions of a Reformed Legalist

Churches of my era led many to believe that Christians were morally superior people because we kept the rules. Obedience was compelled by fear of ostracism. Those whose lives did not match traditional standards of the church were shamed, shunned, or expelled.

This was the mind-set I and many others of my generation grew up with. The result was a tendency to lump together the outright hypocrites (who should have known better) with the spiritually immature who stumbled back into sin.

I abandoned my sense of moral superiority as I grew older. I still acknowledged the fact that there were people in my church who hypocritically hid their private sins. Some of these folks were the quickest to censor and condemn anyone they believed to be breaking the rules. Their legalis-

Visual for Lesson 9. *Use this visual as a basis for a learning activity: form learners into two debating teams, one to take each position.*

tic orientation caused them to be more concerned with controlling the behavior of others rather than repenting of their own secret sins. But I distinguish them from fellow believers who stumble back into sin but then return to the Lord with repentance and humbled hearts.

Rather than jump to judgement, I am determined look to the fruit of repentance. Do I see the fruit of the Spirit in spite of their past failings? Paul says there is no law against this fruit (Galatians 5:22, 23). Make no mistake: I still care about godly behavior. I care deeply about injustice. I seek to live to please my Lord. But I also know I will never live without any sin on this earth. I also realize that others are in the same condition.

I regret having lived as a legalist, and I now attempt to live in such a way that my own fruit is founded on "a broken and a contrite heart" (Psalm 51:17) in keeping with repentance (Matthew 3:8). Such a heart is yielded fully to God. Most assuredly, Philippians 3:13, 14 applies!

B. Prayer

Holy God, although we love Your laws, help us not to fall into the trap of thinking that we are saved by those laws. Forgive us when we have treated rules as more important than people. We pray in Jesus' name. Amen.

C. Thought to Remember

Actions reveal the content of the heart.

INVOLVEMENT LEARNING

Enhance your lesson with KJV Bible Student *(from your curriculum supplier) and the reproducible activity page (at www.standardlesson.com or in the back of the* KJV Standard Lesson Commentary Deluxe Edition*).*

Into the Lesson

Before class, download two or three commercials advertising free credit-score reports from a video-sharing website. Begin class by playing the commercials for your group. *Alternative.* Distribute copies of the "How Do You Rate?" activity from the reproducible page, which you can download, to be completed as indicated by interaction with fellow class members.

After either activity, discuss the idea of ratings with these questions: 1–What is the value of having rating systems? 2–What are some rating systems to which you pay a great deal of attention? 3–In what contexts have you been evaluated by some sort of rating scale? 4–What makes some rating systems more valid than others?

Lead into Bible study by saying, "Rating a movie, evaluating job performance, and assessing the quality of goods are familiar to us. But how do we go about judging the godliness of another person? Jesus has invaluable words of caution on just this question."

Into the Word

Divide students into three groups. Give each group one of the following objects and Scripture assignments: *Judgment Group (Matthew 7:1-6):* a pocket mirror; *Fruit Group (Matthew 7:15-20):* a piece of fresh fruit; *Recommendation Group (Matthew 7:21-23):* a sample letter of reference. Ask groups to read their Scripture passages and discuss how their objects relate to the text.

Expected responses in the whole-class discussion should be similar to these: *Judgment Group*—Before making judgments about others, look in the mirror. It is hard to be taken seriously if you offer advice that you obviously do not follow yourself! Once we do that, we can make clear, helpful judgments, not just condemning remarks. *Fruit Group*—By close examination of an apple, a grape, or melon, one can determine its nature

as healthy or unhealthy fruit. The same is true with people. By examining what they value, how they behave, the reputations they have, and the relationships they form, the "fruit inspector" can reach a valid conclusion regarding someone's suitability as a church leader or teacher. *Recommendation Group*—Job applicants are known to produce glowing letters of recommendations. But only evaluations from those having comprehensive knowledge of a person can be trusted. In evaluating someone's character, care must be taken in discerning the validity of every report. Regarding those who "apply" for eternal life in the kingdom of Heaven, God's evaluation is the one that ultimately matters.

Alternative. Form learners into study pairs or groups of three. Distribute copies of the "True or False?" activity from the reproducible page to be completed as indicated, then discuss.

After either activity, lead into the Into Life segment by saying, "Jesus does not command that we say nothing when someone we know is on the wrong path. Rather, He counsels us not to offer blanket condemnation. Instead, we first evaluate our own behavior so we can offer helpful correction without hypocrisy. We need to respond to evil wisely. Let's see how that might look."

Into Life

Ask the class to name common sinful behaviors; jot their responses on the board. Then ask a volunteer to select an item from the list and offer one example each of blind acceptance, blanket condemnation, and godly counsel. *Example:* for abortion, **blind acceptance** might be to support unthinkingly the "right to choose" argument; **blanket condemnation** might be to stand outside an abortion clinics merely to yell at those trying to enter; **godly counsel** could be to refer those with unplanned pregnancies to a local crisis pregnancy center (which you support) for counseling.

A Covenant
Between Friends

DEVOTIONAL READING: John 15:12-17
BACKGROUND SCRIPTURE: 1 Samuel 18–20

1 SAMUEL 18:1-5

1 And it came to pass, when he had made an end of speaking unto Saul, that the soul of Jonathan was knit with the soul of David, and Jonathan loved him as his own soul.

2 And Saul took him that day, and would let him go no more home to his father's house.

3 Then Jonathan and David made a covenant, because he loved him as his own soul.

4 And Jonathan stripped himself of the robe that was upon him, and gave it to David, and his garments, even to his sword, and to his bow, and to his girdle.

5 And David went out whithersoever Saul sent him, and behaved himself wisely: and Saul set him over the men of war, and he was accepted in the sight of all the people, and also in the sight of Saul's servants.

1 SAMUEL 19:1-7

1 And Saul spake to Jonathan his son, and to all his servants, that they should kill David.

2 But Jonathan Saul's son delighted much in David: and Jonathan told David, saying, Saul my father seeketh to kill thee: now there-

fore, I pray thee, take heed to thyself until the morning, and abide in a secret place, and hide thyself:

3 And I will go out and stand beside my father in the field where thou art, and I will commune with my father of thee; and what I see, that I will tell thee.

4 And Jonathan spake good of David unto Saul his father, and said unto him, Let not the king sin against his servant, against David; because he hath not sinned against thee, and because his works have been to thee-ward very good:

5 For he did put his life in his hand, and slew the Philistine, and the LORD wrought a great salvation for all Israel: thou sawest it, and didst rejoice: wherefore then wilt thou sin against innocent blood, to slay David without a cause?

6 And Saul hearkened unto the voice of Jonathan: and Saul sware, As the LORD liveth, he shall not be slain.

7 And Jonathan called David, and Jonathan shewed him all those things. And Jonathan brought David to Saul, and he was in his presence, as in times past.

KEY VERSE

The soul of Jonathan was knit with the soul of David, and Jonathan loved him as his own soul.

—1 Samuel 18:1

COVENANT IN GOD

LESSON AIMS

After participating in this lesson, each learner will be able to:

1. Retell the story of the friendship between Jonathan and David.

2. Describe the significance of the covenant between Jonathan and David.

3. Make a plan to be a better Christ-honoring friend to another person.

LESSON OUTLINE

Introduction

A. Promise Keepers

In the 1990s, the Promise Keepers organization took Christian men by storm in the U.S. Tens of thousands from many backgrounds—different denominations, different races and ethnicities, even non-Christians—would drive hundreds of miles to fill football stadiums to praise God together in song, prayer, and preaching. The key theme of the movement was integrity. A Christian man should be a man of his word: a promise keeper to God, family, friends, acquaintances, and everyone else.

Of course, this directive is not just for men. All God's people need to be promise keepers. Spouses need to keep commitments to each other. Children and parents must build trust by keeping their word. Employers and employees must act in accordance with hiring agreements. We can learn from those who went before us how to keep faith in our relationships.

B. Lesson Context

In the Christian arrangement of the books of the Old Testament, 1 and 2 Samuel are included with the historical books (Joshua–Esther). They record the transition from theocracy (being governed by the Lord) to monarchy (being governed by an earthly king). The books of 1 and 2 Samuel can be divided into these sections:

- The end of the period of the judges (1 Samuel 1–8)
- The Lord's selection and rejection of Saul, Israel's first king (1 Samuel 9–15)
- The Lord's selection of David and the fall of Saul (1 Samuel 16–31)
- The establishment of David's throne (2 Samuel 1–10)
- The sin of David and consequent flight from Jerusalem (2 Samuel 11–18)
- The reestablishment of David in Jerusalem (2 Samuel 19, 20)
- The legacy of David (2 Samuel 21–24)

Samuel is a pivotal figure in the history of Israel, being the last of the judges and the first of the prophets (see Acts 3:24; 13:20). The Israelites, tired of the abuses of Samuel's sons, demanded that Samuel give them an earthly king "like all the nations" (1 Samuel 8:1-5). This flew in the face of God's desire for Israel to be a priestly, holy nation under His rule (Exodus 19:6; 1 Samuel 12:12-16).

The Lord required Samuel to proclaim the negative consequences of becoming like the nations by having an earthly king (1 Samuel 8:11-18), but He still chose to grant their request. The Lord selected Saul, but Saul did not faithfully carry out the Lord's commands (13:7-14; 15). Thus the Lord instructed Samuel to tell Saul of His rejection and then to anoint David to be Saul's heir even while Saul still lived (13:14; 16:1).

I. A Covenant Made

(1 Samuel 18:1-5)

King Saul met David for the first time during a confrontation with the Philistines. Young David killed the giant Goliath, leading to a rout of Israel's enemies (1 Samuel 17:1-54). After this great victory, Saul met with David, who formally identified himself as the son of Jesse from Bethlehem (17:55-58). Jonathan, son of Saul, also had seen David's victory over Goliath and presumably was present when David appeared before the king.

A. United in Friendship (v. 1)

1. And it came to pass, when he had made an end of speaking unto Saul, that the soul of Jonathan was knit with the soul of David, and Jonathan loved him as his own soul.

And it came to pass often marks the beginning of a new story or a new scene in a larger story. Here it

HOW TO SAY IT

Abraham	*Ay*-bruh-ham.
Bethlehem	*Beth*-lih-hem.
Deuteronomy	Due-ter-*ahn*-uh-me.
Ecclesiastes	Ik-*leez*-ee-*as*-teez.
Goliath	Go-*lye*-uth.
Leviticus	Leh-*vit*-ih-kus.
Philistines	Fuh-*liss*-teenz
	or *Fill*-us-teenz.

marks the shift from the scene in Saul's court following the death of Goliath to the friendship and covenant between Jonathan and David.

The word translated *soul* occurs three times in this verse. Though it has a relatively wide range of meaning, here it most nearly means "self," one's whole being. With so many nuances, however, there is no reason that the writer could not also intend the reader to note other meanings. For instance, *soul* can also be used to contrast with *body* to include the will and emotions (Isaiah 10:18). This would suggest that Jonathan loves David with his innermost being. The word *soul* can also refer to the life of a creature, suggesting that Jonathan loves David forcefully, as though his life depends on it (Deuteronomy 19:21; Isaiah 56:11). In short, Jonathan loves David as he loves himself.

The word *knit* is the same verb that is translated "bound up in" in Genesis 44:30, describing the relationship between Jacob and his youngest son, Benjamin. Similarly, Jonathan's soul, both will and emotion, is bound to David's soul. This speaks to the commitment of one to the other. Their allegiance is not created merely out of a sense of duty but out of deep emotional and even spiritual attachment.

Together these two Hebrew words *soul* and *knit* demonstrate the genuineness and intensity of the bond between the two men. Though this verse focuses on Jonathan's affection for David, other texts make clear that the feeling is mutual (see 1 Samuel 20:42; 2 Samuel 1:26; 21:7).

❧ *BFFs* ❧

In the shorthand lingo of modern social media, *BFF* stands for "best friends forever." Earlier generations talked about "soul mates." Both terms refer to pairs of people who seem so perfectly matched psychologically and emotionally that they understand each other almost intuitively. Though many examples are fictional, taken especially from love stories, BFFs can also be found in the real world. Some marriages are examples of this; others find their BFF in lifelong friendship.

David and Jonathan seem to have been BFFs. They were united in spirit more deeply than just enjoying each other's presence; they were united in what they knew to be best for God's people. Jonathan was the heir apparent of King Saul, but he later comes to accept that God had chosen another man to put on the throne. The best BFFs, like Jonathan and David, are united in wanting what God wants. How does your BFF relationship spur you on to serving the Lord?   —C. R. B.

> **What Do You Think?**
> How can we ensure that our friendships are genuine and not simply founded in a desire for gain of some sort?
>
> *Digging Deeper*
> Under what circumstances, if any, would it be appropriate to draw up a general rule of friendships that is based on a single bad experience with a "fair-weather friend"? Why?

B. Bound in Service (v. 2)

2. And Saul took him that day, and would let him go no more home to his father's house.

This verse interrupts the story of Jonathan and David to briefly resume the story of Saul's action regarding David. The Hebrew word translated *took* can suggest choosing or selecting—as in Isaiah 44:14, in which certain trees were selected but not removed. This is the idea here; Saul selects David for a place in his court.

The second clause elaborates on what it means for Saul to take David. The king values David's contributions in his court and military and so requires him to remain by the king's side. This marks the end of David's career as a shepherd (but see 2 Samuel 24:17; Ezekiel 34:20-24 regarding David as a shepherd of God's people).

C. Formed in Love (vv. 3, 4)

3. Then Jonathan and David made a covenant, because he loved him as his own soul.

There are two types of formal covenants: those between equals and those between a superior and an inferior. The most significant covenants in the Old Testament are made between people and the Lord (examples: Genesis 9:17; 17:1-22; 2 Samuel 7:1-16). Covenants between various people also

occur: states and their representatives, kings and their subjects, military leaders and their soldiers, and individuals. Within the last category we see marriage portrayed as a covenant between a husband and a wife.

The covenant between Jonathan and David can be argued as one of power imbalance because Jonathan is the son of the king. A strong case can also be made that this covenant is made between equals. Jonathan and David clearly share mutual love (see commentary on 1 Samuel 18:1).

4. And Jonathan stripped himself of the robe that was upon him, and gave it to David, and his garments, even to his sword, and to his bow, and to his girdle.

Formal covenants in the ancient Near East are comprised of distinct parts. These may be enumerated as follows: (1) identification of the giver; (2) the historical prologue; (3) stipulations of the participants; (4) storing and public reading; (5) witnesses of the covenant; (6) blessings for keeping and curses for violating the covenant terms; (7) a ceremony for ratification including a verbal affirmation; and (8) sanctions pronounced on a violator of the covenant terms.

Our passage describes only one of the elements of a covenant, the ceremonial act: Jonathan's giving David *garments* (see a similar act in Genesis 41:41-43). These probably represent various aspects of his royal status. The Hebrew word translated *robe* is an outer garment worn by people of status. That Hebrew word is also translated variously as "mantle" as we see wearing it such people as priests (Exodus 28:4), prophets (1 Samuel 15:27), royalty (1 Samuel 24:4; 2 Samuel 13:18), the wealthy (Job 1:20), and government officials (Ezra 9:3).

The *sword* and *bow* are weapons of warfare. The *girdle* is used to bind up the tunic so that one can be ready for freer movement, especially in battle (Psalm 45:3), and to carry the sheath for the sword (2 Samuel 20:8). Giving these items is more than a symbol of friendship; it is a pledge of Jonathan's military loyalty to David.

❧ THE MEANING OF GIFTS ❧

Gifts can take on many different meanings based on any number of different circumstances.

Sometimes gifts express gratitude, as when dinner guests bring flowers in appreciation for the invitation they have received. Other gifts are meant to manipulate, like when merchandisers offer free items to entice us to buy something. Then there are Christmas and birthday gifts which may be genuine gifts of love or, in some cases, merely offered because it is customary to give something on those occasions even though the giver has no significant connection to the recipient. Sometimes gifts are used to confirm a relationship. The presentation of a diamond engagement ring confirms the love a couple has for one another and the commitment to continue growing in love together.

Jonathan's gifts to David confirmed his loving commitment. Jonathan saw in David a true friend. By his gifts, Jonathan was saying, "I pledge my friendship and loyalty to you." Like Jonathan, we can and should give gifts that honor our promises to our loved ones. What gifts will you give to honor yours?   —C. R. B.

> ### What Do You Think?
> What could be some modern equivalents of the way Jonathan expressed friendship with David? Why?
> *Digging Deeper*
> Think of nonmaterial things as well as tangible objects. Be prepared to explain the nature of the equivalence.

D. Sent in Service (v. 5)

5. And David went out whithersoever Saul sent him, and behaved himself wisely: and Saul set him over the men of war, and he was accepted in the sight of all the people, and also in the sight of Saul's servants.

This verse concludes the scene between Jonathan and David and summarizes the information that follows (1 Samuel 18:6, 7, not in today's text). David's wise behavior shows that the Lord has blessed him. Wisdom is frequently contrasted with foolishness in the Bible—with the assumption that God both gives wisdom and blesses those who demonstrate it (1 Samuel 13:13; Proverbs 1:7; 3:35; Matthew 7:24-27; etc.). as long

as he acts wisely, David can expect to continue to be successful in his service not only to the king but also to the Lord.

The people accept David and approve of Saul's decision to send him out to fight their battles. David's forays habitually result in success (1 Samuel 18:30; 2 Samuel 5:2). Emphasizing that everyone, even Saul and his court, accepts David foreshadows the conflict to come.

II. A Covenant Observed
(1 Samuel 19:1-7)

After the events in 1 Samuel 18:1-5, all seems well. The situation begins to fall apart as Saul grows jealous of David due to the adoration of the nation (1 Samuel 18:7, 8) and as an evil spirit torments Saul (18:10). The king twice attempts to kill David (18:11). But no matter how Saul schemes, the Lord is with David and keeps him safe (18:12-30).

A. A Plot (v. 1)

1. And Saul spake to Jonathan his son, and to all his servants, that they should kill David.

We see again the nature of Saul's fear and jealousy. Notice the progression. First, Saul personally tried to end David's life (1 Samuel 18:10, 11). Then Saul tried to achieve the same result by stealth (18:17). Now Saul openly tells *his son* and *all his servants that they should kill David.*

B. A Plan (vv. 2, 3)

2, 3. But Jonathan Saul's son delighted much in David: and Jonathan told David, saying, Saul my father seeketh to kill thee: now therefore, I pray thee, take heed to thyself until the morning, and abide in a secret place, and hide thyself: and I will go out and stand beside my father in the field where thou art, and I will commune with my father of thee; and what I see, that I will tell thee.

This verse emphasizes Jonathan's positive regard for David, in spite of all the paranoia evident in King Saul, Jonathan's *father.* The covenant that Jonathan has made with David prevents him from obeying his father's orders to kill David. This puts Jonathan in a difficult situation. In order to save his friend, he has to disobey his father. And the king can certainly punish his son any way he sees fit for such an act of rebellion!

Jonathan chooses to honor his covenant with David and makes a plan to protect him. David is told to *hide* himself *in a secret place* in a certain *field*, presumably where Saul commonly goes (see 1 Samuel 20:5, 19). Then Jonathan will do two things. First, he will *go out* with his father, and then he will *commune with* Saul about David. This is to gauge Saul's reaction to the conversation in order to report it to David (see 20:12).

C. A Defense (vv. 4, 5)

4a. And Jonathan spake good of David unto Saul his father, and said unto him, Let not the king sin against his servant, against David;

Jonathan's gives his exhortation in the third person (*let not the king*), which is meant to be deferential rather than commanding. He begins by exhorting his father not to *sin against . . . David* (see 1 Samuel 20:32). Though sin is usually understood as an offense against God alone, those sins against God are frequently also sins against other people (Genesis 42:22; Exodus 10:16; 1 Corinthians 8:12; etc.). Sinning against David would mean bringing him to harm. Jonathan emphasizes his earnest plea using forms of the word *sin* three times in short order while speaking to his father (see 1 Samuel 19:5).

Jonathan's address of his father as *the king* speaks also to the honor and responsibility of that position. The king must do what is right in the eyes of the Lord (Deuteronomy 17:14-20). Jonathan fulfills the command to argue for justice that the king should fulfill (Proverbs 21:8; Jeremiah 18:20).

Referring to David as the king's *servant* makes clear the difference in power and status between those two. But even though the king has the power to do as he pleases with and to his servant, the king must honor the Lord in all decisions. David is loyal to the king, and it would be evil to harm a loyal servant (see 1 Samuel 22:14; 25:21; Proverbs 17:13).

4b, 5a. Because he hath not sinned against thee, and because his works have been to thee-ward very good: For he did put his life in his hand, and slew the Philistine, and the LORD wrought a great salvation for all Israel: thou sawest it, and didst rejoice:

Jonathan gives an insurmountable reason for not harming David: David has done no wrong to King Saul—quite the opposite, in fact! Evidence of David's *very good* work is recounted in that he risked *his life in* killing *the Philistine* giant Goliath (17:50, 51). The result from *the Lord* was *a great salvation for all Israel* (17:52, 53). Jonathan then reminds his father, who was an eyewitness to all this, that he *didst rejoice* when it all happened.

5b. Wherefore then wilt thou sin against innocent blood, to slay David without a cause?

Jonathan concludes his argument by returning to his beginning exhortation and turning it into the rhetorical question we see here. A rhetorical question is designed to make a point rather than get an answer.

The answer itself is obvious: the king should not *slay David without a cause* because then the king himself would become guilty and deserving of death (Deuteronomy 19:10-13). The term *blood* is often used metaphorically of the life force (compare Genesis 9:4 for "life" and 42:22 for "death"). Here *blood* refers to David's manner of living. Jonathan describes David's blood, or actions, as *innocent* because David has acted faithfully as a servant in the court of Saul. David has never given Saul any reason for Saul's anger.

> **What Do You Think?**
> What are some ways we can act to defend an innocent friend without jeopardizing our own credibility in the process?
>
> *Digging Deeper*
> What types of situations might call us *not* to defend a friend, either to protect ourselves or to do what is ultimately best for the friend in question? And if there are limits to loyalty, what are they?

D. A Promise (v. 6)

6. And Saul hearkened unto the voice of Jonathan: and Saul sware, As the LORD liveth, he shall not be slain.

Jonathan's argument has the desired effect. *Hearkened unto* means both to hear and to act in accordance with what is heard, as when the Lord told Abraham to "hearken unto [Sarah's] voice" (Genesis 21:12). Similarly, the exodus from Egypt was initiated because God not only heard but acted on the groaning of the children of Israel (Exodus 2:24, 25).

Saul's obedience to *the voice of Jonathan* culminates in making a vow in the name of *the Lord*: David *shall not be slain*. Making vows is equivalent to making a covenant (Deuteronomy 4:31). The Lord expects the king to keep his vow (Numbers 30:2; see also Matthew 5:33-37). Deuteronomy 23:21-23 declares that vows must be kept, while Ecclesiastes 5:4-6 reminds the reader that breaking a vow angers the Lord. By swearing that David will live, Saul binds himself to do all in his power to protect David.

What Do You Think?
What are some techniques to keep a vouching-for situation from resulting in more emotional "heat" than the "light" of facts and reason?

Digging Deeper
Should you focus on reducing emotional "heat" (and run the risk of appearing defensive) or on increasing the "light" of reason (and run the risk of allowing emotional characterizations to stick)?

E. A Reunion (v. 7)

7. And Jonathan called David, and Jonathan shewed him all those things. And Jonathan brought David to Saul, and he was in his presence, as in times past.

David emerges from his prearranged hiding place after hearing the proper signal. Jonathan informs him of Saul's change of heart and as a result David is in Saul's presence *as in times past*. This phrase calls back to mind how well David and Saul had worked together initially. David's service in Saul's court is no less valuable than his military service (1 Samuel 16:14-23; 18:13; 19:8). At least for the time being, Saul desires that David live and thrive in the king's court as before (but contrast 19:9-15; 20:31, 33).

What Do You Think?
If a church were to have a ministry to reconcile conflicts between friends and family members, what would such a ministry look like?

Digging Deeper
Consider further how churches in a given area could band together to do this.

Conclusion

A. Covenant Keepers

His covenant with David put Jonathan in a difficult situation. When he learned of the king's unjust plot on his closest friend, he risked (at best) alienation from his father and (at worst) death. Nevertheless, Jonathan was true to his covenant with David without being disloyal to his father, reconciling Saul and David. The Lord is pleased when we are covenant-keepers. That's true for simple promises, such as being on time for dinner, or major ones, such as honoring marriage vows.

C. Prayer

Dear Lord, help us follow Jonathan's example of keeping covenant as we are faithful to the promises we make. We pray in Jesus' name. Amen.

D. Thought to Remember

Honoring covenants, commitments, and contracts honors the Lord.

Visual for Lesson 10. *Point to this visual as you ask what elements your learners see that they experience or desire to experience in friendships.*

INVOLVEMENT LEARNING

Enhance your lesson with KJV Bible Student *(from your curriculum supplier) and the reproducible activity page (at www.standardlesson.com or in the back of the* KJV Standard Lesson Commentary Deluxe Edition*).*

Into the Lesson

Distribute handouts (you prepare) with the following quotes on each. Ask class members to mark each sentence with either a + for *agree* or a – for *disagree*. Ask those willing also to mark **!** if they have experienced the statement.

__ 1. "A friend is someone who knows all about you and still loves you" (Elbert Hubbard).

__ 2. "There is nothing I would not do for those who are really my friends. I have no notion of loving people by halves, it is not my nature" (Jane Austen, *Northanger Abbey*).

__ 3. "I would rather walk with a friend in the dark, than alone in the light" (Helen Keller).

__ 4. "Friends are part of the glue that holds life and faith together" (Jon Katz).

__ 5. "Do I not destroy my enemies when I make them my friends?" (Abraham Lincoln).

__ 6. "Wishing to be friends is quick work, but friendship is a slow ripening fruit" (Aristotle).

Alternative. Have each student number 1 through 6 on a blank piece of paper. Then read the statements above and have students mark each as *agree* or *disagree*. Discuss their responses. Then have volunteers tell how one of the sentences has proven true for them.

Alternative. Distribute copies of the "Acquaintance . . . or Friend?"activity from the reproducible page, which you can download. Ask students if they agree or disagree with the quote. Taking no more than one minute, have them complete the "Remembering My Friends" section as indicated.

Lead into Bible study by saying, "Today we'll look at a story of friendship to see how it confirms or contradicts these quotes. Maybe we'll decide something new about friendship in the process."

Into the Word

Briefly summarize the story of David and Saul that precedes today's printed text. Write the following questions on the board or include them on the handout (you prepare) with the quotes above.

The answers in parentheses are given only for the teacher's reference. 1–What was the nature of the friendship between David and Jonathan? *(that of a formal covenant)* 2–How did the two friends seal their covenant? *(by personal gifts to David, indicating Jonathan's complete loyalty to him)* 3–What happened when times got tough? *(Jonathan interceded with Saul on David's behalf to save his life)* 4–What risk did the friend take that demonstrated his friendship? *(Saul could have turned on Jonathan, killing him as well as David)*

Ask a participant to read 1 Samuel 18:1-5 while other class members listen for answers to the questions. Briefly summarize the events from the end of 1 Samuel 18. Then ask a participant to read 1 Samuel 19:1-7 as class members listen again for answers to the questions. Ask volunteers to give their answers.

Alternative. Distribute copies of the "Demonstrating His Friendship" activity from the reproducible page. Ask students to complete this activity in pairs as indicated and share answers.

Into Life

Lead class members to think again about the quotes. Ask, "How does the story of David and Jonathan's friendship reflect the truth or show a problem with [a quote you point out]?" After covering all six, form students into pairs to respond with each other to the following prompts:

• *I have a friend who has stuck with me in tough times.*

• *I know a person who needs the friendship I could offer.*

Challenge class members to (1) find a way to thank a friend for his or her loyalty or (2) take steps to become a friend by reaching out with an offer of help.

Alternative. Ask class members to complete individually the chart in the "Strengthening Our Friendship" activity from the reproducible page. If time allows, ask volunteers to share what they've written.

A MOTHER-DAUGHTER COVENANT

DEVOTIONAL READING: Ruth 4:13-17
BACKGROUND SCRIPTURE: Ruth 1:1-18

RUTH 1:6-11, 14-18

6 Then she arose with her daughters in law, that she might return from the country of Moab: for she had heard in the country of Moab how that the LORD had visited his people in giving them bread.

7 Wherefore she went forth out of the place where she was, and her two daughters in law with her; and they went on the way to return unto the land of Judah.

8 And Naomi said unto her two daughters in law, Go, return each to her mother's house: the LORD deal kindly with you, as ye have dealt with the dead, and with me.

9 The LORD grant you that ye may find rest, each of you in the house of her husband. Then she kissed them; and they lifted up their voice, and wept.

10 And they said unto her, Surely we will return with thee unto thy people.

11 And Naomi said, Turn again, my daughters: why will ye go with me? are there yet any more sons in my womb, that they may be your husbands?

· ·

14 And they lifted up their voice, and wept again: and Orpah kissed her mother in law; but Ruth clave unto her.

15 And she said, Behold, thy sister in law is gone back unto her people, and unto her gods: return thou after thy sister in law.

16 And Ruth said, Intreat me not to leave thee, or to return from following after thee: for whither thou goest, I will go; and where thou lodgest, I will lodge: thy people shall be my people, and thy God my God:

17 Where thou diest, will I die, and there will I be buried: the LORD do so to me, and more also, if ought but death part thee and me.

18 When she saw that she was stedfastly minded to go with her, then she left speaking unto her.

KEY VERSE

Whither thou goest, I will go; and where thou lodgest, I will lodge: thy people shall be my people, and thy God my God. —**Ruth 1:16**

COVENANT IN GOD

Unit 3: Covenant: A Personal Perspective

LESSONS 10–13

LESSON AIMS

After participating in this lesson, each learner will be able to:

1. Recall the dramatic account of Ruth's decision to go with Naomi from Moab to Israel.

2. Explain how the historical context influenced the decisions of Ruth, Naomi, and Orpah.

3. Develop a plan to assist someone who is experiencing loss and/or loneliness.

LESSON OUTLINE

Introduction

A. A Selfless Act

Cameron Lyle was a senior track star at the University of New Hampshire in spring 2013. Just days before he would compete for gold medals in the America East Conference championships, he learned that his bone marrow was an exact match for a 28-year-old leukemia patient who had been given six months to live. The transplant needed to occur right away, so Lyle faced a choice: sacrifice years of personal dreams and cut his athletic career short, or help save another man's life. Without hesitation, he chose to donate.

Such acts of selflessness are commended frequently in Scripture (for example, Philippians 2:4). The Bible contains many examples of loyalty and self-sacrifice. Joshua served as faithful aide to Moses for many years (Exodus 24:13; 33:11). Elisha refused to leave Elijah's side as his master's time on earth drew to a close (2 Kings 2:1-6). The women followed Jesus to His crucifixion and sought to take care of His body (Luke 23:27, 49; 24:1-11). Jesus himself said, "Greater love hath no man than this, that a man lay down his life for his friends" (John 15:13). As we shall see, God uses selfless acts to help those in need.

B. Lesson Context: Period of the Judges

The story of Ruth takes place during the period of the judges (Ruth 1:1), which lasted from about 1370 to 1050 BC. This situates the story in a spiritually dark period of Israel's history. For one thing, divine inspiration through prophets was rare (1 Samuel 3:1). For another, Israel's population at that time routinely abandoned the teachings of the Mosaic covenant in favor of simply doing whatever they thought was right in the moment (Judges 2:10-19).

Israel had no king in those days (Judges 17:6; 18:1; 19:1; 21:25). This statement is often taken as a positive appraisal of the forthcoming kingship in Israel; it suggests that kingly leadership would keep the nation on a better track spiritually (compare Psalm 72:1; Proverbs 16:12; Isaiah 9:7).

An alternate appraisal, however, is entirely negative: the nation's spiritual state was so poor that the people didn't even need a king to lead them down the wrong path (see 1 Kings 16:29-33; 2 Kings 15:27-28; etc.). In either case, the author's observations reflect poorly on the covenant people of God, who regularly snubbed their divine king.

Against this dark backdrop, the story of Ruth provides a ray of sunshine. Self-centeredness and idolatry were not universal. Some people still acknowledged God as they made their plans.

C. Lesson Context: Non-Israelites

The Old Testament preserves accounts of non-Israelites acknowledging Israel's God as being supreme. After hearing of the Israelites' deliverance from Egypt, Rahab acknowledged the Lord as God in Heaven and on earth (Joshua 2:8-11). Upon being cured of leprosy, Naaman the Syrian declared there to be no God anywhere in the world except Israel (2 Kings 5:15). In some instances, foreigners recognized the greatness of Israel's God better than the Israelites themselves did (contrast 1 Kings 16:29-34; 17:7-24; compare Luke 4:25-27).

The book of the Bible in today's study, Ruth, is named after a non-Israelite. Yet the story arguably centers more on the words, actions, and mental state of Naomi, who was Ruth's Israelite mother-in-law.

At the point where today's text picks up their story, the Israelite Naomi had been living in Moab for some 10 years. She, husband Elimelech, and their two sons had had to leave their hometown of Bethlehem due to famine (Ruth 1:1-5).

HOW TO SAY IT

Balaam	*Bay*-lum.
Balak	*Bay*-lack.
Canaan	*Kay*-nun.
Elimelech	Ee-*lim*-eh-leck.
Moabite	*Mo*-ub-ite.
Mosaic	Mo-*zay*-ik.
Naaman	*Nay*-uh-mun.
Nehemiah	*Nee*-huh-**my**-uh.
Orpah	*Or*-pah.
Rahab	*Ray*-hab.
Syrian	*Sear*-ee-un.

The Bible records several famines that prompt people to leave the promised land of Canaan for greener pastures. Most notably, Jacob and his sons relied upon Egypt during seven years of famine and eventually migrated there with their families (Genesis 41–46; compare Genesis 12:10; 2 Kings 8:1, 2). We are not specifically told whether this famine arose from divine wrath, though Israel was warned of this possibility (Deuteronomy 11:13-17; Amos 4:9).

While in Moab, the two sons "took them wives of the women of Moab; the name of the one was Orpah, and the name of the other Ruth" (Ruth 1:4a). However, the passing of a decade finds the husbands of Naomi, Orpah, and Ruth deceased (1:4b, 5). Women without husbands or adult sons usually face desperate circumstances in ancient times. Such is the backdrop of the interaction of the three women—only one of which is an Israelite—in today's text.

I. First Plea
(RUTH 1:6-10)

A. Return to Judah (vv. 6, 7)

6. Then she arose with her daughters in law, that she might return from the country of Moab: for she had heard in the country of Moab how that the LORD had visited his people in giving them bread.

Israel has a troubled history with *Moab*, which occupies the territory immediately to the east of the Jordan River and the Dead Sea. The Moabites are descendants of Lot by his older daughter (Genesis 19:36, 37). They are banned from the assembly of the Lord because they did not come to Israel's aid during their wilderness wandering and because King Balak of Moab hired Balaam to curse the Israelites (Deuteronomy 23:3-6). During the early period of the judges, Eglon, the king of Moab, ruled over Israel for 18 years (Judges 3:14).

While the story's developments thus far have been grim, here we find the first sign of good news. After a decade of famine in Judah, the Lord has now provided *bread* for *his people* once again (see Psalm 132:15; Matthew 6:11), and Naomi plans to *return* home.

Visual for Lesson 11. *Start a discussion by pointing to this visual as you ask, "Why is this statement important for the Christian walk (or run)?"*

7. Wherefore she went forth out of the place where she was, and her two daughters in law with her; and they went on the way to return unto the land of Judah.

With food now more plenteous back in *the land of Judah*, Naomi decides *to return*. She no doubt hopes to find support from her late husband's extended family, though her protracted absence may also leave her estranged from them. She cannot be certain what she will find upon her return (compare 2 Kings 8:1-6).

Naomi's *two daughters in law* have presumably been a part of her household for some years. Familial ties have solidified, and the common experience of loss and widowhood serves to bolster their bonds. The younger women thus initially agree to accompany their mother-in-law back to her homeland. The precise length of the journey is uncertain, since we do not know where Naomi lives in Moab. The journey represented a firm commitment, however, leaving Moab behind forever.

B. Return to Moab (vv. 8, 9)

8. And Naomi said unto her two daughters in law, Go, return each to her mother's house: the LORD deal kindly with you, as ye have dealt with the dead, and with me.

We may imagine that as the women are about to leave Moab, *Naomi* has second thoughts about taking *her two daughters in law* with her. That

Naomi bids them to return to their *mother's house* (rather than father's) may indicate that she feels guilty for asking them to abandon their own mothers in favor of her.

In addition, the mother's house is often associated with marriage (compare Genesis 24:28; Song of Solomon 3:4; 8:2; contrast Genesis 38:11). This gives the younger women another hint about acquiring husbands.

> **What Do You Think?**
> In what way could you show kindness to a person in need of direction in life were you to use God's kindness to you as a model?
> **Digging Deeper**
> How would that expression of kindness differ for a close friend vs. a mere acquaintance?

The word *covenant* is not found in this book. But Naomi's desire for *the Lord* to *deal kindly with* her daughters-in law includes a Hebrew term that is used frequently in Old Testament situations involving covenants or oaths. The term may signify willing devotion, kindness, and/or mercy that an advantaged party extends to someone disadvantaged. Jonathan showed such mercy to David, and took the same in pledge from him (1 Samuel 20:8-15).

The Lord showed such kindness to Israel in general (Deuteronomy 7:12). Naomi here attributes it to Ruth, and Boaz will do the same later (Ruth 3:10). For deeper study, see also Deuteronomy 7:9; 1 Kings 8:23; Isaiah 54:10; 55:3; Psalms 25:10; 89:28; 106:45; Daniel 9:4; Nehemiah 1:5; 9:32; and 2 Chronicles 6:14.

9. The LORD grant you that ye may find rest, each of you in the house of her husband. Then she kissed them; and they lifted up their voice, and wept.

The Hebrew word translated *rest* sometimes describes a place or state of peace, security, and relief from anxiety (compare Deuteronomy 12:9; 1 Kings 8:56; Jeremiah 45:3). Naomi shares in the worries and travails that Orpah and Ruth are experiencing. For a widow to find a new *husband* is the best path toward economic security in this cultural context (see Ruth 3:1). Given the tenuous relations between Moab and Israel, the women's chances of finding husbands among their own people would likely be greater than finding them in Judah.

❧ SETTING OUR CHILDREN FREE ❧

When our children were young, a call came to my wife and me to go to Liberia as missionaries. At the time, we lived about five miles from my parents. My father asked me half-seriously, "Why are you taking my grandchildren so far away from me?" I reminded him that, earlier in his own life, the call of God had led him, my mother, and me to move 2,000 miles away from *my* grandparents. Dad's response was a somewhat pained smile as he gave us his blessing in spite of the personal loss he would be feeling.

As Naomi was returning to her own country, she urged her two daughters-in-law to remain in their home country, even though the emotional cost to her would be great. She wanted Ruth and Orpah to be free to hear God's call. Are we as willing as Naomi was to set our children free?

—C. R. B.

C. Widows' Resolution (v. 10)

10. And they said unto her, Surely we will return with thee unto thy people.

The younger women both at first express their desire to *return* with Naomi to her *people*. Perhaps their statement here reflects genuine resolve. However, it may have been expected for the women initially to refuse to leave Naomi, regardless of their true wishes. After all, to turn and leave Naomi too readily would dishonor her. As a result, Naomi must now press her case even further in order to afford her daughters-in-law an honorable exit from the situation, if they were looking for one.

> **What Do You Think?**
> What circumstances call for helping that takes the form of loyalty? Why?
>
> **Digging Deeper**
> In what situations, if any, might an expression of loyalty do more harm than good? Why?

II. Second Plea
(RUTH 1:11, 14)
A. Widow's Desperation (v. 11)

11. And Naomi said, Turn again, my daughters: why will ye go with me? are there yet any more sons in my womb, that they may be your husbands?

Naomi has been away from her hometown for some 10 years by this time (see the Lesson Context). Naomi also cannot guarantee that she will be able to provide *husbands* for Orpah and Ruth from among her own kinsfolk. And Naomi certainly cannot provide future husbands from her own *womb*!

All this underlines the fact that finding new husbands is a top priority. But more than their own security is at stake here. Their first husbands died, leaving no male heirs. The law stipulates that if a man dies and leaves no sons, the man's brother must marry the widow and produce a child in the deceased brother's name (Deuteronomy 25:5, 6). This custom, known as "levirate marriage," ensures the continuation of the dead brother's family line. Moab likely has a similar law or custom.

Unfortunately, Naomi herself is also widowed. Whether or not she is past menopause is uncertain. But even if she is still of childbearing age, she would first have to find a husband before more sons could be forthcoming. Were she able to find a husband and conceive more sons, however, Orpah and Ruth would not want to wait all the years until they reached marriageable age (Ruth 1:13, not in today's text; compare Genesis 38:11).

B. Daughter's Departure (v. 14)

14. And they lifted up their voice, and wept again: and Orpah kissed her mother in law; but Ruth clave unto her.

Faced with an excruciating choice, *Orpah* finally yields to the strength of Naomi's case, bids her in-law goodbye, and takes her leave. In her situation, this decision represents a wise earthly choice. She is setting herself up to find a new husband and the security that marriage provides.

Ruth, however, decides to stay with Naomi and sticks close to her. The word translated *clave* here is the same Hebrew root used in Proverbs 18:24 to describe the "friend that sticketh closer than a brother." The word also describes the commitment that a man has for his wife (Genesis 2:24) and the faithful adherence that God requires of Israel (Deuteronomy 10:20; Joshua 22:5).

> **What Do You Think?**
> What should you do for and/or say to someone who is about to make a major life-decision while under emotional distress?
>
> *Digging Deeper*
> To what extent, if any, should your answer take into account his or her personality? Why?

III. Third Plea
(RUTH 1:15-18)

A. Mother's Counsel (v. 15)

15. And she said, Behold, thy sister in law is gone back unto her people, and unto her gods: return thou after thy sister in law.

Naomi is still not entirely convinced that Ruth really wants to stay with her, so she must give her one last chance to turn back. She reminds Ruth once again that to go to Judah means leaving *her people* and everything she knows. She would also be leaving those who worship the *gods* of her native land (see Joshua 24:14).

It is clear that Naomi still adheres to worship of the God of Israel, and likely wants Ruth to do so as well. Even so, Naomi at least understands why Ruth may want to continue worshipping her Moabite gods. By outward appearances, they seem to have provided for their people better than Israel's God has provided for them. An implicit challenge, therefore, is that of basing a decision merely on outward appearances. In that regard, Orpah's decision is understandable. But *understandable* isn't the same as properly *justifiable*. We live with such a tension yet today.

B. Daughter's Resolution (vv. 16-18)

16. And Ruth said, Intreat me not to leave thee, or to return from following after thee: for whither thou goest, I will go; and where thou lodgest, I will lodge: thy people shall be my people, and thy God my God.

As a Moabite, Ruth has no legal obligation to go with Naomi to Judah. Her offer here reflects only devotion and love for her mother-in-law. She goes beyond the call of duty and declares her intent to adopt Naomi's home, *people*, and *God* as her own (see Psalm 45:10).

Sometimes God's people need to be reminded that foreigners can compare with them favorably in mimicking the character of God. Ruth's selfless pledge of allegiance to Naomi and her God stands in marked contrast to the depictions of rebellion and idolatry in the time of the judges (compare Joshua 24:15).

> **What Do You Think?**
> What should be your next step were you tomorrow to encounter someone who is determined to go "all in" for Christ?
>
> *Digging Deeper*
> At what point would you include the caution of Luke 14:25-33 in your counsel?

17. Where thou diest, will I die, and there will I be buried: the LORD do so to me, and more also, if ought but death part thee and me.

Ruth completes her pledge in the strongest of possible terms: at the risk of a divine curse, she declares that she will remain with Naomi until *death* (compare 1 Samuel 3:17; 20:13; 1 Kings 19:2; 20:10; etc.). So devoted is Ruth to her mother-in-law that she anticipates even joining her in the family tomb at death. In effect, she declares herself Naomi's daughter and shows her determination to care for Naomi as her own mother.

Ruth is aware of at least some of the tenets found in the Mosaic law concerning proper treatment of the poor and widows (Exodus 22:22-24; Deuteronomy 10:17, 18; 24:17-22; Ruth 2:2). Naomi certainly knows the law (3:1, 2, 12, 13) and may have taught her daughter-in-law as her own child in the ways of the Lord (Deuteronomy 6:1-9). Ruth's actions here reflect the character of a God who cares for the weak and vulnerable and seeks to rescue them from life's predicaments.

God often accomplishes these goals through the actions of self-sacrificing people who put the needs of others ahead of their own as Ruth does.

❧ PERMANENT STICKINESS ❧

In 1974, a member of a church choir was looking for a way to hold place markers in his hymnal. Six years earlier, a coworker at 3M company had developed by accident an adhesive that wasn't very good, and the company saw no use for the new formulation. But the first man saw it as the answer to his need. Company leadership came to realize that the not-very-good, temporary adhesive could meet the needs of others as well. The result was the yellow self-stick note!

Sometimes *temporary* is better than *permanent*; but often it's the reverse. The latter is the case in today's text. When Naomi begged Orpah and Ruth to return to their homes, both voiced intention to stick with their mother-in-law. Orpah's stickiness ended up being temporary, while Ruth's was permanent. On the significance of Ruth's decision, see Matthew 1:5-16. Then evaluate the level of your "stickiness" to Christ.   —C. R. B.

18. When she saw that she was stedfastly minded to go with her, then she left speaking unto her.

Naomi graciously and gratefully accepts Ruth's kindness and the "covenant" relationship Ruth offers (see commentary on Ruth 1:8). Naomi may have had doubts initially about Ruth's true wishes to stay or to go. But the strength of her declaration and the invoking of a divine curse put an end to any further discussion (compare Acts 21:13, 14).

> *What Do You Think?*
> What methods can we use to teach others (and ourselves) when to speak up and when to shut up? Or is that something to learn only by personal experience? Explain.
> *Digging Deeper*
> Consider how these texts suggest possibilities: 1 Kings 22:5; Job 2:9, 10, 12, 13; 13:4, 5; 16:1-5; 19:2; Psalm 12:6; Proverbs 12:18; 16:21, 24; 17:27; 23:9; Ecclesiastes 5:2; 6:11.

Conclusion
A. A Selfless Life

An array of related terminology makes apparent that the expressions of loyalty between Naomi and Ruth reflect a covenantal bond (compare Ruth 1:16, 17 with 1 Kings 22:4; 2 Kings 3:7). The story shows the God of Israel as a God who cares for the disadvantaged, sometimes directly (compare Ruth 1:6; 4:13), but often through the actions of obedient people. Today's account concerning actions of a Moabite woman may have confronted Israel in a way similar to Jesus' parable of the Good Samaritan ,with its positive portrayal of a despised neighbor (Luke 10:25-37).

Even if we are not a "despised neighbor," the example of Ruth should be a call to action. I know a widow who lives in service to others. She sponsors a scholarship fund for ministry students. She corresponds with missionaries and former students. Countless members of our congregation have been touched by the encouragement of her prayers, cards, visits, and character.

Not all selfless acts are as dramatic as Ruth's returning with Naomi, nor need they be. The disadvantaged are all around us. They are those who battle with addiction, suffer with grief, struggle to make ends meet, are homeless, are despondent widows and widowers, etc.

Acts of kindness to such folks draw the pleasure of our heavenly Father (Matthew 5:3, 4). Though He involves himself even more directly when He chooses, God often chooses to employ His people as His hands and feet (Isaiah 6:8; etc.). As He uses Ruth's covenant with Naomi, so are we His instruments. And He uses us best when we heed the words of James 1:27: "Pure religion and undefiled before God and the Father is this, To visit the fatherless and widows in their affliction."

B. Prayer

Father, open our eyes to the needs around us, and grant us a selfless heart to reach out and meet those needs. We pray in Christ's name. Amen.

C. Thought to Remember

God uses the faithful to help those in need.

INVOLVEMENT LEARNING

Enhance your lesson with KJV Bible Student *(from your curriculum supplier) and the reproducible activity page (at www.standardlesson.com or in the back of the* KJV Standard Lesson Commentary Deluxe Edition*).*

Into the Lesson

Write the words "Loss" and "Help" on the board. Ask class members to share times when (1) they received help they needed after experiencing significant loss, and/or (2) they offered help to someone else who had suffered significant loss.

After several have shared, ask class members to identify elements their stories have in common. (*Expect responses such as these:* those experiencing loss could not provide for themselves; those offering help did so at personal sacrifice and/or without expectation of compensation; the helper and the helped grew closer to each other and/or already had a personal relationship; and the help was an expression of the importance of that relationship.)

Lead into Bible study by telling students that an ancient story contains many of their experiences. Say, "As we read today's Scripture, think about who was helped, why the help was offered, and what that help said about the relationship of the two main characters."

Into the Word

Summarize the Lesson Context, explaining why today's Scripture comes from a dark period in Judah's history. Remind students of the events recorded in Ruth 1:1-5.

Tell class members that today they'll read part of the Bible story about Ruth and Naomi. Ask half of the class to read and listen as if they were Naomi, while the other half reads and listens as if Ruth.

Read Ruth 1:6-18. Pause at appropriate points (which you've marked in advance) to ask class members to indicate how they think their assigned character is feeling. (If learners have trouble engaging, voice some of the following emotions, asking for a show of hands after each: happy, sad, calm, excited, angry, laughing, sullen, resigned, etc.) Use areas of disagreement as launching points for discussion. Point out at appropriate times that it's not an either/or choice, that emotions can be mixed.

In such cases, ask class members what two or more emotions are most likely at certain points. Discuss what role emotions should and should not play in making major life-decisions. Encourage explanation of minority viewpoints.

Connect the discussion with the Into the Lesson activity by asking which experiences voiced are closest to that of Naomi and Ruth. Ask learners to explain those similarities. (*Possible responses:* an attempt, like Naomi, to be independent; expressing reality, as Naomi told Ruth and Orpah not to expect more sons from her to be their husbands; insistence, as Ruth, on a certain course of action when logic didn't seem to support the decision)

Option. Distribute copies of the "In-law Diaries" activity from the reproducible page, which you can download. Read today's printed text in the segments indicated on the sheet. After each segment, pause for learners to make entries as indicated. After the last entry, cycle back to the beginning as you ask volunteers to share what they've written.

Into Life

Refer again to "Loss" and "Help." Ask class members to voice situations involving significant loss in your church or community. Ask everyone to brainstorm ways the class can help in the situation; make a plan to do so.

Alternative. Ask class members for examples of loss in their families, circles of friends, or neighborhoods. Explore ways to help by "walking alongside" the grieving in some way in the week ahead. End class with prayers for those who volunteer to do so as they attempt to comfort those suffering loss.

Option. Distribute copies of the "Blessed to Be a Blessing" activity from the reproducible page as a take-home exercise. Ask for volunteers to be ready to share in the next class session what they have written and how things turned out.

A Covenant to Marry

Devotional Reading: Hebrews 13:1-8
Background Scripture: Ruth 1:6-18; 3; 4; Matthew 19:1-12

Ruth 3:1-6, 8-12, 16-18

1 Then Naomi her mother in law said unto her, My daughter, shall I not seek rest for thee, that it may be well with thee?

2 And now is not Boaz of our kindred, with whose maidens thou wast? Behold, he winnoweth barley to night in the threshingfloor.

3 Wash thyself therefore, and anoint thee, and put thy raiment upon thee, and get thee down to the floor: but make not thyself known unto the man, until he shall have done eating and drinking.

4 And it shall be, when he lieth down, that thou shalt mark the place where he shall lie, and thou shalt go in, and uncover his feet, and lay thee down; and he will tell thee what thou shalt do.

5 And she said unto her, All that thou sayest unto me I will do.

6 And she went down unto the floor, and did according to all that her mother in law bade her.

. . . .

8 And it came to pass at midnight, that the man was afraid, and turned himself: and, behold, a woman lay at his feet.

9 And he said, Who art thou? And she answered, I am Ruth thine handmaid: spread therefore thy skirt over thine handmaid; for thou art a near kinsman.

10 And he said, Blessed be thou of the LORD, my daughter: for thou hast shewed more kindness in the latter end than at the beginning, inasmuch as thou followedst not young men, whether poor or rich.

11 And now, my daughter, fear not; I will do to thee all that thou requirest: for all the city of my people doth know that thou art a virtuous woman.

12 And now it is true that I am thy near kinsman: howbeit there is a kinsman nearer than I.

. . . .

16 And when she came to her mother in law, she said, Who art thou, my daughter? And she told her all that the man had done to her.

17 And she said, These six measures of barley gave he me; for he said to me, Go not empty unto thy mother in law.

18 Then said she, Sit still, my daughter, until thou know how the matter will fall: for the man will not be in rest, until he have finished the thing this day.

Key Verse

[Boaz] said, Blessed be thou of the LORD, my daughter: for thou hast shewed more kindness in the latter end than at the beginning. —**Ruth 3:10**

COVENANT IN GOD

Unit 3: Covenant: A Personal Perspective

LESSONS 10–13

LESSON AIMS

After participating in this lesson, each learner will be able to:

1. State the purpose of Ruth's visit to Boaz's threshing floor.

2. Explain how, in light of cultural context, the actions of Ruth and Boaz were conducted with complete integrity.

3. Identify one way to show greater integrity in relationships, and make a plan to implement it personally.

LESSON OUTLINE

Introduction

A. Manipulative Models

The movie *How to Lose a Guy in 10 Days* puts its romantic leads at the mercy of one another. The two meet and immediately begin manipulating one another to win secret bets with their friends. Though they enjoy being together, proving their friends wrong consistently trumps kindness and honesty. Both win their bets, but their self-serving tactics leave the couple deeply hurt. In real life, two people would walk away from this broken relationship.

Selfishness abounds in human affairs, and the pages of Scripture contain many examples. In the period of the judges, we find such examples as Abimelech, who sought the kingship for himself (Judges 9), and Samson, whose narcissistic encounters with the Philistines often served himself instead of Israel (Judges 14–16).

Fortunately, though, people are not always selfish. The book of Ruth portrays several characters who demonstrate selflessness and integrity in their relationships. These characters draw their integrity from the character of the God who works through their actions to advance His benevolent purposes.

B. Lesson Context

Because Ruth had left her home country out of loyalty to her mother-in-law (see Lesson 11), Naomi viewed Ruth's future security as her own responsibility. Ordinarily, a woman's father or other male relatives would arrange her marriage and protect her. This unusual state of affairs left the two women to provide for themselves.

Naomi gave her daughter-in-law her blessing to go into the neighbors' fields and seek permission to glean there to provide for them both (Ruth 2; compare Leviticus 19:9, 10). Ruth ended up in the field of Boaz, a close relative of Naomi's deceased husband, whom the text introduces as a man of standing in his town (Ruth 2:1). Spiritually sensitive readers recognize the providential hand of God in the events (2:3). In due course, Boaz met Ruth and praised her acts of kindness to Naomi. He invoked God's blessing on her and made sure she was safe and provided for during the harvest.

Because this lesson focuses on Ruth's proposal to Boaz, we must address the questionable legality of marriage between an Israelite and a Moabite. The law included certain restrictions about a Moabite not being part of "the congregation of the Lord" (Deuteronomy 23:3; compare Nehemiah 13:1). Such exclusion suggests a prohibition against intermarriage because the offspring of this union would never be included in the spiritual life of Israel.

Centuries later during the time of Ezra, intermarriages with non-Israelites were considered a threat to the purity of the covenant people. Following the Babylonian captivity, the returned exiles were especially aware of the importance of remaining separate from idolatrous influences. The leadership of the community took action to dissolve such marriages (Ezra 9:1, 2; 10:1-5; compare Nehemiah 13:23-37). This separation would help ensure that the Israelites would not become guilty (again) of the sins that had led to the captivity (see Deuteronomy 6:13-15; compare Jeremiah 19:4, 5).

Ruth had affirmed without reservation her allegiance to the God of Israel and severed ties with Moab (Ruth 1:16, 17). One might say she had been adopted into the covenant people. Thus, despite her Moabite nationality, there was no danger of her turning the family line of Elimelech (Naomi's husband) to foreign and false gods.

Because she had embraced God alone, Ruth needed to follow His laws for His people. The need for Ruth to remarry stems from the directive to bear a child for her deceased husband (see Deuteronomy 25:5-10). This practice ensured that the dead man's legacy did not die with him. The practice also provided for the widow. She gained both a husband and a child through the practice of levirate marriage (see Lesson 11 on Ruth 1:11).

Though the concept of kinship is important throughout the Bible, the book of Ruth explores extensively themes of covenantal loyalty within the family. Duties within the family include buying back land sold in times of emergency (Leviticus 25:25-27; Ruth 4:2-6), redeeming family members sold into debt slavery (Leviticus 25:47-49), and avenging murder (Numbers 35:19). For Ruth, the most important kinship obligation was that of levirate marriage (see commentary on Ruth 3:9b below).

I. At Home
(RUTH 3:1-6)
A. Naomi's Commands (vv. 1-4)

1. Then Naomi her mother in law said unto her, My daughter, shall I not seek rest for thee, that it may be well with thee?

Naomi responds to Ruth's expressions of loyalty toward her by answering in kind (see Ruth 1:14-17). She embraces her duty to help Ruth find *rest*, a figurative way of speaking about finding a secure home (see Deuteronomy 28:65; 1 Chronicles 6:31; Lamentations 1:3). Security for Ruth means finding a husband. Naomi chooses the harvest season (Ruth 2:2, 23)—a time of fertility, divine favor, and renewed hope—to move to help Ruth.

What Do You Think?
What should be the criteria in a church's benevolence policy for deciding whom the church is and is not obligated to help?

Digging Deeper
In what ways, if at all, would that policy be different from one you would draw up for yourself personally? Why?

2a. And now is not Boaz of our kindred, with whose maidens thou wast?

The text does not say exactly how Boaz is related to Naomi's late husband (Ruth 2:1), but Naomi views Boaz's kinship as fortuitous. The fact that he is a relative makes him a desirable candidate for marriage to Ruth (see comments on 3:9b).

2b. Behold, he winnoweth barley to night in the threshingfloor.

The scene Naomi describes unfolds one night during the barley harvest. Boaz will be winnowing *barley* at *the threshingfloor*. Such a place is located in the open, outside the city (see Judges 6:37). The winnowing process involves tossing threshed grain into the air so that the wind can blow away the chaff (compare Judges 6:11; Isaiah 41:16; Jeremiah 4:11, 12; Luke 3:17).

3a. Wash thyself therefore, and anoint thee, and put thy raiment upon thee, and get thee down to the floor.

Bathing is not an everyday practice in ancient Israel. Boaz and his fellow workers likely do not *wash* after their day's work. To *anoint* oneself beyond bathing marks a special occasion. Naomi further tells Ruth to take care when dressing. Taken altogether, Naomi's instructions signal to Ruth that tonight is the night to shed the attire of mourning (compare 2 Samuel 12:20; 14:2; Isaiah 61:3), put on regular garments, and present herself as an eligible bride (compare Ezekiel 16:8-12).

3b. But make not thyself known unto the man, until he shall have done eating and drinking.

Naomi anticipates that Boaz will celebrate the harvest with food and drink (see Exodus 34:22; Deuteronomy 16:13-16; Isaiah 9:3). A woman approaching a man at night is highly suspect, so Naomi advises Ruth to be cautious, not letting Boaz or anyone else become aware of her presence too soon. Her visit to the threshing floor is only for Boaz to discover, no one else (see Ruth 3:14).

4. And it shall be, when he lieth down, that thou shalt mark the place where he shall lie, and thou shalt go in, and uncover his feet, and lay thee down; and he will tell thee what thou shalt do.

After Boaz has a good meal and is in a good mood, he will fall asleep near the grain. Then the time will be right for Ruth to make her approach. But with what intent exactly? To seduce a drunken Boaz, in a fashion not unlike Lot's daughters, from which Ruth's people descended (Genesis 19:30-38)? Some opt for this interpretation, and not without reason. Besides the historical precedent, the narrative thus far contains several Hebrew words that are often imbued with sexual connotations: *lieth/lay down* and *uncover*. To lie down together is a common euphemism for sexual intercourse. Additionally, the Hebrew term *feet* is used as a euphemism for male genitalia (see 1 Samuel 24:3; Isaiah 7:20). The writer builds tension and highlights the risk involved in this nighttime scene without spelling out exactly what Naomi expects of Ruth.

The narrative as a whole speaks against the possibility that Naomi intends for an illicit encounter to occur. No doubt she uses Ruth's youth and attractiveness to advantage, and the encounter includes an element of sexual allure. Even so, the narrative portrays the characters as exceptionally virtuous, with integrity and faithfulness to God. Nothing in Boaz's actions thus far suggests that he will respond favorably to Ruth if she presents herself as a common prostitute (compare Genesis 38:15, 16).

The sexual overtones of the story notwithstanding, it is better to assume that Ruth presents herself to Boaz as a woman who has moved past her bereavement and is now available for remarriage. Naomi mitigates the risk of proposing the match to Boaz by sending Ruth herself to open his eyes to the possibility of marriage. Because of their common bond of faith in the God of Israel, Boaz and Ruth will not be, to use Paul's language, "unequally yoked" (2 Corinthians 6:14).

> *What Do You Think?*
> What kinds of counseling cases call for direct advice vs. those that don't?
> *Digging Deeper*
> How will you go about improving your ability to discern one situation from another?

B. Ruth's Compliance (vv. 5, 6)

5, 6. And she said unto her, All that thou sayest unto me I will do. And she went down unto the floor, and did according to all that her mother in law bade her.

Though Ruth had earlier refused her mother-in-law's advice and guidance (Ruth 1:8-17), here she consents to follow her instructions fully (see Ephesians 6:1; Colossians 3:20). Both her disobedience and obedience result from her love for Naomi. Ruth recognizes Naomi's rightful role as her matchmaker in this circumstance. Naomi, who earlier found herself at odds with the Almighty (Ruth 1:13, 20, 21), sees Him at work behind the scenes.

❧ TRUSTING WISE COUNSEL ❧

Mentor relationships are both enriching and, at times, challenging. In order to truly learn, the protégé must trust the guidance of the mentor. We see this in the strong-willed mentorship of Anne Sullivan and her deaf-blind student, Helen Keller. Their historic breakthrough came when Anne splashed water over one of Helen's hands and then signed the word *W-A-T-E-R* into her other hand. Helen understood what Anne was trying to teach her! From that day, Helen trusted Anne, and her life was changed for the better.

Trusting the wise counsel of mentors is often essential in obedience to God. Naomi saw the bigger picture of Boaz's being a well-suited match for her daughter-in-law. She directed Ruth to go to him even though Ruth was a foreigner. Ruth trusted Naomi's directives and experienced God's blessings as a result. Who do you trust to help you seek God's ways in your daily life?   —B. L.

II. At the Threshing Floor
(RUTH 3:8-12)
A. Ruth's Proposal (vv. 8, 9)

8. And it came to pass at midnight, that the man was afraid, and turned himself: and, behold, a woman lay at his feet.

Some hours later, Ruth approaches Boaz quietly and uncovers his *feet* or some portion of his lower body (Ruth 3:7, not in today's text). Given his grogginess, the darkness, and the insecure situation of sleeping out in the open, Boaz is *afraid*. But soon he perceives *a woman . . . at his feet*, perhaps after catching the aroma of perfume. But how does Boaz know that his visitor is not a prostitute who has come from town to offer her services?

HOW TO SAY IT

Abimelech	Uh-*bim*-eh-lek.
Boaz	*Bo*-az.
Deuteronomy	Due-ter-*ahn*-uh-me.
Elimelech	Ee-*lim*-eh-leck.
levirate	*leh*-vuh-rut.
Leviticus	Leh-*vit*-ih-kus.
Moab	*Mo*-ab.
Moabitess	*Mo*-ub-ite-*ess*.
Nehemiah	*Nee*-huh-**my**-uh.
Philistines	Fuh-*liss*-teenz
	or *Fill*-us-teenz.

Visual for Lesson 12. *When you come to Ruth 3:10, start a discussion by pointing to this picture as you ask how integrity and kindness are related.*

9a. And he said, Who art thou?

This is the natural question to determine the woman's identity and, along with it, her intentions. That Boaz knows his visitor to be a woman is confirmed by his use of the word *thou*, since it is feminine in Hebrew.

9b. And she answered, I am Ruth thine handmaid.

Ruth gives her name, but does not refer to herself as a stranger (as in Ruth 2:10), nor does she call herself a Moabitess (compare 1:22; 2:2, 21; 4:5, 10). Her self-designation as *thine handmaid* is the position of a female servant (compare 2:13). This is the first signal to Boaz that Ruth desires marriage.

9c. Spread therefore thy skirt over thine handmaid.

This request presumably refers to the gathered portion of clothing that previously covered Boaz's legs. The Hebrew metaphorically calls this garment Boaz's "wing"; thus Ruth plays on his earlier comment that she has found security and refuge under the "wings" of the God of Israel (Ruth 2:12; compare Ezekiel 16:8). Ruth intimates that she has faith in God's provision. Furthermore, she views Boaz as the instrument in the hands of God to protect and provide for her.

9d. For thou art a near kinsman.

This fact makes Boaz eligible for a levirate marriage with Ruth (see Genesis 38:8; Deuteronomy 25:5-10; commentary on Ruth 1:11 in Lesson 11). Since Ruth's husband (an Israelite) died without heirs, a male relative is expected to step in and produce a son to preserve the family line of the deceased.

B. Boaz's Prospects (vv. 10-12)

10. And he said, Blessed be thou of the LORD, my daughter: for thou hast shewed more kindness in the latter end than at the beginning, inasmuch as thou followedst not young men, whether poor or rich.

Boaz discerns Ruth's intentions rightly, blessing her instead of cursing her. On her actions as a *kindness,* see comments on this term at Ruth 1:8 in last week's lesson. He recalls Ruth's kindness to Naomi (1:8; 2:11) and declares the present action an even greater kindness. Ruth could have ventured on her own and charmed a younger man. But in keeping with her character thus far, she honors her mother-in-law's desires and, by extension, Israel's law.

Because of the legal complications and some other differences between the present situation and the scenarios envisioned in Genesis 38 and Deuteronomy 25, some scholars are disinclined to view Boaz's marriage to Ruth as a levirate marriage (see comments at Ruth 3:12 below). Their thoughts along these lines may be warranted. But even if not strictly of the law concerning levirate marriage, Boaz's forthcoming marriage to Ruth certainly falls within the bounds of tradition, ethics, and cultural expectations of the day.

11. And now, my daughter, fear not; I will do to thee all that thou requirest: for all the city of my people doth know that thou art a virtuous woman.

Just as Ruth has agreed to do all that Naomi instructed (Ruth 3:5), now Boaz agrees to do what Ruth seeks to be done. He recognizes both Ruth's risk in approaching him at night and her honorable intentions. His description of her as *a virtuous woman* uses the same two Hebrew words as found in Proverbs 12:4; 31:3, 10. Thus does Boaz assure Ruth that he will vouch for her reputation in *all the city.*

❧ CHOOSING INTEGRITY ❧

When she was 18 years old, Princess Elizabeth convinced her father, King George VI, to accept her bold choice to join Great Britain's military service. The future Queen of England thus left behind royal regalia for overalls in order to train as a mechanic and truck driver. In becoming a member of her country's armed forces, Elizabeth modeled integrity as she shared the burdens of so many others during World War II.

Ruth also modeled noble character that was noticed by everyone around her. She remained with Naomi and worked hard in the fields to sustain them both. She followed her mother-in-law's directives and approached Boaz with patience. Ruth was loyal and selfless in how she honored Naomi and Boaz. In everything, she demonstrated integrity in her commitment to Naomi's God—the only God there is. How are the choices you make today witnessing to your reputation for integrity, or lack thereof?   —B. L.

12. And now it is true that I am thy near kinsman: howbeit there is a kinsman nearer than I.

Boaz accepts Ruth as his Israelite kin even though she is a Moabitess by birth (see Ruth 2:20). He also acknowledges the issues of legality and social custom involved with Ruth's use of the term *kinsman.* Boaz's own integrity will not allow him to proceed until one hurdle is cleared. The duties of the kinsman must fall first to the nearest male relative, and there is someone more closely related to Elimelech than Boaz (see 4:1). Boaz must therefore defer to that man. Because land inheritance is also at stake, the nearest kin has right of first refusal. He must be given the opportunity to act as the kinsman or decline to do so.

> **What Do You Think?**
> How should we handle situations in which doing the proper thing may appear to others that we're just shifting an obligation onto someone else's shoulders?
>
> **Digging Deeper**
> Consider 1 Thessalonians 4:11, 12; 1 Timothy 3:7; 5:21, 24, 25; and Hebrews 4:13 in light of doing right in God's eyes vs. doing right according to people.

III. At Home Again
(RUTH 3:16-18)
A. Ruth's Account (vv. 16, 17)

16, 17. And when she came to her mother in law, she said, Who art thou, my daughter? And she told her all that the man had done to her. And she said, These six measures of barley gave he me; for he said to me, Go not empty unto thy mother in law.

In Ruth 3:13, 14 (not in today's text), Boaz pledges to redeem Ruth if the nearer kinsman cannot or will not do so. Ruth remains with Boaz until just before daybreak. Then she quietly takes her leave, carrying with her the *six measures of barley* that Boaz has given her. Exactly how much barley this is is uncertain. But the context makes apparent that it is a generous amount.

The gift serves at least two purposes: it confirms Boaz's intention to marry Ruth if he can, and it expresses his appreciation to Naomi. He does not want Ruth to return to Naomi *empty*. The word being translated that way is the same one Naomi used to describe herself when she returned to Judah (Ruth 1:21). The implication is that Naomi's empty days are behind her. God thus works through Boaz on behalf of both women (see Psalm 37:3-5).

What Do You Think?
To whom should you express appreciation in the coming week for a help he or she extended to you recently?
Digging Deeper
What are good criteria for deciding whether expressions of appreciation should or should not be in the form of a material gift?

B. Naomi's Advice (v. 18)

18. Then said she, Sit still, my daughter, until thou know how the matter will fall: for the man will not be in rest, until he have finished the thing this day.

Naomi bids Ruth to *sit* tight and be patient, for the final resolution of the marriage possibility will not take long. Within a few hours she expects Boaz will have the matter resolved (see Ruth 4).

What Do You Think?
What are some ways to offer encouragement in life-changing situations that clearly call for "wait and see" inaction?
Digging Deeper
How would you tailor your response for someone who just has to "do something" vs. someone of a "what will be, will be" mind-set?

Conclusion
A. Good Models Are Hard to Find

Marriage is one of the most sacred covenants that human beings can enter into. Sadly, integrity in this hallowed relationship is all too rare. Some cite "irreconcilable differences" after growing apart for years. Others find, too late, that they were not well-suited to each other from the very beginning of their relationship.

Infidelity abounds in all segments of society. Spouses cheat through social media, visiting illicit websites, concealing text messages, hiding money, etc. Abuses of many kinds contribute to broken marriages.

Scripture does not downplay the lack of good role models, whether in the arena of marriage or elsewhere. The actions of biblical characters are not always noble or exemplary. Even the one described as "a man after [God's] own heart"—David son of Jesse (1 Samuel 13:14; Acts 13:22)—failed miserably (2 Samuel 11). The account in today's lesson, however, presents a shining example of integrity and determination to follow God's principles. There was no manipulation to obtain selfish goals. Naomi, Ruth, and Boaz acted as people of God in the best sense. What models they continue to be!

B. Prayer

Father, form in us an upright character that works to advance Your purposes in the world. We pray for this in Jesus' name. Amen.

C. Thought to Remember

God blesses and uses those who show integrity in relationships.

INVOLVEMENT LEARNING

Enhance your lesson with KJV Bible Student *(from your curriculum supplier) and the reproducible activity page (at www.standardlesson.com or in the back of the* KJV Standard Lesson Commentary Deluxe Edition*).*

Into the Lesson

Pose these questions for whole-class response: 1–What is the strangest or funniest thing you've ever seen at a wedding? (Allow an appropriate number of responses to the first question before asking the second.) 2–What is a wedding custom you wish we could abolish?

Alternative. Distribute copies of the "Hidden Message, Helpful Message" activity from the reproducible page, which you can download. After learners work in pairs for several minutes, ask who can read it. Ask volunteers how they've seen this principle played out with positive or negative examples.

After either alternative, lead into Bible study by saying, "Today we're going to look at a prelude to a wedding. The details of this account may seem strange to us in our time and in our culture. But we will see how the actions demonstrated the integrity of everyone in the story."

Into the Word

Use the questions below in one of two ways: (1) copy and distribute them on listening sheets, to be used as such while someone reads Ruth 3 out loud, or (2) copy and distribute the questions on separate sheets of paper so that each class member ends up with at least one question. If using option 2, have the passage read, then say, "This story likely raises some questions. Our class members want to pose some of those." Ask class members to read their assigned questions in the order below.

1–What did Naomi want for Ruth? *(3:1)*

2–What was special about Boaz? *(3:2, 12)*

3–How did Naomi propose that Ruth make herself available to Boaz as a wife? *(3:3, 4)*

4–How did Ruth react to Naomi's proposal? *(3:5, 6)*

5–How did Boaz react to Ruth's actions? *(3:10-15)*

6–What seems unusual or unfamiliar in this story?

7–What do we conclude about the integrity of Naomi, Ruth, and Boaz from this story?

Expected responses may be found here: 1–Ruth 3:1; 2–3:2, 12; 3–3:3, 4; 4–3:5, 6; 5–3:10-15.

Ask class members to name elements of the story that demonstrate the integrity of Naomi, Ruth, and Boaz. (*Possible responses:* Naomi sought what was best for Ruth; Naomi sought to honor her husband by providing him heirs; Ruth trusted Naomi's suggestion for presenting herself to Boaz; Ruth did not present herself to Boaz in an inappropriate way; Boaz did not take advantage of Ruth but honored her and Naomi with a gift of barley; Boaz acknowledged the rights of another kinsman.)

Fill in gaps in students' understanding by sharing information from the lesson commentary.

Into Life

Ask class members to suggest words or phrases that describe actions of integrity. List these on the board. (*Possible responses:* selflessness, consideration, generosity, respect, honoring God)

Ask class members to give examples from the news or their experience in which these qualities would improve relationships. Then distribute paper for the class members to list at least three relationships they have. These may include relationships family members, coworkers, business partners, fellow church members, or neighbors.

Next, ask class members to circle the relationship on their lists that is the most troubled or tenuous. (If they have not listed a troubled relationship, they should add one now.) Direct them to look at the qualities listed on the board. Ask, "Which of these qualities could you demonstrate to heal that relationship or otherwise make it stronger?" Ask class members to write that quality next to the names they've circled on their sheets.

Alternative. Distribute copies of "My Relationship Matrix" from the reproducible page, to be completed as indicated in one minute. Discuss. (*Option.* Distribute as a take-home activity.)

A Covenant of Love

DEVOTIONAL READING: Hebrews 12:7-13
BACKGROUND SCRIPTURE: Ephesians 5:21–6:4

EPHESIANS 5:21-33

21 Submitting yourselves one to another in the fear of God.

22 Wives, submit yourselves unto your own husbands, as unto the Lord.

23 For the husband is the head of the wife, even as Christ is the head of the church: and he is the saviour of the body.

24 Therefore as the church is subject unto Christ, so let the wives be to their own husbands in every thing.

25 Husbands, love your wives, even as Christ also loved the church, and gave himself for it;

26 That he might sanctify and cleanse it with the washing of water by the word,

27 That he might present it to himself a glorious church, not having spot, or wrinkle, or any such thing; but that it should be holy and without blemish.

28 So ought men to love their wives as their own bodies. He that loveth his wife loveth himself.

29 For no man ever yet hated his own flesh; but nourisheth and cherisheth it, even as the Lord the church:

30 For we are members of his body, of his flesh, and of his bones.

31 For this cause shall a man leave his father and mother, and shall be joined unto his wife, and they two shall be one flesh.

32 This is a great mystery: but I speak concerning Christ and the church.

33 Nevertheless let every one of you in particular so love his wife even as himself; and the wife see that she reverence her husband.

KEY VERSE

[Submit] yourselves one to another in the fear of God. —**Ephesians 5:21**

COVENANT IN GOD

Unit 3: Covenant: A Personal Perspective

LESSONS 10–13

LESSON AIMS

After participating in this lesson, each learner will be able to:

1. List ways that being a Christian affects one's role as husband or wife.

2. Explain why the "everyone to everyone" theory of Ephesians 5:21 is false.

3. Explain why Christian marriages are unique and commit to honoring that uniqueness.

LESSON OUTLINE

Introduction
   A. Not Like the Movies
   B. Lesson Context
I. Transition (EPHESIANS 5:21)
II. Wives and the Lord (EPHESIANS 5:22-24)
   A. What to Do (v. 22)
   B. Why Do It (vv. 23, 24)
      If I Could Turn Back Time
III. Husbands and Christ (EPHESIANS 5:25-32)
   A. Pattern to Repeat (v. 25)
   B. Results to Anticipate (vv. 26, 27)
   C. Fact to Accept (vv. 28-32)
IV. Summary (EPHESIANS 5:33)
      Perfect Union
Conclusion
   A. A Beacon of Light
   B. Prayer
   C. Thought to Remember

Introduction

A. Not Like the Movies

Year after year, star-studded romantic comedies are released by Hollywood for public consumption. People meet, at first hate each other, then share experiences, grow as human beings, and fall blissfully in love. Usually, though not as often as once was the case, the couple's adventure ends in their marriage.

This, the entertainment industry tells us, is what marriage is. Two people are "meant for each other" in their mutual fulfillment. Their romance makes everything right. Their marriage serves as nothing except the exclamation point on their romantic experience of self-fulfillment.

Of course, most married people, and probably most unmarried people, will say that this view of marriage is nonsense. Yet the focus on romantic self-fulfillment still powerfully shapes people's understanding of marriage.

In New Testament times, marriage was as much misunderstood as it is today, though the misunderstanding then was not like ours now. Today's text has much corrective for both.

B. Lesson Context

Our text comes from Paul's letter to the Ephesians. This is known as one of Paul's four Prison Epistles, written while he was in the custody of the Roman military. (The other three epistles designated as such are Philippians, Colossians, and Philemon.) Ephesians was written to Christians in the city of Ephesus, a large, grand city on the west coast of Asia Minor. Paul chose Ephesus as a base for evangelistic efforts in that area. He spent nearly three years in the city (Acts 20:17-21, 31).

The letter itself falls into two parts: a discussion of the nature of the gospel (chapters 1–3) and a discussion of how to live in light of the gospel (chapters 4–6). The second section makes clear that the Christian life is an outgrowth of the Christian faith. It begins with an exhortation to "walk worthy of the vocation wherewith ye are called" (Ephesians 4:1). That is, the recipients were to live according to the gospel message by which God made them members of His people. The story of Jesus—the one who gave His life for the sake of those alienated from Him, the one who now reigns in the heavenly places—determines the life of the Christian. To walk in a manner worthy of the Christian calling is to live as did Jesus, imitating Him by living to bless others, not oneself (5:1, 2).

Our text falls in the middle of this practical discussion, as Paul sets forth what many refer to as a "household code." He discusses each of the common roles in a household—the family and any servants who worked in it—of his time. Throughout the discussion, Paul speaks within the relationships that people commonly knew in that period. But he does something far different from merely affirming the common social order: he infuses every household role with the story of Jesus.

I. Transition
(EPHESIANS 5:21)

21. Submitting yourselves one to another in the fear of God.

This statement concludes a discussion of Christians' shared life in which they (we) instruct and encourage one another as empowered by the Holy Spirit (Ephesians 4:17–5:20). Thus Paul introduces the household code (see the Lesson Context) seamlessly from the discussion he has just concluded.

Paul uses the word translated *submitting* a total of 23 times in his letters. It occurs in contexts of relationships with God (Romans 8:7), with the higher powers of earthly authorities (Romans 13:1, 5; Titus 2:9; 3:1), with spiritual leaders (1 Corinthians 16:15, 16), of Christian wives with husbands (1 Corinthians 14:34; Ephesians 5:24 [below]; Colossians 3:18; Titus 2:5), and others.

HOW TO SAY IT

Corinthians	Ko-*rin*-thee-unz (*th* as in *thin*).
Ephesians	Ee-*fee*-zhunz.
Ephesus	*Ef*-uh-sus.
Epistles	Ee-*pis*-uls.
Leviticus	Leh-*vit*-ih-kus.
Philippians	Fih-*lip*-ee-unz.
tabernacle	*tab*-burr-*nah*-kul.

The phrase *one to another* establishes the context. One theory is that this phrase (which is a single word in the Greek text) means "everyone to everyone." But this theory is overturned when we consider how Paul and other Bible writers actually use this word, which occurs right at 100 times in the New Testament. Those uses reveal that the best understanding is "some to others" (examples: Luke 12:1; John 13:14; 1 Corinthians 11:33; Galatians 6:2; and James 5:16).

Submission to others runs counter to our most stubborn impulses. We naturally want to act for our own benefit, which we assume is in conflict with others' benefit. Paul says, however, that it is the realization of God's existence that compels us to submit. Such realization results in *fear,* which is better understood as holy reverence and awe for God rather than terror.

> *What Do You Think?*
> What steps will you take to make Ephesians 5:21 more of a reality in your life?
> *Digging Deeper*
> What changes will others see as you do so?

II. Wives and the Lord
(EPHESIANS 5:22-24)
A. What to Do (v. 22)

22. Wives, submit yourselves unto your own husbands, as unto the Lord.

The expectation for *wives* to *submit* themselves to their *husbands* is not unusual in Paul's time. People from all corners of the ancient world would say the same. What is distinct is that Paul adds *as unto the Lord.* A Christian wife submits not because it is the cultural custom or expectation, but because she also submits to the Lord Jesus. So her relationship with her husband is to be likened, in some sense, to her relationship with the Lord.

Outside of a Christian perspective, a wife might see submission to a husband as something she does so that she will get in exchange what she needs in the marriage. No, Paul says, this relationship is not based on exchange. Rather, the wife's focus on her husband is that of a disciple who is focused on serving the Lord.

We must be on the alert lest the concept of submission be wrongly taken to imply inferiority. All humans are equal before God, and all men and women have equal access to the salvation offered through Christ (Galatians 3:26-29). But such equality does not negate the fact that God has ordained gender roles. Those roles are based in the order of creation (1 Timothy 2:12-14), not cultural practices.

> ### What Do You Think?
> What are some godly ways for a wife to demonstrate submission to her husband?
> ### Digging Deeper
> How do we distinguish between godly and ungodly ways?

B. Why Do It (vv. 23, 24)

23a. For the husband is the head of the wife, even as Christ is the head of the church.

The wife's submission to her husband is to transcend social convention and reflect the relationship of the church to Christ. The church's submission to Christ is complete and unqualified. Earlier in Ephesians, Paul compared the church with a body and Christ with the head of the body (Ephesians 1:22; 4:15). Paul follows a common metaphor that uses this picture of the head and body to illustrate authority.

❧ *If I Could Turn Back Time* ❧

When my husband and I were starting out, he decided to open a trading account and invest in some small companies. He poured over the stock-market section in the newspaper and selected a handful. I thought it was a waste of time, and I never hesitated to tell him.

A financial dispute soon erupted that threatened our marriage. I insisted that he close the account and sell the stock. I felt justified due to the financial jeopardy in which he had placed our family. In reality, I had squashed him just when he was learning how to support us. Worse, I took away every opportunity for him to learn the love of Christ through my submission to him.

Paul explains that the husband is the head of his family, steering it in a way that is analogous to the way Christ directs the church. Are you making the same mistake I did?   —P. L. M.

23b. And he is the saviour of the body.

Again, the point is not to reinforce the cultural norm of submissive wives. Paul reminds us that for Christ and the church, the head of the body is also *the saviour of the body*. Though we often think of the word *savior* strictly as a religious term, in Paul's time it is most common as a political term. Great kings and generals are called savior because of the brave, noble deeds they do to benefit their people.

Christ, of course, is the Savior who displaces all others. But He does so by sacrificially giving His life, unlike all others. We understand from this statement that Paul's picture is of a gospel-shaped relationship between a man and a woman who are both faithful disciples of Jesus. In this way, the wife submits to a husband who imitates Christ's self-giving humility for her benefit. He has authority because He is Savior, not tyrant.

This observation reminds us that Paul is not addressing dysfunctional relationships. Wives of abusive or neglectful husbands are not called to endure their abuse and demonstrate submission to it. Only with the repentance and commitment of both partners, including their commitment to forgive each other, can Paul's description of marriage exist.

24. Therefore as the church is subject unto Christ, so let the wives be to their own husbands in every thing.

Paul repeats his point to make clear that he is describing distinctly Christian marriage, not conventional marriage grounded in cultural expectations. The grateful, lavish service that the church renders to Christ will be the pattern by which the Christian wife submits to the Christian husband.

So as people look at Christian marriages, they should see transformed relationships. Such marriages are based not on social conventions or even mutual benefits. Rather, they are founded on Christ's sacrificial love for the church and the church's response of service. People will see in such marriages a metaphor of the gospel.

III. Husbands and Christ

(EPHESIANS 5:25-32)

A. Pattern to Repeat (v. 25)

25. Husbands, love your wives, even as Christ also loved the church, and gave himself for it.

Now the instructions turn to husbands, as the comparison with *Christ* and *the church* continues. For *husbands,* who have been granted primacy in marriage by order of creation (again, 1 Timothy 2:12-14), their wives' submission to them must draw self-sacrificial *love* in return. That means seeking the wife's good first, even at great cost to oneself. Christ's sacrifice was complete: He gave His life. It was gracious: He died for unworthy sinners. It was generous: it brought blessing to others. This is Christ's full expression of love, and it is the pattern by which the Christian husband loves his wife.

> ### What Do You Think?
> What are some godly ways many husbands can demonstrate loving self-sacrifice in their marriages?
>
> ### Digging Deeper
> How do we distinguish between godly and ungodly ways?

B. Results to Anticipate (vv. 26, 27)

26. That he might sanctify and cleanse it with the washing of water by the word.

Paul continues to use Christ's love for the church as a pattern for the husband's love for his wife. In so doing, he focuses on what Christ accomplished by His love. That love prompted the Lord to give himself in death to make forgiveness possible. The church is made clean (justified) by the loving self-sacrifice of Christ, purged of the stain of sin by Christ's loving surrender in which the innocent one took the penalty of the guilty. This cleansing has made the church a distinct people: we have been and are being set apart (sanctified) to belong to God, by Christ's act. As a bride is set apart in marriage to belong to her husband, so the church is set apart for Christ (Revelation 21:2).

This comparison sets the agenda for the Chris-

Visual for Lesson 13. *Point to this visual to introduce the discussion question that is associated with Ephesians 5:21.*

tian husband. His love for his wife is to aim for the same outcome as Christ's love for the church, that the wife should fully express her purpose and identity as God's person. The husband loves the wife not for his own gratification but to contribute to her growth and maturity as a person of God. The husband's love expresses the good news of Jesus, both in its self-sacrificial nature and its deeply God-focused aim. This makes the Christian marriage distinct from marriage as practiced in any time or culture.

27. That he might present it to himself a glorious church, not having spot, or wrinkle, or any such thing; but that it should be holy and without blemish.

Christ's loving sacrifice makes the church a reflection of Christ's glory—His true, praiseworthy nature that is revealed in His death and resurrection. Like a bride beautifully adorned for a wedding, the church is adorned with the glory of Christ, made His by Christ's gift of grace and mercy. Christ's cleansing of the church and making it whole, can be compared with an animal without imperfection that is offered in sacrifice in the tabernacle (Leviticus 22:21; Numbers 19:2).

The perfection of Christ's own sacrifice becomes the hallmark of the church's identity and life. The church is remade in Christ's image to belong fully to Him, to be *holy* or set apart to belong to God by forgiveness and transformed lives (see 1 Peter 1:18, 19).

This again becomes the focus of the husband's love for the wife. His is not to focus on himself and his own needs. Rather, his focus is to be on his wife's fulfilling Christ's aim that she become fully His in faith, forgiveness, and life. He wants her not to be adorned to enhance his own prestige but with Christlikeness (1 Peter 3:3, 4). Both husband and wife thereby become living sacrifices (Romans 12:1).

C. Fact to Accept (vv. 28-32)

28. So ought men to love their wives as their own bodies. He that loveth his wife loveth himself.

Paul develops another comparison. The church is Christ's own body, as Paul has said before (Ephesians 1:22, 23; 4:15; 5:23). Christ's identification with His people is part of what Paul learned on the road to Damascus. Jesus asked Paul, a persecutor of the church, "why persecutest thou me?" (Acts 9:4). When Paul (as Saul) persecuted the church, it was as if he were persecuting the Lord personally, because the Lord is so closely identified with the people for whom He gave His life and in whom His Spirit lives. Husbands are to view their wives in the same way. As Jesus repeated the command in calling for His followers to love their neighbors as themselves (Leviticus 19:18; Matthew 22:39), husbands have a particular call *to love their wives* as they love themselves. Even more than in other relationships, spouses are identified with each other, belonging to each other as to no other person (1 Corinthians 7:4).

> ### What Do You Think?
> In what ways can your church improve its premarital counseling program in light of today's lesson?
> *Digging Deeper*
> Consider the benefits and drawbacks of such a program being mandatory.

29. For no man ever yet hated his own flesh; but nourisheth and cherisheth it, even as the Lord the church.

Paul appeals to common sense: people naturally take care of themselves. That is conventional. What is unconventional is the Christian's sense of

self. Christ's identification with His church expands our understanding of ourselves. As Christ sees the church as His body, a spouse is to see self in their marriage partner. The focus, then, is not on one's own needs but the needs of the other who is truly one's own self (Philippians 2:1-4). This is exactly how Christ has regarded the church in His humble self-sacrifice on her behalf (2:5-11).

30. For we are members of his body, of his flesh, and of his bones.

Christians are called to identify "self" in others, to treat others with the same love with which they naturally treat themselves, because of common identity in Christ's *body*. All parts of the body live to serve the other parts (1 Corinthians 12:12-26). The unity between Christ and His people is so powerful that it transforms our most basic understanding of ourselves.

31. For this cause shall a man leave his father and mother, and shall be joined unto his wife, and they two shall be one flesh.

Paul now quotes from Genesis 2:24, the explanation that follows the account of the creation of woman from man. There God shows the man that he has no partner who corresponds to him, who is like him (2:18-20). So God creates the woman from the man's own flesh, effectively dividing the human nature into two kinds, male and female (2:21, 22). The man then reinforces his identity with the woman as he exclaims that the woman is his own bones and flesh (2:23).

This creation account explains God's design in marriage. The man and woman form a coequal partnership as two bearers of God's image (Genesis 1:26, 27). Each is fundamentally different from the other, yet corresponding to one another. Their union brings together the two expressions of the image of God, male and female, that God created at the beginning. No other union features this combination of mutual self-identity and difference. No other except one, that is. See the next verse.

32. This is a great mystery: but I speak concerning Christ and the church.

Husband and wife stand as divinely designed entities. They are the same in terms of being created in the image of God, but obviously different as male and female. Together they form a corresponding union, a partnership equal in worth while differing in roles. Although we are not God, His Holy Spirit indwells us (Acts 2:38, 39). The image of God with which we are stamped has been and is being restored.

But the roles of *Christ and the church* are distinct. The partnership between the Lord and His people is that of the Lord's sending and empowering combined with the church's being sent and being empowered (Matthew 28:19, 20) as we are commissioned to do His work. As we do, we complete the mission that Christ inaugurated when He became like us in our humanity, suffered death in our place, and overcame death in His resurrection (Colossians 1:24-26). Paul calls this a *mystery* as he uses that term elsewhere (Ephesians 1:9; 3:3, 4, 9; 6:19). What God had intended from the beginning is now revealed through Christ.

The exclusive covenant bond of partnership between husband and wife points to the greater bond between the Lord and His people. What an extraordinary, solemn, challenging assertion the apostle gives us!

> *What Do You Think?*
> What steps can Christians take to increase the level of love and respect evident in their marriages?
> *Digging Deeper*
> Research these references to biblical characters as you form your conclusions: Genesis 12:10-20; 16:5; 20:1-13; 1 Samuel 19:11-17; 2 Samuel 6:16-23; Job 2:9, 10; Acts 5:1-10; Acts 18.

IV. Summary

(EPHESIANS 5:33)

33. Nevertheless let every one of you in particular so love his wife even as himself; and the wife see that she reverence her husband.

This is Paul's summary to husbands and wives in Christian marriages. Such marriages are to demonstrate the love of Christ, in contrast with the lesser loves that humans have created for themselves. Christian marriages are to be worthy of the calling by which Jesus' followers are called.

A friend called to share with me an amazing story of how God was working in her life. As soon as I hung up, I cried out to the Lord. I was overwhelmed with my son's troubles at school, my daughter's rebellion at home, and my own exhausting work schedule. In that moment, I sensed God telling me I needed to quit my job.

I had two options: I could demand that my husband accept my decision, or I could come to him with respect. In choosing the latter course of action, I told him respectfully what I sensed I needed to do. His response was one of complete support and assurance that it was the right decision. That moment was a turning point in our marriage as well as in our relationship with Christ.

When husbands love and wives respect, they become a mirror image of God's plan for the church.

—P. L. M.

Conclusion
A. A Beacon of Light

This pattern set forth by Paul in today's lesson challenged the ways people viewed marriage in his day. For people of pagan background, marriage placed the wife under the husband's control for the benefit of the husband. The idea that marriage was for something other than the benefit of the husband was foreign. Yet to walk in a manner worthy of the good news of Jesus demanded that the pagan concept be replaced.

Romance is terrific. The Bible celebrates it (see the Song of Solomon). But romantic love is not the foundational stuff of a Christlike marriage. The Christian couple abandons cultural expectations of marriage and replaces them with Christ's expectations. That will mean not the seeking of fulfillment of self but the losing of self.

B. Prayer

Lord, teach us to love as You love, with grace, forgiveness, and persistence. We pray this in the name of the one who died in our place. Amen.

C. Thought to Remember

Love without self-sacrifice—isn't.

INVOLVEMENT LEARNING

Enhance your lesson with KJV Bible Student *(from your curriculum supplier) and the reproducible activity page (at www.standardlesson.com or in the back of the* KJV Standard Lesson Commentary Deluxe Edition*).*

Into the Lesson

Distribute slips of paper and pencils to your class members. Depending on the situation of your class members, give them one of the following sentences to complete.

If your class is composed of middle-age or older adults: My advice for people just getting married is _____.

If your class is composed of young adults: One way my marriage is different from my parents' marriage is _____.

Give this one to any learners who are single instead of the above: My attitude toward marriage is _____ because _____.

Ask learners to complete the sentences, but not write their names on their slips. Collect the slips, shuffle them, and read them to the class. Name or categorize attitudes toward marriage, based on class members' responses. Then ask, "What makes marriage difficult?" Follow up with, "What makes marriage for Christians is easier or more difficult than marriage for non-Christians?"

Alternative. Distribute copies of the reproducible page, which you can download. Point students to the "Marriage Broken" activity at the top of the page. With a time limit of one minute, have students write descriptions of what seems to be happening in each one. (You can use the "Marriage Mended" part of the reproducible page in the Into Life section.)

Lead into Bible study by saying, "Today, we're going to look at a covenant that's personal, a covenant arrangement that has affected each of our lives in one way or another. I'm talking about marriage. The challenge for us is to decide how a Christian marriage can be more pleasing to God than marriages not governed by Christ."

Into the Word

Distribute an incomplete chart (you prepare) that has 5 columns. Have printed the following as column headers, left to right: *Ephesians 5:21-33 / Christ / Church / Husband / Wife.* Directly underneath the column header *Ephesians 5:21-33,* have the words *Attitude / Actions / Purpose* arranged so they are the titles of three rows that extend underneath the remaining 4 columns. The result should be 12 blank intersections where the other 4 column headers meet the 3 row designators. Form learners into pairs to fill in the 12 blank intersections as the column and row designators suggest.

Alternative. Distribute copies of the lesson text, Ephesians 5:21-33, and challenge pairs of students (but not married to each other) to *underline* all instructions to husbands in the text, to *circle* all instructions to wives, and to *place a star* beside sentences that indicate the reasons for what the text is teaching. Have learners share responses in whole-class discussion.

Ask, "What do you conclude from the fact that Paul sets forth more requirements for husbands than for wives?" After an appropriate amount of discussion, follow up with this question: "Who has the more difficult challenge in obeying this Scripture: husbands or wives?" Discuss.

Into Life

Ask class members to think again about the sentences they completed at the beginning of class. Ask which sentences need to be altered to reflect today's text better. (Reread some of the slips again to refresh memories or stimulate discussion.)

Alternative. Point students to the "Marriage Mended" section of the reproducible page. Allow a maximum of one minute for learners to engage the activity as indicated. Ask for volunteers to share thoughts for whole-class discussion.

Write this sentence on the board: *Christian marriages are unique because* _____. Ask class members to volunteer completions to the sentence. End with a prayer for the marriages represented—and to be represented—in your class.

Student Activity Reproducible Pages

·

Fall Quarter 2018 God's World and God's People

GOD CREATES HEAVENS AND EARTH

SAY WHAT?

People have many different ideas about how our world and the universe came into being. How would you use the first sentence in the Bible, "In the beginning God created the heaven and the earth," to respond to the following statements?

"The universe is eternal. It has always existed, and it always will exist." —————————
——

"The beginning of the universe happened in a spontaneous Big Bang explosion that generated the earth, sun, moon, and stars."————————————————————————————————————
——

"We have no way of knowing how the universe came into being." ——————————————
——

PICTURE THIS!

Take a 5-minute walk. Go outside if the weather is good, or walk inside the building. As you go, use your smart phone or your hands to frame pictures of things or people that you think represent the lesson concepts (creation, light or energy, and separation of light and darkness) as you have understood them in Genesis 1. There are no right or wrong answers! You are looking for scenes that speak to you.

Now select your favorite "photo" and write why it is appropriate for the concept you chose it to represent. For example, you may have taken a picture of a big oak tree with the sun shining through the changing leaves because it reminds you of the light or energy in God's creation.

Concept	Photo Example/Why You Selected It
Creation	
Light or energy	
Separation of light and darkness	

GOD CREATES LIGHTS AND LIFE

SIX DAYS OF CREATION

Today's text (Genesis 1:14-25) describes the fourth, fifth, and sixth days of creation. Read the texts listed below that correspond to the first, second, and third days of creation. List what was created on each day. Compare this list to the fourth, fifth, and sixth days.

Day 1: Genesis 1:3-5

_____

Day 2: Genesis 1:6-8

_____

Day 3: Genesis 1:9-13

_____

Day 4: Genesis 1:14-19

_____

Day 5: Genesis 1:20-23

_____

Day 6: Genesis 1:24, 25

_____

What do you notice about the parallels between Days 1 and 4? _____

Days 2 and 5? _____

Days 3 and 6? _____

How does this pattern demonstrate that God brought order to the universe He made? _____

_____

_____

FOR THE BEAUTY OF THE EARTH

The words to this hymn written in 1864 by Folliott S. Pierpoint describe the glory of God seen in both the creation of the heavens as well as the earth. Read the first two verses and the refrain of this hymn below.

Verse 1:
For the beauty of the earth,
For the glory of the skies,
For the love which from our birth
Over and around us lies.

Refrain:
Christ our God, to Thee we raise
This our hymn of grateful praise.

Verse 2:
For the wonder of each hour
Of the day and of the night,
Hill and vale and tree and flower,
Sun and moon and stars of light.

In the space provided below, write a new verse to this hymn to celebrate God as Creator of a universe filled with endless marvels.

_____

_____

_____

_____

GOD CREATES PEOPLE

Lesson 3, Genesis 1:26-31; 2:4-7, KJV

IN HIS OWN IMAGE

Moses records the Spirit's revelation to him of the creation of man (Genesis 1:26-31). The uniqueness of that element of God's creation is best summarized in the phrase, "in his own image." Complete the following by filling in appropriate vowels. Each will highlight an element of being made in God's image.

1. C R _ _ T _ V _ T _

2. L _ N G _ _ G _

3. W _ L L F _ L N _ S S

4. M _ R _ L   D _ S C _ R N M _ N T (two words)

5. R _ L _ T _ _ _ N S H _ P

6. C _ V _ N _ N T   C _ P _ C _ T _ (two words)

Where do you see each of these in today's texts? Write a short explanation of each to the right of the words above.

What other elements of our correspondence to God's nature and character distinguish us from other elements of His creation?
See John 15:9, 17. _____
See Romans 1:18-20. _____
See Psalm 8, especially verses 1 and 5b. _____

POTTER AND CLAY

In the Spirit's words in Genesis 2:4-7, some see in the creation of Adam an image similar to that of the potter throwing a beautiful pot. Accept that image, and then note the similarities and the differences. One suggestion is made for each.

SIMILARITIES	DIFFERENCES
Both are created for a purpose.	God's creation is animate; a pot is inanimate.
_____	_____
_____	_____
_____	_____

Compare and contrast your lists with those of another class member.

GOD CREATES THE FAMILY

FAMILY

In Genesis 2 and 4, God clearly delineates what a family looks like. There is a husband, a wife, and ideally children, to continue God's plan to fill the earth with people to glorify Him. Adam, Eve, Cain, and Abel are an example, the first example, the precedent.

With the many genealogical listings the Spirit provides in the Word, God emphasizes the importance of family in His plans. See those provided for Jesus, the second Adam, in Matthew 1:1-16 and Luke 3:23-38. Use these Scriptures to put the following names in correct chronological order to finish each sentence: Abraham, Adam, Boaz, David, Isaac, Jacob, Jesse, Judah, Noah, Seth, Shem.

1. He worked through the family of _____.
2. Then He worked through the family of _____.
3. Then He worked through the family of _____.
4. Then He worked through the family of _____.
5. Then He worked through the family of _____.
6. Then He worked through the family of _____.
7. Then He worked through the family of _____.
8. Then He worked through the family of _____.
9. Then He worked through the family of _____.
10. Then He worked through the family of _____.
11. Then He worked through the family of _____.

Then He worked through the family of Mary and Joseph (both descended from David, but from different sons) to bring Jesus into the world by means of a virgin birth.

Now you have a historical overview of God's history to bring about the second Adam, Jesus.

How will you allow God to work through your family?

TWO SEXES

A sin-corrupted world wants to throw off the concept of two sexes. It wants to alter God-revealed relationships between the two He created and declared "very good." Look at each of these texts and write a short truth revealed.

Genesis 1:27 _____ Genesis 2:22 _____

Genesis 4:1 _____ Genesis 5:1, 2 _____

Leviticus 20:10 _____ Romans 1:20, 26, 27 _____

ANOTHER FAMILY

Though the New Testament continues its picture of the ideal family and interrelationships with its members, it speaks also of another family, the church fellowship. But the purpose remains the same: to glorify God. Look at Ephesians 5:22–6:4 for the Spirit's comparison of the family to the church. What resembles the physical family in the spiritual family? What is different?

SIMILARITIES
Love is the guiding principle.

_____

_____

_____

DIFFERENCES
The human family has "spots and blemishes."

_____

_____

_____

GOD CONFRONTS SIN

A TREE AND A TEMPTATION

Today's text (Genesis 3:8-17, 20-24) describes the events following the woman and man eating fruit from the tree of the knowledge of good and evil. Using the texts provided, answer the questions that provide the background for today's text.

1. According to Genesis 2:8, 9, what did God plant in Eden?

2. According to Genesis 2:16, 17, what was God's command to the man about the trees?

3. According to Genesis 2:17, what was the punishment if the man ate from the tree of the knowledge of good and evil?

4. According to Genesis 3:1, how did the serpent twist the command of God in Genesis 2:17?

5. According to Genesis 3:3, how did the woman change the command of God in Genesis 2:17?

6. According to Genesis 3:4, 5 how does the serpent tempt the woman?

7. According to Genesis 3:6, why does the women eat the fruit?

8. According to Genesis 3:7, what was the result of the woman and her husband eating the fruit?

CONFESSION AND REPENTANCE

Sin is a reality. All have sinned. We cannot hide our sins from God, yet we do try. Believers accept the responsibility for their sins and seek reconciliation with God and others through confession and repentance. Silently reflect on the answers to the following questions.

What sins have you committed? Which sins do you commit regularly?

What is a consequence for your sin?

How has your sin affected your relationship with God?

Who else have you hurt as a result of your sin?

What sin do you need to repent of today in order to restore your relationship with God?

What relationships do you need to restore? What can you do to restore those relationships?

Read Psalm 51:1-14.

Ask God to forgive your sin and give you guidance in restoring the relationships damaged by your sin. Thank God for His forgiveness and provision.

THE RIGHTEOUSNESS OF NOAH

Lesson 6, Genesis 6:9b-22, KJV

WARNING SIGNS FOR TODAY

The people of Noah's day were not following God. What caution or warning signs might God post on the earth TODAY to direct people to abandon sin? Complete possible warning signs below and list a possible Scripture reference for each.

**STOP WARNING DO NOT CROSS   DO NOT ENTER   DANGER
CAUTION   KEEP OUT TOXIC DO NOT TOUCH 404**

Possible Scripture References

1. Slow! _____   _____

2. Beware! _____   _____

3. Wash Hands! _____   _____

4. Caution! _____   _____

5. Warning! _____   _____

6. No Lone Zone _____   _____

7. Danger! _____   _____

8. No Entrance! _____   _____

Which signs might God post primarily outside the church? Which might He post primarily inside the church? Why?

_____

_____

_____

_____

▼▼DO NOT CROSS▼▼DO NOT CROSS▼▼DO NOT CROSS▼▼DO NOT CROSS▼

Graphics: © adekvat | iStock | Thinkstock©

THE CALL OF ABRAM

Lesson 7, Genesis 10:1; 11:10, 27, 31, 32; 12:1-4, KJV

FAMOUS ANCESTORS

Match the celebrity on the right with his or her famous ancestor on the left.

Ancestor	**Descendant**
___ 1. Abraham Lincoln	A. Katherine Hepburn
___ 2. Benito Mussolini	B. Ozzy Osbourne
___ 3. Thomas Jefferson	C. Lee Marvin
___ 4. Jesse James	D. Brad Pitt
___ 5. King Louis IV of France	E. Sophia Loren
___ 6. King Henry II of England	F. Tom Hanks

PROMISE SEARCH

Find the following words related to the word *Promise* in the Word Search below.

```
A R M Y H P O H R T K O E P G
I C E K L M F C N I A H Y S P
P B F P K L E E H E I F E W H
T A A W O V M J H H A T E C X
K C I B G T T N P B Y H T A O
T H T P I J K X L C Z Z N G G
H J U M R A U K E E Q B A S P
S E M X A O Y O D Y U B R L Q
M O V O U U M Z G D H D A F K
C X H X M P X I E I Q Y U X F
K W X C P B B K S K P V G B X
C O V E N A N T L E G K L N I
```

Commitment

Covenant

Guarantee

Oath

Pact

Pledge

Promise

Vow

What has been the impact of God's promises in your life?

_____

_____

_____

_____

THAT'S IMPOSSIBLE

Match the quote on the left with its source on the right.

__1.	"It always seems impossible until it's done."	A. Lewis Carroll (author of *Alice's Adventures in Wonderland* and *Through the Looking Glass*).
__2.	"Sometimes I've believed as many as six impossible things before breakfast."	B. Sir Walter Scott (Scottish novelist, playwright, and poet).
__3.	"To the timid and hesitating everything is impossible because it seems so."	C. Walt Disney (Animation pioneer).
__4.	"It's kind of fun to do the impossible."	D. Marcus Aurelius (Emperor of Rome).
__5.	"Because a thing seems difficult for you, do not think it impossible for anyone to accomplish."	E. Nelson Mandela (President of South Africa).

BIBLE BABIES

Isaac wasn't the only baby in the Bible who was predicted or about whom information was made known before birth. Try to identify each one without looking up the reference.

Information	Reference	Who was this baby?
1. His parents were to never cut his hair.	Judges 13:2-7	1.
2. He leaped in the womb when his cousin (who was also in the womb) came close.	Luke 1:44	2.
3. He was consecrated by God before he was born	Jeremiah 1:5	3.
4. He was covered by God in his mother's womb	Psalm 139:13	4.
5. Of His kingdom there will be no end.	Luke 1:26-33	5.

THE MARRIAGE OF ISAAC

Lesson 9, Genesis 24:12-21, 61-67, KJV

TRUST AND OBEY

Work in groups of two or three to compose a new verse to the hymn "Trust and Obey." Write a verse that is specific to today's challenges. The meter is 6.6.9, which essentially means two lines of six syllables each followed by a line of nine syllables. Each verse has two sets of those.

The Current Verses:

1	When we walk with the Lord In the light of His Word, What a glory He sheds on our way! While we do His good will, He abides with us still, And with all who will trust and obey.	4	But we never can prove The delights of His love, Until all on the altar we lay; For the favor He shows, And the joy He bestows, Are for them who will trust and obey.
2	Not a shadow can rise, Not a cloud in the skies, But His smile quickly drives it away; Not a doubt or a fear, Not a sigh or a tear, Can abide while we trust and obey.	5	Then in fellowship sweet We will sit at His feet, Or we'll walk by His side in the way; What He says we will do; Where He sends, we will go, Never fear, only trust and obey.
3	Not a burden we bear, Not a sorrow we share, But our toil He doth richly repay; Not a grief nor a loss, Not a frown or a cross, But is blest if we trust and obey.	Chorus	Trust and obey, For there's no other way To be happy in Jesus, But to trust and obey.

The New Verse

_____

_____

_____

_____

_____

_____

Siblings' Rivalry

What's Your Family's Conflict Style?

Examine the conflict styles listed below. For each method identify a family member who uses that one. Be sure to pick one for yourself!

Conflict Style	Description	Who?
1. Avoidance	Refuses to bring up or discuss difficult topics.	
2. Accommodation	Gives in to everyone's wishes for the sake of peace at any price.	
3. Competition	Stands ground; must come out on top, even if the other person loses out.	
4. Compromise	Gives up something in order to resolve the issue.	
5. Collaboration	Seeks win-win solutions where what's important to each person is addressed.	

Conflict in Scripture

Where do the situations in the following references fit, if at all, in the above five categories? Which, if any, fit in more than one?

Scripture	Avoidance	Accommodation	Competition	Compromise	Collaboration
Genesis 26:19-22					
Genesis 30:25-34					
Matthew 17:27					
Acts 6:1-7					
Acts 15:36-41					
Philippians 4:2, 3					

JACOB'S DECEPTION

Lesson 11, Genesis 27:5-10, 18, 19, 21-29, KJV

HOW NOT TO BE SCAMMED

Jacob pulled a fast one on his father, Isaac, and deceived him. Here are some of the common scams or deceptions we must beware of today.

Identity theft: Someone wrongfully uses another person's personal data fraudulently. This can involve bank accounts, credit cards, medical expenses, or tax returns.

Fake charities: Instead of helping people in need, these fakes keep the money for themselves. Some crooks try to fool people using names that are similar to those of legitimate charities.

Have you ever been the victim of a scam? How did it turn out?

Did you ever use any of the following in order to protect yourself from being deceived?

- **Know who you're dealing with.** Call the Better Business Bureau or consumer protection agency to see if the organization is credible.
- **Guard your personal information.** Don't provide your credit card or bank account number unless you are paying for something and know the organization is valid.
- **Be cautious about unsolicited e-mails.**   • **Don't believe promises of easy money.**
- **Fully understand every offer.**   • **Check your credit reports regularly.**

DECEPTIVE EXCUSES

Look at the common deceptive excuses below. Suggest polite but truthful replacement answers.

Deceptive Excuse	Truthful Response
1. "I was late because of traffic."	
2. "I'd love to go to the baseball game, but I've got something else planned."	
3. "I didn't think you'd mind if I borrowed your sweater without asking."	
4. "That dent was there when we picked up the car."	
5. "I'm too full to eat another bite."	

JACOB'S DREAM

TOO BUSY TO REMEMBER?

Below each column of boxes, there is a column of letters. Choose from the letter column to fill in the boxes directly above it. Mark off each letter as you use them. (Hint: Start with the columns with single letters.) The quote is a paraphrase of a prayer by Lord Jacob Astley.

Created by puzzlemaker. discoveryeducation.com

```
        U              E            F S O
   H O L    R D    Y Y O I    U O R G B T
   T O W A B D S I F O U    F N R G E T
   Y O D O Y U O M N I T M K O T W E E
```

TABLE OF BLESSING

Plan a night to celebrate God's blessing in your life!

Who will you invite, and why? _____
_____
_____

How will you explain the evening to your guests?_____
_____
_____

How will the menu items illustrate the theme of the celebration? _____
_____
_____

How will your acknowledgement of God's blessings be like and unlike Jacob's acknowledgement in Genesis 28:20-22?_____
_____
_____

GOD'S BLESSING

Lesson 13, Genesis 30:22-32, 43, KJV

WHAT EACH GENERATION WANTS FROM WORK

While sociologists debate the exact years for the following generations, these parameters are general descriptions for characteristics of those born in certain years and their attitudes for what they want from their work environment.

Name of Generation	Years Born	Desires from Work Situation
Millennials	1983 to 2004	Mentoring, flexible hours, work-life balance, the chance for overseas assignments
Generation X	1965 to 1982	Career development services, flexible hours to accommodate families, access to information networks
Baby Boomers	1946 to 1964	Financial planning services, wellness initiatives, and recognition programs
Silent or Greatest Generation	1920s to mid-1940s	Phased retirement options

Does this description match your personal experience?

Speculate on why each generation values the work benefits it does.

Is it easy or difficult to view your salary and benefits as coming from God's hand?

How might a Christian and a non-Christian have differing attitudes toward work?

HOW GRATITUDE CHANGES US

Gratitude changes us! Reflect on how that happens in the four areas below.

	How It Happens	When It Happens	Where It Happens
Thoughts			
Attitudes			
Relationships			
Worship			

This is one step I can take to increase my gratitude this week: _____

Lesson 2

Six Days of Creation, Part 1: Day 1=Light was created and God separated light from the darkness. Day 2=Waters were separated above the earth to create the sky above. Day 3=Water gathered together into seas to create dry land. God created plants and trees. Day 4=Sun, moon, and stars were created. Day 5=Animals were put in the sky and the seas. Day 6=Animals were made for the land.

Six Days of Creation, Part II: Day 1=God creates light and on Day 4 God creates that which provides the light. Day 2=God creates water above and below and on Day 5 God fills both with animals. Day 3=God creates land and on Day 6 He fills the land with animals. There is a specific order in which God creates. First He creates the space and then in the same order creates that which fills the space.

Lesson 3

In His Own Image, Part 1: 1=Creativity. 2=Language. 3=Willfulness. 4=Moral Discernment. 5=Relationship. 6=Covenant Capacity. Further explained in the following: 1=the desire to make something new and glorious. 2=sophisticated speech. 3=ability to decide. 4=knowledge of good and evil. 5=desire to be in communion with other people. 6=the ability and desire to enter agreements with others.

In His Own Image, Part 2: John, capacity for love; Romans, awareness of God's existence and expectations; Psalms, ability to analyze and appreciate the intricacies of the creation; learners may also suggest such characteristics as desire for communion with others, thinking/cognition, and an understanding of death and its inevitability.

Potter and Clay, possible answers: *Similarities*: both are thoughtfully planned; both are entirely at the will of the one who creates; both have aesthetics and function. *Differences*: man is filled with a God-breathed soul, the pot only empty space; the one—man—was created to be eternal, the pot, temporal; man was declared "very good," perfectly made, but pots are sometimes recast because of flaws.

Lesson 4

Family: 1=Adam. 2=Seth. 3=Noah. 4=Shem. 5=Abraham. 6=Isaac. 7=Jacob. 8=Judah. 9=Boaz. 10=Jesse. 11=David.

Another Family: *Similarities*: There is a structure of responsibility and authority; the more mature have responsibility to the less mature; one must be born into both. *Differences*: The physical family has "spots and blemishes," the true church is completely glorious; physical birth does not automatically make one a part of the spiritual family. That necessitates "new birth."

Lesson 5

A Tree and a Temptation: 1=A garden, all kinds of trees, tree of life, tree of the knowledge of good and evil. 2=Free to eat from any tree, but must not eat from the tree of the knowledge of good and evil. 3=Death. 4=He said they weren't allowed to eat from any tree. 5.=Not allowed to touch the fruit of the tree. 6=Tells her she will not die, her eyes would be open, she would be like God. 7=She sees it is pleasing to the eye, desirable for gaining wisdom. 8=Eyes were opened, realized they were naked, covered themselves.

Lesson 6

Warning Signs for Today: *Possible Scripture references* 1=Slow–James 1:19. 2=Beware–Colossians 2:8. 3=Wash Hands–James 4:8. 4=Caution–1 Timothy 5:14. 5=Warning–Hebrews 11:7; 12:25. 6=No Lone Zone–Hebrews 10:25. 7=Danger–Matthew 5:22. 8=No Entrance–Revelation 21:27.

Lesson 7

Famous Ancestors: 1–F; 2–E; 3–C; 4–B; 5–A; 6–D.
Promise Search:

```
                    T
                 N
         P     E              E
     A W O V M              E E
   C     T     P       H T A O
 T   P I       L           N
     M R       E           A R
     M         D     M     A U
   O           G     I     R A
 C             E     S     U G
 C O V E N A N T   E
```

Lesson 8

That's Impossible: 1=E. 2=A. 3=B. 4=C. 5=D.
Bible Babies: 1=Samson. 2=John the Baptist. 3.=Jeremiah. 4=David. 5=Jesus.

Lesson 10

What's Your Family's Conflict Style: Responses will be subjective.

Lesson 11

Deceptive Excuses: Possible Answers. 1="I'm sorry for being late; I should have given myself some extra time." 2="No thank you. I don't enjoy sporting events." 3="I'm sorry. I should have asked you first." 4="That dent was caused when I backed into a pole." 5="The spices in this dish don't agree with me."

Lesson 12

Jacob's Dream:

Lesson 13

What Each Generation Wants from Work: https://www.recruiter.com/i/what-each-generation-wants-from-employers/

Student Activity Reproducible Pages

·

Winter Quarter
2018–2019
Our Love for God

LOVE AND OBEY GOD

LIKE-MINDED

Rate how much you enjoy the objects or activities below using this scale:

                    5 = really enjoy
                    4 = like
                    3 = feel indifferent
                    2 = dislike somewhat
                    1 = really don't like

__ dogs	__ auto races	__ pizza
__ music	__ cats	__ movies
__ honey	__ football	__ flowers
__ milk	__ Bible study	__ anchovies

If time allows, compare and contrast your results with those of your classmates.

FAMOUS FAREWELL ADDRESSES

Whether you are a world political leader or an everyday servant of God, what you pass on to others can significantly shape their lives and their futures. Read the following Bible verses and famous speech quotations. In the blank below each quote, write your best guess of who gave the farewell address.

1. "As we peer into society's future, we . . . must avoid the impulse to live only for today, plundering for our own ease and convenience the precious resources of tomorrow. We cannot mortgage the material assets of our grandchildren without risking the loss also of their political and spiritual heritage. We want democracy to survive for all generations to come, not to become the insolvent phantom of tomorrow."

_____

2. "Now unto God and our Father be glory for ever and ever. Amen. Salute every saint in Christ Jesus. The brethren which are with me greet you" (Philippians 4:20, 21). _____

3. "I go the way of all the earth: be thou strong therefore, and shew thyself a man; and keep the charge of the Lord thy God, to walk in his ways, to keep his statutes, and his commandments, and his judgments, and his testimonies . . . that thou mayest prosper in all that thou doest, and whithersoever thou turnest thyself" (1 Kings 2:2, 3). _____

4. "Teaching them to observe all things whatsoever I have commanded you: and, lo, I am with you alway, even unto the end of the world. Amen" (Matthew 28:20). _____

5. "The lesson of all this was, of course, that because we're a great nation, our challenges seem complex. It will always be this way. But as long as we remember our first principles and believe in ourselves, the future will always be ours. And something else we learned: Once you begin a great movement, there's no telling where it will end. We meant to change a nation, and instead, we changed a world." _____

LOVE AND SERVE GOD

SERVE THE LORD

In the word search puzzle below, find these 10 words taken from the Joshua 24:1-3, 13-15, 21-24 passage.

Abraham
Canaan
Choose
Gods
Israel

```
C K V T E I O B E Y R S
E A K J S V W L D U E A
F N N R W J R K I S L T
O P A A Y P V E S F S V
X E K L A S T E S F D E
L C K D R N N U Q X O D
W H R I I T O Q X V G L
C O B O I A B R A H A M
L O X W A U H S O J A F
E S Z D X G G Y F R D I
J E U P W E H L M A A R
N U A X N E D B W V D K
```

Joshua
Lord
Obey
Serve
Witnesses

Puzzle made at puzzlemaker.discoveryeducation.com

SIGNS OF YOUR FAITH?

Evaluate the potential usefulness or harm of using Christian products as self-reminder and to a witness to your service to God in light of today's key thought: "As for me and my house, we will serve the Lord" (Joshua 24:15).

	Helpful self-reminder	Harmful self-reminder	Useful as a witness	Harmful as a witness
Bumper sticker	___	___	___	___
Wristband	___	___	___	___
T-shirt	___	___	___	___
Plaque	___	___	___	___
Other	___	___	___	___

LOVE AND WORSHIP GOD

SATISFIED WITH GOOD THINGS

Unscramble these words found in Psalm 103. Copy the letters in the numbered blanks to the blanks at the bottom to figure out the message.

1. HERTAF

__ __ __ __ __
1

2. SESSADEI

__ __ __ __ __ __ __
4 13 11

3. TINBEEFS

__ __ __ __ __ __ __ __
8   7

4. TOSRUESSHENGI

__ __ __ __ __ __ __ __ __ __ __ __ ' __
6   3   12 16

5 GEART

__ __ __ __ __
15   5

6. RITNLASVEEG

__ __ __ __ __ __ __ __ __ __
10   9   2 14

__ __ __ __ __ __ __ __ __ __ __ __ __ __ __ __
1 2 3 4 5 6 7 8 9 10 11 12 13 14 15 16

PRAISE JOURNAL

In Psalm 103 David begins by praising the Lord and listing many reasons why He deserves praise. Now it's your turn to praise Him!

Bless the Lord, _____, bless His holy name!
                  (your name)
Bless the Lord, and don't forget all of the reasons why you are praising Him!

List three reasons why you praise Him.

I praise You because _____.

I praise You because _____.

I praise You because _____.

Lord, You have been merciful and gracious to me. I have seen Your mercy and love when . . .

_____

_____

LOVE GOD FOR THE GIFT OF JESUS

THE BIG ANNOUNCEMENT

There are 15 incorrect words in the mangled reproduction of Luke 1:26-31 below. With Bibles closed circle the incorrect words and write the correct word(s) above the words you circled.

In the seventh month the angel Michael was sent from God unto a city of Galilee, named Bethlehem, to a widow espoused to a man whose name was Simeon, of the house of Levi; and her name was Martha. And the angel came in unto her, and said, Hail, thou that art barely favoured, the Lord is with thee: blessed art thou among peasants. And when she saw him, she was comforted at his saying, and cast in her mind what manner of farewell this should be. And the angel said unto her, Fear much: for thou hast found favour with God. And, behold, thou shalt conceive in thy womb, and bring forth a daughter, and shalt call her name Immanuel.

THE GIFT OF JESUS

Simeon received a magnificent gift by being permitted to see and recognize Jesus, the Lord's Christ, the Messiah. As you think about things we know about Simeon, consider in what ways these things do or do not apply to you.

What We Know About Simeon	Does/Doesn't Apply to Me
Guided by the Holy Spirit (Luke 2:25a, 27)	
Just and devout (Luke 2:25b)	
Waiting for the Messiah, "the consolation of Israel" (Luke 2:25c)	
Realized the purpose of his life (Luke 2:26, 29)	
Able to recognize the fulfillment of God's promises (Luke 2:30-32)	

LOVE GOD AND SERVE OTHERS

Lesson 5, Matthew 25:31-46, KJV

VIGNETTES OF KINDNESS

Vignette 1

MARIE *(hearing a knock on her door)*: Hi, Denise.

DENISE *(talking hurriedly)*: Hi, Marie. I'm sorry to bother you, but I was wondering if I could borrow a stamp.

MARIE: Sure, no problem. Come in out of the cold. I have a stamp right here.

DENISE: Oh, that's great. After I wrote checks and used up all my stamps to pay bills this morning, I remembered I had a personal letter to mail as well, and I was one stamp short.

MARIE *(handing her a stamp)*: Here you go.

DENISE *(reaching out her hand)*: And here's the money for it.

MARIE: Oh, forget about it. You can lend me a stamp when I run out.

As Denise lays the envelope on the table to attach the stamp, Marie peeks down at it, then exclaims: What! You're writing to that Ruthford guy in prison? He's the one who broke into both of our houses! Why would you write to him?

DENISE: I just feel sorry for him. I found out his mother is very ill right now, so she isn't able to visit him.

MARIE: He should have thought about that before he became a burglar. How did you find out about his mother?

DENISE: Oh, I stopped by to find out which prison he's in, and there she was, sick from chemo.

MARIE: Poor lady. What a jerk her son was to get in trouble and leave his mother in the lurch. Why are you writing to him?

DENISE: I wanted to let him know I forgive him. I may even go visit him. He's barely out of his teen years. I thought he could use some encouragement.

MARIE: Well, you're a better person than me. I say, "Good riddance to bad rubbish!"

DENISE: Thanks again for the stamp. See you later.

MARIE: Sure thing. Bye, Denise.

Vignette 2

ALONSO *(waving hello)*: Hey, Derek. I'm trying to finish up snowblowing before I go to work, and I just ran out of gas. Do you have any I could borrow?

DEREK: Sure thing. I got the gas can right here. My snowblower's all filled up, so help yourself.

ALONSO: Oh, that's great. Thanks so much. I'll fill it up tonight and bring it back.

DEREK: Sounds good. But why are you still snowblowing? Your driveway is clean as a whistle.

ALONSO: Yes, but I always do my neighbor's driveway whenever I do mine. And he won't be able to get out if I don't finish.

DEREK: You don't mean old man Jackson's driveway, do you? He's the grouchiest man around. I try to stay as far away from him as possible. Does he pay you to do it?

ALONSO: Oh, no. I just do it to help him out. He's got arthritis real bad and can't do it himself. And he needs to drive his wife to dialysis several times a week.

DEREK: Well, I hope at least he appreciates what you do.

ALONSO: Whether he does or not, I know he needs the help. Got to dash. Thanks, Derek.

DEREK: You bet. Bye.

Walk in Love

CAN YOU SPOT A LIAR?

According to FBI interrogation experts, there are telltale clues that a person is lying. Indicate whether each statement is a good sign that the person is Lying (L) or Truthful (T).

__ 1. They can tell their story chronologically forwards and backwards.

__ 2. They use a lot of words and tell their account in considerable detail.

__ 3. They use mostly first person pronouns (I, my) rather than third person pronouns (he, she, it).

__ 4. They say the word *no* with a drawn-out sound (noooooo) or in a singsong voice.

__ 5. They speak faster and more loudly than usual.

__ 6. They are obviously infuriated at being accused.

__ 7. They answer questions simply and directly.

__ 8. They point their feet toward the exit.

WHAT'S LOVE GOT TO DO WITH IT?

Paul prays for the Thessalonians that their hearts will be directed "into the love of God." John states that Christians are to "love one another" and "walk in [love]." Yet other things these apostles say may seem very unloving (compare 2 Thessalonians 3:6, 14; 2 John 10). Within the heart below explain why the directives of Paul and John are indeed based in love.

Paul identifies some people as "wicked," and he prays to be delivered from them.

John identifies certain people as "deceivers" and "antichrist." He tells the Christians not to take them into their houses or even greet them.

Graphic: © RedlineVector / iStock / Getty Images Plus

IMITATE CHRIST

Lesson 9, Philippians 2:1-11, KJV

LEVELS OF AUTHORITY

Put the following designations in order of rank, from lowest (8) to highest (1).

__ Major   __ Colonel
__ Captain   __ Brigadier General
__ Master Sergeant   __ Lieutenant
__ Major General   __ Lieutenant General

In what ways does a person's rank or status have the potential of interfering with his or her relationships?

_____

_____

_____

HIDDEN MESSAGE

Cross out words in the following categories to reveal a hidden message that gives the first step in getting along with others.

Vegetables   Words that have more than one "o"
Words that rhyme with "dark"   Animals
Furniture   Words with double consonants

carrot	mark	care	dog	chair	look
about	chest	pig	lark	opposite	bear
peas	what	loony	is	lettuce	stark
beginning	meaningful	table	to	sofa	happen
park	other	giraffe	annoyed	people	desk

Hidden message:

_____

_____

_____

ULTIMATE PRIZES?

Match the world-famous prize with its description.

___ 1. Nobel Peace Prize	A. For achievements in newspaper, magazine, journalism, literature, and musical composition.
___ 2. Academy Award	B. For outstanding achievement in music performance.
___ 3. The Pulitzer Prize	C. One of the five awards, the other four being for work in chemistry, physics, medicine, and literature.
___ 4. Grammy Award	D. Honors a living person who has made an exceptional contribution to affirming life's spiritual dimension, whether through insight, discovery, or practical works.
___ 5. The Templeton Prize	E. Any one of 24 awards for artistic and technical merit in the American film industry.

LOSSES AND GAINS

What have you lost or gained since becoming a Christian? Read and consider Matthew 10:39; Mark 10:28-31; and Luke 14:26 in your responses.

Category	What have you *lost* because of your faith in Christ in this area of life?	What have you *gained* because of your faith in Christ in this area of life?
Relationships		
Vocation		
Purpose		
Dreams		

OUR LOVING GOD

FOLLOW THE LEADER?

List the country with which each leader on the left is associated. Each country on the right can be used only once.

Alexander the Great   _____   A. Canada

Catherine the Great   _____   B. France

Genghis Khan   _____   C. Greece

Gustavus Adolphus   _____   D. India

Joan of Arc   _____   E. Mongol Empire

Mahatma Gandhi   _____   F. Russia

Nelson Mandela   _____   G. South Africa

Pierre Trudeau   _____   H. Sweden

Queen Victoria   _____   I. United Kingdom

BE AN OVERCOMER

What things about modern culture tend to block a truthful view of God's being in control and protecting us? Rank-order the following list from 1 (most serious) to 8 (least serious).

___ A. National nightly news reports   ___ B. Local nightly news reports

___ C. Talk shows   ___ D. Entertainment choice and temptations

___ E. Vested interests   ___ F. The court system

___ G. Overt persecution of Christians   ___ H. Redefinition of truth as personal to the individual

Where do you most agree with your fellow students? Why?

_____

_____

_____

_____

Where do you most disagree with your fellow students? Why?

_____

_____

_____

_____

OUR MIGHTY GOD

Lesson 12, Psalm 66:1-9, 16-20, KJV

SING AND SHOUT

Read Psalm 66. The hidden words for the puzzle are the answer to the clues.

```
H U P O W E R S W A K D
A A E T V E I R O N Y E
P B T E I N W E U C S Y
C Z Z Y G K F Y A I A X
B V Q A H W C A A C C N
S E I M E N E R O N U Z
E E I X A C P P L O U N
M W A C R K I T L G K N
H S J R T X J O U H X K
T M H S T W I T J O R Y
S M Y K U H A F A E Z U
E U Y L Z K J J U I R W
```

Discoveryeducation.com/free-puzzlemaker

Clues

1. Talking to God _____
2. Strength or might _____
3. Personal opponents _____
4. Populated planet _____
5. Expressing approval _____
6. Produce melodious sounds _____
7. To be glad _____
8. Center of emotions _____

BOASTING ABOUT GOD

Psalm 66 celebrates God's supreme name, power, and works. Use that as inspiration to suggest ways "all the earth" (v. 4)—including you—can brag about God and "make his praise glorious" (v. 2) today. See also Psalm 44:8.

_____
_____
_____
_____
_____
_____
_____

"In God we boast all the day long, and praise thy name for ever."

(Psalm 44:8, KJV)

OUR RESCUING GOD

Lesson 13, Psalm 91:1-8, 11-16, KJV

METHODS OF PROTECTION

Make the single best match between the list of protective things on the left with the thing protected from on the right. Each entry on the right is to be used only once.

__ 1. Sunscreen

__ 2. Air bags

__ 3. Barry Manilow songs played over speakers

__ 4. Bike helmet

__ 5. Digital Rights Management

__ 6. Doormat that says "The neighbors have better stuff"

__ 7. Deep mountain bunker

A. Copyright infringement on software

B. Nuclear war

C. Burglars

D. Loitering teenagers

E. Brain injury

F. Traffic accident

G. Sunburn

While people are able to protect themselves from some dangers, God is able to protect and rescue from all threats, no matter the circumstances. When was a time He protected you?

_____

_____

IN NEED OF PROTECTION

Find the words on the right that describe things from which we need God's protection and rescue.

```
D F T D Z W R C E H V V Z R C
M E B T J R O P S E X Q O A Y
M O P E B N X Y O A I C N E F
Q C Z R F M W O P R N P N O R
X N U L E B Y C R T G O I G T
Q H I F U S F Z U A M C Q P J
N C Q W C H S S P C W V K D H
T S L D D X V I S H A N D L W
P I H S D R A H O E J P F E O
T J S A I A L J V N N Y R B D
K K O L G J U F E A R K V R N
L W W B L J D F A W H G C W V
B W F J Y D B J R A J R I I S
T H J X G Y K K K S M C R G S
U N C E R T A I N T Y K C U W
```

Conflict
Depression
Fear
Hardship
Heartache

Job
Money
Purpose
Sickness
Uncertainty

When finished, pick one area with which you struggle most. Exchange thoughts with your puzzle partner and commit to pray for each other in the week ahead. During those prayers, remind yourself of the Lord's willingness to watch over and protect you in all circumstances.

Lesson 1

Famous Farewell Addresses: 1=President Dwight Eisenhower. 2=Apostle Paul. 3=King David. 4=Jesus. 5=President Ronald Reagan.

Lesson 2

Serve the Lord:

```
C + + + E I O B E Y + S
+ A + + S V + + + + E +
+ + N R + + R + + S + +
+ + A A + + + E S + S +
+ E + + A + + E S + D +
L C + D + N N + + + O +
+ H R + + T + + + + G +
+ O + + I A B R A H A M
L O + W A U H S O J + +
+ S + + + + + + + + + +
+ E + + + + + + + + + +
+ + + + + + + + + + + +
```

Lesson 3

Satisfied with Good Things: 1=father. 2=diseases. 3=benefits. 4=righteousness. 5=great. 6=everlasting. **Message:** Find the blessings.

Lesson 4

The Big Announcement: Change: <u>Seventh</u> to **sixth**. <u>Michael</u> to **Gabriel**. <u>Bethlehem</u> to **Nazareth**. <u>Widow</u> to **virgin**. <u>Simeon</u> to **Joseph**. <u>Levi</u> to **David**. <u>Martha</u> to **Mary**. <u>Barely</u> to **highly**. <u>Peasants</u> to **women**. <u>Comforted</u> to **troubled**. <u>Farewell</u> to **salutation**. <u>Much</u> to **not**. <u>Daughter</u> to **son**. <u>Her</u> to **his**. <u>Immanuel</u> to **Jesus**.

Lesson 6

Can You Spot a Liar? 1=T, since liars have rehearsed the story one way but get confused when telling it in reverse order. 2=L, since they are working hard to convince you and give you more information than needed. 3=T, since liars use third person to put distance between themselves and what they are saying. 4=L. 5=L, since they are working hard to convince you. 6=T, since this is how innocent people act. 7=T, but liars are more likely to use complex sentences. 8=L, since they are hoping to leave as soon as possible.

What's Love Got to Do with It? Paul's love is evident in his desire that the gospel be preached unhindered (2 Thessalonians 3:1, 2), so that many more can receive eternal life. He also wants those who have already believed not to fall under the destructive influence of wrong teaching (3:6-10, not in today's lesson text). The latter is also the basis of John's love (2 John 7-11).

Lesson 7

Prideful Heart vs. Humble Heart: adultery / desires / double-mindedness / enmity / envy / fighting / friendship with the world / lust / wars connect with the **prideful heart**; affliction / cleansing / grace / mourning / purification / resistance to the devil / submission connect with the **humble heart**.

Lesson 8

God's Redemptive Work: 1=C. 2=A. 3=E. 4=B. 5=D.

Lesson 9

Levels of Authority (lowest rank to highest): 8–Master Sergeant. 7–Lieutenant. 6–Captain. 5–Major. 4–Colonel. 3–Brigadier General. 2–Major General. 1–Lieutenant General.

Hidden Message: Care about what is meaningful to other people.

Lesson 10

Ultimate Prizes? 1=C. 2=E. 3=A. 4=B. 5=D.

Lesson 11

Follow the Leader? Alexander the Great, C–Greece. Catherine the Great, F–Russia. Genghis Khan, E–Mongol Empire. Gustavus Adolphus, H–Sweden. Joan of Arc, B–France. Mahatma Gandhi, D–India. Nelson Mandela, G–South Africa. Pierre Trudeau, A–Canada. Queen Victoria, I–United Kingdom.

Be an Overcomer: Responses will be subjective.

Lesson 12

Sing and Shout: Prayer in vv. 19, 20. Power in v. 3. Enemies in v. 3. Earth in v. 4. Praise in vv. 2, 8. Sing in v. 4. Rejoice in v. 6. Heart in v. 18. KJV and NIV.

```
+ + P O W E R S + + + +
+ + + + + + I R + + + E
+ + + + + N + E + + S +
+ + + + G + + Y + I + +
+ + + + H + + A A + + N
S E I M E N E R + + + +
+ E + + A C P P + + + +
+ + A + R + I + + + + +
+ + + R T + + O + + + +
+ + + + T + + + J + + +
+ + + + + H + + + E + +
+ + + + + + + + + + R +
```

Lesson 13

Methods of Protection: 1=G. 2=F. 3=D. 4=E. 5=A. 6=C. 7=B.

In Need of Protection:

```
D + + + + + C E H + + + +
+ E + + + + O + S E + + + Y
+ + P + + N + + O A + + E +
+ + + R F + + P R + + N + +
+ + + L E + + R T + O + + +
+ + I + + S + + U A M + + +
+ C + + + S S P C + + + + +
T + + + + + + I S H + + + +
P I H S D R A H O E + + + +
+ J + + + + + + N N + + + +
+ + O + + + F E A R K + + +
+ + + B + + + + + + + C + +
+ + + + + + + + + + + + I +
+ + + + + + + + + + + + S
U N C E R T A I N T Y + + +
```

Student
Activity
Reproducible Pages

—— • ——

Spring Quarter
2019
Discipleship
and Mission

Student Activity Reproducible Pages

·

Summer Quarter 2019 Covenant in God

Jesus Institutes the New Covenant
Lesson 1, Mark 14:17-25; Hebrews 8:6, 7, 10-12, KJV

A Jewish Holiday

The Israelites had various feasts and observances that we would refer to as holidays, each having specific traditions. Match the below list of Jewish traditions on the right with their associated holidays on the left. There are three traditions for every one holiday, and each tradition is only used once. The definitions may help you to make the correct associations.

JEWISH HOLIDAYS	TRADITIONS
1. Pesach (Passover)	__ a. Challah (egg-rich, yeast-leavened bread)
	__ b. Haggadah (the book of readings for seder)
2. Yom Kippur (Day of Atonement)	__ c. Hametz (leavened food banned during this holiday)
	__ d. Machzor (or Mahzor, a Hebrew prayer book containing the Jewish liturgy for festivals)
3. Shabbat (Sabbath)	__ e. Seder (a ceremonial dinner held to commemorate the exodus from Egypt
	__ f. Shamor (Observe or watch)
	__ g. Shofar (a ram's-horn trumpet)
	__ h. Tzom (Fasting)
	__ i. Zakhor (the ethical duty to remember)

The Lord's Supper

The Lord's Supper is a reminder of Christ's sacrificial death that allows us to be under the new covenant, under God's forgiveness. This new covenant is to define us as Christians, living with Christlikeness and anticipating Jesus' return. To gain more personal insight into the significance of communion, write down all the associations you have with each of the elements.

Bread:

_____

_____

Fruit of the vine:

_____

_____

JESUS SEALS THE NEW COVENANT

Lesson 2, Mark 15:6-15, 25, 26, 33-39, KJV

VARIOUS VIEWPOINTS

Distribute copies of the script below to seven learners before class, with one person each for the Narrator, Pilate, Jesus, and the Centurion and three students to read in unison for the Sanhedrin.

NARRATOR: Reads Mark 15:6-10.

PILATE: These Jewish leaders tax my patience. Why do they insist on bothering me with their petty religious issues? I'll show them. I'll release this Jesus as a goodwill gesture to the people. They love Jesus; they will not want Him to die.

THE SANHEDRIN: The only way to get rid of Jesus is to have Pilate declare Him a threat to Rome and to Caesar. We must stir up this crowd against Him, so Pilate has no choice but to condemn Jesus to death.

JESUS: These men behave as though they are in control of this situation. They do not realize that they are fulfilling God's plan. I stand here willingly and I will die willingly, not out of submission to Rome but in submission to my Father.

NARRATOR: Reads Mark 15:11-15, 25, 26.

PILATE: These people are idiots. Don't they realize they are pawns in the hands of their religious leaders? Yet while I don't really think Jesus is guilty, I will have to listen to them or risk my position. But I will have my revenge. I will place the title of "The King of the Jews" over Him for all to see. Let's see how they like that.

THE SANHEDRIN: Finally, we will be free of Jesus. His followers will all scatter at His death, and we can resume life as usual. God shall surely reward us for guarding His law.

NARRATOR: Reads Mark 15:33-39 and Psalm 22:14, 15.

THE CENTURION: I do not know who this man is, but I know what people say about Him. He was kind and forgiving; He healed people's diseases, and they say He even brought the dead back to life. I've never seen a man die the way He did. I think He must really be the Son of God.

JESUS: Father, I am poured out like water, and all my bones are out of joint. My heart is like melted wax. My strength is gone, and my tongue cleaves to my jaws. You have brought me into the dust of death; into your hands I commit my spirit. Be not far from me.

MY RESPONSE

How would you personally respond to the questions below?

1. In what ways is Jesus my king? _____

2. What actions evidence this to others who see me on a daily basis? _____

3. In what ways do I rely on God's power rather than my own?_____

4. What actions evidence this to others who see me on a daily basis? _____

5. In what ways am I willing to share the good news of Jesus' death and resurrection with others? _____

6. How can I do that this week? _____

The New Covenant's Sacrifice

Day of Atonement Match

Match the suggested feature of the Day of Atonement (see Leviticus 16; 23:26-32; Numbers 29:7-11) on the left with its counterpart on the right from the lesson.

Day of Atonement

_____ 1. Once a year

_____ 2. First covenant or testament

_____ 3. Blood of animals

_____ 4. Temporary cleansing

_____ 5. Offered by humans

_____ 6. Holy Place

_____ 7. High priest

_____ 8. Purified flesh

Jesus' Sacrifice

a. Jesus Christ

b. Heaven

c. Eternal redemption

d. One time only

e. Through the Holy Spirit

f. Blood of Christ

g. Purged or cleansed conscience

h. New Testament

Hebrew Parallelism

Hebrew poetry is known for its parallelism—repetition of the same thought with different words in consecutive lines of poetry. Using some of the main ideas below from today's lesson text, construct a poem using parallelism to praise God for His sacrifice of Jesus. (See Psalm 24 for a good example of parallelism.)

Write your poem on the lines below.

Christ is a superior high priest.

_____

Jesus was a superior sacrifice to those that

_____

were offered in the Old Testament.

_____

Christ entered into a sanctuary superior to the tabernacle.

_____

Christ instituted a better covenant.

_____

God made a better promise through Jesus' sacrifice.

_____

HEARTS UNITED IN LOVE

CHRISTIAN PERKS

Find the benefits of being a Christian as listed in Colossians 2:1-15. Use the clues below to help you find the correct answers. Circle the benefits in the puzzle.

1. A treasure hidden in Christ

2. What binds us together

3. A result of full understanding

4. Though absent in body, Paul is present in this

5. The person in whom God's fullness dwells

6. Jesus is the head of all ___

7. We are ___ and raised with Christ

8. Where our sins are nailed

9. What Paul hoped to comfort and encourage

10. Paul wanted them to know the ___ of God

11. They were no longer ___ in their sins

12. Those over whom Christ triumphed

```
J V C Z I M M C T B E W
F T I R Z I Z Z B L E K
J M P R O X A U S J F H
D S D O T S R M C U H M
Z A O H T I S H R I W L
J F E H E T R E G Y S P
S I B D R I L I H K B S
F R X A S D V G P C C B
Y R E T S Y M O D S I W
X H V W R B T H I W K R
L T O J O T J O M E S R
S S L Q N P S R F O H X
```

GROWTH SYMBOLS

Create a different symbol (such as Æ § © ‡ √ ≠ Ø ∞ # & Δ † Σ) for each of the spiritual growth tasks below. Then place the symbols on a calendar as shorthand reminders to guide you in a month of committed habits that will help you develop a more steadfast faith.

Bible study

Daily devotional time

Prayer time

Life conversations with a mentor or accountability partner

Family devotions

Sunday	Monday	Tuesday	Wednesday	Thursday	Friday	Saturday
					1	2
3	4	5	6	7	8	9
10	11	12	13	14	15	16
17	18	19	20	21	22	23
24	25	26	27	28	29	30

RIGHT ATTITUDES

WHAT'S IN A NAME?

Match each of the following names with a description. You may not be familiar with all the names, but this quiz will be easier once you understand its theme!

_____ 1. Curly Howard

_____ 2. Lady Antebellum

_____ 3. Honest John

_____ 4. "Sweet" Saraya Knight

_____ 5. Little John

_____ 6. Michael Ende

_____ 7. Don Black

_____ 8. Frank Beard

a. Con man in *Pinocchio*

b. Gigantic member of Robin Hood's Merry Men

c. White supremacist

d. Country group that is mostly male

e. Author of *The Neverending Story*

f. Only clean-shaven member of the band ZZ Top

g. Member of the Three Stooges with a crew cut

h. Loudmouthed, obnoxious professional wrestler

UNEXPECTED WORDS

Place the words below into the grid. How are these words unexpected descriptions of a person blessed by God?

Word bank:

poor

mournful

meek

hungry

thirsty

merciful

pure

peacemakers

persecuted

slandered

FULFILLING THE LAW

BIG CLAIMS

Below the names of companies are scrambled, followed by their advertising slogans. Unscramble the names to find out who is making these big claims. What are they promising? How factually accurate are they?

1. earlhy-vaddsion—American by Birth. Rebel by Choice. _____

2. krallham—When you care enough to send the very best._____

3. trawaml—Save Money. Live Better. _____

4. sheetawi—Breakfast of Champions. _____

5. dailydensn—The happiest place on earth. _____

6. grubre gink—Have it your way. _____

7. armhonat—Fueling the American Spirit _____

8. stribhi sawyira—The world's favorite airline. _____

9. acoc alco—It's the real thing. _____

10. tegiltel—The Best a Man Can Get _____

PASS THE SALT, TURN ON THE LIGHT

Evaluate your "saltiness" or "bright-lightedness" by choosing a metaphor found below that best fits you. What changes do you need to make to be saltier or brighter?

Popcorn Salt—My world would just not "taste" the same were it not for my presence. I add a godly influence that has stirred spiritual thirst in my friends.

Rock Salt—I have a potent presence, but I tend to present truth in too big of chunks. My influence is too easily brushed off without penetrating the surface.

Garlic Salt—Salt is salt, but sometimes my actions leave a bad taste in the mouths of others.

Candlelight—My glow for God is alluring, but in a romantic, mystical sort of way. It can be so subtle that others do not see God in every detail and in all His glory.

Strobe light—My pulsating beams draw attention, but because my godly behavior is on again, off again, I am more of a distraction than an illuminator.

Crystal chandelier—The light of my life is refracted through the prisms of God's eternal truth. I am there, but people do not really see me. Rather they view God's radiance showering my world with beautiful points of light.

LOVE ONE ANOTHER

CRIME CLASSIFICATION

Which of these crimes are usually considered felonies (F), and which are considered misdemeanors (M)?*
What are some factors considered when classifying crimes in this way?

_____ 1. Health insurance fraud

_____ 2. Tampering with an odometer

_____ 3. Cruelty to animals

_____ 4. Witness tampering

_____ 5. Escape from custody

_____ 6. Using a fraudulent cigarette tax stamp

_____ 7. Delivering liquor to a minor

_____ 8. Obstructing mosquito control

_____ 9. Receiving kickbacks

_____ 10. Selling fireworks without a permit

*These examples are taken from the Connecticut General Statutes.

DISSECTING THE TEXT

Take apart our Scripture verse for today by filling in these blanks with words or paraphrases from the cited
verses.

Big Sin #1 (Matthew 5:21) _____

Source of that sin (Matthew 5:22)_____

Remedy (Matthew 5:23, 24)_____

Danger if not remedied (Matthew 5:25, 26) _____

Big Sin #2 (Matthew 5:27) _____

Source of that sin (Matthew 5:28)_____

Remedy (Matthew 5:29, 30)_____

Danger if not remedied (Matthew 5:31, 32) _____

TRANSFORMING LOVE

Lesson 8, Matthew 5:38-44, KJV

CONSEQUENTIAL QUOTE

Place or copy the puzzle tiles into this grid to form a quote about the consequences of vengeance.

—*Mahatma Gandhi*

PERSECUTION MAP

The countries listed below are considered to be those most likely to persecute Christians. Choose a country and pray for its leaders this week.

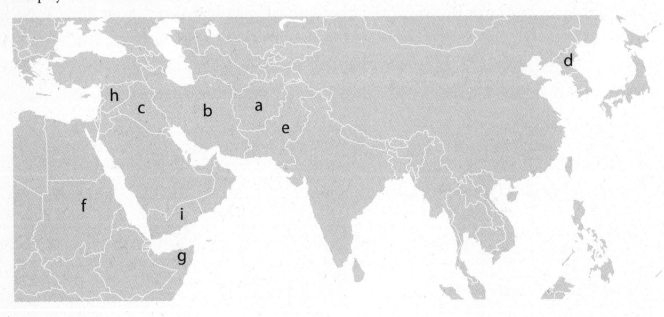

a. Afghanistan
b. Iran
c. Iraq

d. North Korea
e. Pakistan
f. Sudan

g. Somalia
h. Syria
i. Yemen

SPIRITUAL DISCERNMENT

Lesson 9, Matthew 7:1-6, 15-23, KJV

HOW DO YOU RATE?

Ask your fellow class members about their experiences with rating systems. Try to have various class members initial each one of these statements about ratings.

_____ 1. Had a 3.0 or better grade point average in high school.

_____ 2. Knows credit score.

_____ 3. Last movie seen was rated PG.

_____ 4. Has never eaten at a five-star restaurant.

_____ 5. Has recently had a performance review at work.

_____ 6. Reads book reviews before reading a book.

_____ 7. Owns a car with a high MPG rating.

TRUE OR FALSE?

This is an easy true/false test—because all the following statements are false according to our lesson text! But just to make it a challenge, be ready to explain why the statement is false and correct it.

___ 1. Being a critical person has no negative consequences for the critic (vv. 1, 2).

___ 2. Since we are imperfect, "Do as I say, not as I do," is good advice (vv. 3-5).

___ 3. When someone refuses to listen to your advice, keep giving it until they surrender (v. 6).

___ 4. Of course, you can judge a book by its cover! (v. 15).

___ 5. There is really no good way to tell whether a person's advice and teachings are worthy of being followed (vv. 16-20).

___ 6. We should accept a person's spiritual testimony at face value (vv. 19-21).

___ 7. Miraculous signs and grand accomplishments are a sure sign that a person walks with God (vv. 22, 23).

A Covenant Between Friends

Lesson 10, 1 Samuel 18:1-5; 19:1-7, KJV

Acquaintance . . . or Friend?

Novelist S. E. Hinton once wrote, "If you have two friends in your lifetime, you're lucky. If you have one good friend, you're more than lucky." She spoke to the fact that we may have many acquaintances we call friends, but a "good friend" is more than a pal or a regular dinner companion. A good friend demonstrates loyalty and may even take risks on your behalf, just as Jonathan did with David.

Remembering My Friends

In this space, list all the people who would think of you as their friend. Write as many names as you can in this space in one minute. _____

_____

Now go back and circle the one or two people whose loyalty to you over time makes them more than an acquaintance. How is your friendship with this person or two people different from your relationship with the others? Write two or three answers here. _____

_____

Demonstrating His Friendship

Read 1 Samuel 18:1-5 and 19:1-7. In this space, write attributes of Jonathan's friendship with David.

_____

How did Jonathan show that David was more than his pal?

_____

Strengthening Our Friendship

Notice that Jonathan reached out to David to promise his friendship to him. What actions could you take to demonstrate your friendship to someone who is or could be close to you?

My Friend's Name	What I'll Do

A Mother-Daughter Covenant

In-law Diaries

Pretend you are Ruth or Naomi. What would you record in your diary after the events recorded in each of the Scripture paragraphs indicated below?

Ruth 1:1-5	
Ruth	*Naomi*
Ruth 1:6, 7	
Ruth	*Naomi*
Ruth 1:8-10	
Ruth	*Naomi*
Ruth 1:11-14	
Ruth	*Naomi*
Ruth 1:15-18	
Ruth	*Naomi*

Blessed to Be a Blessing

In the space below, jot the names of people or situations you know where great loss or loneliness has been experienced. Try to think of at least 10 examples.

1. _____
2. _____
3. _____
4. _____
5. _____

6. _____
7. _____
8. _____
9. _____
10. _____

In which of these situations could you bring comfort or demonstrate love? Circle at least one of them. Decide what you can do this week to be a blessing with the person or need you have circled.

A COVENANT TO MARRY

Lesson 12, Ruth 3:1-6, 8-12, 16-18, KJV

HIDDEN MESSAGE, HELPFUL MESSAGE

Solve the following cryptogram to reveal a truth we can take away from the story of Naomi, Ruth, and Boaz.

A Lesson for All of Us

A	B	C	D	E	F	G	H	I	J	K	L	M	N	O	P	Q	R	S	T	U	V	W	X	Y	Z
	19					4	21					11					24	14	9						

G _ _   B L _ S S _ S _ S   T H _ S _   _ H _   S H _ _
4 23 15   19 11 13 14 14 13 14   9 21 23 14 13   25 21 23   14 21 23 25

_ _ T _ G R _ T _   _ _   T H _ _ R   R _ L _ T _ _ _ S H _ _ S
2 7 9 13 4 24 2 9 12   2 7   9 21 13 2 24   24 13 11 3 9 2 23 7 14 21 2 26 14

After you have completed the sentence, talk with another class member to reflect on this principle. Share either a positive or negative example from your experience.

MY RELATIONSHIP MATRIX

Write your name in the center of the circle below. On each line write the name of someone with whom you have a regular relationship, such as a coworker, family member, neighbor, or friend.

- Make the line a solid line if you feel your relationship with this person is healthy and strong.
- Circle the name of the person whose relationship causes the most stress. How could improved integrity—on their part or yours—make this relationship healthier?
- Pray about a plan for improving your relationship with this person.

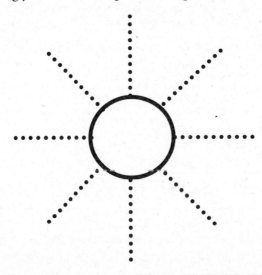

MARRIAGE: A COVENANT OF MUTUAL LOVE

Lesson 13, Ephesians 5:21-33, KJV

MARRIAGE BROKEN

Look at the four pictures below. What's going on in these marriages? Choose one and write a paragraph or story to describe the problems this marriage is facing.

Photos: © omgimages / Ridofranz / alexsokolov / djedzura / iStock / Getty Images Plus

_____

_____

_____

MARRIAGE MENDED

What principles from Ephesians 5:21-32 could help and heal these marriages? Write a paragraph of biblical counsel to the couple whose picture above you described.

_____

_____

_____

_____

_____

_____

Lesson 1

A Jewish Holiday: 1=Pesach (see Exodus 12): Haggadah (b), Hametz (c), Seder (e). 2=Yom Kippur (see Leviticus 23): Machzor (d), Shofar (g), Tzom (h). 3=Shabbat (see Exodus 31): Challah (a), Shamor (f), Zakhor (i).

Lesson 3

Day of Atonement Match: 1=d. 2=h. 3=f. 4=c. 5=e. 6=b. 7=a. 8=g.

Lesson 4

Christian Perks: 1=wisdom. 2=love. 3=riches. 4=spirit. 5=Christ. 6=power. 7=buried. 8=cross. 9=hearts. 10=mystery. 11=dead. 12=powers.

Christian Perks solution::

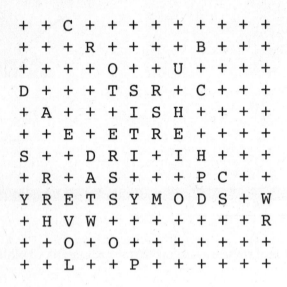

Lesson 5

What's in a Name? 1=g. 2=d. 3=a. 4=h. 5=b. 6=e. 7=c. 8=f.
Unexpected Words solution:

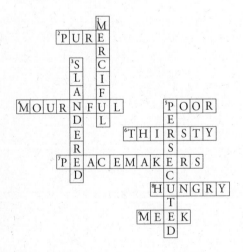

Lesson 6

Big Claims: 1=Harley-Davidson. 2=Hallmark. 3=Walmart. 4=Wheaties. 5=Disneyland. 6=Burger King. 7=Marathon. 8=British Airways. 9=Coca Cola. 10=Gillette.

Lesson 7

Crime Classification: 1=F. 2=M. 3=M. 4=F. 5=M. 6=F. 7=F. 8=M. 9=F. 10=M.

Dissecting the Text (suggested answers): Big Sin #1=murder. Source of that sin=uncontrolled anger. Remedy=reconcile with the person. Danger if not remedied=feud will continue until someone pays. **Big Sin #2**=adultery. Source of that sin=lust for another. Remedy=avoid the temptation at all cost. Danger if not remedied=destruction and devaluation of marriage.

Lesson 8

Consequential Quote solution:

A	N		E	Y	E		F	O
R		A	N		E	Y	E	
W	I	L	L		O	N	L	Y
	M	A	K	E		T	H	E
	W	H	O	L	E		W	O
R	L	D		B	L	I	N	D

Lesson 9

True or False? Answers can be drawn from the lesson text.

Lesson 12

Hidden Message, Helpful Message: God blesses those who show integrity in their relationships.

Lesson 13

Broken Marriage: arguing, distant/unengaged, raised voices, marriage counseling.